READER'S DIGEST

HOW TO
PAY LESS
FOR JUST ABOUT
EVERYTHING

HOW TO
PAY

PUBLISHED BY THE READER'S DIGEST ASSOCIATION LIMITED
LONDON • NEW YORK • SYDNEY • MONTREAL

LESS

FOR JUST ABOUT EVERYTHING

CONTENTS

THE 6 'PAY LESS' PRINCIPLES

If you want to enjoy the best things in life without paying more for them than you need to, then it makes sense to learn how to spot – and secure – a bargain on everything you buy. **HOW TO PAY LESS FOR JUST ABOUT ANYTHING** is a modern shopper's bible, full of insider information and thousands of ideas, tips and resources to help you make wise decisions and get a better price, whether you are buying from a large store or a market stall, or paying for professional advice or a tradesman's services.

1 DEVELOP THE 'PAY LESS' ATTITUDE

Approach every purchase with the belief that you can do better than the asking price, and you're half way to doing just that. Train yourself to look for the money-saving angles in every situation, no matter how large or small the potential savings may be. Assume that other people are getting a bargain, so why shouldn't you? And remember that most goods and services have a healthy profit margin so there is usually plenty of room for manoeuvre.

2 FIND THE CHEAPEST PRICE

Do your research. There are now so many businesses vying for your custom with discounts and special offers that you can almost always find something cheaper if you know where to look. Check out our Resources boxes for recommended suppliers and information sources and, if you can, get onto the Internet to track down those good deals. It's a user-friendly virtual marketplace that really has brought bargain-hunting into the 21st century.

3 TAKE YOUR TIME

Don't be forced into a situation where you have to make a rushed purchase. You'll get the best deals if you book tickets in advance, or wait until that bathroom suite goes on sale, or keep a constant eye on camera prices so you can pounce when they drop. Give yourself time to shop around, weigh up your options and buy when the moment is right.

4 ASK THE RIGHT QUESTIONS

Learn the magic phrase that may get you a bargain: 'Is that the best you can do?' In other words, ask the seller to be resourceful on your behalf. You may find that you qualify for a discount, simply by paying cash. Or that a cruise will cost less if you go in May. That your insurance premiums will be lower if you meet certain criteria. Or that the coat you covet is going on sale next week. Most people really do want to help you – especially if you are friendly and smile.

5 USE YOUR BARGAINING POWER

Be prepared to haggle. Ask yourself how much the seller wants your business. Is he overstocked? Is he desperate to make his quota or his commission? Are you his only customer? Assume he wants to do a deal – you're probably right! Offer to buy more if he'll give you a discount. See if you can take a reduced service and pay less. Spot a flaw in the item and suggest a lower price. Find a rival offer and ask him to match it. On the other hand, bargaining also means being willing to walk away.

6 THINK CREATIVELY

If the price is still not right, don't give up. Be flexible. See if you can get a workman to lower his charges by offering to do part of the job yourself. Go in with friends to get a discount on bulk buys for everything from theatre tickets to vintage wine. Do a neighbour's gardening in exchange for free baby-sitting. That way, everybody wins – and everyone gets something for less.

HOW TO USE THE INTERNET TO

Today, the Internet is a vital tool in the battle to cut costs and get the best available deal. Used effectively, it can save you a fortune on everything from clothes and food to insurance or utility bills. It is now faster, safer and easier to use, giving you access to an enormous range of products and making it quick and simple to compare prices. This has been aided by the growth in comparison sites that, effectively, do our research for us (we list a wide range in our Directory). Here, we show you how to navigate one such site.

    If you don't own a PC, visit an Internet café or local library and use their computers to get information on goods and services – plus contact details.

HOW WEBSITES WORK

When you visit a website, the first page will usually offer a list of options. **moneysupermarket.com**, shown here, directs you to sections on **MONEY**, **INSURANCE**, **TRAVEL**... Click on the bar at the top, or icons shown below, for sub-sections. Motoring subdivides into new cars, loans, car hire, insurance, reviews, and more. Each of these is a link to an individual section, which you can access.

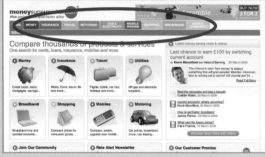

JUMPING FROM PAGE TO PAGE

Click on the category you require, such as **SHOPPING**, and this will present you with a number of other options. Here, on the left, you could choose from 'Cameras & Photography' or 'Fashion & Accessories' that then subdivide further into more specific areas, such as *Binoculars* or *Men's Shoes*. This website also highlights Hottest and Newest products – sometimes a quick route to a good deal.

GETTING MORE INFORMATION

As you delve further into a website, you will find that there's often a lot more information than you would typically find in a shop or printed catalogue. This page offers in-depth product details – including dimensions and power consumption – plus there are links to 'Retailer Offers' plus useful 'User' and 'Expert Reviews' – you can even add your own. Always check Terms and Conditions, delivery details and returns policy before committing to a purchase.

EMAIL FOR CORRESPONDENCE

If you decide to buy online, most online shops will ask for your email address as part of the payment process – it's used for sending order confirmations, delivery notes and other correspondence. If you don't have an email address and want to shop via an Internet café or local library, you'll need to set one up in advance.

Some services are set up specifically to help out in this situation: if you join a web-based email service, such as **www.yahoo.co.uk** or **googlemail.com**, you get an email address of your own and you can use it to send and receive email messages from any PC – from a Internet café, for example. Most such services are free.

PAY LESS FOR EVERYTHING

STRAIGHT TO THE STORE

Once you've found the product you want at a price you are happy with, the 'Go to site' button will take you to the relevant retailer's website. The page for this TV gives full specifications, shows how much you save (over £110 off the RRP here) and suggests some accessories. There are also links to 'Terms and Conditions', 'Ordering, Returns', 'Warranties', 'Customer Services' and 'Contact Us' – which, helpfully, gives an address and phone number.

DECIDING TO BUY

If, after studying the relevant pages, you decide to proceed with the purchase, there should be easy, step-by-by instructions to follow. Here, you would head to the section on the right headed 'Want to buy this?' It offers warranty options and a choice of delivery dates before you click 'Add to basket' (other options here could be 'Proceed to checkout'). Finally, click 'Buy Now'. If you have second thoughts or get confused, just quit and come back later – there are no sales people to apply pressure!

ORDERING AND PAYING

From 'Add to Basket', you arrive at a page that confirms what you have ordered, the price and delivery charges. Follow this page to the checkout, where you will be asked to type in your address (for delivery) and payment details – you will be asked several times to confirm your command before your purchase goes through. Almost all online shops offer credit cards as a payment option, and it's a good idea to use this (see below, 'Is ordering online safe?')

HOW TO PAY

Q Do I have to pay for delivery?

A Some websites may offer free delivery for larger orders. In other cases, the savings you make almost always make up for the delivery cost.

Q Is ordering online safe?

A Online ordering is much like mail order: you are covered by distance-selling legislation, and if you pay by credit card you are protected from losing your money if the goods or services you buy are defective.

Q How do I ask a question about my order?

A Look for a link to a 'Frequently Asked Questions' (or 'FAQ') page – this may address your query. If not, look for a 'Contact Us' or 'Help' page – it may contain a telephone contact number, or an address for sending questions by email.

Q What sort of receipt do I get?

A At the end of the purchase process, there will usually be a confirmation page with an order reference – print it out and keep it. The online shop may also send you an electronic receipt by email and a printed receipt with the goods you've ordered.

Eat healthily and well while sticking to a budget by assessing your culinary needs before you hit the supermarket. Learn when and where to shop, at home and abroad, and how to equip your kitchen without paying a fortune.

Food and drink

SHOPPING SENSE

Before you go food shopping, write down what you need. Searching for inspiration not only wastes time but you'll also end up buying too much. And never shop on an empty stomach. Munch on a banana or cereal bar on your way to the store – it will take the edge off your appetite, and you're more likely to save money by buying only what you need.

STICK TO YOUR LIST

Making a shopping list and sticking to it are two different things. Research shows that the average shopper buys one unlisted item from every supermarket aisle every time he or she goes shopping. If the store has ten aisles, that adds up to at least ten items every week of the year. If each item costs £1, that's an extra £520 you could have kept in your pocket.

TOP TIPS SHOPPING-LIST SECRETS

■ **Make a note** Keep a notebook and pen in your kitchen. As soon as you deplete your stock of a storecupboard item or are getting close to using up a necessity such as tea or milk, add it to the list. If you have a preference for a particular brand or store, note that down, too.

■ **News items** When you see local newspaper ads with special prices on foods you buy regularly, circle the dates and clip them to your list, or make a note directly on your list for that store noting the sale item and sale dates. That way, you won't buy something only to discover later that a similar item was on sale for much less.

■ **Group your list** Organise your shopping list in the same way as the store is laid out to prevent wandering – and possible impulse buying (see page 21). The more you wander up and down the aisles to pick up the next thing on your list, the more you'll be tempted by extra items. This simple organisational trick could save you 15% on shopping bills.

CASE STUDY

FAMILY MEALS PLANNED AROUND THE SPECIAL OFFERS

Diane Harding, with a family of four young boys and an athletic husband, plans her weekly shop around on-sale items she sees advertised in flyers and the local press. At first, she would pick up just a few sale buys that she would then make for that evening's meal — but now she's found a way to save even more. If, for example, minced beef is on sale, she'll buy enough for three meals: chilli con carne one night, beefburgers another night and shepherd's pie for the third. If yoghurt is on special offer, she'll buy enough for breakfast and dessert for the whole week to mix with fruit or honey. By

planning her meals around sale items and paying special attention to deals on meat and fresh produce – which account for half of her purchases – Diane can save 30% on her weekly food bill.

Stock up on store-cupboard items

These common staples and ingredients have a long shelf life. Buy them whenever you see them on sale, and be sure of getting the best price.

- Baking powder
- Breadcrumbs
- Caster sugar
- Cocoa
- Coffee
- Cornflour
- Couscous
- Flour
- Fruit (tinned)
- Herbs (dried)
- Honey
- Ketchup
- Mustard
- Olive oil
- Pasta (dried)
- Pepper
- Pet food
- Rice
- Salt
- Soup (tinned)
- Soy sauce
- Spices
- Stock cubes
- Sugar
- Sunflower oil
- Tabasco sauce
- Tea
- Tomato purée
- Tuna (tinned)
- Vegetable oil
- Vegetables (tinned)
- Wine vinegar
- Worcestershire sauce

■ **Weekly visit** Don't visit any store more than once a week. Generally, aim for a once-a-month big shop at a discount warehouse, such as Makro or Costco (see page 24), or place a large online order (see page 25) to stock up on storecupboard items. You'll probably need to visit your regular supermarket about once a week for things that you buy in smaller amounts and every two or three days for perishable items such as milk, fresh fruit and vegetables. But remember, the more you shop the more you will buy.

THE CHEAPEST TIME TO SHOP

You may be able to save money on some of the items on your shopping list if you shop late in the day, when retailers, especially market stallholders, are likely to discount perishable items they want to shift. This can mean anything from half-price tomatoes to chilled soups, pasta sauces or yoghurts nearing their sell-by date.

DISCOUNT DELI

Check the deli counter for ends or offcuts of cold meats and cheeses and get a discount of 50% or more. The high turnover of such items ensures that the end bits won't be stale or past their best, just psychologically less appealing than a slice from a new joint or a wedge of uncut cheese. If you buy more discounted meat or cheese than you need at the time, you can freeze the surplus.

ANALYSE YOUR PURCHASES

Most people are shocked by their food bills – and would be even more dismayed to see where the money really goes. You may find that more than 20% goes on non-essentials.

Record impulse buys Every time you pick up an item that's not on your shopping list, note it down in a different coloured pen. If you add more than six items, you are in danger of losing control of your spending.

Use a zapper to avoid checkout surprises If your supermarket has a bar-code reader that you can use, check your total as you shop. Reconsider any impulse buys.

Add up all your receipts Each time you buy food – including sweets for the children, a sandwich for lunch or a bag of apples on your way home from work – keep the receipt. Save them all together and total them at the end of the week to see how much you are really spending on food and drink. Do this for a couple of weeks and then sit down and decide whether you can do without some of the items.

Separate miscellaneous from food items When you return home from a major shopping trip, categorise what you have bought. Tick off essential non-food items such as toothpaste, kitchen and cleaning supplies, clothing, stationery and pet food – that alone could account for a third of your bill.

Cutting down your food bill Take a look at your remaining food bill and use coloured markers so you can see what you have spent in different areas. Pick out snacks, biscuits and appetisers. Then highlight fizzy drinks, bottled water, alcohol, tea and coffee, followed by extravagant items such as desserts and expensive convenience meals. Highlight storecupboard items, which are a form of investment in your larder. What you should be left with is the fresh, healthy food you and your family will eat at mealtimes during the week. You can now work out what you can do without. This exercise could save you 20% on your food bill.

SAVE ON LAST-MINUTE BUYS

If you've forgotten something on your shopping list, consider whether you can wait until your next supermarket shop rather than picking it up at your local convenience store.

You will usually pay for the privilege. Even some supermarket mini-shops have higher prices than their larger equivalents. Here's how the prices for the same items compare.

	CONVENIENCE STORE	SUPERMARKET MINI-SHOP	SUPERMARKET MAIN STORE
1 PINT MILK	£0.49	£0.45	£0.45
SMALL LOAF	£0.87	£0.75	£0.75
250g BUTTER	£1.25	£1.26	£1.25
TIN OF CAT FOOD	£0.61	£0.56	£0.55
230g CHOCOLATE	£1.58	£1.37	£1.35

Prices correct at time of going to press

BEST BUYS ON EVERYDAY FOODS

Make a list of basic foods you use regularly, and buy them in quantities suited to your needs. For example, if your family eats a lot of bread, it's worth stocking up when prices are low and freezing the excess for later.

SAVE WITH SEASONAL FRUIT AND VEG

Seasonal, locally grown produce tends to be cheaper and better quality as it can be grown more naturally with less reliance on expensive greenhouses or pesticides – it is also likely to taste better as it hasn't been picked and flown into the UK before it has fully developed its flavour. Locally grown fruit and veg will have clocked up less 'food miles', too, helping the environment as well as the local economy. Buy fruit and vegetables from an outlet or greengrocer where you can select and weigh your own. You'll be able to buy the exact quantity you need and check more easily that the produce isn't bruised or damaged than if it's in a sealed pack. Loose fruit and vegetables also keep for longer.

FROM THE MARKET STALL

If possible, avoid shopping for fruit and vegetables at the supermarket. Producers select individual, unblemished items of a similar size to look more attractive in the package, and this costs more. Smaller greengrocers and market stalls receive a lower-grade produce, which is just as good but less visually perfect. It will be cheaper, but you should select your individual items with care. Avoid market stalls where traders put items into a brown paper bag from a box at the back.

Get more per kilo

If you're planning to eat raw fruit, buy the smallest pieces as you'll get more per kilo. But, if cooking, buy larger (and fewer) pieces to avoid waste when they're peeled and prepared for the pot.

SMART MOVES

FRESH, FROZEN, TINNED OR READY-PREPARED?

Fresh is not necessarily the most expensive but you will pay a premium for vegetables that are both fresh and peeled, chopped or otherwise ready-prepared. Remember, though, that when you prepare vegetables such as peas yourself, you'll reduce the overall weight. Frozen vegetables are often good value, particularly when out of season.

VEGETABLES	FRESH	FROZEN	TINNED	READY-PREPARED
Green beans	£3.54/kg	£0.95/kg	£1.48/kg	£5.62/kg
Mushrooms	£2.96/kg	£2.00/kg	£2.52/kg	£3.56/kg
Cauliflower	£0.99 each	£0.94/kg	–	£3.80/kg
Peas	£2.30/kg	£1.67/kg	£1.26/kg	£5.80/kg
Carrots	£0.78/kg	£0.99/kg	£0.97/kg	£1.56/kg
Sweetcorn	£0.25 per cob	£0.97/kg	£1.20/kg	£7.65/kg

Prices correct at time of going to press

CHEAP FOR CHUTNEY

Discounted fruit needs picking over carefully. It may be cheap because it's fully ripe and needs clearing to make room for a new delivery. This is fine if you'll be eating the fruit on the same day or plan on making preserves and chutneys, but if it has ripened too far it is more likely to go to waste. Check reduced-priced vegetables carefully: green vegetables such as beans and broccoli should look bright and fresh; root vegetables such as carrots or potatoes should be firm; and, lettuces and leaf vegetables should be crisp.

SALAD SENSE

Pre-packed bags of prewashed salad can be 50%–70% more expensive than mixing ingredients and making your own salads. A 200g bag at £1.76 is a similar price to two large iceberg or romaine lettuces, or four small little gem lettuces – each enough for several salads.

WHAT'S IN SEASON?

Although fresh fruit and vegetables are less seasonal these days as crops are flown in from far and wide, many items are still much cheaper at their British seasonal times.

FRUIT AND VEGETABLES	PRICE IN SEASON	PRICE OUT OF SEASON
SPRING		
1kg BROCCOLI	£1.34	£1.68
1kg ASPARAGUS	£5.76	£7.96
1kg MINI CARROTS	£1.30	£2.27
SUMMER		
1kg RUNNER BEANS	£2.94	£7.50
1kg STRAWBERRIES	£3.10	£6.56
AUTUMN		
1kg PLUMS	£5.04	£5.98
1 CAULIFLOWER	£0.70	£0.99
1kg COURGETTES	£1.66	£1.97
WINTER		
1kg BRUSSELS SPROUTS	£1.78	£5.24
1 CABBAGE	£0.78	£0.99
1kg LEEKS	£2.48	£3.18

PICK YOUR OWN

■ Picking your own will save you money – fruit and vegetables can be 30%–50% cheaper than shop-bought. To find local farms where you can pick your own produce visit **www.pickyourown.info/**; for farm shops go to **www.farmshopping.net** or ring 0845 45 88 420 ✉.

■ Although it's no longer possible to pick wild flowers, these rules don't apply to hedgerow fruits such as blackberries and elderberries, nor to vegetables such as wild garlic and samphire grass.

■ British woods and forests are full of edible mushrooms that few people bother to pick. The Collins Gem *Mushrooms* (£4.99) is a handy guide to help you indentify mushrooms and toadstools. However, if you are in any doubt as to whether a mushroom is safe to eat, leave it alone.

■ There should be space even in a small flat to grow herbs on a sunny windowsill, saving you pounds on the expensive pre-packed herbs sold in supermarkets. Basil, coriander, chives and parsley are easy to grow. A packet of parsley seeds costing £1.59 will yield a constant crop for cutting that would have cost £50 or more in the shops.

TALKING TURKEY

Many people only think of cooking turkey at Christmas, but it is an economical choice all year round – a 4.5kg bird will feed about a dozen people. You don't have to buy a whole bird, since turkey is available in supermarkets and at butchers as oven-ready joints, breasts, cubes, steaks and mince and is good value for family meals and barbecues.

THE TENDER TOUCH

Flank steak, stewing beef and other less-expensive cuts of meat are 10%–30% cheaper than choicer cuts, but they need longer cooking to make them tender. Plan in advance if you are going to use them; an Irish stew needs to cook for 2 hours, for example, though marinating for as little as 20 minutes will help to tenderise and add flavour, too.

FALSE ECONOMY?

Cheaper minced beef may not necessarily be higher in fat than prime minced steak (the fat content of both will probably be less than 10%) but it's likely to have been made from a cheaper cut, such as shin or skirt. The meat will also have been hung for a shorter period so will need longer cooking to make it tender. Economy mince is fine for slow-cooked chilli con carne or a bolognese if you add plenty of herbs, wine and tomato purée for extra flavour. But buy prime mince for quick-cook homemade burgers.

CHICKEN PIECES

You can save on chicken pieces if you buy a whole chicken and cut it up yourself – all it takes is a good knife and a systematic approach. Whole chickens range from between £4 to £6 for a 2kg bird, compared to about £3.29 for 1kg of chicken thighs or more than £11.50 for 1kg of boneless, skinless breasts. Use the bones and leftovers in stocks and soups. Roasted chicken wings make excellent party nibbles.

Add your own extras and save 40%

Many brands instantly bump up the price of a basic product by adding other ingredients such as sugar, seasonings and sauces, which you can easily mix in yourself, should you want to.

■ Avoid sweetened cereals – frosted cornflakes can cost almost 40% more than the unsweetened variety.

■ Salads with added dressing or croutons can be over 30% more expensive than salads that have no dressing or other additions.

ARE READY-MADE MEALS WORTH IT?

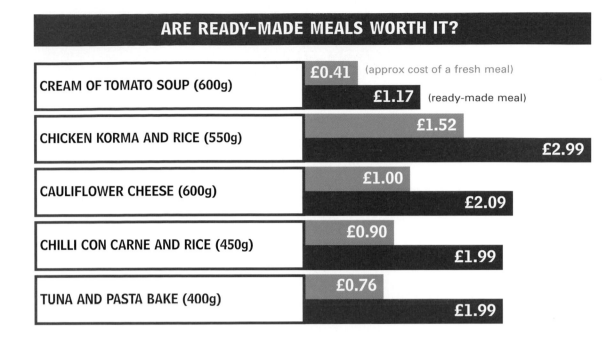

	Fresh meal	Ready-made meal
CREAM OF TOMATO SOUP (600g)	£0.41 (approx cost of a fresh meal)	£1.17 (ready-made meal)
CHICKEN KORMA AND RICE (550g)	£1.52	£2.99
CAULIFLOWER CHEESE (600g)	£1.00	£2.09
CHILLI CON CARNE AND RICE (450g)	£0.90	£1.99
TUNA AND PASTA BAKE (400g)	£0.76	£1.99

SOMETHING FISHY

Although expensive, fish is an economical buy as it has little waste. Fresh fish should have plump flesh and bright eyes.

Avoid pre-skinned fillets The price of 1kg of skinned and boneless cod is £11.49 compared to £8.97 for unskinned. To remove the skin, grasp the tail firmly and hold a knife vertically while running it the length of the fish.

Pricing your prawns Unpeeled prawns cost around £1.55 for 250g; the same quantity of peeled prawns would be £1.99. As peeling prawns is time-consuming, for convenience buy a smaller portion of peeled prawns than you need for a recipe and then chop and add cheaper seafood sticks (88p for 250g) to make up the weight.

Buy whole and bag up A whole 2kg–2.3kg salmon on special offer might cost £3.50 a kilo. If you cut it into fillets and freeze the surplus in individual bags, you will save nearly 40% over pre-cut fillets, which cost over £10 a kilo.

TOP TIPS SPOTTING A BARGAIN

■ **Package appeal** One brand of jam might look appealing in its rustic jar, but check the weight on the label before you buy. The jar may contain only 400g of jam but cost the same as the plainer jar on the lower shelf weighing 500g.

■ **Staple diet** Fill spare freezer space with kitchen staples such as milk, cheese and bread on special offer. (See Can You Freeze It? on page 19.)

■ **Slice by slice** If you buy a lot of cold cuts such as salami and garlic sausage, invest in a meat slicer and buy them in a piece to slice at home. Unsliced, the meat will stay fresher for longer and you'll save around 15% on flat-packed slices.

■ **Get grating** Bags of pre-grated cheese cost around 30% more than a block of cheese. Look for reduced-price offcuts of cheese and grate your own. Freeze or keep in the fridge in self-seal plastic bags and make up mixes of different cheeses such as red Leicester, Cheddar, Edam and Gouda to add colour and variety to sauces and gratin dishes.

SAVE ON ETHNIC INGREDIENTS

If you cook a lot of curries, stir-fries or other Far Eastern dishes and have an ethnic store nearby, buy your staples such as rice, noodles, spices and sauces there. Basmati rice is expensive in an ordinary supermarket, where a 500g box of a popular brand is likely to cost around £1.50 compared to £4 for a 5kg bag from an Indian grocery store. You can make similar savings in Chinese or Asian stores on stir-fry sauces, chilli sauces and pastes, soy sauce and noodles.

BULK BUY FOR BARGAINS

Take advantage of the seasonal glut of fresh produce and meat by buying it in bulk. Pay the lowest prices for as much of your favourite fruit and vegetables as you can store or freeze, and then give your taste buds a treat by eating fresh-from-the-freezer summer raspberries in January.

SEASONAL PRODUCE FOR STORAGE

Long-lasting vegetables and fruit can be bought in bulk from pick-your-own centres or farm shops at a fraction of the price per kilo in supermarkets.

Fruit and veg to keep A sack of potatoes or onions can be stored through the winter. You can also store garlic, apples, pumpkins, marrows and root vegetables such as carrots. Green vegetables can't be stored but freeze well. Tomatoes can be made into soups and sauces, then frozen.

How to store You need space in a cool garage or shed to ensure the produce doesn't go bad before you use it up. Root vegetables should be stored in crates, separated by sand or sieved soil. If you are short of suitable space, ask nearby friends or family if you can share with them.

YOUR FREEZER WILL PAY FOR ITSELF

Costing from £120, a large chest or upright freezer can be a money-saving asset, as the reductions on bulk-bought meat, jointed and ready-to-freeze, are significant. And you can cook double portions of meals, one for now and one for later, store seasonal fruit and vegetables and take advantage of supermarket discounts on perishable staples. Freeze food in single, double or family-size portions to suit your lifestyle.

TOP TIPS FREEZER FACTS AND FALLACIES

Don't waste frozen food by not caring for it properly. But there is no need to throw away what you can safely keep.

■ **Prevent freezer burn** Food will stay in better condition if you wrap it before you freeze it, excluding as much air as possible. This is particularly important when freezing meat which, if 'burnt' by ice, will become dry and tasteless.

■ **Use up quickly** Strong flavours such as spices, chillies and salt become more pronounced when frozen, and the fibres of meat, fish and poultry begin to break down. So smoked bacon and salted butter both have a shorter freezer life than unsmoked bacon and unsalted butter.

■ **Don't throw it away** A common myth is that food kept frozen beyond its recommended time is unsafe to eat. If properly frozen, food will never go 'bad' in a freezer, but over time its texture and taste will deteriorate. Use over-date food immediately on thawing and cook it thoroughly.

■ **When you must throw it out** Cooked dishes that thaw during power cuts and breakdowns but still feel cold should be transferred to the refrigerator and used as quickly as possible. Fresh food or cooked dishes that have thawed and no longer feel cold must be discarded.

---

keep it simple

USE YOUR LOAF
If you live alone, a loaf of bread frequently turns mouldy before you have a chance to eat it all. For fresh bread daily and no waste, buy a whole loaf and freeze it. The slices can be toasted from frozen or you can defrost them quickly in a microwave if you fancy a sandwich.

LOVE FOOD HATE WASTE

Around one-third of the food we buy is thrown away, costing the average family an estimated £8 a week – or £420 a year. This not only dents your budget but is bad for the environment. Simple measures to reduce waste include using a portion planner (such as a spaghetti measurer or weighing scales) so you don't cook too much, careful meal planning and shopping, keeping a close eye on use-by dates and making good use of leftovers. The campaign website, **www.lovefoodhatewaste.com** provides great advice on eliminating waste. Visit the WI **www.thewi.org.uk** for lots of tasty recipes that use up leftovers.

■ **Refreeze safely** Bread, plain cakes and raw pastry can be refrozen safely even if they have thawed, but will quickly become stale on rethawing. Fruit should be cooked before being refrozen, and will then be useful for making purées, coulis or jam.

FOR CHEAP YEAR-ROUND PRODUCE
Freeze fruit and vegetables as soon after harvest as possible.
Freezing fruit Rinse fruit (except soft fruit); leave stoned fruit whole, or stone and chop. Skin or peel peaches, apricots, mangoes and nectarines and freeze them in a light syrup with lemon juice added to prevent them from discolouring in the freezer. Spread currants, blackberries, raspberries and gooseberries out on trays, open freeze until solid and then pack into freezer bags and seal.
Freezing vegetables Peel and chop vegetables as required, and blanch for 2–3 minutes in a basket immersed in a pan of boiling, unsalted water to preserve their colour, flavour and nutritional value. Once blanched, plunge the vegetables into iced water, then drain, dry, cool and pack for the freezer immediately. Blanching times vary according to the vegetables being frozen but, as a general rule, the younger and more tender the variety, the less time it needs.

CAN YOU FREEZE IT?

It is not always clear what will and will not freeze successfully and safely, as these lists of similar items demonstrate. When in doubt, freeze only items that have been cooked. Although freezing halts almost all spoilage, bacteria in meat, and some enzymes that can cause further deterioration in fruit and vegetables (for example, potatoes when frozen raw), are only destroyed by cooking at high temperatures.

FREEZES WELL	DON'T FREEZE
RASPBERRIES	WHOLE MELONS, BANANAS
SKIMMED, SEMI-SKIMMED MILK AND DOUBLE CREAM	FULL-FAT MILK AND COTTAGE CHEESE
EGGS (lightly stirred or separated)	EGGS (in their shell)
TOMATOES (for soups and sauces)	TOMATOES (for salad)
SPINACH	LETTUCE
POTATOES (fully cooked, or blanched in hot oil as chips)	UNCOOKED POTATOES
FRESH MEAT, POULTRY, FISH AND SHELLFISH	PREVIOUSLY FROZEN UNCOOKED MEAT, POULTRY, FISH & SHELLFISH (but once cooked they can be refrozen)
CREAMY DESSERTS (soufflés, mousses and cheesecakes set with gelatine)	FRUIT JELLIES, FRESH EGG CUSTARD

SUPERMARKET SAVERS

BUY MORE FOR LESS?

They are commonplace now, but it is still worth taking advantage of some supermarket best buys.
- Buy-one-get-one-free
- A larger quantity for the same price
- Trial sizes at low prices
- Jumbo or multipacks – but make sure you are buying something you know you'll use or will be able to finish by the 'best before' date.

BUT BEWARE

- Avoid the three-for-the-price-of-two offers unless you really need three of the item – if you want one of something, don't let the supermarket tempt you to double your bill.
- Make sure two-for-the-price-of-one deals aren't just a ploy for getting rid of old or unwanted stock.

For many people, the most convenient way to shop is to buy their groceries, fresh produce and household goods under one supermarket roof. If your store is open 24 hours, try shopping when the aisles are clear.

WATCH POINTS TRICKS OF THE TRADE

Once you walk through their doors, supermarkets want you to spend, spend, spend, so be aware of the tricks they employ to part you from your hard-earned cash.

- **Getting the runaround** The chiller cabinets containing basics, such as milk, juices and butter, are invariably at the back of the store, forcing you to walk past magazines, confectionery and countless other distractions to pick up a pint of milk. If you only need a couple of items, go to a store where you are familiar with the layout and leave with what you came in for.
- **On the edge** Essential foodstuffs are usually displayed around the perimeter with the more costly ready-meals and prepacked items on the centre aisles. The more you shop in the outer aisles, the more you'll save.
- **The eyes have it** Supermarkets have a trick of placing higher-priced goods at eye level. Look up, or down, to spot the regular-price items on the top or bottom shelf.
- **All change** Just when you've mastered the layout of your local store, everything is rearranged. Avoid being tempted by unfamiliar displays and ask a member of staff to tell you where you can now find the items you're looking for.
- **Wits' end** If you think the items displayed at the end of aisles are being sold at a reduction, think again. The eye-catching banners and signs are often masking excess stock selling at regular prices.

CHECK THE UNIT PRICE

When comparing price tags, look for the lettering saying 'price per 100ml' or 'price per kilo'. This is useful for fresh produce or any item where pack sizes vary. Larger packs are often, but not always, better value than smaller ones, so check the unit price to make sure. Here are some prices we found in one shop on one day.

	EXPENSIVE OPTION	BETTER OPTION
Dried pasta shapes	500g size @ £1.56p per kilo	3kg size @ £1.15 per kilo
Mature cheddar	sliced @ £9.04 per kilo	whole, unpackaged @ £7.50 per kilo
Vine tomatoes	packaged @ £5.63 per kilo	loose @ £1.99 per kilo
Baking potatoes	loose @ £1.38 per kilo	prepacked @ 96p per kilo
Sweet potatoes	packaged @ £1.68 per kilo	loose @ £1.28 per kilo
Coke	12 x 330ml cans @ 16.2p per 100ml	2-litre bottle @ 7.9p per 100ml

BEAT THE SUPERMARKET PLANNERS AT THEIR OWN GAME

Supermarkets are laid out the way they are for one very specific reason – to make you part with your money. They are carefully designed by experts who use every marketing trick in the book to slow you down, tempt you with impulse buys and inspire you with delicious-looking and smelling food – we've all been enticed by the bakery smells pumped to the front of the store or the gleaming, colourful piles of peaches and red peppers. Next time you shop, see how many tricks you can spot – and don't play their game.

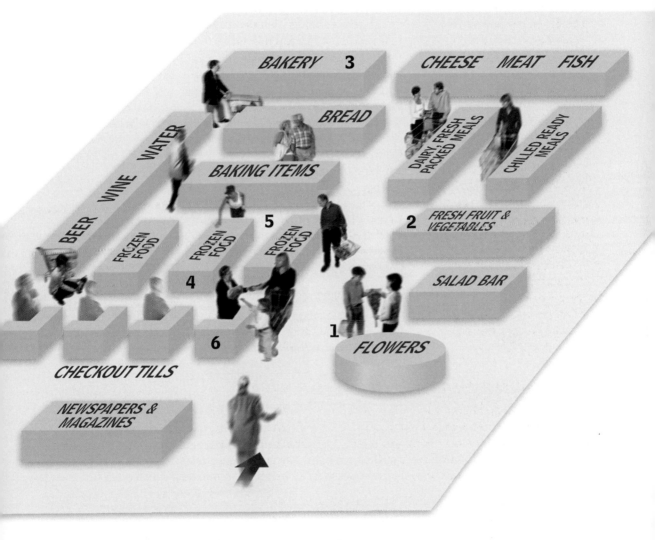

1 Flowers, fresh fruit and the salad bar entice you in and immediately gratify your senses. Wait to the end to see if you really need them.
2 Make smart decisions between prepacked and loose in the fruit and veg section. Don't be tempted by the salad dressing and dips, as often the most expensive are placed beside comparatively inexpensive produce.
3 If you have only come in for a loaf of bread, don't pick up a basket – you may become waylaid and end up filling it.

4 The chock-a-block end-of-aisle displays are made to look like a bargain dump bin, but don't be fooled – they may be full-price items.
5 Frozen food cabinets are positioned to block your path on the way to the checkout. Ready meals whet your appetite and are a convenience, but they're expensive.
6 Waiting in a queue can be boring, so don't even look at the checkout till items – they are impulse buys you don't need and they usually have a high mark-up.

OWN LABELS ADD VALUE

Own-label goods are rarely prominently displayed – they may be stacked on the top or bottom shelves. The packs may look less interesting but remember, dried and canned goods don't need fancy packaging.

Tasty copycats Own-label ranges are unlikely to be made by the market brand leader but by reputable companies that are often household names (even if the supermarkets are reluctant to reveal their source).

Significant savings Percentage savings on own label against the market leader are considerable, typically: 12 x 330ml cans of cola (50% less), pasta (50% less) and self-raising flour (40% less), (see table, right).

CUT OUT THE COUPONS

Flick through the supermarket's own magazine before you start shopping to judge whether you'll use the money-off coupons or offers inside. The coupons will be in the same place in the magazine each month. If you buy the products featured you could make substantial savings, in addition to recouping the price of the magazine.

Reap the rewards If there is a special offer on any food on your list, check for a coupon that will give you even more savings. Combining special offers with coupons will reward you the most.

Cross competition In order to entice you away from your regular supermarket, some stores will take their competitors' coupons. So even if you are shopping at Tesco, you may be able to use Sainsbury's vouchers.

BE A LOYAL CUSTOMER

Most supermarkets offer customers loyalty cards with which you earn points every time you shop. You won't save a fortune collecting the points – usually for every £1 you spend you earn one point and when your tally reaches 500 you're given a voucher worth £2.50 – but if you shop in the store anyway, why not?

Double up Look out for offers of bonus points on items you regularly use, but don't get carried away buying things you don't need.

Go further Vouchers can be used to reduce future shopping bills at the store but many cards also allow you to convert points into Air Miles (see *Good-value travel*, page 180).

STORE BRAND

Posh Nosh

DISCOUNT DEALS

Supermarkets usually have at least one basket or shelf of discounted stock somewhere in the store. Cans with torn lables, ends of lines, or packets or boxes with minor dents will all be heavily marked down – by as much as 60% or more – and are worth investigating. Buy cans without labels only if you're feeling adventurous. Never buy badly dented cans from any outlets as their seal may be damaged and the contents could be spoiled and highly dangerous.

SAVE MORE THAN 50% WITH SUPERMARKET OWN BRANDS

This table shows how much you can save by choosing a supermarket's own brand instead of nationally advertised brands. The savings vary but are always worth making. You could have saved £9.40 on this sample shopping list alone.

ITEM	SIZE	NAME BRAND PRICE	OWN BRAND PRICE	SAVED	SAVING
Low-fat spread	500g	£1.42	£1.08	£0.34	24%
Aluminium foil	300mm x 10m	£1.89	£1.16	£0.73	39%
Baked beans	4 x 420g cans	£2.18	£1.49	£0.69	32%
Tea bags	80 bags	£1.79	£1.29	£0.50	28%
Butter	250g	£1.21	£0.94	£0.27	22%
Cat food	12 x 100g	£3.37	£2.19	£1.18	35%
Cornflakes	500g	£1.69	£0.95	£0.74	44%
Fish fingers	300g	£1.79	£1.49	£0.30	17%
Dried mixed herbs	9g/14g	£1.08	£0.68	£0.40	37%
Herbal tea	40 bags	£1.62	£1.49	£0.13	8%
Instant coffee	100g	£2.65	£1.49	£1.06	40%
Olive oil	500ml	£3.39	£1.96	£1.43	42%
Lemonade	2 litres	£0.94	£0.44	£0.50	53%
Kitchen towels	double pack	£1.68	£1.09	£0.59	35%
Washing-up liquid	500ml	£0.98	£0.44	£0.54	55%

SELL-BY DATES

Health and safety laws govern sell-by dates and responsible retailers abide by strict procedures for clearing stock, but just how much importance should consumers attach to these dates? Fresh food, such as fish and meat bought loose by weight, has no sell-by date stamped on its wrapping so it is left to the customer's common sense to store it properly and use it up quickly. Loose fruit and vegetables have no sell-by date, but even before you purchase it's easy to spot yellowing leaves, mould, shoots or shrivelled skin, indicating the produce is past its best.

Shelf life To bag a bargain, head straight for the supermarket bin containing a selection of items just about to pass their sell-by dates. Take advantage of these offers if you know you can use the items quickly. Sugar, salt and dried pulses will keep for a long period, as will canned food.

When small is best Olive oil and vegetable oils keep well after the bottle has been opened, but walnut and other nut oils become rancid within two to three months. This is why nut oils are sold in small bottles. Dried fruit also stores well (should it become over-desiccated it can be revived by an overnight soak in a little brandy, tea or water) but nuts need to be used up, particularly pine kernels, which quickly lose their flavour.

SHOPPERS' CHOICE

THE DISCOUNTERS

Discount supermarkets such as Aldi, Netto and Lidl can often be a good place to grab a food bargain. They are not usually located in central areas, have basic fixtures and fittings and most only accept cash and debit cards. They also don't tend to carry the range of products that the major supermarkets do. But where you gain, if you buy goods as and when you see them is on real bargains with their weekly specials, which tend to change on Thursdays and Mondays. Recent good deals have included top-quality wines, fish and meat. They can also be ultra-cheap for basic branded products. You can sign up to receive weekly offers by email.

FARMERS' MARKETS

Farmers' markets are now found all over the country and are good for seasonal fruit and vegetables. They may be cheaper than a supermarket. Goods such as cheeses, bacon, honey, sausages and game from small local suppliers can be expensive due to their quality and flavour and the labour-intensive way they are produced. Farm shops are a good place to look for seasonal fruit and vegetables, as well as eggs and meat. Prices are highly competitive, especially if you buy in bulk, such as a large sack of potatoes or a whole lamb portioned and packed for the freezer.

Cash-and-carry outlets and discount warehouses are a popular way to shop in the US and are becoming increasingly popular over here. Check out how they can save you money.

JOIN THE CLUB

Cash-and-carry outlets sell primarily to a business clientele and the stock is purchased with them in mind. Members of certain professions can also shop there if they have authorisation, as can local community groups such as PTAs (Parent/Teacher Associations) and playgroups.

Makro UK To shop at Makro, businesses need to supply documents such as a copy of their VAT registration, copies of invoices over £50 and personal identification of the proposed cardholder before a trade card is issued.

Costco Wholesale This is a member-only cash-and-carry, offering trade membership for companies at an annual fee of £20 plus VAT, which includes a spouse card. Membership is also available to individuals over the age of 18 who currently work in or are retired from a variety of professions, including finance, local government, education, police, civil service, health service and the legal profession. The annual fee is £25 and, again, proof of identity is required such as employee ID card, payslip or certificate of professional qualification, plus a bank statement or current utility bill.

Buying in bulk Cash-and-carry stores are mainly designed for large-scale purchases. Tomato ketchup will be sold in a pack of two of the largest size bottles and fizzy drinks in packs of six 2-litre bottles. The savings are significant but you have to be able to store goods for use over several weeks, and the ranges are limited and not in constant supply. Cash-and-carry outlets stock some regular items, but you may find that you visit for a specific type of food and it isn't in stock. If you can afford to buy in bulk, the meat, fish and delicatessen food is of high quality.

Club together Ask a neighbour who is a member of a cash-and-carry to consider buying in bulk for a group of local friends, who could then all take advantage of discounts of up to 30% on many everyday items.

TOP TIPS GET ONLINE

If you buy bulky items, such as bottled water, pet food, potatoes, soft drinks, baked beans, kitchen rolls or jumbo bags of snacks, it's worth thinking about shopping online.

■ **Compare prices** Browse retailers' websites to compare prices and services and then shop when it suits you. Most large online websites are geared to people's routines and will deliver at a time when you can be there to receive the goods.

■ **Avoid temptation** If you shop online, you're less likely to be tempted to impulse buy. Although many retailers charge a delivery fee, you'll almost certainly still save money when the cost is compared to visiting a supermarket.

■ **It pays to stay loyal** Once you've signed up, stores will be keen to keep you loyal. Watch out for special online prices, mail shots offering discounts and free delivery.

WHERE TO SHOP ONLINE

Most sites offer delivery over a wide area, but enter your postcode before ordering to check you're covered, especially if you live in a remote area. To make sure you are getting the best value for money, use a price comparison website such as **www.mysupermarket.co.uk** or **www.trollydolly.co.uk** – just select the type of goods you are interested in and a list of supermarkets and current prices appears.

■ **www.tesco.com** ✉ It costs £4.85 for next-day delivery or £6.85 for a two-hour delivery slot, which include the cost of a personal shopper to select goods from shelves.

■ **www.asda.com** ✉ The number of stores offering home delivery is increasing, and costs between £4–£5. You can book a two-hour delivery slot up to three weeks in advance and add items up to 5pm on the day before delivery.

■ **www.waitrose.com** ✉ WaitroseDeliver operates in selected areas – just enter your postcode to check which services are available. The minimum order is £50 and the delivery charge is £3 for instore collection or £5 for home delivery.

■ **www.ocado.com** ✉ A company working in partnership with Waitrose, Ocado offers a wide range of branded goods as well as the goods that appear in Waitrose stores. There are one-hour delivery slots and free delivery over £75.

■ **www.sainsburys.co.uk** ✉ Type in your postcode to check they deliver in your area. The delivery charge ranges from £3.50–£6.50, although is free on all orders over £100. A service charge of £6 applies on all orders below £40.

■ **www.marksandspencer.com** ✉ Delivery is limited to certain items, including clothing, cases of wine, hampers and homeware. Delivery starts at £3.50 and is free on certain items – including clothing – if you spend more than £30.

CASE STUDY

STRAWBERRY FAIR

When Liz Saunders was planning a summer lunch for her 50th birthday party, she wanted to provide strawberries for dessert for her 70 guests. First she weighed a single portion, then multiplied it to work out that she needed 8 kilos (17lb) for the party.

As a member of Costco, she made this her first stop. The packs of strawberries there contained eight large, identical fruits. There was no weight on the pack, so she didn't know how many to buy and suspected that these perfect specimens would not be especially tasty. Next she checked her local supermarket, where strawberries were on special offer at £1.75 a punnet. The small print indicated this to be £4.36 a kilo but she could not be sure that the offer would be available on the day of the party. At the local farm shop, where there were also pick-your-own fields, the price was £3.30 a kilo, and

it was possible to order exactly what she wanted. This was much nearer to her home than Costco and cheaper than Sainsbury's. Being farm-fresh, the produce was delicious and she was also supporting a local supplier.

MEALS ON A BUDGET

Cheap meals can be both delicious and nutritious. You just need to know what's value for money and how to make the most of everything to hand.

DIY ALTERNATIVES

Buying everyday ingredients in larger quantities and preparing your own dishes at home is always less expensive than pre-packaged smaller portions. Mix and match your favourite ingredients for foods you eat regularly – and save up to 50% on the cost of ready-made items.

Salad dressings Make up a basic vinaigrette with three parts olive oil to one part wine vinegar, then add your own flavours, such as mustard, honey, sun-dried tomato paste, pesto, balsamic vinegar, light soy sauce or chopped herbs. Cut the cost further by replacing half the olive oil with a cheaper oil such as sunflower.

Muesli Buy large bags of oats and wheat flakes from health food shops and add a selection of nuts and dried fruits.

Couscous Avoid packs with added flavourings, which can cost up to six times more than plain couscous. Buy your couscous unflavoured and add your own extras.

Tinned tuna A 400g can of plain tuna in oil or brine will save you around 50% on the cost of a smaller tin with added flavourings. Buy the larger tin and use in weekday family bakes and healthy main-meal salads.

TOP TIPS SPREAD THE COST

Make expensive meat and fish go further by mixing them with cheaper ingredients.

■ **Full of beans** Try replacing half the quantity of minced beef in a shepherd's pie with canned borlotti, black-eye or haricot beans.

■ **Veggie-value** Increase the quantity of vegetables and cut back on the chicken or prawns in a stir-fry, or make a vegetable-only version.

■ **Sensible substitution** Tofu is high in protein but only about half the price of good-quality braising steak. It absorbs the flavours of the food it is cooked with, so make a hearty casserole using half cubed beef and half cubed tofu.

■ **Curry flavour** Replace half the lamb in your favourite curry recipe with diced vegetables such as cauliflower, carrots and sweet or ordinary potatoes.

■ **Satisfying soups** Inexpensive green and brown lentils keep their shape when cooked. Simmer them in a well-flavoured stock, with chunks of gammon and baby onions.

LESSONS IN LEFTOVERS

Think of all the bread you casually throw away as throwing money in the bin. You wouldn't dream of doing that, so learn to transform leftovers into tasty bites and snacks.

Melba toast Remove the crusts, toast lightly under the grill on each side and then cut each slice in half horizontally. Return to the grill and toast until the slices curl. Cool, store in an air-tight container and serve with pâtés.

Rescue a disaster

Most people have experienced a bad cooking moment and probably thrown the results out in disgust. Being budget-wise means knowing what to do in a culinary emergency.

■ Heavy-handed with the salt when boiling vegetables or making soup or a casserole? Add a couple of peeled, raw potatoes or drain off half the liquid and replace with fresh water or stock.

■ Is your curry making your eyes water? Stir in some natural yoghurt to cool it down and serve as soon as it's ready. Longer cooking encourages spicy flavours to develop.

SMART MOVES

Breadcrumbs Make breadcrumbs using a food processor. Freeze in plastic bags, or spread out and leave until dry and crisp, turning over occasionally. Once dry, store the crumbs in a screw-top jar. The remnants at the bottom of your biscuit barrel are another good source of tasty crumbs. Crush to an even crumble with a wooden spoon and use as a biscuit base for desserts.

Croutons Cut a slice of toast into small squares and serve with soup or on salads.

Desserts Make a bread-and-butter pudding, summer pudding or an apple charlotte.

Bread bites Cut into squares, or slices if French bread, toast and spread with pesto, sun-dried tomato paste or simply drizzle with olive oil. Top with slices of mozzarella, goat's cheese, olives, cherry tomato halves, anchovies or other ingredients and serve as a snack.

GREAT-VALUE INGREDIENTS

Fortunately, the least expensive ingredients often turn out to be the most healthy, a bonus when it comes to making nutritious family meals (see recipes on page 28).

Tinned fish Sardines, mackerel and pilchards make tasty patés, and tuna is a favourite stand-by for casseroles; all can cost less than 80p a tin. The slightly more expensive salmon and mussels still make an economical treat.

Pulses At under 50p a tin, lentils, peas and beans are an inexpensive mainstay for vegetarian dishes. Dried pulses work out even cheaper, but the long cooking that some of them require adds to their cost.

Turkey cuts Because it is so low in fat, turkey is becoming more popular. The meat-to-bone ratio is quite high, so the price of fresh turkey compares favourably with chicken.

RESOURCES

RECIPE OF THE DAY
■ Find inspiration for your cooking by checking the recipes for budget meals on these websites:
www.sainsbury.co.uk/food/
www.netmums.com/food/
www.goodtoknow.co.uk/
www.recipes4us.co.uk
■ The Vegetarian Society offers a good selection of vegetarian recipes
www.vegsoc.org/cordonvert/ recipes 0161 925 2000 ✉.
Budget vegetarian recipes can be found at:
www.mealsonabudget.co.uk/
www.frugal.org.uk/recipes
http://allrecipes.co.uk/

TUNA FISH CAKES

COST FOR EACH PERSON: 80P
SERVES 4

450g mashed potato
400g canned tuna in brine, drained
2 tablespoons tomato ketchup
6 spring onions, finely chopped
1 teaspoon dried mixed herbs
1 egg, beaten
salt and pepper
85g dry breadcrumbs
oil for frying or grilling

1 In a bowl, mix together the potato, tuna, ketchup, onions, herbs and beaten egg. Season and divide the mixture into eight equal portions. Shape each portion into round flat cakes and coat with the breadcrumbs.
2 Chill for 30 minutes to firm up the cakes and then shallow fry for 10 minutes until golden on both sides.
3 Alternatively, brush the cakes with a little oil and grill. Serve with a green vegetable or salad.

POTATO AND SAUSAGE FRITTATA

COST FOR EACH PERSON: 60P
SERVES 4

450g potatoes, peeled and cut
   into small chunks
4 large sausages
2 tablespoons oil
6 large eggs
salt and pepper

1 Cook the potatoes until just tender and then drain.
2 While the potatoes are cooking, grill the sausages until cooked. Cut into bite-size pieces.
3 Heat the oil in a large frying pan and fry the potatoes until lightly browned. Add the sausages and stir well to mix with the potatoes.
4 Beat the eggs, season and pour into the pan. Cook until the eggs set on the bottom, then put under a hot grill to set the top.

FEED A FAMILY FOR UNDER £5

VEGGIE BEAN SOUP

COST FOR EACH PERSON: 75P
SERVES 6

2 tablespoons oil
2 leeks, thinly sliced
200g carrots, finely chopped
250g swede, peeled and cubed
600ml tomato juice
600ml vegetable stock
230g can chopped tomatoes
400g can kidney beans, drained
400g cannellini beans, drained
salt and pepper

1 Heat the oil in a large pan. Add the leeks, carrots and swede, cover the pan and cook over a low heat for 10 minutes, stirring occasionally.
2 Add the tomato juice, stock and tomatoes and bring to a simmer. Cover the pan and cook for 20 minutes or until the vegetables are tender.
3 Add the beans, season and simmer for a further 10 minutes. Serve with warm crusty bread.

CHEESE, BACON AND BEAN PIE

COST FOR EACH PERSON: £1.18
SERVES 4

700g potatoes, peeled
    and cut into small chunks
1 tablespoon oil
420g gammon steaks,
    cut into bite-sized pieces
1 leek, thinly sliced
100g mushrooms, quartered
2 x 420g cans baked beans
    in tomato sauce
2 tablespoons warm milk
salt and pepper
75g Edam cheese, grated

1 Cook the potatoes in a pan of boiling water until tender.
2 Meanwhile heat the oil in a frying pan and fry the cut gammon for 5 minutes. Drain any excess liquid from the pan, add the leek and mushrooms and fry for a further
5 minutes. Stir in the baked beans and spoon into an ovenproof dish.
3 Drain and mash the potatoes with the milk, seasoning and cheese. Spoon the potato mixture over the gammon mix and spread out in an even layer.
4 Preheat the oven to 190°C/375°F/gas mark 5 and bake the pie for 30 minutes until golden brown. Serve with peas or sweetcorn.

MASALA VEGETABLES

COST FOR EACH PERSON: 85p
SERVES 4

2 tablespoons oil
1 large onion, peeled and chopped
3 carrots, chopped
450g pumpkin or squash, peeled and cut
    into chunks
1 red pepper, deseeded and chopped
2 courgettes, cut into chunks
2 tablespoons curry paste
400g canned chopped tomatoes
    with chilli
300ml vegetable stock
2 teaspoons cornflour
150g natural yoghurt

1 Heat the oil in a large pan. Add the onion and carrots and fry for 5 minutes. Add the squash, red pepper and courgettes and fry for a further 5 minutes, stirring occasionally.
2 Stir in the curry paste, tomatoes and stock, bring to a simmer, cover and cook for 15 minutes or until the vegetables are just tender.
3 Mix the cornflour with the yoghurt and stir into the pan. Simmer over a low heat for 5 minutes. Serve with rice.

GOURMET GOODIES

If you enjoy the good things in life but want to avoid paying top prices, it's worth finding suppliers who give substantial discounts, and timing your shopping for seasonal savings.

LUXURY CHOCOLATES AT SWEET PRICES

By keeping an eye on specialist chocolate retailers and shopping at the right places, you can bag a bargain. In particular, look out for sales offers just after Christmas, Easter and Valentine's Day.

Discounts online On the web, the Chocolate Trading Company **www.chocolatetradingco.com** ✉ and Hotel Chocolat **www.hotelchocolat.co.uk** or 08444 933 933 ✉ both offer discounted and sale items for stock that they want to clear quickly, which can be reduced by nearly 40%.

For true connoisseurs Mail-order chocolate clubs can also be worth joining if you are a dedicated chocolate lover who already spends a lot on your favourite indulgence. Hotel Chocolat's Chocolate Tasting Club offers an introductory selection at £9.95, then a monthly selection at £16.95 if you join. Or apply for free membership of the highly regarded Chocolate Society **www.chocolate.co.uk** or 0845 230 8868 ✉ for a 10% discount on all online purchases, together with access to exclusive promotions.

LOWER THE COST OF QUALITY COFFEE

Your local supermarket offers reasonable-quality coffee for around £2 to £2.50 for 225g (8oz), but for an unusual or higher-grade product try a specialist supplier and get together with coffee-loving friends for bulk discounts.

Free delivery For an online supplier who offers quality products and free delivery on all orders, try Red Monkey Coffee **www.redmonkeycoffee.com** or 0870 207 4831 ✉.

Wholesale discounts Although you can make savings at most coffee suppliers through mail-order or the web, Discount Coffee **www.discountcoffee.co.uk** or 0845 225 5000 ✉ offers exceptional value. There is no delivery charge on orders over £50 (delivery on smaller orders starts at £2), and up to 60% off wholesale prices for large orders – such as cases of 50 sachets of ground coffee or 4kg–6kg (10lb–14lb) of beans. The emphasis is on bulk buys but they also have special offers on smaller orders.

Limit storage time Although you will save by buying in bulk, it isn't sensible to buy more freshly roasted coffee than you will use in under a fortnight as it will lose its flavour.

GET VALUE ON GOURMET MEAT AND GAME

For top-quality meat and game it's hard to beat Scottish butcher Donald Russell **www.donaldrusselldirect.com** or 01467 629666 ✉. Prices reflect the high standard but watch out for adverts for seasonal bargains and Value Boxes (such as six fillet steaks for £34 – reduced from £63) or try the butcher's line for daily offers. Delivery is free on orders over £80. Find producers of organic and free-range meat on **www.alotoforganics.co.uk** ✉ and **www.foodfirst.co.uk** ✉.

Seasonal prices Wait to buy game until the shooting season is well under way to make big savings, as prices are higher at the beginning of the season. The season for grouse runs from August 12 to December 10; for duck (inland) from September 1 to January 31; for partridge from September 1 to February 1; and, for pheasant from October 1 to February 1. In a good year you can save even more by waiting until the end of the season when there is a glut and by buying directly from a local game dealer. For details of game dealers near you visit the British Association for Shooting and Conservation's Game's On website **www.basc.org.uk/content/games_on_test** ✉. You will tend to pay less for a large (usually tougher) bird than a young one.

SAVINGS ON SUPERIOR SEAFOOD

Seafood enthusiasts can benefit from specialist online or mail-order suppliers who offer value on larger orders.

Long-distance savings Try a mail-order company such as The Fish Society **www.thefishsociety.co.uk** or 0800 279 3474 ✉, which supplies over 200 kinds of frozen fish and seafood. Their stock is of high quality and environmentally friendly, and their special deals offer good value. A supplier of similarly high quality is Martin's Seafresh **www.martins-seafresh.co.uk** or 0800 0272066 ✉. This Cornwall-based company offers freshly caught seafood and will post anywhere in the UK. Postage is £7.95 (minimum order £25), and regular customers are entitled to discounts.

Buy in season Even if you are buying fresh fish in smaller quantities from a local supplier, you can still make savings by avoiding buying just before or after the low season in spring, when prices are higher. Crab and lobster are more expensive from January to March and mussels from April to August, but the price for prawns should be stable all year round.

CHANNEL HOP FOR CUT-PRICE CHEESE

You can buy a wide variety of high-quality cheeses by mail-order from companies such as House of Cheese **www.houseofcheese.co.uk** or 01666 502865 ✉, but for the best value make the most of your trips abroad. Prices can be an amazing 75% lower in France. For more on bargains abroad, see page 34.

FAIR TRADE BARGAINS

Many Fair Trade foods are worth buying for their gourmet qualities alone, and their prices are reasonable, too. Highly recommended are Divine chocolate bars from Oxfam, Green & Black's Organic Cocoa and Fair Trade mangoes, both available from Waitrose and other supermarkets, and Traidcraft organic Seville marmalade, available online at **www.traidcraftshop.co.uk** ✉.

GIFT HAMPERS

For special occasions or impressive gifts that don't cost the earth, you can't go wrong with a hamper from one of Britain's top suppliers. Prices for ready-made hampers can be well over £100 a person, but you can order good-quality, reasonably priced hampers from Freshampers (**www.freshampers.com** or 01962 773771 ✉). Hampers start at £16.95 a person (minimum order is for four people), plus delivery from £10. (Orders are restricted to within 100 miles of Winchester.) You can reuse the packaging and the plastic cutlery, which can also be recycled. To order a hamper nationwide, contact Deli Rosslyn (**www.delirosslyn.co.uk** or 020 7794 9210 ✉), whose picnic hampers start at £21 a person.

GOOD DEALS ON WINE AND SPIRITS

Wine sales have grown rapidly in the past 20 years, but as few of us are connoisseurs, how do we decide which bottle to select from the crowded shelves?

KNOWLEDGE IS BUYING POWER

Don't assume that a high price necessarily indicates high quality. Although this is often true, some wines command higher prices than others for historic reasons or because of trends. If you learn about wine, you will be in a better position to spot the best-value vintages. Consider taking a course or setting up a wine club with friends or colleagues. You can arrange regular tastings at which everyone brings a bottle of a particular type of wine.

CHEAPEST ISN'T BEST VALUE

If supermarkets have a wine on special offer at a knockdown price, it's worth giving it a try. However, with UK tax at more than £1 a bottle regardless of the quality of the wine, plus the cost of making and shipping it and the bottle itself, a wine costing around £2.99 is likely to be significantly inferior to one at £5, where a higher proportion of the cost relates to the wine itself.

SUPERMARKET WINNERS

In a 2003 *Which?* survey, Tesco's non-vintage Premier Cru Champagne triumphed over a variety of other champagnes, both supermarket brands and non-branded varieties, some of which cost up to £5 a bottle more. So don't be disparaging about own-label brands on any type of wine; due to their desire to appeal to more upmarket customers and to their huge buying clout, own brand is often cheapest – and best.

HALF-PRICE BIN ENDS

These are odd bottles left over from a particular vintage or producer that the off-licence wants to shift. There are usually fine wines that can be picked up at bargain prices.

COMPARE PRICES OF WINE, BEER AND SPIRITS

Supermarket prices are generally better than those in off-licences, but keep an eye out for special promotions and bargains. Warehouse prices are the most competitive, and by choosing carefully you can save at least 20% on every bottle of wine you buy.

	OFF–LICENCE	SUPERMARKET	WAREHOUSE*
HARDYS STAMP CHARDONNAY SEMILLON 75cl	£7.49	£6.19	£6.19
CAMPO VIEJO CRIANZA (RIOJA) 75cl	£9.49	£6.97	£5.49
YOUNGS SPECIAL BITTER 500ml	£1.99	£1.69	£1.75
BOMBAY SAPPHIRE GIN 70cl	£17.99	£15.99	£16.42
DOW'S LATE BOTTLED VINTAGE PORT 75cl	£10.49	£11.99	£9.99

* Warehouse wine prices are for bottles bought by the case, not individually.
UK prices correct at time of publication

WAREHOUSE DEALS

Wine warehouses, such as Majestic, offer some great deals. They sell by the case of 12 bottles, although these do not all have to be the same type of wine. Check **www.majestic.co.uk** ✉ to find the location of their stores or order online.

LET'S PARTY

Investigate good deals, such as 'wine of the month' or '11 bottles for the price of 12' at supermarkets.
Sale or return To calculate how much wine to buy, bear in mind that a normal 75cl bottle will give six glasses of still wine and eight to ten glasses of champagne or sparkling wine. Arrange to return unopened bottles to your supplier.
Free glasses Wine shops normally lend glasses and offer a delivery service free of charge if you buy wine from them.

DRINK NOW NOT LATER

Most table wines sold in supermarkets and off-licences are designed to be drunk within one to two years rather than laid down. Store wines stoppered with corks on their sides or the corks will dry out, let in air and spoil the wine.

INVESTING FOR THE FUTURE

If you are lucky enough to get your hands on wines suitable for laying down, you can look forward to a treat later.
Conditions apply To ensure your wine is drinkable, let alone improved by laying down, you must have a suitable cellar or well-insulated area – an unsuitable environment will ruin it. Be prepared to store bottles for decades.
Which wines? Suitable wines include top-quality claret and vintage champagne or port – usually obtainable from a specialist auction house by the case, rather than from the local supermarket. If you are looking for wines to buy as gifts that can be enjoyed now or laid down, visit **www.wine2laydown.com** ✉.

AVOID WASTING LEFTOVER WINE

Pour leftover wine into a smaller bottle and seal with a tight-fitting cork. Or use a pump that removes the air from a half-finished bottle so the wine returns to its unopened state.

LET IT BREATHE

You can improve an inexpensive bottle of red wine by opening it two or three hours before drinking.

RESOURCES

BUYING ONLINE
www.laithwaites.co.uk
0845 194 7711 ✉
everywine.co.uk
0800 072 0011 ✉
www.virginwines.com
0870 164 9593 ✉
www.uk.chateauonline.com
0800 169 2736 ✉

WINE CLUBS
http://www.decanter.com/
specials/68176.html ✉
www.sundaytimeswineclub.
co.uk/ ✉

WINE COURSES
■ For an eight-week evening introductory course in Aberdeen, Birmingham, Haywards Heath (Sussex), Manchester and London (London £210, elsewhere £199) visit **www.wine-education-service.co.uk** ✉.
■ For courses from the Wine & Spirit Education Trust, call 020 7089 3800 or try **www.wset.co.uk** ✉.
■ Try the free online course at **www.freewine course.com/** ✉.

ONLINE GUIDES
■ For wines, log on to **www.wineanorak.com/**
■ For Scotch whisky, **www.scotchwhisky.net** ✉.

BEST BUYS ABROAD

Discovering new foods and tastes is one of the highlights of travelling overseas. If you find local produce, or even authentic cooking equipment, that you particularly like, buy some to bring home. You can almost guarantee the price will be less than that of the same items for sale in the UK.

WHERE TO SHOP AND WHAT TO BUY

Follow locals to the food shops, off-licences and market stalls they patronise and so avoid buying obviously overpriced items aimed at tourists.

France Visit French markets for a tempting choice of cheese, honey and olive oil from the producers. Jars of mustard, cooking chocolate and strings of garlic are also good buys. Look out, too, for local produce, such as walnut oil from the Charente region. Stock up on table wine, local aperitifs and *digestifs*, and sweet muscat fortified wines.

Belgium Bring back chocolate – the quality is high and prices can be 60% lower than at home.

Italy Save money on food such as salami, Parmesan, Parma ham, panforte, sun-dried tomatoes, single-estate olive oils, aged balsamic vinegar, dried porcini mushrooms and perhaps a pasta maker. Take home wine, aperitifs (such as Campari and Limoncello), and even an espresso coffee maker.

Spain Pick up saffron, a paella pan, Pata Negra dried ham, dulce pimenton (smoked paprika), turron (nougat), olives, manchego cheese, sugared almonds and sherry at a fraction of the price they are in supermarkets in Britain.

Asia Ordinary Chinese or Indian teas will taste fresher than anything bought back home. Stock up on unusual whole and ground spices from local markets and bottled condiments that can be difficult or expensive to obtain in Britain, such as fish sauce, chilli paste and oyster sauce. You can find decorative and inexpensive china and wooden serving bowls and kitchen utensils, such as wooden steamers and strainers.

Middle East and North Africa Buy whole and ground spices from local markets, herbal, floral and fruit teas, honey, olives, Turkish delight, whole nuts in honey, dried fruits, and tagine dishes and Greek or Turkish coffee pots.

BUY YOUR DRINK ABROAD

Take advantage of trips abroad to stock up your wine cellar and buy cheaper spirits and fortified wines. If you don't have time for a vineyard visit, a trip to the local supermarket can yield bargains.

Direct from the vineyard If you're spending several days in a region, visit different vineyards and sample local wines in restaurants, noting what you like. On the last day, go back to your favourites to stock up. Make sure you can keep the temperature down on the way home – heat spoils wine.

From the supermarket Local wines will be the best buys, so try a variety during your stay, including aperitifs and *digestifs*. Avoid the cheapest as something quite palatable in the sun will seem to have lost its appeal when drunk back in Britain. Go for a mid-range wine abroad and you will have

RESOURCES

FOREIGN FIELDS

■ Find more information on the type of food you are allowed to bring back to Britain from abroad on the Food Standards Agency's website at **www.food.gov.uk** ✉.

■ For general advice, information on ferries and price guides on food bargains abroad (mainly France) try **www.day-tripper.net** ✉.

■ To arrange a vineyard visit, contact Arblaster & Clarke at their website **www.winetours.co.uk** or phone 01730 263111 ✉.

BRING IT HOME FOR LESS

Be sure to get the best value in the countries you are visiting by knowing what food and drink to bring home. The chart below shows some examples of good buys in commonly visited destinations – see what you can find! The prices in the purple-shaded bars are the sterling equivalent of what you would pay for the goods abroad and the red-coloured bars give the price of similar goods in Britain.

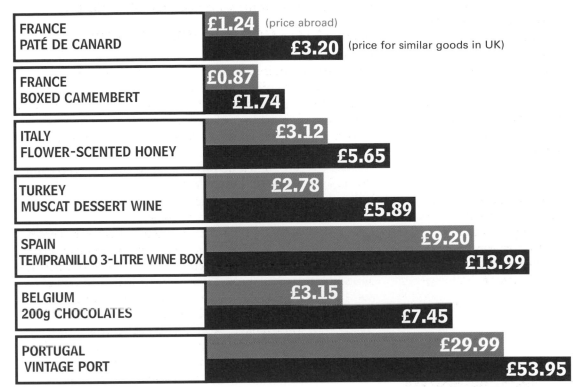

	Price abroad	Price for similar goods in UK
FRANCE PATÉ DE CANARD	£1.24	£3.20
FRANCE BOXED CAMEMBERT	£0.87	£1.74
ITALY FLOWER-SCENTED HONEY	£3.12	£5.65
TURKEY MUSCAT DESSERT WINE	£2.78	£5.89
SPAIN TEMPRANILLO 3-LITRE WINE BOX	£9.20	£13.99
BELGIUM 200g CHOCOLATES	£3.15	£7.45
PORTUGAL VINTAGE PORT	£29.99	£53.95

brought home a bargain. In France, for example, a bottle of good Haut-Médoc wine can cost under £3.

Spirit savings European supermarkets sell spirits at much lower prices than in the UK due to the very low French excise duties. It is easy to save 30% on whisky and Cognac – even more if you buy the larger 1 litre bottles. Much of the French own-brand drink to good value, too.

KNOW YOUR IMPORT RESTRICTIONS

Don't go to the trouble of shopping, packing and carrying only to find you have bought too much, or the wrong things.

Alcohol limits Travellers within the EU can bring back, duty free, up to 90 litres of wine and 10 litres of spirits, provided the alcohol is not for resale (the limits are 4 litres and 1 litre from outside the EU). See the Customs and Excise website at **www.hmce.gov.uk** ✉ for up-to-date information on imports from EU and non-EU countries or phone the National Advice Service on 0845 010 9000.

Other restrictions Always check what you can take out and bring in. Recent epidemics in Britain have resulted in restrictions on the importation of meat and milk products from many parts of the world. You can bring back any food on sale in an EU country, but nothing of animal origin from non-EU countries.

KITCHEN SENSE

A well-equipped kitchen needn't break the bank. Simply decide exactly what equipment you need and then invest well, buying the best quality you can afford.

TOP TIPS BUY VALUE-FOR-MONEY PANS

A set of three or four top-quality saucepans plus a robust frying pan will save you money in the long run, as cheap pans wear out quickly and need replacing.

■ **Hob matters** The type of pan you need depends on your hob – be particularly careful to select the right pans if you have an induction hob as these require pans to have a magnetic core, so only cast iron and enamel-coated steel pans are suitable. See the Cookware Buying Guide at **www.johnlewis.com/Magazine/GuideDepartments.aspx** ✉ for the correct pan for your hob.

■ **Choose the right pans** Copper pans are highly regarded as the best conductors of heat, but they are expensive and require a lot of maintenance. Stainless steel pans are cheaper and easier to care for. The steel should have a chrome/nickel content of at least 18/10. Brands to look out for are Stellar (around £110 for a 5-piece set including a frying pan, **www.hartsofstur.com**, 0800 371 355 ✉) and Fissler (around £450 for a 5-piece Pro set, **www.fisslercookware.co.uk**, 0845 6800 258 ✉). Aluminium pans are flimsier but less susceptible to wear and tear if coated. Hard anodised pans are made from treated aluminium but because the material is often coated, the surface is easily damaged. Cast iron is heavy but suited to long, slow cooking on an Aga-type range. Enamel-coated steel is also heavy, but more versatile.

■ **Sets are better value** You can save up to 50% by buying entire sets rather than individual components. Check out the twice-yearly sales in department stores when top manufacturers sell boxed sets at knockdown prices.

CUTTING THE COST OF KNIVES

A set of good kitchen knives is a once-in-a-lifetime investment, and they are not cheap. To minimise the cost, know how to judge quality and shop around for a bargain.

Reliable makes A good-quality knife will be made in one piece with the metal going right the way down the handle, which should be securely fixed. Brands that are noted for their quality include Sabatier (around £33 for a carving knife), Henckels and Global (from £64 and £75 for a carving knife), (**www.cooks-knives.co.uk** 01877 332703 ✉). However, Kitchen Devil knives were commended by *Which?* as the 'best value for money buy'; their carving knife is around £25, from hardware and kitchenware stores.

Mail order with caution You can find good mail-order deals but make sure you can test the feel of the knife in your hand and send it back if it's not right. Culinaire on 01293 550563 or **www.kitchenknivesdirect.co.uk** ✉ offers good deals on quality makes, including free postage and packing. It is worth spending money on a recommended brand as the knives will serve you well and may never need replacing.

ECONOMICAL STARTER PACKS

For people equipping their first kitchen, starter packs can be a good way to provide the basic tools and, like most bulk buys, can be good value for money. Just don't expect them to last for ever – they will eventually need to be replaced. But by then their owners should have learned how to care for their kitchenware and can buy more expensive, higher-quality products. You can buy a set that includes kitchen knives, three saucepans and a frying pan plus other utensils for £17 from Tesco Direct **http://direct.tesco.com** ✉ or an entire 45-piece kitchen starter set with chopping board, storage set and more for £39.99 from Argos at 0845 640 2020 **www.argos.co.uk** ✉. Students can often buy kitchen starter packs through their university Accommodation Office.

SAVING WHILE COOKING

Saving fuel doesn't just make financial sense, it also helps the environment by conserving precious energy. Make full use of your oven by cooking several dishes at the same time and maximise hob heat by placing steamers over pans.

OIL RESOURCES

Leave vegetable oil that has been used for deep-frying to cool completely before straining it through a coffee filter or fine sieve and pouring it back into a bottle for recycled oil. If it was previously used at a high enough temperature, it won't have picked up food flavours and so can be used again. Oil used for frying fish should be kept separate.

JUST A CUPPA

When making tea, boil only the water you need instead of filling the electric kettle. According to the Energy Saving Trust, if we all did this we'd save enough electricity to power almost all our street lights.

PUT A LID ON IT

Speed up cooking time by covering pans and casseroles with a tight-fitting lid. To make a loose lid tighter, put a sheet of foil under it.

A COLD START

If a roast or casserole needs to cook for more than an hour, start it in a cold oven and cook for the prescribed time. Reserve preheating for baking only.

SAUCEPAN SAVVY

Ensure the base of your pan covers the electric or gas ring so heat cannot escape up the sides of the pan.

ON THE BOIL

The cheapest and fastest way to bring water to the boil for cooking in a saucepan is to use your electric kettle.

DOUBLE UP

Steam fast-cooking vegetables in a basket over a pan in which you are boiling slower-cooking ones, such as potatoes, to save turning on a second ring.

PILE ON THE PRESSURE

Pressure cookers reduce cooking time by almost two-thirds. They are better than microwaves for tenderising tough cuts of meat and for cooking large quantities.

SLASH OVEN COSTS

Heating in the oven costs the same whether you're cooking two portions or ten. Maximise oven heat by cooking several dishes at the same time, especially cheaper cuts of meat that require long, slow cooking. Remove large joints and whole chickens or turkeys from the fridge an hour or so before cooking so they come to room temperature. If the centre of the meat is very cold, the joint will take longer to cook.

Looking good

The idea that you need plenty of money to look good is an outdated concept. There are even advantages to a small budget: limitations stretch the imagination and force you to think hard about how much you really want everything you buy.

MAKING THE MOST OF YOUR WARDROBE

Success with today's fashion relies more on individual style than a big bank balance. And style isn't about rushing out to buy a new season's look. A different approach to what you already own can be just as effective as a shopping spree – and more satisfying.

MAKE REALISTIC CHOICES

Common sense should be your first guideline. Before buying anything new, think about your lifestyle and select only items you'll wear often enough to justify their purchase. Make sure any additions will complement what you already own, choosing fabrics and styles that are easy to wear and maintain for maximum versatility.

Avoid dry cleaning As a rule, try not to choose fabrics that need dry cleaning. This is especially true of garments that will need frequent cleaning – you'll pay from around £2.50 upwards each time you need to get a shirt cleaned.

Linen lasts Linen is more resistant to deterioration when exposed to sunlight and high temperatures than cotton, but buy a linen blend if you like your clothes crease-free.

Buy denim for value Denim is one of the most comfortable and cheapest materials. It gives you lots of wear for your money – and grows in style with age.

Hard-working luxury Silk may be luxurious but it is also durable and hard-wearing. It keeps you cool in summer and, because it is breathable and light, keeps you warm in winter – particularly if layered with other clothing.

Artificial fabrics have their place Fabrics such as viscose are hard-wearing and can be rolled for ease of packing without creasing. More recent materials like Tencel® have many of the advantages of natural materials – such as comfort, drape and strength – but with added ease of care and durability.

TOP TIPS BUILDING BLOCKS TO STYLE

A good clearout lets you start to acquire the building blocks to looking good. Look at your wardrobe as a whole. To maximise the number of outfits you can put together, focus on items that relate to each other.

■ **Simplicity pays** The most versatile clothes are simple – well-cut trousers or skirts and plain shirts and T-shirts.

■ **For all seasons** Try to choose fabrics that will take you through different seasons. Soft and crisp cottons, lightweight wool, soft knits, silk and fabrics with a hint of stretch will all work well throughout the year.

■ **Sartorial style** Traditionally, men have tended to have a smaller wardrobe and to buy clothes with a longer-term approach. This can be a helpful model for women, too. A good tailored suit is a perfect example – it may cost a little more initially but it will last for ages and you can ring the changes by wearing it with different jackets, skirts and trousers and adding accessories to dress it up.

---

keep it simple

A NEW START
To revamp your wardrobe, pare it down to the clothes you actually want. This way, you'll avoid buying items that coordinate with clothes you no longer wear. Begin by separating clothes into three piles: dustbin; charity shop; pieces you want to keep.
Be ruthless and get rid of anything you haven't worn for the past two years. Don't keep something in the hope that you will lose weight or that it will come back into fashion.

keep it simple

SPEND LESS
These items will boost your morale and give a new lease of life to your wardrobe for little outlay:

- T-shirts: white T-shirts are invaluable neutrals that go with anything. Coloured vests or T-shirts will add a dash to a simple outfit.
- Cheap, colourful belts
- Metal, wooden, tin and enamel jewellery
- Beaded necklaces
- Costume jewellery
- Pretty flip-flops
- Patterned/plain scarves

WHEN TO SPLASH OUT

Spend a little more on the essential ingredients of a basic wardrobe – they will repay you in more ways than one.

Good-quality shirt Go for a simple, well-cut design in cotton or silk. It works well in the day with jeans or a casual skirt; at night with a slinky skirt or trousers; and, as a summer jacket over a vest or camisole.

Quality mainstays When buying tailored winter outfits, be prepared to pay more for good-quality items, particularly with jackets and tailored trousers. Check they are lined and well finished, too. You'll be rewarded with a better fit and clothes that stay looking good for longer.

The best accessories Your shoes, bags, scarves and belts should work with most of your wardrobe. Buy quality accessories in the sales to add style to more basic outfits.

BUY CHILDREN'S CLOTHES AND AVOID VAT

Petite shoppers (up to 5ft 4in/1.63cm and up to size 10) can benefit from the zero VAT rate on children's clothes. These days, children's ranges are imaginative enough to appeal to most adults. Children's shoe sizes generally go up to a size 5 or 6 (38 or 39), and clothes intended for 14- to 15-year-olds may fit small adults.

DON'T SKIMP ON LINGERIE

When it comes to planning a wardrobe, underwear is often overlooked. Ill-fitting lingerie can ruin the final effect of an outfit. However, you don't have to spend a fortune on designer lines.

Free fitting Before buying a bra, check out the styles available and take advantage of the professional measuring service offered by many department stores free of charge. Find a brand and style that suits you, then check online sources and catalogues for the same item at a cheaper price.

Slinky or sensible For a list of websites offering lingerie, ranging from low-priced to luxury, log on to **www.somucheasier.co.uk** and look for Lingerie under Clothes. You'll find favourites like Marks & Spencer alongside specialists such as Sexy Plus, which caters exclusively for larger ladies, or **www.needundies.com**, which offers underwear for men and women with a multibuy scheme on well-known ranges. Check each website for special offers. For a real bargain, try Primark, where it is possible to get a set of bra and knickers for £3–£5.

DESIGNER OUTFIT — LOW COST ALTERNATIVE

£120 — £15
£45 — £8
£350 — £130
£200 — £20
£150 — £30
£225 — £35

TOTAL £1,090 — TOTAL £238

DESIGNERWEAR ON THE CHEAP

Knowing where to go for your designer suit can mean savings of up to £232 (new) or over £400 (nearly new) on a Jaeger ladieswear wool suit (November 2008).

DESIGNER SHOP	£498
DESIGNER OUTLET	£145
SECONDHAND	£85

BESPOKE SUITS AT HALF THE PRICE

If you would like a bespoke suit but don't want to pay Savile Row prices, try using a visiting tailor from the Far East before paying expensive prices at home. Tailors from Hong Kong – such as Raja Fashions – frequently hold fittings in hotels across Britain. They email your design and measurements back to Hong Kong, and the suit is made and sent to you within four weeks. It can cost as little as £169, but check the details in advance – linings, for example, may not automatically be included in the price. For information on visiting tailors, see page 57.

Fabric choices Although pure wool is normally the recommended choice for a quality suit, a wool/synthetic blend is a good substitute and costs about 20% less.

HIRE OR BUY FORMAL WEAR EX-RENTAL

If you are put off wearing a formal suit by the price, consider hiring one or even buying an ex-rental outfit. For example, at Hire Society (**www.hire-society.com** or 0871 437 0271) a traditional black dinner suit costs £150 to buy new, £34 to hire for 48 hours (plus delivery and collection) or £100 to buy ex-rental.

BUY MENSWEAR – SAVE UP TO 50%

Men's clothing tends to be less expensive and is often better quality than women's. If your style is casual, try the men's rails for a bargain but check the fit. Basic shirts, T-shirts and sportswear can be as much as 50% cheaper when bought in the menswear department.

ASK YOURSELF

BEFORE YOU BUY
When you're making a purchase make sure you get value for money by asking these 'three by three' questions:
- What three things can I wear it with?
- What three places can I wear it to?
- What three ways can I accessorise it?

DESIGNER OUTFIT

LOW COST ALTERNATIVE

£120   £20
£65   £10
        £120
£300
£200   £40
£140
        £40
£240   £50

TOTAL £1,065   TOTAL £280

HIRE A HAT

Don't waste money buying a ladies' hat for a formal occasion. Try a hire company such as Get Ahead Hats. Visit **www.getaheadhats.co.uk** or 01254 889574 ✉ for a list of branches. Hire from £40 a week.

BAGS OF STYLE

Look out for old leather handbags from charity shops or the family attic. Vintage handbags saved by your mother or aunt have a timeless appeal, and a secondhand Chanel bag would be a real style find. Camera cases and satchels also make unusual but stylish accessories. Clean up old bags with saddle soap, then use shoe polish and buff well. For a quick shine, rub with hand cream and wipe off with a tissue.

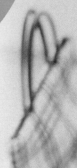

BEST FOOT FORWARD

■ If you need shoes to match a dress for a special occasion, buy plain satin pumps and have them dyed instead of spending time and money searching for the right colour.
■ Strappy summer sandals bought in the end-of-season sales can double for evening wear.
■ Sew beads or sequins on plain canvas shoes for fun casual wear.

PRICE WATCH

For good deals on men's watches, cufflinks, wallets, belts, hats, gloves and scarves, plus clothing and gadgets, try **www.menkind.co.uk** 01306 646311 ✉.

ACCESSORISE FOR ADDED VALUE

Accessories add variety to your wardrobe, transforming clothes from casual to sophisticated or upgrading a simple outfit from day to evening wear. A few well-chosen items can make an inexpensive outfit look like a designer creation.

QUICK FIXES FOR SECONDHAND JEWELLERY

■ Repair gold or silver-plated jewellery with a fine paint brush and gold or silver spray paint. Spray a little paint onto a piece of cardboard, dip in the brush and touch up the chips.
■ To unknot a chain, lay it on a piece of wax paper. Put a drop or two of baby oil directly onto the knot. Use two needles to untangle the knot gently then blot the oil with tissues.
■ If the post on a pierced earring has broken, use a nail file to smooth off any residual glue from the back, then mount a new post with permanent glue.
■ If the pin on the back of a brooch is broken don't throw it away – put it on a chain to make a necklace, sew it to a jacket or repair it with permanent glue.

WINNING WAYS WITH SCARVES

A scarf is one of the most versatile accessories in your wardrobe.
■ Use a large woollen one as a winter shawl or poncho instead of a coat.
■ Twist a wide cotton scarf into a bikini top for the beach, or use a big scarf as a sarong.
■ Wear a narrow scarf or a necktie as a belt with jeans or casual trousers.
■ Use a small scarf to tie up long hair into a pony tail.

BUTTONS AND BOWS

The buttons and other trims used on designer or vintage clothes are sometimes worth more than the garment itself. Look for damaged secondhand designer outfits going for a song in charity shops, snip off the buttons and use them to give a touch of class to a plain jacket or sweater.

MONEY OFF DESIGNER SHADES

If you hanker after a pair of designer sunglasses and you don't need prescription lenses, you can usually save 15% on a stylish pair for men or women through designer websites and outlets (see pages 45 and 48), or save 15% by buying them VAT-free at an airport shop (see page 57). For the best protection, look for a sticker that specifies 100% UV blockage.

SOS (SAVE ON SHOE LEATHER)

Men's shoes are expensive, but you can find bargains without pounding the pavement:
■ Get up to 70% off well-known brands (for men and women) plus free delivery on selected items at www.shoe-shop.com 0844 844 0809 ✉.
■ Invest in a pair of handmade shoes that could last for 10 years or longer. Shoes from Tim Little's collections start at under £200, bespoke made-to-measure shoes at £1,550 with a second pair from £675. Visit www.timlittle.com,

A GIRL'S BEST FRIEND

If you are looking for jewellery made of precious stones or metals, visit a wholesaler in London's Hatton Garden for the best prices. Get the names and numbers from the British Jeweller's Association, www.bja.org.uk 0121 237 1110 ✉.

BAUBLES AND BEADS

Jewellery doesn't need to be pricey. You can find colourful beads in craft shops such as Creative Beadcraft www.creativebeadcraft.co.uk 01494 778818 for under £1 a pack and make your own.

BARGAINS BY POST AND ONLINE

Shopping online is growing in popularity, although many shoppers still like to receive a catalogue to browse at their leisure and to pay by post or phone.

MAIL ORDER FOR 20% SAVINGS AND MORE

Mail order offers all the choice of the high street, often with more competitive prices and no hassles. Catalogues are also the perfect solution for men who hate shopping.

Stress-free shopping Browse a catalogue or website, then order by phone or online to cut out the hassle of the high street and try on clothes in the privacy of your own home.

Price advantage Prices are often lower than those in the shops because you can order direct from suppliers or from discount specialists. Some companies offer free postage and packing. (See Resources, right, for contact information.)

WATCH POINTS MAIL-ORDER PITFALLS

The main problem with mail order is that you have to rely on a catalogue (print or online) to judge an item's suitability. This can result in having to pay to return unwanted items.

■ **Try for size** Sizes aren't always standard; you may have to try on a few garments before finding the right size. To counteract this, use a company that offers a free or heavily discounted first order in case you have to return anything.

■ **Check the cost of returns** Check terms and conditions before ordering. You may have to pay postage and packing if you need to return or exchange an item. Some companies offer free returns, but watch out for the time limit.

SAVE TIME AND MONEY SHOPPING ONLINE

The Internet has transformed the way we shop, saving us both time and money – and increasing choice significantly.

RESOURCES

CATALOGUES

For convenience you can't beat catalogue shopping. Compare prices to discover the best deal.

■ At **www.catalink.net**, you can sign up free to receive catalogues by post or view online.

■ **http://buy.uk.shop.com/** has links to catalogue, online discount and clearance websites.

■ **www.somucheasier.co.uk/ clothes-catalogues.html** has information and links to the most popular mail-order catalogues. Alternatively, order a free catalogue direct via the company's own website (see Resources, page 45) or call direct:

Freemans 0844 556 4444
Kays 08448 111 800
La Redoute
0844 842 2222
Next 0844 844 8000
Lands End
0845 0123 000
M&M Direct
0871 664 1333
Fashion World
0871 231 4000

Favourite shops and niche suppliers can all be found at our fingertips, with at-a-glance information on products, discounts, special offers and money-off vouchers.

Spoilt for choice Websites such as www.somucheasier.co.uk provide a directory of popular and secure online shops. Under 'Clothes', categories include women's and men's clothing, lingerie, sports gear, maternity clothes, and more.

Special offers Try a site such as www.vouchercodes.com, which lists all the latest discounts, voucher codes and exclusive offers available at thousands of online stores.

Auction sites New or nearly new designer clothes – as well as vintage items, wedding clothes, fancy dress and more – can be found on auction sites such as eBay. But remember – your rights against a private seller are considerably reduced.

Plus sizes The Internet is a great place to hunt for competitively priced clothes in larger and non-standard sizes. Visit Yours for size 14–32 women's clothing, while Sexy Plus offers underwear for 'Big Beautiful Women'. Big For Men offers clothing and footwear for the larger man.

> ## COMPARE PRICES ONLINE
> To make sure you are getting a bargain, use a price comparison website such as
> www.kelkoo.co.uk
> www.dealtime.co.uk
> www.pricerunner.co.uk

RESOURCES

HOT WEBSITES FOR MEN AND WOMEN

■ **www.kays.com** Fashion brands at affordable prices. Discounts of up to £15 off the first order, free delivery, free returns and 14 days approval. Brands include Adidas, Animal, Miss Sixty, So Fabulous and Ted Baker.

■ **www.freemans.com** Substantial savings on clothes, footwear and sportswear.

■ **www.next.co.uk** Inspirational ideas from the Next Directory online.

■ **www.redoute.co.uk** A stylish collection of clothes at affordable prices.

■ **www.landsend.co.uk** Smart, comfortable casual clothes including petite and plus ranges for women and a tall range for men.

■ **www.debenhams.com** The popular high street department store online with a wide range of men's and women's clothing including own brands and designer labels.

■ **www.bbclothing.co.uk** A designer clothing site, Brown Bag Clothing has discounted designer labels, including Aquascutum, Armani, Boss, Diesel, Lacoste, Prada, Paul Smith, Timberland and Versace.

■ **www.yoox.com** Reductions on last season's designer collections, from coats and suits to bags and shoes.

■ **www.asos.com** Dress like a celebrity for a fraction of the price.

■ **www.kitbag.co.uk** Money-saving deals on top brands such as Nike, Adidas, Reebok and Umbro.

■ **www.mandmsports.com** End of ranges from names such as Adidas and Bench.Up to 75% off high street prices.

■ **www.my-wardrobe.com** Well-edited designer clothes at competitive prices. They have frequent sales and special offers.

■ **www.vouchercodes.com** Information on vouchers, discounts and special offers on your favourite brands.

■ **www.brandalley.co.uk** Sign up and receive frequent offers – discounts are typically 30-70% off a range of designer brands.

JUST FOR WOMEN

■ **www.topshop.co.uk** Inspired by the catwalks, fashionable clothes can be found here at reasonable prices.

■ **www.fashionworld.co.uk** Affordable fashion in sizes 12–32 with a free returns policy.

FOR SIZE 16 AND OVER, CHECK OUT:

■ Elvi at **www.elvi.co.uk**
■ Evans at **www.evans.co.uk**
■ Dorothy Perkins at **www.dorothyperkins.co.uk**
■ Lingerie for the larger lady at **www.sexyplus.co.uk**

JUST FOR MEN

■ **www.bigformen.com** Clothing and footwear at competitive prices.

■ **www.designerdiscount.co.uk** Savings of 50% or more off designerwear

■ **www.ebay.com** Buy and sell clothing and accessories.

■ **www.topman.com** The latest trends, plus seasonal offers.

PLAN YOUR SALES FOR GREATEST SAVINGS

Organise your sales shopping to make the most of the bargains at certain times of year. Some items are particularly cheap according to the season, such as end-of-summer ranges in July and end-of-winter ranges in January.

SALES SHOPPING – SAVE OVER 40%

Coats and outerwear A good time to buy a winter coat is in the January or February sales as department stores often do good reductions before spring fashions arrive. 'Classic' items – particularly in black – are not always put in the sales, but if you're flexible about the style and colour you want, you may get a great bargain.

Summer savings If you can wait to buy summer clothes until July or August, you will benefit from reductions of up to 40% on the prices at the start of the season. This also applies to the season's swimwear, which will be on sale at reduced prices by mid-summer.

January sales All items of clothing are slashed in price in the post-Christmas sales so that retailers can make room for the new season's stock. Remember that the sales often start before the New Year. Check in advance to see if an item you have been coveting will be reduced in the sales.

50% OFF IN THE HIGH STREET

The selling point of high street stores like Gap (find a local branch in your phone directory) and New Look (0500 454094) is their up-to-the-minute fashions. Turnover is expected to be rapid, and items that remain unsold for more than two months are relegated to the sale rail where you can grab them for as little as half their full price.

DISCOUNT OUTLET SALES – SAVE 80%

Big savings can be made in the sales merely by visiting your local high street, but for the real bargains try factory shops at sales time. Here, prices can be as much as 80% less than the nonsale high street price.

HEAVILY DISCOUNTED HAUTE COUTURE

If your taste runs to the glamorous and expensive but your wallet doesn't, the designer sales may be for you. If you live in London, you're in luck because almost all of them are held in the capital – if you live elsewhere, it may be worth the cost of travelling to London for the day to pick up bargains at up to 90% less than the normal retail price. But be warned – if you are over a size 12, you may not find much of interest. Supermodel-sized shoppers (6–8) may pick up a real bargain. Be prepared to wait in long queues, to forgo the luxury of a dressing room and to jostle with the crowds for the best deals. In most cases, you may need to add your name to a mailing list at the shop or fill in a form online, through the relevant website, to be notified about future sales.

GETTING FURTHER DISCOUNTS

If you find an item of clothing you like that has a button or two missing or a loose thread, you may be able to get it at a further discount. Remember that you may be asked to waive your statutory rights if you buy a garment in the full knowledge that it has a fault.

BUY A CLASSIC FOR 70% LESS

Sale discounts at designer shops can vary from 25% to an enormous 70%. But although they're quality-brand goods, the choice may be limited so don't be tempted to buy something ultra-trendy if it isn't exactly what you're looking for. Use this kind of shopping to boost wardrobe basics with good-quality names and special items that will give a touch of designer style to the rest of your clothes.

SALES ARE ONLINE TOO

When hunting for seasonal bargains, don't forget that the online retailers also hold sales at the same times as those on the high street. Here, too, items that have not sold during the season are heavily discounted – by as much as 50%, for example, at La Redoute. For more tips on buying over the Internet, see page 44.

 **RESOURCES**

RECOMMENDED DESIGNER SALES

■ **The Designer Warehouse Sales** (North London, 020 7697 9888, or go to **www.dwslondon.co.uk** ✉) Entrance fee £2. More award-winning designer labels under one roof than any other outlet in the UK. Held over three days, 10 times a year, they hold a major London sale for women and men. You can buy Galliano, Alexander McQueen and Vivienne Westwood, plus Philip Treacy millinery, shoes from Gucci and Mui Mui at 60–80% less than retail. New and local designers are also featured.
■ **Designer Sale UK** (East London, 01273 470 880 or **www.designersales.co.uk** ✉) Substantial discounts can be found here for both women and men. Recent bargains include a Biba dress for £55 reduced from £295, and a Vivienne Westwood skirt for £50 reduced from £245. Some items go for as little as £10.
■ **The London Fashion Designer Sale** (Hampstead and Chelsea, visit the website at **www.designer fashionsales.co.uk** ✉) Reductions of up to 75% on items from today's newest designers, including East to West, Planetude and The Sheepskin Company. Tickets are £3 on the door. The company also runs the Cabbages and Frocks Market in Chelsea on Saturdays and Hampstead on Sundays. Items from new designers, retro and vintage clothing mix with cupcakes and cappuccinos.
■ **London Fashion Weekend** (West London, 020 8948 5522 or see their website at **www.londonfashionweekend.co. uk** ✉) Entrance is £10 but you can find big reductions on women's and men's designer clothing and accessories at the spring and autumn events. Many London designers are here, including Ally Capellino and Lulu Guinness – and many of the smaller labels.
■ **Wahl Fashions** (Central London, 020 7349 5222) Designer clothing for women from Beppe Bondi, Votre Nom, Tuzzi and others. Sales twice yearly – usually April and October – with items often for sale at 50% of their usual retail price.

BUY HALF-PRICE AT FACTORY OUTLETS

For a bargain from both high-street and designer names, try visiting a shopping centre where discount outlets are gathered together in one place.

TOP TIPS SHOPPING WITHOUT DROPPING

Get the best value from your shopping trips by careful planning. Check purchases thoroughly and ask about the returns policy before buying apparent bargains on impulse.

■ **Big-name stores** To save on travelling, look for outlets that are anchored by well-known names, such as Gap, and have at least three stores you're interested in.

■ **Check first** Always telephone factory and outlet villages first to ensure they are still trading.

■ **Flawless** Check for flaws that may have caused their rejection. Sometimes garments are manufactured specifically for factory outlets and the quality isn't as good.

■ **Avoid impulse buys** Be clear about what you want. Don't be seduced by the low price if an item is out-of-date.

 **RESOURCES**

FACTORY OUTLETS IN LONDON

■ **The Burberry Factory Store** (Chatham Place, Hackney E9, 020 8328 4287) Sells top-quality clothing, shoes, jewellery and accessories. In the sale, men's shirts from £19, plus 20-30% off slight seconds.

■ **Clark's Factory Shops** (Rye Lane, Peckham SE15, 020 7732 2530 and Powis Street, Woolwich SE18, 020 8854 3163) Sells footwear end-of-line styles.

FACTORY OUTLETS OUTSIDE LONDON

For a list of factory outlets see **www.shoppingvillages.com**

■ **Alexon sale shops** (Batley, 01924 423172; Belper, 01773 881408; Cardiff, 01443 402615; Colne, 01282 856 200; Dover, 01304 226616; Fleet, 01252 815027; Grantham, 01476 591001;

High Wycombe, 01494 464214; Hornsey, 01964 535441; Luton, 01582 399854; Newcastle, 0191 297 2420; Ramsgate, 01843 589860; Ross-on-Wye, 01989 769000; Rotherham, 01709 382491; Southport, 01704 531281; Street, 01458 841831; Swindon, 01793 431854; Tamworth, 01827 310041); Walsall, 01922 618200.

■ **Aquascutum factory shops** (Corby, 01536 205086)

■ **Bicester Village Oxon** (01869 323200 and at **www.bicestervillage.com**) Savings of up to 60% on the previous season's branded goods for women and men.

■ **Clarks Village** (Street, Somerset, 01458 840064 and at **www.clarksvillage. co.uk**) Up to 60% off famous brands for women and men.

■ **The Galleria outlet centre** (Hatfield, 01707 256860, **www.thegalleria.co.uk**) The stores here usually offer up to 50% discounts.

■ **Laura Ashley discount shops** (Hornsea, 01964 535196; Newtown, Powys, 01686 623730; Taplow, 01628 550360; Thurrock, 01708 860750)

■ **McArthurGlen** (020 7535 2300, **www.mcarthurglen.com**) Designer outlets in seven UK locations offering up to 50% discounts: Ashford, Bridgend, Cheshire Oaks, Livingston, Mansfield, Swindon and York, .

■ **Mulberry factory shop** (Somerset, 01749 340583) The latest designs substantially discounted.

■ **The Original Factory Shop** (nationwide, 01282 833222, **www.theoriginalfactoryshop. co.uk**) Outlets nationwide offering up to 75% off well-known high street brands.

■ **Peak Village Outlet** (Rowley, Derbyshire, 01629 735326 at **www.peakvillage. co.uk**) Stores offer up to 70% off a full range of fashions. Open 364 days a year.

BARGAINS AT CHAINS AND SUPERMARKETS

A growing number of discount chains offer great bargains on brand-name clothing. And various supermarkets have added their own fashion ranges to the goods they stock at some very competitive prices.

DISCOUNT CHAINS OFFER UP TO 60% OFF

Chains of stores that offer hugely discounted clothing for all the family have spread nationwide. If you have web access, you can use their websites to find a store near you.

Matalan (01695 552400 and at **www.matalan.co.uk**) Matalan is a large chain of discount stores offering low prices on a range of fashion. Pop into your local branch to pick up a free membership card. As well as saving you up to 50% off high-street prices, they'll send you regular updates on new collections and special offers.

T K Maxx (**www.tkmaxx.com**) T K Maxx offers famous-label womenswear and menswear up to 60% less than recommended retail prices. You'll find big savings on a variety of genuine designer wear – from wardrobe basics such as jeans and shirts, to cashmere sweaters – if you're prepared to hunt through rails of clothes.

Primark (**www.primark.co.uk**) A low-cost chain rather than a discount store, Primark stores offer items at up to half the price of even the cheaper high-street shops. They sell low-cost everyday clothing, with a good selection for children.

PICK UP A BARGAIN WITH THE FAMILY

Many supermarket chains now have their own clothing ranges – including designer labels such as F&F, Cherokee and Stone Bay at Tesco and Tu Clothing at Sainsbury's. Both George at Asda, Debenhams and Littlewoods Direct offer very competitive rates, especially on schoolwear.

RESOURCES

BARGAINS GALORE
Dedicated bargain hunters will find a great source of information and comprehensive lists of secondhand and factory shops and other value outlets in *The Good Deal Directory*, available by phoning 01367 860016 or by visiting their website at **www.gooddealdirectory. co.uk** ✉.

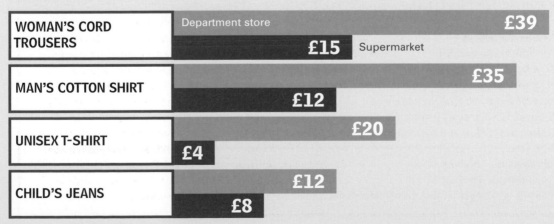

SUPERMARKET BEST BUYS

The top bargains at the supermarket are everyday classic items such as white shirts and sportswear – you can save as much as 90% over department store prices.

	Department store	Supermarket
WOMAN'S CORD TROUSERS	£39	£15
MAN'S COTTON SHIRT	£35	£12
UNISEX T-SHIRT	£20	£4
CHILD'S JEANS	£12	£8

Prices correct at time of publication

BUY SECONDHAND FOR FIRST-RATE DEALS

If you are prepared to rummage through old clothes in vintage shops and markets, special bargains may await you. You could find nearly new designer dresses for as little as 10% of their original price.

FINDING MARKET BARGAINS

It is quite acceptable to haggle for a better discount when buying from street markets. First find out the seller's asking price to determine how low a price you can reasonably offer.

BEST MARKETS FOR SECONDHAND BARGAINS	
MARKET	**WHAT TO BUY**
Camden Lock, London NW1 **Tube: Camden Town, Chalk Farm** **Open daily 10am–6pm (7pm on Thurs)**	Designer clothes Also good for new and secondhand clothes and jewellery. Avoid the crowds at weekends.
Petticoat Lane, London E1 **Tube: Aldgate, Aldgate E., Liverpool St.** **Sun 9am–3pm**	Mainly new but some secondhand street fashion and footwear, bags and leather goods.
Portobello Road, London W11 **Tube: Ladbroke Grove, Notting Hill** **Mon–Sat 8am–6.30pm (closes at 1pm Thurs); main day Sat**	Clothes, footwear and jewellery. Best bargains at Ladbroke Grove end. Best secondhand clothes are on streets alongside the Westway and under the canopy at the junction with Portobello Road.
Old Spitalfields, London E1 **Tube: Aldgate, Liverpool St., Whitechapel** **Sun–Frid 9.30am–5pm (Thurs 8am)**	Designer and vintage clothing.
Affleck's Palace **52 Church Street, Manchester** **Mon–Fri 10am–5.30pm; Sat 10am-6pm**	A large indoor market selling 'alternative' fashion and vintage clothing, with lots of retro styles and new designers.
The Barras **4–6 Stevenson Street, Glasgow** **Saturday and Sunday 10am–5pm**	Clothing (new and secondhand) – check designerwear is genuine! – accessories and more.
Quayside Market, **Quayside, Newcastle** **Sundays 9am–2.30pm**	Secondhand clothes, amongst many other items (it's one of the largest Sunday markets in England), new clothing and accessories.
Rag Market (St Martin's Market) **Edgbaston Street, Birmingham** **Tues, Thurs, Fri and Sat 9am–5pm**	Vintage (some designer) clothes, accessories, fabrics and makeup.
St Nicholas Market **Corn Street, Bristol** **Mon–Sat 9.30am–5pm; some Sundays**	Clothing (new and vintage), jewellery, fabric and beads.

DRESS AGENCIES FOR DESIGNER DISCOUNTS

Dress agencies are the places to find secondhand designer clothes, bags, shoes and other accessories at savings of up to 75% and more. They are also an excellent way of recouping cash on garments you no longer wear. Agencies usually offer between a third and a half of the original price to sellers, and some allow you to reclaim or donate to charity clothes that are unsold after a couple of months. Most agencies won't consider clothes that are more than two years old, and the smarter ones accept only big names.

TOP TIPS FINDING CHARITY SHOP BARGAINS

Local charity shops can be an excellent source of bargains, but be prepared to set aside some time to look. And if you want designer goods, pick your area carefully.
■ **Ready to rummage?** Many charity shops including Oxfam, Scope and Age Concern are updating their image to make it easier to find designer bargains. But for real finds, you may still have to hunt through less-desirable items.
■ **Exclusive neighbourhoods** Naturally, the best bargains are more likely to be found in affluent areas. Pick the right shop and you may find a Nicole Farhi outfit for £25. Shops in West and Central London tend to yield high-quality goods but can also command higher prices – the smarter parts of other cities and suburbs may offer better value. Shops in the commuter belts and wealthier areas such as parts of Cheshire and the Home Counties can also be a good bet.

 **RESOURCES**

LONDON DRESS AGENCIES
■ **Bang Bang** (Goodge Street W1, 020 7631 4191) Offers a good selection of younger styles, from cheap street fashion to designer labels.
■ **L'Homme Designer Exchange** (Blandford Street, near Baker Street W1, 020 7224 3266) Get men's designer wear here, plus ties, cufflinks and more.
■ **The Loft** (Monmouth Street, near Covent Garden and Leicester Square WC2, 020 7240 3807) This shop offers items from contemporary designers for a third or so of their original price and a well-stocked £5 basket.
■ **Wellingtons** (Wellington Place, St John's Wood NW8,

020 7483 0688) Find a wide range of clothes and accessories for women, such as leather and suede jackets from £20; lots of Dolce & Gabbana; high-street labels and a bargain rail for under £20.
■ **The Anerley Frock Exchange** (Anerley Road SE20, 020 8778 2030) Large shop stocking women's clothes from Next and Gap to Versace.

DRESS AGENCIES OUTSIDE LONDON
■ **The Danbury Dress Agency** (121 Main Road, Danbury, Essex or **www.danburydressagency.co.uk**) All designer stock is sold at discounted prices, although around half is new. Also wedding outfits, swimwear, bags, shoes and more.

■ **Designer Exchange** (3 Royal Exchange Court, off 17 Royal Exchange Square, Glasgow, Scotland, 0141 221 6898) Nearly new designer clothes and accessories from Gucci, Louis Vuitton, Armani, Max Mara and more.
■ **Elite Dress Agency** (35 King Street West, Manchester, 0161 832 3670; Altrincham, 0161 9285424 or **www.elitedressagency.co.uk**) The largest dress agency in Europe, this shop offers clothes for all the family. Labels include Gucci, Versace and Paul Smith.
■ **Seconds Out** (High Street, Cookham, Berkshire, 01628 850371 or **www.secondsout. org.uk**) Numerous designers with new stock arriving daily. Also offers a range of accessories, including hats.

■ **Best-value shops** Cancer Research and Oxfam are at the more expensive end of the charity clothing market. Prices at other nationwide charity shops and those run by smaller local organisations tend to be cheaper. But this does not mean that you won't still find bargains at the larger shops.

■ **Re-fashioned chic** Traid (Textile and Recycling for Aid and International Development) shops in London and Brighton are also worth a visit. Traid was once described as 'the hippest charity chain in the UK' by GQ magazine. Its staff pay a great deal of attention to the selection and organisation of their secondhand and customised clothing. Traid's re-fashioned and customised garments and accessories, such as shirts, sportswear and bags, are now fashion must-haves.

■ **Children's couture** Look out for real finds in children's clothing, including designer names. These are often little-worn and a fraction of the original price.

WATCH POINTS USED CLOTHES

When shopping for secondhand goods, don't get carried away by the bargains. Be realistic about the item's suitability and the repairs and improvements you can make.

■ **Stain removal** If the garment is stained, assess whether you or a good dry cleaner would be able to deal with it.

■ **Costly repairs?** Try to judge whether you would be able to repair any damage yourself or whether you could pay someone else to do it and still save. Problems that are easily tackled include moving buttons and shortening the length. More tricky problems that are better left to the experts are alterations around the shoulder area and where the material is difficult to work with, such as leather or velvet.

■ **Avoid a fashion faux pas** When considering a vintage item, make sure it is in keeping with your personal style. And to avoid spending on something you will be unable to wear, keep current trends, colours and shapes in mind.

 **RESOURCES**

CHARITY SHOPS NATIONWIDE

Check out charity shops in your area.

■ Barnardo's **www.barnardos. org.uk** 020 8550 8822 (includes a dress agency and bridalwear collection)

■ British Heart Foundation **www.bhf.org.uk** 020 7554 0000

■ Cancer Research UK **www.cancerresearchuk.org** 020 7121 6699

■ Oxfam **www.oxfam.org.uk** 0300 200 1252

■ Sue Ryder **www.sueryder care.org** 020 7400 0440

■ Traid **www.traid.org.uk** 020 8733 2580

LONDON CHARITY SHOPS

■ **Cancer Research UK** (Hill Street, Richmond, 020 8940 4581) Great for modern, stylish clothes at moderate prices.

■ **Crusaid** (Churton Street SW1, 020 7233 8736) The first place to go for quality high-street names as well as designer labels.

■ **Fara** (Fulham Road SW6, 020 7371 0141) Find designer cast-offs and handmade shirts.

■ **Oxfam** (Goodge Street W1, 020 7636 7311) Many designer labels among the selection upstairs.

■ **Salvation Army Charity Shop** (Upper Street N1, 020 7359 9865) One of London's best charity shops.

■ **Traid** (61 Westbourne Grove W2, 020 7221 2421) Find good-quality secondhand goods and inspired customised clothes and accessories. Traid has eight branches in London and one in Brighton.

VINTAGE VALUE

Although vintage clothes shops tend not to be as cheap as charity shops, you can still find good secondhand bargains in them. Many are stocked from the charity shops so will already have creamed off the pick of the garments. If you're short of time, it can be worth starting at one of the better-quality shops to find real retro chic.

NETWORKING – EVERYONE WINS

It's always satisfying to get a new item for your wardrobe or accessory drawer for nothing, or next to nothing. Organise like-minded friends and acquaintances to meet regularly to sell your unwanted items. Set a few basic rules, such as all clothes, accessories and jewellery must be of good quality and in excellent condition. Then, get selling to each other at knockdown prices. Guide prices could be:
■ Under £15 for big items such as coats, weather-proof/activity gear and shoes.
■ Under £10 for trousers, skirts and handbags.
■ £5 for tops and sweaters.
■ £2 for small accessories such as costume and other non-gold/silver jewellery, scarves and belts.

SWAP SHOPS FOR FUN AND GREAT VALUE

Swap shops are even more fun than network parties, but you need to work out what constitutes a fair swap. The best way is to put items into different categories and swap like for like – not just similar items but ones that are of approximate value. For example, if you had an expensive piece of jewellery that you don't wear any more you could swap it for top-quality, well-cut trousers; or you could trade an upmarket jacket for a skirt and top.

RESOURCES

SECONDHAND SHOPS
■ **Oxfam Originals**, (0300 200 1252), **www.oxfam.org. uk/shops** ⊠) Boutiques in Manchester, Liverpool, Leeds, Nottingham, Preston, Rochester and York offer retro and vintage clothing.
■ **Beatnik Emporium** (Southampton, 023 8063 3428, **www.beatnikemporium.com** ⊠) Secondhand, retro, vintage and new items.
■ **Armstrongs**, (Edinburgh, 0131 220 5557, **www.armstrongs vintage.co.uk** ⊠) From Victorian times to today.
■ **eBay** (**http://clothes.shop. ebay.co.uk**) This auction website offers a wide range of clothing.

ESSENTIAL READING
Bargain Hunters' London by Andrew Kershman £6.99, ISBN 0952291428
How to Sell Clothing, Shoes, and Accessories on eBay, Entrepreneur Press, £7.99, ISBN 1599180057

LOOK AFTER SWEATERS

Don't spend money on little shavers for sweaters. Gently remove bobbles with a cheap disposable razor.

TIE RESCUE

If you get a water spot on a silk tie, let the spot dry and then rub the spotted area vigorously with a hidden part of the tie. Small spots can be removed with soda water.

THE RIGHT HANGERS

Hang silk clothing on plastic or padded hangers. Wooden ones may cause snagging. Don't use thin metal dry cleaner's hangers for any of your clothes.

MAKING CLOTHES LAST LONGER

Whether you wear jeans and T-shirts, jumble-sale finds or tailored separates, treat everything in your wardrobe as if it cost five times the price. That way, your clothes will look good for longer.

SUEDE SHOES

■ To get rid of scuff marks, rub gently with very fine sandpaper.
■ Steam clean suede shoes by holding them over a pan of boiling water. Once the nap is raised, stroke the suede with a soft brush in one direction. Let the shoes dry before wearing them.

SPONGING SUEDE

Restore the nap on a suede garment by rubbing a dry sponge over it after each wearing.

GET THE MOST FROM YOUR LINGERIE

Ideally, all fine lingerie should be hand washed. If you don't have the time for this, enclose it in a bag to prevent it from getting tangled in the washer and use the delicates setting. Do not use a dryer as this will damage the garments. If possible, dry lingerie naturally, away from direct sunlight.

SWIMWEAR CARE

To give your swimwear a longer life, rinse in cold water after each use to remove salt or chlorine, which weakens the stretchy fabric. Then hand or machine wash on a gentle cycle. Do not twist or wring out or hang to dry in direct sunlight.

EASY ON THE STARCH

Most manufacturers recommend that you don't use starch on clothes as it damages the fibres. If you have your clothes cleaned, ask for a light starch only. And if you apply your own starch, use a dry iron and make sure you clean it after use as starch build-up can stain clothes.

STAIN REMOVAL

Treat new stains by dampening a soft cloth with soda water and sandwiching the stained area between two layers of the cloth. This lessens staining, but wash or dry clean the garment as soon as possible.

PRESSING MATTERS

Dry cleaning is actually bad for clothes, as well as for your bank balance. If clothes are creased, not dirty, have them pressed instead. This is much less likely to weaken fabrics and will help to prolong the life of good-quality garments. To do your own pressing at home, use a damp cloth and a hot iron and keep the iron moving constantly. Or, to remove creases from most fabrics, hang the garment in the bathroom for 5–10 minutes, just after you've had a hot shower. The heat and steam will make the creases drop out without subjecting the fabric to chemicals.

SPILT WINE

Red wine spills needn't mean waving goodbye to a garment. Act quickly and either saturate the stain with white wine, or pour on plenty of salt followed by soda water. This should wash out the worst of the mark. Blot, and launder immediately.

PERFECT FINISH

If a silk garment has lost its finish and looks crumpled, try a little steam heat. Hang it in a steamy bathroom or lay a damp cloth over it and gently pass the iron over it.

SHOP ABROAD FOR BIG SAVINGS

Both the Internet and budget airlines have made purchasing goods from abroad increasingly popular. Get best value for money by knowing which countries offer the real bargains.

WHERE TO FIND THE BARGAINS

Paris is renowned as the fashion Mecca but try looking for bargains farther afield, such as in Hong Kong, or in lesser-known shopping areas, such as Florence.

Hong Kong Fashion prices can be less than half those in New York, and diamonds are half the British price. For cheap clothes, try Stanley Market – a half hour's bus ride away from town, to the south side of the island. More discounted clothing and footwear is for sale in central Hong Kong at The Lanes (Li Yuen Street, East and West). It's also a great place to get favourite garments copied by a tailor.

United States In New York hunt for bargains in the Garment District in lower Manhattan. Try Century 21 for discounted designer clothes, with 40–70% off many big names. Filene's Basement and TJ Maxx are also worth a visit. If you are prepared to travel out of town, you can shop at Woodbury Common – a huge outlet mall full of bargains from top-name designers – about an hour from Manhattan. Other centres, such as Orlando in Florida, also offer great deals on clothing. Prices for brands such as Gap and Banana republic are often the same in dollars as they are in pounds which gives you a good discount whatever the current exchange rate. Remember: American sizes are more or less two sizes bigger than British ones so if you are women's size 12 you will normally take an American size 8.

Athens Leather goods are particularly good value in Athens. Visit the sales in Athens in August and February for the best bargains. Try Ermou Street, off Syntagma Square, Eolou Street and Agiou Marou for clothing bargains and Kolonáki for designer clothes and accessories.

Italy The country is especially good for shoes and other leather goods such as gloves and handbags. Remember that most shops close for siesta from 2pm until evening so time your shopping accordingly. If you're after cutting edge design, go for Milan; Rome is probably tops for glamour. Tuscany and the area north of Milan are some of the best places for designer outlet shops including Prada, Gucci and Armani. If you're in Florence, try The Mall, which offers substantial savings on designer brands such as Fendi and Valentino. Other mall-type outlets include McArthur Glen Serravalle (Piedmont), and Fashion District (south of Rome).

Paris Visit during the January or July sales for bargains at the big department stores such as Galeries Lafayette and the big-name designers such as Louis Vuitton. Try the Rue St-Placide where you can find both new young designers and discount stores that carry last year's stock from fashion houses.If you're a shoe fan who loves to dig for treasure try

CHOOSE YOUR SHOPPING SPOT

If you are after a particular item, it's worth taking heed of prices around the world – your chosen holiday destination may not offer the best value. An Expedia.co.uk survey in 2003 found that leather jackets of the same quality varied in price by as much as 1200% depending on where they were bought. A jacket bought for just £66 in Hong Kong might cost £750–800 in Paris or Milan but just over half that cost in New York.

Rue Meslay in the 3rd district which is packed with shoe wholesalers, some ultra-cheap and tacky, but others offering recent and current designs at big discounts.

CHRISTMAS SHOPPING ABROAD

A weekend shopping package in New York costs from around £480 a person (based on two sharing), including flights and a three-star hotel (room only). Combine this with a strong exchange rate, and you may discover that a sight-seeing holiday with treats like eating out and entertainment alongside your bargain-hunting will still be cheaper than buying the same goods in Britain.

BEWARE OF IMPORT DUTIES

If you are importing goods from non-EU countries such as Hong Kong or America you may have to pay import duties (payable on any purchase over £340), VAT and a handling charge, adding around 20% to the purchase price. But there is no duty or VAT on books, no VAT on children's clothes and no duty on computers. For up-to-date information and advice, check the Import & Export section of the Government's Customs and Excise website (see right).

HIDDEN COSTS OF INTERNET BARGAINS

Duties and VAT apply to goods bought over the Internet, as well as those you bring back yourself. When calculating the price of items ordered from abroad, remember to add in the cost of postage and packing which, for bulky or heavy items, can be quite considerable, plus the import duty that may be applicable from some countries. Your items may get stuck in Customs for several weeks if import duty is due – and it add a substantial amount to your original purchase price. Always make sure that you are ordering from a reputable company with a secure website. If you are not sure, don't order.

WATCH POINTS VAT-FREE SHOPPING

Shopping for fashion items at the airport can be a good idea if you are short of time, but be aware that with a bit of hunting you can probably find a better bargain at home.
Do a price comparison Decide what you want before your trip abroad and get some idea of prices locally. Note that the airport VAT-free price is based on the full high-street price, so you may get a better price at home in the sales.
Reserve your goods At the airport you can use the Personal Shopper Service to find your goods. Go for value, like Prada sunglasses at 15% less than high-street prices.
Leave bargains behind If you are travelling in the EU don't take your goods with you on holiday – use the free Shopping Collection Service to leave your purchases at the airport, to be picked up on your return (see below).
Avoid taxes If you take your VAT-free bargains with you while travelling outside the EU, and then bring them back with you to the UK, you may end up having to pay tax on them. Collect them on your return and save the tax.

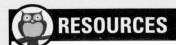

RESOURCES

SHOPPING ABROAD

■ Before importing goods, check the Customs and Excise website at **www.hmrc.gov.uk** ✉.
■ Find information on buying goods within Europe and over the Internet at **www.adviceguide.org.uk** and **www.tradingstandards. gov.uk** ✉.
■ For information on airport duty-free shops in the UK, visit **www.baa.com/shopping** ✉.

VISITING TAILORS

■ Raja Fashions (see Bespoke Suits on page 41) on 00852 2366 7624. For full details, visit **www.raja-fashions.com** ✉.
■ Ash Samtani Clothing Ltd on 00852 2367 4285 or visit the website at **www.samtani.com** ✉.

HEAD-TO-TOE BEAUTY

An effective daily skincare regime can be yours for literally pennies. Check out DIY alternatives to expensive creams and treatments or find a supplier who offers real value.

LOW-COST TREATMENT FOR BLEMISHES

Rather than paying for special shop-bought treatments, which range in price from around £4 to over £20, use a variety of tried-and-tested remedies for blemishes that cost just a few pennies.

Witch hazel or calamine lotion Dab on the cleansed, affected area before bedtime. Both treatments work just as well as more costly products.

Honey treatment Dab a little honey onto a blemish and cover it with a plaster. Honey kills the bacteria and aids the healing process.

Lemon juice healer Blemishes heal quickly if you dab them with a little lemon juice.

Potato cleanser To clear blackheads, rub your face with a slice of raw potato after cleansing.

TOP TIPS BEAUTY ON A BUDGET

By using inexpensive but effective products and household ingredients, you can avoid paying inflated prices for more slickly packaged beauty remedies.

■ **Star buy** A top London model agent happily admits to using E45 cream as her night-time moisturiser. At £3.99 for a 125g tub, it's one-tenth the price of more upmarket creams, and it works just as well.

■ **Soft as silk** Baby oil – at £2.57 for 300ml – can be just as effective as expensive cosmetics at removing make-up and softening skin. Olive oil is another great moisturiser at £1.29 for 250ml. You can also use it to bathe chapped hands, brittle nails and torn cuticles.

■ **All-purpose moisturiser** Vaseline jelly is great for slicking eyebrows and dabbing on dry skin under the eyes. For a plumper pout, mix it with sugar and massage it into your lips. Coat rough hands in Vaseline then put on gloves;

doing this for a few nights makes a big difference. The handbag-size pot for £0.87 is still one of the best beauty products on the market.

■ **Pennywise toner** Remove every last trace of cleanser with witch hazel. Keep a £2.14 200ml bottle in the fridge for a cheap, quick pick-me-up.

■ **Anti-ageing therapy** Instead of laser treatment and expensive creams, dab vinegar on age spots daily until they fade, or rub them with the inside of banana skins.

SWITCH SUPPLIER – SAVE OVER 60%

By buying your favourite beauty products from a cheaper shop or online you can make worthwhile savings without having to switch brands.

Lower prices High street discount stores like Superdrug and supermarkets such as Asda and Tesco give good deals on fragrances with savings of up to 70% on department store prices as well as good deals on many other own-brand and name-brand beauty products.

Web bargains Online suppliers offer huge savings and free delivery on orders over £25. At **www.buycosmetics.com** you can yield savings of over 60% on top brand skincare. Great bargains at **www.saveonmakeup.co.uk** included a Christian Dior lipstick at £1.99, reduced from £14.50 (December 2008). Try **www.fragrancedirect.co.uk** for discounted perfumes (£20 off Joop Homme Eau de Toilette), aftershaves and more.

Holiday savings If you holiday or take occasional shopping trips to France, you can pick up skincare, perfume and cosmetics for 20%–40% less than in Britain (look out for French brands like Chanel and Clarins).

TOP TIPS SAVE £20 ON A PEDICURE

Instead of heading for the local beauty salon where it can cost over £30, try a home pedicure for under £10.

■ Using a massage brush or roller, massage the soles of your feet from the toes to the heels and then the instep.

■ Give your feet a footbath, then rub off hard skin with a pumice and push back the cuticles with an orange stick.

■ Finally, refresh your feet with a tincture such as lavender, thyme or sage.

LOWER THE COST OF MEN'S GROOMING

Men's grooming is big business, but you don't need to go overboard on designer products to look and feel your best.

Choose with care As with women's beauty products, you can reduce your spending by buying a cheaper brand that still does the job and choosing a more economical supplier. A mid-range brand of aftershave lotion from a high street retailer is a mere £6.84 – a good buy compared with a similar designer-branded product costing £30 or more from department stores. Good-value mail-order companies such as Yves Rocher (**www.yves-rocher.co.uk** or 0870 049 2222), may also be worth trying for products you use every day.

Save on aftershave balm To save on a favourite designer balm, use a neutrally scented low-cost balm from the supermarket as a base and add a little of the expensive balm, which will fragrance the entire bottle.

RESOURCES

ESSENTIAL OILS
■ Neal's Yard Remedies
www.nealsyardremedies.com
0845 262 3145 ✉
■ Essentially Oils
www.essentiallyoils.com
0845 130 4400 ✉

BEAUTY ONLINE
■ Check out these useful websites for beauty products and tips:
www.makingcosmetics.com advice and ingredients to make your own
www.ivillage.co.uk/beauty for women
www.ebay.co.uk for beauty items and great deals on top brands
www.catwalk-queen.net for great beauty tips

SITES FOR MEN
■ Keenly priced shaving and skincare products are available at
www.shave.com ✉.
■ Find special offers and grooming tips at
www.lookmantastic.com ✉.
■ For grooming products and advice go to
www.menessentials.com
01273 425262 ✉.

FRUIT FACIAL
COST 40P PER FACIAL

1 tablespoon mashed strawberries
1 tablespoon of organic natural
  yoghurt

1 Mix the strawberries with the
yogurt.
2 Apply the mixture to your face and
neck, cover with a warm cloth and
leave it for a few minutes.
3 Rinse with cold water.
4 This is not suitable if you are
prone to allergies.

FIRMING MASK
COST 48P PER MASK

2 carrots
1 tablespoon of potato flour
1 egg yolk

1 Finely grate the carrots, add
the potato flour and egg yolk
and stir thoroughly.
2 Wash your face and neck and
immediately apply the paste.
3 Leave for 20 minutes.
4 Wash off with warm water
and rinse with cold.

PAMPERING FOR PENNIES

**Use inexpensive storecupboard ingredients for natural,
old-fashioned, homemade beauty preparations that
contain no harmful additives, smell delicious and
save you buying expensive branded products.**

MASK FOR OILY SKIN
COST 28P PER MASK

Juice of half an orange
8 tablespoons of flour

1 Squeeze the juice into a bowl and stir
in enough flour to make a thick paste.
2 After cleansing, apply the mask
with a soft brush and leave it on
for 20 minutes.
3 Wash off with warm water.

IVY MASSAGE OIL
COST £5 FOR A 2-3 MONTH SUPPLY

1 handful of fresh ivy leaves
100ml of wheatgerm oil
1 drop of rosemary oil

1 Put the ivy leaves in a jar and add the wheatgerm oil.
2 Seal and leave for two weeks in a warm place.
3 Strain through a fine sieve, add the rosemary oil, then pour the massage oil into a bottle and seal.
4 Massage into areas of cellulite using circular movements.
5 See warning below.

EXFOLIATING BODY SCRUB
COST 15P PER TREATMENT

2 tablespoons of double or whipping cream
1 tablespoon of salt

1 Put the cream and salt in a bowl and beat to a smooth paste.
2 In the shower or bath, gently rub the paste over your body using circular movements.
3 Shower or sponge off the body scrub afterwards.

MOISTURISING MASK
COST £2.45 FOR 3-4 MASKS

1 tablespoon of lanolin
1 tablespoon of petroleum jelly
3 drops of chamomile oil
3 drops of geranium oil

1 Combine the lanolin and petroleum jelly in a bowl, add the oils and stir in until thick and creamy.
2 Transfer to a small pot with a lid and store in a cool place for future use.

DEEP CLEANSER
COST 20P PER APPLICATION

1 Stroke on milk of magnesia with cotton wool balls, avoiding the eye area.
2 Leave for 10 minutes.
3 Gently remove with warm flannel and apply a moisturiser.

WARNING
Do NOT use rosemary essential oil if you are pregnant, have high blood pressure or suffer from epilepsy. Always consult a qualified aromatherapist if in doubt.

DRY HAIR SHAMPOO
COST £1 PER TREATMENT

1 egg white
2 egg yolks
1 teaspoon of honey
1 tablespoon of olive oil
Juice of 1 lemon

1 Whisk the egg white and fold in the yolks.
2 Stir the honey, olive oil and lemon juice.
3 Massage the shampoo into the scalp and thoroughly coat the hair.
4 Leave for a few minutes and rinse the hair, using plenty of water until all the shampoo has gone.

PATCH TEST
Essential oils are highly concentrated and can irritate the skin, so always take care, especially with a new oil. Dilute one drop in one teaspoon of carrier oil and test on your skin. Except for lavender and tea tree oils, pure essential oils should not be used on the skin.

BE CREATIVE WITH MAKE-UP

Don't spend money unnecessarily on expensive make-up. Often, a cheaper substitute will do just as good a job, or you can invest in a good-quality, multi-purpose product. Keep costs down by knowing how to make your make-up last.

BUY MULTI-PURPOSE AND SAVE

It is in the cosmetics manufacturers' interests to sell you a separate product for each make-up stage. But it makes economic sense to use cosmetics with a double or treble life.

An eye pencil pays its way A soft, light-brown good-quality eye pencil costing around £12 can be used for outlining lips, defining brows, shaping round the eye socket and putting a soft line under the lower lid. If you buy a separate lip pencil, brow pencil, eye shadow and eye pencil, the total could be over £25.

Cost-cutting colour A blusher can act as eye shadow and be used for cheeks and lips. Or you can pay around £11 for a quality lipgloss that can also be a blusher and brow highlighter (total cost for separate products is around £20).

Dual-use bases Buy a foundation or moisturiser that also acts as a sun block. A good-quality foundation with UV protection costs from £10–£30.

Budget compacts Look out for a combination foundation and powder compact for little more than the price of a powder alone.

GOOD-VALUE SUBSTITUTES

You can make further savings by buying some products from non-cosmetic counters.

Low-cost powder Baby powder at around £1.50 for 500g costs less than translucent powder; apply finely with a large make-up brush.

All-round sheen Vaseline is a multi-purpose bargain at around £1.90 for 225g. It conditions lips, adds a subtle glow to cheek bones and defines eyelashes.

RESOURCES

FRUGAL BEAUTY

■ To order leading brand beauty products online at a discount, try www.buycosmetics.com www.cosmetics4less.net www.saveonmakeup.co.uk or www.slapiton.tv (some offer free UK delivery and no minimum spend, others free delivery on orders over £25 minimum).

■ For recipes and ingredients on making your own cosmetics, check out the website www.makingcosmetics.com

FACING THE FACTS ON MAKE-UP

For beauty essentials, check out supermarket own-brands, such as Tesco and Asda, and online discount websites such as www.saveonmakeup.co.uk. The price difference between these and the name brands from the top cosmetics houses is significant.

BRAND	LIPSTICK	FOUNDATION	BLUSHER	MASCARA	TOTAL
Designer name	£16.50	£27.00	£24.50	£17.50	£85.50
Mid-range	£7.82	£10.27	£7.33	£8.31	£33.73
Low-cost	£3.95	£4.95	£3.50	£3.95	£16.35
Supermarket	£1.83	£1.83	£1.83	£1.83	£7.32

AVOID WASTING MAKE-UP

Don't waste money by throwing away expensive cosmetics before you've used them up. Use every ounce of the product to make your budget stretch.

Lipstick first aid If a lipstick breaks in half, salvage it by softening the ends over a flame, joining them together and leaving them to set in the fridge.

Use a lip brush Invaluable for rescuing the last of a lipstick and for creating a clean, professional outline. They cost from around £2.50, or buy an inexpensive brush set from £1.99.

Revive old pencils Dried-up eye and lip pencils can be softened overnight by putting them point down in a jar containing an inch of baby oil.

Nail varnish When nail varnish is past its best, dip the wand end into a jar of very hot water for five minutes.

Rescue crumbly powder Cakes of powder blush or eye shadow that start to crumble can be ground into loose powder and decanted into small jars.

TOP TIPS LONGER-LASTING MAKE-UP

A little know-how helps you to save money and time by avoiding having to reapply makeup constantly.

■ **Everlasting eyeshadow** Before putting on eye shadow, apply a light coat of cream foundation, blending with your little finger. The powdery shadow will bind to the foundation and stay in place longer than if applied directly.

■ **Longer lived lipstick** Your lipstick will last longer if you pat face powder over your lips, apply the lipstick, blot and powder again and reapply a final layer of lipstick.

■ **Nail varnish tricks** Make your nail varnish last longer by keeping it in the fridge. Bring it back to room temperature before applying to nails.

RESOURCES

HOME SHOPPING
Some companies specialise in a shop-at-home service. They all offer good-value hair and beauty products delivered to your door by a trained beauty consultant. Prices tend to be lower than those in the shops, and you can browse their range at your leisure.

■ **Avon** Contact them for a brochure on 0845 601 4040 or at **www.avon.uk.com** ✉.

■ **Body Shop** Call 0800 0929090 for details of their 'at home' service or visit the website **www.thebodyshop.co.uk** ✉.

■ **Virgin Vie** To receive a catalogue, call 0845 300 8022 or go to **www.virginvieathome.com** ✉.

REDUCE THE COST OF HAIRDRESSING

Don't be persuaded to get a haircut from an indifferent hairdresser, however cheap. The key to good-looking hair is a good cut, but you don't have to pay inflated salon prices.

CUT THE COST OF SALON VISITS

To reduce the cost of good hairdressing, keep salon treatments to a minimum, watch out for recommended freelances or offer to be a model for a hairdressing salon or school.

Minimise costs If your only alternative is a visit to an expensive salon, get the cut and skip the blowdry.

Hire a freelance If you hear of a good freelance hairdresser who will cut your hair at home for a fair price, book an appointment immediately.

Become a model Check out special deals at hairdressing schools or trainee nights at established salons that are looking for models. The cut costs around £5 – at some salons it's free – while the colouring and perm cost up to £15 each. These deals are often advertised in the local press. The ads will state the requirements for a cut – in most cases you must be over 18 – and appointments are restricted to certain times. Often the stated booking fee is around £5, but the ad doubles as a voucher so showing it means that the booking is actually free. It is best to phone well in advance, book and turn up early. Make sure that you allow plenty of time as a trainee will take a lot longer than an experienced hairdresser.

TOP TIPS BUYING SHAMPOO

A recent report by *Which?* untangled some myths about shampoos. It tested a range of shampoos from the cheapest to the most expensive.

■ **Buy the best-value product** All shampoos tested cleaned hair efficiently but the cheapest shampoos did a better job than the more expensive salon products. The survey concluded that much of what we pay for is packaging, advertising and sophisticated fragrances.

■ **Supermarkets for savings** It established that it is cheaper to buy shampoos in the high street than in the salon, but even then not all outlets are equal, with supermarkets giving the best value. In the *Which?* test, Asda and Tesco charged the least for shampoos (all brands) and Boots charged the most.

■ **Salon products** If you are after specialist products that aren't available in supermarkets, try **www.salonlines.co.uk** ✉ and take advantage of the reductions.

CASE STUDY

CUTTING HAIR COSTS

Kirsty Wallace normally had her hair cut, styled and coloured at a good-quality local salon for around £100. As she had recently quit her job and returned to college, she was short of cash and had to cut back on her hairdressing costs. She knew what she wanted done to her hair, so she contacted a local hairdressing school. She had to wait over a week for an appointment and was warned to allow plenty of time on the day. A cut and colour with a Level 3 student cost her £22, a saving of £78, so it was worth the wait.

MODEL DEALS AT THE SALONS

SALON	SERVICES	COST
L'Oreal Technical Centre, Hammersmith Road, London W6 020 8762 4292.	First appointment (Basic cut, colour or perm) Second appointment Call for a consultation appointment.	Free £15
Trevor Sorbie, Floral Street, London WC2 0844 44 56901	Cuts and colouring on Monday and Tuesday from 6.30pm. Supervised students style your hair.	Free
Manchester College Seven campuses around the city 0161 614 8000 (**www.ccm.ac.uk**)	Cut and finish from Colour (full head) from	£5.60 £10.20
Toni and Guy academies Branches throughout the UK. See **www.toniandguy.co.uk** or phone 020 7836 0606	Cuts Colouring or highlights	from £5 £15–£30
Sassoon Academies Four branches in London (three in W1 and one in Knightsbridge SW1). See **www.sassoon.com** or phone 020 7399 6901	Cuts (discounts available) Colouring and highlights You must book in advance.	up to £12 price on request
Southampton City College St Mary Street, Southampton See **www.southampton-city.ac.uk** or phone 023 8057 7249	Cuts Quasi colour Cap highlights The college's Transformation salon offers a range of hair and beauty treatments	£4–£6 £10 £16

AVOID HIGH PRICES

Even if you are attached to your professional hair-care brand, try to avoid buying hair products in salons as you will normally pay the full price. Many brands that were formerly available only in salons are now on the shelves in the high street. Try supermarkets, chemists and online retailers for better prices. For 300ml of a well-known 'professional' shampoo, the price can vary from £8.95 in a salon to £7 from an online retailer.

DYE IT YOURSELF – SAVE OVER 90%

If your hair is in reasonably good condition and you fancy a colour change, consider doing it yourself, or with the help of a friend at home. The difference in price is striking – you can pay over £80 in a salon for highlights to long hair, but products such as L'Oreal Couleur Experte allow you to achieve a similar effect at home for under £10.

INVEST IN CLIPPERS

For men or boys who like short, cropped hair, invest in clippers at under £20. With a haircut costing over £10, the clippers will repay the investment in two cuts.

RESOURCES

DIY HAIR

Follow the step-by-step guides to creating a range of styles at **www. ukhairdressers.com** ✉. A 5-disk *Hairdressing DVD* set takes you from Fundamentals to Transient techniques, at **www.hair-dvd.com** ✉. Books available include *How to Simply Cut Hair Even Better* (£6.99) or *Haircutting for Dummies* (£9.90) both at **www.amazon.co.uk** ✉.

Healthy living

Investing in your long-term health need not be an expensive option. Instead, take a balanced approach to diet and exercise, and stay up-to-date with what conventional and alternative medicine have to offer. You'll reap the benefits.

HEALTHY LIFESTYLE ON A BUDGET

Diets, fitness regimes, health plans – the complexities and potential expense of a healthy lifestyle can seem daunting. But the essentials for health are simple: a good, balanced diet and regular exercise of a type you enjoy and will continue to pursue. Both are a lot less financially draining than following health fads or paying for expensive treatments.

EIGHT ECONOMY WAYS TO GOOD HEALTH

Before you embark on a new health and fitness regime, keep in mind a few important points:

Healthy food can be cheaper Look at your diet and decide on the changes you want to make. A diet beneficial to your health can also be good for your bank balance – fresh fruit, vegetables, pasta and pulses are all much cheaper than convenience foods, which tend to be high in unhealthy salt, fat, sugars and starches.

Buy fresh This is a rule worth learning to live by. The longer your food has been stored, the less nutritional value it has and the worse it tastes.

Healthy ingredients Consider natural alternatives to shop-bought remedies and add vegetables and pulses to meals to make them healthier.

Drink more The average adult needs to drink 2 litres (3½ pints) of liquid a day. This can be made up of water, soft drinks, tea and coffee, but doctors recommend a maximum of three or four cups of tea or coffee a day.

Use the freezer If you buy and cook your own fresh food, you don't have to give up the convenience of an instant meal altogether. Make soups and stews in batches and freeze for occasions when you don't have the time to cook a full meal.

Think before joining a gym Never join a gym without considering the alternatives. Gyms aren't for everyone and they are expensive – consider walking, swimming, gentle stretching or cycling instead.

Set realistic goals Be sensible and tailor your fitness regime to your lifestyle. Aim for five 30-minute exercise sessions a week – if necessary, some of these can take a form that will fit into your ordinary activities, for example vigorous housework or a brisk walk to the shops. And you don't need to do the whole 30 minutes at once – you can vary your routine on some days by doing three 10-minute sessions.

Don't be a fitness fashion victim Avoid the temptation to think health and fitness is a goal that has to come with a hefty price tag (you don't need a £90 pair of trainers to find out if jogging is for you). But if looking fashionable is an urge you can't resist, then check out companies like M and M Direct (**www.mandmdirect.com** ✉), which offers a range of top-name clothing and goods at up to 75% of high street prices. Companies such as Sportzwear (**www.sportzwear.com** ✉) and Sportsdirect (**www.sportsdirect.com** or 0870 333 9400 ✉) offer a great selection of brands at competitive prices.

RESOURCES

GENERAL HEALTH

www.eatwell.gov.uk ✉ offers advice on a healthy diet, food labelling and keeping food safe plus interactive games, quizzes and useful calculators.

www.takelifeon.co.uk ✉ offers good advice on healthier eating and how to increase activity.

YOU ARE WHAT YOU EAT

A healthy diet helps to keep you well and reduces the risk of serious illnesses such as cancer and heart disease. The good news is that there are lots of ways of introducing beneficial foods into your diet without making big, unpalatable changes, and at minimal cost.

HEALTHY DIET, HEALTHY WALLET

Although choosing the healthier alternative can save you money, a few foods that offer the best nutritional value can be expensive, but you need only use them sparingly.

Go easy on meat Make meat go further by cooking it in casseroles or stir-fries bulked out with cheaper ingredients such as beans, pulses or seasonal vegetables.

Cheap, healthy ingredients Basing meals on starchy foods such as rice, pasta and bread is not only good for a balanced diet but offers excellent value for money.

FIVE A DAY FOR LESS

Doctors agree that we should all eat five portions of fruit and vegetables each day. Here are the best-value ways of ensuring those five portions are a part of your daily diet.

Canned and frozen count too Your daily intake can include fresh, frozen, chilled, dried and canned foods; the health properties of some (like tomatoes) are even better in a canned form, as well as often being cheaper. Save more by buying the supermarket's own brand – it's just as nutritious.

FISH AND MEAT vs VEGETARIAN ALTERNATIVES

Although you may not want to become fully vegetarian, consider dropping fish or meat from your diet for at least one day a week. A 2004 study for National Vegetarian Week revealed that vegetarians visit hospital 22% less often than their meat-eating friends. Reducing your meat intake can be healthier and mean big savings on your food bill.

PRODUCT	DESCRIPTION/USES	PRICE PER PERSON
BEEF	Fillet steak	£5.50
CHICKEN	Whole roasting chicken	£2.00
TOFU	Soya bean curd. Rich in protein, calcium and vitamins. Useful in stir-fries.	£0.25
FISH	Cod fillets	£1.80
QUORN	Mycoprotein (derived from mushrooms). Low in fat, readily absorbs flavour, so useful in casseroles.	£0.75
NUTS	As homemade or pre-prepared tinned nutloaf. Can be roasted, grilled or fried.	£0.50
BEANS	Dried, tinned or fresh. For use in stews and casseroles.	£0.26

BEST-VALUE SUPERFOODS

Certain 'superfoods' provide excellent health benefits as well as offering great value. Include them in your diet regularly for maximum protection against disease.

FOOD	BENEFITS	PRICE
Broccoli	Full of goodness whether fresh or frozen. A good source of vitamin C, folate, iron, potassium and cancer-fighting compounds, it is useful in stir-fries and as a basis for homemade soup.	£1.68 per kilo
Citrus and other tree fruit	Juice or eat whole for fibre and Vitamin C. The antioxidants in some citrus fruits (including pink grapefruits and blood oranges) contain lycopene, which can help to reduce the risk of breast and prostate cancers.	Oranges £1.93 per kilo
Soya/tofu	May help to reduce the risk of breast and colon cancer. Although soya milk can be an acquired taste, it is easy to introduce tofu occasionally as a cheap alternative to red meat and chicken.	Tofu from £1.45 for 250g
Spinach	Rich in antioxidants that help to protect against cancer; folate, essential for a healthy nervous system and proper brain function; and, lutein, which is good for eye health. Steam lightly or eat small leaves raw in salads.	98p per kilo (frozen)
Tomatoes	Like citrus fruit, tomatoes contain lycopene and antioxidants that protect the immune system. Lycopene occurs in higher quantities in canned rather than fresh tomatoes.	£1.65 per kilo

Just juice One – but only one – of your portions of fresh fruit can be taken in the form of juice.

KEEP THE GOODNESS IN

Don't squander your money by making the effort to buy fresh fruit and vegetables and then carelessly destroying their nutritional benefits.

Fresh is best Eat fresh fruit and veg as soon as possible rather than storing – or use frozen.

Minimal cooking Don't cook vegetables for too long as you will overcook them. Cover to keep in steam.

Don't dilute vitamins Boil vegetables in as little water as possible without boiling them dry, then use the water as a nutritious stock for making soup.

Clever storage Cover and chill cut fruit and veg and don't soak or vitamins and minerals can dissolve away.

GROW YOUR OWN

Even if you don't have a vegetable plot, you can make savings by growing fruit and vegetables in your garden.

Be selective Don't grow vegetables you can buy cheaply in the shops; go for those that are sold at a premium, take up little space, yet are simple to grow. French beans, mangetout, sugar snap peas and cut-and-come-again (or 'loose leaf') salad, such as 'Salad Bowl', will net you the biggest savings, especially if you grow them from seed.

Pot-sized plot If you have a courtyard or very small garden, you can still grow some fruit and vegetables in pots. In a 23cm–25cm (9in–10in) pot you can grow one aubergine, pepper or tomato plant; four climbing French or runner bean plants; 32 carrots; or three strawberry plants.

Save on herbs Grow the herbs you use most frequently in a window box, pot or a garden bed by the kitchen door so you can harvest them as and when they are needed. Many have nutritional and therapeutic benefits (see pages 75–77).

GET YOUR ESSENTIAL FATS FOR LESS

The omega-3 essential fatty acids are beneficial fats that can reduce the risk of a heart attack or stroke. You can increase the amount in your diet at minimal extra cost.

Swap meat for fish Replace at least one meat meal a week with oily fish. You don't have to go for expensive fish such as tuna or salmon; mackerel, sardines or herring are just as good, and canned sardines have the bonus of being high in calcium, too, as the bones are edible.

Vegetarian option Top up your omega-3 oils by scattering a handful of pumpkin seeds on a salad or eating a few walnuts. Or eat 1–2 tablespoons of ground flax seeds a day: buy the seeds and mill or grind them yourself rather than taking expensive flax oil or ground flax seed supplements.

WATER ON TAP

Aim to drink up to 2 litres a day – and the more of it that is water the better as this ensures good circulation and digestion and prevents dehydration and the fatigue and mental fuzziness that usually accompany it.

Tap water is just as good According to the Drinking Water Inspectorate, there are no health benefits from drinking bottled water. By drinking tap water instead of bottled you could save 70p a day – that's £21 a month.

TOP TIPS BEST BUYS

To make sure you don't end up paying more for your healthier diet; you may have to make a few modifications to the way you shop.

■ **Bargains at the wholefood cooperative** Although supermarkets often offer value for money, wholefood cooperatives (see Resources, left) can be cheaper for healthy alternatives. We found cashew nuts at half the price bought in 1kg packs from a wholefood cooperative compared to the price in the supermarket, where it is hard to find packs bigger than 300g. The same applies to many popular herbs and spices.

■ **Buy dried not canned** Pulses such as kidney beans, chickpeas and lentils work out about 50% cheaper if you buy them dried rather than canned. But you do need to remember to soak them before cooking.

■ **Buy fruit not fizz** A can of a fizzy drink may contain up to 8 teaspoons of sugar, which encourages weight gain and is bad for your teeth. For a healthy alternative that contains valuable vitamins, mix 500ml of unsweetened fruit juice (orange or apple), with 500ml of water, chill and serve. It will cost just a quarter of the price of a canned fizzy drink.

RESOURCES

HEALTHY EATING

■ Use the website **www.foodstandards.gov.uk** ✉ to check out official Food Standards Agency advice on food, its supply and preparation.

■ For a list of wholefood cooperatives, farm shops and organic outlets near you, contact Big Barn Ltd 01234 871005 or visit **www.bigbarn.co.uk** ✉.

GO ORGANIC THE COST-CONSCIOUS WAY

The organic food industry has grown significantly in recent years, with sales of organic goods now topping £2 billion a year and four out of five families buying some organic produce. Although organic food is still generally more expensive, by buying selectively you can keep costs down.

CHECK OUT THE CHEAPEST SOURCES

The big supermarkets supply over 80% of the organic food we buy but their prices vary considerably. A *Which?* survey in 2004 found that the price of a basket of 13 organic foods, including chicken, beef, milk, vegetables and general groceries, varied by more than £12 between six major high street supermarkets. To ensure you get the best prices, look on the different supermarket websites or phone to check current prices before shopping.

Specialist shops Although buying from producers in smaller quantities than the supermarkets, small independent organic shops are not necessarily more expensive. Keep checking them for value buys.

Buy direct from the supplier Some larger organic farms have their own shops or farm gate sales, or attend farmers' markets (see pages 24–25). Others sell by mail order. To find organic producers in your area, or those who supply a particular product mail order, visit the Soil Association's website **www.whyorganic.org** ✉ and select the Organic Directory. Save by comparing producers' prices online before making an order: prices for organic rump steak, for example, can vary by £7 per kg or more.

SELECTIVE BUYING

Going completely organic could increase your food bill by 40%–50%. But you can make your budget go further by buying just those foods that are most commonly subjected to, or contain, high levels of pesticides. They are:

- apples
- bananas
- green beans
- milk
- peaches
- strawberries
- oats
- peppers
- rice

COMPARE BOX SCHEMES

Run by an organic farm or delivery company, a box scheme puts together boxes of seasonal organic vegetables or fruit, or a mixture of both, for a fixed price and delivers it to your door. Some schemes list what will be included each week on their website and allow you to indicate what you don't like. Often eggs and other products can be requested, too.

Avoid paying extra Prices start from £9, but a box for a family of four is more typically £15–£20. Box schemes are listed in the Soil Association Organic Directory (see Resources, right). Look for a company that delivers free in your area to get better value for money. Some schemes charge £4 or more to deliver unless you order boxes over a certain price, which may be more than you need.

RESOURCES

GOING ORGANIC

■ For information on organic food and farming, including producers, farm shops and box schemes, contact the Soil Association on 0117 314 5000 or 0131 666 2474 (Scotland) or visit **www.soilassociation.org** ✉.

■ **www.alotoforganics.co.uk** is an organic search engine with links to a wide range of organic websites.

■ *The Organic Directory 2007–2008*, published by the Soil Association and Green Books, price £8.95 plus postage, is a guide to organic products and services, from shops and box schemes to restaurants and holiday accommodation in Britain.

FITNESS FOR ALL

ASK YOURSELF

BEFORE YOU JOIN A GYM

■ What do you want from your fitness routine? Is a gym the best way to obtain it?

■ How close is the gym to your home or work? It should be easy and cheap to get there.

■ Have you looked at the alternatives? Compare a local authority gym (from under £40 a month) with private facilities.

■ How long are you committing to? Joining for a whole year could be an unwise financial decision.

■ Check what is included. Is this a place that guarantees to update your fitness programme every 12 weeks or is subsequent contact with an instructor unlikely?

Industry statistics show that the average person who joins a gym attends for just 12 weeks before reducing, or stopping, their visits. Private gym membership can cost over £800 a year – plus a joining fee – and some clubs insist on annual membership, so think carefully before signing up.

TOP TIPS JOINING A GYM

Having decided that a fitness gym or health club is for you, consider a few points before joining.

■ **Check out the venues** Try at least three suitable gyms, preferably within 10–15 minutes of work or home. Book a viewing appointment, avoiding 5pm–7pm on weekdays.

■ **Don't be hasty** Never sign up after just one visit. Make a second visit at a busy time and question other members about the facilities, including the square footage of the gym (ideally a ratio of space to members between 10:1 and 15:1).

■ **Haggle for a bargain** Don't be afraid to negotiate, it is a fiercely competitive market. Avoid the post-Christmas and pre-summer rush to sign up and look out for special promotions. During quiet periods you are sure to find trial memberships for a set number of weeks at a reduced price.

■ **Membership options** Consider reduced-rate, off-peak packages. These give restricted admission (8am–4pm excluding weekends, for example) but are ideal if you are at home during the day and could save you up to 60%.

■ **Get a group discount** Gather a group of friends or colleagues and get a discounted corporate membership – most health clubs offer them for groups of 10 or more.

■ **Pay as you go** Many local authority gyms have a pay-by-session option. This could work out cheaper if your number of visits per month is likely to vary significantly.

ANNUAL FITNESS COSTS – THE COMPARISONS

Even a modestly priced local authority gym could cost you around £400 a year. So what are the alternatives?

A regular swim is good all-round exercise, excellent value for money and can burn up 500–700 kcals/hour; a pair of trainers will get you on the road for a regular run, burning 600–1000 kcals/hour; or you could invest in walking shoes and explore the countryside (130–240 kcals/hour).

PRIVATE HEALTH CLUB	£850
LOCAL AUTHORITY FITNESS GYM	£400
YOGA CLASS (once a week)	£390
SWIMMING (assuming two visits a week)	£380
RUNNING	£85
COUNTRY WALKING	£50
EXERCISE DVD	£15

RESOURCES

BUYING BIKES ONLINE

■ You can pick up bargain bikes of all kinds, used and unused (sometimes factory rejects), on **www.ebay.co.uk** ✉. If you want to collect your bike in person (and many sellers prefer this), search the cycling category by region.

■ The Police Property Disposal website **www.bumblebeeauctions.co.uk** ✉ auctions unclaimed property held at police stations around the country. Check which station the bike is at before bidding, as you will have to collect it. (See *Leisure and hobbies*, page 167.)

INEXPENSIVE FITNESS ALTERNATIVES

If you aren't a gym person but still want to keep fit, there are many low-cost alternatives.

Walking is free Get off the bus or train one stop earlier and walk. If you work in an office, take a turn round the block or visit the nearest park in your lunch hour. If you enjoy the countryside, make walking your weekend hobby. A brisk walk uses around 240–300 kcals an hour.

Step up to fitness Use the stairs instead of the lift or escalator and you'll burn up to 1,000 kcals an hour.

Try a taster Look out for introductory or taster sessions to fitness classes. Don't commit to a 26-week yoga or Pilates class before trying it.

Good team work Team up with a group of friends and hire a village or community hall. You can get somewhere for a couple of hours that will cost about £20 and – if there are enough of you – you could even hire a freelance instructor.

Free recuperation If you have had a long illness or are recuperating from surgery, ask your GP if there is an arrangement with a local fitness centre whereby they can prescribe a set number of free sessions.

On your bike Cycling is one of the best cardiovascular exercises and burns around 400–600 kcals an hour. Look out for secondhand bicycles advertised in your local paper, or buy from a local cycle auction – sometimes organised by schools or the police – or an online auction (see Resources, above).

SPORT TO ENTERTAIN

Much has been written about today's unhealthy lifestyles, however sport is social and can offer great entertainment as well as exercise – much of it free or for a nominal fee.

■ **After-school and holiday clubs** Check with your child's school or local authority to discover what is on offer. Education departments are responsible for many local sports facilities, including swimming pools, which may offer special holiday rates, playschemes or even holiday camps (**www.direct.gov.uk**).

■ **Free sport sessions** Watch out for schemes such as Asda's Sporting Chance initiative. Vouchers available instore give children across the UK access to free sports sessions during school holidays (not Christmas), including fencing, football, basketball and trampolining. Visit **www.asda-sportingchance.co.uk** for details.

■ **Group activities** Many swimming pools offer free, or discounted, sessions for the over-60s, as well as yoga and exercise classes. Older residents in Blackley, Manchester can visit the UK's first purpose-built playground for the elderly, which features specially designed fitness equipment. More playgrounds are planned.

RESOURCES

BUY TRAINERS FOR LESS
You'll find bargain trainers in factory outlet stores and on the Internet. But remember cost is not the only factor: you must be sure they fit correctly and are comfortable. If buying online always check the returns policy.
Get discounts of up to 60% at **www.mandmdirect. com** (0871 664 1333) ✉ and money off well-known brands at **www.sportsshoes.com** (01274 530530) ✉.

HOME WORK-OUTS

If it's difficult to get to the gym or an exercise class, or you'd rather exercise in the privacy of your home, there are various options. The key to successful home exercising is to be realistic about what you are likely to enjoy and so will continue to do. Otherwise any outlay, however small, will be a waste of money.

Use a DVD Invest in an exercise video/DVD and devise your own programme. Before deciding what to buy, look on **www.reviewcentre.com** to compare users' ratings and reviews of different DVDs – a frank 'this was definitely not for beginners' could save you a £15 mistake. The site also tells you what to expect to pay. It's also worth checking **www.amazon.co.uk** ✉ for new and secondhand prices.

Simple props work Invest in a few inexpensive pieces of equipment. A skipping rope (from £3) will give you a great cardiovascular workout, or get a fitball (from £10–£16 from **www.fitball-training.com** ✉) – a superb piece of equipment recommended by fitness professionals to develop muscles in the trunk. Hand weights at around £10 are good for toning the arms, or you can improvise with two same-size cans of baked beans (or whatever you have in your storecupboard).

TOP TIPS EXERCISE MACHINES

The two most popular exercise machines bought for home use are the exercise bike and cross (or elliptical) trainer. Although these require more space and outlay than the equipment above, you can get bargains if you know where to look, and they'll cost much less than annual gym fees.

■ **Discounts on line** Look at **www.powerhouse-fitness.co.uk** ✉ for a good range of discounted trainers and **www.fitness-superstore.co.uk** ✉, which offers a price guarantee and big reductions on ex-demo stock; the company also offers an onsite warranty, so will send out an engineer if there's a fault. Visit **www.argos-sports.co.uk** ✉, which guarantees the lowest internet prices in the UK and a 14-day money-back guarantee; call 0845 465 0846 for expert advice.

■ **Don't go for the cheapest** It's better to buy a discounted or secondhand machine (look in your local paper or on **ebay.co.uk** ✉) than a cheaper new one that isn't as solid or has fewer programmes. Not only will you get a better machine for the price, but you'll also be able to resell it – should you want to – without losing much money.

■ **Must-have features** If you are to keep using your machine it has to give you an interesting workout. Look for one with a variety of programmes that vary the resistance level. Also go for a machine with a heart monitor.

BEST-VALUE SPORTSWEAR

You don't need to have the latest in fitness clothing in order to exercise. An old T-shirt and shorts or tracksuit bottoms are perfectly adequate to start with.

Brand names for less If you do decide you need specialised clothing, buy at factory outlet shops or on discount days at department stores such as Debenhams. You're likely to find the best discounts online; sites such as **www.mandmsports.com** ✉ and **www.littlewoodsdirect.com** ✉ allow you to search by brand and give discounts of as much as 75%.

HOMEMADE REMEDIES

The average medicine cabinet probably costs around £30 to stock every three or four months. So save money by remembering that many foods, herbs and spices can be used as inexpensive medicines for a variety of ailments.

ACHING FEET

Add 3 tablespoons plain mustard to a bowl of warm water and stir until dissolved. Soak your feet for at least 15 minutes or until the water has cooled completely.

COLDS

Drink echinacea tea, a natural antibiotic that also strengthens the immune system. Or make a hot drink with the juice of half a lemon and a teaspoon of honey in a glass of hot water. The lemon is rich in vitamin C and the honey has antiseptic properties. (Do not give honey to children under 2 years old.) Garlic fights infection so use it in your diet to build resistance to colds and flu. It also helps combat coronary heart disease by cutting the levels of fatty deposits in the blood.

BAD BREATH (HALITOSIS)

Chew fresh parsley or mint leaves, or make your own herbal mouthwash. Boil 2 cups of water in a small pan, remove from the heat and add fresh parsley and 2 teaspoons each of whole cloves, ground cinnamon and peppermint extract. Leave the mixture to infuse for an hour then strain into a jar. Seal and keep in the fridge for up to two weeks, using after meals to freshen the breath.

ACNE

Nasturtiums are a natural antibiotic. Make a tea from a handful of chopped leaves and boiling water and drink three times a day. Use as a face wash when cooled.

HANGOVERS

Honey – taken with vitamin C, plenty of water and a little caffeine – helps the body eliminate alcohol and overcome the effects of drinking too much.

COUGHS

To make a cough syrup, combine 3 tablespoons lemon juice and 1 cup honey with ¼ cup warm water. Take 1 or 2 tablespoons every three hours. Do not give to children under 2 years.

PMT

To ease pre-menstrual tension, two weeks before your period increase your intake of fruit, vegetables and low-fat dairy items and reduce caffeine and alcohol; eat at least every three hours and exercise regularly.

HEADACHES

For a nervous headache, drink a weak infusion of rosemary or basil. Infuse 1 teaspoon fresh rosemary leaves in a pint of boiling water for 5–10 minutes, then add lemon and honey to taste. For basil, infuse 1 teaspoon fresh chopped leaves in a cup of hot water. Drink once or twice a day. For a tension headache, place a hot compress (a heating pad, hot water bottle or hot towel) on the neck to relax the muscles.

EAR WAX

Flush out ear wax with a 50/50 mixture of hydrogen peroxide and warm water. Repeat twice a day until the wax softens and washes out.

INDIGESTION

To counter the discomfort of indigestion, drink a cup of mint or fennel tea, which you can buy as herbal tea bags. To make your own fresh mint tea, put 2 teaspoons chopped fresh mint leaves in a cup of boiling water and leave for 5–10 minutes to infuse. Strain, then sip slowly after meals. Alternatively, put 1 teaspoon sodium bicarbonate in a glass of water, stir to dissolve, then drink. The alkaline solution neutralises the acid in your stomach.

HEARTBURN

Bananas have a natural antacid effect, so if you suffer from heartburn – caused by excessive acid refluxing into the oesophagus from the stomach – eat a banana. If you are pregnant and suffer from heartburn at night, eat an apple before bed.

INSOMNIA

Drink a cup of chamomile tea in the evening, or a sweetened milk drink. The sugars in the drink help the brain cells to absorb more tryptophan (in the milk protein) from the bloodstream. The brain converts tryptophan to a soothing chemical called serotonin.

MIGRAINE

Eat a couple of fresh feverfew leaves in a sandwich each day to reduce – and in some cases even prevent – migraine attacks. Do not eat the leaves directly as they can cause mouth ulcers. CAUTION: Pregnant women should not eat feverfew.

INSECT BITES

Relieve the itching and pain of all bites and stings by applying ice to the area. Treat bee stings by flicking out the sting horizontally (to avoid squeezing in more venom from the sac), then apply a paste of bicarbonate of soda and water. Treat wasp sings with vinegar. CAUTION: Allergic reactions to insect bites can be severe. If in doubt, get medical assistance immediately.

ARTHRITIS

Fill self-sealing food bags with ice and hold them against the affected joints for 15–20 minutes. Repeat several times a day until the swelling goes and the pain is relieved. Alternatively, rub in a little plain mustard.

MOTION SICKNESS

Peel some fresh root ginger and chew before and during travel. Or chew candied ginger. Ginger is more effective in preventing travel sickness than some over-the-counter remedies and does not cause drowsiness.

SORE THROAT

Ease a sore throat with one of these homemade gargles.
■ Dissolve 1 teaspoon table salt in a cup of warm water.
■ Infuse 1 teaspoon dried sage or 2 teaspoons chopped fresh sage in a cup of boiling water. Cool before use.
■ Combine 2 tablespoons plain mustard and 1 tablespoon each of lemon juice, salt and honey with 1½ cups boiling water. Allow to cool.

CONSTIPATION

For a natural laxative, soak five prunes in orange juice or water overnight. Eat the prunes and drink the soaking liquid before breakfast. Or combine 2 cups tomato or vegetable juice with 1 cup sauerkraut juice and 1–2 cups carrot juice. Drink 1 cup at a time, refrigerating the rest.

OSTEOPOROSIS

For an inexpensive supplement, take sodium-free antacid tablets – they are just as effective as traditional calcium supplements but less expensive.

SUNBURN

Wrap ice cubes in a towel and apply to the sunburn to reduce soreness and swelling. To make a cooling solution, put 4 tea bags, 2 cups fresh mint leaves and 4 cups water in a saucepan. Simmer for 5 minutes, strain and cool. Apply with a face cloth.

NASAL CONGESTION

Garlic and onions are natural alternatives to over-the-counter decongestants. Eat as many as you can, either raw in salads or in cooked dishes. Inhaling steam is also a good remedy. Pour boiling water into a bowl and cover your head and the bowl with a towel. For extra benefit, add 6 drops of eucalyptus oil. Drink elderflower tea, which eases catarrh and relieves sinus problems.

TOOTHACHE

Soak a sterile cotton ball or piece of gauze with oil of cloves and apply to the area. If the ache has just started, a hot drink may help; for on-going pain, suck an ice cube for relief.

SAVE ON SUPPLEMENTS

With a few exceptions, a healthy diet should remove the need for vitamin and mineral supplements. But if you need to take supplements on a regular basis, you can still do something to reduce the cost.

DO YOU NEED THEM?

The sale of vitamins and minerals represents a multi-million pound industry. Those most likely to benefit are:

Pregnant women If you are trying to conceive or are already pregnant, a supplement of 400 micrograms of folic acid is recommended up to the 12th week of pregnancy. Vitamin A supplements should not be taken (and foods high in vitamin A, such as liver, should be avoided) to prevent damage to the baby's development.

Children Young children aged between 6 months and 5 years may need vitamin A and D supplements if they don't like dietary sources such as liver, fish, leafy green vegetables or red or orange fruit and vegetables, or if they have minimal exposure to sunlight.

Menopausal women Women who are going through the menopause or are post-menopausal may need calcium and Vitamin D supplements to help prevent osteoporosis. To get good value for money, buy calcium citrate, which is more expensive but is absorbed well by the body, instead of calcium carbonate, which is cheaper but not easily absorbed and can lead to kidney stones. Vitamin E is also useful.

Those on restricted diets If you are a vegetarian or are following a restricted diet for medical reasons, you may need supplements such as vitamin B12, vitamin D, calcium, iron and zinc.

DISCOUNTS IN THE HIGH STREET

Look for promotions run by leading high-street retailers such as Superdrug and Boots, or health food chains such as Holland & Barrett. Three-for-two deals are often the cheapest way of buying supplements, and you can make considerable savings by buying in bulk. Be careful to check the best-before dates and calculate how many you'll use within this period of time.

Supermarket savers Most supermarkets now stock a wide range of own-brand and branded supplements and often run discounts or buy-one-get-one-free offers.

ONLINE BARGAINS

Check Internet sites such as **www.hollandandbarrett.com** 0870 606 6605 ✉, as its own-label products usually offer some savings; **www.zipvit.com** 0800 0282875 ✉, which has permanently reduced prices and challenges the shopper to find cheaper vitamins elsewhere; and, **www.biovea.co.uk** 0800 612 9600 ✉, which offers free postage and packing on orders over £29.

Price comparisons You can also use a site such as **www.savebuckets.co.uk** ✉ or **www.bestshopsearch.co.uk** ✉ to find advice, comparisons and information on where to go for the

ASK YOURSELF

DO I HAVE A DEFICIENCY?

■ Do you have muscle spasms, cramps or aches?

■ Are you suffering from fatigue, apathy, poor concentration or depression?

■ Are you anaemic?

■ Do you have bone pain or osteoporosis?

■ Is your skin dry or scaly, or does it heal slowly?

If the answer is yes to any of these, it could be that you have a vitamin or mineral deficiency. Consult your GP, who may recommend supplements.

NATURAL SUPPLEMENTS VS CONVENTIONAL TREATMENTS

There are a number of vitamins, minerals and natural remedies that are proven to help with certain conditions. They also tend to work out cheaper than the equivalent conventional pharmaceutical products that provide the same benefits.

SUPPLEMENT	GOOD FOR	COST	PHARMACEUTICAL PRODUCT
Acidophilus	Settling the stomach when travelling abroad or when taking a course of antibiotics	£17.57/60 caps 29p a day	£4.69/10 sachets 47p–£1.17 a day (*Resolve Extra*)
Aloe vera	Healthier hair, skin and nails	£8.32/180 caps 5p a day	£21.52 for 90 tabs 24p a day (*Perfectil*)
Cod liver oil	Healthier joints	£7.50/180 caps 4p a day	£12.71/90 tabs 15p–45p a day (*Seven Seas JointCare*)
Evening primrose oil	Pre-menstrual tension	£6.80/120 caps 6p a day	£3.11/20 tabs 31p–93p a day (*Feminax*)
Korean Ginseng	Helping the body resist all types of stress	£11.70/180 caps 7p 13p a day	£5.86/75 tabs 16p a day (*Stressless*)
Lavender oil	Relieving stress and insomnia	£6.36/30ml (dose 2–3 drops a day)	£4.69/16 tabs 29p a day (*Nytol One-a-Night*)

best buys (select the Health & Beauty category on the Home page, then Vitamins to display the vitamin categories). Visit the Food Standards Agency's Eat Well, Be Well website at **www.eatwellbewell.gov.uk** ✉ for information on vitamins and minerals, including where they are found, how much you need and what they do (find advice under 'Healthy diet' then 'Nutrition essentials').

SAVE ON A YEAR'S SUPPLY
If you need a particular supplement, look into discounts for buying a year's supply at once. At **www.healthydirect.com** 0800 107 57 57 ✉, a bottle of 360 capsules of own-brand Evening Primrose Oil costs £16.99, a saving of nearly 30% over a 4-month online supply and over 50% cheaper than the equivalent (full-price) product in a high-street chemist.

VITAMINS AND MINERALS ON TRIAL
If in doubt, and after consultation with your GP, buy a small amount of a supplement that might be helpful. Don't go for multi-buys or a yearly supply until you have monitored your response. Keeping a diary of your diet and physical and emotional well-being can be a useful indicator of their effectiveness.

**RESOURCES**

TAKING SUPPLEMENTS
■ To check the safe limits for supplements, visit **http://www.food.gov.uk/multimedia/webpage/vitandmin/** and download the report by the Expert Group. Recommended daily vitamin and mineral intake and information on what happens if you take too much are given at **www.eatwell.gov.uk**.
■ For a good all-round reference, try *Reader's Digest Guide to Vitamins, Minerals and Supplements*, £14.99, ISBN 13 9780276429309.

ALTERNATIVE THERAPIES FOR LESS

Complementary and alternative treatments are now widely used and in some cases are available on the NHS. But there are also ways of enjoying the benefits of those that are not without breaking the bank.

ACUPUNCTURE FOR FREE

Long regarded as a mystical Chinese practice, acupuncture won the approval of the British Medical Association in 2000 and is now the fastest-growing complementary therapy used within the NHS. So before looking for a private acupuncturist, who typically costs £35–£50 a session, visit your GP: more than 2,000 GPs and hospital doctors are trained in acupuncture techniques and many physiotherapy departments in NHS hospitals now offer acupuncture.

ALEXANDER TECHNIQUE

If you have breathing disorders, joint or muscular problems associated with poor posture, difficulties with movement or coordination, you may have considered the Alexander Technique. A one-to-one session can cost £25–£35 an hour (with a series of sessions being needed), but you can sign up for group workshops and classes for much less. A single day class can cost under £30, for example. Go to the Society of Teachers of the Alexander Technique website **www.stat.org.uk** ✉ or phone 0845 230 7828 for details.

AROMATHERAPY OILS FOR 40% LESS

While you may not want the outlay of going to an aromatherapist, you can benefit from using aromatherapy oils at home (but take advice if pregnant, as some oils can be harmful in pregnancy). Many essential oils are thought to enhance mood – lavender and neroli aid relaxation, while bergamot and grapefruit are energising, for example. Others can help certain conditions. Though these oils can be expensive, the Internet provides some bargains – **www.essentialoilsdirect.co.uk** sells 10ml of lavender oil for £2.65, compared to the £6.65 you'd pay in a highstreet chemist. Compare prices including p&p carefully.

OVER-THE-COUNTER HERBALISM

A consultation with a medical herbalist costs £25–£40 a session (expect to pay £10–£15 more for the initial consultation) and may help certain chronic complaints (see Resources, left). But for minor imbalances you can save by treating yourself – you'll find remedies in chemists, health food shops and on the Internet. Find a range of remedies, herbs and tinctures at **www.thinknatural.com** 0845 601 1948 ✉ or go to **www.nealsyard remedies.com** 0845 262 3145 ✉.

HOMEOPATHY

The Society of Homeopaths has a list of qualified
practitioners who are registered with them on
www.homeopathy-soh.com 0845 450 6611 ✉. An initial
consultation costs £55–£65 (less for follow-up sessions),
although there are often reductions for families and
jobseekers. But check out these cheaper options:

Homeopathy on the NHS Some GPs take a course in
homeopathy and practise as GP homeopaths (with the
initials MFHom). Check with your local NHS Trust to
see whether there is a GP homeopath in your area.

Homeopathic hospitals There are National Health Service
homeopathic hospitals in Bristol, Glasgow, Liverpool,
London and Tunbridge Wells. A GP homeopath can refer
you to a consultant at these hospitals.

Homeopathy at home Many symptoms can be treated
at home. Homeopathic remedies are widely available in
high-street chemists and health food shops. Weleda have a
guide to remedies on their website **www.weleda.co.uk** or you
can obtain copy of their *Mind Your Body* catalogue by
phoning Weleda on 0115 944 8222 ✉.

MASSAGE ON A BUDGET

There is nothing quite as relaxing as a massage, but the
average session costs from £30 an hour. However, those
in the know can pay a lot less.

Free treatment Massage – like many other complementary
therapies – has seen a surge in popularity, with professional
training courses, schools and courses at local adult education
establishments cropping up all over the place. They often
need 'subjects' on which students can practise, so find one
locally and offer your services.

Make money from massage Consider training yourself –
you will learn a skill to practise on family and friends and
could even make a profit from it.

MEDITATION

We all know that when we are stressed we are more likely
to succumb to illness, and recent research suggests that
meditation can boost the immune system and reduce blood
pressure, heart and breathing rates and muscle tension.

Joining a class Check in your local library, health food
shop or adult education centre for meditation classes, which
are inexpensive. Or join a yoga class, which incorporates an
element of meditation at the end of the session.

Going it alone Meditate at home and it will cost you
nothing except time. Set aside 20 minutes a day when you
won't be disturbed and can sit comfortably and quietly.
Concentrate on your breathing, or a certain word or phrase,
or focus on the flame of a candle placed in front of you.

REFLEXOLOGY

An hour's session with a reflexologist costs £20–£45, but
someone who is still training may be happy to practise for
free. Approach a college accredited to the Association of
Reflexologists (listed at **www.aor.org.uk** 01823 351010 ✉) to
volunteer yourself for a training session.

RESOURCES

**AROMATHERAPY AND
MASSAGE**

■ Contact the
International Federation
of Professional
Aromatherapists for a
list of schools and
practitioners on
01455 637987
www.ifparoma.org ✉.

■To buy good-value
aromatherapy oils, try
websites that sell direct
to the public such as
**www.youraromatherapy.
co.uk** ✉ and
**www.essentialoilsdirect.
co.uk** ✉.

■ For information on
training in massage,
www.massagetherapy.co.uk
✉ lists professional
associations and
governing organisations.

A BETTER DEAL ON MEDICINES

Whether you go to the doctor and come away with a prescription or treat yourself with an over-the-counter preparation, there are savings to be made.

GET THE BEST FROM YOUR PRESCRIPTION

Although no expense should be spared when it comes to your health, you can avoid spending money unnecessarily. Just because you have a prescription, this doesn't mean you will get the cheapest remedy.

Consult the expert Prescription medicines can be more expensive, so the first thing you should do is to seek advice from the pharmacist – sometimes it is cheaper to purchase the same drug over the counter rather than paying the prescription charge.

Prepay and save If you have a long-term illness or condition, consider buying a Prescription Pre-payment Certificate (PPC). These act like a season ticket and cost £102.50 a year (1 April 2008) or £27.85 for three months. A PPC is worth having if you need more than 14 items a year or three items in three months. Apply for one online at **www.nhsbsa.nhs.uk**, phone 0845 850 0030 or fill in form FP95, available from pharmacies and doctors surgeries, and send it to the PPC Issue Office.

Prescriptions may be cheaper If you have to purchase medication over a period, it can be cheaper to get a single prescription from the doctor that covers the whole time, instead of buying a pack of the medication each week. For example, hayfever tablets for two months cost £7.10 as a single prescription from the doctor, whereas even unbranded antihistamines can cost around £10 from the chemist for sufficient tablets for the same period.

GET FREE PROFESSIONAL ADVICE

NHS Direct is a free, 24-hour-a-day health advice service so, if you are concerned about an ailment that doesn't need immediate attention, make it your first port of call out of surgery hours and at weekends or on public holidays. Trained medical practitioners can be reached on 0845 4647, or use the website at **www.nhsdirect.nhs.uk** to search for information and advice on treatment. Also, NHS Choices at **www.nhs.uk/Pages/homepage.aspx** provides medical advice, a Health A–Z of conditions and treatments, information on how to Live Well, and a Find Services section, which lists hospitals, dentists, pharmacies, special clinics and more.

SAVE BY BUYING GENERIC DRUGS

We are all familiar with the brand names of popular drugs, such as Panadol, Nurofen, Imodium and Clarityn. When a drug is developed, the manufacturer takes out a patent for exclusive rights to produce and sell it for a set period of time, normally 20 years, to help recoup their research and development costs. When that period elapses, other

companies can produce their own versions. These are known as generic drugs and are usually sold under the name of the active ingredient. Sold in bulk by major chemists and supermarkets, generic drugs are often much cheaper.

BUY MEDICINES FOR UP TO 80% LESS

You can save a considerable amount of money by buying generic medicines, which are just as effective as their branded equivalent. For example, hay fever sufferers could save £4 a week over the course of the pollen season. Branded medicines such as Zirtek, Benadryl, Clarityn and Piriteze all cost between £3 and £4.50 online for a supply of seven tablets (a week's worth). Generic equivalents available in chemists, supermarkets and some discount stores cost from as little as 56p for the same length of treatment.

Name dropping To be able to ask for and recognise generic equivalents of common branded medicines, it helps to familiarise yourself with their names. See right for the names of generic drugs sold for common complaints and the chart below for potential cost savings.

TOP TIPS FINDING THE RIGHT DRUGS

To make sure you buy the products you want, you may need to ask for help and check the labelling.

■ **Ask a pharmacist** You will often find generic drugs readily displayed in supermarkets, but they will probably not be on display at the chemist's. You may need to tell the pharmacist specifically that you want the generic (or cheapest) version.

■ **Compare ingredients** If you're unsure of what you are considering buying, check that the name and amount of the active ingredients are the same in both the generic and the branded packet.

■ **Ignore the packaging** Don't let the often understated packaging of generic drugs put you off buying them. Supermarkets and major chemists aim to produce them as cheaply as possible, and this doesn't affect the effectiveness of the drug. All drugs are tested by the Medicines and Healthcare products Regulatory Agency and have a PL (licence) number on the box.

GET TO KNOW GENERIC NAMES

These are the non-brand names for medicines that you can buy over the counter to ease everyday ailments.
Allergies Loratadine, chlorphenamine, ranitidine (antihistamines)
Antiseptic Potassium permanganate solution, sodium chloride (salt)
Colds Benzocaine (spray, for sore throats), pseudoephedrine, xylometazoline (for nasal congestion), codeine linctus (for coughs)
Heartburn Aluminium hydroxide (antacid)
Muscular pain Ketoprofen (gel)
Oral hygiene, ulcers Chlorhexidine

A BITTER PILL TO SWALLOW?				
CONDITION	**GENERIC**		**BRANDED**	
HEADACHE	16 x paracetamol	£0.65	16 x Panadol	£2.30
MUSCLE PAIN	24 x ibuprofen	£0.89	24 x Nurofen	£3.99
HAY FEVER	30 x cetirizine	£6.99	30 x Zirtek	£13.90
DIARRHOEA	12 x loperamide	£2.99	12 x Imodium	£5.50
THRUSH	1 x fluconazole	£5.35	1 x Diflucan	£10.68
TOTAL		**£16.87**		**£36.37**

LOWER-COST DENTAL CARE

If you are lucky enough to be registered with an NHS dentist – only around 50% of the the UK's adult population are – then you hold the key to low-cost care. A shortage of dentists – especially those accepting new NHS patients – means that many of us will have to fund private treatment.

FINDING AN NHS DENTIST

Although it can be tricky to find an NHS dentist, for routine treatments you will save significantly (see chart, right).

Contact NHS Direct Ring NHS Direct on 0845 4647 or search their website **http://www.nhs.uk/servicedirectories** for details of local practices offering NHS dental care.

Waiting lists Try phoning around local dentists, and if any practice is keeping a waiting list put your name down.

Dental Access Centres In some areas, people who aren't registered with an NHS dentist can get treatment at a Dental Access Centre. Contact your local NHS Trust for details.

Keep your dentist If you are registered with an NHS dentist, go regularly. Many will take you off their list if you do not attend for a stated period (typically 12–18 months).

FREE NHS DENTISTRY

If you are eligible for free treatment, use your entitlement. If not, check the price of treatment before proceeding.

When is treatment free? Treatment is free: if you are under 18; if you are aged 18 but in full-time education; if you are pregnant or had a baby in the 12 months before

---

COSMETIC DENTISTRY FOR LESS

Most practitioners offer a discount for early payment. None are shy about advertising their prices – a search on the Internet will reveal scores of practitioners – so compare costs carefully. If you want your teeth to be whitened, ask whether a home whitening service is available. This costs about half as much as the price of surgery-based procedures, although it is not quite as effective. Always check the dentist is experienced in cosmetic dentistry. Has he or she taken advanced courses in current techniques? Can you see before and after pictures and testimonial letters from clients who have had similar treatment? Does the dentist have imaging or presentation devices to help demonstrate how the procedure is done and what results might be expected?

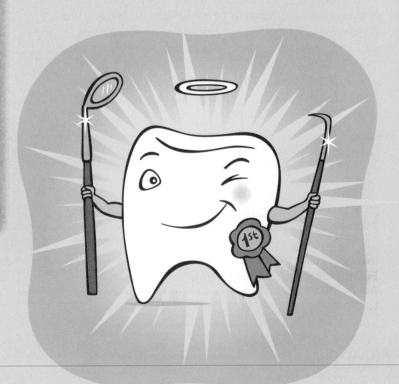

DENTAL CHARGES FOR COMMON TREATMENTS

Private treatment charges can vary widely so it is worth obtaining several quotes, particularly for more complicated procedures such as crowns and implants.

TREATMENT	NHS	PRIVATE
BASIC EXAMINATION	£16.20	£33–£64
SCALE AND POLISH	£16.20	£36–£47
SMALL FILLING	£44.60	£57–£104
SMALL X-RAY	£16.20	£20–£39
ROOT FILLING	£198.00	£202–£670
CROWN	£198.00	£312–£490
IMPLANT	NA (not available)	£949–£2,585

Private figures from Whatprice (**www.whatprice.co.uk**), December 2008.

treatment stated; if you are an in-patient in an NHS hospital and treatment is carried out by an NHS dentist; if you (or your partner) get income support, have a valid NHS tax credit exemption certificate or are named on a valid HC2 certificate for people entitled to help with NHS charges.
What do you pay? Since 1 April 2008, NHS dental treatment is divided into three 'course of treatment' bands. Band 1 covers an examination, diagnosis, advice and a scale and polish (£16.20); Band 2 includes everything in Band 1 plus fillings, root canal work or tooth extraction (£44.60); Band 3 includes everything in Band 1 and 2 plus crowns, dentures or bridges (£198). You will be charged £16.20 to book an urgent appointment.

BEST-VALUE PRIVATE DENTAL TREATMENT

If you have to go private, there are two schemes commonly used to help fund treatment.
Capitation and maintenance schemes These schemes involve the payment of a set monthly amount that is determined after your current level of dental health has been assessed. The scheme should then cover the costs of basic treatment. Be careful taking this route as the service is often tied to your dentist, who will in turn be tied to one of the main schemes available. This may present a problem if you move to another part of the country as you may need to be assessed again by your new dentist and start a scheme anew.
Full cover plans The other option is full cover (or cash and full medical plans) which, for a monthly premium, cover you for a stipulated amount of treatment during the course of a year, and some will also offer cover for work following an accident. Make sure you check the level of cover as well as terms, conditions and any exclusions. Under these schemes, dental cover is sometimes an add-on to full private medical insurance.

RESOURCES

PROVIDERS OF DENTAL PLANS
For capitation and maintenance schemes:
www.denplan.co.uk
0800 401402 ✉
www.practiceplan.co.uk
01691 684145 ✉
For full cover plans:
www.hsa.co.uk
0800 085 0203 ✉
www.bupa.co.uk
0800 600 500 ✉.
To search for a good deal, go to: **www.lookfor health.co.uk** ✉.

ECONOMY EYE CARE

The market for glasses and contact lenses is fiercely competitive, with local opticians, high street stores, mail-order companies and Internet suppliers all vying for custom. Use this to your advantage to find the best deal.

GETTING AN EYE TEST

Having your eyes tested every two years will identify eye diseases before they affect your sight and can pick up health problems such as high blood pressure, diabetes and brain tumours. Optometrists charge between £17 and £30 for an eye test, so shop around.

Free checks Check whether you are entitled to free NHS eye tests (see box, left). If so, ask your optometrist for a NHS sight test form (GOS1) before you have the eye test.

Company perk If you use a computer or display screen at work, your employer be required to pay for your sight test. Check with your HR department.

Scot free If you live in Scotland, you won't have to pay for a sight test as free NHS eye examinations were introduced in April 2006.

LOW-COST GLASSES AND CONTACT LENSES

If you need glasses or contact lenses you are not obliged to buy them from the optician where you had your eye test. Take your prescription and buy more cheaply elsewhere.

Savings on the Internet Online suppliers sell products at substantially lower prices than most high street shops. You can find reading glasses for as little as £2 on the Internet, while the starting price at one leading high street franchise is £59 (including prescription lenses).

Major discounts Some larger high street stores will match Internet prices, so phone to check before ordering online. Some also give interest-free credit and offer advantage cards. Watch out too for special offers and voucher codes.

Free trials Look out for promotions run by major contact lens manufacturers offering free contact lenses as a means of introducing potential customers to new products such as daily disposables, coloured contact lenses or bifocals.

French bargains Combine a day trip or holiday with a visit to a French optician and save about 20% on glasses and 50% on disposable contact lenses. Check prices at home before you travel to ensure you get a bargain.

WATCH POINTS BUYING ON THE INTERNET

Make sure your Internet savings don't cost you dear.

■ **Compare like with like** Manufacturers make a range of different quality products at different prices. Check your Internet bargain isn't a cheaper alternative before buying.

■ **Check overall costs** Just because lenses are cheap doesn't mean you'll get the best overall deal. Compare the price of cleansing materials and postage and packing.

■ **Follow-ups** Internet purchases don't include the normal follow-up service you get from an optician, such as adjustments to frames or a contact lens check.

GET THE BEST-VALUE MEDICAL HELP

If you have an acute or life-threatening illness, you can usually depend on prompt treatment from the National Health Service. But many debilitating conditions have long waiting lists. So how do you get the treatment you need when you need it without paying to go private?

TOP TIPS GETTING THE BEST FROM THE NHS

If you don't have private health insurance and you want to avoid paying to beat the queues, you need to know the system so you can get the best from it.

■ **Check the waiting list** The government has targets for the maximum time a patient should have to wait for treatment under the NHS. Find out what the target is for your condition and how long you are likely to wait for local treatment.

■ **Ask for another referral** If the waiting time is longer than the government target, ask your doctor to refer you to a different hospital or area with a shorter waiting list. He may need to check that the local health authority will fund the treatment at another hospital.

■ **Contact the hospital of your choice** The Patients' Association Helpline (see Resources, right) may be able to help you identify a good hospital; your GP should be able to help or point you in the right direction, and it is also worth talking to your local Primary Care Trust (PCT) as well as their counterparts in surrounding boroughs or counties.

■ **European partnership** In some cases your local PCT may have identified a need for certain types of elective surgery that can't be met by its own hospitals and set up an agreement with a European provider. Check with your NHS Trust to see whether any such schemes are active.

■ **NHS private treatment** If you have a scheduled operation that is cancelled and the hospital is unable to offer you another date within a specified time, you may be able to be treated in a private hospital paid for by the NHS.

NHS TREATMENT ABROAD

If all else fails, you could take advantage of a European Court ruling that patients are entitled to seek treatment in other member states of the European Union (EU) if there is an excessive waiting list for NHS treatment.

Conditions apply Treatment abroad is only possible when a local health authority has money in its budget but does not have the capacity in its hospitals. You are far more likely to be referred to a private hospital than get sent abroad.

Getting authorisation You'll need the support of your consultant and an E112 certificate authorising payment to the overseas hospital by your local health authority. The main criterion is whether there has been any 'undue delay' in the provision of treatment. This may be taken to mean anything from four months to a year, depending on how painful or debilitating the condition is.

CASE STUDY

FRENCH LEAVE
Jack Simms, 73, had been waiting for a hip replacement for nearly a year.
'My daughter wanted me to go private, but without health insurance it was going to cost over £7,000 and there's no way I could afford that. Then when I moved to live near her we found that her local NHS Trust had an arrangement with a hospital in Lille and I got priority treatment. I was in hospital for two weeks to make sure everything was OK before I came home, and travelled back through the Channel Tunnel by ambulance. All my expenses were paid by the NHS Trust. But Jenny had to pay for her trip when she came to visit me.'

PRIVATE TREATMENT ABROAD – SAVE OVER 30%

If you are considering paying for private treatment, it pays to look abroad. Many European hospitals charge considerably less than private facilities in the UK. The chart below shows the comparative costs of four common elective operations. Prices include accommodation, food, surgery and post-operative care in hospital, but not travel costs.

OPERATION	UK COST (PRIVATE)	COST IN FRANCE	COST IN GERMANY
CATARACT	£1,800	£1,300	£1,200
HIP REPLACEMENT	£7,000	£5,000	£6,500
KNEE REPLACEMENT	£8,500	£5,700	£7,150
PROSTATECTOMY	£3,650	£4,700	£5,400

Locating a hospital You'll need to identify the overseas hospital and the consultant who will oversee the surgery. This is best done by your NHS consultant, although an application to any European Union teaching or university hospital should give successful results.

TOP TIPS PRIVATE MEDICAL INSURANCE

Private Medical Insurance (PMI) usually means you get medical treatment when you need it, but policies can cost as much as £3,000 a year. There are ways to make savings on PMI premiums – however these will limit your choices and the type of service you receive.

■ **Decide how much to pay** Decide in advance what you can afford. With PMI, you get what you pay for so it is important to make the right decisions at the outset.

■ **Flexible patients save** Insurers will usually give you a choice of three bands (typically A, B and C) ranging from a bed in the most expensive private hospitals through to medium-priced private hospitals and most provincial teaching hospitals.

■ **Large excess, lower premiums** Selecting a larger voluntary excess is another way of keeping the costs down, and you will be given the choice of paying the first part of any claim (anything from £100 to £2,000). There are different types of excess clauses, so check carefully.

■ **Budget policies** Budget or low cost policies specify a limit to the number of days in hospital or the range and extent of treatments for which you are covered.

■ **Direct debit for 5% savings** Pay by direct debit. Most insurers will reduce your annual bill by, typically, 5%.

■ **Join a group scheme** Group cover is cheaper. Some employers run schemes for staff and their immediate family, while certain professional institutions, trade unions and other bodies will also offer group schemes or pass on a discount to their members. This is a benefit worth having.

■ **Check the exclusions** Check that you understand the list of exclusions, which can be lengthy. You are unlikely to be covered for pre-existing conditions.

RESOURCES

ARRANGING PRIVATE TREATMENT
Some independent companies have set up their own partnerships with hospitals in Europe and farther afield to provide a service for people looking for treatment abroad. To find out more about private treatment options in Britain and abroad, look at **www.privatehealth.co.uk** or its sister website **www.treatmentabroad.net** ✉.

■ **Don't pay for travel** Make sure the policy you choose enables you to be treated at hospitals near your home.

■ **Join online** Insurers have got wise to the operational savings they can make by encouraging customers to register and then manage their cover on line. Savings can be significant. One such provider is **www.xshealth.co.uk** ✉.

■ **Seek professional advice** As always, if you are thinking of committing to a big montly outlay it is worth talking to an independent financial adviser before you make a decision.

LOW-COST HOSPITAL CASH PLANS

Hospital cash plans are a less expensive alternative to PMI (costing from £4.50 per week) designed to help with medical expenses rather than paying them in full. Cash payouts are small (they may pay £15–£90 for each day you are in hospital) but are useful if you are on a tight budget. Cash plans can also help towards optical and dentistry expenses, or visits to the chiropodist.

COSMETIC SURGERY ABROAD

Over 100,000 people from Britain now travel abroad each year to take advantage of cheaper cosmetic surgery deals. For example, liposuction in the UK can cost £1,500–£5,000, while in Belgium it would be around £900 and in Hungary just £500. However, aftercare and follow-up appointments are difficult, and UK surgeons are treating an increasing number of patients whose operations have gone wrong.

■ **Guide to procedures** Contact the British Association of Aesthetic Plastic Surgeons for advice and information on cosmetic procedures 020 7405 2234 **www.baaps.org.uk** ✉.

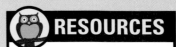

RESOURCES

HEALTH INSURANCE
For details of private medical insurance plans and cash plans, contact: Western Provident Association on 01823 625230 or **www.wpa.org.uk** ✉ HSA on 0800 072 6712 or **www.hsa.co.uk** ✉. For information on hospital cash plans, contact: Barclays on 0800 7316 2825 or **www.barclays.co.uk** ✉ HealthSure on 0800 085 0630 or **www.healthsure.co.uk** ✉.

COMPARING PRIVATE MEDICAL INSURANCE

Monthly premiums vary considerably, depending on the excess and the treatments excluded. The last two schemes are for hospital cash plans, shown for comparison, but these are very different policies and do not offer the same level of cover as PMI.

PROVIDER	EXCLUSIONS	BENEFITS	COST/MONTH
INSURER A (PMI)	Psychiatric care Most outpatient care	Minor surgical procedure	**£20.03** (£350 excess)
INSURER B (PMI)	Psychiatric care	Nursing at home, private ambulance, NHS cash	**£41.99** (£500 excess)
INSURER C (PMI)		Nursing at home, private ambulance, NHS cash, minor surgical procedure	**£51.50** (£100 excess)
HOSPITAL CASH-BACK SCHEME A	Pays a yearly max of £300 for dental and optical care, £1,500 for birth of a child, £105 per night in hospital, £525 for specialist consultations, £675 for complementary therapies, plus personal accident cover.		**from £6.50** eight levels of cover available
HOSPITAL CASH-BACK SCHEME B	Pays a yearly max of £280 for dental and optical care, up to £800 for physio, osteopathy, acupuncture, chiropractice or homeopathy, £240 towards allergy testing and chiropody, and £150 for health screens.		**from £2/week**

Prices from Moneysupermarket.com, December 2008.

All figures are based on a single, non-smoking female, aged 45.

Practical parenting

According to recent research, the average cost of raising a child from birth to age 21 is over £186,000. And that's just for one child. There are some costs, such as childcare, that you may not be able to cut, but in areas such as baby equipment, clothing, food and outings you can make significant savings.

NEW BABY ON A BUDGET

From the moment you discover you are going to have a baby, you'll be deluged with information on what you can't possibly live without. Beware of such guidance; there are only a few things you really need, and many of these can be sourced at a discount.

BEG, BORROW OR BUY?

To avoid making expensive mistakes, don't rush into buying things for your baby.

Ask for advice Once you have had your 'anomaly' scan – about halfway through your pregnancy – start talking to friends and relatives with babies about what they have found most useful and what was a waste of money. Write a list of what you think you'll need at the outset and don't be tempted to stray from it.

Secondhand is good enough Save on large items such as prams, carry-cots and cots by borrowing them from friends whose children have outgrown them, or by buying them secondhand through the classified section of your local paper, from ads on supermarket noticeboards or via one of the many online marketplaces such as eBay (**www.ebay.co.uk** ✉) or My Mummy and Me (**www.mymummyandme.co.uk**). Also go along to a National Childbirth Trust (NCT) nearly new sale – enter your postcode on the 'share your experiences' section on the home page at **www.nctpregnancyandbabycare.com** for the address of your nearest sale or contact the NCT on 0300 33 00 770 ✉.

SLEEPING SOLUTIONS

Dispense with the cost of buying a crib or Moses basket, which your baby will outgrow in a few weeks, by putting your newborn in a full-size cot. This is safe, as long as you position your baby with his feet at the end of the cot and his head half-way down (which stops him from burrowing under the sheets and overheating). Before buying secondhand, read the Smart Moves box on page 92.

SAVE ON BABYWEAR

You will be confronted with an enormous array of gorgeous babywear, but choose what's practical and good value – and accept offers of used baby clothes from friends.

The bare essentials For the first two or three weeks your baby will spend much of the time asleep, so vests and sleepsuits are the most practical clothing. They are comfortable, easy to wash and don't need ironing. Buy a few sleepsuits and vests in the 'newborn' size and some more in size '0–3 months' before your baby is born. Look for good-quality fabric as they need to withstand frequent washing, but don't pay a fortune. Supermarkets or high-street stores such as Argos, British Home Stores and Marks & Spencer are usually the best value for multipacks, or buy in the sales; check specialist shops such as Mothercare, too.

Before buying secondhand, read the Smart Moves box on page 92.

---

keep it simple

BASIC EQUIPMENT
Basic baby needs are:
- A place to sleep
- Clothes to wear
- Something to drink
- Something to be transported in
- Nappies

FREE OFFERS

After your first trip to hospital for an ultrasound scan, you will begin to receive promotional literature and samples of goodies for you and the baby. Once you're confident about the health of your baby, sign up for anything that promises money-off vouchers and free samples. If you want to avoid being inundated by all and sundry, tick the 'don't pass on my details' box that all these leaflets must carry by law.

SMART MOVES

The low-down on cots

Buying a secondhand cot could save you more than £100.

You will need to check that:
- the cot hasn't been painted by the owner. The paint may have been lead-based, and as lead is toxic it's not worth taking the risk;
- the teething rail is in a reasonable condition – these can be replaced, but make sure you can get the correct part before buying such a cot;
- none of the screws and bolts are missing;
- the slats aren't damaged and are no more than 6cm (2in) apart;
- the catches on the drop-side are secure, and the base fits properly.

Whether you buy a new or secondhand cot, it is essential to purchase a new mattress. Research by the Foundation for the Study of Infant Deaths (FSID) has found that instances of cot death are increased with the use of a secondhand mattress, especially if the mattress comes from another home.

keep it simple

BE WISE: IMPROVISE

- You can make your own crib using a laundry basket or even a dresser drawer. As long as babies have a firm mattress and suitable blankets, they really don't mind where they are.
- If friends or other family members are due to give birth a couple of months before or after you, why not halve the cost of a crib by sharing one? But you will still need to buy separate mattresses.

TOP TIPS BEST-BUY BABY CLOTHES

Many people enjoy giving baby clothes as presents, but they usually buy the small sizes that won't fit for long. Take advantage of this by not buying too many before your baby is born, then buy wisely to get the best value for money.

■ **Get the most wear** Always choose one size ahead of your baby's actual age. Sizes can be on the small side and babies grow quickly. Most 6-month-old babies can wear clothes size 9–12 months, 1-year-olds wear size 2 and so on. But do take account of the season – lightweight summer clothes are no use in the winter, and vice versa.

■ **Stock up** When sales shopping, get clothes for the coming months. If your child is 9 months old in January, buy clothes for 18–24 months in anticipation of the following winter. In 'expensive' baby shops, head for the sale rails – there's nearly always one in Baby Gap, and bargains of up to 50% off – sometimes more – can be had.

■ **Designer modes** Be selective when buying up-market babywear. There's little point in paying top price for vests, plain tops or tights, for example – just mix in cheaper labels with some branded goods and you'll give the impression of full designer wear but pay a fraction of the cost.

■ **Good investments** If you are tempted by expensive clothing for your baby, consider whether it is good value for money. Trousers and practical dresses may be worn enough to justify the outlay, but avoid paying top price for an outfit for special occasions – it might only get one airing. See if you can borrow a special occasion outfit instead.

■ **Nearly new** For some real bargains, go along to nearly new sales and secondhand babywear shops. Babies grow very quickly and favourite clothes are often outgrown long before they're worn out. You can benefit from what other people have had to throw out; some items may still carry the original shop tag, indicating that they've never been worn.

■ **Web buys** Good deals can be had on **www.ebay.co.uk** ✉. Select 'Home, garden & family', then the baby and clothing categories. You'll find secondhand and brand new designer and high-street baby clothes being sold for next to nothing. There are a number of links to websites selling clothing at the UK Children's Directory **www.ukchildrensdirectory.com** ✉.

FEEDING, BATHS AND NAPPIES

Whether you breastfeed or bottle-feed, or opt for terry nappies or disposables, you'll be faced with a whole gamut of equipment to make your life easier. But the old ways are often the simplest (and the cheapest), as our mothers and grandmothers will tell us.

BREAST IS BEST – AND CHEAPEST

If you can, breastfeed your baby. Breast milk is free, convenient and has health benefits for you and your baby.
The costs of breastfeeding Don't be lured into spending unnecessarily. As a minimum you'll need two nursing bras and breast pads (washable ones are more economical than disposables). Wear loose T-shirts or blouses, and only invest in a (secondhand) breast pump if you are returning to work or you want your partner to share feeding with you.
The costs of formula You may not want to breastfeed or maybe you can't. If so, you will need to use formula milk, the cost of which mounts up (from £400 a year, plus bottles, teats, etc). Ask your baby clinic for their prices, and remember that if you receive income support you may be able to buy formula at the clinic at a reduced rate. Otherwise, keep an eye out for multibuy savings in chemists and supermarkets and stock up when you can – your baby will need formula milk for most of the first year.

SAVE ON STERILISING

Even if you breastfeed, you'll need to sterilise any bottles you use and, in the first stages of weaning, ensure that spoons and bowls are scrupulously clean.
Low-tech equals low cost The cheapest option is cold water sterilisation. You can buy sterilising tablets cheaply at a chemist's; simply add them to water and submerge your bottles in it.
High-tech alternatives Both electric and microwave steam sterilisers are more expensive options that may be worthwhile if you are bottle feeding. If you feel the time-saving benefit they offer is worth the extra outlay, shop around for the best deal before your baby is born. Also, keep an eye out for promotional packs that include free extras such as bottles and teats.

TOP TIPS BABY FOOD BONUSES

Between four and six months, your baby will be ready to begin supplementing her milk feeds with other foods that are cheaper than conventional baby foods.
■ **Frozen purées** To save money on shop-bought jars, buy a few flexible ice-cube trays and make your own purées (see Smart Moves, page 94). Freeze the purée as you would ice-cubes, then defrost the exact quantity you need for each meal, eliminating waste.
■ **Refilled jars** Recycle any empty shop-bought jars of baby food by sterilising the jar and its lid and then filling it with

RESOURCES

WEANING WISDOM
For general advice on weaning and recipes to make for your baby, see:
■ **www.nctpregnancyand babycare.com**
Breastfeeding line 0300 33 00 771 ✉
■ **www.babycentre.co.uk**
■ **www.forparentsbyparents .com** ✉
■ *New Complete Baby and Toddler Meal Planner* by Annabel Karmel, Ebury Press, £14.99 ISBN-10 0091880882

ASK YOURSELF

DO I REALLY NEED A HIGH CHAIR?
A baby can be fed in a portable car seat set in its upright position or simply held in your lap. Once your baby is able to sit upright, you can buy an inexpensive three-in-one booster seat (from about £20). This seat, which has a seat belt and removable tray, can be strapped onto a sturdy kitchen or dining-room chair. The tray has a high position and a lower position to accommodate the child's size as she grows. When the tray is no longer needed, it can be removed and the seat can be used as a booster seat at the table.

homemade food. These small jars are ideal for taking out and about with you.

■ **Uses for cow's milk** Reduce the cost of formula milk by introducing diluted cow's milk to your baby's diet from the age of six months. It can't replace formula, but it can be used on cereal and in cooking.

■ **Safe leftovers** When using jars, spoon only the required amount into a bowl so you can use the remainder later.

EXTENDING THE JUICE

Don't waste your money on baby juices. Buy plain juice concentrates (the least expensive, but be sure they are marked 100% juice with no added sugar) and reconstitute according to the package directions. When you are filling a bottle or sipping cup, fill the container about one-third to half full, then top it up with water. Your juice will last longer and your baby will consume less fruit sugar, which can contribute to early tooth decay.

BATHING YOUR BABY

Every baby store has a wide selection of goods and products devoted to cleaning your baby. What should you buy?

Baby bath alternatives When considering whether to buy a baby bath, bear in mind that your baby will only fit in it for a few weeks, and most health visitors recommend that you only bathe your baby twice a week during the first six weeks. So instead of paying out for a bath that will get little use, why not bathe your newborn in the kitchen sink? She'll be quite safe and you won't have to bend over so awkwardly. Clean the sink thoroughly and line it with an old towel to prevent your baby from slipping. Then pull on

---

Make your own baby food

It's easy to save money by making food for your baby.

Homemade purées These work out much cheaper than shop-bought jars. Start off by introducing one taste at a time: puréed carrot, potato, parsnip, turnip, apple, pear, mashed banana or avocado. Later you can mix purées to make new flavours – apple and mango, for example, or carrot and courgette. As they grow,

don't be afraid to make your own concoctions using flavours you know they like. Babies generally love sweet potato, so try mashing sweet potato, salmon and broccoli together to make a delicious and nutritious meal. Just blend it down, using milk or water to get the right consistency, then freeze in meal-size containers.

Baby rice and cereals These are expensive, but did you know that baby rice is simply ground rice? Use a coffee grinder or a super-

efficient blender, pour in the rice grains, grind away and store the powder in the freezer in a resealable plastic bag.

Family food As your baby grows and you feel more relaxed about what they eat, structure mealtimes to fit in with your own – if you eat a sandwich lunch and a proper dinner, do the same for your baby. That way, your baby can eat a little of the family food instead of you having to buy and prepare different meals at different times of the day.

SMART MOVES

a pair of cheap white cotton gloves so you have a good grip on your little one. If you'd prefer to bathe your baby on the floor, look in discount shops for a rectangular washing-up bowl – it will do just as well.

Potions and lotions Save on the expense of baby toiletries: general guidance is just to clean your baby with water, since it is thought that baby bath and talcum powder can contribute to skin complaints.

Bath toys Plastic bowls, cups and spoons from the kitchen provide endless entertainment in the bath and help your baby to learn; and plastic sieves or funnels of different sizes make interesting water toys. Not only are these playthings free, but they often have the edge on expensive bath toys that are funny to look at initially but are soon ignored by your infant because they don't allow actual play.

TOP TIPS WHICH NAPPIES?

You will have to decide which side to take in the great nappy debate. You have three options: traditional, terry-towelling nappies with plastic pants and disposable liners; the new, shaped reusable nappies; or disposables.

■ **Terry-towelling nappies** These are usually considered the cheapest, since after you have made the initial outlay for nappies, pins and pants, you can use them until your toddler is potty trained. But there is still the cost of disposable liners and washing and drying the nappies to be considered. If you go down this route, look out for nearly-new nappies that have been abandoned in favour of disposables. Because drying terries can be difficult,

keep it simple

BE PENNYWISE AT BATH TIME

■ Forget forking out for antislip mats or baby seats for the bath – one of the best ways of ensuring that your baby is safe in the bath is to get in too. You can join in the bathtime play and relax a little yourself.

■ You probably have the perfect substitute for costly baby talcum powder sitting in a kitchen cupboard: cornflour. It works just as well as baby powder to keep your baby dry, and it won't irritate her lungs if it gets breathed in – a big plus.

BABY CLUBS

Some supermarkets and high street stores – including Tesco and Boots – operate baby clubs, 0–5 clubs or parenting clubs. Join up and you'll receive newsletters or magazines with details of baby products, special offers in store and money-off vouchers. Check their websites, too, for baby bargains, recipes and expert advice.

RESOURCES

NAPPY LAUNDERING

■ Consult the National Association of Nappy Services (NANS) at **www.changeanappy.co.uk/** 0121 693 4949 ✉; the NCT (see page 91), to find out about laundering services in your area; or the Real Nappy Campaign **www. realnappycampaign.com** 0845 850 0606.

■ Your local authority may provide a nappy laundering service.

especially in winter, and tumbledryers are expensive to buy and run, invest in an old-style drier that pulls up to the kitchen ceiling.

■ **Shaped reusable nappies** These are three times as expensive as terries to buy and also need cleaning. Find out if your local council offers a financial incentive for reusables; some give a rebate for not adding more nappies to a landfill site.

■ **Disposable nappies** These are the most popular option, and the most expensive. You can save as much as 4p a nappy by buying own-brand nappies, but if they don't fit as well or are not as absorbent, they'll be a false economy. Reduce the cost of branded nappies by signing up with the manufacturers so you benefit from money-off vouchers. And look out for multibuy offers in supermarkets, chemists and online.

■ **Nappy service** A laundering service for reusable nappies will collect your dirty nappies and drop off clean ones every week. But this can cost around £35 a month (a staggering £1,050 over two and a half years).

WIPE OUT EXTRA COSTS

You do not need to buy wipes for your baby. Instead, you can make them yourself.

Disposable wipes Cut a roll of strong paper towels in half crosswise. Put a half roll in a plastic container with a tight lid. Combine 1½ cups of water with 1 tablespoon of liquid baby bath soap. Pour the mixture over the towels to saturate them and cover the container. When you need a wipe, tear off a sheet from the roll.

Washable wipes If you use terry-towelling nappies, save more money by using washable wipes as well. Buy a bundle of flannels at a discount store or price club, such as Makro or Costco, and keep them in the bathroom near your baby's changing area. When it's time to change your baby, dampen a clean flannel in the sink and use that to wipe your baby's bottom. (If the baby has a really dirty nappy, dampen one flannel and rub a little soap over it, then dampen a second to rinse.) Toss the dirty flannels in your nappy bucket to wash and sterilise with the nappies.

NAPPY OPTIONS: COSTS OVER 2¹/₂ YEARS*

TERRY TOWELLING	Start-up £40 Flushable liners £98 Detergent £90 Electricity £46 Washing machine depreciation £25	**£300**
SHAPED NAPPIES	Start-up £165 Flushable liners £98 Detergent £90 Electricity £46 Washing machine depreciation £25	**£425**
DISPOSABLES	Size 1 nappies at 27 for £3.67; size 2 at 35 for £5.97 Size 3 at 31 for £5.94 and size 4 at 68 for £11.98 All the same popular brand	**£760**

* This is the average time of a child in nappies. Costs calculated on the basis of six nappies per day.

BABY TRANSPORT

The choice of car seats, prams, pushchairs and sophisticated travel systems that combine all three is extensive. Don't be tempted to buy more than you need – with careful planning you can keep the costs down.

CHOOSING CAR SEATS

Legislation introduced in September 2006 makes it compulsory to use the correct child restraint from birth until the child is 12 or 13 years old, or 1.35 metres tall.

Seats that fit It is essential that a seat fits your car securely. The best way to ensure this is to go to one of the RoSPA (Royal Society for the Prevention of Accidents) centres – contact the Road Safety Department at your local council or visit **www.rospa.com** or phone 0121 248 2000 ✉ for details of your nearest centre – and find out which seats fit your car. Once you know, look at the many websites that sell baby goods to check out the cost – you can save up to 30% on high street prices. Go to the RoSPA website **www.childcarseats.org.uk/links/manufacturers.htm** for a list of manufacturers' websites, which give recommended prices; and **www.childcarseats.org.uk/links/retailers.htm** for links to retailers' websites and their prices.

Stick with the basics Don't pay over the odds for gimmicks or glamorous fabrics. They won't make any difference to your baby.

Travel in the rear It is illegal to use a rearward-facing baby seat in the front if there is a passenger airbag. Only put a forward-facing child seat in the front if it is unavoidable.

WATCH POINTS CAR SEAT SAFETY

If you are offered a used car seat that fits your car, be very cautious. Your baby's safety is the top priority even if it costs a few pounds more.

■ **Take care with used seats** The protection offered by child car seats is reduced if it has already been in an accident or thrown around. Consider a used seat only if you can be sure of its history – if it comes from a friend or relative. Do not buy from the small ads or secondhand.

■ **Follow instructions** Make sure the manufacturer's instructions are with the seat, so you can be sure you are fitting it securely.

■ **Check standards** The seat must meet the United Nations ECE Regulation 44.03 or later standard 44.04. It should have an 'E' mark.

■ **Look for ISOFIX points** The most secure car seats have ISOFIX (International Standards Organisation FIX) fitting points. If your car takes an ISOFIX car seat, buy this type.

PRAMS AND BUGGIES

The most economical choices for a newborn are either to buy a traditional pram secondhand and then go on to a buggy later, or to buy a two-in-one pushchair with a seat that adjusts from flat to upright, accommodating your child until he is happy to walk everywhere.

ASK YOURSELF

ARE BABY SLINGS WORTH IT?
These are great for carrying your newborn, and invaluable if you also have a young toddler as they avoid the need for a double buggy. But as your baby gains weight, too much strain will be put on your back and you will have to stop using it once the baby weighs about 9kg (20lb). If you have a friend with a baby sling – especially one with head and neck support – ask if you can borrow it. Unless she is already pregnant, you can be sure you'll have finished with it before she needs it back.

CHANGING BAGS FOR HALF PRICE
When you are buying your first pram, you'll be enticed by the matching changing bag. These can be overpriced and are often quite impractical. Instead, look in sports shops or school outfitters for a roomy and comfortable backpack or bag that will accommodate all your paraphernalia (make sure you include a waterproof mat). You should end up with something at around half the price of a purpose-made changing bag.

PRAMS vs BUGGIES

When choosing a pram or pushchair consider your lifestyle. If you walk long distances (to the shops or friends), a traditional pram or three-in-one pushchair with carrycot might be the best option.

If you rely on public transport or travel by car look for a two-in-one that folds easily to go on the bus or put in the boot. Umbrella buggies (or strollers) are not suitable for newborns.

Think it through A pram will be cost-effective only if you have given some thought to what you really need. One with big wheels, for example, may look great but if it fills every inch of the boot, you'll end up buying a smaller one as well.

What to look for Make sure you know what's included in the price. Some prams come with raincovers and parasol, while with others you will have to buy these as extras.

Lightweight buggies Also known as strollers, these are suitable for babies from three or six months, depending on the model. If you will be using it occasionally, buy a sturdy, cheap model. If the buggy is for everyday use, be prepared to pay a bit more but shop around for the best deal.

Double buggies These are often a necessary evil but rarely receive much use, so it's always advisable to buy secondhand – but make sure that you find one with swivel wheels.

Resale value There is a thriving secondhand market (check the ads in your local paper or visit a website such as **www.baby-things.com, www.preloved.co.uk** or **www.ebay.co.uk** ✉). If you make a wrong choice sell it on, whether it's a new pushchair or secondhand pram. Don't hang on to them – styles change and as they get older their value will drop.

BEST-BUY CAR SEATS

Car seats are described by stage or group when you buy them in the shops. Consider your options, bearing in mind your plans for future children. Buying group 0+1 and 2/3 combination will keep your child safe from birth to 11 for £200. Group 0+ and 1/2/3 combination will keep your child safe from birth to 11 for £155.

STAGE	GROUP	TYPE OF SEAT AND WEIGHT		APPROXIMATE AGE	PRICE FROM
1	0 0+	Rear-facing	birth to 13kg (29lb) [Group 0 (birth to 9kg/22lb) is no longer produced on its own]	birth to 12–15 months	£80
2	1	Front-facing	9kg–18kg (20lb–40lb)	9 months to 4 years	£80
1 and 2	0+1 combination	Rear and front-facing	birth to 18kg (40lb)	birth to 4 years	£130
3	2	[Group 2 (15–25kg/ 33–55lb) is only produced in combination with other groups, e.g. 2/3]			
4	3	Booster seat cushions	22kg–36kg (48lb–79lb)	6–11 years	£15
2, 3 and 4	1/2/3 combination	Front-facing booster seat	9kg–36kg (20lb–79lb)	9 months to 11 years	£100
3 and 4	2/3 combination	Front-facing booster seat	15kg–36kg (33lb–79lb)	4–11 years	£40

Prices given are for the lowest rrp (recommended retail price) available for products recommended on the website of nursery equipment company Baby's Mart in December 2008. Most equipment sold via the website for less than the rrp stated.

SAFETY AT ANY PRICE

Safety is something you don't want to take any chances on, but you don't need expensive equipment. Many people get by without stair gates and cupboard locks, but the success of this depends on your child. It's better to be safe than sorry.

WATCH POINTS HAZARDS AT HOME

The best method is to deal with situations as they arise, while keeping an eye on the obvious dangers. For example:

■ **Get a fireguard** If you have an open fire (real or gas), you will need a fireguard as soon as your child becomes mobile. Look out for secondhand guards, ask friends who have an older child and check out catalogue and DIY stores as they will often be cheaper than baby stores.

■ **Put away dangerous substances** Ensure that cleaning materials and medicines are kept well out of reach.

■ **Use safety devices** If your child is into everything, or you want to take every precaution, look out for special packs in DIY stores that include plug covers, cupboard locks and door stops. These starter packs work out much cheaper than buying individual packs of safety devices.

SAFETY CHECKS

Whether it's new or secondhand, before you buy equipment for your baby you want to be sure it has not been recalled. The Royal Society for the Prevention of Accidents website **www.rospa.com** ✉ lists products that have been recalled by the manufacturers for safety reasons. (Select 'Product Safety' from the main menu, then The Trading Standards Institute product recall list or phone 0121 248 2000 for more information ✉.) The products listed include cribs, baby furniture, clothes, childproofing items, baby foods and formulas, over-the-counter medicines, car seats and buggies.

RESOURCES

SAFETY ADVICE
Although we all try hard to prevent injuries, each year more than 1 million children need hospital treatment in Britain after an accident in the home.
■ The Child Accident Prevention Trust website at **www.capt.org.uk** or 020 7608 3828 ✉ has factsheets on aspects of child safety you can view online, and publications that can be ordered.
■ Government information on safety at home can be found at **http://www.direct.gov.uk/en/ Parents/Yourchildshealthand safety/index.htm**, including chemical safety, how to reduce trips and falls, and fire safety.
■ For more useful advice go to **www.safekids.co.uk**, including sections on Around Water & Garden and Childproofing.

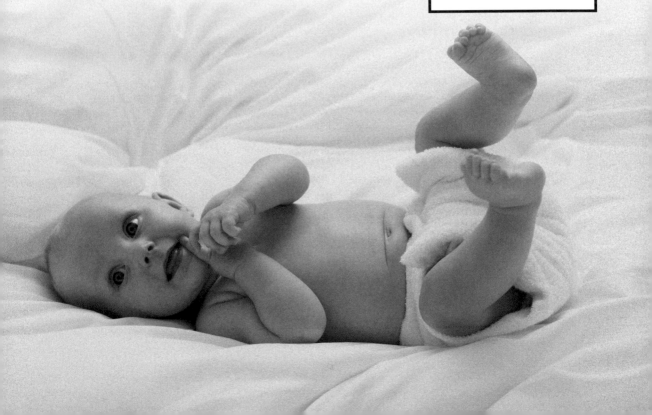

CUT THE COST OF CHILDCARE

For most working parents, the major outlay for the first five years is childcare. While it's essential to find a form of care that suits you and your child, cost is also a key factor. There are different ways of paying less, depending on your income and whether or not you work full time.

EXAMINING THE OPTIONS

If you have relatives who live nearby and will look after your baby, you will make substantial savings on childcare. If not, you may have to consider one of the following.

Sharing childcare If you have a job-share or work part time, you may be able to join forces with another part-time worker and take it in turns to look after each other's children. Check your legal position with your local Children's Information Service; if you look after someone else's child for more than two hours a day for payment you have to register as a childminder. Even if you don't need to register, you may have to increase your insurance.

Workplace nursery If your employer provides the site and is actively involved in the running of the nursery, you pay no tax on the benefit provided and have the reassurance and convenience of having your child nearby. Your employer gets full tax relief on the costs of running the nursery or play scheme, as well as happier employees. If you don't have a workplace nursery, ask if your employer will set one up.

Day nurseries These cost £110–£200 a week, but once your child is three years old he'll be entitled to free early years education, which allows your child 12.5 hours free nursery education for 38 weeks of the year. To claim, fill in an Early Years Application Form, available from the nursery or local Children's Information Service.

Childminders vs nannies Depending on where you live, childminding rates range between £2.50–£4 an hour for each child. Childminders can work out cheaper than a nanny if you only have one child. An experienced, full-time nanny will cost around £200–£300 a week (£300–£400 to live in), but you'll need to pay your nanny's tax and national insurance contributions on top. A nanny is only really cost-effective if you have more than one child, or if you can arrange a nanny share with another family. Check with your local National Childbirth Trust group to see if they run a nanny share register, or visit **www.nannyshare.co.uk**.

CLAIMING BACK CHILDCARE COSTS

If you use registered childcare (a childminder or nursery, not usually a relative or nanny unless they are registered), you may be entitled to help with the cost through the Working Tax Credit (up to a maximum of £175 a week for one child and £300 for two or more children). To find out if you qualify, get the leaflet WTC1 'Child Tax Credit and Working Tax Credit: An Introduction' from your local tax office or phone the Tax Credits helpline on 0845 300 3900.

RESOURCES

WHAT'S AVAILABLE
- For details of childcare options in your area, visit **www.childcarelink.gov.uk** or phone Childcare Link on 0800 2 346346 for details of your local information service. (In Scotland, visit **www.scottishchildcare.gov.uk**). Childcare Link will also have details of local places that are registered to provide free nursery education.
- The National Childminding Association can give advice and information on childminders. The NCMA helpline is 0800 169 4486; their website is **www.ncma.org.uk**.
- For general Information on childcare and benefits, visit the Working Families website **www.workingfamilies.org.uk** or phone 020 7253 7243.
- For information on the Working Tax Credit, visit **www.hmrc.gov.uk** (0845 300 3900), or the Citizens Advice Bureau website **www.adviceguide.org.uk** or your nearest branch. See *Tax and benefits*, page 312.

HOLIDAY CHILDCARE

Once children have reached school age, full-time child care is no longer a priority for working parents. But there's still the problem of how to keep your children occupied once the holidays come around.

ORGANISED HOLIDAY ACTIVITIES

Summer and Easter camps are a boon to working parents, giving them peace of mind that their youngsters are being well supervised and learning new skills. Privately run day camps are expensive, charging from £200 a week, but there are plenty of other organisations that provide excellent supervised activities for much less.

Local authority schemes Holiday play schemes, organised by local councils, are run by qualified playworkers and offer daily fun for the kids from 8.30am to 6pm. They cost from £75 a week, depending on the type of activity.

Camps and courses Don't book your summer holiday until you've found out what camps are on offer for any organisations your child belongs to, such as Guides, Scouts and Woodcraft Folk. Army, sea and air cadets organise residential courses, many for well under £100 a week.

YMCA holiday activities YMCAs organise holiday and summer activities for children aged 5–14, offering sports, art and crafts and day trips. Week-long camps start at around £100 and may include transport, and there are discounts for booking early. Find your local YMCA at **www.ymca.org.uk**.

Sports-based activities Local sports or leisure centres are likely to have a full programme of holiday activities, ranging from free half-day sessions to football weeks costing from around £60. For water sports fans, Surrey Outdoor Learning and Development organise 2–3 day kayaking and canoeing course from £60–£100 (**www.surreycc.gov.uk** or 01372 378901 ✉). The King's Sports Camps (**www.kingssportscamps.com** or 08700 429 324 ✉) – run by The King's Foundation – offer one-week courses costing £79–£139; parents or carers on a low income may be eligible for help under the Assisted Places Scheme.

Arts and crafts Local museums and art galleries often put on free holiday activities. Check your local theatre, too, as some run drama classes for under £20 a day, or £100 a week. Most churches also run holiday clubs for children.

ARRANGING CHEAPER CHILDCARE

Even if your children go to organised activities for part of the holidays, they need to be taken there. And there will be times when they are at home and need supervision.

Share the care Enlist the help of relatives and friends to drop off and pick up your children at their activities, or look after them at home. If possible, split your leave with your partner, so that you can each spend time separately with the children. Or arrange to share the services of a nanny or au pair with friends in the same position as you are.

Cheaper nannies Trainee nannies may welcome the chance to practise their skills with a family for a lower rate than a qualified nanny. Try advertising on a college notice board.

SPREAD THE HOLIDAY COSTS

During term-time, put a little money away into a short-term savings account for the children's holiday activities. In this way, not only will you spread the load of the inevitable extra expense but you will earn some interest on your money, too.

---

keep it simple

PICK A PROJECT

Save money on activities outside the home by getting your children started on an inexpensive project to last them over the holiday, such as mega Lego building, putting together a large scrapbook or planting and tending a garden. This makes it easier for other people to cover for you as the children have a specific interest to occupy them.

 **RESOURCES**

Select seconds

Buy secondhand when you can – there are nearly-new bargains in many shops and sales.

- **Coats and jackets** Usually well made, and last a while.
- **Dressy dresses** Often good enough for resale once they are outgrown. This applies particularly to those for younger children.
- **Never say no to hand-me-downs** Even if these items have seen better days, there are times when you need clothes for rough wear. Family and friends with older children will know you appreciate anything they can pass on.
- **Teenage styles** Bygone styles sometimes appeal to teenagers. Visit car boot sales and flea markets together – you may make great finds.

SMART MOVES

GOOD-VALUE CLOTHES

Before long, fashions and branding will become important to your child. But there are plenty of ways to keep him happy, while looking after your wallet.

TOP TIPS EASY WAYS TO PAY LESS

- **Storecard benefits** Sign up for storecards from the big department and chain stores, such as Debenhams, Bhs and Monsoon. You could gain 'points' to redeem against future purchases, advance notice of sales, or money-off vouchers and discounts. But avoid the high interest charges by always paying off your bill in full every month.
- **Sales online** Many online catalogues start their sales ahead of reductions offered by post, and the same goes for the online outlet of some high street stores. Register your email address to get advance notice of sales and any special offers.
- **Get in the club** Look out for bargains in 'club' stores, such as Matalan and Costco, where you will find many items of clothing at rock-bottom prices.
- **Discounted designers** Department stores such as Debenhams and discount stores like TK Maxx offer good-value ranges by top designers. If your child must have branded gear, look for it here or try shopping sites such as **www.littlewoodsdirect.com** to get discounts.
- **Branded sportswear** You can make savings on clothes and trainers at a factory outlet shop or on the Internet (try **www.sportzwear.com** and **www.mandmdirect.com**).
- **School uniform** Most schools nominate a preferred outfitter, but don't accept that you must buy every item there. Look for high-cost items such as blazers at school sales. Blazers are often bought and not worn, and a secondhand one can look as good as new. Buy school shirts in multipacks at high street stores and supermarkets. Grey, black or navy skirts and trousers in a non-specific style can also be bought from high street stores.

CASE STUDY

DRESSING FOR LESS

Anna's 9-year-old son, Harry, had outgrown his wardrobe. Faced with the expense of reclothing him, she started to shop around. First stop was the online auction site eBay, where she picked up a pair of trousers, long-sleeved top, T-shirt and unworn swim shorts – all designer-branded – for £17.60 (including postage). She found four T-shirts for £2.50 each and a parka for £16 at Tesco (£26), and a hooded top, pack of 3 long-sleeved T-shirts and pyjamas, totalling £20, at the budget store Peacocks. Catalogue company Freemans (**www.freemans.com**) provided a Nike T-shirt and shorts set, socks and briefs (7 pairs of each), and jeans for a total of £52, giving a final total of £115. Similar clothes in high street shops would have cost twice as much.

A SEWING MACHINE CAN SAVE YOU MONEY

Because sewing machines have little resale value, you can usually pick up a used one cheaply. Consider a reconditioned model from a sewing machine shop. You should be able to get a good brand for £70–£125. Check out newspaper ads and car boot sales, but bear in mind machines bought this way will probably need an overhaul at a cost of £60–£75.

STYLISH REVAMPS

Bring old clothes right up to date by:
- cutting off cotton trousers below the knee to make cropped ones;
- turning a summer dress into a skirt and a crop top;
- cutting the arms to three-quarter length on a top or cardigan and adding a ribbon trim.

LONGER SKIRTS AND DRESSES

If you sew, you could buy a remnant of fabric that matches or contrasts with the dress fabric and stitch an additional panel to the hem.

Use simple sewing skills to give your children's clothes a new lease of life. Simple makeovers can help you to stretch your clothes budget, but do consult with your children as they get older or your idea of stylish may be their idea of embarrassing.

NEW CLOTHES FOR NOTHING

PARTY CLOTHES MAKEOVERS

Unless there is a grand occasion such as a family wedding, your daughter won't need a proper party frock. Simply jazz up an inexpensive plain jersey or cotton dress, or a skirt or cropped trousers and a matching T-shirt, with some sparkly sequins. Glue more sequins to a pair of canvas sandals and she'll have a designer outfit.

CONCEAL STAINS AND SMALL TEARS

Cover them with a shop-bought motif such as a skateboard or a butterfly. You don't have to sew them on – use iron-on bonding fabric to hold them in place.

LENGTHEN SLEEVES AND TROUSERS

If the sleeves on a shirt or sweater get too short at the cuff while the body still fits well, transform the shirt into a short-sleeved version of the original (or, in the case of a sweater, into a sleeveless vest). To add length to girls' trousers, buy a selection of braid, ribbon or trimmings and sew several strips of different ones to the hem on each leg.

NO-FUSS FOOD

As with clothing, children become pickier and more brand-aware as they grow older. But a few tactical moves should make the shopping bill easier to swallow.

SHOPPING STRATEGIES FOR LOWER BILLS

Shop by yourself Taking the children around a supermarket, as well as being a logistical nightmare, will inevitably add to the bill items you wouldn't have bought if you were alone. So leave the children at home if you can – 24-hour supermarkets make this possible for many families.

Online shopping If the prospect of a late-night supermarket run is too much to contemplate, shop online. You'll follow your list far more closely and you should more than save the delivery charge, especially if you make use of the many money-off vouchers sent out by supermarkets in their bid to win new online customers.

Fill the freezer Stock up your freezer once a month at a good-value freezer store. The same items are often cheaper than at the supermarket, and you'll cut the weekly trip down to just fresh items.

Support your local market Make a saving on fresh fruit and vegetables by buying at a local market. Eggs may be less than half the supermarket price, too.

BUY IN BULK, SERVE IN SMALL PORTIONS

Food producers love to offer small sizes of a product to entice parents – and children – with miniature portions. Don't be fooled by cute packaging – you're paying over the odds. For example, a small bag of crisps typically costs 38p, while a 14-pack bag of the same brand is on sale for £2.23 – 16p a bag. Always buy the largest packet of raisins,

---

FEEDING THEM WHEN YOU'RE OUT

The best way to save money on food when you're out is to take a packed lunch. But when you're struggling with kids, buggies and bags, you might not want to add flasks and sandwiches to the load. On a fine day when you can eat outside, go to a bakery or supermarket for filled rolls and a greengrocer for some fruit. You'll fill your children up with healthy food and should make a reasonable saving compared to eating in a fast-food restaurant.

Bake in bulk

crackers, biscuits and so on, but then transfer the contents to small plastic containers or bags that can be brought out when needed.

FOOD SIZE MATTERS, TOO

There are ways to feed your children morsels that match their size and still hold down food costs. Blocks of cheese are less expensive than cheese sold in slices, but your children will enjoy the cheese more if you cut it into sticks or cubes. Baby carrots – less expensive when bought in big bags – look friendlier than big carrots. Alternatively, you could cut larger carrots into sticks yourself. For no-cost fun, cut sandwich bread with cookie cutters or roll narrow strips of bread spread with a filling into pinwheels.

JUST LIKE GRANDMA USED TO MAKE

While you may not always have the time to make meals from scratch, doing so will save money and it's healthier, too. Make it easier on yourself by thinking ahead.

Cook twice as much Whenever possible, make double the quantities and freeze half for future use. You can do this with pasta sauces, stews, savoury mince for shepherd's pie or lasagne, and stewed fruit for pie fillings or crumbles.

Bake in bulk Take a tip out of your grandmother's book and have a baking day. Biscuits, fairy cakes, muffins and sponges are all quick and easy to bake, and cost a fraction of shop prices. If you combine your baking day with cooking a roast lunch you'll use your oven to the full and save on electricity, too. Involve the children in order to develop good food habits.

> **keep it simple**
>
> **SAVE 50% ON JUICE CARTONS**
> Individual juice cartons may be handy, but they are expensive and create a lot of waste. Instead, use a reusable plastic bottle (sports bottles work well) and fill that with the juice of your choice. If you make it up from a frozen concentrate and dilute it with water you'll reduce costs even further. For a special treat, use half juice and half sparkling water.

FEEDING CHILDREN: PROCESSED COMPARED WITH FRESH

SMALL CARTON BRAND-NAME SQUASH	£0.39
BRAND-NAME SQUASH, DILUTED AT HOME	£0.09
SNACK PACK WITH CHICKEN AND CHEESE	£1.20
2 BREAD ROLLS WITH CHICKEN OR CHEESE	£0.85
READY-MADE SAUSAGES AND MASH	£1.89
HOME-COOKED SAUSAGES AND MASH	£0.90
READY-MADE RICE PUDDING	£0.54
HOME-MADE RICE PUDDING	£0.21
READY-MADE SHEPHERD'S PIE	£1.85
HOME-COOKED SHEPHERD'S PIE	£1.10

Prices are for each serving, and are taken from a leading supermarket in December 2008. Products used for both ready meals and fresh food are average for those available – neither premium nor value.

'MUST HAVE' TOYS AND FURNITURE

Babies and toddlers don't need fancy toys – most of all they need things that are age-appropriate and interesting. As your child grows there'll be ever more demands on your purse – for more toys, fancy kids' furniture and some way to accommodate their growing number of belongings.

TOP TIPS THRIFTY TOYS

■ **Simple ideas for babies** Don't buy soft toys, because your baby will be given lots and they provide little stimulation for very young children. It is better to buy the small but perennially popular items such as stacking cups, balls that rattle and wooden blocks. A baby gym is useful, and you can look for this in nearly-new sales and on eBay (**www.ebay.co.uk**).

■ **Sharing in the fun** Swap toys with friends to give your child maximum variety without spending a fortune. Alternatively, join a toy library where you can borrow toys for nothing (or a nominal fee). For details of local toy libraries, ask at your local library, check your local council website or visit the National Association of Toy and Leisure Libraries' website **www.natll.org.uk** (020 7255 4600) ✉.

■ **Secondhand buys** Visit car boot sales and local school fêtes and Christmas bazaars. There is always a toy stall, and you'll find games, puzzles and toys, often in pristine condition. Trikes and bikes are quickly outgrown and can be picked up secondhand for a fraction of their original cost. Look out for bike auctions at local schools, where your child can try them before you bid. There's also a wide range of bikes available via the police property disposal website Bumblebee Auctions (**www.bumblebeeauctions.co.uk**).

TOYS FOR FREE

Making toys for your baby needn't take the skill and ingenuity of a *Blue Peter* presenter.

■ Make a shaker by half-filling an empty water bottle with dried lentils or rice. Ensure the lid is screwed on tightly.

■ Cover a cereal box with plain paper and then stick on pictures of animals, flowers or family photographs and cover with sticky plastic. Babies love looking at the pictures and will turn the box over and over.

■ Make a ball from scraps of different-textured material stitched together and stuffed with old tights. For extra interest, include a bell inside the ball.

Pay less for educational toys and books

There are ways to reduce the expense of these valuable learning tools.

Toy libraries Toys designed to develop your child's imagination and reasoning powers are at the core of most toy libraries (see above for more information).

NCT sales The National Childbirth Trust holds annual nearly-new sales of toys and books in towns all over Britain. (For more details, see page 91.)

School fairs and sales Stalls run by parents often include toys that have been outgrown by their original owner, and are generally in excellent condition.

Discount bookshops Chains such as The Works offer hefty reductions on the retail price of books.

The Internet E-bookstores – such as **www.amazon.co.uk** or **www.countrybookshop.co.uk** – offer a huge range of titles often heavily discounted (check the cost of delivery).

Libraries Don't forget to borrow books from the local library – they are also a great source of videos, DVDs and CDs.

High-street stores Monitor stores for sales and spot discounts. This applies not just to the Early Learning Centre, but to more general retailers – such as WH Smith – as well.

Museums Shops at museums such as the Natural History Museum include many great toys and books – and reduce prices from time to time.

SMART MOVES

FURNITURE

Today you can kit out your child's room with fabulous child-size furniture. While it may be worth buying a small table and chairs (which you can find secondhand), remember that by the time he starts school he'll already be growing out of them. To get value for money, it's much better to buy full-size furniture your child will grow into.

Bedding and curtains You can soften the feel of full-size furniture by choosing child-style fabrics for bedding and curtains, and decorating the walls with a fun border. All of these can be changed at a later date at little extra cost.

DOUBLE-DUTY BEDS

When it's time to buy a big bed for your child, consider one with a mattress set on a frame that has drawers underneath. If space is limited or children are sharing a room, this is a real space saver, providing storage and a sleep space in one. Alternatively, there are storage boxes on wheels that can be kept under beds. Some beds come with extendable legs, so can be turned into a high sleeper when it is safe to do so.

Onwards and upwards For older children and teens, consider a loft bed with a storage or a study area below. You'll find a wide variety of prices and styles available in DIY superstores, furniture stores and online. Prices including bed, wardrobe and desk start at about £270. If it is a long-running line, you can buy the initial bed and then add the optional extras later to spread the cost.

TOP TIPS CREATING PRIVATE SPACES

If you have two children sharing a room, you probably face demands for more privacy than your house allows. Here are some low-cost suggestions for room dividers that give children some space of their own.

■ **Cheap bookcases** Place a free-standing bookcase, ranging from waist height to ceiling height, between the two beds. Or look for open metal bookcases (available at office liquidation stores), and bolt one side to the wall to prevent it tipping over. Your children will have more privacy and somewhere to store their belongings.

■ **Folding screens** Make simple wooden frames or use lightweight interior doors, and join them with hinges. Cover with fabric, or turn them into free-standing bulletin boards and let each child decorate their side of the screen.

■ **Curtain between the beds** Save money on a curtain by dyeing an old sheet, or use a 1960s-style curtain of beads.

keep it simple

CUSHION COMFORT
Instead of spending money on child-size chairs that are soon outgrown, try some penny-wise cushion ideas.

■ Buy a large foam cushion form and make a simple cover for it. Floor cushions allow a child freedom to cuddle up wherever they wish, and they are safe and easy for children to move.

■ Create a pile of old decorative pillows – if you don't have any, pick them up at car boot sales or in charity shops and have them dry-cleaned. Let your child make his or her own little nest for reading or listening to music.

OUT AND ABOUT

While toddlers and young children are easily entertained with water, a sandpit and swings in the park, older children demand more. Take advantage of low-cost entertainment for your children and make your money go further.

OUTDOOR FUN

Contact your local tourist office or consult the website of your local council for details of local places that offer the timeless attractions of tree-climbing, duck-feeding or an adventure playground for free. Most heathlands and parks are free to access. You will also find information on cycle routes, walks, events and free activities such as sports and drama sessions – often specially run by local authorities for children in the school holidays.

Join the National Trust Consider joining the National Trust ✉ or English Heritage ✉ – whichever has properties closest to you. The grounds provide exciting settings for outdoor play and you can look around interesting houses and castles as well. Some National Trust properties have tracker activity packs to help children explore. Find listings of family days and children's summer activities at the Family Visits section of the website (under Information for Visitors): **www.nationaltrust.org.uk** or phone 0844 800 1895 ✉. It's worth looking online for savings – a sizeable discount can sometimes be had if you pay by direct debit.

CULTURE VULTURES

Children's workshops There are children's workshops covering many different arts and crafts activities, from jewellery-making and mask-making to T-shirt decoration, and many more besides. Some workshop venues have individual websites, and others can be found by going to your local council website and selecting the children's events link. Local libraries and museums should also have useful information.

Theatre and dance Some theatres run special children's workshops. The Tricycle (020 7372 6611; **www.tricycle.co.uk**) offer such events as a finger-puppet workshop for 3- to 5-year-olds (£4–£6), and dance, movement and mime for older children (£8–£10). Mayhem Theatre Arts in Hoddesdon (01992 465100; **www.mayhemtheatrearts.co.uk**), Hertfordshire offer a 4-day holiday workshop for around £80. Children may also enjoy open-air theatre, such as productions at Regent's Park or Edinburgh Castle.

Check out museums Entrance fees to museums are generally reasonable, especially family tickets and groups. Many are free – including some of the biggest, such as the Science Museum ✉ and the National History Museum ✉ in London, and the National Railway Museum ✉ in York. The larger museums and those with interactive exhibits and activities provide a whole day's entertainment. Some sports clubs, such as Manchester United and Lords, have museums at their stadiums or there's the National Football Museum in Preston (**www.nationalfootballmuseum.com** ✉).

RESOURCES

NEWSLETTERS AND INFORMATION COVERING CHILDREN'S ACTIVITIES

■ The National Trust **www.nationaltrust.org.uk/** 0844 800 1895 ✉.

■ English Heritage **www.english-heritage. org.uk**/0870 333 1181 ✉.

■ For details of local events, visit your library or local council website. Alternatively, visit **http://news.bbc.co.uk/ local/hi/default.stm** ✉ and search by region. There are several dedicated websites, including **www. familiesonline.co.uk** or **www.kidsdaysout.co.uk** ✉.

■ To find museums of interest near you, visit **www.museums.co.uk** ✉ where you can search by location or type.

■ For information on loyalty card deals, visit **www.tesco.com/clubcard** or **www.nectar.com** ✉ (Sainsbury's).

EXTREME ADVENTURES

Day trips to theme parks are a treat for the children although they are pricey. But there are ways around this.

Pay in advance Make savings by buying tickets in advance and booking online. Legoland (**www.lego.com/legoland** ✉) offers a 10% discount on tickets booked online, or phone 0871 2222 001 for more information. The Alton Towers website (**www.altontowers.com**) offers a 20% online discount or 35% saving on family tickets (phone 08705 20 40 60 ✉).

Use loyalty points Supermarkets such as Sainsbury's and Tesco have schemes whereby you can exchange loyalty points for tickets to theme parks and other attractions for as little as £5 (in vouchers).

FAMILY FARE REDUCTIONS

Buy a family railcard By paying just £24 a year, you can save a third on most adult rail fares and 60% on child fares. There is also a railcard available to 16- to 25-year-olds, again priced at £24, and entitling the bearer to a third off rail fares. These cards pay for themselves within a few trips, depending on the length of the journey.

Reduced fares Even if you don't have a railcard, anyone under the age of 16 is entitled to reduced railway fares (14- and 15-year-olds may be asked for proof of age).

Travel by tube Children under 11 who live in London can now travel for free on the Tube, Docklands Light Railway and London overground with a free 5–10 Oyster photocard. Children visiting the capital can travel for free when accompanied by an adult with a valid ticket (a maximum of four children per adult passenger). For information, visit **http://www.tfl.gov.uk/tickets/** ✉.

Around Britain There are comparable travel offers in many other parts of Britain. In Manchester, you can buy a one-day Wayfarer ticket that will give four people (two of whom can be over 15) unlimited travel by bus (at any time) or by train and tram (after 9.30am on weekdays) throughout much of the northwest for £18.40. Visit **www.gmpte.com** ✉.

Plan ahead By using other travel websites such as **www.thetrainline.com** ✉ you can make substantial savings, as long as you specify your travel dates, avoid peak travel times and book at least a week in advance.

keep it simple

WHEN TO LEAVE THE CAR AT HOME
If you're taking the children out for the day, check at your local rail or coach station for family deals to places of interest and major attractions. These deals often include money-off vouchers or even the full price of admission. At **www.daysoutguide.co.uk** you can register for days out ideas, special offers and 2FOR1 entry into London's top attractions – including Madame Tussauds and the London Dungeon – when you travel to the capital by train.

Family affairs

It is vitally important that your family is financially protected from unexpected events, and you are secure in old age. Find out about ways of reducing insurance and other costs, and entitlements that can help you.

LIFE AND HEALTH INSURANCE

If you have a family, or anyone who would suffer financially if you died, it is essential to take out life insurance. And death isn't the only threat to your family's financial security. Serious illness or injury, either to the main earner or whoever is looking after the children, can be a major financial blow. Compare insurance providers to find policies that cover your needs and the most competitive premiums.

LIFE COVER OPTIONS

Life insurance is essential if you have dependants, such as a partner or children. It is one of the few financial products that has got cheaper in recent years, so if you haven't got a policy already signing up could cost less than you think. And if you already have cover, you could save money by replacing it with a cheaper plan – but make sure you have a new policy in place before cancelling your existing cover.
Term insurance This is the simplest, cheapest and most popular form of life cover. You are charged premiums for a set term, typically 20–25 years or until retirement, and your dependants receive a tax-free payout if you die within that period. There is no cash in value, so if you outlive the plan you'll get nothing back. You are free to cancel at any time.
Whole-of-life cover Life insurance that lasts as long as you do, paying a tax-free lump sum whenever you die, is less common and more expensive. If you took out a policy some time ago, see if you can find a new, more competitive one.

TOP TIPS GET THE POLICY YOU NEED

Make sure you aren't paying for more insurance than you require by getting the right sort of policy at the right price.
■ **Unnecessary cover** If you don't have any dependents, you don't need life insurance.
■ **Shop around** It's worth shopping around for the lowest rate, either online, by telephone or using a specialist insurance broker. Don't just accept a plan that your bank or existing insurance company is offering. Do some research and get independent financial advice to help you decide which product is right for you.
■ **Pick the right policy** If you are covering your mortgage, consider a 'decreasing' term policy where the amount of insurance and your monthly premium falls steadily as your outstanding repayment mortgage is paid off. Alternatives are 'level' term, where your monthly premiums and insured amount remain fixed, and 'increasing' term, where both premiums and the amount insured increase every year.
■ **Be honest** Tell the insurance company about any medical conditions you have. If you don't, you could be left without cover and it may not pay out when needed.
■ **Avoid inheritance tax** Write the policy into trust (see page 115). This will ensure your tax-free payout falls outside your estate for inheritance tax purposes. Most insurance companies will provide the relevant trust forms.

INSURANCE FOR THOSE AT HOME

It's worth considering how the working parent would look after their children if something happened to the person looking after the kids – probably worth around £30,000 a year in unpaid housework and informal childcare. Most working parents couldn't afford to pay that from their salaries, and could be forced to give up work to look after their family.

 **RESOURCES**

COMPARING INSURANCE POLICIES

Although comparison sites are a good way of comparing the cost of life and protection insurance you should get advice before buying. Find an independent financial adviseradviser at **www.unbiased.co.uk** and 020 7833 313 ✉. For life and protection insurance **www.lifesearch.co.uk** 0800 316 3166 ✉; and **www.directlife.co.uk** 0800 980 9801 ✉. For people with medical problems or who are having trouble getting insurance try **www.the-insurance-surgery.co.uk** 0800 083 2829 ✉ and **www.totallyinsuredgroup. co.uk** 08450 77 40 30 ✉.

HEALTH INSURANCE OPTIONS

The two most popular insurance policies to cover illness are income protection (IP) and critical illness insurance (CI). IP is the insurance that most people should have, but few do. IP provides a tax-free income if you are unable to work because of illness. CI pays out a tax-free lump sum if you are diagnosed with one of a list of life-threatening illnesses.

INCOME PROTECTION

Also known as permanent health insurance, IP pays a tax-free monthly income if you fall ill and are unable to work. Unlike CI, it pays if you are off work due to stress or back trouble, two common causes of workplace absence.
Long-term benefits The income will continue until you recover and return to work or reach retirement age. This means if you fall seriously ill the policy could pay out for many years. As a result, IP may be more expensive than CI.

CRITICAL ILLNESS COVER

CI pays out a tax-free lump sum if you are diagnosed with one of a list of serious, life-threatening illnesses, such as cancer, heart disease or a stroke. However, only serious illnesses are covered – even some cancers are excluded.
Combine life and CI Many people buy CI to cover their mortgage with life insurance. You can save money by taking out a combined life and CI policy over a set term. However, the policy will only pay out once, either if you suffer a serious illness or in the event of your death. Shop around to find the best deal, and write your policy into trust to avoid inheritance tax if you should die (see page 115).

REDUCING INCOME PROTECTION PREMIUMS

Be sure of a payout

■ **Extend the deferral period** You can opt to receive income protection payouts 4, 13, 26 or 52 weeks after you stop work, living on your savings or cover from work in the interim. This cuts your premiums but still gives you protection from long-term sickness absence.

■ **Save on sickness benefits** Check how much the state and your employer will pay if you fall sick, as this will reduce the amount you need to fund yourself.

■ **Don't overinsure** Because the payout is free of tax, you only need to cover around half of your salary. Work out how much you need to live on each month.

■ **Fixed premiums** If you can, choose a policy with guaranteed or fixed monthly premiums. Reviewable policies are cheaper initially, but could become much more expensive over time as premiums are reviewed every few years.

■ **High-risk jobs** An age-related policy could be cheaper for people in high-risk jobs or smokers. However, premiums start cheaper than guaranteed or reviewable policies but increase each year as you get older.

■ **Get advice** Getting the right cover can be complicated so see an independent financial adviser before buying a policy.

MORTGAGE PAYMENT PROTECTION INSURANCE (MPPI)

Also called accident, sickness and unemployment (ASU) cover, MPPI covers monthly mortgage repayment for a limited period, so you don't lose your home following illness or redundancy. Payouts are tax-free as they are sent directly to your lender and do not affect state benefits.

Costs Cover ranges from around £1.50 to £6 for each £100 of mortgage repayment you protect – so if your mortgage bill is £500 a month, expect to pay between £7.50 and £30.

Limited cover MPPI typically covers you for 12 or even 24 months. If you are ill or unemployed for longer, MPPI will stop paying out. Income protection covers you for much longer, although it doesn't protect against unemployment.

One or the other You can buy an MPPI policy to cover accident and sickness cover without unemployment cover – and vice versa.

MONEY FROM THE STATE

Before buying any sort of illness insurance, you should check how much you will get from the state. If you are employed you will usually get statutory sick pay (SSP) of £75.40 a week for up to 28 weeks (2008/2009) if you are off work for four or more days. After 28 weeks, you will be assessed for Employment and Support Allowance (ESA). You will be assessed in a 13-week period and during this time you will receive around £60 a week if you are over 24. If you are deemed to be able to do some work you can claim ESA of £84.50 a week until you can get back to work. You will receive £89.50 indefinitely if you are deemed unfit to return to work. If you are self-employed you don't get SSP and are assessed for ESA instead.

MONEY FROM YOUR EMPLOYER

If you are off work ill your employer only has to pay you SSP, but many employers pay more than this. When taking out insurance, take money you will get from the state and your employer into account.

HELP PAYING YOUR MORTGAGE

If you have a low income or are unemployed you may get some help paying the interest on your mortgage. Income Support Mortgage Interest benefit (ISMI) which started on 5 January 2009 will cover interest on your mortgage up to £200,000 after 13 weeks of claiming.

Support scheme In December 2008 the Homeowner Mortgage Support Scheme was announced to help people who suffer a temporary loss of income. Mortgage interest payments can be deferred for up to two years with some lenders, and paid back when finances improve; the mortgage term will be increased to keep payments manageable.

ASK YOURSELF

DO I NEED MPPI?

To find out whether you need Mortgage Payment Protection Insurance (MPPI) with accident and sickness cover, or unemployment cover, or both, ask yourself the following questions:

■ **If I'm made redundant, will I struggle to find a new job?** If there are plenty of opportunities in your field, you can probably do without the unemployment element.

■ **Am I eligible for MPPI unemployment cover?** You can't claim unemployment cover if you are self-employed, take voluntary redundancy, resign from your job, take early retirement in lieu of redundancy or work in temporary employment.

■ **What other insurance do I have?** If you have income protection, or access to a good sick pay scheme, you may only need unemployment cover, or no cover at all.

■ **Is my mortgage lender offering me a good deal?** If you are offered a policy where you pay more than £5 for each £100, you will probably find a better deal with another MPPI provider.

■ **When can I claim?** Some policies won't pay for the first 30 or 60 days of unemployment or illness, by which time you may have recovered or found a new job. Others allow immediate claims. Read the small print carefully.

WILLS AND INHERITANCE TAX

Dying intestate – that is, without leaving a will – means you lose your chance to divide your estate to make it more effective in avoiding inheritance tax (IHT) and to make sure the people you want to benefit from it.

TOP TIPS SAVE ON WRITING A WILL

You can produce your will in a number of ways, varying in complexity and cost. Choose the method that is most suited to your circumstances and budget. But be warned: self-penned testaments spark the majority of court cases.

■ **Do-it-yourself: £0** If you have very simple financial affairs and feel able to master the complexities of will writing, you could get a couple of books from the library and draw up your own. You will need to include the essential wording and you may be able to find your way through the subject well enough to write out your instructions. But you must make sure that it is properly witnessed and your executor knows where it is kept.

■ **Use a template: £10** Wills that have been preprinted, with blanks for the essential information you need to insert, are available for as little as £10 from places like Tesco and WH Smith. First of all, you will need to calculate the worth of your 'net estate', which is the amount remaining in your name after funeral expenses and any outstanding debts have been deducted. Write down the full names of everyone you wish to benefit and how much they should receive, and make a gift of any residue – otherwise it could go to the Crown, or the wrong relative. While this is undoubtedly the cheapest means of drawing up a will, it is probably not the best if your affairs are at all complex. Similar services are available online for £10 to £30.

■ **Online will writers: £30 to £75** Anyone can draw up a will for you. Online will writers will produce a will for around £30 to £75. Choose one that is a member of a professional body, such as The Institute of Professional Willwriters or The Society of Will Writers, as these have codes of conduct and indemnity insurance.

■ **Online will writing checked by a solicitor: £50** Some online will writers produce wills that are checked by a solicitor.

■ **Solicitors: £80 to £300** If in any doubt, go to a solicitor, who will charge from around £80 for a relatively straightforward single person's will, or up to £300 for a couple. Take comfort from knowing that this outlay could save your family thousands of pounds after your death. If you don't have a solicitor, contact the Law Society for recommendations. You can keep the time – and therefore cost – to a minimum by having a clear idea about what you want to achieve. Filling out a will template before visiting the solicitor will often help to clarify your thinking, even if the solicitor draws up the final version.

RESOURCES

WILLS AND INHERITANCE TAX

■ You can find a low-cost expert online. The Will Site, for example, can prepare a single will from £59, checked by a solicitor. Find it at **www.thewillsite.co.uk** or phone the helpline on 0845 126 0891 ✉).

■ For information on making a will, contact The Society of Will Writers on 01522 687888, **www.willwriters.com** ✉) or The Institute of Professional Willwriters on 08456 442042, **www.ipw.org.uk** ✉).

■ To view the Inland Revenue's information on inheritance tax, go to the website **www.hmrc. gov.uk/inheritancetax**).

INHERITANCE TAX PLANNING

Inheritance tax (IHT) is paid by your estate on your death if the value of your assets exceeds the nil-rate threshold of £312,000 (at the 2008–2009 rate). Anything above this threshold is taxed at 40%, unless it is left to your spouse or charity, in which case no tax whatsoever is payable. The tax should be paid within six months, and your friends and family cannot benefit from your estate until the duty has been cleared.

Not just for the rich Many people regard IHT as a problem for the seriously wealthy, but millions of homeowners are likely to be caught in the net, because the value of their properties counts as part of their estate. With house prices rising in recent years much faster than annual increases in the IHT threshold, more and more people will face an IHT bill. But with a little planning and a simple procedure you can slash the tax you pay.

NEW RULES FOR COUPLES

Since 2007, couples and people in civil partnerships have been able to share their inheritance tax allowances on death. As before, when one partner dies they can leave an unlimited amount to the surviving partner, or up to £312,000 to anyone else, without tax being due. When the surviving partner dies they can use their allowance plus the remaining allowance from their partner. This means that up to £624,000 can be passed on without any tax being liable.

Discretionary trust A flexible type of trust that gives trustees 'discretion' as to how the income from it can be used, although they are usually guided by a 'letter of wishes' attached to the will. There is now little need for a discretionary trust – which was previously used to save loved ones from having to pay tens of thousands in tax – now that any unused nil rate band can be transferred to the surviving spouse or civil partner. However, there are circumstances where it could still be worthwhile. This includes: complex succession plans, especially if there has been a second marriage and/or stepchildren; where the value of assets in the trust is likely to grow faster than the nil-rate band allowance; and, estates containing assets eligible for business or agricultural property relief.

CASE STUDY

COUPLE GAINS FROM NEW RULES

John and Nancy Williams were married and owned a house together that was valued at £400,000. They had other savings worth £100,000, giving them total assets of £500,000. John died in August 2008, and all of the assets passed to Nancy without any IHT being due. When Nancy dies she can leave the full £500,000 to her children without any IHT being due because the value of the estate is less than the total value of John and Nancy's tax-free IHT limit £624,000 – £312,000 for Nancy and the unused £312,000 for John. If Nancy died in the same tax year as John (2008-2009) and the estate was worth more than £624,000, then tax would be payable at 40% on the amount above the tax-free limit.

PENSIONERS' BENEFITS AND ENTITLEMENTS

Almost every pensioner is entitled to some benefits. Several may apply to you, to boost your income or offset the costs of care at home or in a residential or nursing home.

TOP TIPS COMMONLY MISSED BENEFITS

Don't be one of the huge number of pensioners who are missing out on benefits – Age Concern ✉ estimates that almost £5 billion in pensioner benefits remain unclaimed each year. Make sure you keep up to date with the benefits systems. Even if you have savings or a large house, you should still check out your entitlements.

■ **Pension Credit** The government estimates that nearly two million pensioners could be entitled to Pension Credit but aren't claiming it. Pension Credit has two parts. The first part is a Guarantee Credit that gives a minimum income guarantee if you are aged 60 or over – it tops up income to £124.05 a week for a single person and £189.35 for a couple (increasing to £130 and £198.45 in 2009-2010). The second part is a means-tested Savings Credit that provides extra money to many people aged 65. You may be eligible for the Guarantee Credit or the Savings Credit, or both. Contact The Pension Service for help in filling out your claim on freephone 0800 99 1234, or see **www.thepensionservice.gov.uk/pensioncredit** ✉.

■ **Housing Benefit** Although this is means-tested, people over 60 may still be able to claim – even if they have some savings – and get help paying their rent.

■ **Attendance Allowance** One of the few benefits for the elderly available usually irrespective of income or savings, the Attendance Allowance is available to people aged 65 and over who need help with everyday tasks such as washing and dressing. The Department for Work and Pensions ✉ decide whether you are eligible or not; get specialist advice from Age Concern ✉ or a similar agency on how to fill out the form so as to present your case in the best way. In 2008-2009, the allowances are £44.85 a week for help day or night, and £67 for help both day and night.

keep it simple

HOW TO APPLY FOR BENEFITS
Pick up information leaflets at your post office, Jobcentre Plus ✉, HM Revenue and Customs ✉ or The Pension Service ✉. For help with your entitlements, contact your local Jobcentre Plus or the Department for Work and Pensions (DWP). Visit the DWP website at **www.dwp.gov.uk** ✉ for information and to download relevant application forms, and **www.direct.gov.uk** ✉ for information about all government services.

CASE STUDY

INFORMED ADVICE NETTED £19.71 A WEEK
Valerie Roberts reaped the benefits of accepting help from the Pension Service in making her claim. A single woman living on her own, she was already receiving the Guarantee Credit part of the Pension Credit, which topped up her weekly income to £124.05. When she turned 65 in 2008, she became eligible to apply for the Savings Credit element of the Pension Credit, but was not sure whether she would gain anything by doing so, because the calculations seemed so complicated. An Age Concern fact-sheet advised her: 'You are likely to be entitled to Savings Credit if as a single person your income is less than £174 a week and if as a couple your joint income is less than around £255 a week.' Encouraged by this, she decided to claim with the help of the Pension Service and was delighted to discover that she would receive an additional £19.71 each week.

WATCH POINTS **HELP FOR YOUR HOME**

In addition to the usual benefits, pensioners can also get help with costs relating to maintaining their home.

■ **Heating and insulation** If you are 60 or over, your household is eligible to receive a tax-free Winter Fuel Payment. In 2008/2009, this was £250 if you were the only eligible person in your household, £125 if others were also eligible, and £250 for those receiving Pension Credit or Jobseeker's Allowance. People over 80 are entitled to more.

■ **Maintenance and repairs** Local housing authorities can provide assistance in repairing and improving housing, in the form of grants, loans, materials and labour. Contact your local authority or nearest Citizens Advice Bureau to see a copy of the local authority's Housing Renewal Policy.

FINANCIAL HELP WITH HEALTH CARE

Although some concessions – such as dental treatment – are means-tested, there are entitlements available that are automatic. Those aged 60 and over are entitled to free prescriptions and eye tests regardless of any savings they may have, although the cost of glasses is not subsidised.

TAKE ADVANTAGE OF TRAVEL ENTITLEMENTS

If you know your entitlements, you can benefit from the special rates offered to pensioners for many products and services on different types of transport.

Free bus travel If you live in England and are 60 and over you are entitled to free off-peak local bus travel (between 9.30am and 11pm Monday to Fridays and any time at weekends and public holidays).

Save up to 33% on train fares The Senior Railcard costs £24 a year(or £65 for three years) and provides fare reductions to anyone aged 60 or over. This saves a third off most rail fares in Great Britain. For details, visit **www.senior-railcard.co.uk**, 08448 714 036 ✉ or phone National Rail Enquiries on 08457 48 49 50 or **www.nationalrail.co.uk** ✉.

Save up to 50% on coach fares Up to half-price coach fares are available to anyone aged 60 or over on National Express coaches if you can prove your age (**www.nationalexpress.com** or 08717 818181 ✉). Use Yellow Pages to check with smaller local participating coach companies. (See *Good-value travel* page 182.)

CHEAPER TV VIEWING

Watch TV for free If you are aged 75 or over you are eligible for a free television licence for your household. You just need to apply for it. See **www.tvlicensing.co.uk** or call 0844 800 6790 ✉ for further details.

Concessionary licence The Accommodation for Residential Care (ARC) concessionary TV licence, costing just £7.50, is for those who are aged 60 plus and living in sheltered accommodation or a care home. Residents aged 75 or over are entitled to a free television licence. The full TV licence fee is paid for a television in a communal area. You can also apply for a 50% concession on the cost of your licence if you are blind or severely sight impaired.

RESOURCES

GREY POWER

■ Britain's two largest organisations working with and for older people are Age Concern **www.ageconcern.org.uk** 0800 00 99 66 ✉ and Help the Aged **www.helptheaged.org.uk** 020 7278 1114 ✉. Both produce fact sheets on a wide range of subjects, including benefits, entitlements and care in old age.

■ The Saga Group **www.saga.co.uk** ✉ provides services for people aged 50 plus. As with any financial product, shop around and get independent financial advice if you need help choosing the right product.

CUT THE COST OF CARE IN OLD AGE

Plan for the future and consider your options, so that if you or a relative needs to go into care, you can make an informed choice and know how to get the best deals.

TOP TIPS THE BEST DEALS ON CARE HOMES

There are essentially two categories of homes: local authority homes and independent care homes (either private homes or voluntary homes often catering for particular professions or religions). For local authority homes, contact your local council.

■ **Get subsidised care if you can** The amount you pay for a place in a local authority care home is means-tested and subsidised where appropriate. The same holds true for independent homes if they accept residents on local authority funding. An average residential care home is around £500 per week and a nursing care home between £600 and £700 per week. Having part or all of your fee paid will make a big difference to your finances, as a residential care home could cost £26,000 a year and a nursing home between £31,200 and £36,400 a year.

■ **Try for a reduction at an independent home** If you are not receiving local authority funding, but your independent care home of choice takes local authority subsidised residents, find out what your local authority pays for a place; it may well be less than what a self-funding individual pays, and you may be able to use this information to negotiate a price reduction.

FUNDING CARE

Your local authority will examine your finances to determine whether or not you will have to pay towards the cost of care.

Property included For 2008–2009, if you have capital or savings over £22,250 (including the value of your home unless it's still occupied by your partner or a dependent relative) you will be expected to meet the full costs of care.

Council loans If you don't have a partner or dependent relative living-in, and must sell your home, and your capital and savings other than your home amount to less than £22,250, you can claim the right to have your local authority pay your fees for the first 12 weeks of care. After that time, if your house is still unsold, the local authority will lend you the amount of your fees, but you will have to repay them once you receive the proceeds of the sale.

TRANSFERRING ASSETS

Be careful if you are considering transferring assets to someone else in anticipation of your move into a care home (see left). There are now strict rules about 'deliberate deprivation of capital' and you could end up costing yourself and your family a great deal more than you were attempting to save.

Separate your assets

If you are living with a partner and one of you needs to move into a care home, the local authority will divide your income to calculate your contribution to care-home fees.

■ As long as one of you lives in your home, its value won't be taken into account, so make sure your local authority is aware of the remaining resident.

■ Only 50% of any private pension should be taken into account.

■ Your savings will be divided equally. It's best to split your assets before the local authority becomes involved, and to make sure that any care-home costs are paid from the accounts of the person in the home.

SMART MOVES

LONG-TERM CARE INSURANCE

With care home fees escalating rapidly, it's a good idea to consider care fee payment plans that will pay your fees. There are two types of plan, both regulated by the Financial Services Authority ✉: prefunded long-term care insurance, which you buy in anticipation of future need; and, an immediate care annuity, which is suitable if you have to move into a home and don't have any other provision. **What's in it for you?** The main benefit of these schemes is peace of mind that the care home fees will be paid for the rest of your life, and not just until your capital runs out. In addition, you will hopefully still have some assets remaining after buying the annuity, which can cover any other expenses or can be left to benefit your family.

HELP WITH THE COST OF CARERS

There is a benefit called Carer's Allowance that is available to those who look after someone else in an informal way – they might be a relative, a friend or a neighbour. To get it, the carer has to spend at least 35 hours a week giving personal care.

Find out if you qualify The carer has to be at least 16 years old, and the person being cared for has to be receiving an Attendance Allowance or a Disability Allowance. The Carer's Allowance is £50.55 a week (2008–2009 rates), but it can vary depending on any other benefits the carer receives. It is not generally available to those who earn more than £95 a week (in 2008–2009). Contact your local Jobcentre Plus ✉ office for a form or call the Benefit Enquiry Line 0800 882 200 ✉, or claim online at **www.dwp.gov.uk/carersallowance** ✉. For more details, go to **www.direct.gov.uk** ✉ and look under 'Caring for someone'.

RESOURCES

HELP WITH CARE
■ Age Concern and Help the Aged have useful fact sheets (see Resources, page 117).
■ The Nursing Home Fees Agency **www.nhfa.co.uk** ✉ also has guidance on benefits and entitlements to help fund the cost of care 0800 99 88 33.
■ Find out which are the best care homes by contacting the Commission for Social Care Inspection, which registers and inspects care homes. See **www.csci.org.uk** 0845 015 0120 ✉ for the address of your nearest office.
■ Carechoices at **www.carechoices.co.uk** 01223 207770 ✉ has listings of care homes nationwide.

GETTING THE BEST CARE

These are the main types of care available for the elderly, both at home and in a residential facility. How much you pay for each level of care is affected by a number of personal circumstances and other relevant factors.

■ Your income, savings and capital (which may include the value of your home) are all taken into account when local authority social services calculate how much they expect you to pay towards your care.

■ Local authorities vary in their interpretation of relevant regulations and guidelines, and so differ in how much they will contribute, and their charges.

■ In addition, England and Wales, Scotland and Northern Ireland all differ in what they ask you to pay towards the cost of your care.

■ All the costs shown below may be reduced after means-testing.

TYPE OF CARE	SERVICE PROVIDED	COST
Domiciliary care	Household tasks and general care	£8–£14 an hour
At-home nursing	Nursing and personal care	£18+ an hour
Residential homes	Room, board and personal care	£500+ a week
Nursing homes	Room, board and personal care	£600–£700+ a week

Animal matters

No one would claim that keeping a pet is primarily a question of cost. But why spend more than you have to when there are so many money-saving ways of obtaining and caring for a much-loved member of the family?

AFFORDABLE ANIMALS

Don't pay more than you need, but take care that an inexpensive pet does not bring long-term expenses.

RESCUED PETS ARE A DOUBLE BLESSING

Offering a caring home to an unwanted animal is a satisfying experience and it can save you money, too.

Benefits Animals offered through charities have normally been vet-checked, vaccinated, neutered and sometimes even microchipped. Some charities expect adoptive owners to pay towards these costs – the cost of adopting a vaccinated, microchipped, vet-checked, wormed, neutered dog from the RSPCA (Royal Society for the Prevention of Cruelty to Animals) is £80–£130. You will also receive free expert advice on the animal's care.

Potential problems Although many animals rehomed in this way make excellent pets, some come with ingrained behavioural problems. Be prepared to spend some time on retraining if necessary.

FRIENDS MAY NOT CHARGE AT ALL

If an acquaintance has an animal that has given birth, this can be an inexpensive way of acquiring a new pet.

Benefits You will usually be charged a fraction of the going price – if anything – though you should offer the cost of a similar animal (see Resources overleaf). This option lets you visit the animal many times before buying so you get to know your pet before making a commitment.

Potential problems Get a written guarantee if you pay a near-market price. If the animal is ill, or turns out to have congenital problems, it may be embarrassing to make a complaint, and having a guarantee document makes the situation clearer if you need to seek legal redress later.

FREE ADVICE BEFORE BUYING

If you have queries on types of pet, breeds or general care, take advantage of free resources.

Pet shops A good pet shop – though not a cheap option – can give you valuable guidance on buying a first pet, and you can get your money's worth if you ask for plenty of free advice, including after your pet is at home.

Rescue centres Organisations such as the RSPCA ✉, Cats Protection ✉, and Dogs Trust ✉ offer free advice to potential pet owners to help to prevent problems they may not have foreseen.

RESCUED PEDIGREE ANIMALS

If you want to adopt a rescued animal but have set your heart on a particular breed, it is quicker to contact a breed-specific rescue than to wait for your chosen animal to turn up at your local general rescue centre. Websites such as The Dog Rescue Pages at **www.dogpages.org.uk** ✉ list specialist canine rescues. For cats, try The Cat Rescue Resource on CatChat at **www.catchat.org** ✉, which has a similar list for cats.

---

keep it simple

COSTLY ERRORS

■ Don't buy an animal you don't have time to look after properly. Paying someone else to exercise and care for your pet can be costly – dogs need up to five hours a day to exercise, feed, groom and train.

■ Check bloodlines and avoid animals with a family history of ailments. Many pedigree dogs have inbred health problems, such as labradors with dodgy hips, cocker spaniels with autoimmune disease, bulldogs with breathing difficulties and dachshunds with bad backs. Owning these breeds can result in hefty long-term vet bills.

■ Don't buy an unhealthy animal. A dog or cat should have a glossy coat, bright eyes, clean teeth and an alert manner. A rabbit or other small mammal should have a rounded shape, a bird should be alert and fish should swim easily and have no lumps or fungal growths.

SPECIALIST BREEDERS

If you are after a particular breed of animal, or if you want to breed or show your pet, buying directly from a specialist breeder is probably the best option. Use a resource such as **www.breederdirectory.co.uk** ✉ to select a dog breed and locate a suitable breeder. Alternatively, you can contact the Kennel Club (0870 606 6750 or use their website **www.the-kennel-club.org.uk** ✉) to find registered breeders.

Benefits The price you pay will not have the percentage that is added by a pet shop, and you will have details of the background of the animal you are buying.

Potential problems There should be none if you make sure that the breeder sells animals registered with the accepted authority for the breed – the Kennel Club for dogs or the Governing Council of the Cat Fancy for cats (**www.gccfcats.org**; 01278 427575 ✉) – and that the animals are vaccinated and healthy. Ask if tests have been carried out for genetic disease or whether there is a history of skin or joint problems, and try to see the parents as they should give you a clue to the animal's eventual size and temperament.

PEDIGREE PETS FOR LESS

A pedigree animal can be expensive, but there are savings to be made if you ask the right questions.

Not for show If you don't intend to show your animal, ask for a 'pet' standard rather than a 'show' standard. There may be a slight 'defect' in colour or posture that is unacceptable in a show animal but won't make the slightest difference in a family pet. You could get a pet standard Burmese cat, for example, for £400 rather than £600.

Golden oldies Animals that are too old to breed are also considerably cheaper but no less lovable. Opt for one in good health and with plenty of energy.

Don't follow the herd Popularity in breeds and colours changes from year to year, but this is purely subjective. If you opt for a less popular breed you could get yourself a fine animal and a real bargain.

SHARE A PET

If you can't afford the time or money for an expensive pet, you can still enjoy their companionship.

Horses and ponies These are beyond the reach of most households, but a particularly keen youngster could try volunteering at a local stable. Your child will learn about horses, get to feed and groom them and possibly be able to ride occasionally for free.

Volunteer pet care Local animal rescue centres, as well as many community schemes to help senior citizens, need people to walk animals and take care of pets' routine needs. By volunteering to help, you will gain much of the day-to-day pleasure of a pet for free.

Dog walking for the blind Sign up with your local charity for this worthwhile way to spend time with an intelligent, well-bred, well-trained dog.

Petsitting for the holidays Advertise locally or contact pet-owners' clubs to offer your services. Most owners would be glad to share their pet with you.

MEALS ON A BUDGET

Pet food outlets and discount Internet sites are a cheaper source of tinned and dry food than your local supermarket or pet shop. But there are other sources of cheap – and even free – pet food you should consider.

BUYING IN BULK

Check out the online shop at **www.petplanet.co.uk** (0845 345 0723) ✉, which offers special deals on all types of pet food, or **www.pet-supermarket.co.uk** (0870 626 02 19). Also, **www.petsathome.com** (0800 328 4204) ✉ advertises its latest offers, though you will need to visit a store to buy. If you buy in sufficient bulk, you will often avoid delivery charges. If you don't have room for storage, share with a friend.

CHEAP CUTS FROM THE BUTCHER

High-quality protein is essential to a healthy diet for cats and dogs, and meat is a great source. Unlike humans, pets don't object to offcuts and the cheaper, less meaty cuts that cost little, such as pigs' trotters and oxtail.

Raw or cooked Any fresh meat fit for human consumption can be fed raw, but any other meat must be well-cooked.

Cheap meat Meats such as offal and chicken wings are nutritious and cheap.

Bones for health Raw bones are great for teeth and a good source of calcium. Don't give cooked bones – especially chicken bones – to dogs (see right).

FREE VITAMINS FROM WEEDS

Garden weeds can be nutritious for rabbits, guinea pigs and small rodents. Wash them well before feeding to your pet.

BEWARE FALSE ECONOMY

You should never give these foods to your pet, no matter how cheap

Dogs Cooked bones may splinter and cause injury or choking. Raw chicken bones, or chocolate in quantities, can kill.

Cats Vegetarian diets can't supply adequate nutrition. Milk can cause gastro-intestinal problems.

Rabbits Large quantities of dandelion can act as a laxative.

Birds Chocolate and avocado can kill parrot-like species such as budgies. A seed-only diet can also shorten your bird's life.

HOW COSTS OF PET FOOD COMPARE

A 1999 *Sunday Times* survey found that feeding your dog human-grade food from a supermarket, while not providing a complete diet, could actually work out cheaper than a conventional diet that was specifically manufactured for dogs. A *Which?* survey found that mid-range and even cheap complete diets for pets were just as nutritious as the most expensive ranges of pet food, at a saving of up to 75%.

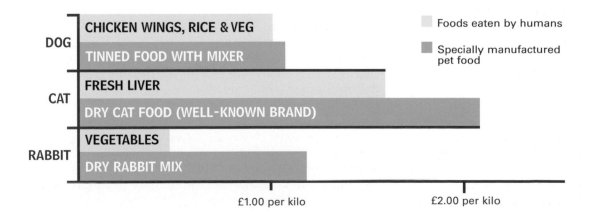

DOG — CHICKEN WINGS, RICE & VEG / TINNED FOOD WITH MIXER
CAT — FRESH LIVER / DRY CAT FOOD (WELL-KNOWN BRAND)
RABBIT — VEGETABLES / DRY RABBIT MIX

■ Foods eaten by humans
■ Specially manufactured pet food

£1.00 per kilo   £2.00 per kilo

Delicious homemade treats

DIY DOG CHEWS
Don't buy your dog expensive rawhide chews – give him or her a carrot full of healthy vitamins.

Pennywise As a medium dog chew costs about £1 and a carrot costs only 8p, even if you have to replace the carrot frequently, this is a major saving.

BUDGET CAT TREATS
Instead of buying cat treats, make your own for a fraction of the price. Mix the following ingredients, and place ¼ teaspoon dollops onto a greased baking tray.
- 185g tin of mackerel or tuna in oil
- 1 cup of wholemeal breadcrumbs
- 1 beaten egg
- ½ tsp brewers' yeast
Bake at 180°C/250°F/gas mark 4 for eight minutes. The treats can be kept for three weeks in the fridge or even longer if frozen.

Pennywise Cat treats cost around 80p for a 50g bag, whereas the recipe above gives you four times as much for less outlay. Fish provides valuable proteins, and the brewers' yeast contains fatty acids and B-complex vitamins for a glossy coat, healthy nervous system and fewer fleas.

NATURAL RABBIT TREATS
Although you can buy treats for rabbits, they're often not beneficial. Try the following instead – they're cheaper and better for your pet, too.
- Herbs, such as oregano, mint, parsley and thyme.
- Alfalfa (in moderation).

Pennywise Rabbit treats cost around £2 for a 100g bag, so growing your own treats is much cheaper.

BUDGIE RECIPE
Give your budgie a snack that will provide hours of chewing fun plus valuable vitamins by offering produce from your garden.
- Fresh eucalyptus or fruit tree twigs or branches.
- The heads of seeding grasses.

Pennywise You'll save the cost of manufactured budgie treats.

FEED FISH CHEAPLY
Save money on fish food by supplying your own.
- Fish love live foods and their condition improves when fed on them. Buying these from pet shops is expensive, so catch your own mosquito larvae, water fleas and daphnia from local ponds and water butts.

Pennywise Live foods cost from 40p for a small bag or £1.30 for pond size, whereas home-caught food is free.

RESOURCES

PET DIETS
Upgrade your pet's diet:
- *Natural Nutrition for Dogs and Cats: The Ultimate Diet* by Kymythy Schulze, 2003, price £6.99, ISBN-10 1561706361.
- *Dr Pitcairn's Complete Guide to Natural Health for Dogs and Cats*, 1995, price £12.04, ISBN-10 0875962432.
- *Give Your Dog a Bone: The Practical Common-sense Way to Feed Dogs for a Long Healthy Life* by Ian Billinghurst, 1993, price £21.50, ISBN-10 0646160281.

Plants to include are chickweed, clover, coltsfoot, comfrey, cow parsley, groundsel, goosegrass, mallow, meadowsweet, plantains, sow thistle, vetches and yarrow.

TOP TIPS AVOIDING WASTE
You can get a great deal on the pet food you buy only to find it goes to waste because you don't serve it properly. Here are some canny ways of making food go further.
- **Cats eat more of lower-grade food** Cats tend to regulate their intake of vital nutrients. Feeding a cheaper, less-nutritious brand of cat food is not necessarily a cost saver – the cat has to eat more to derive the same benefit. Cat food should contain around 26% protein, in the form of meat, chicken or fish (vegetable protein isn't as useful).
- **Dogs are greedy feeders** Find out the best weight for your dog (your vet can advise you). Feed your pet a regime that suits its weight to avoid wasting food and making it fat.
- **Rabbits pick and choose** If you give a rabbit a commercial rabbit mix consisting of grains, seeds and cereals, your pet will pick out the parts it likes and leave the rest. For less waste, feed your rabbit a good-quality pellet – which combines all these ingredients – instead.
- **Fish are usually overfed** Fish kept in tanks are usually overfed, which causes polluted water. Skip feeding your fish for at least one day a week for healthier fish.

PAMPER YOUR PETS

It's natural to want to buy your pet the finer things in life, from a luxury cage to a basket full of entertaining toys. Don't bother to feel guilty though – if you know where to look, you needn't break the bank providing for your pet in style.

DESIGNER LABELS AT DISCOUNT PRICES

It's true – Gucci has gone to the dogs, along with a few other top designers. If you hanker after a Burberry dog bed or a Louis Vuitton collar and lead, factory outlet stores (check the Directory ✉ for designer names) are the best place to indulge your tastes. You can snap up bargains at eBay (**www.ebay.co.uk** ✉) and there are also a number of websites offering designer pet ranges, such as the online pet boutique Puchi at **www.puchipetwear.com** ✉ and the delightfully stylish **www.urbanpup.com** ✉. If you must dress your pet, check for special offers and sale discounts.

DES RES FOR POSH PETS

If you have any carpentry skills and your pet needs a wooden hutch or cage, you can easily make your own or adapt a secondhand cupboard. If you sew, make inexpensive luxuries such as catnip mice or a dog blanket from luxurious fabric remnants such as brocade or velvet, or copy ideas on the cheap from upmarket glossy magazines.

RECYCLE YOUR OWN BELONGINGS

Dogs love to chew on cotton towels, knotted socks, cotton rope and old stuffed toys – but check these for safety before handing them over (see below). Cats enjoy chasing ping-pong balls or plastic golf trainer balls. Dogs and cats don't need a vast array of toys – let them play with a couple at a time and change them round every few weeks.

USE UP HOUSEHOLD WASTE

You can give rodents the cardboard middles from toilet and kitchen towel rolls to gnaw and use as tunnels.

keep it simple

CHEAPER BEDDING

For bedding for your rabbit or other small mammal, buy a straw bale from a farmer or wood shavings and sawdust from a carpenter. This is half the price of buying the same thing in small packs in the pet shop. If you own a paper shredder, use shredded paper for your pet's bedding. As long as you are shredding good quality, non-toxic paper, your pet will be happy.

JUST ONE CAREFUL OWNER

Local newspapers, classified ad magazines such as *Loot,* and websites such as eBay can be great sources of good-value secondhand cages and equipment. If you can afford to wait, keep an eye on these sources until the right deal comes along. Just make sure you disinfect carefully anything that has been used by another animal.

WATCH POINTS DANGEROUS TOYS

When recycling household items for pets, take the following precautions:
- **Cut off dangerous bits** Remove buttons and zips from clothing used as bedding, as well as eyes and any small plastic parts that could be swallowed from old soft toys.
- **Check any wood** Ensure wood has not been treated with a toxic varnish or paint – if necessary, sand down to remove the surface, then re-treat.

LOWER VET BILLS

Of course, you should never stint on veterinary care when it is needed. But it makes good sense to shop around for a reliable vet with reasonable charges, and to learn when a trip to the vet isn't necessary after all.

CATCH PROBLEMS EARLY
Make a habit of checking your pet's physical condition every day. If it is a tame animal, feel it all over for any lumps or bruising, and keep an eye on anything that seems unusual.

PICK A VET BEFORE YOU NEED ONE
Research conducted by pet insurance provider Intune during 2008 found that prices for routine veterinary treatments varied by a massive 86% depending on the vet consulted and the area you live in. A standard consultation, too, ranged from £21.95 to £40.92. So it pays to find a vet you can afford before you need one in a hurry.

Compare costs As there is no national structure for vets' fees, find out the costs of common treatments, such as vaccination, dental care and neutering, from several local vets. Ensure the vet you choose offers good value.

Get a quote Even if you already have a vet, get more than one quotation for any expensive treatment even if you feel it's best to go with your regular practitioner.

SHOP AROUND FOR MEDICINES
You can ask your vet for a prescription and take it along to a high-street pharmacy, where it may be filled more cheaply. Most chemists stock products commonly prescribed for

ASK YOURSELF

SHOULD I TAKE MY PET TO THE VET?
Here are a few signs that indicate a prompt visit to the vet is in order:
■ the animal is lethargic;
■ it is shivering when asleep or has its eyes shut most of the time;
■ your pet is having trouble breathing;
■ the animal won't eat;
■ it has a severe wound, can't walk, is crying or is sensitive to touch.

An ounce of prevention is worth £££ of cure

Get regular checkups Nip problems in the bud with a yearly checkup, costing £25–£40 for a cat or dog.

Think ahead Get to know what health problems your breed is prone to and be on the lookout for them. It is thought that there are 400 hereditary diseases in dogs alone. The Kennel Club publishes a list of breeds and conditions for which DNA tests are available at **www.doggenetichealth.org** ✉.

SMART MOVES

The tests cost £50–£65 each.
It pays to vaccinate Protect your cat or dog from expensive, even fatal, diseases by getting the vaccinations recommended by the British Veterinary Association. Start in the first weeks of life and follow up with annual boosters.

Monitor weight Stand above your dog or cat and feel its waist. A healthy animal has an indentation behind its ribs. If you can't feel the ribs, chances are your pet is overweight. Ask your vet how much it should weigh, give it more exercise and don't overfeed.

Keep fur clean to avoid disease Rabbits, for example, are prone to fly strike caused by flies laying their eggs in soiled fur.

Check teeth Tartar, plaque or gum disease can lead to trouble and eventual tooth loss. You can brush the teeth of a cat or dog with a human toothbrush and pet (not human) toothpaste to prevent problems and avoid expensive descaling. You can also buy dental chews.

Diet watch Dry food (as opposed to semi-moist) can lessen digestive problems, maintain healthy teeth and prevent obesity.

keep it simple

NURSE KNOWS BEST
For minor procedures, such as clipping claws, see a veterinary nurse rather than the vet. This should save you the cost of a full veterinary consultation, which is unnecessary for simple or routine treatments.

RESOURCES

CHECK OUT THE CHAINS
Though it's comforting to have a vet down the road, regional chains such as Midlands-based Pet Vaccination Clinics (**www.petvaccinationclinic. com**, 01564 823825 ✉) specialise in cut-price vaccinations (complete puppy course £34.24), neutering (£68.52–£78.29), microchipping (£12.24). Independent vet's fees can be double.

■ For free or subsidised pet care, contact one of these veterinary chains or charities:
RSPCA low-cost neutering vouchers and subsidised vet treatment **www.rspca.org.uk** ✉;
PDSA low-cost neutering vouchers and subsidised vet treatment **www.pdsa. org.uk** ✉;
Blue Cross free means-tested veterinary care **www.bluecross.org.uk** ✉;
Cats Protection half-price neutering vouchers and subsidised vet care **www.cats.org.uk** ✉.

veterinary treatment and will order others for you. According to the Competition Commission, British vets add up to 68% to the price when dispensing medicines.

FREE OR ASSISTED VETERINARY CARE

If you can't afford veterinary care, you may be able to take your pet to an animal charity treatment centre such as those run by the PDSA (People's Dispensary for Sick Animals), RSPCA or Blue Cross for free or assisted treatment. Also, the RSPCA's Vetfone can provide advice about general pet-care issues on 01728 727 673 (fixed fee of £9.59) or 09065 00 55 00 ✉ (£1.50 per minute).

Are you eligible? You must normally live in the centre's catchment area and be receiving either Housing Benefit or Council Tax Benefit. The number of pets treated may be restricted and some procedures excluded.

Special offers from private practices If you live outside a charity's catchment area, your pet may still be treated if you register with a private practice offering an assisted treatment service, such as the PDSA's PetAid scheme; or you may apply for a grant from the PDSA Special Request Scheme. Telephone 0800 731 2502 ✉ for more details.

Watch for free offers Contact your local council or visit its website for free treatment offers. Its Animal Welfare service may offer free microchipping, vaccinations or neutering. Free or reduced-cost neutering is available from the RSPCA, Cats Protection and many small, independent rescue groups.

THE RIGHT INSURANCE

Some say it is better to save the money you might have spent on insurance premiums and pay your own vet's bills. Only you can weigh up the pros and cons of insuring your pet and decide which, if any, policy is best for you.

MODERN TREATMENTS AND BIGGER BILLS

Medical advances mean that it's now possible to extend a pet's life in ways that were once undreamt of. Today, a dog with a heart condition can be fitted with a pacemaker (the operation and care could cost £8,500), while a dog with arthritis can have a £2,500–£4,000 hip replacement. And that is not all: one insurer reported a claim of £36,000 made by the owner of a dog which caused a road accident. Insurance might meet the expense of medical treatment or injury to a third party, but a lifetime's insurance cover can also mount up to several thousand pounds.

WATCH POINTS INSURANCE PITFALLS

Figures given on Moneysupermarket.com show that the owner of a one-year-old labrador retriever living in Hampshire could expect to pay from £84–£312 to insure the dog annually, and £46–£170 for a crossbred kitten. Most pet insurance will cover vets' bills for illness and injury, third-party or accidental damage, replacing a deceased pet and disposing of its body, and advertising and paying a reward for a lost pet. Some bargain policies have restrictions, such as on cover or payout, or a large excess. Others may vary the fees depending on your locality and the breed of animal insured. Insurance companies will not pay for routine treatments such as vaccinations or neutering.

■ **Maximum claim limit** Check that the maximum claim for one incident falls within a reasonable limit for your pet. For example, a dog that is involved in a traffic accident can cost thousands of pounds to restore to health. When a four-year-old labrador was hit by a car, his owner paid over £800 for X-rays and surgery to treat the dog's injuries. Had the dog been insured, this would almost certainly have been fully covered as the maximum claim limit for most pet insurance policies is generally between £1,500 and £7,000.

■ **Restrictions on cover or payout** Some policies restrict the length of time you can claim for the cost of treating a long-term condition, or put a ceiling on how much money you can claim. This could mean that if your pet is insured and then becomes chronically ill, you may eventually find yourself paying the treatment costs even though your pet is insured. Choose an insurance policy that will pay out for an indefinite period of time for an ongoing medical condition.

■ **Age limit** Many older pets are uninsurable unless they have been covered by the same insurer from an early age. If an older pet is taken on by an insurance company, the owner will have to pay much heftier premiums. In addition, you may have to pay a percentage of the total cost of each claim.

■ **Excess payment** Check the amount of the excess and whether it's payable for each claim. Excess fees for

keep it simple

THE BEST POLICY
■ Insure pets from an early age.
■ Insure more than one animal with the same company.
■ Choose a policy with relevant discounts – for senior citizens, for example.
■ Make sure the company has the General Insurance Standards Council (GISC) stamp.

BETTER DEALS FOR CITY DWELLERS

If you live in an urban area, choose an insurer that does not price its policies according to where you live. Because vet bills tend to be more expensive in the city, if you choose an insurer that varies fees according to location, you will pay a higher premium for urban living.

veterinary treatment are £50–£90 for each claim for a single condition in one year. The excess for third party liability is generally higher – normally £75–£250 for a dog.

■ **Increase in premiums and limited claims** Many policies automatically increase your premium once you have made a claim. In addition, there may be a limit to the number of claims you can make each year.

■ **Exclusions** All policies exclude expenses arising from medical conditions that existed before the policy was taken out. For example, the owner of a cat with diabetes took out a pet insurance policy, but as the diabetes was classed as a pre-existing condition the owner still had to bear costs of £100 a month for treating the diabetes. Had she insured her pet before the condition developed, the insurers would have paid for the diabetes treatments, although they may have increased the insurance premium.

■ **Switching to another insurer** Because a new policy will exclude all pre-existing conditions, changing to a different insurance company means that the new insurer will not cover the cost of treatment for any conditions for which the old insurer was paying.

 **RESOURCES**

COMPARE INSURANCE RATES
■ Get links to insurance companies offering competitive quotes on **www.find.co.uk** ✉.
■ Compare insurance rates on **www. moneysupermarket.com** ✉.

CHOOSING THE BEST-VALUE PET POLICY

These policy terms are based on a pedigree labrador retriever in the Home Counties, aged 3–4 years. Pedigree animals carry a higher premium as they can have more problems; policies for a pedigree cat or a young mongrel in a city would be different.

Policy Example/ Annual Premium	Maximum annual Vet fees/ Excess each claim	3rd Party Liability/ Excess each claim	Death benefit	Holiday cancelled	Reward if lost	Most suitable for
A £84	£1,500/£69	£1m/£250	£350	No	£100	Owners who don't take expensive holidays
B £112.55	£1,500/£49	£1m/£75	£350	No	£100	Older dogs (8 years plus)
C £125	£3,500/£75	£1.25m/ £250	£500	£750	£450	Pedigrees/valuable dogs
D £169.64	£2,000/£49	£1.5m/£75	£750	£1,000	£600	More than three pets (5–10% discount)
E £175	£5,500/£75 (doubles if claim £1,000+)	£1.75m /£250	£1,250	£2,000	£750	Dogs likely to need expensive vet treatment
F £259.81	£4,000/£49	£1.75m/£75	£1,000	£1,500	£800	Cover for life; discount for three or more pets covered
G £312.69	£6,000/£49	£2m/£75	£1,500	£2,500	£1,000	Valuable dogs; cover for life

Rates correct at time of publication. Prices courtesy of www.moneysupermarket.com

CAREFREE HOLIDAYS

Your holiday will be anything but relaxing if you have to worry about your pets while you're away, or pay nearly the cost of your own holiday on their sojourn at the local kennel. Luckily, there are answers both at home and abroad.

TAKING PETS ABROAD

Although taking cats and dogs to Europe is easier than it was pre-2000, it is still expensive. Travelling with your pet by car is the most convenient and cheapest option. But you will have to pay for microchipping, vaccination, a blood test, and a PETS (Pet Travel Scheme) certificate before setting off, and tick and tapeworm treatment before you return – costing from £160 to over £300 (shop around for the best deal). Most of this expense will have to be repeated each year you travel. But this may be a cost-effective option for longer stays abroad, especially if you take trips regularly. Visit the Pet Travel Scheme page, under Animal Health & Welfare, on DEFRA's (Department for Environment, Food and Rural Affairs) website, for details **www.defra.gov.uk** or call the PETS helpline 0870 241 1710 ✉.

Countries in the PETS scheme European countries to which you can take your pet under PETS rules include Austria, Belgium, Denmark, France, Germany, Greece, Italy, the Netherlands, Norway, Spain and Sweden. Non-European countries include Australia, Canada, New Zealand and mainland USA. The DEFRA website has an up-to-date list.

PETS WELCOME HERE

If you are taking a holiday in the UK, it often makes sense to take your pet with you. Use an online resource such as **www.k9directory.com** ✉ or a book such as *Pets Welcome!* by

---

CASE STUDY

A PERFECT SOLUTION

When Peggy Sharp had to go to Canada for two months to take care of her elderly aunt, she didn't know what to do with Buster, her old cat. As a pensioner herself, she could not afford professional carers, nor the cost of taking him with her. Luckily, two school-age sisters in the block of flats opposite her house doted on Buster and longed for a cat of their own, which they could not have in their flat. All Peggy had to do was ask and they were only too delighted to come to her house several times every day, under their parents' supervision, to feed Buster, play with him and groom him. By this simple neighbourly act, they saved Peggy more

than £1,200 – as well as the worry she might have felt if she had not known that Buster was in safe and friendly hands.

Anne Cuthbertson, 2007, ISBN-10 1850554064, or the AA publication *Pet Friendly Places to Stay*, ISBN-10 074954922X, to find suitable accommodation.

BETTER BOARDING

Boarding may be the best option for dogs who need daily exercise, and for pedigree animals where having a vet on call is a service worth paying for. Prices are from around £15 a day for a dog (depending on its size) and from £8.50 for a cat. You may be able to ask for a reduction in rates if you book more than three months in advance, if you are a frequent customer or if you are boarding more than one animal.

Get recommendations If possible, use a boarding service recommended by friends or seek the advice of your vet who should know of reputable local ones.

Contact the council Your local council can give you the names and rates of boarding kennels in your area. There are no national or even local guidelines on charges, but the Competition Commission is more critical of inflated kennel charges than any other pet-care cost, so be aware that some kennel charges are way out of line.

See for yourself Always visit a boarding kennels before deciding that this is where you want to leave your pet.

RESOURCES

REGISTERED PETSITTERS

If you have to use a petsitter, be sure of a reliable, value-for-money service by checking that they are registered with the National Association of Registered Petsitters. In addition, always ask for and check references.

■ You can find more information about petsitting services at **www.dogsit.com** 0845 2308544 ✉ and **www.ukpetsitter.com** ✉.

■ Some housesitting agencies also offer petsitters who will look after your pet in your home, making sure it is fed and exercised.

TOP TIPS CHEAPER PETSITTING

Petsitting prices ranges from being totally free to costing more than boarding. The main advantage is that your pet can stay in familiar surroundings.

■ **Home visits** Getting a pet carer (often a qualified veterinary nurse) to come to your house is affordable but not cheap at £8–£18 a visit. Your best bet for finding such a person is to contact your local vet or friends with pets.

■ **Get live-in petsitting for free** You'd be surprised how many animal lovers would relish the chance to stay in a nice house or area in exchange for looking after your pet. If you have to pay for this service, on the other hand, it could cost you £25–£65 a day, plus travel expenses. If this is your choice, make sure you use someone who is registered and worth the fee you are paying.

■ **Go halves with a neighbour** If you find that neighbours are going away at the same time, you may be able to share their care arrangements.

■ **Swap petsitting for babysitting** It may be easier to ask a neighbour to petsit if you can offer something they would value equally in return – babysitting, for example, lawn mowing or ironing.

■ **Form a petsitting club** Team up with pet owners who live near you and work out a petsitting rota. Local pet clubs should be able to put you in touch with like-minded individuals.

■ **Ask a friend** Pet-loving friends who have none of their own may be willing to come and stay with your animals.

You can make your parties memorable affairs and still watch the budget – a little careful planning will leave you with more to spend on the things that really matter.

Special occasions

GETTING IN THE MOOD

Setting the scene is one of the most important aspects of planning a party, as the right decorations and lighting will put guests in a festive mood. With imagination and canny shopping, you can transform your home for very little.

BARGAIN DECORATIONS

Look at your social diary and plan ahead – having a stock of cheaply sourced party goodies and decorations will save you from expensive last-minute shopping.

Gift and craft shops Prices at gift and knick-knack shops can be more reasonable than at specialist party shops. Scour card shops for balloons, banners and celebration confetti. Craft and fabric stores often have all sorts of party décor. Watch out for sales and cheaply priced oddment bins.

Chains and supermarkets Discount superstores such as TK Maxx and Matalan, DIY stores and supermarkets stock many items that can be transformed into decorations, as well as partyware. Supermarkets offer discounted items after an event such as Halloween and Christmas; buy them and save for the following year. Brightly coloured plastic plates and cups can be snapped up at the end of the barbecue season – great for children's parties year after year and you save on the themed cardboard tableware that ends the day in the bin.

TOP TIPS ATMOSPHERIC LIGHTING

Appropriate lighting creates a welcoming ambience. Use party lights and a selection of taper-style and column candles to help give a party atmosphere with a minimum of expense.

■ **Change colour** Swap plain light bulbs for coloured ones for about £1.50 each. Warm colours give a flattering soft glow to a room, while cool colours can help conjure up a mood for themed occasions such as a Halloween party.

■ **Reusable party lights** Start snapping up strings of indoor/outdoor Christmas lights during post-festive sales. These tiny lights, costing from under £15 for a string, add enchantment to any party scene, indoors or out. You can reuse them and they can be left unattended, unlike candles.

■ **Grab bargains** Tealights cost as little as £5–£6 for 100, and larger candles are not expensive when bought in bulk. IKEA's white Jubla candles are £3.22 for 20. Leading candlemaker Price's (**www.prices-candles.co.uk** 01234 264500 ✉) has factory outlets in Gretna, Street and Fareham.

■ **Make the most of singles** If you have leftover single candles in a variety of shades, place them in a matching pair of candelabras on the dining-room table or mantelpiece for a colourful display. Buy candelabras cheaply from a street market or in secondhand and charity shops.

■ **Cooler candles** To save even more money on candles, store them in a sealed box in the fridge and light them when cold. They will burn more slowly.

■ **Bargain garden lights** If you are throwing an evening party, place tealights in old jars and use wire to hang them in trees or along a fence. Or set them in paper bags half-filled with sand and position around a patio.

RESOURCES

PARTY PLANNING
■ For free online invitations, visit **www.evite.co.uk** ✉.
■ Find Internet bargains for your party at **www.partystuffonline.co.uk**
■ For good-value bouquets from £9.99 online, try **www.bunches.co.uk** ✉ or phone 0800 626249.
■ Buy cheap candles online from **www.just-candles.net** ✉.
■ For cheap party lights, try **www.christmastimeuk. com** or phone 01427 667270 ✉.

COMPARE THE COST OF ROSES

If your heart is set on roses, here's what you could pay for a dozen. The more expensive roses are arranged with foliage and tied with attractively presented cellophane and ribbons, so choose cheap bunches and make your own floral arrangements.

MARKET	£6
TESCO	£9.99
WWW.BUNCHES.CO.UK	£29.99
INTERFLORA	£40.98
WWW.BLAKESFLOWERS.COM	£41.95

Prices correct at the time of publication and include delivery, except for the market and Tesco

FRUGAL FLOWERS

Flowers always add style to a party, but can be expensive. Committed money savers grow their own flowers for cutting, or ask a green-fingered friend who is coming to the party to donate some. Even if you have to buy shop-bought flowers, you can still keep down costs.

Bunches in season Only buy flowers in season, as the more exotic the bloom, the higher its cost. Buy flowers in bunches of the same variety as flower arrangements tend to cost more and will limit your options.

Choose your supplier Supermarkets are a source of cheap flowers, especially when the blooms are near their sell-by date. Avoid buying flowers at petrol stations where prices can be extortionate and the flowers may not last.

Save at street markets Street markets always have flower stalls and their blooms are reasonably priced and cheaper at the end of the day when the flowers need to be sold.

Bulk buys at flower markets Search your local directory for flower markets in your area. You will have to buy in bulk, but the savings are definitely worth it (see *Homes and gardens*, page 215).

FLORAL FILLERS

Use greenery – preferably from your own garden – to make floral displays go further. Herbs such as rosemary or lavender last well and give arrangements a wonderful scent.

Artful artifice Combine paper, silk or ceramic artificial flowers with fresh greenery. They can be used year after year.

Fruit and nuts When making a table centrepiece or wreath for a door, use fresh fruit, vegetables and nuts for an inexpensive arrangement.

Bowers of green For a stunning effect, lop off branches from shrubs or trees such as bay or fir, wash off any insects and place them on bare walls or on a buffet table. Remember, however, that you are not permitted to take greenery from public places.

GILDING THE LILY

Flowers are lovely on their own but you can make them look more special, or even tie them in to your party theme, by adding a few finishing touches.

■ Cut or buy seasonal foliage to fill up the vases. Or use good artificial foliage – no one will be able to tell the difference.

■ Add stems of gypsophila or carnations, which are inexpensive and complement roses. Mixed displays always look more opulent.

■ Add some seasonal decorations: ribbons, ears of corn, small glass ornaments, paper or wooden shapes glued to the end of lengths of wire. Your party theme will suggest other options.

■ Finish your bouquets with a wrap of coloured cellophane or tulle.

THEMED PARTIES

Building your party menu and decorations around a theme or specific event will help you to make a big splash for less money. Why? Because the choices of food and décor will be clearer, allowing you to tailor the party for effect rather than expense.

70S FLASHBACK

Dress in hot pants, flares and psychedelic clothing. Dance to Gloria Gaynor, the Bee Gees and the Village People. Lava lamps and disco balls make great decorations. A perfect meal is a cheese fondue, and then get your guests to play charades and guess the '70s personality. This retro-style party theme can be adapted to suit any era and any music, and so is ideal for someone with a milestone birthday.

MONOPOLY PARTY

Meet up with friends at a café or bar in the morning and divide into teams. Each team is given tasks to perform at various Monopoly-style sites and must prove they have been there. Community chest and Chance cards are dares to be done at designated times. Meet back at home in the early evening. Give prizes to the winners, then prepare easy, hearty food such as baked potatoes with a selection of fillings.

STAR TURN

Rent a karaoke machine, or buy a 'Karaoke Classics' CD for £5 and let your friends do their best Elvis Presley or Cher impersonations. Just warn your neighbours first, or invite them. Serve a punch of fizzy wine and fruit juice, with finger food such as chicken wings.

ETHNIC POTLUCK

Ask each guest to choose a different country and bring an appropriate dish. As the host, you provide beverages, tableware and linens. Play CDs of appropriate music and ask a travel agency or the tourist board for posters or brochures to use in decorating.

MEXICAN NIGHT

Create a Latin fiesta by decorating your venue with strings of lights, cacti, colourful balloons and streamers in red, green and yellow. Dance to sounds of the mambo, samba and tango. Serve tortilla chips with salsa, wraps filled with chilli, re-fried beans, sour cream, guacamole, cheese and lettuce, and ask your guests to bring bottled beers.

CATERING ON A BUDGET

Whether you are planning simple nibbles for a few friends or a formally catered event on a large scale, there are plenty of ways to save on the costs of the party food without skimping on style.

TOP TIPS MAKE FOOD GO FURTHER

Choose and serve food in the right way and you can provide a sumptuous spread while sticking to your budget.

■ **Save with spreads and dips** Expensive ingredients such as smoked salmon will go further if combined with dressings, cream cheese and vegetables in dips and spreads. Serve spreads with crackers and breads, or use them as fillings for puff pastry shells and wraps.

■ **Two for the show** Even at a formal sit-down meal you can drop a course and serve two rather than three. This suits many people's appetites, and as long as the serving is leisurely your guests will still enjoy time at the table. Either serve a main course and dessert with a good selection of bread to start, or starter and main course only with chocolates and coffee to finish.

■ **Avoid too many choices** Most people will have one or two slices of meat, but if they are offered fish as well they may choose both – and then eat only half of each. Serve the main dish on a plate – whether the fish or the meat – to prompt guests to choose one or the other.

■ **Serve on a platter** For a sit-down dinner, serving side dishes family-style on a platter in the middle of a table – rather than as restaurant-style individual portions – makes them go about 20% further.

A FORMAL AFFAIR

Many people like to make celebrations such as significant birthdays, wedding anniversaries and christenings formal affairs with a slap-up sit-down meal or lavish buffet. If you want to have a special party, getting caterers in could be the solution – and it could be less expensive than you think.

Choosing a caterer Shop around for different packages until you find one that suits you, as prices vary considerably – some simply bring the food, while others will also supply linen, crockery, a marquee, waiters and more.

Draw up a budget To avoid a larger bill than you were planning for, set a budget and stick to it. Don't be persuaded to have any extras, or a more 'sophisticated' menu, unless they are within your price range. Unnecessary frills could add up to 25% to your overall costs. Agree what is included and get a written quote.

Work with your chef If you are dealing with a large firm, find out if they have flexible deals – ask if altering the set menu will cost more, or whether it can save you money. If your caterer is a one-woman band, see what cost-cutting suggestions she can make or whether you can save by helping her prepare some of the food.

Delivered to your door Party delivery services bring finger foods or party meals to your door ready to pop in the oven

---

CALCULATING QUANTITIES

Get your quantities right and you will avoid wasting food or appearing stingy.

■ If you are serving buffet food alone, allow 8–12 pieces for each person.

■ 450g (1lb) of pasta serves 4–6 people at a sit-down meal or 8–12 at a buffet.

■ For a mixed buffet, allow 110g–170g (4oz–6oz) of meat, fish or cheese for each person.

■ A sit-down meal should contain 140g–170g (5oz–6oz) of meat or fish for each person and three vegetable dishes.

A MOUTH-WATERING MENU YOU CAN AFFORD

The two impressive menus below are for a self-catered formal summer dinner party for 10 people, but Menu B is half the price of Menu A because it is based around seasonal and other inexpensive ingredients and cuts out unnecessary extras.

MENU A

Scallops served in chicory cups
with a creamy wine and
ginger sauce

Roast duck with foie gras stuffing
served with kumquat and brandy sauce

Shredded sprout and
cabbage sauté

Roast pumpkin and sweet potato

Individual chocolate truffle tortes
served with a foaming
Cointreau sauce and candied
cape gooseberries

Irish coffee and luxury Belgian
chocolates

cost for each person: £22.50

MENU B

Steamed asparagus bundles served with
shrimps in lettuce cups with a tangy
lime hollandaise sauce

Tender chicken breast fillets filled with
goats' cheese, tomato, spinach,
courgette, peppers and walnuts,
rolled and baked and served with
watercress sauce

Green vegetable medley – runner
beans, garden peas and spring onions,
stir-fried in a balsamic dressing

Potatoes Normandy

Individual summer puddings served
with a foamy lemon syllabub sauce

Fresh coffee served with homemade
mocha truffles

cost for each person: £11.00

for a fraction of the price of getting caterers in. A luxury three-course dinner for 15–20 people might cost from around £14 a head, whereas bringing caterers in to cook at your venue would cost over £30 a head.

Cut costs by helping out See if you can reduce your bill by doing some of the chores, such as picking up the drinks. Using your own linen, glasses, china and cutlery could save more if you don't mind doing the washing up. Some supermarkets and off-licences offer free glass hire if you don't have enough of your own.

Hiring tables and chairs Look in the Yellow Pages under Catering Equipment Hire for local companies and compare their price lists. If you have access to a van, save on delivery charges by picking up the equipment.

Coordinated approach Save on hiring damask tablecloths by draping white sheets over the tables so they come almost to the ground. Then lay your own smaller coloured cloths on top or make some from fabric remnants. Add good-quality paper napkins in a matching colour.

Save 50% on waiting staff For formal occasions where waiting staff are required, ask your friends or neighbours if their teenage sons and daughters might be willing to work for some extra cash.

DEALS YOU CAN DRINK TO

STOCK UP ON HOLIDAY

If you are planning a large party, make significant savings by visiting wine and beer warehouses in France on your way home from a holiday. These are situated in convenient stop-off points near ferry or shuttle terminals and are open seven days a week for most of the year. You can expect to save at least £2 per bottle on still wines and £3 on a bottle of bubbly – a saving of around £300 if you were providing for 150 wedding guests. It could even be worth making a special trip. (See *Eating and drinking*, pages 32–34.)

RESOURCES

ONLINE DRINK SUPPLIERS

■ Try the following websites ✉ to compare prices:

www.co-opdrinks2u.com
www.dealtime.co.uk
www.discountwines.com
www.majestic.co.uk
www.normandie-wine.com
www.oddbins.com
www.tesco.com/winestore
www.virginwines.com
www.wine.shopping-finder.co.uk

■ Glass hire: some supermarkets, including Tesco, offer a free service; off-licences Oddbins and Majestic offer free hire if you order wine from them.

Alcohol can be an important part of a social event, but do not feel obliged to offer a full bar or any spirits. Beer and wine are usually sufficient, or stick to one spirit in keeping with your guests' tastes or a seasonal theme, such as a fruit rum punch in summer or eggnog with brandy in winter.

TOP TIPS FINDING A BARGAIN

The cost-conscious party-giver should make it a rule never to pay full price for wines. Take advantage of discounts given for buying in bulk. Watch out for retailers that offer other services that help you cater for guests – for example, free glass loan and a sale-or-return policy.

■ **Wine warehouses** Wine warehouses are large stores around Britain or on the Internet, that offer substantial discounts on a wide selection of alcohol. There are usually a number of special deals available offering further savings. Some sell wine or beer by the case only and offer additional party services such as free glass loan, chiller bins and ice. They usually have a sale-or-return facility, which is useful as it can be difficult to judge how much alcohol you will need at a party – this way, you only pay for what you drink.

■ **Cheap wine online** Search the net for good deals when planning your party (see Resources, left). Many companies offer wine, cocktail mixes and champagne at enticing prices.

■ **Supermarket savers** The big chains now dominate the drinks market and can offer party planners impressive savings, both instore and online. Visit 'Discounter Bonanza' at the Tesco Wine Club, for example, for savings of up to 50% and free delivery on orders over £99. Keep an eye open for instore offers (or check at **www.mysupermarket.co.uk**), and buy over a period of time – you can also collect loyalty points. Many supermarkets now offer free glass hire, too.

ALCOHOL-THEMED PARTIES

Planning a party around a particular beverage is an easy and low-cost party idea as friends can bring a favourite tipple.
Wine and dine When asking guests to bring a bottle to a dinner party, specify that it should go with a particular course or dish, then make sure you drink the donated wine.
Bring on the brew With the explosion of microbreweries, there is now an exciting variety of beers available. Host a beer-tasting party and invite your friends to bring a six-pack of their favourite brew. Mexican, Indian and Chinese foods especially are enhanced by beer.

DISCOUNTED READY-MIXED DRINKS

There are plenty of ready-mixed drinks to choose from in supermarkets and off-licences, as well as cash-and-carry stores where they can cost under £1.50 a bottle. They have a shorter shelf life than wines and spirits, so when stores over-stock you can buy at half price or on a buy-one-get-one-free basis. Check that you will use them by the use-by date.

NON-ALCOHOLIC FRUIT FIZZ

MAKES 10 SERVINGS

■ In a large saucepan, combine 25g each frozen raspberries and strawberries, 1.3 litres water, 350g sugar, 10 whole cloves, ½ teaspoon ground cardamom, six strips orange zest and 1 split vanilla pod.

■ Bring to a boil over a medium-high heat; reduce the heat and simmer, uncovered, stirring occasionally, for 10 minutes.

■ Strain through a fine sieve and discard the solids. Cool to room temperature, and then stir in 450ml orange juice and chill.

■ Just before serving, stir in 450ml chilled sparkling water.

■ Serve over ice and garnish as desired.

ANNIVERSARY FRUIT PUNCH

MAKES 8 SERVINGS

■ Drain the liquid from a 215g can of apricot halves, reserving half the juice.

■ Mix the juice with a bottle of sweet white wine, 450ml orange juice, 200ml pineapple juice and 1 tbsp lime juice.

■ Dice half of the canned apricots.

■ Fill one-third of a large jug with crushed ice. Pour the wine mixture into the jug and top with the diced apricots.

■ Garnish with sprigs of mint.

CLASSIC SANGRIA

MAKES 12 SERVINGS

■ In a large pitcher, mix 1.7 litres fruity red wine such as burgundy, 225–450ml brandy, Cointreau, cassis, or other fruit-flavoured liqueur, and 6–8 tbsp lemon juice.

■ Stir, and add 225ml of sugar syrup.

■ Add orange and lemon slices, pitted cherries or pineapple rings. Chill well.

For white sangria, use dry white wine such as Chablis, Grand Marnier or other orange-flavoured liqueur, and lemon or lime-flavoured tonic.

HOMEMADE PARTY DRINKS

Making your own refreshing drinks costs much less than ready-mixed drinks or even wine and beer. Served in a pretty jug or punch bowl, they add a festive spirit to any party.

BASIC SUGAR SYRUP

(FOR SANGRIA AND SUMMER WINE CUP)

■ Combine 450g sugar and 600ml water in a heavy-bottomed saucepan. Cook over a moderate heat, stirring often, until the mixture comes to the boil and the sugar dissolves.

■ Remove the pan from the heat, cover and leave for 10 minutes to dissolve any remaining crystals, and let stand to cool.

■ Pour into a jar or bottle with a tightly fitting lid. Makes 600ml–700ml.

■ Make up to two days before use and store in the fridge.

SUMMER WINE CUP

MAKES 24 SERVINGS

■ In a large punch bowl, mix 4 bottles of dry white wine with 1 bottle of dry sherry.

■ Add 225ml of sugar syrup and stir.

■ Top up with 1.5 litres lemonade and add ice cubes.

■ Garnish with sprigs of mint, sliced apple and a few strawberries.

CHILDREN'S PARTIES FOR A SONG

It is easy to get carried away when it comes to your children's big day. When planning their party, ask them what they want – it may surprise you – and keep them involved. Imagination can count for more than pounds spent.

LOW-COST INVITATIONS

Children love to make their own birthday fliers. If they have access to a computer, they can design and print off as many invitations as they need. Older children can email them to save on paper and postage. Or you could photocopy or print a photo of your child onto card and write a message by hand on the back.

TOP TIPS PARTY ENTERTAINMENT

Hiring a magician, juggler or face painter can be expensive, ranging from £95 for 45 minutes to £160 for two hours. Party games that you organise yourself can be just as much fun for younger children and cost next to nothing. Visit **www.netmums.com** for lots of good ideas.

■ **Classic games** Old favourites, such as Musical Bumps, Musical Chairs, Blind Man's Buff and Charades don't require any special equipment and are perennially popular.

■ **Dressing up** Children love dressing up, so put a selection of colourful clothes, hats and shoes into a large box and let them create their own costumes, with a prize for the best.

■ **Treasure hunt** Write clues on slips of paper and send the children off to hunt for treasure – such as small sacks of chocolate coins – in your house or garden. Older children might prefer a supervised scavenger hunt in a local park.

CASE STUDY

HAVING A GREAT TIME OUT OF DOORS

Helen Pearce was determined to disguise the fact that the birthday party she organised for her 7-year-old daughter, Katy, wasn't going to be as lavish as some of her friends' events. Katy was born in May, so it was a pretty safe bet that the weather would be fair so a Sports Day party – where the children would be perfectly happy to make their own entertainment – seemed the ideal option. Helen and her husband, Michael, turned their lawned garden into a professional-looking venue by painting white lines on it for a mini-running track and other athletic events, which really impressed Katy's classmates. Now that the stage was set, Helen planned a simple picnic and let the children make their own ice-cream creations (with supervision!) for dessert. When choosing items for the party bags, Helen thought like a child. She found inexpensive toys, such as 99p cars for the boys and 55p bracelets for the girls. She also included a metallic balloon (99p for 10), a home-baked biscuit and a small packet of sweets (bought at 75% off the usual price in a post-Easter sale). The party was such a success that Katy's 9-year-old brother, Scott, wants to do the same. Though his birthday is in October, Helen is planning an outdoor barbeque and lots of athletic events to keep the children warm.

PARTY OUTINGS FOR LESS

When children get too old to have in-house parties, amusement parks, adventure playgrounds and swimming pools are popular venues.

Home catering Party outings will be much cheaper if you can take your own food, cake and party bags.

Get the numbers right Find out if there is a minimum number of guests you have to invite. Many places offer group discounts, including Longleat, Wiltshire (01985 844400, **www.longleat.co.uk** ✉), Madame Tussauds, London (0870 400 3000, **www.madametussauds.com** ✉) and Thorpe Park (**www.thorpepark.com**, 0870 444 44 66 ✉).

Minimise the price You can usually save £2–£3 a head by booking in advance rather than paying on the day. Some venues, such as Alton Towers (**www.altontowers.com** 08705 20 40 60 ✉), offer a 20% discount if you book over the Internet. You could also save up your supermarket loyalty vouchers and use these. And some attractions, such as bowling alleys, charge less during the slow summer months.

Free and low-cost outings Visit free museums or events, such as the Changing of the Guard in London, and low-cost venues such as art galleries and small open farms. Try Forestry Commission parks (**www.forestry.gov.uk** ✉) for a picnic or barbeque, or go to the seaside by train. Many children never travel by train so this will be a double treat (see *Practical parenting*, page 108).

 **RESOURCES**

CHILDREN'S PARTIES
■ For ideas and a directory of suppliers, visit **www.kidspartysurvival guide.com** ✉.
■ These books give plenty of ideas: *'Practical Parenting' Party Games* £5.99, ISBN-10 0600606945; *Annabel Karmel's Complete Party Planner* £12.99, ISBN-10 0091875268.
■ Look at **www.cadbury. co.uk** ✉ for recipe ideas for chocolate party cakes and biscuits.

COMPARING PARTY BUDGETS (FOR 10 CHILDREN)

TYPE OF PARTY	VENUE	FOOD	CAKE	PARTY BAG	PRIZES	ENTER-TAINMENT	TOTAL
At home with homemade food, games	£0	£29	£2.45	£15	£10	£0	£56.45
Soft play centre, bought cake	£70	incl.	£8	£15	£0	£0	£93
Swimming pool, homemade cake	£125	incl.	£2.45	£15	£0	£0	£142.45
Hired hall, face painter, bouncy castle, bought cake	£40	£29	£8	£15	£0	£80 + £70	£242
Hired hall, entertainer (2hrs), homemade food	£40	£29	£2.45	£15	£0	£160	£246.45
Legoland (inc. 2 adults), picnic, bought cake	£240	£29	£8	£0	£0	£0	£277
Themed party with cheerleader in hired hall	£40	£29	£8	£24	incl.	£225	£326

Prices correct at time of publication

*£20 for each guest based booking online in advance.

GLAD TIDINGS AT CHRISTMAS

Although it does not feel right to be miserly during the festive season, you don't have to spend lots of money to have fun. Get the whole family involved in the preparations and approach Christmas as a family activity – you will enrich your time together as well as saving money and adding a personal touch to your decorations and cards.

SPEND LESS ON DECORATIONS

If you are willing to be adventurous and shop away from the high street, you can save a small fortune on decorations – leaving you more to splash out on presents.

Car boot and garage sales You can pick up a bargain just before or just after Christmas. Look for unused tablecloths, candleholders, strings of lights, ornaments, boxed presents and artificial trees. Scour sales advertised in local papers throughout the year, especially from September.

Fabric and craft shops Watch for sales, usually just before and after Christmas, as well as end-of-line or old-stock bins. You should be able to pick up glitter glue, fabric remnants (a piece of red cloth to cover a small side table, a piece of velvet to embellish a cushion, or a holly print fabric to wrap up a present), shiny ribbon, foam stamps and shaped scissors. You may also find decorations at 50%–70% off the full price.

DECORATE LATE – SAVE OVER 50%

Start a family tradition of buying and decorating a tree on Christmas Eve and you will be surprised at the bargain-basement price you can get. Visit your local street market on the weekend immediately before Christmas and the traders will be practically giving away the trees.

Make your own decorations

Be creative and get back in tune with the spirit of Christmas.

Recycle old decorations Pile inexpensive glass ball ornaments into a bowl or basket to decorate a windowsill or shelf.

Cut out paper snowflakes Fold a square piece of white paper in half, then in half again. Now fold the square into a triangle. Cut out shapes along the outer edges of the triangle. Open up the paper and you have a snowflake. Tape to windows or hang as ornaments.

Make Christmas oranges Using double-sided tape, stick a strip of festive ribbon around the circumference of an orange. Repeat the other way, so you have a ribbon running vertically and horizontally all round. Push whole dried cloves into the outer skin of the orange and place in a bowl, or hang up using a looped ribbon.

Fill a bowl Use bright red and green apples, golden oranges and satsumas bought cheaply from a street market. Tuck in sprigs of holly and small conifer boughs. Include Brazil nuts, walnuts and hazelnuts, which can be nibbled throughout Christmas.

Use tree trimmings Cut off the lower branches from your Christmas tree before setting it in a holder and use them to make a wreath or a swag for the mantelpiece.

Go for natural beauty If you have a cotoneaster or holly bush in your garden, cut branches to make inviting natural decorations. Add a bow and fairy lights strung through the branches. Or pick up nuts, bare twigs and fir cones on a walk through the woods. Leave them plain or spray paint gold, silver or white. Arrange the nuts and cones in bowls, or tuck them along the mantelpiece or on shelves and windowsills.

SMART MOVES

COMPARE THE COST OF CHRISTMAS TREES

TREE TYPE	SIZE IN METRES (FEET)			
	1.2-1.4M (4-4½FT)	1.5-1.7M (5-5½FT)	1.8-2M (6-6½FT)	2.1-2.4M (7-8FT)
ARTIFICIAL TREES				
Fraser Fir	£39.95	£49.95	£64.45	£84.45
Killington Pine	–	£66.25	£101.50	£135.85
North Valley Spruce	–	–	£49.95	£64.95
Black and Silver	–	–	£99.95	£119.95
Dunhill fir with decorations	–	–	–	£119.95
REAL TREES				
Norway spruce	–	£22	£27	£35
Nordman fir	£24	£25	£32	£36–£48
Fraser fir	–	£35	£42	£49–£56
Pot-grown Norway Spruce	£32 (2ft from £16)	£38	£44	–

Information **www.christmastreeland.co.uk**; prices correct at time of publication

BARGAIN CHRISTMAS TREES

For many people, a home at Christmas needs a tree, but an expensive natural tree is not the only choice available.

Tree farms for value If you want a fresh tree, your best bet is a tree farm (see Resources, right). The prices are good, and the tree is fresh and so will last longer and look better. Selecting and chopping your tree can be fun for all the family. Many tree farms offer hot chocolate or mulled wine to warm you up while you chop and shop.

Choose a cheaper variety Nordman firs have excellent needle retention (some don't drop their needles at all), but they will set you back 30% more than an ordinary Norway spruce. Limit needle drop on a spruce by slicing off the top when you bring it indoors and watering the tree well – a 1.8m (6ft) tree drinks 600ml (1 pint) of water a day.

Artificial trees The most economical approach is to invest in an artificial tree. Though the better-looking trees cost more, this is a one-time investment that should pay for itself within a few years. You can buy the trees plain, with lights or completely decorated, depending on your budget. They go up in minutes, will serve you well for years and are cheap if you buy them during post-Christmas sales.

Mini-trees If you live in a flat, or if putting up a full-sized tree is more trouble than it is worth, consider a miniature tree, either artificial or real. At Christmas, prices rise according to height, so small trees can be a bargain.

Deep-rooted trees The most expensive but environmentally friendly option is to buy a container-grown, rooted tree from a nursery and plant it in the garden after Christmas. If you have the space, you can do this every year. Or start with a fairly small tree and repot it after Christmas in a bigger pot with fresh compost – it can be brought in for several years until it grows too big, making it a worthwhile investment.

RESOURCES

CHRISTMAS TREES THROUGH THE NET
■ Try these websites for Christmas trees:
www.birstall.co.uk or 0800 085 0005;
www.xmastreesdirect.co.uk or 0845 3700 333;
www.christmastreeland. co.uk or 01577 865500 ✉.
■ The British Christmas Tree Growers' Association offers a list of growers who sell quality trees. Call them on 0131 664 1100, or visit **www.christmastree. org.uk** ✉.

Fun and inexpensive gift baskets

Gift baskets full of lots of little treats are often more pleasing than a single present costing double the amount. Try to tailor-make them to the recipient for an even more delighted response.

Young baby Fill an inexpensive basket with practical items the parents will appreciate, such as sleepwear, vests, bottles, bibs, nappies, a snuggly, booties or socks – plus a rattle and a cuddly toy.

Young children Line a basket with a bright T-shirt, then add a packet of coloured pencils, a box of crayons, safety scissors, stickers, comics, a small car or doll and packets of favourite sweets.

Older children Line the basket with a T-shirt printed with a favourite band's logo. Add some suitable toys or games, and a computer-printed 'certificate' offering to take the child to a local 'splash slides' pool, to the cinema to see a latest release or on a shopping trip.

Older relatives Line a basket with velvet, then fill it with accessories for his or her favourite hobby, such as golf tees, balls and a shoe brush; a trowel, packets of seeds and a mini watering can; or a book on world travel, sun lotion and brochures for cruises.

Almost anyone Put decorative fabric covers over the lids of small jars of homemade jam, lemon curd or chutney, or a selection of luxury foodstuffs, and secure with a ribbon. Tuck into a basket lined with gingham and straw.

Recycling is free When Christmas is over, recycle your tree by taking it to the Christmas tree skip at a local council household recycling centre or a local garden centre, where it can be shredded and recycled as mulch.

SEASON'S GREETINGS

The cost of sending greeting cards can soar to over £1 a card, but you can share seasonal cheer for much less.

Shop after Christmas Cards are reduced by up to 70% in January, so shop for next year's cards in the sales and then tuck them away.

Create cards for free Some of the cards you receive are just too beautiful to throw away. Using last year's cards, cut off designs and motifs, and glue them onto card blanks either as a central feature or a pattern. Embellish the cards with glitter or embossed lettering. Or make gift tags by cutting the central motifs from cards, punching a hole at one edge and tying on a ribbon. Cards can also be made cheaply from note cards with suitable illustrations – why pay extra for a printed Christmas salutation?

Transform old cards for decorations For attractive paper garlands, cut the front of old cards into strips and make interlocking chains to hang on a tree, edge a mantelpiece or brighten a staircase. For unique napkin rings, cut 5cm (2in) strips from the cards, form them into a circle and glue or staple the ends together.

The last post Posting your cards on time allows you to send them second class instead of first. This is especially cost-effective for cards going overseas.

Email greetings Bypass the Post Office altogether and create cards on your computer to send by email. The website www1.egreetings.com offers ready-designed cards you can send free to family and friends at home and abroad at just the click of a button.

PURCHASING POWER

Smart Christmas shopping means buying presents you think a person will like when you spot them, and when the price is right. Look for gifts throughout the year. Holiday trips, craft and country fairs, gift shops at museums and botanical gardens, auctions and flea markets are all excellent sources of one-of-a-kind presents. Earmark a drawer or the back of a cupboard as a designated gift store. Then, when Christmas – or birthdays and other special occasions – approach, you can reach in and produce the ideal present for anyone on your list.

MAKING MEMORIES

For a unique Christmas present – as well as for a milestone birthday, wedding anniversary, graduation or retirement – make a scrapbook or collage. Use photographs, decorative papers and other memorabilia. Ask friends, family members and colleagues to contribute a written memory of an event or conversation shared with the recipient to include in the present. Or make a personalised calendar featuring 12 photographs that show a special moment in the person's life. The recipient can then enjoy your gift all year long.

PERSONALISED GIFT WRAP

With wrapping paper costing £1 a sheet or more, decorating your own gift wrap is a rewarding project, as well as a creative way to add a personal touch to a present. Using thin brown parcel paper or another type of paper with the equivalent thickness, paint with acrylic paint and sponge, potato print, stencil, fingerpaint or draw designs to create one-of-a-kind wrapping paper. Fabric also makes an excellent wrap, especially for awkward shapes, and can be bought very cheaply (£1 a metre for sheer fabric or tulle, £2 a metre for cotton) in fabric warehouse sales, end of lines or on street markets. Tie with satin ribbons.

SAVE ON SEASONAL PLANTS

Don't wait until the last moment to buy poinsettias or forced bulbs, when they will cost double and have suffered from sitting too long in heated shops. Buy them early and keep in a cool spot until you need them.

Garden centres DIY stores with garden centres, such as B&Q and Homebase, tend to offer good deals on Christmas flowers and bulbs.

Web bargains Scour the Internet for florists offering inexpensive bouquets for same or next-day delivery – for example, bouquets from **www.bunches.co.uk** ✉ start at £9.99 (including first-class delivery), while at **www.crocus.co.uk** ✉ they're priced from £29.35 (including courier delivery).

Pots of fun Pick up cheap flower bowls or pots during the summer sales and then plant them up with bulbs yourself in plenty of time for Christmas. Or buy terracotta pots from the garden centre and let your children decorate them first with acrylic paint or by sticking on shells or mosaic tiles with PVA glue – especially good for grandparents.

WEDDINGS FOR THE (PRICE) WISE

You don't have to splash out on a lavish ceremony and reception – some of the most memorable weddings are simple, elegant and affordable affairs.

SPENDING TO SAVE

A little initial outlay can save a lot of unnecessary expense – planning and prudence are worth it.

Coordinated discounts A wedding planner costs from £800 (or 10–15% of the total budget) but could save you big money by negotiating discounts from preferred suppliers. Find one in the Yellow Pages, in wedding magazines and at wedding fairs, or log on to **www.weddingguide.co.uk** ✉.

Wedding insurance If you are planning a lavish wedding, it is worth protecting your big day. Wedding insurance costs from £50 to over £300 for different levels of cover. This could include wedding cancellation, loss of rings, failure of the photographer, public liability and even stress counselling. If you are planning a more modest affair, insurance may not be necessary. Check your home insurance – wedding presents, dresses and jewellery may well be covered by this. And pay for everything by credit card, which entitles you to compensation from the card provider if, for example, you pay a deposit for a venue that then goes bust.

Bank on it A dedicated bank account for wedding funds will stop you from eroding your funds with unofficial spending. Set aside 5% extra for any unforeseen expenses.

Facts on file A wedding file in which you keep a running total of all expenditure will help avoid any nasty surprises.

Move the date Instead of getting married on a Saturday in June, which is popular and so costs more, choose another month and day. January, February, March and November are quieter times so you'll get a much better rate – you could save 50%. Your honeymoon will cost less, too, if you go out of season.

INVITATIONS, THANK-YOU GIFTS, SURPRISE BILLS
10%

ENTERTAINMENT
10%

PHOTOGRAPHY
10%

FLOWERS
10%

ATTIRE
10%

SERVICE AND RECEPTION
50%

CONTROLLING YOUR BUDGET

Professional wedding organisers advise that the best way to control your budget is to decide how you are dividing it up. These are the proportions they recommend.

GETTING VALUE FROM YOUR RECEPTION

The cost of the ceremony itself is predictable: £30 to give notice in advance, then £40 at a register office, plus £3.50 for a marriage certificate (there will be further charges for a civil ceremony on approved premises, such as at a hotel). A Church of England wedding can cost up to £700 if you want all the extras (bells, choir, video, etc). The reception is where you can be creative, choosing to spend a little – or a lot.

LOCATION	WHAT YOU CAN EXPECT	POSSIBLE SAVINGS	TYPICAL COST*
Outdoor beauty spot	A beach or country park is ideal for an informal party. Ask the local council or park authority if there's a charge; you might need public liability insurance.	Plan an old-fashioned picnic or hire a barbecue to keep costs to a minimum. Take hampers full of cold food, plus rugs and a few small tables and chairs.	£0 venue £40 insurance £60 BBQ hire £80 car park (10 cars) plus picnic
Church hall	Hire of a church hall could cost up to £360, including a kitchen. You may need to hire tables, chairs, linen and crockery and pay for flowers and decorations.	There is often access to a kitchen with crockery and glasses, so you can do your own catering as well as your own decorations and flowers.	£360 plus catering
At home	An economical solution if you have a large house. You may have to hire caterers, a marquee, chairs and tables, and temporary toilets.	For a small party (70–80), save on caterers by having a barbeque in the garden, with casual seating.	£700 marquee £150 tables and chairs £110 BBQ plus catering
Restaurant	For a medium-sized affair, hire a private room. The cost of the meal can be fixed.	For a smaller reception, a large table in the main dining area is a cost-effective solution, although you will lose privacy.	For 50 guests: from £600 (buffet) from £1,800 (sit-down meal)
Caribbean resort	A wedding package, added to the cost of a week in Antigua, includes the registrar, wedding co-ordinator bouquet, sparkling wine and cake.	Tour companies may provide wedding packages free if you stay for 14 nights or if your guests book rooms. Guests will need to pay their own costs.	£2,260 plus catering
Botanical garden	Lush landscapes all year, perfect for photos. Many are equipped for functions, such as London's Kew Gardens or Hestercombe Gardens in Somerset.	Smaller gardens or the orangery of a country house offer an attractive backdrop at a lower price. Member discounts may apply.	£2,500 plus catering
Country club or hotel	Usually includes catering and decorations, so you pay for convenience. If you hire the whole hotel, you'll pay more for exclusivity.	Save by limiting numbers. Choose a Friday or Sunday, which are cheaper than Saturday. Get a discount for overnight guests.	from £2,700 (50 guests)

*before any savings

TOP TIPS A SWELL PARTY

Even with limited resources, which effectively rules out a formal sit-down dinner, you can treat your friends and family to a stylish and elegant reception.

■ **Buffets may be better** A sit-down meal requires one server for every three to four tables, and you pay for every one. A buffet requires servers only at the serving tables.

■ **Alternative meal times** A morning wedding lends itself to a champagne brunch or a light lunch. An early afternoon ceremony could be followed by high tea with lavish sandwiches and strawberries and cream. A late afternoon service is perfect for a cocktail party with finger foods.

■ **Healthy desserts** Because you will be serving cake, do not feel you must offer other desserts. A platter of fresh fruit is an attractive and refreshing finish to any meal. If you want to dress up fruit such as strawberries or raspberries, offer whipped cream on the side.

■ **Discount catering** Look in the Yellow Pages under Schools and Colleges – Further Education to find a catering college and ask them for a quote for waiting staff and food.

BUDGET FOR BEVERAGES

Wine, beer, and a good selection of non-alcoholic beverages, plus champagne or sparkling wine for the toasts, is a less pricey and more satisfying approach than an open bar.

Bring your own The mark-up on alcoholic drinks is steep, so to save money buy your own rather than getting it from the caterer. But for a reception in licensed premises, such as a hotel or country club, check the corkage charge – it can range from £5 to over £30 for each bottle of champagne.

Toasting the bride Champagne or another sparkling wine really makes the toasts special, but not everyone wants to drink it throughout the reception. Save the bubbly for the toasts, and you can then invest in a better-quality wine.

Best of the bubbly If champagne rather than sparkling wine is your drink of choice, shop around for the best deal. During an end-of-winter wine offer, one supermarket offered Pol Aimé champagne in cases of six for £73.99 (under £12.50 a bottle).

Alternative drinks For an afternoon reception, Pimm's or a fruit punch may be cheaper and more appropriate than champagne. A winter wedding could lend itself to mulled wine or spiced cider; the heat of summer calls for jugs of white sangria.

GOOD DEALS ON CHAMPAGNE

CHAMPAGNE TYPE	COST/BOTTLE (12-BOTTLE CASE)
Lanson Brut Rosé NV	£9.49
Bredon Brut NV	£11.39
Lanson Black Label	£13.76
Piper-Heidsieck Brut NV	£24.69
Moët & Chandon Vintage	£35.14

Source: Prices from Waitrose Wine Direct, correct at time of publication

HIGH STYLE ON A LOW BUDGET

When Julia and Richard Millbank were planning their summer wedding, they looked at where they could make savings without losing out on style. For invitations, they bought A5 parchment paper and 50 envelopes for under £40 and asked Richard's father if he would write them in his neat italic handwriting, saving at least 50% on printed cards. Julia looked in bridal boutiques for a dress but her favourite cost £1,500, so she asked a local dressmaker to alter her grandmother's gown for £180. Richard decided to buy an ex-hire morning suit for £120, which would come in useful for future formal occasions and eventually pay for itself in hire fees saved. The couple opted for an outdoor buffet reception in Julia's aunt's large garden. They decorated trestle tables with 10 sumptuous brocade curtains bought on eBay for £65, adding pots of orchids at £5 each from a local flower market. As the evening drew in, mini-lanterns (£28.50 for 10) strung through the trees gave a magical light.

Non-alcoholic options Offer plenty of non-alcoholic drinks too. Sparkling water, lemonade, fruit juices or punch are all appropriate and will save you money.

LET THEM EAT CAKE

These days, you are not limited to the traditional fruit cake. You may want to try a more modern and less extravagant option, such as a lighter sponge.

Traditional fruit cake This is the most expensive cake to buy or make, but it can be cut into modest squares to make it go further. Choose a small fruit wedding cake for you and your partner to cut, and keep a second, simpler iced cake ready to be served out of sight.

Keep it square When you are working out portions, take into account that a square cake will provide more portions than a round cake of the same size.

Finish it yourself A two-tier iced wedding cake from a commercial bakery could cost from £130 or more; ask the baker for a less elaborate 'occasion cake' – the same fruitcake and icing, but much cheaper. Then ask a relative or friend to personalise it as your wedding gift. Marks and Spencer sell plain luxury iced occasion cakes ready to decorate and build into tiers – a 3.85kg fruit cake providing 60 portions costs £55, and a 2.6kg cake (40 portions) £38.

Individual fairy cakes A delightful alternative to make or buy, little fairy cakes are becoming popular with modern brides and will add a light-hearted touch to any reception. They can be personalised with guests' names or decorated to suit your colour scheme, and displayed in a tower or on tiered stands.

Keep it simple Intricate decorations can be expensive. Instead of sugar flowers, pop some of your bouquet flowers in a tiny vase and use that as a topper for your cake.

THE DRESS OF YOUR DREAMS

Looking – and feeling – like a million dollars is, fortunately, not determined by the amount you spend on your dress.

Something old Visit antique shops and charity shops, as many brides wear their dresses once and then give them away. Also try the local papers and the eBay website.

Something new Try wedding warehouse sales or wedding fairs. Bridal dresses from £99 can be found at events organised by theweddingsale.com (**www.theweddingsale.com** ✉). If you want a traditional designer gown, a less expensive route is to rent it. Check the Yellow Pages or the ads at the back of wedding magazines for hire shops.

Sew simple You may be able to make a simple style yourself, or have it made up from a pattern. Ask a friend or relative to help as their present to you.

Family heirlooms If it is in good condition, the gown worn by a relative can work well. Pay a good dressmaker to alter it to fit you for around £180. Look in the Yellow Pages or ask your local dry cleaners if they have an alteration service.

Low-cost options An elegant ivory suit, a knee-length antique lace gown, or a dress in your favourite style can all be suitable wedding attire. Or choose a wedding dress that could easily be adapted for other occasions in the future.

Designer dresses at 25% off Oxfam have 11 shops with their own bridal departments (Bracknell, Bradford, Cambridge, Chippenham, Coventry, Eastbourne, Heswall, Leatherhead, Leicester, Poole and Southampton); you may have to telephone to make an appointment. They sell both new (the average cost of an Oxfam wedding dress is £250) and secondhand wedding dresses; and they can even find something special for your guests, from pageboys to mother of the bride. Visit **www.oxfam.org.uk** or call 0300 2001 333 ✉.

Off the peg Keep an eye on your favourite clothes shop as you might find a dress suitable for your bridesmaids. One bride bought stylish silk dresses in the Monsoon sale for just £33 each for her two bridesmaids in their early twenties. They loved them and wore them to parties later.

A SPECIAL INVITATION

Instead of choosing traditional engraved invitations, look at the options at your local stationers. If these are still too expensive, consider the homemade approach.

Printing versus engraving Good printing looks handsome and costs about half as much as engraving. Paper quality affects cost, too – a pretty, lightweight paper can be 70% cheaper than heavy card.

Your own fair hand A hand-written invitation is much more intimate than a printed one, and costs little except time. If you cannot hand-write your invitations, ask a friend who is good at calligraphy. You can buy exquisite stationery and even good-value do-it-yourself invitation kits.

Special effects To dress up plain invitations, add wax seals, embossed stamps, foil or ribbon. Sprinkle a little confetti or potpourri inside the envelope before you seal it.

Hi-tech invites Design and print your invitations on a computer – you can download graphics from the web and use a fancy font. You could also scan in images of the venue.

CUTTING A DASH

■ Hiring a morning suit and accessories costs from £70, although wedding website **www.weddingguideuk.com** suggests you allow £150. Look out for offers, such as free hire for the groom if six or more members of the party hire from the same company.

■ Consider buying rather than hiring. At most rental outfitters, you can buy a secondhand or ex-hire morning suit for only two or three times the single hire fee, which means it will pay for itself once you have worn it for just a few more formal occasions.

■ Don't be stifled by tradition or feel pressurised to wear a frock coat and top hat. If you already have a smart suit or dinner suit, wear this and spend the money saved on a new shirt, tie or waistcoat.

BUDGET BLOOMS

Flowers are beautiful in their own right and don't need to be extravagant to look elegant.

The bouquet Use only flowers in season and either arrange them yourself or ask a friend or relative to help. You could even use a kit, available from florists, to make a silk flower bouquet.

Decorations for the ceremony and reception Buy pot plants, which cost less than cut flowers and will not wither and die. Tie ribbons around the pots and let guests take them home.

TOP TIPS FINAL FLOURISHES

You can give your wedding an individual, stylish touch without breaking the bank by using local amateur talent rather than paying for professionals.

■ **Classic cars** Hiring a Rolls-Royce limo to get the bride to the ceremony is a time-honoured but expensive tradition that could set you back over £300. Ask through your local vintage car club to see if a proud owner would like to show off his prized horseless carriage for the day.

■ **Making music** Check with local music schools or universities to hire a good cellist, organist or soprano for the ceremony. Or play a CD of birdsong or other music that has a special meaning for you as background music. For the reception, check colleges for student dance bands and vocalists who might meet your needs and be less expensive than professional musicians.

■ **Photography deal** Ask the photographer if he or she will just deliver the negatives and proofs, or supply digital images on a disk. You will make big savings if you print the photos and create a wedding album yourself.

■ **Candid camera** Hire a professional photographer just for the formal line-ups, and ask a friend to shoot informal photos at the reception. If you use a digital camera, you can email photos to your guests.

■ **Hidden cameras** For informal moments you'll treasure, put a disposable camera on each table. Online suppliers offer coloured cameras from under £3 each with flash, and there is usually a discount for bulk purchases. Some also include an envelope for special processing deals.

RESOURCES

WEDDING ADVICE AND INFORMATION ONLINE

■ For information about wedding planning, try **www.weddingguideuk.co.uk**, **www.weddingchaos. co.uk** or **www.confetti.co.uk**

■ For wedding dresses, **www.theweddingsale.com** or **www.oxfam.org.uk**, and discount bridesmaids' dresses **www.gawwk.co.uk**

■ To record the event, **www. disposable camerashop.co.uk**

■ For wedding flower ideas, **www.mywedding flowerideas.co.uk**

■ To compare drink prices, go to **www.champagne-cellar.co.uk**, **www.virginwines.com** and **www.waitrosewine.com**

■ Visit eBay for wedding supplies **www.eBay.co.uk**

■ Wedding insurance and advice: **www.which.co.uk/advice/ wedding-insurance/index.jsp** or **www.weddingcover. co.uk** ✉.

Leisure and hobbies

Make your money go further so you can enjoy more of the good things in life – whether it's trips to the theatre, dining out with friends, pursuing hobbies or expanding your horizons.

DINING OUT ON A BUDGET

Although eating out is a luxury, you can treat yourself without breaking the bank. Take advantage of special deals and plan in advance, so you have time to find the right offer.

CASH IN ON OFFERS

Keep an eye out for special offers that will make your meal a real steal – such as two for the price of one.

Newspaper deals Watch both local and national newspapers such as *The Times* and *The Daily Telegraph* for special offers and coupons, especially early in the year when business is slow. You will generally have to choose from a set menu, and drinks are often extra, but you could find yourself enjoying a two-course meal at a good restaurant from just £5 a head.

Watch the web Check websites such as **www.lastminute.com** ✉, **www.toptable.co.uk** ✉ and **www.bookatable.com** ✉ regularly. These sites offer special deals throughout the year; for example, lastminute's set meals for two in many major cities range from around £15 for two courses. Lastminute also has 'Eat out for under a tenner' or 'under £15' pages and a half-price dining section. Toptable has a similar page of low-price deals and a 'Special offers' link, giving users exclusive deals such as free wine or free dessert when you use their services to book. And **www.5pm.co.uk** has many offers such as £10 for two courses. You will need to register, which is free, to book a table, and you collect loyalty points with each booking.

AVOID HIGH WINE PRICES

One of the major expenses when eating out is the wine, so you can make a substantial saving by bringing your own bottle to establishments that allow this.

The unlicensed option Although unlicensed (or Bring Your Own) restaurants, where you can drink your own wine with your meal, are more common in America and Australia, there is a growing trend for them in Britain. To find a BYO restaurant near you, look at the Bring Your Own Bottle Directory website **www.wine-pages.com/byoblist.shtml** ✉.

Beware of the corkage charge Most BYO restaurants levy a 'corkage charge' – a charge decided by the management for serving wine brought by customers – on BYO wine. It is normally charged by the bottle and can be anything from a few pounds upwards, so check before you dine to avoid paying more than you bargained for, and instead of taking two bottles take one large one.

Budget eating Most BYO restaurants are small and inexpensive, so they won't stretch the budget when it comes to paying for the food.

TIMING IS EVERYTHING

Save up to half the cost of a meal by visiting a restaurant for lunch instead of dinner. The average cost of a three-course meal and a glass of wine in London is £40, but some

---

keep it simple

STILL WATER FROM THE TAP

When you order still water with your meal, order a glass or carafe of tap water rather than bottled water. For a very slight taste difference you will save the cost of the bottled water, which is not only expensive to begin with but also carries a high mark-up in most restaurants.

RESOURCES

RESTAURANT DEALS

To help you plan your value-for-money meal in London, look at:
■ *Time Out London Cheap Eats Guide*, £6.99, ISBN 9781904978961.
■ **www.lastminute.com** ✉, **www.toptable.co.uk** ✉, **www.5pm.co.uk** ✉ and **www.bookatable.com** ✉, all offer special-value meals nationwide.
■ For BYO restaurants go to **www.wine-pages. com/byoblist.shtml** ✉.

 **RESOURCES**

MOTORWAY ALTERNATIVES

To avoid the high prices for eating at motorway service stations, research your stops before starting a journey. Phone local tourist offices for good places to park and eat, then plan a short detour into a small town.

■ **www.5minutesaway.co.uk** ✉ lists restaurants, pubs and other facilities five minutes' drive from motorway junctions.

■ Good Guides publish both *The Good Pub Guide* at £15.99 (ISBN-10 0091922518) and *Great Food Pubs* at £5.99 (ISBN-10 0091885167). There is a new website at **www.thegoodpubguide. co.uk**, or text 'goodpub' to 87080 from your mobile phone to get details of the nearest pub on their list. The cost is 50p plus standard call charges.

■ *AA Afternoon Tea* at £9.99 (ISBN-10 0749549866) is published by the AA.

restaurants offer up to 50% off if you eat at lunchtime. Or dine in the evening during the week, when cut-price set menus may be on offer, instead of at a weekend.

BE A PIONEER DINER

One way of paying less for a gourmet meal is to visit new restaurants soon after they have opened – prices are naturally lower before a new venue develops its reputation. This can be a bit of a gamble, but if you watch the reviews in the dining sections of the local and national papers and at sites such as Dine Online (**www.dine-online.co.uk** or **www.restaurant-guide.com**), you can get some idea of what to expect and a price guide.

TAKE THE SET MENU

To reduce the bill, it's worth giving the restaurant's set menu a try instead of choosing your own dishes. Set menus are designed to allow the restaurant to charge a little less for meals and still give you a delicious culinary experience. Restaurants that only offer a set menu are even better value as they have far lower overheads.

AVOID THE TIPPING TRAP

Don't automatically tip at restaurants. First, make sure that service isn't included in your bill and don't be embarrassed to ask if it's not clear – for groups of six or more diners, it is often added. Give tips to reward good service: 10% is usual or 15% if the service has been exceptional. It is worth checking that the tips are actually paid to the staff.

MOTORWAY MADNESS

Avoid motorway service stations where refreshment prices can be double non-motorway equivalents (£8 for fish and chips, for example). And petrol is more expensive there, too. Take a few extra minutes to drive to somewhere cheaper. Pubs and cafés in nearby towns will have better food at a lower price (see Resources, left). Check guide books such as *The Rough Guide to Britain*, available in libraries, and make a note of eating places they recommend.

Bring-and-dine clubs

SMART MOVES

If eating out is beyond your means, or you don't want to travel far to find fine dining, get together with like-minded people to organise a bring-and-dine club. This will save on costs and still create a real sense of occasion. Arrange to meet up regularly with a group of friends or neighbours – perhaps once a month – at someone's home and each bring a different element of a three-course meal: one of you can organise a starter; someone else the main course; and, a third person brings the dessert. Other people can take charge of the table decorations and wine, or bring coffee and mints. You all get to try new foods and wines in different settings and the costs are split between all the participants, allowing big savings. Even a lavish meal in a carefully arranged setting will cost much less than the normal restaurant equivalent. For example, a sirloin steak at a Harvester restaurant costs £11.95, while a similar home-cooked meal bought from the supermarket can cost as little as £4.50–£5.

BARGAIN-BASEMENT EATING

If your budget is really tight but you still want to enjoy the luxury of eating out, there are other ways to experience very cheap or even free meals.

The proverbial free lunch Look out for luncheon vouchers, which may be offered to you by your employer or on training courses and seminars, when trains or flights are delayed, as part of a tourist package or as compensation for bad service. You can use them towards the cost of a meal at over 33,000 outlets in Britain, including restaurants, cafés sandwich bars, fast food outlets and most big supermarkets. You can even pick up luncheon vouchers free for agreeing to complete surveys for some research companies; for example, PineCone Research **www2.pineconeresearch.co.uk** offers a £4 voucher when you complete a survey for them.

Vouchers for discounted dining If you don't object to participating in surveys, keep an eye on websites such as **www.Vouch4me.com**, which offers rewards such as 25% off weekend bed-and-breakfast stays or a two-for-one ticket to Jongleurs. Other websites, such as **www.vouchercodes.co.uk** (look under 'Printable Vouchers'), offer a selection of discount vouchers for cheap eating out.

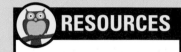

RESOURCES

LUNCHEON VOUCHERS
For information on luncheon vouchers, contact **Accor Services** 0845 3304406 **www.luncheonvouchers. co.uk** ✉.

PRE-THEATRE DINING

To get value for money while enjoying an indulgent evening out, consider a dinner-and-show package, available from **www.lastminute.com** ✉. We found a package that included Grand Circle seats for *The Lion King* and dinner at a nearby restaurant for £38 per person; another deal offered tickets to an English National Ballet production and brasserie meal for just £20 each. In the summer, take an up-market picnic and eat it in a nearby park or on the riverbank.

THE WINE LIST: GETTING VALUE FOR MONEY

Each restaurant has its own pricing policy, with mark-ups typically ranging from 200% or 300% upwards. The mark-up covers the expertise of the buyer, so get value from your spending by trying a wine you don't know, then checking it out at a wine store.

TYPE OF WINE	RESTAURANT PRICE	RETAIL PRICE (TYPICALLY)	MARK-UP
House wine	£14	£6.50	100%-200%
Mid-range	£35	£12	200%
Superior	£50+	£16–£25	100%-300%

TIPS
■ Don't order by the glass: if two or more of you are drinking a few glasses of wine it can work out 20% cheaper to order by the bottle.
■ Unless you spot a wine you know, opt for one from the same region as the restaurant's cuisine: these should have been chosen with more discernment.
■ Discuss the choice with the sommelier or waiter. Ask for their recommendation within your price bracket.
■ If in doubt, pay a few pounds more for wine, then skip the coffee.

LOW-COST ENTERTAINMENT

THEATRE DEALS
The following websites will keep you up to date with special ticket offers and theatre information:
- *The Times* website **www.timesonline.co.uk**
- To use *The Telegraph* website at **www.telegraph.co.uk** – click on 'T offers' and 'Telegraph Box Office'.
- **www.whatsonstage. com** gives national listings and special offers, including meal deals and two-for-one tickets.
- **www.londontheatre.co.uk** – sign up to receive a weekly e-newsletter or monthly e-listing with details of ticket deals.
- **www.theatresonline.com** lists all theatres in the UK and Ireland, offering the latest reviews, previews and information.

Evenings out at the theatre, trips to the cinema and days out with the family visiting places of interest need not be occasional treats. Find out about cut-price ticket deals so you can make your money go further.

TOP TIPS CUT-PRICE THEATRE TICKETS

If an evening at the theatre appeals but the price of a ticket puts you off, make use of cut-price offers and special deals.

- **Preview deals** Book for previews before the show has been reviewed – these first few performances are normally offered at a reduced rate and sometimes even half price.
- **Off-peak shows** Look in national and local newspapers for adverts offering discounts on major shows at quiet times of the year. By quoting a reference number from the paper when booking through the box office, you can benefit from as much as a 50% reduction or a two-for-one offer.
- **On-the-day reductions** Buy tickets for West End theatres half price on the day of performance at the official booths in Leicester Square (Monday to Saturday 10am–7pm; Sunday 12 noon–3pm) and Brent Cross shopping centre. At Leicester Square, queues start forming from 9am in summer, so get there early. Visit **www.officiallondontheatre.co.uk** ✉ and select 'tkts' to see what will be on sale each day. And check websites such as **www.discounttheatre.com**, **www.lastminute.com** or **www.TheatreTicketsDirect.co.uk** for cheap deals.
- **Lend a hand** Volunteer for a scheme such as Shape Arts **www.shapearts.org.uk** 0845 521 3457 ✉ to be an escort-driver and accompany an elderly or disabled person to the theatre – you'll have expenses paid and watch the show free.
- **Just the ticket** If you plan to travel to the theatre by National Rail, check their website **www.daysoutguide.co.uk**, which details special 2FOR1 entry deals to many of London's top attractions, including West End shows.
- **Save up to 70%** At some theatres, standby tickets are offered two hours or less before a show starts. However, sales may be restricted certain groups, such as senior citizens or students only. And there is a chance you might not get in.

CASE STUDY

THEATRE WONDERLAND
Retired teacher Sonia March lives in north London and the theatre and musicals have always been the love of her life. Now she has time to indulge herself, but with a limited income she makes sure she gets value for money. One week she went with a friend to the preview of a Noel Coward play at Hampstead Theatre on Tuesday, each paying just £15 by booking well in advance. On Wednesday, they got tickets for a matinée performance of *Sunset Boulevard* at almost half price through the Leicester Square ticket booth. Then to round off the week, they took advantage of the 'Tickets for a tenner' offers at **www.lastminute.com** ✉ and saw *The Sound of Music* from the upper circle during its final days at the London Palladium. In total, Sonia paid £60, a saving of around £35 on normal prices.

JOIN A MAILING LIST

If you're a keen theatre-goer, it's worth getting on the mailing list of your favourite venues. If possible, book direct rather than through an agency, which will add a hefty fee.

Direct from the theatre Membership of the National Theatre ✉, Royal Shakespeare Company ✉ and many other theatres nationwide costs from around £12 a year, for which you will receive performance schedules, get priority booking and discounted ticket offers. It is possible to sign up for email newsletters or alerts from many theatres for free. For an online listing of UK theatres, see **www.theatresonline.com** ✉. And for less than £1 a week, members of **www.theaudienceclub.com** ✉ can see fringe shows, previews and some West End performances for just £2 each.

Web mailing lists Ticketmaster **www.ticketmaster.co.uk**, **www.latestevents.com** ✉ and SeeTickets **www.seetickets.com** ✉ all provide details of forthcoming events to subscribers.

Check the paper *The Sunday Times* and London *Evening Standard* in particular often carry adverts offering discounts for major shows, especially at quieter times of the year. Also check the *Evening Standard* website **www.thisislondon.com** ✉.

LITERARY EVENINGS

Look out for special events at nearby bookshops. Many now host literary evenings or poetry events, which are free or charge a nominal fee that may include a glass of wine. You could hear your favourite authors read their latest work or discover some exciting new writers.

TOP TIPS MUSIC FOR A SONG

To find cheap tickets for the opera, contact the venue to find out whether they are offering any special deals. The easiest way to do this is to browse their website or phone their enquiry line before booking.

■ **For opera lovers** Not as easy to find special deals, but check the websites of The Royal Opera House ✉, The English National Opera ✉ and the Welsh National Opera ✉ just in case. Scottish Opera ✉ have a £10 Tix deal to encourage under 26s to attend. Opera North ✉ have a SeeMore deal – see three operas and save 25% on one; book for the entire eight-opera season and see one free.

■ **LSO** The London Symphony Orchestra (020 7588 1116 ✉) offer up to 20% off standard ticket prices for groups of 10 or more. They also offer discount for multi-buy booking – book three or more concerts and save 10%. They also give regular free lunchtime recitals at LSO St Luke's, Old Street, London ✉, in addition to free public rehearsals.

■ **Outdoor culture** Many local groups put on free or inexpensive events during the summer when audiences can be seated outdoors. Churches, pubs and parks are the usual venues. Check church notice boards and local papers.

■ **Visit a music school** Many music schools, such as London's Royal Academy of Music ✉, allow observers to listen in on rehearsals for students, as well as giving free entrance to public recitals undertaken as part of their degree. These are often of an exceptionally high standard. Look in the Yellow Pages to find music schools in your area.

RESOURCES

OPERA AND CONCERT TICKETS

Look at the following websites to find a discounted deal for a night at the opera:

■ Click on 'Theatre' then 'Dance & performance' at **www.lastminute.com** ✉.

■ Check the Arts and Theatre section for opera listings and offers on **www.ticketmaster.co.uk** ✉.

■ For listing of opera and concerts nationwide, including minor venues, go to **www.concert-diary.com** ✉. Contact the venues direct for tickets.

CHEAP CINEMA TICKETS
Whether you are a dedicated film buff or an occasional cinema-goer, there are ways you can see a film for far less than the full price.

'Early bird' deals For films starting before 5pm, tickets can cost slightly less than the standard price.

Cheap days Check with your local cinema to see if they have discount days. Many cinemas offer cheaper tickets if you go before 6pm, or on Monday to Thursday. Fridays and weekends are almost always more expensive.

Become a member Cinema chains such as Odeon ✉ encourage visitors to their cinemas and websites to register with them and receive exclusive offers and film news. Many also offer free membership to Odeon Kids. Once you join, you can take a child to the cinema during weekends and school holidays for £2.50, and an accompanying adult gets in free. Students also often qualify for discounts and Senior Screen deals entitled older cinema-goers to cheaper tickets and a free tea or coffee for certain screenings.

DISCOUNTED EXCURSIONS
Many organisations and schemes offer discounts to members, so if you already belong to any of them, take advantage of your entitlement. If not, you may find it worthwhile joining.

Supermarket days out Large supermarket chains, such as Tesco and Sainsbury's, reward customer loyalty through their points schemes. Points can be exchanged for tickets to all kinds of attractions and museums, saving you up to 75% off the normal price (see *Practical parenting*, page 108).

Two ways to save Young Smart to Save account holders with Nationwide Building Society can choose from a wide range of 'rewards'. Savers can enjoy such things as: a free tour of Wembley Stadium with a paying adult; two-for-one entry to Camelot Theme Park in Lancashire; or, buy one game of tenpin bowling and get a second game free. Check for current deals at **www.smartreward.co.uk** ✉.

Banks offer discounts Many high-street banks offer current accounts whose monthly fee entitles holders to discounts on days out and other types of entertainment. The Royal Bank of Scotland's Royalties current account, which costs £6.95 a month, gives holders discounts on days out and dining. If you hold this type of account with a high-street bank, take full advantage of these offers.

HERE Savings for frequent visitors The Art Fund Card offers its members free entry to 200 museums, galleries, historic houses and castles across the UK. It also provides 50% off entry to major exhibitions at the Tate galleries, V&A, The National Gallery, and others. Single membership costs £31.50; double membership is £40.50; and, family membership costs from £45. For details call 0870 848 2003 or visit **www.artfund.org** ✉.

Print your own coupons A number of websites offer discounts for family days out, such as two-for-one deals. The website **www.daysoutuk.com** ✉ has over 300 member discount vouchers. To benefit from offers, just print out your own coupons and take them along to your chosen venue.

The group solution

Save 20%–50% on ticket prices by forming a group of eight or more people.

■ Contact the venue to check their policy on group booking: the number of people needed to qualify as a group and the discount applied varies.

■ To assemble enough people, try placing an advert on the notice board of your local club, school or church.

■ The larger the group, the lower the prices should be.

If you don't feel the discount is large enough, don't be afraid to haggle.

FREE EXTRAS

■ Extra concessionary rates are normally given to certain groups – in particular children up to 16 and pensioners – for midweek matinées.

■ If your group contacts a venue in advance, you may get more free extras. For example, Clyne Gardens and the Botanical Gardens in Swansea will provide either a guided tour or give an informative talk to members of your group if you arrange this with the gardens before the visit.

COACH TOURS

■ If you can't find a large enough group to qualify for big discounts, try joining a coach tour. Check your local paper or information centre for offers.

■ Transport costs, parking charges and show tickets are included in the price.

■ The whole package often costs less than the price of a ticket alone.

FREE TO THE PUBLIC

Many museums, galleries and tourist attractions in major cities do not charge entrance fees and merit several visits.

Public museums Most public museums are now free and offer both adults and children an educational as well as an entertaining day out.

Free art Entry is free to the permanent collection of most regional art galleries as well as famous London art museums such as the National Gallery and Tate Modern.

Visit the House of Commons British residents can participate in free guided tours, which are available on some weekdays by contacting their MP. Phone the House of Commons information service on 020 7219 4272 (**www.parliament.uk** ✉) if you don't know who your MP is and they can find contact details for you. To round off the day, you could visit Westminster Abbey, which is free for evensong. For details of other free attractions in the capital, visit **www.londontourist.org/free.html** ✉.

Local government websites Websites run by your local authority (which will end in **.gov.uk**) often list free attractions and events in your area, as well as other cheap days out.

Free walks As walking is not only free but a convenient way to see the sights, work out an itinerary that includes some spectacular scenery or historical landmarks. Maps are often free at local transport centres and tourist offices. Enjoy England, the official tourist board for England, offers destination guides, ideas, accommodation deals and savings on family days out at **www.enjoyengland.com** ✉.

DAYS OUT AT A DISCOUNT

Visiting in low season, using special-offer coupons or seeking out smaller venues can cut the price or tickets for days out to popular attractions such as gardens, zoos and theme parks.

VISITING GARDENS
Check magazines such as *BBC Gardeners' World* for occasional money-off vouchers for gardens around Britain.
RHS members free Members of the Royal Horticultural Society ✉ get free entry to the Society's gardens and other privately run gardens, as well as reductions on tickets to major horticultural events such as the Chelsea Flower Show ✉. Individual membership costs £48 a year.
Private views For a list of allotments and private gardens open to the public for charity, contact the National Gardens Scheme or look in *The Yellow Book* (see Resources, left), published annually by the National Gardens Scheme ✉.

HERITAGE SITES FOR ALL
If you enjoy visiting Britain's wealth of heritage sites on a regular basis, join organisations that give you free entry.
National Trust sites The National Trust ✉ has more than 300 properties and gardens in its care. Yearly membership including free entry and parking costs £46 (or £34.50 if you pay by direct debit) for an adult. For membership details, call 0844 800 1895 or visit **www.nationaltrust.org.uk** ✉ (see *Practical parenting*, page 108).
A sense of history English Heritage maintains over 400 historic sites. For £41.50 a year, you get free entry to castles, monuments and fine homes. Call 0870 333 1182 or visit **www.english-heritage.org.uk** ✉ for details.

TOP TIPS A DAY AT THE ZOO
As with many other days out, visiting the zoo needn't be an expensive experience as long as you are aware of the pitfalls.
■ **Avoid high season** Some zoos offer lower admission at low season. Woburn Safari Park ✉ offers winter tickets at substantially less than high season prices; London Aquarium ✉ and many other attractions ofer 10% discount if you

book online, and others offer entry for a reduced price if you arrive after a certain time.

■ **More is cheaper** Many zoos offer reductions to groups (for London ✉ and Whipsnade ✉ zoos, this is for 10 or more).

■ **Try smaller attractions** Lesser-known wildlife parks and animal experiences such as butterfly farms are cheaper than bigger zoos. Use the Internet or local tourist office to find these smaller sites.

CHEAP THRILLS

Theme parks are not cheap, but you can save by buying tickets in advance.

Coupons and loyalty points Keep an eye on newspapers for special offer coupons and also on your supermarket's loyalty points scheme. Sainsbury's and Tesco's schemes allow you to buy tickets to many theme parks with your points, reducing the cost by up to 75%.

Website bargains Check on eBay **www.ebay.co.uk** ✉ for cut-price tickets for many major attractions; sometimes they are available at a third of the normal price. You can also save up to 20% by booking on the theme park website.

SAVE ON THEME PARK TICKETS

The chart below shows how much a family of four can save by buying a family ticket instead of individual tickets, and visiting off-peak. If you are likely to visit three times a year (or four times for Thorpe Park), it pays to get an annual pass.

PARK	CONTACT DETAILS	INDIVIDUAL	FAMILY	ANNUAL
ALTON TOWERS	Alton, Staffordshire 08705 204060 www.altontowers.com	£126 £102 (online)	£100 £81 (online)	£240
CHESSINGTON	World of Adventures, Surrey 0870 999 0045 www.chessington.com	£110 £78 (advance)	£92 £78 (online)	£195.74
LEGOLAND	Windsor, Berkshire 0871 2222 001 www.legoland.co.uk	£123.34 £81.30 (online)	none	£202.80 (4 tickets)
THORPE PARK	Chertsey, Surrey 0870 444 44 66 www.thorpepark.com	£112 £80 (online)	£92 £72 (online)	£385

Prices given for individual (four tickets) and family tickets on the day, and annual family passes, are costed for a family of four with two children under 12. Prices correct at time of publication.

CUT THE COST OF HOBBIES

Hobbies needn't cost a fortune. Even if you are collecting or need specialist equipment or materials, you can buy secondhand and take advantage of special deals.

ANTIQUES AND COLLECTABLES
The price-conscious collector can save money by knowing where to shop and using free resources.
Secondhand bargains When starting a collection, don't head for big auctions. Browse the classified ads in your local paper, or visit car boot sales and house contents auctions. The Yellow Pages lists local salesrooms. Also check websites such as **www.antiqueswebsite.co.uk** ✉ or **www.preloved.co.uk** ✉.
Free expertise Gain free insider know-how from web pages such as **www.antiquestradegazette.com** ✉, which gives guide prices and other trade information.

STAMP-COLLECTING BARGAINS
Most stamp-collecting begins as an inexpensive hobby, using stamps found on envelopes. Keep costs under control as you expand your collection.
Contact an office Besides asking friends and relatives for used stamps, ask anyone who sorts the mail in an office – large, international companies are ideal.
Collect together There are groups that can help you collect stamps economically: The Great Britain Philatelic Society **www.gbps.org.uk** ✉, The National Philatelic Society **www.ukphilately.org.uk/nps** ✉, Stamp & Coin Mart at **www.collectors-club-of-great-britain.co.uk** ✉ and Linn's Stamp News stamp magazine website **www.linns.com** ✉.
Find bargains in magazines Buy a philatelic magazine, such as the *GB Journal*, the magazine of the Great Britain Philatelic Society, which also organises postal auctions; *Stamp Lover*, the magazine of the NPS; or *Stamp & Coin Mart* magazine. All carry ads for swaps wanted.

KEEP GARDENING COSTS DOWN
Let your garden grow without incurring large costs by finding ways of getting discounts on supplies and equipment.
Cheap supplies Let nature provide what you need for your hobby. Collect seeds one year to grow the next, take cuttings and swap them with other gardeners you know and save your vegetable waste to make compost.
Group discounts Joining your local horticultural society to take advantage of discounts on garden chemicals and supplies. Membership charges tend to be low and are recouped in savings. Phone your council or check in your library for local societies, or ask other gardeners.
Garden deals Check your local garden centre for end-of-season deals, or magazines such as BBC Gardeners' World for special offers on plants and equipment **http://www.gardenersworld.com/offers/** ✉.
Rent an allotment If you want more space for

Read more for less

If you love reading, keep the costs of your hobby down by not paying the full price for books.

Secondhand books For a wide range of books try secondhand bookshops. Many have their own websites and an online catalogue, such as Barter Books, www.barterbooks.co.uk 01665 604880 ✉.

Discount books For new books and secondhand titles, search the big online suppliers, such as Abebooks www.abebooks.co.uk ✉ and Amazon www.amazon.co.uk ✉. You could save more than 50%. Amazon offers a book either new or secondhand – for a best deal take secondhand. BooksPrice is a free service that compares prices among online bookstores for the best deal available. Go to www.booksprice.co.uk ✉.

Book clubs If you are a regular reader, it may be worth joining a book club. The Book People www.thebookpeople.co.uk 0845 602 30 30 ✉ offer discounted books online or from their catalogue.

Book groups If you have friends who enjoy reading, form a reading group and assemble a private library.

---

growing your own vegetables, rent an allotment. Apply to your local council (parks and leisure department) who will advise on locations and availability. The cost of a plot varies from £6 to £50 depending on size and facilities. The average cost is £17–£30 a year for a 5 rod plot (125m²). Some local authorities offer concessions if you are over 60 or receive benefits. For advice contact National Society of Allotment and Leisure Gardeners www.nsalg.org.uk 01536 266576 ✉.

SEWING AND KNITTING ON A BUDGET

With a bit of searching, needlework enthusiasts can find bargains that will save them the cost of several new patterns.

Bargain fabrics Search in secondhand clothes shops and charity shops for unusual textiles for cushions and throws. Markets and discount fabric outlets are another inexpensive source, as are bargain bins with roll ends. Keep a note of how much fabric you need for your favourite patterns so you can buy the right amount when you chance on a bargain.

Patterns for pennies Look in charity shops and car boot sales for secondhand stitching books and dress patterns. Many embroidery and knitting patterns, for items such as Aran sweaters, don't date. Search www.ebay.co.uk ✉ for patterns as cheap as 99p, many of them vintage.

Stitching showcases Visit needlecraft shows, advertised in stitching and craft magazines, where you find a lot of suppliers with special promotions.

ECONOMICAL ART AND CRAFT SUPPLIES

If your hobby requires craft-related material, get together with like-minded people to benefit from group discounts.

High-street bargains High-street arts and crafts suppliers often offer discounts to art society members and students. Find details in your local library or on your council website.

Online marketplace Numerous suppliers such as Craft Depot www.craftdepot.co.uk ✉, www.artdiscount.co.uk ✉ and www.artandcraftworld.com ✉ offer craft-related materials online, often at discounted prices, particularly you buy in bulk. If you want a return on your outlay, the website Etsy is the place to buy and sell handmade things www.etsy.com ✉.

RESOURCES

NEEDLEWORK FOR NEXT TO NOTHING

For free patterns and cut-price fabrics look at:

■ www.cross-stitch-club.co.uk ✉ has an Internet Club where members can share ideas and tips.

■ www.cross-stitchers-club.com ✉ has free embroidery patterns.

■ www.woolworks.org ✉ offers free knitting patterns.

■ For designer fabrics and wallpapers at up to 60% discount contact www.discount-fabric.com 0870 241 3683 or visit www.homeinteriors.co.uk ✉.

■ For silks, satins and sequined fabrics, contact Online Fabrics Special www.online-fabrics.co.uk or 024 7668 7776 ✉.

MAKING MUSIC

The cost of musical instruments can be enough to deter some would-be players, but you needn't allow financial considerations to put paid to your dreams.

CHECK THE CLASSIFIEDS

Good deals can be found in the classified ads or at Cash Converters stores or auction site **www.cashconverters.co.uk** ✉. Check **www.prepal.com** ✉ for secondhand market prices.

STRINGS FOR BUDDING PLAYERS

A stringed instrument for a child, such as a violin, is better rented than bought because a child will quickly outgrow quarter or half-size versions. When your child is big enough to handle a full-size instrument, purchase a good-quality secondhand one. Take expert advice from a tutor or knowledgeable friend to ensure you make the right purchase.

BE WARY WITH PIANOS

Restoration of a badly treated piano can cost up to £4,000, so take expert advice before buying secondhand.

WHEN TO HIRE

If you are taking private lessons, consider hiring your equipment until you are sure you have made the right choice. Many music shops offer hire schemes for new and used instruments, and you can offset the hire fees paid against the purchase of the instrument should you wish to buy it.

ARTS COUNCIL 'TAKE IT AWAY' SCHEME

Ask your local instrument retailer if they participate in Arts Council England's 'Take it away' scheme. This was launched to make musical instruments and lessons easily affordable, and allows you to apply for an interest-free loan of up to £2,000 for an instrument to pay off over nine months. Visit **www.artscouncil.org.uk/ takeitaway/** or call 020 7973 6452 ✉.

SPECIALIST SOURCES

For good deals on instruments, try: Dawkes Music 01628 630800 **www.dawkes.co.uk** ✉ John Packer Ltd 01823 282386 **www.johnpacker.co.uk** ✉ SigNetMusic 0800 542 1566 **www.signetmusic.com** ✉ Denmark Street, London WC2 has many music shops. Visit **www.denmarkstreetonline. co.uk** ✉.

ADDED EXTRAS

Always ask if the carrying case is included in any price quoted. Often it isn't. Be prepared to haggle with the retailer. Ask if he'll throw in some extras for free – wood polish, reed, extra strings, tube cleaners, straps or even a music lesson.

GREAT-VALUE OUTDOOR PURSUITS

Hobbies such as birdwatching, cycling and rambling, require little outlay once you have bought the basic equipment. Although this may be expensive, you can keep costs down.

WATCH PENNIES ON BIRDWATCHING

Before investing in a pair of binoculars or telescope, contact the RSPB (The Royal Society for the Protection of Birds, **www.rspb.org.uk** ✉). They organise events where you can try them in the field and give advice on choosing equipment.
Magazine ads The RSPB's members' magazine *Birds* and most photographers' magazines carry adverts for new and second-hand equipment. Many of the listed specialist suppliers will part-exchange your old items.
Try a dealer Specialist high-street dealers such as Jessops (**www.jessops.com** 0800 083 3113 ✉) or Kay Optical (**www.kayoptical.co.uk** 020 8648 8822 ✉) can be good for new and secondhand binoculars. A basic pair costs from £50 upwards new, and a better-quality pair from £300 – though the same pair could be as little as £50 secondhand. Find binoculars in your local paper or at websites such as **www.acecameras.co.uk** ✉ or **www.at-infocus.co.uk** ✉.

SAVE ON FISHING

By avoiding the peak season and finding cheap sources of equipment and bait, you can enjoy fishing on a budget.
Buy secondhand Both eBay and your local paper can be a fruitful source of cheap, almost-new items, sold by people who have quickly upgraded their fishing equipment.
Mail order Bait from a local tackle shop can be expensive, but the mail-order companies that advertise in publications such as *Angler's Mail* and *Angling Times* often offer a better deal, especially if you buy in bulk. Team up with friends or join your local fishing club to save money. For listings of fishing clubs in Britain, go to **www.fishingnet.com** ✉.

> **keep it simple**
>
> ### HIRE, DON'T BUY
> If you want to avoid the cost of buying all your equipment, or aren't sure whether you'll continue with a new-found hobby (such as camping or skiing), consider hiring it, at least until you are sure you want to continue. Beans of Bicester offer winter sports wear, camping equipment and water sports equipment for hire by the day as well as equipment for sale. Contact Beans of Bicester 01869 246451 **www.beansonline.co.uk** ✉.

> ### FISH FOR A DISCOUNT AT THE POST OFFICE
> If you are over 65 or registered disabled, take advantage of the discounted Environment Agency Rod fishing licences available only at Post Offices.

Go low-season to cheaper waters Buy off-season day tickets for lower prices – game (fly) fishing waters often charge less at non-peak times (that is, before 31 May). Although fly fishing is generally more expensive than coarse fishing (both for equipment and for tickets), game fishing in man-made lakes is generally cheaper than river fishing.

Fishing on the net Subscribe to the Environment Agency's *Reel Life* e-zine for features news, information and special offers on fishing four times a year. Alternatively, call 08708 506 506 for a print version of your annual regional fishing magazine. In July, National Fishing Week offers hundreds of locally organised angling events – this includes the offer for non-anglers to be taught how to fish free of charge. Details at **www.nationalfishingweek.co.uk** or 07957 673579 ✉.

SPORTS EQUIPMENT AT A DISCOUNT

Buy secondhand if you can. The difference in price between a barely used and a full-price item from your local sports shop can be as much as 70%.

High-street shopping High-street shops such as Argos (**www.argos.co.uk**) often carry cheap sports and fitness equipment, particularly in their sales.

Internet bargains For expensive specialist items, search online for sites that offer discounts, such as Jags Online **www.jags-online.co.uk** ✉, **www.powerhouse-fitness.co.uk** ✉ or **www.sportdiscount.com** ✉. You can save more than 50% on clearance and sale items.

WALKING AND CAMPING

Specialist camping dealers are not always the cheapest for basic equipment. Check other sources to bag a better deal.

High-street bargains Find cheap camping equipment in high-street shops such as Argos, Nettos or Halfords.

Discount shops The Outdoor Megastore **www.outdoormegastore.co.uk** ✉ is an online clearance warehouse for many top-name brands of outdoor clothing and equipment. The online shop World of Camping **www.worldofcamping.co.uk** ✉ have good sales discounts.

Make do and mend Walking boots should never be bought secondhand as they will never be comfortable. If your old boots are worn out, have them repaired by a company like Feet First (**www.feetfirst.resoles.co.uk** 01246 260795), who specialise in resoling outdoor footwear. A resole repair costs £35–£45, whereas a new pair of men's walking boots costs from £50 to over £130.

Used maps and guides Book sites such as Amazon sell secondhand maps and guide books on all parts of Great Britain. For a list of those available, see the Explore Britain website **www.xplorebritain.com** ✉. For details of walking routes, many free, go to **www.walking-routes.co.uk** ✉.

Cut-price tents Attend camping exhibitions (such as the National Boat, Caravan & Outdoor Show ✉ at the NEC Birmingham in February, or one of the smaller events held during the summer), where you can try out equipment and pick things up at reduced prices. If you're looking for a tent, wait until the end of the show – you may make substantial savings by buying one of the exhibition models.

RESOURCES

CAMPING AND WALKING
For information and equipment on camping and walking, consider:
■ *AA Caravan and Camping Britain and Ireland*, £9.99 (ISBN-10 0749550678)
■ *Cade's Camping, Touring and Motor Caravan Site Guide*, £5.99, **www.cades.co.uk** 0844 504 9500
■ **www.uk-sites.com** ✉ lists campsites and has links to individual campsite pages so you can compare facilities and prices.
■ World of Camping **www.worldofcamping.co.uk** 01209 203220 ✉
■ Feet First (outdoor footwear repairs) **www.feetfirst.resoles.co.uk** 01246 260795 ✉
■ Ramblers' Association 020 7339 8500 **www.ramblers.org.uk** ✉

CLUB BENEFITS
Join a specialist club for your particular sport – that way you have access to items sold secondhand by other club members, usually at a much cheaper rate than you'd pay from a commercial supplier.

GOLF EQUIPMENT AT A DISCOUNT

Brand new golfing equipment is expensive – a full starter set costs from around £100 at Argos. Secondhand shops, websites and your local golf club can help soften the blow.

Sourcing secondhand Many general secondhand shops carry golfing equipment discarded by their original owner. Online auction sites such as eBay can also be a source of bargains, as are local papers and boot sales. It is also worth asking friends who are keen golfers and are upgrading clubs if they are thinking about selling their old set.

Go to the specialists Specialist online shops such as Online Golf www.onlinegolf.co.uk ✉ also have special offers and clearance bargains on discontinued lines.

Shop abroad Take advantage of business trips and holidays to stock up on golfing equipment. The website Which? Advice suggests that not only can you find golf clubs available in the USA six months before the appear in shops in the UK, but they can be 50% cheaper. Research comparative prices on the web or at specialist golf shops in the UK before you go.

BETTER-VALUE BICYCLES

Buying a bicycle secondhand can be good value but if you don't know much about them, take along a friend who does.

Go private Buy secondhand from a private seller (through a newspaper or bike magazine ad). It's generally cheaper than buying from a retailer who stocks used models.

Bike auctions These can be excellent places to pick up bargains. Local schools and the police often run them. Look at local ads, ask at your local police station for details or go to **www.bumblebeeauctions.co.uk** for police property disposal auctions.

Buying new For good advice, look for shops that are Association of Cycle Traders (ACT ✉) members and have staff that are Cytech accredited. The best times of year for bargains are autumn, when shops make room for new stock, and January and February when there are sales.

Cheap and cheerful Buying a low-cost basic model for about £100 rather than opting for a lower range of specialist bike that will be £340 or more, can be a sensible option if you're not sure how much you'll use it. Once you have a couple of years of cycling experience you'll know how you want to spend your money.

keep it simple

MUNICIPAL VS CLUB
Many local councils run golf courses and charge from around £10 for 18 holes. Private clubs charge a minimum of £30 a round, and you have to be a member or be playing with one. Rules and etiquette on municipal courses also tend to be more relaxed, so they are good places for beginners or youngsters to start.

SAVING ON SPORTS

If you enjoy spectator sports, you can get great discounts for big matches or make savings by watching good amateur teams instead. And if you prefer to participate, you can save money on even the more expensive sports.

TAKING PART AT LOCAL LEVEL

If you enjoy sport, join a local club or team. Membership at local level isn't expensive and you will have access to the club's equipment and coaching. At a rowing club in Avon, members pay £19 a month while in Southampton the cost is £150 for a year (**www.ara-rowing.org** ✉). Contact Sport England ✉ to access a wide variety of local clubs, from aikido to wrestling. Or visit your local government office's website or your library for more information.

SPECTATOR SAVINGS

Save on the price of a ticket to a sports event by organising a group of friends, or an outing from your sports society, school or work. Ticketmaster offers discounts of 50% or more to organisers of groups, and other ticket sellers offer similar discounts. If you go as part of a group you can expect to save 10%–20%.

Take a cheap seat Buy one of the cheaper higher seats in a stadium, where you will have all the excitment of the game and still get a good view of the action if you take binoculars.

MEMBERSHIPS AND SEASON TICKETS

If you are a fan of a particular sport or team, or have friends with whom you can share the costs, a year's membership or a season ticket could be a worthwhile investment.

Do you need a season ticket? For truly dedicated football fans, being a season ticket holder saves you money if you intend to watch most of the games and assures you of a seat at the big matches. For example, a premier league club currently charges around £25–£50 a match and from £400 to over £900 for a season ticket. If, as a season ticket holder, you attend every home game of a premier league club, you can generally save £300 for the season.

Alternative packages Some football clubs, such as Northampton Town FC, offer a multi-match discount for supporters who don't want to fork out for a season ticket. Many others, including West Ham United, Aston Villa, Stoke City, Fulham and Nottingham FC have introduced reduced-price half-season tickets for the final part of the season's fixture list.

Going local Joining a local or county-level cricket club can bring big savings if you are likely to watch a lot of matches. For example, a year's club membership of Lancashire County Cricket Club costs £155 (with large discounts available for pensioners, students, the disabled and children), for which you get free access to home matches and other benefits. Contact England and Wales Cricket Board ✉ for details of Twelfth Man, the new fans' service that gives access to interactive benefits and services.

AVOID THE FINALS

Avoid the most popular events, such as finals, and instead attend one of the earlier events in the sporting calendar. For 2009, first-round Wimbledon tennis tickets for Centre Court booked in advance (through a ballot) cost from £40–£62, whereas tickets to the finals were £92–£100. If you want to go to Wimbledon for the experience or just to watch tennis, rather than to see the champions, then there are cheaper ways still. If you are not averse to an early start and queuing, you can buy your ticket on the day and pay as little as £8 for ground tickets. Or purchase a resold ticket after 5pm for just £5. See **www.wimbledon.org** ✉.

 **RESOURCES**

SPORTS CLUBS AND EVENTS

■ Sport England
020 7273 1551
www.sportengland.org ✉
■ Sports Council Wales
0845 045 0904
www.sports-council-wales.org.uk ✉
■ ScottishSport, online only, includes hillwalking and snowsports
www.scottishsport.co.uk ✉.
■ **www.uka.org.uk** ✉ lists local athletics clubs and sells tickets to many athletics events.

Membership perks If rugby union is your sport, you may find it worthwhile joining a rugby union football club. You will receive a preferential discount on tickets, as well as discounts on all rugby paraphernalia. Find your local club listed in the telephone directory. For match and ticketing details, visit the national club websites www.rfu.com ✉, www.wru.co.uk ✉ and www.scottishrugby.org ✉.

SAVING ON SWIMMING
Whether you fancy the occasional quick dip or are keen to start a keep-fit regime, swimming is an inexpensive hobby. Most public swimming pools charge £2–£4 for use of the pool, although swimming lessons cost more. You can often save money by purchasing blocks of swim sessions in advance, which can be used at your convenience.

RUNNING REDUCTIONS
Running is free if you simply don a pair of trainers and run around your local park. For a little extra cost you could join a running club and benefit from discounts as well as the social aspects and the competition. Most running clubs cost around £20–£30 to join, with concessions for the young and old, and include entrance fees to races, the use of an affiliated sports centre and discounts at local sports shops. Find a club near you at http://www.runnersweb.co.uk/ or http://www.runtrackdir.com/ukclubs/ ✉.

HORSERIDING AT A DISCOUNT
Although riding lessons are expensive, costing around £70 an hour for a private lesson in London and from £30 an hour in the country, there are ways of avoiding a big outlay.
Student membership If you are a student, join the university or college riding club for cheaper riding deals.
Offer your services If you are an experienced rider, contact local livery stables and private horse-owners. Many people don't have the time to exercise their own animal and would welcome an experienced, trustworthy rider. Find your local stables at www.abrs-info.org ✉.
Fair exchange Some local stables will even give free lessons in exchange for regular help from a volunteer.
Pay by the month Some riding schools will give you a reduced rate if you pay by the month for weekly lessons.

DIVING FOR LESS
If you want to learn to dive, taking a course in Britain may not be the cheapest option.
Dive on holiday If you book a diving course while you are on holiday, you can save up to 75% of the cost of a course in Britain – which normally costs over £300 for a basic five-day course. Avoid school holidays to bag a bargain, but look out for PADI-certified centres (Professional Association of Diving Instructors ✉) worldwide to ensure expert tuition.
Dive in the UK For value for money, search dive magazines and websites for discounted courses. For example, the Dive-In Centre in Cambridgeshire has a Scuba Introduction session for £49 before you commit to a course. Visit www.ukdiving.co.uk ✉ to find a diving school near you.

SMART MOVES

How's that?
Tickets for the last day of a Test Match are not sold far in advance, in case play has ended. But if the match does run into the fifth day, then the tickets are cheap – or even free. Tickets at Edgbaston for days 1-4 of the 2008 Ashes Series cost £75, but for the fifth day were just £20. If you have bought a Sunday ticket and the game runs over, you can attend the Monday game free.
■ Tickets for the new 20/20 day-night matches are £40 for an adult, compared with over £60 for one-day matches.
■ Watching cricket at a local match is free. In country areas just take a deck chair and some refreshments, although many clubs, even village ones, have a bar.

A NEW SKILL FOR LESS

Whether you want to learn a new skill simply for your own satisfaction or to add an impressive extra to your CV, there is often a way to avoid paying full price for the privilege.

BACK TO SCHOOL

Education authorities, clubs and societies offer adult learning opportunities at many local schools and colleges. Check when you book whether you qualify for reduced fees – which can be as little as £10 a term – or even a free place.

Jobless freebies If you are unemployed and the subject of the course is work-related, you may be eligible for free training and assistance with associated costs, including travel, equipment, books and childcare. To find out more, contact your local Jobcentre Plus (**www.jobcentreplus.gov.uk** ✉) about the New Deal programme, which offers help and support for people looking for works, and Work Based Learning for Adults (**http://www.dwp.gov.uk/asd/wbla.asp** ✉), a voluntary full-time training programme.

Low-wage discounts If you are receiving a means-tested benefit such as Working Tax Credit, or are on a low income, you may be eligible for discounted fees – ask your college.

Learndirect courses This government-sponsored initiative offers a range of courses that, depending on your circumstances, are free, subsidised or full price – though they start from as little as £19.99. The courses are designed to allow you to work at your own pace, and can be undertaken at a local centre or from home or work. Subjects include maths and English, home and office IT, and business and management. For more information call 0800 101 901 or visit **www.learndirect.co.uk** ✉.

Over-50s courses You may find your local college runs special over-50s courses with a social element built in. If you are over 60, you'll also benefit from reduced fees.

TRY A MODULE

Many colleges offer modular courses for those unsure of whether they want to commit to long-term study. You can enrol and pay for one module, which you can use towards a qualification if you decide to continue – a good idea if you are not sure if a course will suit you.

KEEP STUDY COSTS DOWN

Benefit from student castoffs by buying educational books from secondhand bookshops. Many specialise in course books so you shouldn't have far to look, particularly if you live near a university or college. Discounts of over 50% on new prices are common. Or post a message on the college notice board saying what you need and offering to buy.

SEARCH THE WEB

Save money by taking advantage of inexpensive learning resources and information on the web. Just enter the subject that interests you into a search engine, such as **www.google.co.uk** ✉, and see what comes up.

COMMUNITY LEARNING CENTRES

If you are seeking low-cost classes, find out about adult learning courses at local learning centres and further education colleges. Visit the Education and Learning section at Directgov **www.direct.gov.uk** ✉ to find a college or learning provider near you. Many of these centres are subsidised and extremely good value. Some courses, in computing and languages for example, may be given for free.

Learn from your peers Use an Internet search engine to find a forum, email list or bulletin board to join, and receive the benefit of other students' learning experience in your chosen subject. Your college may also have a forum or email list you can join.

Online courses Many websites offer free online courses, such as the BBC's short language courses for holiday-makers in European languages. Visit **www.bbc.co.uk/languages** and **www.bbc.co.uk/learning** for other courses. Courses in IT, business development and personal development are at **www.freeskills.com** ✉ for £99 for a year and with a 'try before you buy' facility. And see learndirect (page 170).

Global learning Employment expert Manpower offers employees free access to over 1,100 web-based courses. A few of the courses from their Training Development Centre (look under 'Jobseekers') are available to anyone at **www.manpower.co.uk** ✉.

International courses Because courses are online, you are not limited to those based in Britain. For example, you can enrol for up to three courses at the Virtual University (**www.vu.org**), based in America, for $18 each term.

Distance learning colleges If a course at your local college is too expensive, find out whether a college specialising in distance learning offers the same course. Prices are often considerably cheaper and the courses even more flexible than the part-time or evening courses offered at local colleges and universities. Find a course at **www.icdl.open.ac.uk** ✉ or **wwwdistancelearninginfosite.com**.

TAKE ADVANTAGE OF EVENING CLASSES

Prospectuses are usually available at your local library or distributed via the local paper before the start of term, but you can contact the course provider at any time for advice.

Artistic value Evening classes that require potentially expensive equipment and materials, such as pottery and art, are often particularly good value. Schools are able to take advantage of educational discounts that are not available to the general public and you benefit from the discounted rates.

Special deals for starters Some classes offer first-timers' deals, such as the first two classes for the price of one.

Term discounts Some organisations give a discount for paying for the whole term's classes in advance, which is worth considering if you know you'll like the course.

OLD-FASHIONED PURSUITS

Take a step back in time to discover some old skills and you will find yourself a rewarding hobby.

Flower power Many flower-arranging clubs exist in towns or villages where you can buy equipment cheaply and attend demonstrations. Find out more about your local club from NAFAS (National Association of Flower Arrangement Societies) on 020 7247 5567 **www.nafas.org.uk** ✉.

Ring those bells Most people in England live within a short distance of a church with a ringing band. There is rarely any fee to join and you will be taught to ring. If you are asked to ring for a wedding, you get paid. Contact the Central Council of Church Bell Ringers on **www.cccbr.org.uk** ✉.

RESOURCES

FINDING A COURSE
To find out about courses in your area and fees:
■ Contact your local colleges or visit **www.learndirect.co.uk** ✉ or **www.lifelonglearning. co.uk** ✉.
■ For information on short courses visit **www.hotcourses.com** ✉.
■ Adult learners can find out about the courses available to them and funding at **www.direct.gov. uk/en/EducationAndLearning /index.htm** ✉.
■ For free basic IT, business and personal-development courses see **www.freeskills.com** ✉.
■ Full-time, part-time or summer courses in London are covered by *Floodlight*; either buy the magazine guides at bookshops or visit **london.floodlight.co.uk/** ✉.

Good-value travel

Spending more on a holiday doesn't always mean having a better time, especially if you have to check your wallet constantly. Armed with this suitcase of tips, you can make the most of your hard-earned cash and get more from your holiday experience.

KEEPING THE HOLIDAY BUDGET IN CHECK

According to the Association of British Travel Agents (ABTA), holidays are "the last thing people give up". Luckily you can cut costs without reducing enjoyment by taking advantage of the many great deals available – or take the plunge and try something different!

WAYS TO KEEP THE COSTS DOWN
The cost of a two-week summer holiday for a family of four increased by around £400 in 2008, and ABTA suggests it could average over £2,500 in 2009. However, there are a number of ways for the savvy traveller to make savings.
Visit the sales January to February is the busiest booking period – and also a great time to look for bargains as tour operators are eager to attract customers. In January 2009, one operator offered £200 off summer bookings, low deposits, free child places and no flight supplements.
Lower hotel rates Airlines cutting back on holiday flights means fewer travellers, so hotels desperate to fill empty beds tend to lower their prices. Check for top deals and the latest offers at **www.hotels.co.uk** or 0871 200 0171 ✉.
Late room deals If you are prepared to risk waiting until the last moment before booking, there are some great savings to be had. Discount hotels specialist LateRooms offers up to 70% off room prices and no booking fee at **www.laterooms.com** or 0870 300 6969 ✉.

INSIDE OR OUTSIDE THE EUROZONE?
The weakening of the pound against the euro and the dollar has made traditional destinations such as Spain, Greece and the US significantly more expensive. Consider destinations where you will get more for your money.
Good exchange Check to see which currencies are faring worse. At the beginning of 2009, for example, your pound would have gone 25% further in Iceland and 10% further in Serbia, Poland, Hungary or South Africa.
Deal or no deal? Turkey and Egypt are great destinations for UK holidaymakers escaping the eurozone. However, research by the Post Office reveals price hikes at these destinations as local businesses cash in on the boom. By contrast, it reports that Spanish restaurants have been dropping prices to tempt back travellers.
Caribbean steal It might sound extravagant, but great deals can be found to more exotic locations like the Caribbean. Reductions of over £2,000 for a couple for a one-week stay have been found at **www.caribbeanconnection.com** ✉.
France by ferry Despite the strong euro, ferry deals mean a family can travel to France for just £100. Living expenses will be higher, but an increase in the duty free limit to £340 means you can fill up the boot with bargains on the way back. (See Import Restrictions, page 35.)
Backing Britain Or why not forget currency worries and take advantage of the great holiday deals available at home?

RESOURCES

PRICE COMPARISON
These websites make it possible to compare a wide range of holidays and deals.
■ Holiday, car hire, travel insurance comparison and more at **www. travelsupermarket.com** ✉.
■ Kelkoo is one of the UK's most popular shopping comparison websites at **http://travel.kelkoo.co.uk** ✉.
■ Teletext Holidays vets suppliers and offers a price match guarantee **www.teletextholidays.co.uk** ✉.

Group holidays and shared accommodation

Real savings can be made by organising holidays that lend themselves to sharing accommodation.

Skiing holidays Chalets are perfect for groups, small or large, although it is obviously cheaper if you use all the available space. A self-catered apartment for six in Meribel, France, cost from £134 per person for a week, while a catered chalet at the same resort cost £389 per person in January 2009.
See **www.chaletfinder.co.uk** 01453 766094 ✉.

Villas in the sun Prices for villas vary hugely, but if it accommodates more people, the price per person will be cheaper.
For holidays in September 2009, **www.villastogo.com** ✉ were advertising a villa for 10 in the Algarve for £858 a week (£86 each); a similar villa sleeping 2–6 people was £1,296, (£211 each). To save money – and ensure the children have playmates – look at villas that accommodate two families.

Gites in France Similar economies can be made on larger properties in France. Rural properties are cheaper than those near a beach, so consider a gite inland with a pool at **www.holidaygites.co.uk** ✉.

TOP TIPS ACTIVE HOLIDAYS

If you are seeking an active break or want to take in the sights, then package holidays catering for specific interests are often both fulfilling and good value.

■ **Coach travel** If you are keen to take in the scenery of your chosen destination, a coach tour offers cost-effective travel. A ten-day trip to the Austrian Lakes costs from £489 a person at **www.consorttravel.com** ✉. The price includes coach travel, accommodation at a 3-star hotel on a half-board basis, excursions and entertainment.

■ **Walking holidays** For a seven-day holiday walking part of the pilgrimage route of St James from Le Puy in France to Santiago in Spain, including half board accommodation, maps and transport of luggage, see **www.worldwalks.com** or 01242 254353 ✉. Their prices are from £445 a person.

■ **Seeing the world** Attractive deals can be found at **www.travelsphere.co.uk** for escorted holidays worldwide. A seven-day tour of Beijing and Xian including flights, half-board accommodation and excursions costs from £899.

■ **Family deals** Specialising in holidays in Scotland **www.familyholidays.biz** ✉ is an ideal site for families with young children who like activities to search. A golf package for two adults and two children including seven nights accommodation, four family golf lessons, 9-hole golf round, seven-day course pass and car rental costs from £1,800.

■ **Adventure on a budget** Budget adventure holidays across the globe can be found at **www.responsibletravel.com** or 01273 600030 ✉, offering inspiring treks and activities as well as making a real difference to local people. A camel safari in Morocco, for example, costs from £358.50 for 8 days (excluding flights).

FREE SIGHTSEEING SPECIALS

When you travel to a city, visit the tourist office to find out about any free tours the city sponsors. Before you set off, check out a directory of tourist offices around the world by going to **www.tourist-offices.org.uk** or telephoning 0870 241 9084 ✉.

Walking tours Many towns and cities have inexpensive walking tours with excellent guides that charge far less than big tour operators do. Guided walks around London cost as little as £7 each, paid on arrival. For more information see **www.walks.com** or phone 020 7624 3978 ✉. Alternatively, visit **www.londonforfree.net/walks/index.shtml** ✉, which includes information and maps for a number of self-guided walks, including The Ripper Walk and The Bridges Walk. The website also has sections on indoor (historic churches and pubs) and outdoor activities (markets, Victorian cemeteries), that offer an inexpensive alternative to official tours.

History hounds If you are interested in architecture or history, the tourist office can direct you to the relevant local societies. They may be sponsoring tours or educational programmes and you can further your education in a way that you enjoy for little or no cost.

Civic amenities Don't forget that city parks, museums, universities and libraries often have free or discounted tours on specific days or at special times. With careful research

and planning, you may be able to coordinate dates and find several tours for free.

WATCH POINTS
RIP-OFFS ON LOCAL TOURS

■ **Reps on commission** When your holiday reps bully you into that welcome meeting, bear in mind that they make significant commissions on every trip they sell to you.

■ **Shopping sprees** If you do go on a trip with your tour operator, the chances are it will be in a coach full of tourists from home. You may also get taken to shops for souvenirs where your rep will get a percentage of everything you buy.

■ **Go local for half the price** Tour operators can charge two or three times the price of a tour with a local company. On a trip to Egypt, you could get a tour of nearby temples in an air-conditioned, chauffeur-driven car with a guide for less than half the price of a trip with your tour operator. Ask for contacts at your hotel, try information centres, or look for details at an Internet café when you have a better idea on arrival.

■ **Comfort zone** Despite the cost advantages, there may be a language problem with a local, so if something goes wrong it may be easier to deal with your tour operator. And, of course, take care and make sure the local guide is legitimate and authorised to conduct a tour.

Holidays that pay their way

THE NATIONAL TRUST
Visit **www.nationaltrust.org.uk** or call 0844 800 3099 ✉ to find out about NT working holidays – anything from carrying out a survey of moorland plants to herding goats – which cost from £60 a week.

SMART MOVES

They include food and hostel-style accommodation throughout Britain. Participants also receive the bonus of one year's free entry to National Trust properties around the country, worth £46 (see

Practical parenting, page 108, and *Leisure and hobbies*, page 160).

WORKING ABROAD
If you want to go farther afield, you could try grape picking in France or protecting a nature reserve in Nicaragua.

■ To find out more about paid and unpaid work in the UK and abroad, check **www.anyworkanywhere.com** ✉.

■ A directory of opportunities for volunteer environmental work in 150 countries, including Costa Rica, Ecuador, Grenada and Nevada, USA is at **www.workingabroad.com** ✉.

There is an allowance based on the local cost of living for some of these destinations, but it is only payable if you have two years' relevant experience in the line of work that you are planning to undertake. Most volunteer programmes provide you with room and board, the amount of which depends on the country.

■ The Overseas Job Centre is aimed mainly at young Britons, and includes information on fruit picking, ski jobs and working in tourism or catering.
Go to **www.overseasjobcentre. co.uk** ✉.

BE YOUR OWN TRAVEL AGENT

More than 50% of British travellers now use the Internet to book their getaway, and the savings can be substantial. However you book, check exactly what is, or isn't, included.

ONLINE REVOLUTION

The Internet is an invaluable tool for the independent traveller, allowing you to take control of your plans and search out a bargain.

Internet versus brochure *Holiday Which?* compared four leading travel companies and found that online bookings were cheaper than the brochure price every time. It also found a big price difference between brochures, so shop around if you book this way. Many promotions – especially late deals – are only available online, and using the Internet to gain access to companies around the world saves you the cost of international telephone calls.

Cheap hotels The website **www.cheeptravel.co.uk** ✉ claims to list the cheapest hotel rates from many cities worldwide, securing huge discounts at some destinations. For more discounted rates, try **www.totalstay.com** or 0844 493 9115 ✉.

Flights and car hire Many sites enable you to book flights and car hire (see Resources, left). Travel sites suggest that you book car rental as far in advance as possible and consider renting for a full week to get special package rates (see page 183). There are also Internet sites where you can buy insurance (see page 194) and book airport parking (and save up to 20%, see page 181).

AGENT OR INTERNET?

The explosion in Internet travel companies and low-cost airlines has led to a serious decline in the traditional package holiday. But book-it-yourself (B-I-Y) holidays won't necessarily get you the best bargain.

B-I-Y versus package A 45% increase in B-I-Y holidays is predicted over the next five years, and there is no doubt that big savings can be made on brochure prices. However, the slump in the industry has led package holiday providers to offer some amazing deals to counteract falling demand. And booking through a tour operator protects you against such things as cancellation – you will need to buy insurance that covers this as well as ill health if you book your own.

On the cheap Numerous Internet providers will help you put your holiday together without travel agents. Cheap flights can be found at **www.cheapflights.co.uk** ✉, while there are great rates on rooms at **www.laterooms.com** ✉ or **www.lowcostbeds.com** ✉.

Late is best Many of the best deals are to be had on late bookings at websites such as **www.lastminute.com** or **www.latedeals.co.uk.** But not everyone is in a position to be this flexible and late choice can be limited. Don't be afraid to haggle with operators, either – you could save an extra 15% on late deal prices, says the MoneySavingExpert.com.

TOP TIPS MAKE THE MOST OF THE WEB

■ **Check the market** Look at five reputable websites before making a booking.

■ **Be one step ahead of your agent** Check out a travel agent's website first, even if you do end up calling them. Search facilities are far more sophisticated now, but pricing structures in the travel industry are complicated and you may need the help of an agent to get things straight.

■ **Website savvy** To make your research faster and easier, bookmark your favourite sites for bargain travel, hotels and cars on your computer. It will make comparison shopping much quicker and simpler.

■ **Watch out for booking charges** Hidden charges, such as taxes, may only be added on at the time of booking. Check totals carefully.

GET INVOLVED

If you want to do more than save money and would like to foster international friendships, there are various ways.

Join the club Women Welcome Women World Wide (01494 465441 or **www.womenwelcomewomen.org.uk** ✉) is a unique organisation. Offering cross-cultural experiences and insights into different lifestyles, 5W has around 2,500 members in 70 countries. Members must be female, aged 16–80, and either request to be hosted or undertake to host another member for a period to be agreed. There is no membership fee, but a donation of £35 is suggested.

Town twinning Contact your local council to find out if your town is twinned with towns in Europe or farther afield. If so, get involved in the twinning association and take advantage of the exchange visits organised.

GET THE BEST FROM YOUR AGENT

If you don't have the time and energy for making your own travel arrangements, then use a travel agent.

Look for unbiased advice An agent you know and trust can be an indispensable source of information and good fares. Discuss all your requirements with the agent and make sure they understand what is important to you. However, remember that many airline companies offer bonuses to the travel agencies that sell the most tickets.

Read 'the guide's guide' Before you commit, ask to see the *Gazetteer* (**www.gazetteers.com**) – the 'insider's guide' to your destination. Every agent has a copy of this valuable reference book under the counter, which carries detailed independent information about holiday destinations.

WATCH POINTS AGENCY CHECKS

■ **Hidden extras** Read the small print of brochures and travel agreements to make sure you don't miss added extras. Watch for additional charges, such as taxes.

■ **Be safe rather than sorry** Bear in mind that even if a smaller agent offers a cheaper price, they may pose a financial risk. Seek out the ABTA (Association of British Travel Agents) or ATOL (Air Travel Organisers' Licensing) symbols. That way, you'll have financial protection if the tour operator goes bust.

RESOURCES

FREE ACCOMMODATION

If you are keen to travel but don't want to fork out for accommodation, then organise a holiday exchange with someone who lives at your chosen destination.

■ **Stay4free** (**www.stay4free.com** ✉) is an organisation founded by world travellers for everyone from businessmen to backpackers. Without charging a fee, the site puts you in touch with people offering free accommodation.

■ If you don't mind the idea of another family living in your house while you are on holiday, consider a house swap. You can find a suitable exchange partner through well-established agencies (see page 185).

Look for unbiased advice

CUT-PRICE FLIGHTS

With intense competition among airlines on many routes and reduced-price tickets available from both airlines and travel companies online, you can often pick up a real bargain. Do your research thoroughly before booking and consider all the available options.

FLIGHTS ON THE INTERNET

A 2008 survey by webTV travel site Holiday '09 revealed that six out of ten British people now book their flights online. But with sites such as **www.trailfinders.com** ✉, **www.travelbag.co.uk** ✉, **www.worldtravelguide.net** ✉ and many more, the options online can seem overwhelming. That's where **www.skyscanner.net** ✉ – a dedicated flight search engine – comes in. It compares budget air travel worldwide, with an easy-to-use search engine that enables you to look at both budget and scheduled flights. Skyscanner doesn't take bookings, but it provides links to the relevant airline.

No frills versus comfort On a day in January 2009 we searched travelsupermarket.com for a price on a flight from London to Malaga and it came up with 10 flights, including a best price of £64.99 on easyJet. A flight with British Airways at £160.30 offered more comfort and free food, which is often not included with the cheaper airlines.

TELEPHONE MANNERS

If you decide to call the phone reservation numbers given on travel or airline websites to buy a flight instead of booking online, learn these tricks to make the most of your phone time:

Do your homework first Check newspapers or online sources to get a sense of the best fares and which airlines are offering specials. You can use this information to spur the agent into topping the deals you've already found.

Call early or late If you catch a ticket agent at a time when they're having fewer phone calls, you're more likely to get their full attention and their help in finding the best fares. What if BA is offering a great deal, but you prefer Virgin? Ask the Virgin agent if they can match the rival offer.

Last but not least Use every ounce of charm you have. We've found that a good strategy is to get the agent on your side by being a relaxed, humorous customer.

CONSOLIDATORS AND CHARTERS

If you're planning a trip to a popular holiday destination, it always pays to check the following options:

Consolidators A consolidator buys up blocks of air tickets and then sells them at a large discount. You will see advertisements for consolidators in the travel section of most large Sunday newspapers. This can yield excellent prices on tickets to major overseas destinations, including the Caribbean, Australia and New Zealand, and Asia. But you'll find a number of restrictions on the tickets, so you must be willing to be flexible to maximise savings if you plan to buy tickets this way.

TAXES, FEES AND EXTRA CHARGES

On top of the air fare, expect to pay:

■ Air Passenger Duty: an excise duty levied by the UK Government. Current rates can be found at Excise & Other, Information & Guides at **www.hmrc.gov.uk** ✉. At the time of publication, the standard rate of duty was £20 for Europe and £80 for elsewhere.

■ UK Passenger Service Charge: the element of the fare that the airline pays to UK airports for the use of their facilities, now shown separately.

■ Insurance and security charge: levied by many airlines since 9/11 to cover increased costs of insurance and security.

■ Fuel surcharge: usually shown on tickets as YQ or YR, it can be well over £100 on long-haul flights.

■ Other taxes, fees and charges: on international flights there may be duties levied by other states, as well as airport charges.

In May 2008, the extra charges on a BA flight from London to San Francisco were:

Ticket	**£287**
Fuel surcharge	**£218**
Tax	**£80**
Credit card surcharge	**£3.50**
Insurance and security charge	**£2.50**
Total	**£591**

Charter flights These can be purchased as 'air only' or in combination with tour packages that offer discounts on hotels. They almost always fly non-stop to highly popular holiday destinations and, as with consolidators, there will be fewer options on seating and availability. Use a knowledgeable travel agent to protect yourself from scams and last-minute cancellations.

TIMING IS EVERYTHING

In many travel guides, the virtues of making reservations early to save money are extolled over and over again. They are right. You'll usually get a better price if you make reservations several weeks in advance, and you're more likely to get the flights and seats you want.

Wait and gamble But booking early isn't always best. Most airlines don't offer a supersaver fare until close to the departure date. Do you wait, hoping the airlines drop their fares, or take the safe route and buy tickets well in advance? It depends on the nature of your trip and the strength of your nerves.

The smart approach Keep an eye on normal low fares to destinations you're interested in so you get to know the range of prices. Then, if you really need to travel at a certain time, on a specific date, start checking fares about six weeks before your trip. When you see one that you know is reasonable and meets your needs, go ahead and book it.

Eco friendly and economical

Going green can be good value as well as good for the planet.

Voluntourism A combination of travel and volunteering, have fun while benefitting local communities. The Expedia Community Service Program organises volunteers to help at World Heritage sites. Go to **www.friendsofworldheritage.org** ✉. Volunteer for projects in Belize, Malawi, Nepal and elsewhere with Personal Development Overseas at **www.thepodsite.co.uk** ✉. Projects Abroad has volunteering roles for a range of professions at **www.projects-abroad.co.uk** 01903 708300 ✉.

EcoHolidaying Find over 50 articles on the subject at **www.ecoholidaying.co.uk** ✉. The Ecotourism Resource Centre acts as a guide for ecotravellers at **www.ecotourdirectory.com** ✉. (See **www.responsibletravel. com** on page 174.)

Our green and pleasant land Taking your holiday in England saves on costly fares as well as emissions. For great ideas and offers go to **www.enjoyengland.com** 020 8846 9000 ✉.

Let the train take the ecostrain According to Eurostar, flying between London and Paris or Brussels generates 10 times more CO_2 emissions than going by train. Visit **www.eurostar.com** ✉ (and see page 183).

Making the upgrade

It's hard to get an upgrade on a flight, but there are still some tricks that might work.

Frequent flyer points These are the best way to get an upgrade.

Use your charm Be polite, non-demanding and even humorous to the person at check-in.

Cause to celebrate Bring proof of a birthday, anniversary or honeymoon – and make it known.

Dress well Clean and neat is essential.

Popular airline You're more certain of success if the airline is likely to be oversold in economy.

Quiet days Monday to Thursday is usually the best time.

Single seat You have a better chance if you are travelling on your own.

SMART MOVES

Be flexible If you wait until the last minute, you may get a further discount but you'll often have to be flexible about things such as non-stop flights, dates, times and seats.

High-street bargains Check to see if flights are cheaper from one of the larger high-street travel agents than if you contact the airlines direct, especially on long-haul trips.

BE CONTRARY

Do the opposite of what everyone else is doing. Not only will you escape the crowds and higher accommodation prices but you are more likely to get a better deal.

Fly off-peak It is usually cheaper to depart on a Tuesday, Wednesday or Thursday and stay over one Saturday night. Flying late at night or early in the morning may also save you some cash, although the price reductions are often negligible and the inconvenience considerable.

Off-season success Wherever possible, travel outside the main holiday periods. If you are travelling to Sydney, Australia, for example, you could fly in May for under £700, whereas it may cost you over £1,000 in December.

WATCH POINTS HIDDEN COSTS

■ **Taxes** Many airlines do not include the price of taxes and other charges until the flight is actually booked. Airline Passenger Duty (APD) on economy flights now ranges from £10–£40, and there will also be fuel surcharges (this was £109 one-way on a BA economy long-haul flight in January 2009). The Advertising Standards Authority rules that print adverts have to include all non-optional charges, but this does not apply to websites.

■ **No refunds** If you cancel a trip, taxes and charges should be refunded. But many airlines, including easyJet, do not make refunds after 24 hours of booking, and only issue credit in exceptional circumstances.

■ **Inconvenient airports** No-frills airlines often fly to airports in an out-of-the-way city. For example, Ryanair fly to Girona. To get to Barcelona from there, it is a 21 return coach trip taking an hour each way.

■ **No public transport** If you decide to save money by flying very early or late, bear in mind that public transport may not be running, so that the money you save on the flight may be spent on a taxi to the airport.

■ **No meals** Budget airlines often cut costs by not providing in-flight meals. Avoid buying food in-flight, which is sold at a hefty mark-up, by bringing your own.

■ **Long stopovers** If money takes precedence over time, it may be worth having a stopover. You could save money opting to do this, although this is not always the case.

TOP TIPS MAKE THE MOST OF AIR MILES

There are now over 120 million travellers globally with frequent-flyer accounts, but many of us don't make the most of them – there are an estimated 14 trillion unused air miles piling up. Airlines generally award one air mile for every mile flown on a full-price flight, and some airlines even give a reduced allocation on discounted flights. If you are a frequent flyer, these miles will soon accumulate.

■ **Choose your route** Only use air miles for expensive routes, certainly not one covered by a budget European airline. That said, to earn the 10,000 BA Airmiles you would need to fly to Sydney would involve spending £3,500 a month in Tesco for a whole year.

■ **Partners make prizes** Check out the list of partners for each programme. Gone are the days when you just got air miles for flying. Supermarkets, hotels, car hire, energy companies, credit cards and other services often offer air miles as part of their loyalty incentives. Check for partnerships between airlines – many allow miles to be used towards the purchase of tickets on other carriers.

■ **Play the field** Look at other airlines involved in air miles schemes. Many people mistakenly think that they can only use air miles for the airline that issued them. Don't presume this airline is the best one to save with. *Holiday Which?* suggests joining the loyalty scheme of foreign airlines that have two-way agreements with the carrier you want to gain benefits from.

■ **Stay on top** Remember to ask about extra miles and always keep your boarding card to prove your entitlement if the air miles are not credited. Book as far ahead as possible as there is often limited availability.

PARKING PLUSES

If you are driving to the airport, remember to book ahead – which can save you 60% – or, if you have an early start, take a room in a nearby hotel that includes holiday parking as part of the package.

Long-term bonuses Most airports have adequate long-term parking provision, and frequent shuttle buses run between parking lots and the departure gates. But the cheapest option is an independent satellite parking lot near the airport. They charge up to 75% less than the on-airport car parks, offer a shuttle bus service and are usually fenced in as well as guarded.

Parking plans on the net We checked prices for a week's pre-booked parking in April 2009. The site **www.parkandsave.co.uk** 0870 733 0542 ✉ offered space at Heathrow for the week in question costing £46.95 off-airport and from £76.80 on-airport. But if you stay in one of its suggested hotels for one night the inclusive price starts at £102.35 for a double room. This compares with the full BAA (British Airports Authority) car parking charge of £120.80, but by booking a day ahead this charge drops to £76.80. Call 0870 850 2825 or visit **www.baa.com** ✉. The helpful site **www.airport-parking-shop.co.uk** ✉ searched six parking companies and gave transport time from each to the terminal, along with the frequency of transfers. Again, the lowest price for our dates was £46.95.

Short-term losses The closer the car park is to the airport, the higher the parking fees tend to be. Never leave your car in short-term parking for more than an hour or two. Some airports have a free period if you are just picking someone up. Glasgow airport offers free parking in the short-term lot for 10 minutes but if you go over your free time it costs £2.50 for up to 30 minutes and £5.60 for up to 3 hours.

RESOURCES

FREQUENT FLYER FACTS

■ Use the collection calculator at **www.airmiles.co.uk** ✉ to work out how to collect air miles.

■ For an annual fee of €129, **www.globalflight.net** ✉ provides independent analysis of 180 frequent flyer schemes.

■ For which credit cards accumulate the most air miles go to **www. creditchoices.co.uk** ✉.

BUDGET AIRLINE BONUS

The no-frills airlines now offer accommodation and cruises, such as easyHotel. In January 2009, Flybehotels was offering rooms in Prague from £17. Look at: easyJet **www.easyjet.com** ✉; Flybe **Flybe.com** ✉; Ryanair **www.ryanair.com** ✉.

BY LAND AND BY SEA

With low-cost air fares, travelling overland or by ferry can be more expensive. The trick is to book as early as possible as cheaper tickets are sold on a first-come-first-served basis.

COACHING SESSIONS

Taking the coach is one of the cheapest ways to travel long distances both in Britain and farther afield.

Go to the 'funfare' National Express offers 'funfares' via its website **www.nationalexpress.com** ✉ only, although m-Tickets can be sent to your mobile. Fares start at £5 (plus 50p booking fee) for travel between London and 60 destinations around the country. As 'funfares' are only made available a month in advance, expect a late or early departure.

Golden-age benefits Most people know about discounts for students, but over-60s can travel up to half-price on most National Express services without a discount card.

DON'T GO OFF THE RAILS

Thankfully, new names have been introduced for rail fares across the National Rail network: Anytime – buy and travel when you like; Off-Peak – buy anytime and travel outside peak times, plus Super Off-Peak (cheaper but more restrictions); Advance – book ahead and travel on a specific service (see chart below). Call National Rail Enquiries or see their website **www.nationalrail.co.uk** ✉ for rail tickets and information and contact details for all train companies.

Group or family discounts Some operators, such as South West Trains, offer GroupSave, a '2 pay, 4 travel' off-peak discount for small groups. Additionally, up to four children can travel with the group for £1 each. Check with your train company to see if have a large group scheme – for ten or more travellers – offering even greater discounts.

RESOURCES

TRAIN TRAVEL
■ Ticket information, a journey planner and links to train companies can be accessed at **www.nationalrail.co.uk** 08457 48 49 50 ✉.
■ If you are not sure which company you need, a good site that covers them all is **www.qjump.co.uk** ✉.
■ **www.infotransport.co.uk** ✉ has a full timetable for all companies as well as listings of rail websites, including Eurostar.
■ Contact Eurostar at **www.eurostar.com** or call 08705 186 186 ✉.

PLAN AHEAD AND SAVE OVER £200

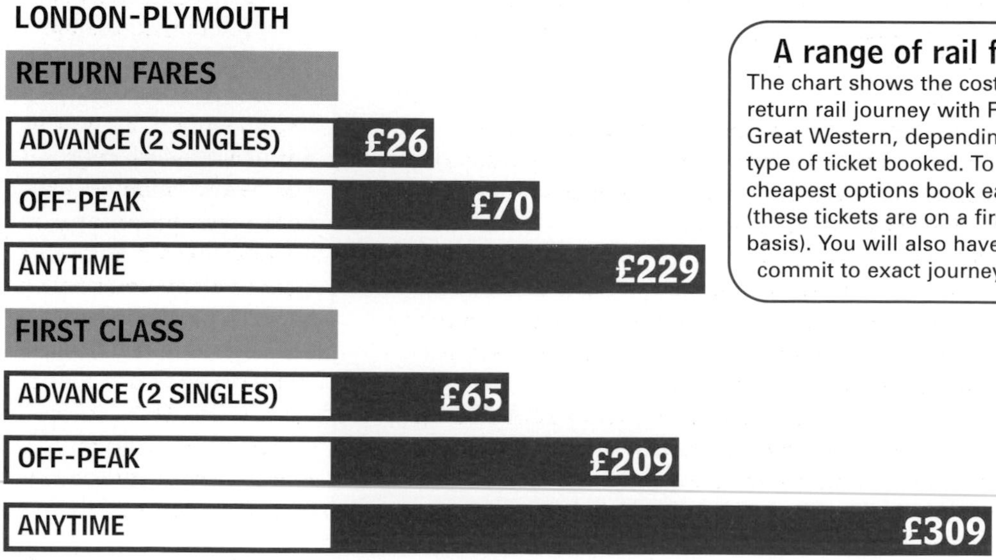

LONDON-PLYMOUTH

RETURN FARES

ADVANCE (2 SINGLES)	£26
OFF-PEAK	£70
ANYTIME	£229

FIRST CLASS

ADVANCE (2 SINGLES)	£65
OFF-PEAK	£209
ANYTIME	£309

A range of rail fares
The chart shows the cost of a return rail journey with First Great Western, depending on the type of ticket booked. To get the cheapest options book early (these tickets are on a first-come basis). You will also have to commit to exact journey times.

Take the train to Europe Transforming short-haul travel to Europe, Eurostar has doubled trips from London to Paris and Brussels. It offers links to 100 destinations. Check the website **www.eurostar.com** ✉ for Latest Deals, such as London to Paris or Brussels for £59 return in January 2009. They also guarantee that you will save on separate bookings if you book Eurostar and hotel together.

FAIRER FERRIES

In common with other modes of transport, cross-channel ferry travel has undergone a transformation. Again the rule is to book early to get the best deals, or look for special offers and late deals.

Sail through online bookings It is no longer complicated to book via the Internet, whether you use an independent site or the website of the ferry company. Sites such as **www.ferrysavers.co.uk** ✉ offer a 'Compare the fare' search facility and, they say, the cheapest ferry prices online. We checked the price of a July sailing on Brittany Ferries (**www.brittany-ferries.co.uk** or 0871 244 0744 ✉) from Poole to Cherbourg in January, and found it was exactly the same, £35, at both Ferrysavers.com and on Brittany Ferries' site. The company offers no discount for booking online.

Stay for more than a day A high-season day return to France by ferry can cost under £40, but if you want to go for longer two singles can work out at £70. Companies claim that this is prohibited, but in practice they are unlikely to charge you the difference.

Special offers Companies eager for custom offer discount of 15% or more for bookings made well in advance. On the other hand, be flexible and stay on the lookout for last-minute offers. The cheapest option is to travel mid-week – Saturdays are most expensive – on an overnight ferry.

CLEVER CAR HIRE

Free upgrades Taking a chance by booking the cheapest car going, which is usually also the smallest. Because these cars are limited, the rental agency will sometimes offer you an upgrade. If they initiate the upgrade, don't pay more for it, especially if you reserved ahead with a credit card.

Get extra insurance? In Britain, many car rental offices will try to sell you insurance but it will be almost duplicating the cover you are already paying for. Check with your own car insurance agent or your credit card company. But when hiring overseas make sure you are fully insured – in this instance the rental company's insurance will probably be the best and most convenient deal.

Fill her up? In the past, the car you rented would have a full tank and it would save you money to return the car full of cheap petrol. Now you'll often be getting a car with only a half tank, so put in no more fuel than necessary. Ask for details, then follow the cheapest option.

Hire online Easy booking and special offers – such as 50% off – can be found at **www.holidayautos.co.uk** ✉, part of Lastminute.com. Get an instant quote at **www.holidaycarsdirect.com** or 0870 112 8101 ✉. Or for pan-European car hire try **www.ebookers.com** 0871 223 5000 ✉.

ASK YOURSELF

DO I NEED TO PICK UP MY RENTAL CAR AT THE AIRPORT?
If you arrive late in the day and are staying in the city near the airport, consider taking the shuttle to the city centre and renting the next day. This will save you a day's hire cost and the trouble of finding your way in an unfamiliar city when you're tired after a flight.

CAR HIRE WATCH POINTS

■ Ask when you book if it's cheaper to pay in local currency at your destination, or in sterling at the time of booking.

■ In America you will need supplemental liability insurance (SLI), typically to $2 million, collision damage waiver (CDW) and loss damage waiver (LDW). You can buy SLI cheaper from **www.worldwideinsure.com** before you travel, and your credit card may cover CDW. Check if an excess is charged.

■ Check that the rental is for unlimited mileage, or you risk an additional bill when you return the car.

■ Local taxes may apply; check when you book.

■ An extra driver, a different drop-off location and a driver under 25 may cost more. Only pay for what you need and compare deals offered by different companies.

ROOM FOR RENT

For some people, a luxury hotel is the only place to stay. But many others know that the money saved on a hotel room leaves more for food, sightseeing, shopping and other enjoyable activities.

DISCOUNT BOOKINGS

Decide how much time you will spend in your room, then book accordingly. If you're staying in a resort, the quality of the room matters more than if you're touring several cities.

Discount booking sites The directory website **www.ukhotels-net.com** ✉ lists hotel rooms in Britain, many of them discounted. Late booking is effective: in January 2009, this site offered a three-night special in a 4-star Mayfair hotel for £119 per person. Other sites worth checking are **www.roomstobook.co.uk** ✉ (B&Bs and hotels in the UK) and **www.cheaphotelsworldwide.co.uk** ✉, which claims to give up to 70% discount.

Budget chains Hotel chains such as Premier Inn (**www.premierinn.com** ✉) and the international chain Ibis (**www.ibishotel.com** ✉) offer good-quality accommodation at reasonable prices. You are guaranteed a clean, en-suite room with amenities such as a television, climate control and an Internet connection. Their independent counterparts are likely to be more expensive. For example, a double room at a Premier Inn or an Ibis hotel in Edinburgh costs, on average, £65 a night. A double room in an independent hotel of the same standard can cost from around £90.

TOP TIPS SAVE ON ACCOMMODATION

■ **Save 50% at weekends** Most hotels cater mainly for business travellers and have tempting deals for the weekend. Time your big-city escapes and go half price.

■ **Ring late at night and save 10%** Reserve a room when the person at the reservation desk will have time to talk to you. A friendly chat may lead to a better deal.

■ **Ask for a lower room rate and save 10%** Simply asking politely, 'Is that the best you can do?' can often lower the price.

■ **Ring from the lobby and save 25%** If you arrive without a reservation at a big hotel, don't go to the front desk. Ring from the lobby instead – the desk clerk won't know you're already in the hotel and may feel he has to offer you a better deal to get you to make a booking. With smaller hotels, ring from outside on your mobile.

■ **Get the corporate rate for 15% less** If you find yourself staying at a hotel more than once, even if you're not on business, ask if the hotel has special rates for frequent guests or corporate travellers.

■ **Pay with a credit card and save up to 15%** If you're travelling abroad, wholesale exchange rates give companies better deals than individuals. By paying your hotel bill with a credit card you should find you're quids in when you get your statement.

Ring from the lobby and save 25%

NOT JUST FOR YOUTH

If you want a comfortable bed and good meals service in an excellent location from just £8 or £12 per person per night, depending on location and time of year, contact The Youth Hostel Association of England and Wales (**www.yha.org.uk** or 01629 592700 ✉). It's open to all, including senior citizens, families and couples. Or there's Scottish Youth Hostels (**www.syha.org.uk** or 01786 891400 ✉), which, like YHA, is a member of the International Youth Hostel Federation (IYHF) Hostelling International.

Join and save Joining the YHA saves having to pay temporary membership of up to £3 a night each time you stay. For adults it costs £15.95 a year, family/joint membership is £22.95 and group just £25.50. SYHA is £9 for an adult, £13 for family and £25 for a group. Benefits include discounts on travel and attractions, and access to more than 4,000 youth hostels in more than 80 countries through Hostelling International.

Royal living for pauper prices Many youth hostels are in characterful buildings or locations. At Derwentwater in the Lake District you will stay in a 200-year-old manor house from just £15.95 a night.

APARTMENTS AND VILLAS

Instead of staying in a hotel, look at renting a house or apartment; it offers greater flexibility and could be cheaper.

Trawl the net The Internet is the best place to find personal rentals. With Daltons holidays **www.daltonsholidays.com** ✉ you can rent a two-bedroom apartment for four people off season on the Costa Blanca for £100 a week. Apartments in city centres are good value. Attractive holiday apartments in the centre of Prague can be found at **www.apartments.cz** ✉, costing from just £25 a person, or at **www.holiday-rentals.co.uk** ✉ from £33 per property – or £186 for the week.

STAY ON CAMPUS FOR HALF PRICE

Many universities and colleges rent rooms during the holidays when few students are around. The bathroom may be down the corridor, but the savings will more than make up for that. For a list of low-cost university accommodation go to **www.europa-pages.com/uk/budget_accommodation.html** ✉. At Kings College London, for example, the Vacation Bureau offers rooms at four campuses around the city: Great Dover Street, Hampstead, King's College Hall and Stamford Street (**www.kcl.ac.uk** 020 7848 1700 ✉).

House swap

SMART MOVES

Fair exchange How about swapping your family home in Hampshire for a modern house in Christchurch, New Zealand for a fortnight for free? The UK's biggest home-swap agency, Home Link, expects to organise over 13,000 exchanges in 2009 (**www.homelink.org.uk**, 01962 886882 ✉). You can choose from 13,500 homes in over 65 countries, and the company runs offices in more than 20 of them. View their homes online before you register. Many house-swap agencies can be found online, most of which charge a fee of £25 to £115 to register, which includes one listing. You can also swap through a private group, such as a teachers' organisation, but won't get the same advice or support.

Swapping details When you write up the listing for your entry, include all the amenities that would make your home appealing, such as access to public transport, historic sites or cities nearby and areas of natural beauty. If you have regular access to a health club, golf club, beach or special parking, include this.

Check the contract The home exchange networks have standard contracts available. It should include a guarantee that swappers will pay replacement value for any damage. You must inform your insurance company of the swap – and your motor insurer if you plan to swap cars, too.

CouchSurfing The leading network of its kind connects global travellers needing a sofa to sleep on with local communities. There are safety tips and a vouching system, but no guarantees. Have a look at **www.Couchsurfing.com** ✉.

FAMILY FUN WITHOUT PAYING A FORTUNE

Entertaining the children and having fun on holiday needn't come with a hefty price tag.

PACK UP YOUR TENT

Depending on the weather (although the children will love it rain or shine), one of the best family holidays is also the cheapest: camping. If you already own equipment, the major outlay is food and petrol.

Low-cost rentals If you don't own any equipment, try to hire or borrow some from friends for the first outing or two, to see if you enjoy the camping experience; or start out on a site where everything is provided. For a family of four, this can cost 60% less than buying your own tent if you only use it for one year.

Pick and choose Campsites range from remote settings to privately owned grounds that have a full range of facilities including shops, entertainment rooms and swimming pools. Fees vary considerably, too. At some municipal sites you can pitch a tent for under £10 a night, while private grounds can charge over £25. There's a useful UK campsite directory at **www.bigfreeguide.com** ✉, and the Camping and Caravanning Club at **www.campingandcaravanningclub.co.uk** or 0845 130 7632 ✉ publish *Your Big Sites Book* annually for members with 4,000 sites listed. Annual membership costs £35 (2009 price) plus a £7 joining fee – unless you pay by direct debit.

Thrifty campers Keep costs down by bringing your own food and storing it in a cool box – or even a mini fridge with a car adapter if you have one. You can also save money by organising your own entertainment and keeping excursions to a minimum.

RESOURCES

CAMPSITES

■ For child-friendly camping holidays in Britain and Europe, consider the following:
www.canvasholidays.co.uk
0845 268 0827 ✉
www.eurocamp.co.uk
0844 406 0402 ✉
www.haven.com
0871 230 1930 ✉
www.siblu.com
0871 911 22 88 ✉
■ For a list of campsites across Britain, try
www.camping.uk-directory. com ✉. Its search engine allows you to find facilities such as electric hook-ups.

RESPONSIBLE TOURISM

If you are concerned about the impact your family holiday has on the environment as well as the cost to your pocket, consider the following.

Responsible Travel Marketing carefully screened holidays in the UK and abroad, **www.responsibletravel. com** ✉ has links to the tour companies, lodges and hotels who take your booking. Under the budget travel section you can get B&B in the Cairngorms from £25 a

night, or rent a caravan or chalet in Snowdonia sleeping 4–6 from £99 a week. A self-catering cottage for four on Turkey's Lycia coast will cost £250–£380 a week, excluding flights (book early and save 15%).

Responsible rambling If you have older children who enjoy walking, Ramblers Holidays on 01707 331133 or **www.ramblersholidays.co.uk** ✉ offer walking holidays worldwide for all budgets. They try to use local resources and facilities, and put profits back into the community.

Package tour operators Major companies such as Thomas Cook ✉, Cosmos ✉, Virgin Holidays ✉ and First Choice ✉ often advertise free child places, but you'll need to book early as they are limited. These companies are all members of the Federation of Tour Operators ✉, who agreed in 2004 to report on their commitment to sustainable development.

EXPLORE BRITAIN

You need not travel overseas to find an interesting diversity in landscape and culture.

Walking is free Go walking in the Welsh hills or visit the remote craggy islands in the west of Scotland. Holidays from Hillscape at **www.wales-walking.co.uk** or 01974 282640 ✉ start at £275 a person for a six-day break, including bed and breakfast, a packed lunch, tea and evening meal. And **www.oontours.co.uk** or 01768 480451 ✉ offers self-guided walks from place to place, including the Herriot Way.

Stay on a farm Young children love the experience of a working farm. For inexpensive B&B and self-catering farm accommodation, visit Farm Stay UK at **www.farmstayuk.co.uk** ✉. A Cumbrian cottage for six costs from £180 a week.

Family adventures For a fee of £14.95 a year you gain access to plenty of well-researched, up-to-date holiday information at **www.family-travel.co.uk** ✉.

Visit Britain The official website for travel and tourism in the UK at **www.visitbritain.com** ✉ claims to have Britain's largest online accommodation directory, plus travel and transport information and lots of practical advice.

CHILD-CENTRED RESORTS

Many companies offer children's programmes with child-friendly play areas, clubs and even a baby-sitting service.

Cost versus convenience These resorts often have a high price tag but shop hard, think off-season and you'll find a programme and price to suit your family. Mark Warner (0871 703 3880 or **www.markwarner.co.uk** ✉) offers a free child's place on bookings made before the end of January.

Packing the pram Mistakes can be costly, but there's now plenty of good advice to be found online about travelling with children. BabyGoes2 (**www.babygoes2.com** ✉) provides a comprehensive guide for parents, and its growing popularity has meant it can negotiate with top operators for special offers and discounts on holidays and services. Kids In Tow (**www.kidsintow.co.uk** ✉) details family activity and adventure holidays, offering discounts such as £100 off Eurocamp summer holiday breaks. And Take the Family (**www.takethefamily.com** ✉) offers great deals on family holidays, such as 15% off Le Boat holidays in Europe.

GOLDEN AGE PASSPORT – SAVE UP TO 35%

If you are over 60 and retired, both the National Trust (**www.nationaltrust.org.uk** 0844 800 1895 ✉) and English Heritage (**www.english-heritage.org.uk** 0870 333 11812 ✉) offer special membership rates. You can buy a National Trust lifetime membership at a special price of £735 (against £1,125) or £890 for a joint pensioner membership. The equivalent English Heritage fees are £640 and £965. To make these lifetime memberships pay for themselves you would have to use them for 23 and 22 years respectively. Both organisations offer yearly pensioner rates. English Heritage charges £29.50. The National Trust requires you to have held membership for at total of at least five years to qualify. To buy pensioner membership, phone the National Trust on the number above.

CONSIDER A CRUISE

Sailing off into the sunset sounds romantic but can be pricey. Although cruises may seem expensive at first, just about everything is included. So the real savings can be made on land, with wise buying before you embark.

GET ONBOARD WITH A BARGAIN

Using your computer to check out specials can save you big money, even if you end up having to use a travel agent or booking directly through the cruise company.

Get an overview Visiting several sites can give you a good feeling for the cost of a cruise and how to save a few hundred pounds – such as free parking at the port included.

Dream deals The site www.cruisecontrolcruises.co.uk ✉ provides links to a number of cruise operators, including a section on cheap cruises and late offers – this included savings of up to 50% at Cruise118.com. A 13-night Mediterranean cruise was available from £899 (plus £70 to spend on board) through www.cruisedirect.co.uk (0800 093 0622 ✉), while www.cruisedeals.co.uk (0800 107 2323 ✉) showed a Red Sea Magic seven-night break with Thomson for £549 exclusive – a saving of £210 on the brochure price.

CONSOLIDATED SAVINGS

Consolidators are the middlemen between the cruise lines and the consumer. Each cruise line will usually provide a consolidator with a number of cabins for each cruise. The consolidators' deals can be as much as £600 cheaper than those offered by travel agents (we found one offering a maximum saving of £1,510), and include bonuses such as an upgraded cabin or £50–£100 onboard spend.

Scour the newspapers You can find advertisements in the travel section of most major newspapers under either 'consolidators' or 'discounters'. There are several websites now in operation, too, such as www.bestatholidays.co.uk (0871 282 4304 ✉) and the website for the Association of Special Fares Agents www.specialfares.net ✉, which is the platform for discount travel specialists and consolidators.

Vouch for it Voucher codes aren't limited to high street shopping or nights out. Check discount code sites such as www.vouchercodes.com ✉ and www.myvouchercodes.co.uk ✉ for coupons offering money off cruise bookings.

CRUISE CONTROL

A travel agent that specialises in cruises can save you money. They buy up space on certain cruises in bulk at a hefty discount and are therefore able to offer a better bargain.

Assess the agencies Check with more than one agency that specialises in cruises. Try the ones listed under Dream Deals above or, alternatively, www.cruisepeople.co.uk (020 7723 2450 ✉) or www.voyanacruise.com (0800 970 4509 ✉). Some agencies will push one cruise line more than another to get a bonus for extra sales, so to get what you want, find an agent that is willing to review all your options. The

---

SAVE £100 ON DISCOUNTED AIR FARES

Most cruise packages include just about everything but the air fare. Many lines will offer you a discounted fare with an airline partner, but don't automatically buy into this. Use all the tricks for cut-price flights (see page 178) to find the best price to fly to your port of departure. You may save yourself £100 or more. Or you may find that the air fare the cruise line offers is indeed the best. One advantage of booking a flight with a cruise line partner is that if the flight is delayed or cancelled, the line will honour your booking and get you to the ship another way.

Passenger Shipping Association ✉ runs a retail agents' accreditation scheme for high-street travel agents who are experts on cruise holidays. To find an accredited agent, visit **www.discover-cruises.co.uk** or 020 7436 2449.

Be either early or last-minute Cruise lines give a big discount to those who pay well ahead, netting you a saving of up to 50% on the brochure price. (For P&O, 2009 bookings made by 31 January offered 47.5% off plus an additional 5% for booking online.) The same goes if you wait until the last minute and book close to the sailing date, when the cruise line may have cabins it needs to fill. We found a last-minute deal on **www.iglucruise.com** ✉ for a seven-night cruise on one of P&O's most popular liners for £616 – over 50% less than the regular price.

TOP TIPS **ON-BOARD ECONOMIES**
Here are a few before-you-embark tips to keep extra costs from spoiling your cruise experience.

■ **Tips, trips and tipples** Food and entertainment are included but tips are not – and they can add up to over £30 a week for each person. Many shore excursions are extra, bumping up the cost by another £50. So are drinks other than coffee and tea. Check what is included carefully.

■ **Go your own way** Don't limit yourself to the planned excursions from the ship. Contact the tourist bureaux of the ports you'll be visiting beforehand and see what they can offer you. Doing your own land tour can be more fun, better tailored to your interests, and a lot cheaper. Just be sure to get back on time so the ship doesn't leave without you.

■ **Room without a view** Inside cabins are just as spacious as outside ones and generally cost about 60% less. The only thing you'll miss is the view from your room, but if you plan to be out and about most of the cruise, this shouldn't be a problem. Spend the money you'll save on the cabin on treats such as beauty treatments and extra excursions.

RESOURCES

DIRECT LINES
After checking the bargain travel sites, it might save you money to check each cruise line directly. Even if the sites don't book travel, you can get a better idea of the ships and the amenities they offer before you buy.
Royal Caribbean
www.royalcaribbean.com
0845 165 8414 ✉
P&O
www.pocruises.com
0845 678 0014 ✉
Fred Olsen
www.fredolsencruises.com
01473 746175 ✉
Cunard
www.cunard.co.uk
0845 678 0013 ✉
Norwegian Cruise Line
www.uk.ncl.com
0845 658 8010 ✉

Freighters – low costs on the high seas

Alternative cruise If you are adventurous, look into taking a cruise by freighter. On average these cost £70 a day for each person, plus any dues and taxes. Voyages normally take 40–120 days, although segmented trips are available so it is possible to take a 14–day cruise.
Select company Freighters generally carry no more than 12 passengers, but they don't usually allow children under 13 or seniors over a certain age.
Level of comfort There are fewer amenities than a luxury cruise ship but you may find a small pool, a library, a lounge and deck chairs. Life on board is more casual; there are no formal dinners, casinos or organised activities.
Varied routes Freighters have an itinerary, but they are subject to change depending on the cargo. The trips are generally longer and they visit more unusual ports of call than a normal cruise ship.
British departures Travelling on a freighter costs half as much as on a regular cruise ship. The fee covers everything onboard except alcohol. If you want to look into freighter cruises that start from British ports, contact:
Andrew Weir Shipping
020 7575 6480
www.aws.co.uk ✉ or
The Cruise People Ltd
(click on 'Freighters')
020 7723 2450
www.cruisepeople.co.uk ✉.

SMART MOVES

SPENDING POWER

Invest some time and effort before your trip looking for the best travel money deal – you could end up with 10% more to spend and also greater security.

CURRENCY CREDITS

The best deal on foreign currency depends on when and where you are going on holiday. However, there are cheaper options and commission-free currency available.

Post Office pluses The Post Office charges no commission or handling fees on foreign currency orders. They even offer free home delivery on orders over £500. Order at a branch, **www.postoffice.co.uk** or call 08458 500 900 ✉.

Travel agents Larger groups like First Choice and Thomas Cook offer commission-free currency and travellers cheques.

Free for all Lloyds TSB offers commission-free foreign currency to customers and non-customers. Marks & Spencer offers commission-free travel money at its in-store Bureau de Change (find a list of bureaux at **www6.marksandspencer.com**), or over the phone or online to cardholders. Retail foreign exchange specialist Travelex allows you to collect your money at the airport, offers 0% commission and promises not to be beaten on price at **www.travelex.co.uk** ✉.

TOP TIPS GET THE BEST RATES

■ **Taking local currency** Some countries, such as India, will not let you take currency in or out or the country. However, if possible take some currency with you in case there is no ATM ('cash' machine) nearby on arrival. It could cost almost 10% more to exchange at the airport. If you are in a rush, order currency online and collect it at the airport.

■ **Shop around for the best deal** To compare charges made by banks and other travel money providers, go to the Travel section at **www.moneysupermarket.com** or look at **www.moneyfacts.co.uk** and select the Provider Surveys link.

■ **Check the offer** If you are offered an exchange with no commission, check the rate isn't really poor. If the deal includes commission-free buy-back of any surplus when you return, keep all receipts. It may be convenient to change money at your hotel, but the exchange rates tend to be poor.

■ **Cash and carry** If you have a debit card with the Cirrus or Maestro logos, you should be able to use it in ATMs internationally. Find an ATM near your destination at **www.mastercard.com** ✉. If your bank has a branch nearby – or alliance with a local bank – you may be able to withdraw cash without charge. If not, you could be hit with the bank's exchange rate, a foreign exchange fee and an ATM fee of £2-£3 per withdrawal.

■ **Take traveller's cheques** Travel insurance only covers cash up to £200-£500, so traveller's cheques are a safer way to take money abroad. Sign them and make a note of the numbers, and they will usually be replaced by the provider within 24 hours if lost or stolen. Lloyds TSB, Nationwide and Tesco, among others, don't charge commission or handling charges for Sterling traveller's cheques.

ASK YOURSELF

AM I GETTING THE BEST RATES?

■ Always check current exchange rates in a newspaper or on the Internet before buying foreign currency.

■ Look for a provider offering commission-free currency at a competitive exchange rate; a commission-free deal can be poor value if the rate is unfavourable.

USING YOUR PLASTIC CAN BE DRASTIC

British holidaymakers paid credit and debit card issuers £686m in fees and other charges to use their cards abroad during their summer holidays in 2008, according to comparison and switching service uSwitch.com. Make sure you are not paying over the odds for card convenience.

Credit card charges In January 2009, price comparison site Moneysupermarket.com (**www.moneysupermarket.com** ✉) was showing credit card rates of up to 2.99% charged on overseas transactions – almost £30 extra if you spend £1,000 on plastic while overseas. One advantage of using a credit card is that purchases are covered by the Consumer Credit Act, so if anything is faulty when you get it home the cost can be recovered.

Rare exceptions The best-value credit cards shown on the site were the Nationwide Building Society Gold, Post Office Platinum and Thomas Cook Credit Card, which have no foreign usage loading; Saga Platinum charges nothing in EU countries and 1% for the rest of the world.

ATM extras Many banks and building societies also charge customers extra for using their debit cards to withdraw cash while overseas. You could find yourself paying the bank's exchange rate, a foreign exchange fee and an ATM fee. If you must withdraw cash this way, take out larger amounts to reduce the impact of withdrawal fees.

Beware of conversion rates If you use your credit or debit card abroad, some merchants will offer to convert your bill into your home currency for you. This is a process known as 'dynamic currency conversion'. While this allows you to see the exact price in Sterling, you will be charged a higher exchange rate for the service as the merchant will benefit from foreign exchange commissions. Check your bill, and if it appears in Sterling ask to be charged in the local currency.

A NEW CARD FOR TRAVELLERS

A pre-paid foreign exchange card is a new way of paying for your holiday purchases in eurozone countries or the USA. These cards act as a pay-as-you-go debit card, and you can load money onto the card online, over the phone or by SMS.

The advantages Because the cards cut out the middle man – such as a currency bureau – they can offer good rates on euros and dollars. As they can be cancelled like any bank card, they offer greater safety than if you were carrying cash. Also, there is no debt risk as you can control how much you spend while you are away. However, as the concept is relatively new, watch out for application fees, ATM withdrawal fees and charges for top-ups.

Take a card Moneysupermarket.com listed 67 prepaid cards in January 2009. Of these, the FairFX currency card came out best (**www.fairfx.com** ✉). There was no application fee, no fees on purchases and an ATM fee of £1.12 (dollars) or £1.25 (euros) per withdrawal. FairFX claims its currency cards will save consumers up to 10% on travel currency and 5% on the cost of using their UK debit/credit cards. On 26 January 2009, it was offering US$1.36 to the pound, compared with 1.3043 at Lloyds, 1.3043 at M&S, 1.3117 at the Post Office and 1.2672 at Travelex (airport).

CONFIDENCE TRICKS

Scams, thefts and rip-offs often take place in urban areas in less-developed countries. Most happen in the first day or so (you may think you blend in but you probably don't), and the majority are opportunist. This means you can avoid them.

■ Be wary of anyone who approaches you, particularly around popular tourist sites.

■ Always agree a price for taxis (if there is no meter) and tour guides in advance.

■ Watch out for porters who take you to unofficial taxis that overcharge you. Don't use unlicensed cabs in any city.

■ Take care of your bags and money especially in crowded areas and when you are distracted, for example when trying to find your way around on a strange metro. Take your time and zip up bags and pockets.

MOBILE RATES

Before you travel, find out your network provider's rates for making and receiving calls abroad. Orange (**www.orange.co.uk** 07973 100 150/450 ✉) offers their clients this information free. Text 'FROM' followed by the country you are visiting – for example, 'FROM FRANCE' – to 159, and you will receive a text detailing the costs of using your Orange phone in that country. However, your network provider's partner networks in that country may not charge the same rates. Mobile phones connect with the strongest signal, so you may end up paying the fee from any of these foreign networks. You can't dictate which network you connect with, but check the rates with your network provider before you travel so you know how much it is costing to make calls.

SAVING ON HOLIDAY ESSENTIALS

Even before we leave the country, we will spend over £250 preparing for our summer break, according to research by travel insurer Churchill in 2006. But it is simple to reduce the cost of holiday expenditure on basic items.

Special offers Stock up on sun protection in October when prices are cheaper, but bear in mind that its effectiveness diminishes after a year. Alternatively, look out for buy-one-get-one-free promotions in major chemists or supermarkets.

Holiday photos Digital cameras tend to be easier and cheaper. There is no worry about carrying or buying films, you only need print your best pictures, and processing tends to be cheaper. Bonusprint charges £4.99 to process up to 40 postcard-size prints, or 10p each for digital images (this drops to 5p a print if you order over 200).

DINNERS FOR PEANUTS

A memorable meal can be a highlight of any holiday. But avoid situations that will leave a nasty taste in your mouth.

Don't act the tourist Always be wary of special tourist menus. They might be cheap, but dishes are often inferior. Pick the restaurant that is full of local office or manual workers and have the dish of the day or set menu, which will be the best value. A la carte eating is the most costly.

Eat early Many countries lunch at noon, and the specials are the first things to run out. Lunch is usually better value for money than dinner, especially in France where lunch is the main meal of the day.

All-inclusive? Check whether taxes and service are included in the bill. It is easier to ask about local practices at your hotel beforehand than to wait until the bill comes.

Leaving a tip What to tip for and how much varies greatly from country to country. Ask locally so you neither insult your waiter nor tip unnecessarily. For a guide to tipping, go to Which? Advice at: **http://www.which.co.uk/advice/how-much-to-tip-abroad/index.jsp** ✉.

TOP TIPS CHEAPER MOBILE CALLS

A European regulation introduced in 2007 has significantly reduced the cost of calling home when we are on holiday – including a new 'Eurotariff'. But 'international roaming' remains expensive for many callers, costing from 20p to £2 a minute. Before travelling, check with your mobile provider that your phone has been enabled to use abroad, and what the tariffs are. Also look at the international packages – and other options – available.

■ **The Eurotariff** Introduced in June 2007, it sets a maximum charge that operators can charge for voice calls from EU countries – around 38p per minute for making a call and 19p to receive one. However, search around as special offers from some providers will work out cheaper still. In January 2009, 3 Mobile was charging 25p a minute to make calls from an EU country and 10p to receive them (**www.three.co.uk** or 0800 358 6946 ✉).

■ **Cheaper roaming** Calls and texts can cost much more when you are away, especially if you have a prepay service (and you will also have to pay to receive calls and access voicemail, too). Consider switching to a monthly contract if you travel regularly, as lower rates will offset the rental cost.

■ **Find the best plan** Use a price comparison site such as www.moneysupermarket.com ✉ to see how the networks' international roaming charges compare. 3 Mobile has topped the list consistently in many countries, including France, Spain and Australia. Ask your provider if they offer special products, such as flat fees or bolt-ons.

■ **Get texting** To send a message costs around 50p – and it's free to receive them.

■ **SIM-ple savings** If you are away for a while and outside the Eurotariff zone, consider buying a local SIM card. This will enable you to receive free texts and calls, and you can make calls on a pay-as-you-go basis. If you are visiting more than one country, a global SIM card – which enables you to roam from network to network around the world – has the potential to save you a fortune (see table below).

■ **With a Rebtel yell** For anyone making frequent calls abroad on a mobile, Swedish company Rebtel has developed a system that uses the Internet to connect local calls around the world, thereby cutting out the expensive international element. Find out more at **www.rebtel.com** ✉.

■ **Skype's the limit** If you are taking your laptop, use Skype or VoIP (Voice over Internet Protocol) to make free calls (**www.skype.com** ✉). If not, use an Internet café.

■ **Global phone cards** Don't forget the old phonebox! Using a holiday phonecard could prove cheaper than an international payphone or mobile. Some Post Office Holiday Phonecard rates are given below (**www.postoffice.co.uk** ✉).

CUT ONLINE COSTS

■ Internet costs in hotels can be extortionate. Ask at reception for the nearest Internet café, or check online before you go at **www.cybercafes.com** ✉. Café rates are cheaper, and you know what you are spending.
■ Many public libraries have free Internet access.

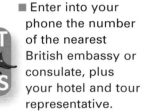

Numbers to note
■ Enter into your phone the number of the nearest British embassy or consulate, plus your hotel and tour representative.
■ Make a note of your phone and serial number and report it immediately if it is lost or stolen.

CUT THE COST OF CALLING HOME

There are big differences in the cost of calling Britain from abroad, depending on whether you use a mobile – and how you use it – a landline or a public payphone. This table compares the two best mobile deals listed by Moneysupermarket.com in January 2009 and a Post Office comparison of phonecard and pay phone prices.

	MOBILE: UK PAY-AS-YOU-GO + PAY MONTHLY		MOBILE: USING LOCAL/GLOBAL SIM CARD				LANDLINE: POST OFFICE PHONE CARD	PAY PHONE
	INCOMING CALLS	OUTGOING CALLS	COST OF PACKAGE	FREE CREDIT	COST OF INCOMING CALLS	COST OF OUTGOING CALLS		
FRANCE	p/m £0.10 p/go £0.10	£0.25 £0.25	L £29.99 G £30	£5 £25	£0.00 £0.00	£0.30 £0.16	13.5p	23.5p
GERMANY	p/m £0.10 p/go £0.10	£0.25 £0.25	L £4.99 G £30	£7.12 £25	£0.00 £0.00	£0.30 £0.18	13.5p	38.5p
AUSTRALIA	p/m £0.00 p/go £0.70	£0.20 £0.75	L £29.99 G £30	£14.44 £25	£0.00 £0.00	£0.17 £0.19	23.5p	23.5p
USA	p/m £0.55 p/go £0.55	£0.55 £0.55	L £19.99 G £15.99	£0.00 £10	£0.18 £0.89	£0.18 £1.19	13.5p	not available

The cost of incoming and outgoing calls is for 1 minute.
p/m = pay monthly; p/g = pay as you go; L - local; G = global

BUY ONLY THE INSURANCE YOU NEED

Holidaymakers spend £1.3 billion more than they need to on travel insurance each year, according to Alliance & Leicester. While we spend time researching the best holiday deal, we don't do the same for travel insurance.

SAVE ON YOUR TRAVEL AGENT'S DEAL

About 60% of us take the easy option and book our travel insurance along with our holiday. However, the insurance sold through travel agents helps boost their profits and could cost you five times more than buying it separately.

TOP TIPS KEEP PREMIUMS DOWN

■ **Free insurance** Some bank accounts or platinum cards offer free travel insurance, however cover levels are often poor and you may have to pay both the deposit and the full holiday cost on the card to qualify.

■ **Home insurance** Your baggage and more expensive personal items, such as cameras and jewellery, may already be covered on your home insurance policy. Check before taking out extra cover.

■ **Multi-trip policies** If you go away more than twice a year, including weekend breaks, you will save money with an annual policy. A European budget policy for a single adult costs from £6.26 for a week at **www.travelinsurance.co.uk** ✉ or £20 for an annual multi-trip policy. You would only need to take four breaks in Britain or Europe to be ahead.

■ **Combined policies** Combining policies for couples or families usually works out cheaper. An annual family European policy costs £42.99 at **www.travelinsuranceweb.com** ✉. At **www.travelinsurance.co.uk** ✉, three children get free cover for every parent covered, so an annual basic family policy for Europe would cost £36 (2 x £18 adult policies).

■ **Buy online** Save 10% or more of the cost of the policy by buying online rather than over the phone.

MAKE SURE YOU CAN CLAIM

Always check the small print of your policy and take a copy with you so you can inform your insurer immediately of any claim you need to make.

Reporting a crime It is vital to make sure you meet the criteria for reporting a crime. Most companies stipulate that the police must be notified within 24 hours of any incident and will expect an official report to validate your claim.

Access to EU healthcare The European Health Insurance Card (EHIC) gives you access to state-provided medical treatment in the country you are visiting. However, it should not be seen as an alternative to travel insurance and you may still need to contribute towards the cost of your care. For information on healthcare abroad look on the NHS Choices website at **www.nhs.uk** ✉. Apply for an EHIC online at **www.ehic.org.uk** ✉ or call 0845 606 2030, or pick up an application pack at your local Post Office.

PENSIONERS CAN SAVE POUNDS

Insurance premiums can double at the age of 65 – some companies increase the premiums at 50 – particularly with annual policies. Fortunately, a number of specialist insurance companies offer cover for older travellers. Check what is available at a comparison site such as **www.travelinsuranceguide. org.uk** ✉, which recommends policies with Bupa, SAGA, Age Concern and Free Spirit for travellers aged over 65.

COMPARE HOLIDAY INSURANCE POLICIES AND SAVE

Don't just compare the cost of the policies, consider details of the relative cover. Look for a policy that provides for medical treatment of at least £1 million in Europe and £2 million farther afield, and £1 million personal liability. You'll need extra cover if skiing or doing extreme sports.

■ Check for any exclusions.
■ Check the company is FSA authorised.
■ Check that you are covered for winter or extreme sports – many policies exclude them unless you pay extra.
■ Make sure you have notified the company of any pre-existing medical conditions.

Multi-trip for one adult (12 months worldwide)

INSURER	COST*	MEDICAL EXPENSES	PERSONAL LIABILITY	BAGGAGE	CANCEL-LATION	EXCESS
TOPDOG	£14.30	£10 million	£2 million	£1,000	£750	£200
INSUREME4	£16.43	£10 million	£2 million	£200	£5,000	£65
DIRECT TRAVEL	£16.70	£10 million	£2 million	£2,000	£5,000	£50–£100
LEADING EDGE	£27/£41	£5 million	£2 million	£1,500	£1,500	£150
AA TRAVEL INSURANCE	£39.63/£52.17	£10 million	£2 million	£1,500	£5,000	£60
YOUR M&S	£44.15/£59.60	£10 million	£2 million	£2,500	£6,000	£50

Single trip for one adult (7 days worldwide)

INSURER	COST*	MEDICAL EXPENSES	PERSONAL LIABILITY	BAGGAGE	CANCEL-LATION	EXCESS
INSURE WITHEASE	£9.83	£5 million	£2 million	£200	£3,000	£150–£250
FLEXICOVER DIRECT	£11.50/£23.50	£10 million	£2 million	£1,000	£1,000	£150
TRAVEL INSURANCE WEB	£12.85/£25.70	£10 million	£2 million	£2,500	£5,000	£60–£200
DIRECT TRAVEL	£16	£10 million	£2 million	£2,000	£5,000	£50–£100
LEADING EDGE	£23	£5 million	£2 million	£1,500	£1,500	£150
AA TRAVEL INSURANCE	£25.38/£38.46	£10 million	£2 million	£1,500	£5,000	£60

Costs show normal rate followed by rate including winter sports. Where a company offers two or more policies, the cheapest is shown. On multi-trip policies, maximum trip length is 31 days

Prices listed by Moneysupermarket.com, correct at time of publication

Homes and gardens

Creating a comfortable, efficiently run home need not be an expensive business. Find out where to buy bargain furniture and appliances on a shoestring, and how to keep your home and garden fresh and welcoming.

FURNITURE BARGAINS

When you are buying furniture, don't just head to your nearest department store – investigate other options and outlets. If you know where, when and how to shop, you can save money on good-quality furniture that will last for years.

TOP TIPS PLACES TO BUY A BARGAIN

There are plenty of outlets where you can save money on buying furniture, whether new or secondhand.

■ **Department and furniture store sales** With astounding price cuts to be found in the sales, find out what is on offer before deciding what to buy. If you have the nerve to hang on, there are often further reductions to be had. In January 2009, Furniture Village was offering a Loft dining table and four chairs for £995 (reduced from £1,995) and interest-free credit. At the end of the month, the set had fallen to £795. Many stores tend to offer clearance bargains throughout the year now, so keep checking at the store or online.

■ **Buy online** Online stores are cheaper than showrooms because their overheads are far lower. Always ask a retailer if they have a website, as prices might be less than in the store.

■ **Bid at auctions** These can be the source of great bargains resulting from house clearances. Look at the catalogue, inspect items you're interested in and register with the auction house. Set a budget and keep to it when you are bidding. Remember there's usually a premium of 15% plus VAT to pay on top of the purchase price.

■ **Online auctions** Bidding online gives you access to a vast array of products at knock-down prices. You are free to browse but will need to register before buying. Compare the price of the item you want to buy with its retail price so you know how much you are saving. Pay by credit card for added security. When we looked, City Furniture Auction at **www.cityfurnitureauction.co.uk** or 01733 208111 ✉ – which sells a huge range of refurbished hotel furniture – was offering Queen Anne mahogany double bedroom sets – including headboard (but no bed), mirror, cabinets, dressing table and more – with a starting bid of £475.

■ **First orders and vouchers** Some mail-order and online retailers give generous discounts on first orders to attract new customers. Check sites such as **www.voucherheaven.com** ✉, which offers voucher codes and discount vouchers for more than 850 retailers. At **www.freeukoffers.com** ✉ you can get 15% off your first order with Littlewoods catalogue.

■ **Buy ex-showhome** Consider buying furniture previously used on display in a showhome (see Resources, right). Prices depend on an item's condition, but you'll usually pay between a quarter and a half of the retail price.

■ **Check ex-display items** Some stores sell ex-display pieces at half price or less, so it's worth asking if there are any on sale. You might be able to get further reductions if they have suffered minor damage you can repair at home.

■ **Factory shops** These sell surplus stock cheaply, including cancelled orders, returns, last season's stock and ends of ranges. Contact a manufacturer or store to see if they have a

RESOURCES

WEBSITES FOR FURNITURE BARGAINS
■ Good-value at **www.argos.co.uk** ✉.
■ Find beds and mattresses at low prices at **www.bedsdirect.com** ✉.
■ Check the biggest online auction house at **www.ebay.co.uk** ✉.
■ Another auction site is **www.ebid.co.uk** ✉.
■ Discounted furniture at **www.furniture123.co.uk** ✉.
■ Brand names such as Jay-Be at **www.furniture busters.com** ✉.

FACTORY OUTLETS
Surplus sale stock, returns and seconds can save you a fortune. Search at these outlets:
■ The John Lewis Swindon Home Outlet **www.johnlewis.com** or 01793 512454 ✉.
■ M&S – 29 outlet stores **www.marksandspencer.com** or 0845 302 1234 ✉.
■ Furniture Village – the FV Outlet is incorporated into certain stores **www.furniturevillage.co.uk** or 0845 0850 480 ✉.
■ Ercol **www.ercol.com** or 01844 271800 ✉.
■ Multiyork – up to 60% off at clearance centres **www.multiyork.co.uk** or 01842 764761 ✉.

EX-SHOWHOME STOCK
Good condition items previously used in a show home at:
■ The Showhome Warehouse **www.showhomewarehouse. co.uk** or 01933 411695 ✉.

factory outlet, but be prepared to travel because most companies only have one. Larger items are discounted the most, so if you are after a sofa, bed or dining table, a long journey may well be worth your while. The Ercol Factory Outlet in Princes Risborough, Buckinghamshire (**www.ercol.com** or 01844 271800 ✉) offers ex-display items, returns and seconds at substantial discounts. For example, a Tortona 5ft bed with a rrp of £1,195 for just £395.

■ **Second-hand sites** A report by Hitwise in October 2008 showed a 22% increase in searches for second hand items over the year, with some sites experiencing a more than 50% increase in traffic. At Preloved there's a wide range of items, including furniture, plus plenty of information and advice. It is free to join at **www.preloved.co.uk** ✉.

■ **Junk and charity shops** Visit shops in affluent areas that are likely to have better-quality furniture. Best buys are items such as large wardrobes or tables that won't fit the average room. Stripping and revarnishing or repainting a useful item could be a good-value option.

■ **Investigate skips** Not for the faint-hearted, but can pay dividends in terms of furniture finds.

■ **Newspaper ads** There are bargains to be had but it pays to do some research. Check what the item costs new and examine it for damage, as you are unlikely to have any recourse if it breaks or won't fit in your room. Include the cost of cleaning in your calculations.

■ **The Freecycle Network** Join one of the 4,670 groups around the globe and exchange your unwanted items for free. Use the 'Find a group near you' facility at **www.freecycle.org** ✉, and get swapping.

■ **Haggle for a lower price** Ask retailers for a discount if you pay cash or buy several items together. They are most likely to agree to this if you're buying items they're keen to shift, such as discontinued lines or end-of-season stock.

WATCH POINTS BUYING FURNITURE

■ **Practicalities** Measure your doors and hall before buying a large piece of furniture. It won't be a bargain if you have to remove windows to get it in.

■ **Hidden extras** Check whether or not delivery is included in the price. Some companies dispatch free but others – particularly stores – charge as much as £50 for large items. If delivery is included in the price, it is worth asking if they will knock something off if you pick it up yourself.

■ **Unwanted goods** Find out if you can return online and mail-order buys without incurring a delivery charge.

INVEST IN THE RIGHT BED

A bed needs to be comfortable and supportive so you get a good night's sleep. The most expensive bed might not be best for you – but spend as much as you can on a good mattress.

Buy just the mattress Even if your mattress needs replacing, your bed base might still be in good condition so you'll save the expense of a whole new bed. There's good advice on buying the right mattress at **www.johnlewis.com** ✉.

Longer-lasting sprung mattresses The more springs a mattress has, the firmer and longer-lasting it will be.

FLATPACKED – NIGHTMARE OR DREAM?

Flatpacked pieces are cheaper than ready-assembled – and easier to get home. But make sure you get value for money by checking the quality and avoiding problems with assembly. Follow these tips to ensure your furniture lasts a long time.

■ Examine the made-up samples in-store for potential problems, such as flimsy drawers.

■ Read the instructions carefully before you start and check you have all the pieces before you leave the store.

■ Make sure that there is a contact for replacement parts.

■ Paint or varnish untreated wood or MDF after assembly to give a smooth surface that is easy to clean.

Pocket-sprung mattresses – where the springs are housed inside individual pockets – are better quality and will last longer than those with open or continuous coil springs.

Don't buy a secondhand mattress However cheap a secondhand mattress is, it will be a false economy as it will have moulded to the shape of the previous owner and won't support you properly. But there's no need to throw out an older, good-quality mattress that has become soft – slip a thin sheet of plywood (around £34 for a double-sized piece from a timber yard or DIY store) underneath for extra support and it will last for another couple of years.

Incorporate storage Divans often have storage drawers underneath, which is often a cheaper option than buying a separate chest of drawers.

VERSATILE SOFABEDS

A sofabed rather than a spare bed is a good compromise if space is tight. Consider how often it is likely to be used.

Buy cheaper for occasional use Less expensive models, from under £500, have a metal mesh base and thin foam mattress and are fine for occasional use. For regular use spend around £700 on a bed with a slatted base and sprung mattress, which is more comfortable and will last longer.

A SOFA TO MEET YOUR NEEDS

Although an expensive sofa will give you years of service (see chart below), you may prefer to opt for a cheaper model so you can buy a new one as fashions move on or your circumstances change.

Smaller means cheaper When considering sofa size, think about how many people are going to sit on it. If it will rarely be more than two, why pay more for a three-seater?

Choose loose covers If you're worried about the sofa showing the dirt, go for loose covers with built-in fabric protection. Machine-washable covers are cheaper to clean than those that are dry-clean only.

> **keep it simple**
>
> **GET VALUE FROM YOUR MATTRESS**
> To prolong the life of your mattress and get better value from it, turn it over and then around lengthways every couple of months. Stick a piece of masking tape on the mattress with the date it was last turned in order to keep track of when the mattress needs turning again.

ARE YOU GETTING VALUE FOR MONEY?

You can pay anything from £200 to over £2,000 for a sofa, so it's important to ensure you are getting value for money. Always ask how the sofa is constructed, because these are the parts you can't see, and go for the best your budget allows. Better-quality, more expensive sofas are built to last and often carry a ten-year guarantee. Bearing this in mind, a £1,000 sofa might not cost much more per year than a £200 one in the long run.

COST OVER TIME	SOFA CONSTRUCTION
£200 SOFA = c.£55 PER YEAR	**£200–£350**: Softwood frame with elasticated webbing and foam padding; foam-filled cushions. Lasts about 5 years.
£500 SOFA = c.£80 PER YEAR	**£500–£800**: Hardwood frame with fibre padding and zigzag springs; feather and fibre or foam cushions. Lasts about 8 years.
£1,000 SOFA = c.£50 PER YEAR	**Over £800**: Hardwood frame with glued, screwed and dowelled joints; coil-sprung seats; horsehair or Dacron padding; feather/down or feather/fibre cushions. Lasts about 20 years.

REVAMP WICKERWORK

You can often pick up wicker pieces for next to nothing, and they look just as good in a bedroom as on the patio or in a conservatory. You'll pay less if the seats are saggy – to tighten them, turn the chairs upside down, wet the underside with a damp sponge and leave for 24 hours to dry and shrink. Give the wickerwork a new-look colour change by spraying with acrylic paint.

FIRM UP A SAGGY SOFA

Make an old sofa more comfy by fitting a piece of plywood beneath cushions for under £10. Or replace foam in cushions – pay about £60 for new foam cut to fit four cushions.

CREATE A HEADBOARD FOR A BED

Give a plain divan bed an instant headboard with a length of fabric, a throw or a lightweight rug hung from wooden dowelling or a broom handle fixed to the wall behind the bed.

REPLACE WARDROBE PANELS

If wardrobe door panels are marked or broken, take them out and use a staple gun (a good investment at around £10) to staple lengths of gathered fabric in their place.

PREVENT TABLE LEGS FROM WOBBLING

Tables usually wobble because one leg is shorter than the others. Lengthen the leg by cutting a piece of cork to the right size and gluing it on with wood adhesive. This is a lot easier than shortening the other legs.

SCRATCHES ON WOOD

Rub small scratches with half a walnut kernel to restore the colour. Repair deeper scratches by rubbing with a wax crayon of the same colour until the crack is filled. Then cover a small piece of wood with a soft rag and rub across the filled scratch to remove surface wax. Buff with a soft cloth and the scratch should be almost invisible. Make white rings fade by rubbing them with toothpaste.

EASY COVER-UPS

Reupholstering a sofa is expensive – around half the price of a new sofa. The easiest and least expensive way to disguise worn-out seating is to drape an attractive bedspread, throw or blanket over it. If you need to buy fabric, the cheapest option is cotton calico that can then be dyed to match your decor. This costs about £2 a metre from a fabric shop. For a more fitted look, use a staple gun to fix fabric to the underside of the sofa to stop it slipping off.

STRENGTHEN FLIMSY SHELVES

Screw battens under the back edges of shelves for extra support to prevent bowing.

TURN PACKAGING INTO FURNITURE

Throw an attractive piece of fabric over a sturdy cardboard box or a plastic or wooden crate for an instant, no-cost coffee table.

DEALING WITH STICKING DRAWERS

If drawers are not sliding in and out smoothly, rub the runners with a candle, a bar of soap or petroleum jelly. If they still stick, rub gently with fine-grade glasspaper or an emery board and re-apply the wax or soap.

STRENGTHEN A CHEST OF DRAWERS

Take out flimsy hardboard drawer bases and back panels, and substitute chipboard to make them more solid. A large sheet costs about £5 from Wickes – half the price of plywood. Alternatively, use wood recycled from old furniture.

INSTANT UPGRADES

With a little imagination and a coat of paint, some different fabric or a change of accessories, you can give your latest furniture bargain a fresh, more stylish look for just a few pounds. Make budget buys look better and last longer, and restore furniture bought secondhand.

USE UP LEFTOVER PAINTS

If you have any leftover paints and are decorating a child's bedroom, try painting each drawer in a chest-of-drawers a different shade, or paint wardrobe doors a contrasting colour to the frame.

TRANSFORM WOOD WITH PAINT

The finish will be far more professional if you sand first or remove old paint with paint-stripper. Streamlined tables and chairs are much easier to strip than ones with fussy mouldings. Ornate chairs may require professional stripping (from around £20), so bear this in mind when buying. Coordinate mismatched wooden kitchen and dining chairs by painting them all the same colour.

NEW HANDLES FOR OLD

Replace plastic knobs or handles on furniture with smart metal or chrome ones, from as little as £2 each.

FIND HOME ACCESSORIES FOR LESS

Soft furnishings, tableware and other accessories help create a stylish, individual home. There are plenty of outlets where you can find these items heavily discounted, so you'll never have to pay full price for anything again.

TOP TIPS WHERE TO BUY

■ **Factory shops** Look out for seconds, last season's designs, ends of lines and surplus stock, at reductions of at least 30% (see Resources, right).

■ **Warehouse sales** Some suppliers of furnishing fabrics hold clearance sales twice a year, including Designers Guild (**www.designersguild.com** 020 7893 7400 ✉) and Osborne and Little (**www.osborneandlittle.com** 020 7352 1456 ✉). Put your name on their mailing lists.

■ **Factory shopping villages** Prices might not be as low as in individual factory shops, but the advantage of shopping at one of these centres is that there are lots of stores under one roof, stocking fashions as well as homewares. Traditional sale times – January and June – are the best times to shop. Two of the biggest are Bicester Village in Oxfordshire and Cheshire Oaks Designer Outlet at Ellesmere Port on the Wirral. For more centres, see **www.shoppingvillages.com** ✉.

■ **Permanent discount stores** TK Maxx and Matalan are the two big names here and each has a wide selection of brand new bedding, towels, curtains, cushions and crockery at great prices. TK Maxx stocks brand names, whereas Matalan sells own-brand goods as well.

■ **Across the Channel** Popular French-made homeware is worth checking out if you are planning a holiday or day-trip to France. Provençal fabrics and Le Creuset pans are just two potential bargains (up to 30% cheaper than in Britain).

BUYING BARGAIN FABRICS

■ Check fabric carefully for quality when you buy at a discount. If you are buying seconds, look out for loose threads, crooked edges and other flaws. Make sure colours of separate items such as towels are a good match.

■ Many sofas and chairs come with an indication of how much fabric is needed for loose covers. If this information isn't provided, take measurements with you so you don't buy too much or too little.

■ If you particularly like a fabric and think you might find various uses for it, buy more of it than you need – you are unlikely to find it again.

CASE STUDY

NEW HOME, GREAT SAVINGS

When newlyweds Sarah and Dan Bell were furnishing their flat, they really made their budget stretch. They netted a sleek leather sofa for just £400 online at the Tesco Direct sale – half the original price. They also got plain voile curtain fabric at 75% off from Terrys Fabrics (**www.terrysfabrics.co.uk** ✉), buying extra to make a cloth to cover a dated but sturdy dining table discovered for £30 in a junk shop and renovated themselves. Crockery came from a Denby Factory Shop (**www.denby.co.uk** ✉), where plates, bowls and mugs were 25% cheaper. For all their bedding and other household linen, they saved 15% by putting in their first order with Littlewoods catalogue.

RESOURCES

FOR LISTS OF SUPPLIERS
■ www.gooddealdirectory.co.uk ✉ has details of factory shops and warehouses with home accessories at discount prices; see also www.homesources.co.uk ✉.

FABRICS
■ **Christy Mill Shop** in Hyde, Cheshire, is the factory shop for Christy towels www.christy-towels.com 08457 585252 ✉.
■ **Knickerbean** has four outlets in southern England for low-priced quality fabrics www.knickerbean.com 01284 704055 ✉.
■ **Fabric Mills** has clearance fabrics at up to 60% off www.fabricmills.co.uk 01285 643111 ✉.
■ **Sanderson** sells fabric and bed linen at up to 75% off www.sandersonfabrics.co.uk 01423 500051 ✉.
■ Suppliers of secondhand curtains, **The Curtain Exchange** has branches all over England www.thecurtainexchange.net ✉; see also The Track House in Warwickshire www.trackhouse.co.uk 01608 682004 ✉.

QUALITY TABLEWARE
■ **Dartington Crystal** has stores nationwide selling discounted glassware www.dartington.co.uk 01805 626262 ✉.
■ **Denby** has ten factory shops plus special offers sold online www.denbypottery.co.uk 01773 740700 ✉.
■ **Spode** has a factory shop for bone china in Stoke-on-Trent www.spode.co.uk 01782 572598 ✉.

■ **Fabric discount shops** These outlets can afford to charge lower prices as they are selling direct to the public with no middleman involved. Fabrics are often manufactured at the same mills as leading brands, but at a fraction of the price (see Resources, above).

■ **Supermarkets** Buy food and furnishings together in the big chains, which now have an impressive range of homewares, bedding and furnishings at competitive prices. Tesco had a 4.5 tog double duvet in its January 2009 sales for £4, while Asda Direct had double plain dye fitted sheets from £5.38 and a pair of matching pillowcases from £2.42.

■ **Secondhand curtain shops** There is a big market in secondhand curtains, with the stock often sourced from showhomes or customers who have simply changed their minds. Prices are a third to a half of what you would pay brand new (see Resources, above).

CHOOSING CHEAP CHINA AND GLASS
Almost perfect Items marked as seconds often have imperfections that are almost invisible. But still examine pieces carefully for chips and cracks before you buy.

Buy in bulk Boxed sets of china or glassware usually cost less than buying individual pieces.

Check on replacements If you are buying a matching set, check whether it is being discontinued. If so, you may still be able to get replacements through a china-matching service, though these can be expensive. If you do need spares, have a look at www.lostpottery.co.uk (0870 732 4462 ✉) or www.tablewhere.co.uk (020 8361 6111 ✉).

PAY LESS FOR CUSHIONS
■ Make your own cushion covers from recycled materials such as embroidered tablecloths, silk scarves and remnants from charity shops.
■ Restuff cushions that have gone flat, using feathers from a pillow.

BEST-BUY KITCHEN APPLIANCES

When you are shopping for domestic appliances, check all the consumer information you can find, either online or at a library. Look for efficiency ratings and repair records, and research what features are available. Make a list of the features you really need and look only at appliances that meet these requirements.

TOP TIPS WHERE TO BUY APPLIANCES

■ **Department stores** Check these out at sale times for the best bargains. Many stores such as Debenhams ✉ have preview days for account customers, and it may be worth opening an account as you will get a further discount on your first purchase. John Lewis ✉ is known for its keen pricing policy and excellent after-sales service – all major appliances have a free minimum two-year warranty.

■ **Electrical superstores** Comet ✉ and Currys (also Dixons online) ✉ are two of the biggest, and you will find even better bargains on their websites.

■ **Independent stores** Small doesn't necessarily mean more expensive, as prices need to be competitive to keep customers. Buyers and Sellers in Ladbroke Grove, London (**www.buyersandsellersonline.co.uk**, 0870 300 2578 ✉) is one of the best independent outlets and offers free delivery.

■ **Buying online** Without the overheads of running a store, online retailers can cut costs on large and small appliances. We found a Russell Hobbs metal kettle on the company's website (**www.russellhobbs.co.uk** ✉) for nearly 40% cheaper than it was at a high street store. And supermarkets such as Tesco ✉ now stock electrical goods at competitive prices.

■ **Old stock** Many manufacturers update their products annually, so you will find last year's models going cheap. Always ask in-store if you can't see any on display, as retailers are often only too pleased to shift them.

■ **'B grade'** Appliances that are ex-display, end of line or customer returns are often substantially reduced. Check the Yellow Pages for local dealers or try specialists such as **www.bgrade.co.uk** or 01452 541105 ✉.

■ **Secondhand** Only buy reconditioned appliances from a reputable retailer. Contact the manufacturer to find out where they are sold. Never buy electrical items from a newspaper small ad, as they could be dangerous.

ARE TOP BRAND NAMES VALUE FOR MONEY?

You pay a lot more for leading brand names than for own-label or lower-end products. Are they worth the extra?

Unnecessary extras The extras you get for greater outlay may be largely cosmetic or more features to choose from. If you are happy with the standard appearance and are not likely to use the extra features, cheaper models are adequate.

Money-saving technology The expensive brands are often the leaders in incorporating cutting-edge technology, which could save you money in the long run. For example, a faster

---

What's worth paying for and what's not

Before you buy a fridge or fridge freezer, think about which features will save you money in the long term – and which ones are not worth paying for.

WORTH IT

■ **Frost-free function** With this function, you won't have to worry about defrosting your freezer.

SMART MOVES

■ **Auto-defrost** Regulates the temperature to prevent frost building up and so keeps the freezer working more efficiently.

■ **Easy-clean shelves** These just require a wipe with a damp cloth, so you won't need to buy expensive cleaning products.

NOT WORTH IT

■ **Chilled water dispenser** Get into the habit of keeping empty bottles filled with tap water in the fridge.

■ **Ice dispenser** Keep ice cubes in a freezer bag so they are always on hand.

■ **Egg and bottle racks** These take up too much room; better to organise the space yourself.

IT PAYS TO SHOP AROUND

APPLIANCE	RRP	CHAIN STORE PRICE	INTERNET PRICE	
Vacuum cleaner	£274	£274	£220	You can make big savings by shopping around for kitchen appliances. The chart shows how you can save over 30% on the RRP (Recommended Retail Price) of well-known brand names by buying at an electrical chain store or Internet shop.
Fridge freezer	£350	£323	£263	
Dishwasher	£299	£306	£270	
Cooker (gas)	£265	£297	£210	
Cooker (electric)	£230	£219	£157	
Washing machine	£370	£367	£299	
Tumble dryer	£415	£350	£320	
Washer dryer	£455	£300	£275	

Delivery charges not included. Information correct at the time of publication

spin speed in a washing machine will leave clothes drier and reduce the electricity needed for tumble drying.

Greater reliability It is worth paying more for reliability. The independent advice offered at **www.uknetguide.co.uk**, for example, lists Neff and Bosch as the most dependable makes of dishwasher. If you have a number of items to buy, it might be worth subscribing to *Which? Advice* ✉ so you can read their reviews; it costs £1 for a trial month and £8.50 a month thereafter. A more reliable product will last longer and save on repair bills, so is a better buy over the long term.

ARE EXTENDED WARRANTIES WORTH IT?

Decline an extended warranty when buying your appliance.
Some retailers charge up to half the cost price for a five-year warranty which is likely to go unused.

Pay for repairs You will be better off paying for repairs as and when needed – and remember that most appliances come with at least one year's warranty, or more if you buy from John Lewis or pay with certain credit cards.

Multi-appliance warranty If you do want the security of a warranty, a multi-appliance one covering several products is better value – the company Warranty Direct ✉ offers breakdown cover on up to three appliances for £10.75 a month.

TOP TIPS BUYING APPLIANCES FOR LESS

■ **Opt for freestanding appliances** These are cheaper than built-in or integrated appliances and you will be able to take them with you if you move.

■ **Smaller size, not price** Most appliances are a standard 60cm (24in) wide, but many ranges have slimline models designed to fit into tight spaces. A smaller size doesn't mean a lower price – they cost as much as full-sized models.

■ **Go for white** A white finish often costs less than chrome or stainless steel, and is easier to keep clean.

■ **Choose two-in-one** Appliances with combined functions, such as a washer-dryer or fridge-freezer, cost less than buying each separately and take up less room in the kitchen.

TOP TIPS FRIDGES AND FREEZERS

The choice of cooling products has never been greater nor has the range of prices. You can pay under £150 for a basic larder fridge up into the thousands for an all-singing, all-dancing American-style fridge freezer. So how can you find the right type of fridge and freezer for your needs without breaking the bank?

■ **Think vertical** A vertical fridge freezer costs less than two separate appliances placed side by side and will make full use of space in a confined area.

■ **How much capacity do you need?** A fridge freezer with a total capacity of about 277 litres (9.8cu ft) is adequate for most families, so there is no point in buying extra space that you won't use.

■ **Freezer on top** Models with the freezer at the top usually cost less than those with the fridge at the top, but are less convenient as you have to bend down to open the fridge.

■ **Economical chest freezer** If you buy frozen food in bulk or freeze your own garden produce, think about investing in a separate chest freezer with a lidded top, which can be stored in the garage. With prices starting from around £120, these cost less and are cheaper to run than upright models.

■ **Buy to suit how you eat** Look at how the fridge and freezer areas are split and buy a model that reflects how you shop. If you eat mostly frozen foods, you will need a larger freezer and smaller fridge, whereas if you are a fan of fresh produce, go for a larger fridge area.

FREEZER CARE

If you look after your freezer, it will not only last longer but also cost less to run.

Keep the freezer full Freezers are more efficient when full, so fill in the gaps with tightly packed newspaper.

Defrost the freezer If your freezer is not frost-free, defrost it once the frost is 6mm (¼ in) thick. The thicker the frost, the harder the freezer has to work and the less efficient it will be. Never scrape the frost away with metal utensils, as you could damage the surface.

DISHWASHER DECISIONS

Unlike most other kitchen appliances, a dishwasher is not regarded as a necessity. But there are benefits in investing in one and they save time standing at the kitchen sink.

DELIVERY AND INSTALLATION

■ Check delivery charges and ask whether the appliance can be installed on delivery. Can the old one be taken away at the same time, and is there a cost for this?

■ By law, gas appliances must be installed by a registered CORGI engineer.

■ You will need to contact your local authority regarding disposal of a fridge, but this is normally free.

ENERGY EFFICIENT

Fridges, dishwashers and washing machines are graded according to their energy efficiency. Buy appliances with an A rating for lower running costs. A fridge-freezer approaching its 10th birthday could be using 50% more energy than a new top-rated model.

What is the best size? Consider how many place settings you need room for. Most standard-sized models take 12 settings – around 76 pieces of crockery and 64 items of cutlery. If you have a large family, a model that takes 14 settings might be more suitable, so you don't have to run the machine so often.

Hygiene and economy Dishwashers are more hygienic and economical than washing by hand. They use half the amount of water and less than 10p of electricity per wash. The best machines have an AAA grade for cleaning, energy efficiency and drying performance.

Keeping the noise down If your kitchen is close to your living area, you will need to check the noise level on cheaper models – more expensive machines have better insulation.

Check the features Choose a machine with programmes and features that suit you, so that you don't pay out for features you don't use.

keep it simple

COOKER CARE
Keep hobs clean, as food won't be cooked efficiently if the area of contact with the pan is reduced by a coating of dirt. Wipe off spills while the hob and oven are still warm to save on elbow grease and detergent.

WATCH POINTS CUT THE COST OF RUNNING A DISHWASHER

Make savings on energy bills by using the most economical cycles to suit your purposes. Operate the dishwasher only when full for maximum energy savings.

■ **Quick wash** Use this cycle for lightly soiled dishes and when there's no time to wait for a full cycle.

■ **Economy wash** Suitable for plates that aren't too dirty, this cycle uses less water and electricity.

■ **Don't use half load** This is a false economy. Running the dishwasher when half full only saves about 25% on energy, so wait until you have a full load.

■ **Timer delay** This function lets you set the machine to come on at a time to suit you – an excellent cost saver if your electricity charges are lower at night.

■ **Don't stint on detergent** Make sure you put detergent in every wash and top up rinse aid and salt as required. Omitting these is a false economy as the machine won't wash properly without them.

■ **Clean the filter** Keep your machine clean by scraping food off plates and removing deposits from the filter after each wash, or debris may coat the next load.

CLEVER COOKER CHOICES

You probably use the cooker more frequently than any other kitchen appliance. There is a wide selection available to choose from, and with a bit of research you will find a good-quality model that suits your needs at a reasonable price.

Freestanding is cheaper As with other appliances, a standard freestanding cooker costs less than a built-in oven and hob. Modern cookers fit in so neatly that you don't sacrifice good looks if you choose this option. Range-type cookers are increasingly popular, but cost upwards of £700.

Gas versus electric Most hobs and ovens run on electricity or gas, or are dual fuel, consisting of a gas hob with an electric oven. Electric cookers are cheaper to buy than gas, but gas cookers are more energy-efficient to run. Halogen and induction hobs are also available, but at a price – expect to pay at least £350 for them.

Fan-assisted ovens It is worth paying a little more for a fan-assisted oven as it cooks more quickly and distributes heat more evenly to prevent food from drying out.

WHAT TO LOOK FOR WHEN BUYING A WASHING MACHINE

A washing machine is a must for most households – it is convenient, efficient and costs far less than a launderette.

Don't be tempted by fancy features Most laundry loads require one of just three programmes: low temperature with a short spin; colourfast/delicates wash with a short spin; hot wash for cottons with a long spin.

Economy features But do look out for options such as half-wash and economy-wash programmes that help you use your machine more efficiently.

Check the grading Washing machines are graded from A to G for wash performance, energy efficiency and spin drying performance, with AAA-rated models the most efficient and economical. Some top-rated machines include 'Fuzzy Logic' – sensor technology that monitors conditions during the wash and makes any necessary adjustments to ensure optimum cleaning, and minimal water and energy use.

Drum capacity Choose a model with a larger drum capacity if you have to deal with big loads of washing on a regular basis. This is also useful for washing bulky items such as duvets, which you would otherwise have to take to the launderette or dry cleaners.

TEMPTED BY A TUMBLE DRYER?

Tumble dryers are expensive to run but are often a necessity in busy households, especially during winter months.

Vented or condenser dryer? Vented dryers, which release the hot air outside, are cheaper than condenser dryers but need to be positioned near a window or exterior wall. Condenser dryers can be positioned anywhere and give better results overall.

Consider a washer dryer This combines the features of both appliances, uses half the space, costs less than buying them separately and doesn't require venting. However, you can't wash and dry at the same time. The drying function is also slower and less efficient than in a separate tumble dryer.

TOP TIPS DOING YOUR LAUNDRY FOR LESS

Set yourself some rules to save water, electricity and money.

■ **Wash full loads** It is more economical to wash a full load so, if necessary, add tablecloths, dishcloths or seldom-washed items to fill the machine. Alternatively, use the half-load economy button if your machine has one.

■ **Use cold water rinses** Rinsing with cold water uses less energy than using warm water.

■ **Don't overdo the detergent** Even very dirty clothes won't wash any better with more detergent and it may leave a film on fabrics.

INVEST IN THE RIGHT VACUUM CLEANER

Buying a good-quality vacuum cleaner can save hours
of cleaning time and add years to floors and furnishings by
removing dirt and grit. Vacuum cleaner prices start at around
£50, but it's probably worth spending more to get the
performance you want. Go for as much motor power as
possible – up to 1,600 watts or so.

Bagged or bagless? A highly debatable point. Bagged
cleaners are usually cheaper than the bagless cyclone type,
but you you will need to buy replacement bags, which can
cost about £1 each. See **www.vacuumcleanerbags.co.uk** 07858
157934 ✉.

Type of flooring The main type of flooring your home has
will dictate the type of cleaner you buy. According to the
John Lewis ✉ buying guide: cylinder cleaners are best for
wooden floors; either model for loop pile carpet, but make
sure the turbo roller attachment is turned off; and, upright or
cylinder with a turbo brush attachment for cut pile carpet.

Reuse bags three or four times When using an upright
hoover with a bag, simply clip off the top, empty out the
dirt, fold the top edge over and staple it closed.

Empty the bag frequently Even a half-full bag can sap up
to 40% of a vacuum cleaner's suction power.

Save wear and tear on your cleaner Pick up hard objects
such as coins and paper clips before you vacuum.

MICROWAVE MAGIC

Microwaves can cook a meal in just a few minutes and so
are much cheaper to run than conventional ovens. A
standard microwave oven that cooks, defrosts and reheats
food costs from about £30, while one with a grill costs from
around £50. A combination microwave with a convection
hot air oven costs from £80 but is still economical to run.

How will you use it? If the microwave is just for reheating
and defrosting, it's not worth paying for extra features. The
models with a grill or fan oven could be perfect in a small
kitchen where space is at a premium.

PURCHASING SMALL APPLIANCES

The only essential small appliances are a kettle, a toaster –
unless your oven has a grill – and an iron.

Check out kettles Plastic kettles cost less than metal ones.
Go for one with a fast boiling time – the fastest boils in
around two minutes. A kettle with a concealed element is
more resistant to limescale, or put a few glass marbles in the
bottom to help prevent limescale from accumulating. Expect
to pay a minimum of £15.

Today's toasters Toasters range from basic models to ones
packed with features, so think what you'll use it for. Prolong
a toaster's life by emptying the crumb tray regularly, and
using wooden tongs rather than a knife to remove trapped
slices (with the toaster unplugged, of course). A basic four-
slice toaster can cost as little as £12.

Select a steam iron Irons range from a traditional dry
model to a high-powered steam generator. Opt for one with
a steam/spray feature, from £15. It will make stiff fabrics
easier to iron so it won't need to be switched on for as long.

RESOURCES

CHECK OUT WEBSITES
■These are some of the
best websites for cheap
kitchen appliances:
www.appliance-direct.co.uk
01332 547580 ✉
www.appliance-world.co.uk
0870 757 2424 ✉
www.comet.co.uk
08705 425 425 ✉
www.dixons.co.uk ✉
**www.buyersandsellers
online.co.uk**
0870 300 2578 ✉
■ For outstanding
customer service, visit:
www.johnlewis.com
08456 049 049 ✉
See also the Home and
Garden section within
www.amazon.co.uk ✉.
■ For spares and
ex-display plus new try
www.bgrade.co.uk 01452
541105 ✉
Bid for bargain, returned
and ex-display items
from Comet at **www.
clearance-comet.co.uk** ✉.
■ To find the best deals
use a price comparison
site such as:
www.unbeatable.co.uk ✉
**www.find-electricalgoods.
co.uk** ✉
**www.moneysupermarket.
com** ✉

CUT THE COST OF CLEANING

Furnishings, flooring and household fittings will last longer if they are cleaned on a regular basis. There's no need to spend much money on proprietary cleaning products, as you can make many of your own for a fraction of the price.

TOP TIPS PAY LESS FOR CLEANING PRODUCTS

You can slash the cost of cleaning products by using the cheap, readily available substances listed below, some of which you will no doubt have around the house already. Each has multiple uses and is effective on a wide range of different surfaces.

■ **Ammonia** Use household ammonia in solution with water on windows, glass surfaces, mirrors, ceramic tiles and cooker hobs. Caution: avoid inhaling fumes and contact with skin or clothing. Cost: under £2 for 500ml.

■ **Bicarbonate of soda** This mild alkaline powder will clean china, stainless steel, fridges and freezers, ovens and plastic furniture. It can be sprinkled on a damp cloth or applied as a paste mixed with water for light scouring; or use as a solution in water when soaking china, for instance, or washing surfaces. Cost: 65p for 200g.

■ **Borax** Domestic or laundry borax softens water and breaks down grease. It's good for cleaning enamel surfaces, ceramic tiles, windows and mirrors, and for dissolving grease in sinks and drains. It will also clear tannin stains in teapots. Use it dry, as a paste with water and vinegar, or in a solution with water. Caution: wear gloves if you have sensitive skin. Cost: £1.70 for 350g.

■ **Lemon juice** Applied neat or added to water, the acidity of lemon juice clears tarnish on brass and copper, removes limescale, rust and stains on marble and plastic worktops, and is effective against unpleasant smells (see page 214). Cost: 50p for 250ml.

ASK YOURSELF

IS IT WORTH BUYING A SUPERMARKET'S OWN-BRAND CLEANERS?

The answer is yes, but the saving is not always very great. Often the difference in price between a famous-name cleaner and the supermarket's own-brand equivalent is 20p–30p. But it's always worth checking the difference. We found a top-brand multi-purpose spray cleaner cost £2.39 for 500ml, but it was £1.25 for the supermarket's own label – nearly 50% less. A leading make of thick bleach cost us £2.70 for 2 litres, against £1.60 for the supermarket's version, and 28p for its value line.

SMART MOVES

Recipes for success

Raid your kitchen cupboards for bicarbonate of soda and lemon juice, and solve cleaning problems for a fraction of the price of branded products.

DRY CARPET SHAMPOO

Sprinkle bicarbonate of soda generously over the carpet, leave for 15 minutes, then vacuum thoroughly.

Cost 65p; cost of branded carpet cleaner: £2.50 plus.

OVEN CLEANER

Mix bicarbonate of soda with a little water to make a thick paste and spread over baked-on grease. Leave overnight, rub with a plastic scrubber and rinse.

Cost 65p; cost of branded oven cleaner: £2.

MILDEW REMOVER

Mimimise mould and remove mildew from a shower curtain by applying a paste of bicarbonate of soda and lemon juice. Soak, then rinse in warm water.

Cost £1.15; cost of branded mildew remover: £2.60.

TAP DESCALER

Rub chrome taps with half a lemon to remove scale and scrub inside them with a toothbrush dipped in vinegar.

Cost 50p; cost of branded limescale remover: £2.

■ **Washing soda** Use to soften water and break down grease, in a hot-water solution. It will clean cooker hoods, extractor fans, hard flooring and drains. It will also clear green corrosion on brass and copper. Caution: wear gloves. Cost: £1.50 for 1kg.

■ **White spirit** A turpentine substitute, white spirit is used neat to clean gilt picture frames and remove wax polish build-up. It can also clear rust spots from acrylic sinks. Caution: it is highly flammable. Cost: £1.64 for 750ml.

■ **White vinegar** Used neat in a solution with water or as a paste with borax and water, vinegar cleans windows, glass surfaces, ceramic tiles and wooden furniture. It can help to remove hard-water deposits from taps, toilet bowls and sinks, and works as a descaler for kettles. (See also Smart moves, page 213.) Cost: £4 for 5 litres.

SAVE BY USING COMMON HOUSEHOLD ITEMS

Proprietary cleaners and stain removers will set you back pounds, but sometimes the solution is much closer to home and costs just a few pennies.

Bread Rub dirty marks on wallpaper gently with a piece of fresh white bread. This also works with Venetian blinds.

Paper Clean grease spots on wallpaper by blotting with a clean paper towel, brown paper or blotting paper and then pressing a warm (not hot) iron over it.

Salt Use salt to absorb red wine spilt on carpet or fabric. Apply immediately after the accident, then brush or rinse away later. Cost of carpet cleaning spray: £2.50 for 500ml.

Talcum powder Pour talc over a grease stain on cloth, leave overnight, brush the talc off and wash the cloth as normal. Cost of a stain remover spray that does the same job: £2 for 100ml.

Baby oil Make stainless steel appliances gleam by gently rubbing them with cotton wool dipped in a little baby oil.

Toothpaste Clean dirty grouting between wall tiles by rubbing with toothpaste, or try a mild bleach solution.

Denture cleaning tablets Use as a kettle descaler. Fill the kettle with cold water, add a couple of denture cleaning tablets, leave overnight, then rinse thoroughly. Cost of a branded kettle descaler: £1.20.

WATCH POINTS **LOOK AFTER FLOORS**

If you take good care of floors and floor coverings, they will reward you with years of service. Protect them from damage, clean regularly and deal with stains promptly.

■ **Use a doormat** The easiest way to keep floor-cleaning costs down is by preventing dirt from entering your home in the first place. Look in IKEA stores ✉ or the £1 shops found in many towns for inexpensive, heavy-duty mats to place outside every exterior door. Put thinner ones just inside the doors to prevent dirt being trodden into carpets and wearing down the fibres.

■ **Clean carpets once a year** Hire a carpet cleaner from a hire shop such as HSS ✉ or get quotes from local cleaning firms. Expect to pay at least £20–£30 a room but look out for special 'whole house' deals. Ask about a discount if you move all the furniture out of the room beforehand, as this

keep it simple

BRIGHTEN LIGHT BULBS
Restore the effectiveness of your light bulbs by dusting them with a dry cloth when switched off. A dust-free bulb shines up to 50% more brightly than one that is dirty.

CLEVER WAYS WITH CLEANING EQUIPMENT

■ **Wipe windows with newspaper**
Rub newly washed windows with crumpled newspaper as the ink will make the glass shine. Cost of a chamois leather: £5.

■ **Cleaning cloths** Cut up old terry nappies, towels, T-shirts, sheets and dishcloths. Cost of a pack of three cloths: £1.50.

■ **Make a polisher for a wooden floor** Tie a duster round a soft broom and use this to apply polish. Cost of replacement head for a floor polisher: £3.65.

will save the cleaners' time and mean they can fit in more jobs that day. For help in finding local carpet cleaning companies, contact the National Carpet Cleaners Association (**www.ncca.co.uk** 0116 271 9550 ✉).

■ **Disguise marks** Rub small scratches on wooden floors with fine steel wool, then mix a little brown shoe polish with floor wax and rub in well. Remove scuff marks on vinyl by rubbing with a clean pencil eraser.

■ **No-cost disguise for a worn area** Disguise a small worn patch on a carpet by filling in with a felt-tip pen in the same colour. Test on an inconspicuous corner first to check for a good colour match.

■ **Attack stains immediately** Soak up spills with a paper towel as soon as they occur, then squirt the stain with soda water, and blot and repeat. Never rub the stain. If the spill discolours your carpet, apply a half-and-half solution of white vinegar and water, then dab and blot with clean rags repeatedly until the mark disappears. Cost of a branded carpet stain remover spray: £2.50 for 500ml.

SAVE ON CARE FOR CURTAINS AND BLINDS

Clean curtains and blinds at least once a year to prevent dirt build-up shortening their life.

Buy machine-washable curtains Wash curtains yourself to save on expensive dry-cleaning bills, which can cost £10 per kilogram of curtain. If the curtains are too large or heavy for your machine, wash them carefully in the bath and hang them to drip dry on a washing line.

New rings for old Boil dirty metal curtain rings in a solution of two parts water to one part vinegar and rub dry with a clean, old towel to make them come up like new.

Cleaning roller blinds A roller blind cleaner bought in a shop costs £7 for 500ml. Instead, unroll washable roller blinds and sponge with a solution of water and washing-up liquid. Or dry clean blinds by laying on towelling and rubbing with flour. Clean Venetian blinds in a mild soapy solution, too.

TOP TIPS A GLEAMING BATHROOM

There's no need to pay out for proprietary bathroom cleaners. Use own-brand washing up liquid (cost: 70p for 500ml) and a little white vinegar instead.

■ **Bathtime basics** If you clean a shower or bath immediately after use, when steam has loosened any dirt, you should only need to wipe over surfaces with a damp cloth plus a small amount of washing-up liquid, or white vinegar for stubborn marks. Wipe soapy film off tiles with a

Ten ways with white vinegar

Vinegar is cheap, at £4 for 5 litres, long-lasting and has myriad uses.

SMART MOVES

Kettle cleaner Fill with equal parts vinegar and water, boil, allow to cool and leave overnight.

Window washer Add a few drops of vinegar to water in a plant mister. Cost of a branded window cleaner: £1.35 for 500ml.

All-round bathroom saviour See below for cleaning baths, tiles, and more.

Plaster perker Mix one part vinegar to three parts water to clean water-stained plaster on walls or ceilings.

Iron restorer Fill a steam iron with a 50:50 solution of vinegar and water. Run the iron on the steam setting until dry and repeat with clear water.

Rust buster Soak rusty screws or nails in vinegar for several days until the rust dissolves, scrub with an old toothbrush and rinse.

Mould preventer Wipe kitchen cupboards and the bread bin with a cloth soaked in vinegar. Branded mould remover: £2.60.

Fabric softener White vinegar makes a great substitute and doesn't affect allergy sufferers as it contains no chemicals.

Vacuum flask reviver Clean a flask by filling with a half water/half vinegar solution, then rinse with clean water.

Hand freshener Rinse hands in vinegar to remove onion, garlic or fish odours.

■ For further advice, go to **www.versatilevinegar.org** ✉ and click on 'Uses & Tips'.

---

mixture of one part vinegar to four parts water. Cost of a branded bathroom cleaner: £1.50 for 500ml.

■ **Cleaning a shower unit** Remove hard-water deposits on shower doors and screens by wiping with vinegar. Leave for 30 minutes, then rinse. Unscrew and soak a shower head in a bowl of warm vinegar to remove scale, using an old toothbrush to clear the holes. Cost of a branded limescale remover, liquid or spray: £3 for 500ml.

■ **Descaling taps** If there is a build-up of limescale on taps, scour with vinegar, then cover with a plastic bag. Leave for a couple of hours, then rinse.

TOP TIPS A SPARKLING KITCHEN SINK AND WORKTOPS

Many kitchen cleaning products can scratch porcelain and stainless steel sinks, so try one of these easy – and much cheaper – ideas instead.

■ **Cleaning porcelain sinks** To remove stains from a porcelain sink, soak paper towels with bleach and spread them over the bottom of the sink. Leave for 30 minutes, remove and rinse with cold water. Cost of a branded kitchen cleaner suitable for porcelain: £1.75 for 290ml.

■ **Keep stainless steel sinks clean** Remove water marks with white vinegar. Rub persistent marks with a paste of bicarbonate of soda mixed with water. Cost of a branded stainless steel sink cleaner: £4 for 500ml.

■ **Remove limescale** Get rid of limescale from around plug holes by rubbing with a piece of cut lemon. Cost of a branded limescale remover: £3 for 500ml.

■ **Hygienic worktops** To avoid the need for a major cleaning job, wipe worktops daily with hot, soapy water, rinse and wipe dry. Rub stains with a damp cloth and bicarbonate of soda. If the stain persists, wipe with a cloth moistened with a little bleach. Cost of a branded kitchen worktop cleaner: £1.25 for 500ml.

NATURAL PESTICIDES

Homemade remedies can work just as well as shop-bought pesticides, and are safer and kinder on your wallet.

INSTEAD OF:
Ant killer
Mothballs
Fly strips

USE:
Dried mint or ground cloves
Cedar chips or lavender bags
Lengths of brown paper soaked in boiled and cooled sugar water

MAKE YOUR OWN AIR FRESHENER

Fill a spray bottle with water and add ten drops of an essential oil – try rosemary, eucalyptus, pine, lavender or citrus.

SIMPLE SOLUTION

Remove unwanted odours from inside the microwave by heating up a slice of lemon in a bowl of water or a bicarbonate of soda solution.

CLEAR SMELLS WITH LEMON

Remove fishy or garlic smells from a wooden chopping board by rubbing the board with a cut lemon. And put citrus peel down an electric waste disposal unit to clear smells.

SCENT OF CLOVES

Simmer cloves in water for a delicious smell that is welcoming in winter.

FRAGRANT BATHS

Pop about eight drops of a relaxing essential oil such as neroli or sandalwood into your bath.

ADD THE SCENT OF BAKING BREAD

Warm brown sugar and cinnamon gently on the stove to fill your home with delicious baking smells. Take care that the mixture doesn't burn.

ABSORB ODOURS

Place a saucer of vinegar next to the cooker to absorb strong odours.

FRESHEN UP AS YOU VACUUM

When you do the vacuuming, put a couple of drops of essential oil into the dust bag and the scent will be dispersed around the house.

KEEP AIR FRESH AND SWEET

Kitchens and bathrooms can harbour unpleasant smells, but there are plenty of ways to get rid of them cheaply or for free. You can make your own air fresheners and room fragrances. Essential oils cost from about £3 a bottle from health food shops, but a little goes a long way and they last well.

LAVENDER SACHETS

If you grow your own lavender, snip the heads off the stalks, let them dry, then make your own sachets to place in drawers using scraps of muslin or thin cotton.

FREE THE FRIDGE OF SMELLS

Put a bowl filled with clean cat litter in a fridge that is going to be switched off for any length of time to absorb smells.

SWEET POMANDERS

Keep wardrobes smelling sweet with homemade pomanders. Stud oranges, lemons or limes with whole cloves, then hang from a piece of leftover ribbon.

FLOWERS AND PLANTS IN YOUR HOME

Add colour to your home with beautiful flowers. Knowing where and what to buy and how to look after them will ensure you get value for money.

SHOPPING FOR FLOWERS

The best bargain flowers are home grown, so plant them in your garden if you can.

Get reductions Supermarkets and street markets are a good source of well-priced flowers – buy at the end of the day when the flowers are often reduced.

Flower markets If you're buying for a special occasion or want exotic varieties visit a flower market, where you'll find flower and plant stalls selling plants at wholesale prices – about half those charged in florists' shops. Prime examples include the Columbia Road Flower Market, in Shoreditch, London (open 7am to 2pm on Sundays only), and Manchester Flower Market, in Piccadilly Gardens in the city centre (open 11am to 5pm, Thursday, Friday and Saturday).

LONG-LASTING BLOOMS

Buy flowers that last a long time, such as chrysanthemums and carnations. Lilies are expensive but last for two weeks and have an intense fragrance that will fill the whole house (but beware: lilies are toxic to cats and dogs). Ensure that you change the water every three days.

Longer-life flowers Cut flowers from the garden just before they are in full bloom. That way they will open indoors and you will need to replace them less frequently.

Delicate scents Sweet peas are easy to grow, have a long-lasting scent, and the more you cut, the more they flower. Freesias are also a good choice for a fragrant flower. Not all colours are strongly scented, so before you buy you may want to sort through and select the most fragrant.

Houseplants Move a pot plant around until you find a spot where it is happy. Don't be tempted to overwater if it looks unhealthy – it could just need stronger sunlight.

TOP TIPS FOR HEALTHY HOUSEPLANTS

Houseplants are a great investment as, if looked after properly, they can last for years. Help keep them healthy with these old-fashioned methods that cost nothing.

■ **Aerating the soil** Mix a few tea leaves or coffee grounds into the plant soil to aerate it.

■ **Tea-time** Give plants a boost by watering occasionally with leftover cold tea.

■ **Leftover water** Add cooled water used for boiling eggs as it is full of nutrients.

■ **String solution** Water small house plants while you are away by using a piece of string. Place one end in the soil and the other in a bucket of water positioned higher than the plant. The string will gradually draw the water from the bucket to the soil.

TRADITIONAL ALTERNATIVES TO FLOWER FOOD

■ Add a couple of aspirin tablets to the vase.

■ Pop a few drops of lemonade into the water.

■ Add a few drops of bleach to disinfect the water, but don't overdo it or you will kill the flowers.

■ Add a couple of coins – the dissolving minerals are believed to extend the life of flowers.

Ways to make cut flowers last longer

■ Buy from a reputable source, and ensure flowers are well wrapped for protection.

■ Choose flowers with firm petals or with buds that are coloured, which shows that they've absorbed enough food to develop fully.

■ Put them in lukewarm water – it has less oxygen, which prevents air bubbles in the stem blocking water uptake.

■ Clean vases thoroughly after use – bacteria kills flowers.

■ Snip stems at an angle to increase the area that can absorb water.

■ Strip off all leaves that would be below the waterline to help keep the water clean.

■ Use flower food as instructed. It contains flower-friendly sugars to feed the flowers and encourage buds to open as well as preservatives to prolong their life.

SMART MOVES

CREATIVE GARDENING ON A BUDGET

Whether you are designing a new garden from scratch or improving what you already have, a lot of work is involved, though with careful planning this can cost surprisingly little. Shopping around and doing the hard graft yourself rather than paying others to do it will reap dividends, both in your garden and for your wallet.

DON'T FIGHT NATURE

Take time to find out about your soil and growing conditions and then select only those plants that will thrive there naturally. Local weeds and wildflowers should also provide clues as to the species of plants that are easy to grow in your garden.

Give plants what they need Identify ways to improve growing conditions to give plants, bulbs and seeds every chance in life.

Choose good stock Buy the best-quality plants you can afford to ensure maximum growth and value for money.

TOP TIPS PLANS FOR PENNIES

A professional garden designer may charge several hundred pounds for a detailed garden plan, plus more again for buying the plants and carrying out the work. But there are ways of keeping the cost of designing a garden down.

■ **Design it yourself** Design your own landscaping and planting plan. There are dozens of books, CDs and websites (see Resources, left) that can help you come up with the right solution for your garden.

■ **Plant it yourself** If you have your garden professionally designed, then do the work yourself. Coblands Nurseries website Best4Plants at **www.best4plants.co.uk** or 01732 350517 ✉ offers advice and sells ready-made borders, such as a 'Winter Border', from £30 to £200 plus.

■ **Hire a student** Contact a local horticultural college to see whether you can hire a student to design your garden.

■ **A garden centre may help** Visit your local garden centre or nursery – staff are often very knowledgeable and may agree to draw up a plan for free, or for a modest fee, on condition that you buy the plants from them.

■ **Visit a DIY store** It is worthwhile trying large DIY chains with garden sections. Watch out for special offers at Homebase ✉ and B&Q ✉, which both offer a good range of reasonably priced garden products. B&Q also has simple, downloadable advice on 'Designing Your Garden'.

LANDSCAPING NEEDN'T COST THE EARTH

Paving stones, soil and gravel can be a major expense, so buy larger quantities for the biggest savings and look out for secondhand bargains.

Buy in bulk It is cost-effective to purchase materials in large quantities, and it is cheaper still to buy them when you can from a builders' merchant or online specialist rather than your local garden centre or a DIY store. Gravel, for instance, costs just £1.65 for 25kg from the builders' merchant Wickes, whereas a bag from Homebase costs £3.29.

Don't go it alone If you are planning to cover large areas of ground, ask neighbours if they plan to landscape their gardens and share the benefits of buying in bulk and split delivery costs. Stone2YourHome (**www.stone2yourhome.co.uk** or 0871 873 2369 ✉) sells loose gravel for under £40 a tonne, plus £20 delivery, with a minimum order of 10 tonnes – enough to cover 140m² if laid 50mm deep.

Bargain paving You may be able to pick up paving stones secondhand. Keep an eye out for anyone renovating their garden, and see if they will sell off unwanted paving slabs cheap. You may even be lucky enough to find some in a skip. They also appear on auction site eBay ✉.

FEATURES FOR THE COST-CONSCIOUS

Ponds, arbours and arches add interest to a garden, but can be expensive to buy and install. With a little know-how you can keep costs down by making your own.

Bargain barrel ponds Ideal for a small garden, a miniature pond made from a half barrel is portable so you can take it with you when you move. Barrels at a garden centre cost from £30, so see if your local pub has any spares.

Arches for the thrifty Rather than paying £75 or more for an arch from a garden centre, save by making your own from flexible plastic plumber's pipe. Key with glasspaper, apply weatherproof paint and attach to wooden supports. Alternatively, reuse timber from a dismantled shed or fence.

BUYING PLANTS ON A BUDGET

Your options for obtaining plants vary from the most expensive garden centre to the humblest roadside stall but, in all cases, make sure you buy viable stock.

Do a deal with friends The cheapest option is to get into the habit of swapping cuttings with friends.

Savings on the road Roadside stalls, where an amateur gardener sells off surplus stock, can be great value – and will suit your soil type if local.

Shop-bought bargains Prices at DIY chain stores and supermarkets can be up to 40% less than at nurseries or garden centres, though the choice might be limited.

Reliability costs Garden centres and nurseries are the most expensive option, but the variety and quality of the plants will be high, so they are less likely to die and need replacing.

Look out for perennials Small perennial plants are good value for money, particularly ones that can be divided easily.

Bulbs for value The most economical bulbs are ones that multiply yearly in the same position. Daffodils and other varieties of narcissi, snowdrops and crocuses are good value.

Avoid cracked containers Don't buy a plant in a cracked container, even if it is reduced, as the roots may be damaged.

MAKE YOUR OWN COMPOST

Since compost from a garden centre can cost from £4 for a 70-litre bag, start making your own compost – it is easy, environmentally friendly and virtually free. You can make a

---

HOW TO MAKE A GARDEN LOOK BIGGER

Create the illusion of size and space in your garden by fixing an old mirror to a wall or fence in a position that gives an attractive reflection, then train plants to conceal the mirror edges.

A LAWN FOR 75% LESS

It is far more economical to sow grass seeds than plant turf, though you will have to wait for the results. Turf for 40m² (432 sq ft) costs around £140 (including delivery), whereas seed for the same area costs £20. You will need a lawnmower if you don't have one – look for bargain buys in summer sales, newspaper adverts, car boot sales and online auctions.

suitable container using a plastic bin with holes drilled round the side. Alternatively, nail together pieces of recycled timber from a wooden palette and wrap with galvanised chicken wire. You can use a piece of old carpet as a lid. Almost any organic kitchen waste can be used for composting, especially vegetable peelings, clothes and furnishings made from natural fibres, egg boxes and lawn mowings.

Council compost Many councils run composting schemes. Go to the Home Composting section at **www.recyclenow.com** ✉ and enter your postcode to see what is on offer in your area. Cheap compost made from green waste is often sold at council recycling and household waste sites.

TOP TIPS PROPAGATE AND SAVE

Propagating your own plants will save you a great deal of money in the long term, and is immensely satisfying.

■ **Savings from seeds** One adult plant can cost as much as a packet of seeds that yields 30–50 plants, so buy seeds or collect them by scooping out from ripe fruit or vegetables, or tying a paper bag round plants and gently shaking. Store dry seeds in small pots until you are ready to plant them.

■ **Cheaper cuttings** Depending on the type of plant, you will need to take cuttings in spring or late summer. Make your own mini cloche by securing a plastic bag over the pot to retain moisture and warmth. Once it has been moved outside, place an upturned jar over the plant for protection against the elements, snails and slugs.

■ **Recycled containers** Rather than paying for plastic plant pots or seed trays, use plastic food containers or yoghurt pots, with lollipop sticks as markers.

■ **Store bulbs** Frost kills non-hardy bulbs, so dig them up once they have finished flowering and keep them in a frost-free garage or shed throughout the winter. Store them inside old tights, tying a knot between each bulb so they are not touching, to minimise the risk of disease.

Improve your soil for free

There are various ways to improve your soil's texture and fertility for next to nothing.

■ Improve drainage in clay soil by working it gently with a fork.

■ Add well-rotted manure. You shouldn't have to pay for this as many stables and farms are only too glad to have it taken off their hands. Make sure it is well-rotted or it will burn your plants. You may have to find somewhere to store manure while it rots down, such as an out-of-the-way corner at the bottom of the garden.

■ Perk soil up with homemade compost.

TOP TIPS CONVERTING CONTAINERS

Virtually anything can be used as a planter, so forget buying pots from the garden centre at a cost of £5–£50. A container should be able to hold enough potting compost for root growth, and have drainage holes to prevent plants becoming waterlogged. Pierce the bottom with a drill or bradawl to make holes before planting.

■ **Add style to plastic** Use leftover paint to add a bright splash of colour to cheap plastic pots, or stick pieces of broken tiles onto waterproof grout for a colourful mosaic finish. Stick shells onto a painted pot or window box for a striking three-dimensional effect.

■ **Antique pots for less** Fashionable antique terracotta pots from exclusive gardening stores are expensive. Create an aged effect on a new pot by painting it with yoghurt to encourage the growth of algae and moss.

■ **Re-use a sink** Old troughs and sinks can make splendid planters. A butler's or Belfast sink works best. Or try a child-size bath galvanised with rust-resistant zinc.

■ **Versatile tyres** Old tyres can be stacked for increased depth. Paint them to improve their appearance.

■ **Drainage included** A metal colander makes a wonderful hanging basket and has ready-made drainage holes. Add a liner if compost is in danger of falling out. Then attach three lengths of chain (from DIY shops) and hang from a bracket.

■ **Transform rubbish** Any of the following containers can look effective when filled with geraniums or other bright flowering plants: a catering-size oil can, ceramic potty or chamber pot, wheelbarrow, terracotta chimney pot, wellington boot or an old mop bucket.

GROW YOUR OWN HERBS

Grow herbs from seed in a pot and make savings on the cost of repeatedly buying them from the supermarket. Plant herbs such as basil, chives, parsley and sage together in a sunny spot, but grow rosemary on its own as it has a tendency to take over. Many varieties will thrive for years if they are pruned regularly.

SAVING WATER

Knowing how to water your garden efficiently and how to conserve water will cut costs, particularly if your water is metered (see *Household finance*, page 298).

Conserve and save Buy an inexpensive water butt or use a plastic bin or other watertight container to collect rainwater. You'll need to place it under a downpipe from the guttering so that the water is channelled into the container.

Re-use water Recycle used water from basins and bath water without much bubble bath.

Beware chemicals Don't use water from the dishwasher. Chemicals in the detergent may be harmful to your plants.

Treat thirsty lawns Spike a dry lawn with a fork to encourage water to penetrate the soil.

Mulch for moisture Old carpet and newspaper efficiently retain water – place around the plants and disguise with soil. Chipped bark, lawn mowings, animal manure and garden compost can also be used.

SPEND AT LEAST 25% LESS ON COMPOST

When planting up containers, reduce the amount of compost you will need by placing an upturned plastic pot in the base, or add pieces of polystyrene packaging to pad out the compost.

 **RESOURCES**

FOR THE THRIFTY GARDENER
Use the following resources to save money on your hobby:

■ For advice on starting your own organic garden, go to the national charity for organic growing site at **www.gardenorganic.org.uk** or 024 7630 3517 ✉.

■ Visit the Home Composting section at **www.recyclenow.com** ✉ for all you need to know about making your own compost.

■ Consider joining an online community, such as the Garden Network, **www.garden-network.co.uk** ✉, which offers free downloads to give inspiration plus member-only discounts on a wide variety of garden products.

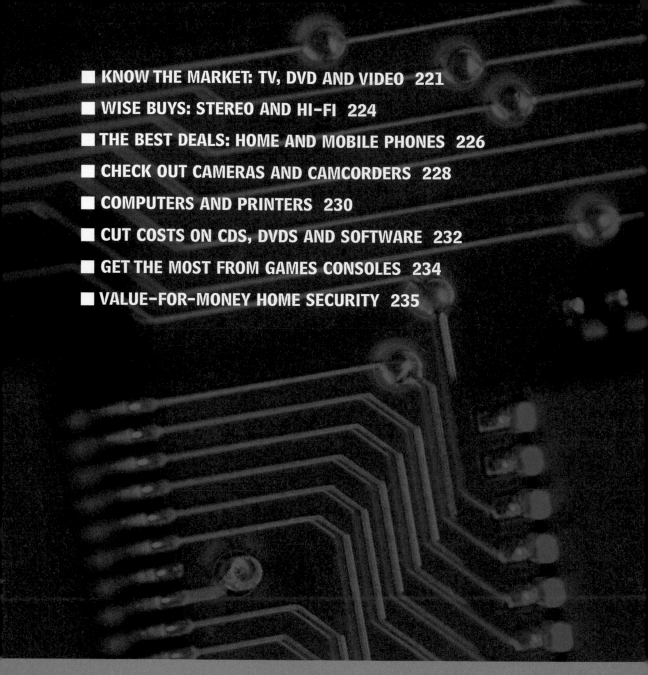

Electronic equipment

With competitive Internet prices and constantly evolving technology, a little homework can add to your enjoyment and save you a lot of money.

KNOW THE MARKET: TV, DVD AND VIDEO

There's huge potential for saving money when you're choosing TV and home cinema electronics. The cash saved by smart buying on just a single item is often enough to justify an extra purchase, such as a surround-sound system or a Blu-ray DVD player, for example.

CHOOSING THE RIGHT TYPE OF TV

Make an informed choice about which type of TV to buy so you purchase the model that suits your viewing habits.

LCD or plasma The quality of LCDs and plasma televisions has improved in recent years. Now there isn't much difference between them in terms of picture quality.

Cost You can get a good-quality 32-inch plasma or LCD for around £400 and a 40-inch for about £600. You can spend twice this for the latest models with extra features and better picture quality.

Size Small flatscreen TVs are available for around £150 to £250 and are a good size for the bedroom or kitchen

Energy LCDs use about a third less energy than plasma TVs. So if you are worried about energy use – which can be high for larger TVs – choose LCD over plasma.

Picture quality HD ready means that TVs are capable of playing high-definition broadcasts. The best TVs are also 1080p, which means that they can make the most out of broadcasts.

For buying advice Magazines like *What Hi-Fi? Sound and Vision* or online reviews can help you choose, or read the test reports at *Which?* Reviews at **www.which.co.uk** ✉.

SAVE ON YOUR SET

If you want to pay less for your next TV, or other home cinema electronics, you will need to look further than your nearest high street or shopping centre.

Shop around The best prices for electrical goods are online. Look out for special offer discounts and free delivery. A quick search on a price comparison site could save you £200 on the cost of a TV (see Resources, on next page).

DIGITAL SWITCHOVER

Between 2008–2012 the government is ending traditional analogue broadcasts across Britain and switching to a digital signal. Before your area's switchover date, you will need to convert your TV to digital. To find out when your area is going digital and what you will need to do to switch, go to **www.digitaluk.co.uk** or 08456 50 50 50 ✉.

HOW MUCH WILL A PLASMA OR LCD COST?

The price of LCDs and plasmas has come down significantly in recent years, but still varies greatly.

The table shows the range of prices for a selection of good-quality LCDs and plasma TVs, and an average price range.

SIZE OF SCREEN	BEST BUY	AVERAGE COST
32-inch	£600–£900	£300–£400
37-inch	£700–£800	£400–£600
42-inch	£900–£1,200	£500–£700
50-inch	£1200+	£800–£1,200

High street and supermarkets You may find that supermarkets often have good deals on TVs, DVDs and other electrical goods. However, beware of brands you haven't heard of which may not offer as good a picture or sound quality as more well-known brands.

Last year's models One way of saving money is to buy last year's TV during the sales. Manufacturers are constantly making minor changes to their ranges and you could pick up last year's model for hundreds of pounds less than the price it was when new and much less than this year's slightly revised model. In this way you can benefit from a much better quality TV at a price that would get you a much lower quality new model. Again, check out product reviews online and in magazines.

Don't buy secondhand LCDs and plasmas aren't as reliable as older standard TVs, so it's best to avoid buying secondhand ones. Look out for companies offering extended warranties on LCDs or plasmas at no extra cost. A free five-year extended warranty could be worth it on a £1,000 TV as long as you are getting a good price.

Local stores It might be worth trying local electrical shops to see if they have any special offers. They may have price promises and free local delivery, but of course make sure you get a good deal. Also look out for a discounted display model, but check how long it has been in the store.

DVD AND BLU-RAY

DVD has all but replaced VHS video now, and a basic DVD player can be bought for less than £20.

Next generation Blu-ray is the next generation of DVD and gives greater storage and better quality than existing DVDs. It also allows the playing and recording of High Definition pictures and sound.

DVD recorders DVD recorders let you record TV on to DVDs as you would have done with video. You need to buy blank DVDs to record on to.

Hard disk drives With a hard disk drive recorder you can record TV on a hard disk. Hard disk recorders can typically store up to 250gb of TV – which is enough space for about 300 hours of television. They also let you rewind and pause live TV.

Choosing a digital provider

SMART MOVES

When choosing a digital TV provider be realistic about what you will really watch, otherwise you could end up paying for a number of programmes or channels that you will never need. You also need to take into account the sort of programmes you want to watch. For example, do you want HD programmes? You will need to have an HD source to make the most of HD's improved picture and sound quality.

Contract flexibility

When you sign up to any digital TV service check the terms and conditions carefully. Check if you can switch to a cheaper package during the contract period.

Access TV online

You can catch up on and download TV programmes you have missed using BBC iPlayer and ITV Player, for example. You can watch the programmes on your PC or download them to your PC or portable device or laptop to watch them whenever you want.

DIGITAL TV

There are hundreds of digital TV channels available in dozens of package deals and tariffs. Subscription fees can wipe out savings made on buying your TV, so choose carefully and read the small print.

Freeview/Freeview+ Freeview is the cheapest option and gives you access to 40 digital channels for no monthly subscription or set-up costs. All you have to do is buy a set-top box for as little as under £20. It is only available in around three-quarters of UK homes, but this should improve as we approach the digital switchover in 2012. Most new TVs now come with Freeview installed already giving you free access to digital TV stations and TV guides. Freeview+ combines a Freeview box with a hard disk recorder. For as little as £80 you can get a Freeview box with 160gb memory for recording programmes and you can also pause live TV.

Freesat ITV and BBC Freesat is a digital satellite TV service from ITV and the BBC with 140 free TV and radio channels. You have to buy an £80 dish and a HD box from £98, but there is no subscription charge or monthly bills.

Freesat Sky This is a digital satellite service from Sky with over 240 free digital channels and 85 radio channels. You will have to pay around £147 for a box, dish, remote and installation. Like Freesat ITV and BBC, there are no monthly fees and no subscription. However, there aren't any HD broadcasts. To get these you need a Sky HD Box costing £99, plus £30 installation and a monthly fee of at least £26.

Top up For TV like Freeview+ you buy a box that includes a hard disk recorder and Freeview. For an extra £10 per month you get access to a further 24 channels.

Bundles You can get digital TV bundled in with phone or broadband from BT Vision, Tiscali TV and Virgin Media. Virgin Media is received through cable and BT and Tiscali through broadband. Prices and services vary so check at their websites or by using a comparison site.

Pay-per-view If you're not sure how many movies you'll watch, don't sign up to the expensive movie channels. Instead, opt for the pay-per-view service.

RESOURCES

DIGITAL TV
To compare the different digital packages available in your area, visit: **www.uswitch.com** ✉; **www.digitalchoices.co.uk** ✉. Or go to the providers' sites:
www.freeview.co.uk 08701 111 270 ✉;
www.freesat.co.uk 0845 313 0052 ✉,
www.sky.com or 08442 411 495 ✉;
www.freesatfromsky.co.uk or 08442 410 595 ✉;
www.virginmedia.com 0845 840 7777 ✉.

CABLED OPTIONS

Not all areas are able to receive cable TV – it depends whether the cables have been laid. If they have, you are sure to know as you will be receiving offers for subscribing to their packages. If you are in any doubt, go to the availability checker at **www.cable.co.uk** ✉.

CHOOSING THE RIGHT DIGITAL TV PACKAGE

The most heavily promoted full packages are those that include movies and sports. These typically cost up to £50 a month and include many channels that you will rarely if ever, watch. If you're unsure whether you'll take full advantage of the movies and sports channels, you might be better off signing up for a basic package. All digital TV companies make it easy to upgrade later, should you find you want to.

	MONTHLY			PER VIEWING
	BASIC PACKAGE	FULL PACKAGE	EXTRA CHANNEL	PAY-PER-VIEW MOVIE
SKY	£16.50	£46	£1 to £19	£3.91
VIRGIN	Free with phone package	£19.50	n/a	£2 to £4.50

WISE BUYS: STEREO AND HI-FI

Whether you want good quality sound from a budget music centre, or want to download the latest MP3 player for a song, spend a little time on research. You can make your hi-fi as easy on your wallet as it is on your ears.

PRICE CHECK

Get an instant survey of prices by going to an online price comparison site such as **www.pricerunner.co.uk** ✉, **www.shopzilla.co.uk** ✉ or **www.kelkoo.co.uk** ✉ (see Resources, page 222 for more options) and using the audio section to browse through hundreds of deals at dozens of dealers. Or try online retailers like **www.play.com** ✉, **www.ebuyer.com** ✉ and **www.amazon.co.uk** ✉.

DON'T BE A FASHION VICTIM

Electronics-makers frequently change the styling of their stereos to make them look up to date without changing the specification. Use this to your advantage by hunting out last season's stereos – look for dealers who specialise in discontinued stock such as Richer Sounds on 0845 900 1230 or **www.richersounds.com** ✉ as well as dealers on auction site eBay (**www.ebay.com** ✉). You'll still get a full year's guarantee and the same sound quality as current models, but you'll make significant savings. An MP3 player that cost £99.95 last year could be bought for as little as £39.95, for example.

BUYING USED

Good quality hi-fi and stereo equipment is usually very reliable, and is therefore a good value used buy because most depreciation happens in the first year. It may even come with a short warranty, too. Steer clear of cheap stereo systems with damage or obvious wear and tear, and look instead for good quality hi-fi separates. If you're buying from a private seller, test the equipment before buying – especially if there are moving parts, such as a turntable, which would be expensive to repair.

UNWANTED GIFTS

It's a fact of life that not all gifts are wanted. Where gifts can't be returned to the original shop, they are often sold through classified newspaper ads or online auctions sites such as **www.ebay.co.uk** ✉ or **www.loot.com** ✉. Browse an auction site shortly after Christmas and you will find plenty of nearly new MP3 players, portable CD players and other electronics gifts – at prices that are lower than those in the January sales.

SYSTEMS VERSUS SEPARATES

For the best sound quality, opt for a system of separates – around £250 will buy a CD player, amplifier and speakers that will be leagues ahead of a similarly priced all-in-one stereo system.

Building a system Begin with a decent amplifier, leads and speakers. Make sure the amplifier has enough inputs – and the right type of inputs – to link up to as many separates as possible, such as a CD player, TV, DVD player, MP3 player and tuner. If you want your amplifier to support surround sound for your TV, then look for an amplifier with 5.1 channel sound.

MP3 PLAYERS

Over the past few years there has been a huge growth in the number and type of MP3 players. These allow you to download music to them or copy music from your computer. A typical MP3 player will have 8gb of memory, which is enough to store 1,000 songs. You can also buy MP3 players that play video. Apple's iPod is one of the most well known MP3 players, but most electronic brands produce several models. Many mobile phones also offer MP3 playback.

WATCH POINTS EXTENDED WARRANTIES

Most retailers offer warranties that insure electrical goods if they breakdown after the manufacturer's warranty period has ended (normally a year). Extended warranties sometimes also cover accidental damage. Consumer groups have criticised extended warranties for being an expensive waste of money as electrical goods are much more reliable nowadays and the cost of repair is often less than the cost of the warranty.

■ **Other legal protection** Under the Sale of Goods Act you could be legally entitled to a free repair or replacement if something you buy is faulty. This important legal protection says that goods should be of 'satisfactory' quality and last for a reasonable length of time.

■ **Right to cancel** If you buy an extended warranty on an electrical appliance for your home you have up to 45 days to cancel it without reason.

UPGRADES CAN SAVE £100s

If your current stereo system works fine but you want better sound quality, think about upgrading part of it. This is one of the biggest advantages of a separates system, but you can do the same for cheaper stereos, too. For example, buying a pair of speakers for £50 to £100 will give a cheap stereo a new lease of life for a fraction of the cost of a completely new system.

CASE STUDY

HI-FI THAT PAYS FOR ITSELF

When Jim Miles wanted to upgrade his old stereo system, he opted for a completely different setup. 'I took one look at the glitzy stereos in the shops and saw that I would be paying for stuff I didn't want – CD and radio tuner. I'd be paying over the odds to get better sound than from my old stereo. 'I mentioned this to a friend at work and he told me he bought old hi-fi separates from online auctions. I checked it out and was amazed to see that some hi-fi was becoming collectible, with buyers from all around the world. I took the plunge and built up a system of separates. I've now got great sound quality and I know that each day my vintage hi-fi actually goes up in value. You can't say that about a new stereo.'

THE BEST DEALS: HOME AND MOBILE PHONES

If phone bills are a constant drain on your finances and you feel you are paying over the odds, it's time to find better mobile and landline deals. Whether your friends and family live nearby or on the other side of the world, there are plenty of phone companies ready to do business with you.

MOBILE MONEY-SAVINGS

Buying and using a mobile phone can be a costly business. Many phones are expensive and the call charges can mount up alarmingly. But there are ways to control these costs.

Assess your needs Before buying a new phone, try to draw up a list of your phone habits – it will help you to choose the right network and tariff. What will the volume and length of your calls be on weekdays and at weekends? Will you be calling landlines or other mobiles? Which networks do your friends and family use?

Pore over the tariff charts or go online It is very difficult to compare mobile networks with their adverts because they concentrate on free talk time, text messages and other incentives. As a result, they rarely cover the cheapest deals – which can be as little as £10 a month. One option is to visit the websites of each company, but a much easier way to compare tariffs is to use a comparison site (See Resources, right).

Cashback deals Some contracts offer money back, usually on the condition that you stay with the network for a year. The money will come as a bill credit, not cash, but this is worthwhile if you are happy with your choice of network.

SAVE £160+ ON YOUR MOBILE

Most new mobile phones are aimed primarily at teenagers and technophiles. If you don't want to take video clips, photos or check email and surf the Internet, opt for a basic phone. With Pay As You Go contracts, the difference between a basic phone and an all-singing, all-dancing model is around £100. With a monthly contract, you can save £160 on the price of a new phone, depending on the subscription deal that you opt for.

CASE STUDY

SWITCHING TO A BETTER TARIFF

Tony Bond was perfectly happy with his mobile phone until he realised how much he was spending on it unnecessarily.

'I'm not actually a big fan of mobile phones but they are a necessity. I got one when I started my own business so that customers can always get in touch with me and I don't lose out on new business. I started out on a £25 monthly tariff with 300 minutes of talk time a month; I thought this would be more than enough. But I've hardly made any calls on it – just on a few occasions, so all those minutes have been wasted.

'When the contract was up, I found a £10 a month deal with 100 minutes of free calls each month. I've used the £15 a month saving to upgrade my broadband connection to a much faster one.'

Be careful of cashback offers that involve you sending in vouchers – it can be difficult to claim the cashback.
Switching made easy Mobile phone companies make it easy to switch to them. Ask your existing provider for your port authorisation code (PAC) and give it to your new phone company, and they will switch your number over as well. It is always worth calling your current supplier, too – see if they will offer an incentive for you to stay aboard.

EXPLORE ALL YOUR LANDLINE OPTIONS

Deregulation of the landline phone means that there are now money-saving UK and international services, and you don't have to switch from BT or change your phone number to take advantage of them (see *Household Finance*, page 301). Use one of the comparison websites to compare all the different deals on offer. Some of the companies work by simply getting you to dial a number charged at a fixed rate, say 2p per minute, and then you dial the number you want to call. With others you have to set up an account and you then call a freephone number and you are billed for each call. Go to a site such as **www.moneysavingexpert.com**  and type 'Callchecker' into the search bar, which will give you up-to-date information on UK and international call charges from the different suppliers who cover your destination. A number of sites such as MoneySavingExpert offer regularly updated advice on choosing a landline provider and how to make the cheapest calls.

Telephone and cable TV Cable TV companies can provide a telephone connection over the TV cable. If you're thinking about signing up for digital TV, too, the combination of digital TV and telephone by cable may work out cheaper than keeping a BT line and subscribing to satellite TV.
Can you switch? Beware of complications if you decide to switch away completely from your BT landline. You can keep your current phone number but you may not be able to transfer other services, such as ADSL Broadband.

TOP TIPS CUTTING CALL COSTS

The charge for each call you make may only be a few pence, but when totted up it can make for a nasty surprise when you receive your monthly or quarterly bill. But you don't have to look hard to find cheap – or even free – options.
■ **Free weekend calls** If you like to chat for hours, wait until the weekend. Some services offer free weekend calls in addition to cut-price weekday calls.
■ **Free calls to friends** You can get free calls to family and friends by getting together and signing up for a service that encourages calling circles. The Talk Together service at **www.talktalk.co.uk** or 0800 049 7802. Once you are a member of TalkTalk it costs nothing to make calls at any time to other people also registered and using TalkTalk. Other calls arecharged at different rates.
■ **Directory enquiries** If you often use directory enquiries to obtain numbers, take some time to find out which is the most economical provider: the cheapest are under half the cost of the most expensive (see *Household Finance*, page 303). There are also free services available.

RESOURCES

COMPARE THE COST OF PHONE CALLS
Phone services, tariffs and call charges change constantly, so check for the best deals regularly at a comparison site.
■ uSwitch (under 'Communications') **www.uswitch.com** ✉.
■ Home Phone Choices **www.homephonechoices. co.uk** ✉.
■ Cheap International Calls **www.cheapest internationalcalls.com** ✉.
■ MoneySavingExpert (under 'Callchecker) **www.moneysavingexpert. com** ✉.
■ Moneysupermarket .com (for mobile deals) **www.moneysupermarket. com** ✉.

CHECK OUT CAMERAS AND CAMCORDERS

The digital age has provided us with an opportunity to save money in still and video photography. Don't let the initial cost of switching over to digital deter you – you will be rewarded with lower running costs and better results.

GETTING THE BEST PRICE

If you visit a high-street electronics shop, you'll see only a fraction of the full range of cameras and camcorders that are available. You'll get a wider choice and lower prices online. You could save as much as £100 buying a typical £200 digital camera online instead of on the high street.

Do your research Before buying any electrical item you should do your research to ensure you choose the right product. The website **www.which.co.uk** ✉ regularly tests camcorders and cameras and the Best Buys it identifies are often head and shoulders above lesser models. Other reviews can be found online or in specialist camera magazines.

Pay the right price Use a price comparison website such as **www.kelkoo.co.uk** ✉ or **www.pricerunner.co.uk** ✉ to get the full picture on prices for any camcorder or digital camera. A good digital camcorder costs from £400 to £500, for example. Cheaper camcorders can be bought for as little as £200. Good HD camcorders that allow you to record in HD on to a DVD or internal memory can now be bought for £500 to £700.

SAVE MONEY WITH DIGITAL

Not only will you save money with digital because you won't have to buy video tapes or film, but digital pictures and films are much more flexible. It's much easier to edit your films on a PC if they are already in a digital format. Once you have transferred digital pictures to a computer, you can email them, edit them or display them in a digital photo frame.

Film costs A digital camera saves on both film and processing costs. If you take many photos, the long-term saving will more than cover the cost of a more advanced digital camera. And you can discard the pictures you don't

---

ASK YOURSELF

DO I NEED TO GO DIGITAL?

■ If you are happy with your analogue compact but would like more control over your prints, consider buying a flatbed scanner instead of replacing your camera. Flatbed scanners can be bought for under £50 from computer stores or online and deliver images scanned from a 35mm print as good as those produced by a digital camera.

SMART MOVES

Accessorising on a budget

For digital camcorders, buy a handful of accessories to maximise the value you get from your purchase.

Memory sticks or memory Most digital cameras or camcorders have in built memory or use memory sticks. You could save money buying these in multipacks. If the camcorder uses DV tapes or recordable DVDs these can be bought in bulk to save money.

Extra battery power Running out of power in the middle of filming is also frustrating. Go online to find an extra rechargeable battery pack (see Resources, right). A regular pack will be about £20, but it is better to opt for the high-capacity battery (around £40) if you are expecting to do longer filming sessions.

Get a tripod A tripod is a must-have for camcorders, and a budget model will only cost around £15 from a high-street camera shop.

GO DIGITAL AND SAVE ON FILM COSTS

One of the benefits of digital cameras is that you don't have to pay to develop film and can delete pictures you don't want, which encourages you to make greater use of your camera. Once you have transferred the images to a PC you can select which images to print either at home or at a processing centre. This chart shows how savings on film can mount up. On this basis, your digital camera could pay for itself in two years.

AVERAGE USAGE	ANNUAL PHOTOS	COST OF FILMS	COST OF DEVELOPING AND PRINTING	TOTAL ANNUAL COST FOR FILM DEVELOPING
Medium	200	£36	£32	£68
High	400	£72	£64	£136

want before printing them either at home or at a processing centre, where they'll cost from 10p–20p a print or less, or at a high-street photo centre such as Jessops or Boots, where you connect your camera and select the images you want. But the cost varies at these centres from 29p to 49p depending on the number of prints.

CAMCORDER RECORDING FORMATS

Before you choose a new camcorder it helps if you understand the different formats for recording.

Mini-DV These are digital video tapes and although they are good quality you have to rewind or fast forward to find clips. Also more tricky to transfer to a computer.

DVD Some camcorders use DVDs to record on to. These can then be played on any DVD player or put into a computer to transfer.

Hard disk drive Your films are recorded on to a hard disk and can then can be transferred to a computer. The benefit of a hard disk is large storage.

Memory card Images are recorded on to memory cards inserted into the camcorder. These can then be transferred to a computer. The benefit is that you can't run out of space as long as you have more cards, unlike a hard disk that can get full until you transfer the images.

CAMCORDER WARRANTY QUESTIONS

Digital cameras are reliable and you're unlikely to need an extended warranty. But digital camcorders have complicated mechanisms and many moving parts, and repairs out of warranty can be expensive.

Insurance policy The most likely risk to a camcorder is accidental damage while you're out and about. Your home contents insurance may already cover this at no extra cost or for an additional premium under personal possessions cover – check your policy before buying extra cover.

Breakdown cover It could cost £80 to take out extended warranty for two years on top of the manufacturer's one-year warranty. Weigh up the benefit of this against the cost of the camcorder and the chance something will go wrong in the first three years. Extended warranties are not normally worth taking out so think carefully before buying one.

RESOURCES

BARGAIN BATTERIES
For the best selection of batteries, order from a battery superstore. But compare costs – they can vary by £5 or more. Go to:
www.budgetbatteries.co.uk 01202 582700 ✉;
www.battery-force.co.uk 01892 888135 ✉;
www.mdsbattery.co.uk 0800 310 2100 ✉.

COMPUTERS AND PRINTERS

Computers, laptops and printers are cheaper than ever, and some good bargains are on offer. You can also save on consumables and get a good deal on an Internet connection.

WHAT TO BUY

Most manufacturers use many of the same internal components in their PCs. This means there is little difference in reliability or cost of parts between companies. The price of computers has dropped significantly in the past few years and so has the price of flat-screen monitors. You can buy a good PC for home use with a flat-screen monitor from as little as £300 to £500.

Check the spec When shopping around, look closely at the specification of the PC. If you aren't sure what to look for do some research online or ask for some help and advice from a high street store or local computer store. Remember to shop around though once you know what you are after.

Look out for returns You could make big savings on computers that have been returned to the manufacturer or reconditioned. They may not even have been used, or even opened – for example, stock returned by bankrupt firms. Check manufacturers' websites (for example Dell, IBM or Compaq) for details of other online retailers.

Avoid used computers Don't bother with used PCs. Older PCs will be slower and are usually poor value.

DON'T PLAY THE WAITING GAME

New generations of PCs tend to feature slightly faster processing power than the last and prices for computers with the latest chips will be higher than older chips. However this shouldn't stop you from buying a computer today as the PCs on sale now have more than enough processing power for all but serious gamers and computer geeks.

UNNECESSARY ADD-ONS

Bundle deals, which often consist of a computer, printer, add-ons and stacks of software, are popular in computer shops. They look tempting, but often hide poor value.

CHOOSE THE RIGHT INTERNET ACCESS			
TYPE	**COST / MONTH (TYPICAL)**	**SPEED (RELATIVE)**	**DOWNLOAD LIMIT / MONTH**
Eclipse Internet	£10.72	24mbps	1gb
Plusnet	£5.99	8mbps	10gb
Three	£10	2mbps	1gb
02	£12.23	8mbps	unlimited
Be*	£13.50	8mbps	unlimited

Source Moneysupermarket.com February 2009. Minimum contracts and set-up fees may apply. Charges do not include monthly phone line rental.

Cut the cost of computer consumables

Today's computers use blank DVDs, CDs, ink, toner and paper. The costs can mount up, so shop around for the best deals.

Compatible ink and toner You don't have to stick to the manufacturer's own brand of ink or toner cartridge. If you have a popular model, check out the prices for compatible alternatives – you will find you can easily cut the cost by up to 40%. Tesco, for example, have a range of own-brand cartridges at discounted prices.

Ink refills Try an ink refill kit the next time your cartridge runs out. Although fiddly to do, by refilling the ink reservoirs you can cut the cost to £5 or less. You can also get them refilled at stores such as Cartridge World (**www.cartridgeworld. org** ✉).

Paper supplies Use copier grade paper for your draft photo print-outs and save the inkjet and photo paper for your final prints only. Go direct to an office supplies company and buy in bulk to maximise the saving: buying five 50-sheet packs of premium photo paper will cut the price by about 25%.

Blank CDs and DVDs (CD-Rs) If you don't use paper or blank discs quickly enough to make a bulk buy worthwhile, get together with family and friends to share the saving. You'll also share the delivery cost, helping everyone out.

Net prices A little surfing on the Internet will save you money on all manner of computer consumables. Try the following general stationery sites:
www.staples.co.uk ✉
www.inkfactory.com ✉
www.viking-direct.co.uk ✉
www.ebuyer.com ✉
www.play.com ✉
www.pcworld.co.uk ✉
www.amazon.co.uk ✉

Unwanted software The bundled software may be advertised as 'worth £500' but it is often outdated or unpopular. If the software isn't exactly what you're looking for, don't let it influence your decision.

Imperfect add-ons The extra hardware included can be a poor choice. For example, the printer may be slow or expensive to run due to high ink cartridge prices. Or you may need an all-in-one printer with scanner and photocopier.

Choose your own bundle Any computer dealer can put together exactly the bundle of hardware and software you want. Give the same specification to two or three dealers and choose the one that gives you the best price. Look out for special offers on the web. It may be cheaper buying exactly what you need separately from different stores if necessary or online.

THE PORTABLE PREMIUM

In the past couple of years manufacturers have introduced many notebook or netbook laptops. These are small, lightweight, affordable laptops that have many of the features previously reserved for much more expensive laptops. For £200 to £400 you can get a laptop with wi-fi, an 80gb internal memory a 10-inch screen and enough processing power to do most of what a more expensive laptop or PC could do. If you want a small laptop to send email, surf the web or for word processing then one of these laptops could be suitable or as an extra computer at home.

BEWARE WARRANTIES

Don't waste money on an extended warranty While it may be worthwhile for a notebook, especially if you use it for work, a desktop PC is relatively cheap and easy to repair.

keep it simple

DIY CAN SAVE YOU £30–£50

PCs are very easy to upgrade – you can swap internal components to make your PC faster or to add more features. By doing it yourself, you'll save the £30–£50 labour fee that many computer dealers charge. Go to the Internet for help: a search on 'upgrade PC graphics card', for example, will turn up lots of advice and even step-by-step guides.

CUT COSTS ON CDS, DVDS AND SOFTWARE

When you've saved a packet by buying your electronic gadgets at the best price, don't blow your savings by buying full-price DVDs and computer software. Make your money go further by using your computer to shop online; half an hour's effective surfing will save money and shoe leather.

BUYING USED DISCS

As long as it plays perfectly, a used CD or DVD is a sensible buy; over time the savings can be enormous. In a typical music collection of 100 CDs, an average saving of £4 for each CD will buy a new TV and DVD player.

Shop locally Local and independent music shops may have a pre-owned section to browse. Oxfam's second-hand store has a CDs, DVDs and Music & Movies section – prices start at under £5 (go to **www.oxfam.org.uk** ✉ and look under 'Shop'). Check out high street charity shops, too.

Look online Online auctions have a far wider selection, with typical CD prices of around £5.

Watch out Before buying at a car-boot sale or temporary fair, check that the disc is legitimate and not a pirated copy.

BUY SONGS INSTEAD OF CDS

If you don't like all the songs on an album, see if the songs you want are available from an online music service, such as **www.apple.com/itunes** ✉ or **www.amazon.co.uk** ✉ rather than buying a CD. You can download individual songs from thousands of albums for around 79p each, build up a music collection on your computer then transfer the songs to an MP3 player or create your own CDs. It's difficult to quantify the savings you'll make if you compare the cost of the downloaded tracks with the same number of tracks on purchased CDs, but you'll have the satisfaction of knowing that you've only paid for those tracks you enjoy listening to.

REPLACING OLD WITH NEW

Are you sitting on a goldmine? If you have a collection of music or film in old formats – vinyl, VHS and CD – they may be worth selling. To find out if any of your old records are valuable, use the Search feature on an auction site such as **www.ebay.co.uk** ✉ to see how much the same records fetch. Online auctions are perfect for getting the best price for items that are otherwise hard to sell and you can reinvest your newly earned cash in more DVDs or MP3s.

Turn your vinyl into digital There's no need to leave those favourite albums gathering dust in the loft – or go out and buy them all again in CD format. You can now buy a USB turntable for around £80 (under £50 if you shop around or look for special offers) and add that cherished vinyl to your digital library to listen to via an MP3 player or burn to a CD. Plug the turntable into a USB port, load the easy-to-install Audacity software and relive those memories.

RESOURCES

MUSIC DOWNLOAD SITES

Steer clear of websites that provide pirated music and buy music from legitimate websites such as:

www.apple.com/itunes ✉
www.amazon.co.uk ✉
www.napster.co.uk ✉

REGIONAL VARIATIONS

Movie studios release DVDs with regional codes to restrict the sale of discs to a particular area – America or Europe, for example. If your DVD player is region-free, you can watch discs bought anywhere in the world and therefore save money by shopping internationally for the best deals – this includes making use of American sites such as American eBay (**www.ebay.com**), where you can get DVDs cheaper than in Britain.

TOP TIPS AUCTION BUYING

Buying online at an auction can be fun, but don't let the excitement get in the way of your better judgement.
■ **Check the seller's profile** To gauge the seller's reliability, check his feedback score. This shows the number of people who have left positive feedback about the way the seller has done business with them. You can read the feedback comments, too.
■ **Bid late** By bidding as late as possible, you avoid revealing your interest to other bidders and help to keep the price down.
■ **Check originality** If the auction description doesn't make it clear that you're buying an original CD or DVD, ask the seller directly in an email sent via eBay. Don't pay £5 for a pirated disc worth 50p.

ACADEMIC DISCOUNTS ON SOFTWARE

Is there a student or teacher in the household? If so, you may be entitled to an academic discount. The savings can be considerable. The most popular office software suite costs around £300 to buy normally, but can be legally purchased for around £100 for students and teachers.

FREE SOFTWARE

There are free versions of lots of software available on the Internet if you know where to look for everything from video-editing software, word processing to security software. You can also download demo versions of software for a month's trial. You can download software for free from sites like **www.download3000.com** ✉, **www.download.com** ✉ and **www.shareware.com** ✉ but there are hundreds more available. For word processing look at Open Office (**www.openoffice.org**) for virus software try AVG Antivirus Free Edition (**http://free.avg.com**) or Firewall Zone Alarm (**www.zonealarm.com**) and for anti-spyware software look at Windows Defender (**www.microsoft.com**).

FALLING GAMES PRICES

When a computer game is new, almost all shops sell it at very close to the manufacturer's list price – typically £30 or £40. Often within a few months, discounts of £5–£10 become common, and within a year it may fall to half-price. After that, the most popular games are often repackaged into a 'classic game' budget line-up with a selling price of £8 or so.

RESOURCES

SUPERSTORE SAVINGS
By shopping for CDs and DVDs online, you could save £5 or more on high-street prices. Online shops also have the advantage of a searchable catalogue that makes it easy to find the most obscure discs. Good sites include:
www.101cd.com
www.amazon.co.uk
www.cdwow.com
www.hmv.com
www.play.com
www.game.co.uk
www.dvd.co.uk

SECOND-HAND SITES
CDs, DVDs, games and more can be found at specialist online sites.
■ Thousands of titles at:
www.secondspin.com ✉ and **www.spun.com** ✉.
■ Most genres plus memorabilia at:
www.moremusic.co.uk ✉.
■ For classical music try:
www.classicalcdexchange. co.uk ✉.
■ Collectable vinyl and CDs at:
www.vinylnet.co.uk ✉.
■ General sites:
www.loot.com ✉;
www.oxfam.org.uk ✉;
www.ebay.co.uk ✉.

GET THE MOST FROM GAMES CONSOLES

A video games console can be expensive and cost more if you are always paying out for new games. By waiting for substantial price cuts and finding alternative means of buying games, you can have fun at a fraction of the cost.

BE WARY OF THE LATEST CONSOLES

You can save some money by not being tempted to buy the latest console as soon as it's launched. Manufacturers are careful to manage supply and demand to try and keep prices high. Consoles get to their natural prices – about 25% lower – after six months or so. After a year or two, they can fall to half their original price. However, demand for the Wii console was so high that it has remained at full price for a couple of years after its launch, although is now being discounted. Xbox 360 was twice the price it is now when it was launched. Sony's PS3 has remained at around £300, £100 less than when it was launched.

AVOID GETTING INTO FORMAT WARS

The three main consoles at the moment are Nintendo's Wii, Sony's Playstation 3 (PS3) and Xbox 360 from Microsoft. All three have been popular and have had a steady supply of new games and accessories – such as PlayTV on the PS3 that turns it into a Freeview box and hard disc recorder.

WHO NEEDS A DVD PLAYER?

Many new consoles work as DVD players, and are able to play back DVDs as well as games. Sony's PS3 has a Blu-ray player, which plays discs in HD. It was one of the cheaper ways to get a Blu-ray player when it was launched.

TOP TIPS BUYING GAMES

■ **Wait it out** If you can bear not to have the newest, must-have game you'll benefit from waiting a few months to decide on whether to purchase or not. Read the user reviews on the Internet (see Resources, left) or in your favourite games magazines to see which games have failed to live up to the hype, and save the expense of buying a dud.
■ **Buying used** CDs and DVDs are immune from viruses so pre-owned copies are worth tracking down. Small local shops are best for pre-owned games – expect to pay half price or less. You can also search Amazon's used section (**www.amazon.co.uk** ✉) and online auctions.
■ **Rent-a-game** Instead of buying games, join a video game rental service. You pay a monthly subscription (£10–£15) to rent the games by post. When you have mastered – or got bored with – the game you have rented, you post it back and choose another game. This gives you the benefit of playing a wide selection of games and, if you're a games fanatic and rent two games a month, you'll pay as little as 25% of the cost of buying them when they're first released. You can also rent games from Blockbuster or other rental companies.

VALUE-FOR-MONEY HOME SECURITY

Installing an effective alarm system will not only give you peace of mind, it can also be the key to paying a smaller insurance premium. But you'll need to do your homework to ensure you make the right choice.

CHECK WITH YOUR INSURANCE COMPANY

To help decide which type of alarm or home security system to install, first call your insurer to find out how much of a reduction in premium you will get for the various types of system you're considering. You may also find they insist on the alarm being fitted by an approved National Security Inspectorate (NSI) ✉ installer.

CHOOSING THE RIGHT TYPE OF ALARM

A professionally installed alarm can cost £400–£1,000, depending on the size of your home.

Siren call The most basic alarm is a bells-only system: if the sensors detect an intruder the alarm sounds, but nothing else happens. You're relying on a neighbour or passer-by to report the alarm bell ringing, so it's a poor investment if you live in a rural or isolated area, and even if you live in a city it may be ignored.

Monitored response The alternative is the same set up of sensors and alarm box, but with an added monitoring system. The alarm is connected to a 24-hour call centre that calls your home to catch any false alarms – before contacting the police. Monitoring can add an extra £5–£20 per month, but is essential for isolated homes.

THE ECONOMY OPTION

If you want to have some additional security you could fit your own DIY alarm system. You could buy a wireless system for a small house for around £100. This would include a bell and alarm box, a couple of infra-red sensors, window sensors and a control panel. Before buying and installing any alarm check with your local Crime Prevention Officer what they would recommend in your area. Although you may have additional peace of mind the police will normally only respond to an alarm that is professionally fitted and monitored.

MULTIPLE DISCOUNT

Save money on having a police-approved system installed by getting together with neighbours in your street and negotiating a discount with an NSI installer.

RESOURCES

FIND AN ALARM INSTALLER
For the police to respond to an alarm both the alarm and installer must be approved, unless a witness has reported a crime taking place. To find an approved alarm installer in your area, visit the National Security Inspectorate at **www.nsi.org.uk** 01628 637512 ✉.

Home repairs and improvements

Doing repairs and maintenance yourself, tackling problems before they get expensive and making sensible improvements helps you to pay less to preserve the value of your home.

PAYING LESS IN AN EMERGENCY

Calling out a plumber or other tradesman in the middle of the night because of an emergency is extremely expensive. But there are ways of keeping costs down.

TOP TIPS PAY LESS TO PROFESSIONALS

Increase your chances of finding a reputable tradesman who will do a good job for a fair fee by adopting these strategies.

■ **Beware the phone book** Unless you have a dire emergency, such as flooding or sparking electrics, try to avoid the emergency plumbers or electricians listed in the phone book. Always ask for a quote before committing – some charge a prohibitive call-out fee, as much as £100 plus high hourly rates thereafter, while others offer a fixed price for specific jobs and no call-out fees.

■ **Keep a list of contacts** Compile a list of local tradesmen who you or your neighbours have used before and can trust, and keep it to hand. If you have a working relationship, they are more likely to come quickly and charge less.

■ **Check existing home insurance** Many home insurance policies include a 24-hour helpline with lists of reputable companies who will send someone in an emergency. Check to see if your policy includes this service.

EMERGENCY DIY

Avoid an emergency call-out fee by making your own repair, temporary or permanent. Plumbing problems are usually the ones that can't wait.

Fixing a leaking pipe If you can spot the leak and it is from a compression fitting – a heavy brass component – tighten the nuts with a spanner. A leak from a soldered fitting – a smaller copper joint – can be fixed using J&B Cold Weld or a similar two-part adhesive, with the pipes drained before you begin. If you are in any doubt about your repair, get it checked by a plumber later.

Drain rods for a blocked drain You can buy a set of drain rods for under £30. Find the manhole and remove the cover. If it's full of water, fit the corkscrew end onto the drain rods and push them into the gulley at the bottom, away from the house. Work the rods backwards and forwards, pulling them out from time to time so you can remove anything the corkscrew has picked up. If the manhole is empty, use the rods in the opposite direction.

Unblocking a sink With a sink plunger, force water down the waste pipe. If that doesn't work, look under the sink for a bowl or U-shaped trap, place a bucket beneath it, then unscrew and flush with water from the taps. Remove residue with an old toothbrush.

Unblocking a toilet Put on a latex glove and feel around the other side of the U-bend. You should be able to remove anything you find there. If you can't find anything, push the head of an old-fashioned cotton mop into the toilet bowl base and work up and down as you would a sink plunger.

ASK YOURSELF

IS EMERGENCY REPAIR INSURANCE WORTH IT?
It is generally worth the premium of around £80. In an emergency, the insurance company will quickly send a tradesman to sort it out. Cover includes problems with central heating, gas, electricity and plumbing. Check what is covered, and what is defined as an 'emergency'.

ALWAYS HAVE A DIY MANUAL ON HAND
Armed with a good DIY manual such as those published by Reader's Digest and Collins, you should be able to cope with many domestic crises yourself.

MAKING A BROKEN WINDOW SAFE

If the glass is still in place or the hole is small, lay strips of duct tape along the cracks to hold it together. If a lot of glass has gone, you'll have to board up the window. Work from the outside if possible, and lay down newspaper to catch the splinters. Wearing gloves and safety glasses, pull out the loose glass, then remove the putty with a hammer and chisel to free the rest of the glass. Cut a piece of hardboard large enough to overlap the putty and secure with tacks or light nails. Seal the edges with duct tape.

CUT THE COST OF EXTERNAL REPAIRS

Water can be highly destructive to flat roofs, brickwork and even interior decoration if you do not maintain the exterior of your house. By catching small problems before they escalate into major emergencies, you'll avoid heavy bills.

KEEP A LID ON ROOF REPAIRS

Felt for a flat roof Repair flat roofs with torch-on roofing felt, £25–£40 for an 8-metre roll. You'll need a blowtorch (from £20) and a gas bottle, but the repair will last indefinitely. Apply the felt when the roof is dry. Cut a patch 15cm (6in) larger all around than the affected area. Heat the shiny side of the felt until the bitumen melts, then position it. Tread down from the centre outwards to avoid bubbles.

Paint over a leak For an emergency repair to a flat roof that is leaking, paint the leaking areas with a bituminous roofing treatment such as Flexacryl from a DIY supplier (£15 for 1kg). You can do this while the roof is wet, or even when it's raining. If the roof has deteriorated all over, buy a 5kg tin (around £60) and paint the whole roof. The same products also work on flashings.

Save on replacement tiles Keep an eye on builders' yards, skips and demolition sites, looking for cut-price or free replacement tiles or slates that match the colour of your roof. Then, when you need to make a roof repair, you won't be forced into an expensive rush purchase.

---

keep it simple

SAFETY FIRST
When working above ground level, make safety your priority. Don't be tempted to save money by taking a chance with an old ladder. Hire or buy the platform or ladder you need to do the job safely. You can hire a folding step-up platform from HSS Hire **www.hss.com** 08456 02 19 61 ✉ at a cost of £40 a week. If you have any doubts at all about working from a ladder or platform, call in a professional.

WHAT YOU SAVE BY DOING IT YOURSELF

CLEANING MASONRY WALLS	HIRED POWERWASH (WEEKEND)	**£66**
	HIRED SPECIALIST COMPANY	**£500** plus
REPAINTING A FLAT ROOF WITH WATERPROOFING SOLUTION	REPAINTING YOURSELF	**£80**
	HIRED WORKMAN	**£150** plus
REPOINTING BRICKWORK	REPOINTING YOURSELF	**£20**
	HIRED WORKMAN	**£20–£25** per m²
APPLYING SEALANT TO MAKE GUTTERS AND PIPES WATERPROOF	APPLYING YOURSELF	**£6**
	HIRED WORKMAN	**£40–£70**
PROTECTING GUTTERING WITH CHICKEN WIRE	APPLYING YOURSELF **£30**	
	HIRED WORKMAN	**£40–£70**

Are you up-to-date with routine checks?

Regular checks cost nothing but can prevent expensive problems occurring.

SPRING

■ Remember to have the chimney swept. Call in a chimney sweep to clear blockages (for around £30–£50) before they cause costly trouble.

■ Check masonry for cracks and fix any that appear by replacing damaged bricks.

■ Check pipes are straight, leak-free and unblocked. Straighten downpipes, clear leaves and flush with water.

■ Check gutters for cracks. Fix with roofing mastic – around £30 for 2.5 litres.

SUMMER

■ Ensure the drive is free of holes. Fill any that appear. A 25kg bag of pre-packed Tarmac costs around £5.

■ Check flat roofs for wear. Paint Flexacryl (about £15 for 1kg) on cracks or tears.

■ Check window sills and fences for rot. Treat if necessary (see page 240).

AUTUMN

■ Check pipes and roofs for leaves, blockages and leaks. Remove leaves, flush out pipes and fix leaks.

■ Check insulation on pipes, especially in well-insulated roof spaces that get cold.

WINTER

■ Check the lower chimney for soot. Clear out if needed.

■ If you go away in winter, remember to leave the heat on low to avoid burst pipes.

MAINTAIN SOUND GUTTERS

Within six months, the effects of rainwater overflowing from a blocked gutter can damage a wall, inside and out.

Install a leaf guard Keep leaves out of gutters by installing a leaf guard costing a few pounds from a DIY store, or make a leaf guard for pennies by bending a piece of chicken wire over the top of the gutter.

Fix cracks and holes Use waterproof exterior sealant to fill small cracks in gutters; fill bigger holes cheaply with self-adhesive flashing. Epoxy-based car body repair paste effectively fills small cracks in metal gutters and downpipes.

Plastic gutters cost less When replacing gutters, choose plastic ones that need no painting and are easier to maintain than metal ones. Use plenty of clips to prevent the gutter bending when full of rain. You may be able to buy a special connector to join the plastic to a metal gutter that is not being replaced. Seal the joint with roofing mastic.

CURING DAMP WALLS

A permanently damp wall costs money by reducing the effectiveness of your domestic heating, and causes condensation that eventually ruins the plasterwork.

Weatherproof walls Bricks in old walls often absorb water, even if the pointing is sound. Having checked that the problem isn't a defective damp course – call in an expert if you're unsure – paint the exterior with two coats of silicon waterproofer (around £20 for 5 litres). A 5-litre 'no name' tin from a builders' merchant could be half the price of branded products, but make sure it's a type that allows condensation to escape. Fill defects in the wall by applying a sand and cement exterior filler, dyed to match the bricks.

Prevent condensation Nine-tenths of interior damp is due to condensation. Improve the ventilation in affected rooms first – this may be enough by itself. Turning up thermostatic radiator valves by 5°–10° may help, too. If these measures don't work, buy a dehumidifier. These cost from £90 to over £300 but are effective and much cheaper than wall insulation, which can cost thousands of pounds.

SMART MOVES

TROUBLE-FREE PATHS AND DRIVES

Paths and drives invariably get covered in weeds and can be damaged by harsh weather. Give them a low-cost facelift.

■ **Save on weedkiller** Use thin bleach (25p a litre) instead of weed and moss-killers (about £5 1kg) for paving. On a sunny day, brush the weeds with the bleach – it will kill shallow-rooted moss and other weeds but won't harm the plants with deeper roots.

■ **Refurbish paving** Cover cracked concrete drives and paths with gravel. Don't pay to remove the concrete – it will help keep the gravel in place and clear of soil.

■ Build a low retaining wall with a row of bricks to retain the gravel. Cut costs by 60% by buying gravel by the metre from a builders' yard instead of in bags.

REPAIRS AND REPLACEMENTS FOR WOODWORK

Wood is the traditional and best material for windows, doors and floors. It is a renewable resource, easily repaired and lasts for a long time if correctly maintained.

WELL-MAINTAINED WINDOWS AND DOORS

Cut costs on maintaining windows and doors by tackling problems yourself in good time.

Use car body filler A cheap way of repairing window sills that have rotted in a few areas is to chisel the rotten wood out, paint the sound bare wood with top-quality wood preservative to prevent more rot, then fill with car body filler. This is less expensive than wood filler – especially if you buy a large tin from a car parts wholesaler – and just as effective. Sand until smooth and paint as normal.

Save 50% on sash window repairs Rattling or draughty sash windows can often be repaired using standard beading and parting beads – around £2 a metre at any good timber yard. If you don't have the skill yourself, a good joiner should be able to overhaul one sash window a day – less if you are lucky, longer if the whole sill has to be replaced. Allow £180–£200 to recondition a sash box and casement; add £80 for a replacement sill. A replacement window will cost £500–£700, or £1,000 plus if a new sash box is needed.

 **RESOURCES**

USEFUL WEBSITES

■ Get DIY advice on maintaining and repairing woodwork and more at **www.diyfixit.co.uk** ✉ and **www.diydoctor.org.uk** ✉.
■ For suppliers of windows and doors, check out **www.homesources.co.uk** ✉.

WINDOWS

■ For reputable glaziers contact the Glass and Glazing Federation at **www.ggf.org.uk** 0870 042 4255 ✉.
■ DIY stores such as Wickes **www.wickes.co.uk** 0845 279 9898 ✉ have low-price PVCu windows, starting from under £80.

■ Andersen Windows **www.blackmillwork.co.uk** 01283 511122 ✉ offers a particularly wide range of windows, plus doors.
■ Protech **www.thebbgroup.co.uk** 01325 310520 ✉ sells windows, conservatories and specialist glazing online.
■ The Original Box Sash Windows Company **www.boxsash.com** 0800 169 3198 ✉ makes casement windows, as well as traditional sash windows.

DOORS

■ DirectDoors.com **www.directdoors.com** 01968 671681 ✉ sells exterior and interior doors.

■ Doors Select **www.doorsselect.co.uk** 01457 867079 ✉ stocks interior doors and timber mouldings.
■ Kershaws Door Warehouse **www.door-warehouse.co.uk** 01274 604488 ✉ sells exterior and interior doors, including manufacturers' seconds.

DOOR FURNITURE

■ Handle World **www.handleworld.co.uk** 01924 481713 ✉ sells door knobs and handles, including cabinet handles, as does online supplier Door Furniture Direct at **www.doorfurnituredirect.co.uk** 0151 652 3136 ✉.

Replace putty the proper way If putty is loose or missing, scrape the old putty out with a chisel, down to the bare wood. Knead fresh putty until workable, then hold it in your palm while you press it in place with your thumb. Smooth the surface and shape it to match the other windows with a scraper or knife dipped in water so it doesn't stick to the putty. When it has hardened, paint the new putty in the same way as wood.

Stop the rot If the bottom of a door or the sill has started to deteriorate, remove paint from the affected area and treat with two coats of wood-hardening resin, then fit a weather bar (£5 from a timber yard). This will divert rain from the door bottom. Paint with two coats of exterior paint.

Strengthen doors Close up loose joints in the corners of a panel door by knocking them together with a mallet, then running two or three one-inch wood screws through the side rails, about 3cm (1½in) in from the edge. Countersink the heads so that they disappear, fill and then coat with paint.

LOW-COST TIPS FOR TIMBER MOULDINGS

You can avoid hiring a carpenter to carry out repairs to internal woodwork by investing in the right equipment. And with a little knowledge, you can keep repairs to a minimum.

Pay less for the perfect fit The main problem when fitting new architraves around doors and windows is cutting the mitres. But if you invest in a chop or mitre saw (about £25 for a manual version or around £70 for a cheap electric one), there will be no need to call in a professional and your corners will be completely accurate and neat.

Rule out replacements When fitting new internal woodwork, always paint the back with wood primer as well as the front. This prevents the wood from splitting as it dries out, so you won't have to replace it again.

EXTERIOR TIMBER REPAIRS

■ Strengthen elderly wooden fences with ready-made metal plates shaped so you can nail horizontal arris rails back onto fence posts. Loose boards and gravel boards – hardwood timber planks fixed to the bottom of panels to stop damp causing the panel to rot – can be nailed back in place with galvanised clout nails, and rotten boards replaced with new from a timber yard. Two coats of coloured exterior wood preservative will protect a fence for five years.

■ Rotten fence posts can be saved by sinking a concrete stub into the soil, then bolting the post to the concrete stub. Or, if enough of the post remains, push it into a spiked metal socket.

TIMBER TROUBLES – PREVENTION vs CURE

PROBLEM	CURE	PREVENTION
Wet rot	Woodwork with extensive wet rot must be replaced – and costs can quickly escalate over the £1,000 mark.	Cure wet rot early yourself with rot killer, wood filler and a coat of paint for under £50 (see opposite).
Specialist woodworm treatment	If woodworm has spread, it can cost from £1,000 to eradicate it from a small house. Specialists have to drill holes in floorboards, joists and stairs to spray in chemical treatments.	You could treat it yourself for under £50. Ask a timber preservation company for a free report on the problem areas – often included with a no obligation quote – then buy your own fluids, such as Cuprinol 5 Star Complete Wood Treatment.
Dry rot	Extensive dry rot can cost thousands of pounds to eradicate from a small house.	Maintain a waterproof roof, sound brickwork and good underfloor ventilation.

GOOD-VALUE FLOORS AND FLOOR COVERINGS

keep it simple

KEEP A WOODEN FLOOR IN GOOD CONDITION
- Stop floorboards creaking by sprinkling talcum powder between the boards to prevent them from rubbing. Or nail them down firmly (check first for pipes below nail positions).
- Protect your floor by using rubber casters or stick-on felt patches beneath heavy furniture, and put down rugs in areas of heavy wear.
- For seriously damaged wood floors, a coat of paint is a cheap and easy cover-up.
- Remove unsightly black heel marks on wood (or vinyl) by rubbing with silver polish on a soft cloth or white appliance wax, available from appliance stores. Remove any excess polish or wax with a clean, soft cloth.

Avoid expensive mistakes by asking yourself a few questions before you buy. Will the flooring receive a lot of wear and tear? Is it important that it's waterproof? Does the floor covering need to muffle sound?

STUNNING SOLID WOOD FLOORS

Save on carpets by exposing wooden floors. With only a little money and effort, your boards can look beautiful.

Sand it yourself Instead of paying hundreds of pounds to have floorboards stripped professionally, hire a heavy-duty sander for around £60 a weekend or £90 a week (plus sanding discs at around £6 for 10).

Save on stripping If you have fairly new floorboards, you may be able to get away with scrubbing them with hot water and detergent before applying a suitable finish.

Do the preparation If you do decide to hire a professional, save money by doing some preparation yourself. Replace any damaged floorboards with boards taken from an area that will be covered by a rug. Then carefully remove protruding nails – or knock them in with a nail punch – that may damage the sander.

CARPET LORE

With carpeting, you generally get what you pay for and high quality will last longer, so buy the best you can afford. Because floors set the tone for your décor, carpeting is an area in which long-term savings should outweigh up-front costs. And with carpet warehouses and department stores competing for business, it is worth visiting several outlets to find high-quality carpeting for a reasonable price.

Fitting a carpet Paying to get your carpet fitted professionally is worth it; it will almost certainly look better than if you do it yourself, unless you are laying foam-back carpet. When looking for the best deal, price the cost of the carpet and fitting together – a more expensive carpet coupled with an in-house fitting service may cost less than buying a cheaper carpet and sourcing the fitting from elsewhere.

Wool or synthetic? Synthetic carpet costs less and should wear well, but wool keeps its looks longer. Consider opting for a wool-synthetic mix that looks good but is less expensive than all-wool.

Pay less for a bedroom carpet A carpet in a bedroom will be less heavily used than one in a living room or hall so you can go for a cheaper option.

COMPARE THE COST OF FLOORING

SOLID WOOD FLOOR	£45–£60
UNTREATED SLATE	£25–£60
WOOL TWIST PILE CARPET	£10–£40
WOOD-EFFECT LAMINATE	£10–£30
SHEET VINYL	£16
VINYL TILES	£8
SYNTHETIC CARPET	£3

These are typical prices per m² for different types of flooring (excluding laying) – though costs vary.

Never skimp on underlay Buying poor-quality underlay is a false economy. A good-quality underlay will extend the life of your carpet by 40% or more and can be reused when the time comes to replace the new carpet on top.

Cut down on waste Make sure your carpet retailer doesn't supply you with a large roll of carpet that may be more than you need once all the awkward corners have been trimmed off. A skilled carpet fitter should use off-cuts to fill in awkward gaps, so you can save by having a carpet properly measured and fitted, especially for areas such as stairs.

Look out for hidden costs Major carpet retailers sell carpet at a reasonable price but inflate the cost of grips and underlay. Ask whether underlay and grips are included, or whether your existing ones can be reused. Check whether you can buy them more cheaply from a DIY store.

WIPE-CLEAN FLOORING

Look out for sales at DIY and high street stores. You can lay most types of laminate and vinyl flooring yourself.

Pay less for a wood floor Wood-effect laminate is the low-cost alternative to laying a solid wood floor. If the surface beneath is flat and in good condition, lay it yourself. Use a specially designed waterproof laminate, such as one with the Aqua Protect logo, in a bathroom or kitchen.

Cheapest for bathrooms Cut the cost of flooring in a bathroom or kitchen by opting for hard-wearing vinyl – the least expensive choice.

Cost-conscious choices for tiles If you want clay flooring, buy quarry tiles – they are half the price of terracotta, which cost over £20 per m². For a real stone floor, which can cost £60 per m² or more, untreated slate is often cheapest but will stain – so use a suitable stain protector (around £15 a litre). Fake a stone floor with laminate tiles (around £15 per m²) or top-quality vinyl that looks like stone (£25 per m² or more) – and both are cheaper than stone to lay.

USE NATURAL-FIBRE FLOORING WISELY

Avoid having to replace natural flooring sooner than you anticipated by taking into account its intended use. Each type has its own strengths. Like carpet, natural flooring looks best when fitted professionally.

■ **For heavy traffic** Buy sisal or coir – the most hard-wearing options – for areas that receive a lot of use. Don't put natural flooring down where food or drink may be spilled, or in a bathroom because damp could make it rot.

■ **For comfort underfoot** Soft, silky jute is a good choice for bedrooms, whereas coir, for instance, may be too prickly.

🦉 RESOURCES

FLOORING SUPPLIERS

■ Some leading suppliers of flooring are listed at **www.homesources.co.uk** ✉.
■ UK Flooring Direct **www.ukflooringdirect.co.uk** 0845 263 6586 ✉ sells a wide range of flooring.
■ Find quality laminates at **www.flooringlaminate.co.uk** ✉.

CARPETS

■ Find local suppliers and useful buying tips at **www.carpetfoundation.com** 01562 755568 ✉.

■ Superstore Carpet Right **www.carpetright.co.uk** ✉ offers 10% web discount and Allied Carpets **www.alliedcarpets.com** 08000 932 932 ✉ has a free survey and estimating service, plus free fitting.
■ The Discounted Carpet Underlay Company **www.discounted-carpet-underlay.co.uk** 01482 215008 ✉ sells low-price underlay.
■ RugsUK.com **www.rugsuk.com** 0808 108 9657 ✉ has many rugs at low prices online ✉.

OTHER FLOORINGS

■ 1926 Trading Company **www.1926trading.co.uk** 0800 587 2027 ✉ for real wood floors.
■ The Tile Warehouse **www.thetilewarehouse.com** 0115 939 0209 ✉.
■ World's End Tiles **www.worldsendtiles.co.uk** 020 7819 2100 ✉.
■ Terra Firma Tiles **www.terrafirmatiles.co.uk** 01264 810315 ✉ for terracotta and more.
■ Natural Slate Company **www.theslatecompany.net** 020 8371 1485 ✉.

SMART DECORATING CHOICES

Painting and decorating is an inexpensive way to give your home a makeover, turning dark spaces into light and airy ones. Here's how to pay less when renovating your existing decorating scheme.

PAINTING POINTERS

Bear in mind that painting a wall almost always costs less than covering it with wallpaper.

Don't skimp on preparation The secret of a successful result lies in the preparation. Make sure your walls are as smooth as possible before starting to cover them with paint, paper or tiles.

Buy match pots Avoid choosing the wrong paint colour by painting sample patches on all four walls of a room, or on large pieces of white paper (lining paper is ideal) that you then stick on the walls. Examine each colour under natural and artificial light to see if you still like it. Match pots cost between £1–£3 each.

Mix your own If you want a bright colour of paint, save money by buying cheap white emulsion and adding a strong-coloured emulsion – a match pot will often be enough –

RESOURCES

DECORATING
- Decorating Direct **www.decoratingdirect.co.uk** sells materials and tools online at trade prices with delivery free for orders over £50 ✉.
- Homesources **www.homesources.co.uk** ✉ lists many suppliers of paints and wallpapers.

PAINT
- A wide selection of paints: Crown Paints **www.crownpaints.co.uk** ✉ Dulux **www.dulux.co.uk** 0870 444 11 11 ✉ B&Q **www.diy.com** ✉ Focus Do It All **www.focusdiy.co.uk** 0800 436 436 ✉ Homebase **www.homebase.co.uk** 0845 077 8888 ✉

- Cuprinol **www.cuprinol.co.uk** 0870 444 11 11 ✉ to protect interior and exterior wood, walls and floors.
- Hammerite **www.hammerite.com** 0870 444 11 11 ✉ for your metal painting needs.
- Technical Paint Services **www.technicalpaintservices.co.uk** 0845 230 1244 ✉ for specialist paints.

WALLPAPER
- Major suppliers: Wallpaperdirect **http://wallpaperdirect.co.uk** 01323 430886 ✉ Harlequin **www.harlequin.uk.com** 0844 5430200 ✉
- Wallpaper Orders UK **www.wallpaperorders.co.uk** 0870 170 9660 ✉ discount online outlet, ranges include Anaglypta and Morris & Co.

- Wallpaper Coverings Direct **www.wallcoveringsdirect.co.uk** 0870 170 9669 ✉ offers a wide range.

TILES
- The Tile Association **www.tiles.org.uk** 020 8663 0946 ✉ provides product and supplier information for wall and floor tiles.
- Topps Tiles **www.toppstiles.co.uk** 0800 023 4703 ✉ is a low-price chain with branches throughout Britain.
- Marlborough Tiles Factory Shop, Marlborough **www.marlboroughtiles.com** 01672 515287 ✉.
- For details of Pilkington's factory outlets visit **www.pilkingtons.com** 0161 727 1111 ✉.

until you get the desired shade. Make a note of exactly which colour you added, and how much, in case you need to make up more paint.

WALLPAPER ECONOMIES

Before you buy expensive wallpaper, check the sales at your local decorating stores, and online shopping outlets that sell designer wallpaper at a discount (see Resources, left).

Try before you buy Just like you would with paint, look at wallpaper samples in the room you intend to decorate in both daylight and artificial light, to be sure that you have made the right choice.

Buy less paper If you select an expensive wallpaper, use it as a focal point and hang it on one wall only.

Paint on paper Combine textured paper with paint for an economical yet stylish look. Textured wallpaper in white or cream is often cheaper than the coloured equivalents.

SAVE THE EXPENSE OF RETILING

Look out for cheap tiles in factory shops and discount warehouses. These outlets have overstock in perfect condition as well as seconds.

Paint over tiles Paint over old tiles for a new look at a fraction of the cost of re-tiling. Clean the tiles and remove all traces of dust, then apply a tile primer, followed by tile paint, both at £13–£15 for 750ml. Alternatively, paint an all-in-one tile paint directly onto the tiles, at a cost of about £16 for 750ml.

Refurbish existing tiling For under £10 you can give ageing tiling a fresh look by regrouting. Scrape out as much of the old grout as possible – you can buy a grout removal tool for around £2 or make your own from an old hacksaw blade. Regrout, using an ice lolly stick to smooth the grout between the tiles.

Replace cracked tiles Save retiling whole areas by just replacing any damaged tiles. Wearing safety glasses, drill a hole in the centre of a damaged tile and chisel it out along with old grout to give a flat surface, working from the centre. Then replace and regrout. If matching tiles aren't available, replace with tiles in contrasting colours.

Salvage not necessarily cheaper When replacing quarry tiles or trying to match old brickwork, try a salvage company such as the Coventry Demolition Company **www.coventry-demolition.co.uk** or 0800 294 8603 ✉, which specialises in reclaiming reusable materials. As the cost of reclaimed materials can be high, also try other sources such as council recycling centres and farm sales.

keep it simple

When decorating, keep waste to a minimum and look after your tools to avoid having to replace them often.

■ Use the smallest possible quantity of white spirit or brush cleaner.

■ Soak brushes in the same jar of white spirit overnight if you plan to use them again next day.

■ After you finish decorating, make sure you clean all traces of paint from brushes and rollers. Prevent damage to brushes during storage by securing paper around the ends.

DESCALE WASHING MACHINES AND DISHWASHERS

Limescale shortens the life of your machine and causes breakdowns, so descale regularly. Remove furring from inside a washing machine by running it on empty with 600ml (1 pint) of white vinegar, followed by a rinse wash. For a dishwasher, add a cup of white vinegar and run the empty dishwasher on a rinse-and-hold cycle. Then add detergent and run through a cycle to clean the machine.

KEEP FILTERS CLEAR

Clean filters in the washing machine and tumble dryer on a regular basis. Similarly, remove food particles from the dishwasher filter once a week.

TIPS FOR TROUBLE-FREE KITCHENS

Save money on calling out the professionals by dealing with minor problems before they become costly repair jobs. Better still, avoid problems occurring in the first place by regular maintenance. It doesn't cost a penny to carry out a few basic housekeeping chores every week or so. These precautions will keep machines running smoothly and save on repairs.

CHECK FIRST

If your washing machine or any other major kitchen appliance starts to play up, run some checks before you resort to calling in the repair men.
- Is the machine properly plugged in?
- Are the sockets and fuses working?
- Check the electrical cord isn't damaged.
- Is there a filter that is clogged up?
- Check that the machine is level.
- Is there some other basic check you could carry out that just might save you an expensive call-out fee?

TOUCH UP PAINT SCRATCHES

A local appliance dealer can sell you touch-up paint. A scratch on a washing machine or fridge quickly creates rust, which spreads the damage. For minor blemishes, paint on a thin coat, allow it to dry and smooth it out with a fine rubbing compound used on car bodies. For deeper gashes and nicks, build up paint in layers, allowing each one to dry before adding the next.

OPEN WINDOWS WHILE YOU COOK

Ensure that you have good airflow through the kitchen. Wash extractor grilles regularly to prevent moisture build-up. If condensation is a problem, install an extractor hood over the cooker.

AVOID BLOCKED PIPES

Put a handful of washing soda and boiling water down the plughole regularly to prevent the U-bend from filling up with food waste. Keep tea leaves, rice and vegetable peelings out of sinks – use a bowl to catch them and prevent them clogging the plughole.

BALANCING ACT

Appliances work best when level, so use a spirit level to check from side to side and back to front. Screw legs or castors up or down as needed.

CHECK THE SEAL ON THE FRIDGE

Put a torch with a beam into the fridge, shut the door and switch off the kitchen lights. Any light leaking out of the fridge is a sign that the seal is damaged. Mend it cheaply with silicon sealant, or buy a replacement seal at an appliance store.

WHEN NOT TO DO IT YOURSELF

Don't attempt a DIY repair if the appliance is still under guarantee or extended warranty. Instead, get the maker or warranty provider to fix it.

A QUICK FIX FOR A WASHING MACHINE LEAK

If the hose on your washing machine springs a leak, fix it cheaply by replacing the faulty hose at your local DIY store.

GIVE YOUR FRIDGE ENOUGH SPACE

Make sure there is enough space between the fridge and the wall for adequate air flow. Keep the coil at the back of the fridge dusted. Check the fridge temperature setting and defrost timer from time to time and adjust as necessary.

DISHWASHER DODGES

■ To check that the spray arm of a dishwasher is working, make a note of its position before you start the machine and then again halfway through a cycle to see whether it has moved.
■ If the spray arm is clogged, you can clear it easily with a skewer or a stiff wire. Then rinse the arm well with water.
■ Fix jammed dish racks by loosening the rollers by hand or unscrewing and replacing them.

LOWER THE COST OF HOME IMPROVEMENTS

A well-chosen new kitchen or bathroom can transform your home and even add to its value. Look in the sales, visit discount warehouses and factory shops and consider ex-display models. Adding more space to your home will also increase its worth. You save more by getting a good deal on materials and managing the building process carefully.

SAVE ON BUYING A NEW KITCHEN

Get 50% off ex-display units As most ex-display kitchens are sold 'as seen', you won't be able to demand a refund if you find a fault, so check well before buying.

Free kitchen planning Many kitchen suppliers will plan your kitchen for you for nothing if you take along a set of detailed measurements, including dimensions of windows, doors and existing appliances.

Cut delivery costs If possible, transport the kitchen units home yourself.

Save on fitting costs Using the supplier's own fitters adds up to 50% to the cost of a new kitchen. There are two ways round this: one is to employ independent fitters you have found yourself; the second is to do a lot of the work yourself, including removing the old kitchen and assembling

---

SERVICE POINTS AND APPLIANCES

Keep existing service points to reduce electrical and plumbing costs when fitting a new kitchen. Also cut out the cost of new appliances by using your existing ones. If you opt for new appliances, remember you are not obliged to buy those offered by the supplier with the kitchen. Sourcing from a discount store could save you anything from 10%–25%.

RESOURCES

KITCHENS AND BATHROOMS

■ For advice on planning and buying a kitchen or bathroom, plus a guide to products, contact The Kitchen Bathroom Bedroom Specialists Association **www.ksa.co.uk** 01623 818808 ✉.

■ For suppliers of kitchens and bathrooms, see **www.homesources.co.uk** ✉.

■ For outlets that sell kitchens and bathrooms at discount prices, visit **www. gooddealdirectory.co.uk** ✉.

KITCHENS

■ Find discount stores and sales offers for kitchens at **www.kitchens.co.uk** ✉ plus details of many other kitchen suppliers and products.

■ You can shop online for cabinet doors at Just Doors **www.justdoors. co.uk** 0870 200 1010 ✉ and Doorsdirect **www.doorsdirect.co.uk** 01423 502040 ✉.

■ Also check out Kitchen Refurbs **www.kitchenrefurbs.co.uk** 0800 781 4798 ✉ for replacement doors and The Kitchen Doctor **www.thekitchendoctor.com** 01689 850000 ✉.

■ National Brands **www.national-brands.co.uk** 01223 835100 or 0151 260 8967 ✉ sell famous-name freestanding kitchen units at up to 70% off at their Cambridge and Liverpool outlets.

■ Good-value kitchens are available from: IKEA **www.ikea.co.uk** ✉

Magnet **www.magnet.co.uk** 01325 744093/4/5 ✉.

BATHROOMS

■ Bathrooms.com **www.bathrooms.com** ✉ is a comprehensive online directory of products and suppliers.

■ The Bathrooms Manufacturers Association **www.bathroom-association.org** 01782 747123 ✉ has an online directory of products and suppliers, including free fact sheets.

■ The Bathroom Discount Centre **www.bathdisc.co.uk** 020 7381 4222 ✉ has an online store and warehouse in Fulham, London.

■ Bathroom Express **www.bathroomexpress.co.uk** 0845 130 2000 ✉ is an online store with keenly priced bathrooms.

the units, and ask the kitchen fitters for a discount. Consider doing the basic installation, too: major retailers such as B&Q will even advise on how to plumb in a new washing machine.

UPGRADING YOUR EXISTING KITCHEN

Pay a fraction of the cost of a new kitchen by adding new doors and work surfaces to carcasses already in place.

Revamp doors Buying new cabinet doors costs from £14 a door, while painting doors that are too good to replace costs just £10 for wood or melamine primer (750ml) plus £10–£15 for 750ml of satinwood or melamine paint. Then fit new knobs or handles – knobs from Screwfix Direct (see Resources, page 253) are about £15 for five, for example.

Replace the worktop A new worktop is another way of making a big change for little outlay. Fitting a worktop is a job for a professional. The price of a new worktop for the average-sized kitchen plus fitting starts at around £300.

Retile the kitchen From around £100, you can retile a kitchen yourself. Alternatively, change the tile colour with tile paint (see page 245).

REVAMPING A BATHROOM

A new bathroom with shower costing from £3,000, including installation, can be a good investment. Do small jobs yourself to maintain its appearance for little cost.

Quick fix Patching up scratches on an enamel bath costs just a few pounds and saves on the expense of a new bath.

Upgrade your taps Elegant taps give an inexpensive bathroom suite a designer look, and cost from about £35 for two from a plumbers' merchant or discount store.

Buy a new suite A new bathroom suite is as little as £250 from a superstore like B&Q. The cheapest bathroom suites at these and similar suppliers are known as 'contract suites'.

Pay less for fitting The cost of bathroom installation is at least as much as the suite itself, so doubling the cost of the job. Some suppliers, such as B&Q, offer an installation service. But you may get a better price if you find your own plumber. Don't use heavily advertised bathroom fitting services – somebody has to pay for all those adverts.

MAKING AN OLD SHOWER GOOD AS NEW

If a shower is sluggish, don't just buy a new one. Mineral deposits from the water may be clogging up the head. Unscrew the head and take it apart. Put all the pieces in a bowl of white vinegar and leave them to soak for a few hours. Use a brush to remove any stubborn sediment and rinse all the pieces well. Reassemble the shower head and screw it back into place. Fitting a new hose often helps as well.

ASK YOURSELF

CAN I GET A GRANT FOR REFITTING MY BATHROOM?

Check with your local council to see whether grants are available. They are generally only available for the elderly, those on benefit or with a disability, or if you live in a deprived area. See *Family affairs*, page 117.

BUILDING AN EXTENSION

Free advice on the cost of extensions is available from the Royal Town Planning Institute and the National Home Improvement Council (see Resources, left) or online at **www.estimators-online.com** (0845 650 2208 ✉).

Get planning permission Skimping on proper checks can prove to be an expensive mistake in the long run. Although you may not need it, always check on planning permission. In addition, ensure that the planned extension complies with Building Regulations by checking with your local authority or the LABC (see Resources, left).

Do you need an architect? Many people assume that architects are only for grand projects and that they cost the earth. But architects' fees are only about 8–12% of the total building cost. For this, you get professional back-up, plans that work, help in negotiating the cost of builders and materials, and supervision of the building project, which can save you thousands. Find a qualified architect through the Royal Institute of British Architects (see Resources, left).

Discount for DIY Adding an extension is of course a job for a professional builder. But you may be able to cut costs in the later stages by tackling the final decorating yourself.

CONVERTING A LOFT

The cavernous space in your loft could be converted into habitable rooms. Doing so might add up to 30% more usable floor area in a two-storey building, and nearly twice as much in a bungalow. A loft conversion costs less than a home extension of the same floor area, because the shell – the roof and floor – is already there.

Don't skimp on advice Check Building Regulations first by contacting the LABC (see Resources, left), and get a surveyor to find out if joists – which are often much weaker than on the first floor – need strengthening.

Make more space cheaply Adding a pull-down ladder to the loft opening and nailing a better floor in place is an economical way of getting more storage space. If you don't need a staircase and don't mind having a ladder, you don't need planning permission. You can add flooring, lighting and a loft ladder for £1,000–£2,000.

Cut the price of stairs You can also save on the expense of having a staircase built – and save valuable space – by choosing a ready-made spiral staircase, if fire regulations permit. These start at under £1,000 and look stylish, too. Check the small ads in the newspapers for low-cost or secondhand stairs, or put in a wanted ad yourself.

Use an independent builder In general, it's cheaper to employ a builder than to go to a specialist loft conversion company that has fixed and promotional costs. But check that the builder you are considering has a good track record in successful loft conversions – ask for a reference and get the builder to obtain permission for you to see other jobs the firm has completed locally.

Do some of the work yourself Depending on your DIY competence, you can make big savings by doing some jobs yourself – from installing a roof window (modern ones don't require scaffolding) to laying floor coverings or decorating.

ADDING A CONSERVATORY

The cheapest way to give your home extra living space is to build a conservatory. It is normally classed as a home extension, which means you need to apply for planning permission, and you should check Building Regulations, too.

Where to buy You can order a conservatory from a specialist supplier or you can buy the components and arrange for assembly yourself. The cost-conscious DIY chain stores such as B&Q (see Resources, page 253) sell conservatories and will install them once the site has been prepared. Buying end-of-line and end-of-season models can slash costs from standard prices, which start at about £2,000.

Low-cost framing PVC-u is the most economical choice for the framing system (aluminium, steel and timber being the other options) and requires less maintenance afterwards.

Install it yourself The bill for professional installation can be over £1,000. But you can save most of the cost of erecting a conservatory by doing it yourself and getting friends in to help, especially if you know someone who is in the building trade and has professional skills. Conservatories come with clear instructions and doing most of the work yourself should not prove difficult, as long as you have had some experience on smaller projects.

RESOURCES

CONSERVATORIES
- For suppliers of conservatories, visit **www.homesources.co.uk** ✉.
- **www.conservatories.co.uk** ✉ is an extensive directory of suppliers and anything to do with conservatories.
- **www.bestquote4 conservatories.co.uk** ✉ lists lower-priced stock.
- **www.conservatories online.co.uk** 0845 603 6078 ✉ offers information on materials, suppliers and special offers.

COSTS AND RETURNS ON HOME IMPROVEMENTS

Check with local estate agents to see what the potential added value of a planned home improvement might be before you go ahead.

Every street has a top price for the value of properties, and no improvement will take house prices beyond that level.

AREA	CONSIDERATIONS AND COSTS
NEW KITCHEN	Costs from around £2,000 to over £20,000 plus installation costs of around 50%. A good kitchen may add 5%–10% to the value of your home, or at least make it easier to sell.
ENSUITE BATHROOM	Costs from around £300 for a basic suite to well over £3,000 to convert a box room with new plumbing; an extra bathroom could add from 0%–5% to the value of your home.
CONSERVATORY	Costs from around £3,000 to £45,000 or more, but increases the light and space in your home as well as improving its saleability. Could add 5% when you sell, but should ideally relate to the overall value of your home. If your home is worth, for example, around £100,000, it isn't worth spending more than £5,000 on a conservatory.
EXTENSION	Costs from £20,000 upwards. An extension makes sense when there is uncertainty in the housing market, giving you more space without the stress and cost of selling and buying a new home. Depending on what to choose to do, it could add 10%–50% to the value of your home.
LOFT CONVERSION	Costs start at around £15,000 and rise to £45,000 or more. A loft conversion will make your house easier to sell but you may not recoup all the building costs. However, it will add value (5–10%) if your home is very small or you are adding a fourth bedroom.

Approximate percentage increases in property value as estimated by the National Association of Estate Agents (NAEA)

BUYING MATERIALS, TOOLS AND FITTINGS

Do some research and compare prices before you buy materials and tools for building work. There are always bargains or discounts to be had if you take the trouble to check various sources.

TOP TIPS SAVE MONEY ON MATERIALS

■ **Shop at DIY chain stores and online** The chain stores and online outlets are often excellent value because of their bulk buying power, and Internet shopping outlets don't have the overheads of retail stores. Compare prices at DIY chain stores. In general, prices are lower at Wickes but their range of products is not as great as that at some other DIY stores.

■ **Save 50% at a builders' yard** Pay less for building materials by visiting a builders' yard rather than a DIY retailer, which can double or treble costs. As a private buyer at a builders' yard you won't be offered items as cheaply as a professional builder, but if you buy in bulk you should be able to negotiate a discount. If you are undertaking a large project, look into membership of BuildStore's ✉ Trade Card scheme, which offers self-builders and renovators discount and benefits on a wide range of products and services.

■ **Negotiate a further discount** If you are buying several items, negotiate further discounts. For example, buy sand and cement with bricks and ask for free delivery.

■ **Look out for money-off days** Some DIY stores hold 10% or 20% discount days for their regular customers and/or senior citizens.

■ **Buy at source and install it yourself** A glazier who comes to measure up and then returns with the correct pane of glass will charge a large call-out fee and for the work on top of that. But you can measure the window yourself, then simply ask him to cut a pane and sell you some putty at a total cost of just a few pounds.

■ **Architectural salvage yards** If you are fixing up an older property or like a period look, reclamation and salvage yards can be sources of inspiration. Look for low-cost materials or interior fittings such as baths, toilets, sinks and fireplaces. Keep your eyes open, too, for good timber, stained glass and ironwork, or root around for unusual door handles or brass knobs to give your low-cost schemes a sense of individuality (see Resources, right).

■ **Check demolition sites** These are a good source of free bricks with a weathered appearance that fit in better with existing older houses and garden walls. But take care – some Victorian brick simply crumbles, and some old bricks may be covered in mortar or they may not be frost-resistant.

■ **Reclaim VAT** If you are self-building, you will need to manage the bookkeeping side of the project as new build is zero rated for VAT. Go to the HM Revenue and Customs website at **www.hmrc.gov.uk** ✉ and type 'Notice 719' into the search box, where there is a facility for non-VAT-registered self-builders to reclaim VAT.

LOWER PRICES: SUPERSTORES vs LOCAL BUYS

■ **Check the superstores** Out-of-town superstores don't have to pay high-street rents and so can pass savings on building materials, tools and fittings to customers. They also cut prices to the bone on popular items and offer loss leaders, too. But you may do better on brushes, paint, door handles and other basics at a neighbourhood hardware shop.

■ **Compare local prices** Check the Yellow Pages for local shops and phone rival stores to compare prices for the same item.

■ **Scour the small ads** You can often find cut-price new or nearly-new items. Some are offered free if you collect them. Local papers also print discount vouchers on certain items.

■ **Place your own ad** Find just what you want on a buyer-collects basis to drive down the price.

■ **Look online** Compare prices online – but watch out for delivery charges if you do spot a good deal. Also, check auction sites such as eBay ✉ for new and secondhand items.

PAY LESS FOR TIMBER

When buying wood in quantity, go to a timber yard. Prices for bulk buys will be lower than a DIY store, and staff can advise you on the most appropriate wood for your needs.

Buy secondhand Reclaimed timber will cost less than new wood, though prices vary according to quality. But be aware that timber yards will refuse to cut secondhand timber because nails, screws and grit damage cutting tools, so you will probably have to cut it yourself.

Keep an eye on skips and building sites Valuable old timber is often junked, and for £10 a builder on the site may even deliver it to your front door.

Old hardwoods You might pick up a beautiful piece of teak or mahogany in an architectural salvage yard in the form of a door, panelling or fireplace surround.

Avoid timber troubles Look carefully for woodworm exit holes, warping and moisture staining before you buy.

Check the ends for quality Some secondhand wood is merely veneer-covered chipboard, and inside it resembles compacted sawdust.

BARGAIN HUNT

■ **Junk shops**
Look for old brass handles, hinges and doorknobs to complement home improvements.
■ **Car boot sales**
Save money on fittings and accessories. The best bargains go early, but it's worth a late afternoon visit to scoop up last-minute discounted items. You can pick up great bargains in affluent areas, where the quality is likely to be higher and the vendors may sell for less.

RESOURCES

PRODUCT INFORMATION

■ Call the Building Centre **www.buildingcentre.co.uk** 09065 161136 ✉; calls are charged at £1.50 a minute.
■ For self-build, renovation and conversion products and services go to **www.buildstore.co.uk** 0870 870 9991 ✉.

DIRECTORIES OF SUPPLIERS

■ Homesources **www.homesources.co.uk** ✉ lists suppliers of products related to DIY and the home.
■ The Good Deal Directory **www.gooddealdirectory.co.uk** ✉ lists discount outlets selling DIY-related products, fixtures and fittings.

DIY CHAIN STORES

■ Argos **www.argos.co.uk** 0845 640 2020 ✉ lets you reserve online, then pay and collect in-store.
■ B&Q **www.diy.com** 0845 609 6688 ✉ has stores and provides an online shopping service.

■ DIYnot **diynot.com** has information from experts as well as an online shop.
■ Focus Do It All **www.focusdoitall.co.uk** ✉ stores and online shop.
■ Homebase **www.homebase.co.uk** 0845 077 8888 ✉.

DIY ONLINE/MAIL ORDER

■ Screwfix Direct **www.screwfix.com** 0500 41 41 41 ✉ huge range of items.

DIY TOOLS SOLD ONLINE

■ DIYtools.co.uk **www.diytools.co.uk** 0870 750 1549 ✉
■ Draper Tools **www.draper.co.uk** 023 8026 6355 ✉
■ Toolbank **www.toolbank.co.uk** 0800 0686238 ✉.

BUILDERS' MERCHANTS

■ Build Center **www.buildcenter.co.uk** 0800 529 529 ✉ has branches throughout Britain, and you can shop online.

■ Buildbase **www.buildbase.co.uk** 01865 871700 ✉ online shopping, many branches plus tool and plant hire.

SALVAGE YARDS

■ Salvo **www.salvo.co.uk** 020 8400 6222 ✉ has lists of local salvage dealers.
■ Billingshurst Building and Roofing Supplies **www.reclaimedbuildingmaterial .com** 01403 782 384 ✉.

PLUMBERS' MERCHANTS

■ Plumb Center **www.plumbcenter.co.uk** 0870 1622 557 ✉.
■ Plumbworld **www.plumbworld.co.uk** 01386 768498 ✉.

LIGHTING SOLD ONLINE

■ Lighting Direct **www.lighting-direct.co.uk** 0844 8044 944 ✉.
■ Lightsaver.co.uk **www.lightsaver.co.uk** 0845 600 3112 ✉.
■ The Lighting Superstore **www.thelightingsuperstore. co.uk** 01225 704442 ✉.

ENERGY-SAVING HOME IMPROVEMENTS

If your utility bills are high, you may be able to lower them by making smart alterations to your home. Being energy efficient need not cost a lot of money – it's possible to make a big difference for very little outlay.

INSULATE FOR THE GREATEST SAVINGS

A sure-fire way to lower your heating bills is to improve the insulation in your property.

Insulate the loft Save heating costs by laying a glass fibre insulation blanket over the joists or filling the spaces between joists with loose-fill granules. Since up to 25% of your home's heat is lost through the roof, you should recoup the cost within a few years.

Check existing insulation Older houses often have only a thin layer of insulation. The recommended depth is 27cm (10½in) deep. If you top it up by 10–15cm (4–6in), you could save as much as £60 in a year.

Lag the pipes Lag hot water pipes with fibre bandage or flexible foam tube, which you can buy from a plumbers' merchant or DIY store. You could save more than just the cost of lost heat – proper insulation helps to stop pipes freezing and bursting in winter.

Insulate the hot water tank Put an 8cm (3in) thick insulating jacket around your hot water tank to reduce heat loss by up to 75%, saving around £40 a year

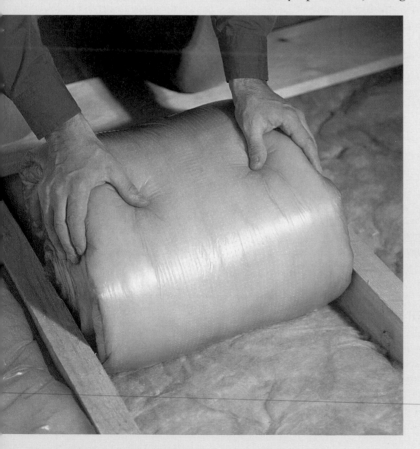

SIMPLE DRAUGHTPROOFING

You can lose up to 20% of the heat in your home through poor ventilation and draughts.

Keep draughts out A brush or PVC seal for external doors costs just a few pounds from your local DIY store. Draught-excluding tape can be used around offending doors or windows. The Draught Proofing Advisory Association at **http://dubois.vital.co.uk/database/ceed/wall.html** or 01428 654011 ✉ offers advice on the right type of draught-proofing material for your home.

Seal up floor cracks Filling cracks between floorboards with newspaper or sealant reduces draughts. If you've just sanded your floor, save the sawdust from the sander to mix with PVC and fill small cracks for a seamless finish.

SEALING WINDOWS AGAINST THE COLD

The average house loses as much as 20% of its heat through the glass in windows; look at ways of reducing this wasteful heat loss – double glazing can cut this by as much as half.

Save £140 a year with double glazing According to the Energy Saving Trust ✉, switching to Energy Efficient Windows will save energy and could reduce your household bills by around £140 a year. The British Fenestration Ratings Council ✉ scheme uses an A–E rating, similar to that given to white goods. The cost of new windows won't be recouped through heating bills alone. However, replacing your old windows could increase the value of your home and make it more saleable, and double glazing provides insulation against noise and smells, and greater security against break-ins. For an average home, initial expenditure on double-glazed windows would be around £5,500, with a projected fuel saving of around £140 a year from the most energy-efficient option. It could also reduce your household carbon emissions by around 720kg a year.

Save up to £65 a year with secondary glazing Generally less expensive than full double glazing, but also slightly less effective, secondary glazing covers existing windows with sealed panels. This type of glazing is worth considering if your windows are sound or you want to keep a period look to your home. The windows have sliding panels and are also available as hinged units, so they can be opened and closed.

Save £30–£40 a year with low-cost options Have your windows professionally treated with Low-E (low-emissivity) film, which costs about £30 a metre, plus installation; this usually lasts about five years. Cheaper still, install sheets of low-E glazing, plastic or vinyl over windows yourself (Low-E film is tinted, so you may prefer one of the alternatives). Cheapest of all, fix insulating film over the windows with adhesive tape. Shrink with a hair dryer until wrinkle-free.

Don't pay for heat you don't need

■ Use your home heating system as efficiently as possible to maximise savings on energy (see *Household finance*, page 298).

■ If your heating is not already controlled by a timer and thermostat, have them installed. If you don't have a thermostat, check the temperature regularly and adjust the heating controls when your house gets warmer. This way, you avoid paying for heating when you don't need it.

■ Having your boiler checked annually can pay for itself, as a well-maintained boiler is less likely to develop costly problems and saves gas by burning it efficiently.

SMART MOVES

HOW MUCH MONEY EACH YEAR CAN YOU SAVE ON ENERGY?

CONDENSING BOILER AND UPGRADED HEATING CONTROLS	**£275**
27cm (10½in) LOFT INSULATION	**£60–£205**
CAVITY WALL INSULATION	**£160**
DOUBLE GLAZING	**£140**
TURNING THERMOSTAT DOWN BY 1°C	**£65**
INSULATING JACKET ON HOT WATER TANK	**£40**
NEW ENERGY-EFFICIENT FRIDGE FREEZER	**£39**
INSULATING HOT WATER PIPES	**£10**

ESTIMATED TOTAL £340

At the start of 2009, the average British household was spending £1,040 a year on fuel. This chart shows how fuel bills – and carbon emissions – can be reduced substantially through energy-efficient measures. The estimated savings of £340 are based on information given by the Energy Saving Trust in February 2009.

HARNESS SOLAR POWER

Save on fuel bills by making use of free solar energy. Whether you have solar panels or not, there are various ways in which you can use solar energy to heat your home.

Install solar panels The most popular way of utilising solar energy is to preheat cold mains water so that less gas, oil or electricity is needed to supply hot water. This is usually achieved by putting a solar panel measuring 3–4m² (3.6–4.8 sq yd) on the roof, facing roughly south. Although solar panels work best in sunny weather, they still function in cloudy conditions and could provide about half your hot water energy needs over the year. An installed system costs between £3,000 and £5,000. DIY kits cost from £1,200. Grants are available through the Low Carbon Buildings Programme (funded by the Department for Business Enterprise & Regulatory Reform) – check their website at **www.lowcarbonbuildings.org.uk** or 0800 512 012 ✉.

Retain warmth in cold weather During winter, allow as much sun as possible into the house. On sunny days, open blinds and shutters, and tie back curtains. Trim evergreen trees and shrubs that shade the windows. As soon as the sun starts to go down, close the blinds or curtains to hold the heat inside.

Keep cool in summer For the summer, take the opposite approach. Plant deciduous trees to shade the house in hot weather, and install awnings over south-facing windows. Close your windows and curtains by mid-morning when the temperature begins to rise, or leave them closed if you'll be out all day. If temperatures cool down after sunset, open up the house to take advantage of any breezes.

TOP TIPS INSTALL BATHROOM FITTINGS THAT CUT HEATING AND WATER BILLS

Install new energy-efficient models when you come to replace bathroom fittings.

■ **Add a shower** Consider putting in a shower if you haven't already got one. A three-minute shower uses a quarter of the water of a bath (excluding power showers). With a low-flow shower-head, you save even more.

■ **Reduce water flow** Fitting inexpensive low-flow shower heads and taps in your home is a simple fix you can do yourself and will reduce the amount of water you use by half, without decreasing the performance of the fittings. Follow the manufacturer's instructions – all you'll need is a wrench or pliers to do the job.

■ **Stop the shower while you soap** Check out shower heads with an off-on switch that lets you interrupt the water flow while you soap up, shave or shampoo and then resume the flow to rinse.

■ **Buy a low-flow loo** When you replace a toilet, get a new low-flow model (which is now required in all new construction). They use only 7.5 litres (1½ gal) each flush, compared with the 16 litres (3½ gal) the old type use.

PAY LESS FOR PROFESSIONAL HELP

Finding good workmen and dealing with them fairly and wisely prevents costs from spiralling out of control.

TOP TIPS GETTING THE BEST PRICE

Always compare prices before settling on a particular builder or workman, and check out other ways of saving money, too.

■ **Ask for written quotes** Collect at least three different quotations (not estimates) for a job, and get them in writing. This gives you some comeback in case of problems. Make a careful list so you can ask each tradesman the same questions. Ask for an itemised quote, so you can compare like with like – 'making good', or replastering and clearing away rubble, should be clearly stated. Make sure the tradesman's full name and address is on the quote, so you can follow up with legal action in case of trouble.

■ **Combine jobs** You may get a better price if the builder who repoints the brickwork on your house also does some work on your garden wall, for example – and you will save on further call-out fees.

■ **Choose a one-man band** Using a VAT-registered builder will automatically add 15% to your bill. If you find a small sole trader who is not registered for VAT, you will save £75 on a £500 job.

■ **Do unskilled work yourself** Cut the price of a job by doing some of the preparation – lifting old floor coverings or removing old tiles, for example – before asking tradesmen for a quotation.

> **DON'T DIY**
>
> Beware of tackling jobs yourself if they:
> ■ require specialist knowledge about gas or electricity – by law, gas appliances must be installed by a Corgi-registered gas fitter (see Resources, page 258), and electrical appliances must be installed according to IEE Wiring Regulations (for details, see the Institution of Engineering and Technology website at **www.theiet.org** ✉);
> ■ are dangerous – for example, working at height from an unsecured ladder;
> ■ are likely to land you with further problems you can't fix yourself – knocking down an interior wall that might be structural, for instance.

> **keep it simple**
>
> ■ When looking for a builder or other tradesman, start by asking for personal recommendations from friends who consider they have had good work done at a reasonable price.
> ■ If it is at all possible, ask to see examples of past work by a builder or tradesman who you are interested in hiring.

RESOURCES

QUALITY CHECKS

Ask trade associations for lists of local members, as most strive to keep standards high and costs down. Check out the following:

■ Federation of Master Builders **www.fmb.org.uk** 020 7242 7583 ✉
■ National Federation of Builders **www.builders.org.uk** 08450 578 160 ✉
■ Council for Registered Gas Installers (CORGI) **www.trustcorgi.com** 0800 915 0485 ✉
■ Electrical Contractors Association **www.eca.co.uk** 020 7313 4800 ✉
■ Glass and Glazing Federation **www.ggf.org.uk** 0870 042 4255 ✉
■ Institute of Plumbing and Heating Engineering **www.plumbers.org.uk** 01708 472791 ✉
■ Painting and Decorating Association **www.paintingdecorating association.co.uk** 024 7635 3776 ✉

DEALING WITH PROBLEMS

The Trading Standards Institute offers help and advice at **www.tradingstandards.gov. uk** ✉. As a last resort, seek redress at the county court. For information on small claims, go to **www.small-claims-court-support.co.uk** 0117 370 4385 ✉.

CHECK OUT GUARANTEES

Look for value-added extras The man who installs your alarm system could offer a year's free guarantee followed by a cut-price annual contract, saving you money on repeated call-outs. And a properly installed and maintained security system could get you a discount on your home insurance.

Read the small print Some guarantees last for just a year and charge an excess after that – so having a 'guaranteed' damp-proof course, for instance, could mean that after one year you have to pay the same firm again if you want them to check their work. If the guarantee is not worth the paper it's written on, ask if there's a discount for doing without it.

HOW TO GET FREE HELP

Many specialists will survey a job for free. Their advice can save you money as, armed with the knowledge, you might then decide to tackle the job yourself.

Measuring up for carpet Retailers will measure up for carpet for free, though some may be wary of handing over the dimensions to you. To estimate the dimensions for yourself, simply divide the total cost of the carpet by its price per square metre. Use graph paper to estimate roughly the area and check their sums.

Timber specialists Specialist companies will assess timber troubles and give you a free estimate. For example, they will track down the source of any woodworm and assess how extensive the damage is. You can then ask the company to sell you the chemicals to do the job yourself much more cheaply – and compare prices in your local DIY store, too.

WATCH POINTS GREAT RIP-OFFS

There are always unscrupulous workmen who are ready to exploit the average person's lack of specialist knowledge.

■ **Passing experts** Beware of the chap who knocks on your door to say he has some Tarmac left over from road

works and will resurface your drive at a cut-price rate. Almost certainly he will do a poor job, and once he has the money you will never see him again.

■ **Eagle eyes** Your suspicions should be aroused by the man who says he has just noticed that one of your slates is loose or missing, but he will fix it for £50. Of course, he has no proper roof ladder or equipment and damages several other slates in the process. Take a long, hard look at the roof yourself, through a pair of binoculars, and only let a local roofer who is well known in your area touch it.

■ **Invisible fixes** Don't believe the workman who services your boiler and then explains that a vital part needs replacing at a cost of several hundred pounds. Decent workmen leave you the packaging, the receipt and the damaged part to show that they really have changed the part they say needed mending. If in doubt, stop the work and get some other free quotes.

■ **Mysterious damage** Watch out for a plumber who works in your loft and then spots discoloured water coming from your taps, or the chimney 'expert' who discovers smoke in the bedroom. Cowboy builders can create problems so that they get paid to fix them. If you suspect this is the case, stop the work and call the council's Trading Standards department right away.

CONTROLLING THE JOB

While your builder will manage the day-to-day running of the job, it is up to you to take control, plan for contingencies and avoid costly misunderstandings.

On schedule Agree a timetable of works and payments, and try to negotiate a rebate for every day the job is late.

Be assured Get proper insurance before you proceed with major work. For any job, check that your workman is properly insured in case he damages your property.

Don't pay too much up front The deposit should be no more than 25% of the total cost. Negotiate a 10% retention at the end to give you, say, two weeks to one month to assess whether the job has been properly done.

Check before you sign If the delivery man won't wait while you check items are in good order, amend the delivery note to say 'goods unseen' before you sign for them.

Record progress Keep a detailed log of the works, and take regular photographs of what has been done. Get receipts for every payment you make.

Job satisfaction Don't sign any satisfaction agreements until you are 100% satisfied. If you are not, ask for a discount or for the job to be completed properly. In case of problems, try to negotiate an amicable solution. If necessary, you can seek advice from your local Trading Standards office (visit the Trading Standards Institute website for advice on dealing with problems with services at **www.tradingstandards.gov.uk** or 08454 04 05 06 ✉), or for redirection to your local office, or contact your local Citizens Advice Bureau. As a last resort, you can take legal action cheaply and simply via the small claims track of the county court. Costs start at £30 depending on the disputed amount, but you may need to hire a solicitor as well.

keep it simple

Communication is the key to a successful and cost-efficient building project.

■ Make sure you understand what is happening at all times. Don't let tradesmen's jargon confuse you – if you don't understand exactly what is meant, ask.

■ If you don't like something that has been done, say so at once – it will be easier and cheaper to change it immediately rather than later on.

■ To avoid the possibility of misunderstandings, write down any changes agreed mid-project.

■ If you start running over budget, let the builder know – he may be able to help by suggesting additional ways of saving money.

Buying and running a car

It's easy to take running a car for granted, but when you realise it's likely to be the second or third most expensive item in your weekly budget, it makes sense to get your priorities and your sums right.

BUYING A NEW CAR

A new car is a luxury, so be sure that a nearly new one would not suit your needs just as well. If you do decide to buy new, getting the right car and the right deal needn't be a hassle if you follow some basic consumer guidelines.

DO YOUR RESEARCH

Save money by doing some background research first. Read car reviews and check prices in magazines such as *What Car?* (**www.whatcar.com** ✉) and *Parker's Car Price Guide* (**www.parkers.co.uk** ✉). Surf the web for good deals and keep an eye on showroom prices.

Set a budget Include tax (see page 267) and insurance (see page 272) in your budget and stick to it. The biggest considerations are the age and model of the car you intend to buy.

Be flexible List the features you want in your new car, such as engine size, number of doors, optional extras and fuel economy, and place them in order of importance. Finding several makes and models that fit your needs will give you more bargaining power – and help you to pay less.

Factor in depreciation You lose thousands of pounds as soon as you drive a new car off the forecourt. Some lose up to 20% of their value the moment you pick them up. But you can cut those losses by choosing models with lower depreciation – a top-of-the range luxury model could lose more than £8,000 immediately, while a mid-range family saloon could cost £1,000 in initial depreciation. If this is a major concern, consider a year-old car – almost as good as new but up to a third less in price.

Compare costs The purchase price may be low but the running costs high. The AA estimates that it can cost £4,000 to run car for a year, including road tax, insurance, breakdown cover, depreciation and lost interest as a result of owning the car. You also need to take into account how polluting the car is as this will affect how damaging it is to the environment and how much road tax you have to pay.

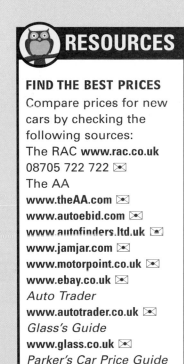

RESOURCES

FIND THE BEST PRICES
Compare prices for new cars by checking the following sources:
The RAC **www.rac.co.uk**
08705 722 722 ✉
The AA
www.theAA.com ✉
www.autoebid.com ✉
www.autofinders.ltd.uk ✉
www.jamjar.com ✉
www.motorpoint.co.uk ✉
www.ebay.co.uk ✉
Auto Trader
www.autotrader.co.uk ✉
Glass's Guide
www.glass.co.uk ✉
Parker's Car Price Guide
www.parkers.co.uk ✉
What Car? Magazine
www.whatcar.com ✉
Which? Magazine
www.which.co.uk ✉

FRANCHISED DEALERS

Most new cars are sold by franchised dealers, who are tied to a particular manufacturer. Although increased competition and government pressure has helped bring down car prices in recent years, franchised dealers' prices can still be higher than prices elsewhere. Save time and money by test-driving a new car at your local dealer and then going for a cheaper deal elsewhere – or haggling (see page 264).

INDEPENDENT DEALERS

Although you'll only get brand new cars from franchised dealers, you may find 'pre-registered' new cars – with delivery mileage – at independent dealerships. They are often cheaper than franchises and you can haggle to reduce prices. Also, some of the online car sites often have better deals from franchised dealers on them.

CONSIDER RUNNING COSTS

Before you put any fuel in the car it will cost you thousands of pounds to own and run.

These figures show the cost of running a new petrol car. Diesel cars cost a similar amount.

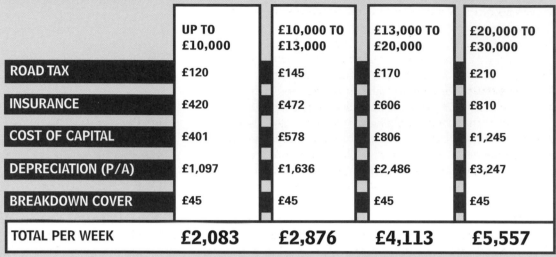

	UP TO £10,000	£10,000 TO £13,000	£13,000 TO £20,000	£20,000 TO £30,000
ROAD TAX	£120	£145	£170	£210
INSURANCE	£420	£472	£606	£810
COST OF CAPITAL	£401	£578	£806	£1,245
DEPRECIATION (P/A)	£1,097	£1,636	£2,486	£3,247
BREAKDOWN COVER	£45	£45	£45	£45
TOTAL PER WEEK	**£2,083**	**£2,876**	**£4,113**	**£5,557**

Source: The AA Running Costs For Petrol Cars 2008

BUY CHEAPER ON THE INTERNET

Online car supermarkets offer worthwhile discounts on new cars and you can bring the price down further by being flexible about the model or colour you buy. Visit websites such as **www.autoebid.com** ✉, **www.jamjar.com** ✉, **www.autofinders.ltd.uk** ✉ or **www.motorpoint.co.uk** ✉ for discounts of 10% to 25%.

• Travelling to another part of the country to pick up a cut-price car you have found on the Internet will cost you the journey, but could save you thousands of pounds on the price of the car. Many dealers will deliver to your home for a relatively small charge.

• Comparison sites – such as **www.kelkoo.co.uk** ✉ and **www.moneysupermarket.com** ✉ – are a good way to search for and compare the prices of new cars.

CUTTING DEALER COSTS ON NEW CARS

Phone several dealers – don't just go to the nearest. But the chances are that you won't get the best possible deal until you're actually sitting in a showroom with the salesman.

Set your price Find the wholesale price of the car you want by using *Glass's Guide* (**www.glass.co.uk** ✉) or the AA (**www.theAA.com** ✉), and read What Car? (**www.whatcar.com** ✉) or Parker's (**www.parkers.co.uk** ✉). Add a small profit for the dealer – say £500. Then ring round different dealers offering that price. Once one offer is made, make a note of it and phone other dealers to see if they can beat it. After you have negotiated the best price, visit this dealer to check that they have the exact car you want to buy.

Plan your timing carefully A good time to buy is just as the new registration models arrive on 1 March and 1 September, because dealers will offer discounts on earlier models to make room for the new ones. Buying at quiet times – just before Christmas or in bad weather when the showroom is deserted – can result in big savings, too.

Hitting the target Closing the deal on a Saturday afternoon at the end of the month can pay off, because selling one more car may help your salesperson hit their target – and make them more likely to give you a better deal. Choose the right time, and you could even get away with offering the cost price without an added profit for the dealer.

Ask for extras Use your bargaining powers to get what you want, such as a CD player, air conditioning, road tax or a higher spec model. Try implying that you will go to the dealer down the road for a better deal and that if they won't throw in the extra you want, the other dealer probably will.

Buy ex-display Pay less by buying an ex-display vehicle or loan vehicle. Make sure you get a new car warranty with it for better protection.

Choose an older model Wait until a new model is just out. Unless you yearn for the latest model, opt for the slightly older one and save enough for a good holiday. But remember that older models will depreciate in value much more quickly than the latest one.

DEPRECIATION

When you buy a new car as soon as you drive it off the forecourt it loses a big percentage of its value as it is now second hand. It will continue to lose value each year; after three years a Ford Focus could be worth 40% less than you paid for it. Other cars could be worth even less.

TOP TIPS LEARN TO HAGGLE

Dealers build in a generous profit margin because they know customers will haggle – and the better you are at it, the more you can save. Take a friend along to keep you from being drawn in to the sales patter.

Don't be put under pressure Don't wait until your current car is failing – being desperate will put you in a poor bargaining position.

keep it simple

DON'T PAY FOR UNWANTED EXTRAS Optional extras such as alloy wheels add significantly to the basic price of a car – make big savings simply by doing without them. But not having the extras could affect the subsequent resale value.

BEST AND WORST CARS FOR DEPRECIATION

Which car you use has a big impact on its value from new after three years. The following percentages are based on a 55 plate with 37,000 miles. The best performing car is still worth almost two-thirds the price it was new, the worst less than a fifth.

BEST PERFORMING		WORST PERFORMING	
MAKE/MODEL	% OF VALUE	MAKE/MODEL	% OF VALUE
Mini 1.4TD	**63.2%**	Alfa Romeo 166	12%
Citroën C1	**61.2%**	Rover 75 Petrol	14.6%
Ferrari F340	**60.9%**	Rover 45/MG ZS	15.9%
Toyota Aygo 1.0	**60.6%**	Saab 9-5 petrol	17.4%
Peugeot 107 1.0	**57.4%**	Kia Magentis 2.0	17.5%

From www.glass.co.uk January 2009.

Be prepared Have your research at your fingertips, with the latest models, prices and options.

Have a starting point When it comes to haggling, start at about 10%–15% off the list price.

Be discreet If you've fallen in love with a car, don't let it show. You'll save more by playing it cool and acting as if you're undecided between several models. And don't let friendly feelings for the sales staff cloud your judgement – you can be pleasant without letting them take advantage.

Don't play the numbers game A salesperson who asks, 'How much would you like to pay each month?' is using one of the oldest tricks in the book. Typical car loan interest rates are between 5%–12% over 1–7 years. Although paying around £200 a month may be affordable, the longer the loan the more interest you pay overall – if you can afford to, take a loan out for no more than three to five years.

Be willing to walk away If you don't feel good about the deal or the dealer, your instincts could be right. And if the dealer asks why, say so – you could see a huge shift in attitude and get a better deal that way.

Go over the details Does the price cover delivery charges and number plates? Are the special features included? If you have agreed a good price, ask the dealer to waive these fees. If he won't, ask for free servicing or complementary extras.

Read the warranty carefully How long does it last, what does it exclude and what conditions are imposed for it to remain valid?

0% deals Look out for dealers offering 0% or low-rate finance – this can save you thousands of pounds in interest. But make sure you are getting a good price on the car, too.

WATCH POINTS FINALISING THE DEAL

Unless you're certain that this is the car you want, don't put any money down until the deal is finalised. Doing so means you lose all your bargaining power.

Don't lose your deposit If you put down a non-refundable deposit and then there are problems, you could lose the money. Ask for a receipt so you have evidence for the Trading Standards office if this becomes necessary later.

Check cancellation terms Check that there is a clause in the contract that lets you cancel it if there is a hitch, such as a delay in delivery.

Make sure the contract is binding Once you are happy with a deal, get the contract agreed and signed.

Test drive your new car When you buy a new car, check every detail and test drive it before finalising the contract. If there are problems, draw them to the seller's attention and ensure minor repairs are agreed in writing before proceeding.

Know your rights If serious faults appear after you have taken the car home, you are normally protected under current legislation. Stop using the car and complain to the seller in writing as soon as possible – you could be entitled to a full refund. See the Trading Standards website at **www.tradingstandards.gov.uk** ✉ or contact your local Trading Standards office for further advice. Also see the advice on buying a vehicle at **www.direct.gov.uk** ✉ and **www.consumerdirect.gov.uk** and 08454 040506

KEEP YOUR OLD CAR OUT OF THE DEAL

You might get a good deal on your new car, and then be fleeced on the trade-in. Fix a price for the new car, then get the best price you can for your old one, possibly by selling it privately.

FINANCING YOUR CAR

Save money by finding the best finance – opting for the convenient deal offered by the car dealer usually means you'll be paying more than you need to.

CHOOSING THE RIGHT DEAL

Broadly speaking, there are four ways to finance the purchase of a car.

Cash If you can afford to pay in cash you won't incur any interest charges and could have some extra bargaining power. However, you may not get the best price as dealers also make money selling finance with their cars.

Loan You could borrow the sum using a personal unsecured loan from your bank or another lender. Shop around for the best interest rate and watch out for early repayment penalties and added payment protection insurance.

Dealer finance Your car dealer may offer you finance on the car. Make sure you are getting a good rate – watch out as dealer finance may require a deposit and rates may be high. Dealers may give you a better price on the car if you take their expensive finance. Some dealers offer 0% finance, but this normally only lasts for up to three years and you will need a larger deposit.

Personal contract plans You pay a monthly amount to lease a car from the dealer. At the end of the lease period, you can either buy the car or return it. Interest rates are usually the highest of all finance options. At the start of the agreement you will be quoted a 'final payment' (or 'balloon payment' figure or GFV – guaranteed future value). This is the amount due if you decide to keep the car after your agreement has ended, and is based on an estimate of your annual mileage. What you pay each month is calculated by subtracting your deposit and the GFV from the car price and then adding interest. There will be a limit on how many miles you can drive each year, for example, 10,000 per year.

TOP TIPS PAYING FOR YOUR CAR

If you borrow money to finance your car, check out websites such as **www.moneyfacts.co.uk** ✉, **www.moneysupermarket.com** ✉, **www.moneynet.co.uk** ✉ or magazines such as *Which? Money* (**www.which.co.uk** ✉), *Moneywise* (**www.moneywise.co.uk** ✉) and *Your Money* (**www.yourmoney.com** ✉) for the best deal.

Check the total cost Compare loans using the APR (annual percentage rate) for the length of loan you want. Make sure you look at the total cost of the loan. Spreading the loan over a longer period may reduce your monthly repayment amount, but will mean you pay more interest overall. For example, £10,000 over three years at 9.9% APR costs £1,528 in interest, but the same loan would cost more than twice as much in interest if repaid over seven years: £3,719.

Credit card 0% deals If you have a credit card with a big enough credit limit and a 0% or low-rate introductory period you could use it to pay for some or all of your car. However dealers may charge you commission of 1% to 3% if you pay by credit card. At the end of the introductory

keep it simple

BUY YOUR COMPANY CAR
If you have a company car and you're about to lose it for some reason, perhaps because it is due for replacement or you are retiring, consider asking your employer if you can buy it. You know its history, and it will have been regularly serviced, so it could be a bargain compared to buying a car elsewhere.

period the interest rate on your card is likely to be much higher, so move it to another card with an introductory rate or to a cheaper loan. Paying by credit card can give you extra protection, see 'Valuable protection' below.

Reduce your debt Bring down the cost of borrowing by paying as large a deposit as you can and borrow any money over the shortest period possible.

Pay cash if you can As new cars depreciate immediately, borrowing money to buy one is a bad idea. Paying cash is the best option, if possible.

Watch out for extras When you take out a loan to pay for a car or use dealer finance watch out for payment protection insurance (PPI). PPI covers your loan or finance repayments if you are unable to work due to illness or unemployment. However there are exclusions and PPI sold with loans and finance can be expensive. If you are worried about making your loan repayments if you are unable to work you should look at alternatives like standalone PPI or Income Protection Insurance (see *Saving, borrowing and investing*, page 324).

VALUABLE PROTECTION

If the dealer provides the finance for your car, Section 75 of the Consumer Credit Act (S.75) gives you valuable protection if something goes wrong with a purchase of between £100 and £30,000 on a credit card or other finance. Under S.75 if the goods are faulty or not as described you can claim a refund from the credit card company or lender instead of the retailer or dealer. You are covered even if you pay a deposit on a credit card and finance the rest by cash.

ASSESS CAR FINANCING CHARGES

LOANS FROM BANKS, MOTOR ORGANISATIONS AND DEALERS

LENDER	LIST PRICE	DEPOSIT	INTEREST	TOTAL COST	MONTHLY PAYMENTS	APR
Best buy unsecured loan	£10,000	n/a	£1,374	£11,374	£316	8.9%
Dealer A finance	£10,000	£1,000	£1,375	£11,375	£288	9.9%
Dealer B finance	£10,000	£2,000	£1,351	£11,351	£260	10.9%

LEASING FROM DEALERS AND MOTORING ORGANISATIONS

LENDER	LIST PRICE	DEPOSIT	ANNUAL MILEAGE	GFV	MONTHLY PAYMENTS	APR	TOTAL COST
Online Personal Contract Purchase	£10,866	£1,087	15,000	£2,883	£240	9.5%	£12,610
Dealer Personal Contract Purchase	£8,881	£1,776	10,000	£3,727	£135	9.4%	£10,363

The charts show financing arranged over 36 months on a small car costing around £10,000. Total cost takes into account purchase price, deposit and interest on borrowing. Figures correct at time of publication.

CAR TAX

In the next couple of years it will get cheaper to tax some cars and more expensive to tax others. The cheapest vehicles to tax are less polluting vehicles with lower CO_2 emissions and those that run on alternative fuels including gas, petrol and gas, petrol and electricity, and petrol/diesel. There will also be lower tax rates from April 2010 for cars in the first year of registration. Older cars registered before March 2001 are taxed based on their engine size. It will cost more than £400 more to tax a polluting car than the least polluting standard car.

Choosing a less polluting car You can find out how polluting new cars are at the Vehicle Certification Agency website **www.vcacarfueldata.org.uk** ✉. You can get more information at **www.direct.gov.uk** ✉ (search for Act on CO_2).

TAXING YOUR CAR – CARS REGISTERED BEFORE 1 MARCH 2001			
ENGINE SIZE (CC)	2008-2009	2009-2010	2010-2011
Less than 1,549	£120	£125	£125
More than 1,549	£185	£190	£205

TAXING YOUR CAR – CARS REGISTERED ON OR AFTER 1 MARCH 2001							
		STANDARD RATES			ALTERNATIVE RATES		
BAND	CO₂ (G/KM)	2008-2009	2009-2010	2010-2011	2008-2009	2009-2010	2010-2011
A	Up to 100	£0	£0	£0	£0	£0	£0
B	101–110	£35	£35	£20	£15	£15	£10
C	111–120	£35	£35	£30	£15	£15	£20
D	121–130	£120	£120	£90	£100	£100	£80
E	131–140	£120	£120	£110	£100	£100	£100
F	141–150	£120	£125	£125	£100	£105	£115
G	151–165	£145	£150	£155	£125	£130	£145
H	166–175	£170	£175	£180	£150	£155	£170
I	176–185	£170	£175	£200	£150	£155	£190
J	186–200	£210	£215	£235	£195	£200	£225
K*	201–225	£210	£215	£245	£195	£200	£235
L	226–255	£400	£405	£425	£385	£390	£415
M	255+	£400	£405	£435	£385	£390	£425

K Includes cars with CO_2 over 225g but registered before 23 March 2006.

BUYING A USED CAR

Buying nearly new is the simplest way to pay less for your car. Since many new models can lose up to half their value in the first two years, buying a two-year-old car gets you a half-price bargain that is still in good shape and unlikely to incur high repair bills.

BUYING FROM A DEALER

You will pay more buying from a dealer but you will also have more protection if something goes wrong. Non-franchised dealers are generally cheaper than the franchises and are more likely to be flexible on price. For extra security, buy from a dealer who is a member of the RMIF (Retail Motor Industry Federation). The conditions of membership require them to provide a good service, and you can go to their National Conciliation Service in the event of a dispute. Contact the RMIF at **www.rmif.co.uk** or 08457 585350 ✉.

Recommended dealers Ask your local garage and friends for personal recommendations.

Check out the warranty Does the car come with a warranty? Check how long it lasts and what it covers. Think carefully before spending a large amount on a warranty and see if you can negotiate a better deal on it.

Bargaining power Since dealers have a wide range of models in stock and tend to be in convenient locations, they give you plenty of bargaining power. If you don't like what you see, you can easily go elsewhere.

LOOK FOR AN AUCTION BARGAIN

Buying at a car auction can get you a real bargain. If you are lucky, you may find a six- to 12-month-old car at a saving of between 20% and 50% off the new car list price.

Have you got the knowledge? As you have just a short time to check the car over, you need to know what you're looking at – or take along someone who does.

Professional organisations For security, only buy from auctions that are members of the Society of Motor Auctions (contact the RMIF, see above, for details).

CAR SUPERMARKETS AND THE INTERNET

Prices at car supermarkets are low because they sell large numbers of cars and have low overheads. Whether you buy from a supermarket or through the Internet, have the vehicle thoroughly inspected and check both the specification and the warranty to ensure you buy a vehicle with a genuine UK specification. Remember to find out how much you will be charged for delivery.

Finding supermarkets Companies to try include: **www.carcraft.co.uk** 0845 094 7000 ✉; Motorpoint **www.motorpoint.co.uk** 0845 4133000 ✉; **www.cargiant.co.uk** 0844 482 4100 ✉. For a list of British car supermarkets, visit **www.car-supermarkets.com** ✉.

Web purchases Buying a car from an online car dealer such as Jamjar (**www.jamjar.com** ✉) can bring even bigger savings than those to be made from ordinary car supermarkets. And

---

keep it simple

CHECK BEFORE YOU BUY

Always check the car you are after doesn't have any skeletons hidden away before you buy. Several companies offer checks for as little as around £4 or £5. The checks will look for things like outstanding finance, if the car has been written off, if is it stolen, if it is a clone of another car, and if the mileage is genuine. You can also pay extra for the vehicle to be inspected by a mechanic and receive a report on any mechanical problems.

These companies offer information on a car's history:

www.autocheck.co.uk ✉
www.theAA.com ✉
www.hpicheck.com ✉
www.rac.co.uk ✉
www.usedcarexpert.co.uk

on auction websites the feedback section gives you opinions on individual sellers – **www.ebay.co.uk** ✉ lets you check the comments of other customers. And **www.autotrader.co.uk** ✉ lets you search for thousands of new or used cars.

CHEAPER FROM A PRIVATE SELLER

Privately sold cars are cheaper than those bought from dealers. View the car at the vendor's home in daylight and in good weather so you can check it over thoroughly and get a feel for how well the car has been maintained.

■ **Try negotiating** You can save a tidy sum by negotiating – many vendors are willing to reduce the price for a quick sale.

■ **When to complain** Although buying privately can be the cheapest way, your legal rights are limited. Cars are sold as seen, so you have no comeback if it is faulty. But if the vendor has described the car wrongly – for example, by saying that it has had only one previous owner when you can prove that it has had more – then you can claim for compensation. But you may not get redress even if you win a legal battle, so check the vehicle thoroughly before buying.

GOOD-VALUE BUYS

You can save serious money over the long term by choosing a used company car, as it is likely to have been well maintained. You can find them at auctions, car supermarkets and some secondhand dealers who specialise in them. Ask to see the log book of the owner.

■ **Used executive cars with a full service history** The first owner of an executive car is often a company, which will have had it serviced regularly and borne the losses of the initial depreciation. The advantage is that you will get a good-quality, well-serviced car at a knock-down price.

■ **High-mileage cars** A car with high mileage could be a bargain, especially if your annual mileage is low. A company car that has been driven for thousands of motorway miles at high speed is usually in better mechanical condition than a smaller car that has spent years on stop-start city driving, which takes a heavy toll on the transmission and brakes.

WATCH POINTS BUYER'S CHECKLIST

Check the car over thoroughly, either yourself if you are knowledgeable or using an expert mechanic or inspector from a motoring organisation for a small fee (see opposite).

■ **Test drive the car** Take the car for a long test drive, including hilly terrain, stop-start town driving and driving at speed. Listen carefully to the engine and use any problems to help you make a decision – or get it checked out, then negotiate a discount.

■ **Look at the service record** Are any parts due to be replaced? For example, a replacement cam belt costs a couple of hundred pounds, but if it fails you might have to buy an entire engine.

■ **Check the MOT certificates** All cars over three years old must have annual tests. Check that the recorded mileage rises steadily each year. If it doesn't, this could indicate that the car has been 'clocked' – the mileometer has been turned back to show a lower figure. If you are suspicious, ask a mechanic

---

DEALING WITH THE TRANSACTION

If making a private purchase, don't be tempted to hand over large bundles of cash. The best way to pay is by a banker's draft or building society cheque; if the vendor has any doubts he or she can call your bank and get it validated over the phone while you are there.

---

keep it simple

CHECK OUT PRICES

Before you start negotiating to buy a new or used car check out how much it is worth. Look at a current copy of *Glass's Guide* or visit **www.glass.co.uk** ✉ (valuation online £3.50) or Parker's **www.parkers.co.uk** ✉, **www.whatcar.com** ✉, **www.autoexpress.co.uk** ✉ and **www.theAA.com** ✉. Use the prices you find to negotiate a better deal on your new car – never pay the advertised price. Compare running costs, performance information, reliability and insurance levels for different makes and models in the *Car Buyer's Guide* at **www.theAA.com** or in *What Car?* magazine.

or inspector to look at whether the recorded mileage fits in with the condition of the car – or just walk away.

■ **Look at the mileometer** If the digits are misaligned, the mileage may have been tampered with.

■ **Examine the interior** Badly worn items such as seats and pedals suggest high mileage more accurately than an odometer reading, especially if there is no service history.

■ **Cheap check for accidental damage** Run a magnet over the bodywork – as it is attracted only to metal, it will show up any dents that have been touched up with body filler.

■ **Look for signs of damage** Damp patches on the carpet could suggest a leak.

■ **Check the tread** Replacing four new tyres is expensive. Check tyres for condition and depth of tread. Anything under 3mm of tread will need replacing.

■ **Ask about the warranty** Dealers may offer a limited warranty – for example, 30 days on a used car. Ask for a longer warranty as part of the deal, and check the terms carefully – most exclude 'wear and tear', and some limit the number of claims.

SAVE MONEY BY SPENDING MONEY

You can avoid expensive repair bills by having a used car checked out by an expert.

■ **Arrange an inspection** The AA ✉ and RAC ✉ offer a range of vehicle inspections. The AA charges £119 or £137 for AA members and £133 or £153 for non members for a visual assessment of the main mechanical areas of a car. However it does not include bodywork or upholstery in its checks. A comprehensive inspection costs up to £260 for members and £290 for non members. But this could be money well spent if it finds significant problems with the vehicle. The RAC offers a similar service and says that three-quarters of vehicles it checks would fail an MOT and 80% of vehicles have faults that would cost more than £200 to rectify. The RAC charges £132 for members and £146 for non members for its cheapest check and £175 and £190 for its comprehensive inspection. You could get your local garage to do a similar check from as little as £50 to £100.

■ **HIP checks** You can pay from £4 to check if your vehicle has a dodgy history (see *Check before you buy*, page 268).

SORTING OUT PROBLEMS

Take advantage of any problems with the car you want to buy by insisting on a better deal.

■ **Negotiate a discount** Take a written report from the AA or RAC back to the vendor to negotiate a discount. Private

SAVINGS TO BE MADE ON BUYING SECONDHAND

Check out the new and used prices of six popular types of car ranging in size from modest to luxury. The used prices (franchised dealer and private) are for a two-year-old car with average mileage (approx 10,000 a year) and in good condition.

CAR TYPE	NEW	DEALER	PRIVATE
SUPER MINI	£10,395	£6,075	£4,955
SMALL FAMILY	£14,125	£5,010	£4,300
LARGE FAMILY	£16,930	£5,350	£4,560
MPV	£21,240	£11,540	£10,145
EXECUTIVE	£26,990	£12,305	£10,485
LUXURY	£56,511	£29,780	£26,670

Prices from *Parker's*, January 2009

vendors will usually reduce the price rather than lose the sale. Most reputable dealers may carry out the work for free, saving you the cost of future repairs – and a good garage should then check that the work has been properly completed without charging you again.

■ **Ask for extras** If the dealer says he can't go any lower, then push for some extras – mud-flaps, or even a tank of fuel. Other extras to negotiate include a CD player, a year's road tax or a better specification.

■ **Getting your money back** If you have a problem with your new or used vehicle take action as soon as possible. Go back to the dealer or car supermarket and notify them of the problem. Depending on the fault you may be covered under a warranty or, if it is a new car, then you have rights under the Sales of Goods Act – see Consumer Direct ✉ or contact Trading Standards ✉ (*see Resources*, left).

Getting a good deal on your old car

Whether you sell your car privately or trade it in, slick presentation increases the chance of a good price.

■ **Put together a seller's pack.** Include details such as service history (a full service history, especially with a franchised dealer, can make your car worth more) and any tyres or engine parts replaced recently. Include details of road tax and MOT.

■ **Check out your local scrap yard** – look in a phone directory or use a parts-finder such as Breakerlink **www.breakerlink.com** ✉ (£1 a minute) **www.breakeryard.com** 0905 232 3000 ✉ or **www.carsparefinder.co.uk** 0907 004 3339 ✉ (£1.50 a minute) to replace missing parts.

■ **Hide paint chips and scratches** with a touch-up stick from your local car-care store, polish the car and replace worn mats.

■ **Find out how much your car is worth** on **www.webuyanycar.com** ✉. They guarantee to buy any car regardless of condition. Complete an online form to receive a price by email. You can also trade your car in at a higher value.

■ **If you have an old car** you may get more for it if you part exchange it. Some dealers will give you a minimum of £1,000, possibly more than the car is worth. But make sure you get a good price on the car you are buying – you may get more if you sell your existing car privately.

GET THE CHEAPEST INSURANCE

Being loyal to your car insurance company will not reward you financially. While you may get a discount as a new customer, premiums will probably go up the following year. You can save money each year by shopping around. Spending a few minutes on a comparison site could save you hundreds of pounds.

CHECK PREMIUMS BEFORE BUYING A CAR

Check insurance premiums before you splash out on a new car. It makes sense to get a couple of car insurance quotes before you buy a new car to make sure you can afford to insure it. The higher the insurance group the more you will pay. Also watch out for imported and modified cars as these normally cost more to insure.

HOW INSURANCE COSTS ARE SET

The amount that you pay depends on several factors.
Insurance group The insurance group reflects the size, specification and cost of repairs to the vehicle. Factors include the car's performance, image and maximum speed. The car's cost when new, the cost of parts and the price and availability of its body shell are also taken into consideration. Each time you go up a group, your insurance costs grow. You can check the insurance group of any car at **www.thatcham.org/abigrouprating.**
Age and occupation of insured driver How old you are and what your job is affects how much you will pay. For example, someone in their twenties will pay more than someone in their fifties, and a publican will pay more than an accountant.

BUY THE RIGHT INSURANCE POLICY

Choose insurance that suits you and your car. Third-party insurance is cheaper, but if you have a valuable car, a comprehensive policy will give you more security.
■ Third-party insurance covers the cost of damage you may cause to someone else, their vehicle or property with your car.
■ A third-party, fire and theft policy also pays out if your car catches fire or is stolen.
■ Fully comprehensive insurance will cover repairs to your vehicle, too, after an accident.

FINDING THE BEST-VALUE INSURANCE

Car insurance premiums vary depending on the insurer and the type of policy you choose. It only takes around 15 minutes to search dozens of insurers using one of the car insurance comparison sites and could save you hundreds of pounds. It makes sense to use one or two of the sites and compare results. Make sure you compare like with like and watch out for excess and cover offered by each policy.

BEST QUOTES FOR COMPREHENSIVE	ANNUAL PREMIUM	EXCESS
Co-op Insurance	£303.49	£100
Budget	£307.69	£200
Policy Shop	£310	£250
Igo4	£312.59	£300
Churchill	£312.90	£100

Source: www.gocompare.com January 2009. Based on a Ford Focus 2008 1.6 for a 38 year old operations manager in manufacturing with a 3-year no claims discount.

Postcode Where you live has an effect on the premium. Some areas, such as inner cities, are more high-risk than others, and whether the car will be parked on the street or in a garage will also be relevant.

Driver's record The past record of the driver, including convictions and insurance claims made, will have an effect.

GETTING A COMPETITIVE QUOTE

The best way to get a good deal on your car insurance is to use a car insurance comparison site. You enter your details once and get a range of quotes from a wide selection of insurers. You can also compare the cover each policy offers. However not all companies are included on comparison sites so it makes sense to compare the results from a couple of sites and possibly go direct to insurers. An insurance broker may be able to get you a good deal so may be worth a try, especially if you are high risk, young, etc.

Go back to your insurer Once you have found some cheaper quotes go back to your insurer and see if it will match or beat the best quote you have found. You may find they offer you a more competitive quote to keep your business.

Compare like with like When shopping around for any insurance make sure you are comparing like with like. Policies offer different features as standard – for example, a courtesy car or legal expenses cover. Also watch out for excesses: the higher the excess (the amount you have to pay if you make a claim) the cheaper the premium. So always check cover and excesses when comparing policies.

Pay in one go If you can, pay your insurance in one go. Most companies will give you the option to pay in instalments but they also charge interest of up to 30%, so it can add almost a third to the cost of insuring your car.

TOP TIPS SAVING ON MOTOR INSURANCE

There are many ways in which you can bring down your premiums, depending on your age and circumstances and the type of driving you do.

■ **Insure through your motoring organisation** You may get a discount from the RAC ✉ or the AA ✉. However, check that you are getting a good price.

■ **Pay the cheapest way** Don't pay in instalments – this can add up to 30% to the cost of insurance.

■ **Opt for a bigger voluntary excess** You'll have to pay more if you have an accident, but you could save in the region of £50 on a £600 premium by increasing the excess from £100 to £250.

■ **Avoid making minor claims** If you claim for minor incidents, you'll simply push your premiums up. You must tell your insurer about all accidents or risk having no cover.

■ **Update your details** Make sure you tell your insurer about your correct details. For example, ensure you give a realistic annual mileage, tell your insurer if you no longer need cover for driving to and from work, use a realistic value for your car. You could save money switching to third party, fire or theft from comprehensive cover.

---

keep it simple

KEEP AN EYE ON YOUR PREMIUMS Check your car insurance premiums yearly – rates do change and you may find that last year's best buy has been undercut.

SMART MOVES

Cut up to 30% off your insurance

Consider taking extra training to cut insurance costs.

■ Newly qualified drivers could save up to 20% to 30% on their insurance by doing Pass Plus extra training costing around £150 (**www. passplus.org.uk** ✉). However, you may get cheaper insurance without the discount so shop around.

■ Experienced drivers could save money on their insurance by taking extra training in advanced driving. According to the Institute of Advanced Motorists (**www.iam.org.uk** 020 8996 9600 ✉) nine out of 10 advanced motorists pay less for their car insurance.

■ **Invest in better security** Tell your insurer if you have an approved car alarm system or immobiliser – not only will it help protect your car, it will bring premiums down, too.

■ **Garage your car** Your insurer will give a discount if your car is garaged at night.

■ **Choose a car in a low insurance group** What car you drive can make a big difference to how much insurance you will pay.

■ **Additional drivers** Adding a partner on to your insurance could save you money. However, adding younger drivers could be expensive. Be careful of adding a younger driver on to your insurance to insure their car. If it's their car the insurance needs to be in their name as the main driver.

■ **Insurance for older drivers** Several insurance companies offer insurance for older drivers – including **www.saga.co.uk** ✉ and **www.ageconcern.org.uk** ✉. However, these may not offer the best deal. Shop around like any other driver and see if you can save.

■ **Don't break the law** Premiums rise steeply once you have points on your licence, and insurance companies won't pay out if an accident results from your breaching the terms of your insurance – for example, if you drive while under the influence of drink or drugs.

RESOURCES

SHOP AROUND FOR INSURANCE
Compare online motor insurance quotes at:
www.moneysupermarket. com ✉
www.gocompare.com ✉
www.confused.com ✉
www.uswitch.com ✉
www.beatthatquote.com ✉
www.tescocompare.com ✉
www.comparethemarket.com ✉
www.autotrader.co.uk ✉

CASE STUDY

HOW A YOUNG DRIVER CUT HIS INSURANCE PREMIUM

Chris Scott got a shock when he received the renewal notice from his existing car insurer. His premium had increased from £300 to £750 after just one year. Chris is 21 and over the past year he had been given six points for speeding and as a result his premium had increased dramatically. Chris queried the premium and was told that his premium may go down after a year if he doesn't have any accidents or get any more points. Chris had also been given a discount in his first year of driving because he had been on a Pass Plus training course.

Chris couldn't really afford the increased premium and decided to shop around for cheaper insurance. Using an insurance comparison site he found similar cover for £500. By increasing his excess to £500 he reduced it down further to £400. Chris saved himself £350 on his insurance in around 15 minutes and from now on will shop around for his car insurance each year.

WATCH POINTS JOB-RELATED INCREASES

Your job affects how much you pay on your insurance. Insurers classify jobs according to risk and their claims experience.

Insure your wife or husband Insurance costs for couples are normally lower than insuring both people separately. However, if you are the main driver of a car make sure that the insurance is in your name.

Park more securely Leaving the car at home or parking it more securely at your workplace can bring down your insurance premiums – let your insurer know.

Tell the truth Changing your occupation to save on car insurance premiums or lying about the number of no-claims years you have is illegal and could leave you out of pocket if you come to make a claim.

Business use Even if you use your car only occasionally for business, make sure you opt for business use. It might not increase your premium at all, and you will be covered if you have an accident on one of those rare business trips.

keep it simple

CAR INSURANCE GROUPS

Insurers classify every car according to its insurance group. You can check the rating of your car at **www.thatcham. org/abigrouprating**. One way of reducing your car insurance premiums is to choose a car in a lower insurance group. It can save you hundreds of pounds a year.

COST-CUTTING DRIVING AND MAINTENANCE

Save money on fuel and avoid large garage bills with these simple strategies and checks.

TOP TIPS MAXIMISE FUEL ECONOMY

Fuel prices have soared in recent years so it makes sense to try and conserve as much fuel as possible when driving.

■ **Don't drive** The best way to save money on your car fuel costs is to leave the car at home. Many journeys are short and you could walk instead, or use public transport.

■ **Think ahead when driving** Rapid acceleration and braking are heavy on fuel – take your foot off the accelerator when you approach a red light, and then brake gently. Accelerate gradually, too. Gentle driving in town can cut fuel costs and emissions by more than 10%.

■ **Select high gears** Once you are moving drive in the highest gear you can.

■ **Turn off your engine** When it's safe, turn off your engine when you stop.

■ **Cut your speed** Save on fuel by driving more slowly. For example, driving at 60mph on motorways instead of 70mph will give you much better fuel economy.

■ **Close windows** Driving with the windows open costs you money on fuel economy.

■ **Remove the roof rack** An empty roof rack pushes up fuel consumption by around 10%, and a fully laden one by up to 30%.

■ **Reduce weight** Empty the boot and roof storage box. Extra weight means fewer miles to a litre.

■ **Don't use unnecessary accessories** Air conditioning can use up to 10% more fuel.

■ **Car sharing** Sharing the car can save you large amounts of money. You can search for car sharing at www.nationalcarshare.co.uk or 0871 8718 880 ✉.

■ **Avoid premium grade** Most cars don't need premium fuels. Stick to cheaper standard fuels and save money.

MAKE THE CHANGE TO CLEANER FUEL

■ Think about converting your car to run on cleaner fuels, including natural gas or liquefied petroleum gas (LPG). LPG vehicles cost about 30% less to run than petrol vehicles and about the same as diesel vehicles. LPG gives about a 10% to 15% reduction in CO_2 emissions compared to petrol.

■ Petrol costs about twice as much as LPG and there are more than 1,200 LPG refuelling sites around the country.

■ Making the change costs over £1,200 to £2,700.

■ You could consider changing to an electric car, particularly if you make mainly short journeys. Petrol/electric hybrids can travel around 60 miles or more on a gallon.

■ Find out more about energy efficient cars at The Energy Saving Trust at **www.energysavingtrust. org.uk** 0800 512 012 ✉ and Friends of the Earth at **www.foe.co.uk** ✉ also has information on using cleaner fuels.

SHOP AROUND FOR CHEAP PETROL

There is a big difference in the price of petrol in your area. Here we show the price of petrol in several garages in West Sussex in January 2009.

	UNLEADED	DIESEL	SUPER	LPG
HIGHEST PRICE	90.9p	101.9p	100.9p	49.9p
AVERAGE PRICE	87.7p	99.1p	93.3p	49.9p
LOWEST PRICE	84.9p	96.9p	87.9p	49.9p

Source **www.petrolprices.com** ✉ January 2009.

LOOK FOR THE CHEAPEST PETROL

Petrol prices vary considerably and supermarkets are often cheapest. Check out the best local prices at www.petrolprices.com ✉.

HAVE YOUR CAR SERVICED REGULARLY

Having your car serviced regularly keeps it in good running order, improves fuel efficiency and helps you avoid large bills – an unchecked minor problem could cause serious damage. Worn-out brake pads, for example, could result in damage to the brake discs, which will then need replacing. For a small family car, new brake pads cost about £30 a set, as opposed to around £130 if you have to replace the discs as well.

Stay local Your local garage may charge less for servicing than a franchised dealer, so ask for quotes before taking your car in. Check and compare the hourly labour charge, which will probably be the largest part of the bill.

WATCH POINTS TOP GARAGE SCAMS

■ **Extra work discovered mid-job** When you take your car for its MOT, the garage may discover major work that needs doing before it will pass the test. You know you should shop around for the best price, but you can't – the car is already stripped down and the MOT certificate is about to run out. The answer is to use an independent MOT-only centre for a £20 to £40 test well before the certificate expires. Once you know what needs to be done, search for the best quote.

■ **Unquoted labour charges** A repair costs £340, but the bill comes with an extra £120 charge for stripping down the engine – two hours' labour at £60 an hour. You've been

Save money by checking your car yourself

Keep your car running well with these checks:

Oil Check the oil every other time you fill up with petrol and top it up when it runs low. Check the other fluids at the same time, including brake fluid and power-steering fluid.

Wipers Check your windscreen wipers – smearing suggests that they are wearing out. Try cleaning them first, checking the edges and smoothing them down with fine-grade glasspaper if they are rough. Or buy new ones to slot into place. Fix a bent wiper by switching off the ignition to stop it mid-stroke, then grip it with two pairs of pliers to twist it gently until straight.

Tyre tread Examine the tread on tyres regularly. Uneven wear suggests that you should ask your garage to fix the tracking and wheel balance. At the same time, get them to switch tyres front and back to maximise their life.

Antifreeze Top up antifreeze in winter to reduce the risk of emergencies and expensive garage recovery.

Lights Avoid emergency replacements by checking all your lights weekly at dusk and replacing any blown bulbs.

Battery Check the battery regularly. If you need a new one, buy the longest-lasting one your car can take – it'll help prevent problems with the starting, charging and electrical systems and save money in the long run.

Tyre pressure Make sure tyres are inflated as specified to ensure fuel economy and safety.

Leaks Puddles under your car can be caused by leaking brake fluid, oil or windscreen wiper fluid. To detect problems early, before any damage has been done, use a small plastic bowl to catch the leaking fluid and examine it to pinpoint the problem.

SMART MOVES

cheated – the bill should include stripping down the engine for the job, or the garage should tell you beforehand that there will be a separate charge. Explain why you feel the bill is unfair, and ask for a reduction. Say you will approach the local Trading Standards office if you aren't satisfied. Always agree in advance what is included in a quote.

■ **Extra work done without agreement** The garage manager tells you that they found a major fault – so they fixed it and doubled your bill. A reputable garage would have called you first. The solution? First, ask friends and neighbours which garage they recommend or, if you're new to the area, use a larger garage that is part of the Retail Motor Industry Federation scheme (**www.rmif.co.uk** or 08457 58 53 50 ✉). In case of trouble, you'll be able to ask the RMIF to arbitrate.

■ **Work not done** Your car has had its major service, but you're suspicious – did they really do the work? Check the oil – if it's black and dirty, they haven't changed it. Check coolant levels, too – if they're low, they haven't done the job properly. Complain to the garage and the council's Trading Standards department (see Resources, page 270), and find a better garage.

CAR CLUBS FOR OCCASIONAL DRIVERS

If you need a car just occasionally – even for as little as an hour at a time – you could join one of a number of car clubs round the country. You can search for clubs near you at Car Plus **www.carclubs.org.uk** or 0845 217 8996 ✉. Once you have joined one of the clubs you can book a car, by phone, text or Internet, then pick it up from a designated parking space less than ten minutes' walk from your home or workplace. There is normally an annual or monthly fee and then you pay by the hour or day.

■ **Save on car expenses** With a car club, you get access to a car without having to own it, so you save on servicing, maintenance and garaging costs.

■ **Reasonable rates** Rates vary but you could save money on owning and running a car with clubs like WhizzGo (**www.whizzgo.co.uk** or 08444 77 99 66 ✉) and Zipcar (**www.zipcar.co.uk** or 020 7669 4000 ✉). Zipcar charges an annual fee of £25 and hourly rates from £3.95 and daily for £29 during the week. At the weekend the hourly rates are

CAR CLUBS: HOW MUCH COULD YOU SAVE?

Car Plus (**www.carplus.org.uk** ✉) estimates people could save thousands of pounds by giving up their family car and using a car club instead. Based on a medium family car, driving 10,000 miles per year with annual insurance of £250, and a three-year-old car club car you could save £2,139 a year.

	ANNUAL COST
OWN CAR	£4,659
CAR CLUB	£2,520
TOTAL SAVING	£2,139

£4.95 and £45. Fuel, insurance and 60 free miles are included. As Zipcar is in London it includes the congestion charge. Whizzgo has cars in large cities, including Leeds, Liverpool, Brighton and London. It charges a monthly fee of £5, hourly rates from £5.99 and £49.99 for 24 hours.

JOIN A CAR POOL
Being part of a car pool can enable you to share costs between several drivers. In some parts of Britain, such as Leeds, you can use special lanes for cars carrying more than one occupant.

■ **Cheaper insurance** The ABI (Association of British Insurers ✉) say that if you are a driver in a car pool scheme, your normal motor insurance still applies, but if in any doubt, contact your insurance company. Some insurance companies offer reductions for people in a car pool.

■ **Cheaper parking** Check with your employer or car park operator. They may offer better spaces, discounts or even free spaces for car pool drivers.

■ **Tax breaks** Ask your accountant what you can deduct for car pooling expenses.

TOP TIPS: DIY VALET SERVICE
Keeping your car looking clean and shiny needn't involve expensive trips to the car wash or valet service, or investment in special car-cleaning products. Soapy water, baking soda and vinegar are natural cleaning agents that do an effective job and cost next to nothing.

■**Save money on de-icing** If your windows and windscreen ice up overnight in winter, pour a jug of hot (but not boiling) water over them and switch the wipers on for a few seconds. Any ice that re-forms can then be cleared easily with a scraper, and you'll save on cans of de-icer. Avoid ice in the first place by covering your windscreen at night.

■ **Removing insects** Squashed insects on the windscreen and bodywork can be removed simply with one or two cups of baking soda mixed with two cups of warm water in a clean spray bottle. Soak the insects for a couple of minutes, then rinse with a hose, using a sponge to remove the insects.

■ **Demist your windscreen** Buy a blackboard rubber for under £1 and keep it under the front seat. It's handy for wiping the windscreen if it gets steamed up.

■ **Homemade window cleaner** Save money on ready-made window cleaning solutions by mixing warm water with a little white vinegar in a clean spray bottle.

■ **Removing oil stains** Remove oil from the garage floor with white spirit and a layer of cat litter. Once the litter has absorbed the oil, sweep it up and use white spirit on remaining stains.

■ **Wash your car** Save up to £5 a week at the car wash by doing the job yourself. Always wash a car in the shade and when the engine is cool – a hot surface dries the water too fast, leaving unsightly spots. Rinse the car with a hose to loosen dirt, then turn the tap off to save water. Use one bucket of soapy water – dishwasher detergent is fine – and one bucket of clean water. Use the hose for the final rinse.

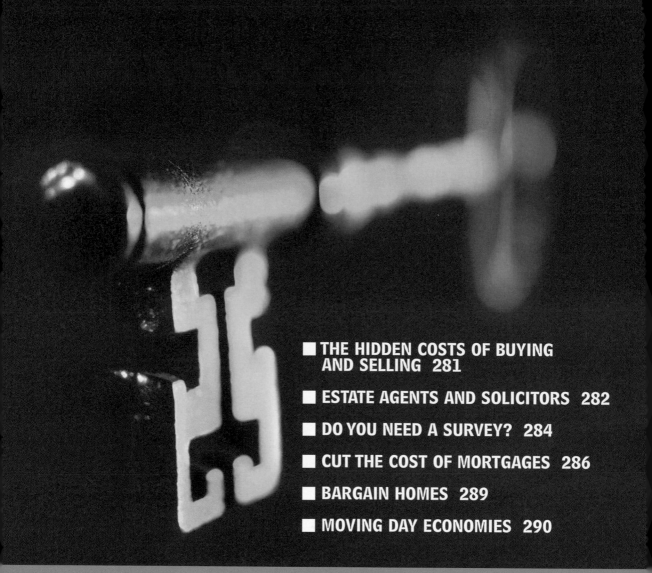

Buying and selling property

After a decade of dramatic rises, house prices have stalled or even fallen as a result of the global credit crisis in 2008. So it is more important than ever that you explore all the financial options and keep the costs of buying and selling property in check.

THE HIDDEN COSTS OF BUYING AND SELLING

House buying and selling is expensive. Before you even consider the cost of your mortgage, there are fees, taxes and other charges that can run into thousands of pounds. The table below shows typical costs, but you can make savings.

TOP TIPS LEARN WHERE YOU CAN SAVE

Although some costs, such as stamp duty, are unavoidable, many other expenses are variable. Good research can result in considerable savings if you do some of the work yourself.

Explore all options Estate agents' fees vary, so shop around – and look into selling your house yourself (see page 283).

No stamp duty Although you normally have to pay stamp duty on properties valued at more than £125,000, up until 2 September 2009 this has been increased to £175,000. After 2 September 2009 once again property in some disadvantaged areas will be free of stamp duty up to £150,000. See **www.hmrc.gov.uk** or phone 0845 603 0135 ✉ to find out whether your purchase qualifies.

Cut conveyancing costs Solicitors' fees have become more competitive in recent years, so get several quotes. If the sale is simple, you could cut costs substantially by doing your own conveyancing (see page 283). However, you won't be able to get compensation if anything goes wrong.

Save on surveys If the property is in good repair, you may not need a full structural survey but a more limited homebuyer survey may be sufficient (see page 284).

Cheaper moves Removal firms' charges vary, so be sure to get several quotes. You can also save on removal fees by doing some of the work yourself (see page 290).

Do your own research Look online for information about house prices, the local area and property for sale. Prices achieved can be found at **www.nethouseprices.com** ✉ and **www.houseprices.co.uk** ✉; both sites are based on information from the Land Registry. Get a valuation of your property from **www.zoopla.co.uk** ✉ and **www.propertypriceadvice.co.uk** ✉.

STAMP ON COSTS

You can't avoid stamp duty, but you can avoid paying more than is necessary.

■ Look for a house priced under the closest stamp duty band limit (see below). A house at £250,001 attracts a 3% rate of stamp duty, whereas one at £250,000 incurs 1% stamp duty.

■ When you are selling be aware that a price a little above a stamp duty threshold is very likely to be reduced to below the threshold. But beware: don't try to evade stamp duty by cutting the house price and bumping up fixtures and fittings: HMRC take steps to prevent this.

■ For a free online stamp duty calculator, go to HMRC **http://sdccalculator. hmrc.gov.uk**

House value	Stamp duty rate (until 2 Sep 2009)
0-£175,000	0%
£175,001-£250,000	1%
£250,001-£500,000	3%
Over £500,000	4%

Information January 2009

HOW YOU CAN SAVE ON FEES AND TAXES

Estimated cost savings on a property priced at £260,000.

	TYPICAL	COULD REDUCE TO
ESTATE AGENT'S FEE	£6,500 @ 2.5%	£2,600 by negotiating a 1% fee
STAMP DUTY	£7,800	£2,500 or less by negotiating price below 3% threshold
SOLICITOR'S FEES	£1,500	£750 by using online solicitor
SURVEYOR	£600	£250 by getting a report and valuation only
REMOVALS	£600	£400 by doing some of the work yourself
TOTAL	£17,000	£6,500 – a saving of £10,500

ESTATE AGENTS AND SOLICITORS

Professional help, although expensive, can save you worry and hassle. But save money by negotiating fees, and consider cutting costs by doing your own advertising or conveyancing.

DO IT ONLINE

Cut out the estate agent and sign on with an Internet sales site (see *Resources*, right). Costs are likely to be £20–£199 to advertise your house online. HouseWeb (**www.houseweb.co.uk** 0845 003 0717 ✉) with its £199 Platinum service offers an online advert with up to 20 photos, a For Sale board, email and phone number to receive enquiries, an online map and printable flyers. It charges just £47 for an online advert with one photo, email, map and printable flyers.

WATCH POINTS SNAGS WHEN SELLING

Be aware of the pitfalls when selling your house, otherwise your money-saving efforts may be counter productive.

■ **The right price** A problem with DIY selling is under or overpricing. Check that the price you set is reasonable (see *Do your own research*, page 181).

■ **Paper money** Newspaper ads give limited exposure, and you might pay £100 for just one week's insertions.

■ **Contract length** Do not tie yourself to a long contract with an estate agent in case you want to change agencies.

■ **Check the charges** You should be given written details of charges and when they are payable at the outset (see below).

■ **Advertising costs** Some estate agents make additional charges for advertising and For Sale boards.

■ **Official bodies** Only use an estate agent that is a member of National Association of Estate Agents ✉ or Royal Institute of Chartered Surveyors ✉. Since October 2008, all estate agents have to be a member of a redress scheme. Check that your agent is covered by the Ombudsman for Estate Agents ✉ or the Surveyor's Ombudsman Service ✉.

Choose the right agency deal

Estate agents' charges vary from 0.5% to 4% depending on the deal. As increases in house prices in recent years have far outstripped rises in agency costs, you are justified in arguing for the lowest rate.

Sole agency This is normally the cheapest option. You make an agreement for a set period. The agent cannot claim commission if you sell privately but if you sell through another agent, both get commission.

Joint sole agency Two agents work for you on a sole agency contract. This is usually a little more expensive than a sole agency agreement.

Multiple agency A number of agents work for you and the one who gets a sale takes the commission. This is often the most successful,

and expensive, option.

Sole selling rights The agent gets commission however the house is sold – even if you sell it to a friend or colleague. This is obviously unfair, so avoid it.

'Ready, willing and able purchaser' If the agent finds a purchaser able to buy, commission is payable, even if the sale does not go through. So again, avoid signing agreements that include this type of deal.

TOP TIPS GET £5,000 MORE FOR YOUR SALE

You are likely to achieve a quicker, more profitable sale by showing your home in its best light to potential buyers. Good presentation could add thousands to the selling price.

■ **Declutter** Put into storage any items that make the place look crowded or untidy. The house may look spartan for a while, but a tidy, spacious appearance will attract buyers.

■ **Redecorate** Spruce up any areas that look worn – the cost of a lick of paint and a little elbow grease can add several thousand pounds to a sale. Finish any half-completed DIY jobs – a well-maintained house is always worth more.

■ **Clean and sweeten** Give the entire house a thorough clean, eliminating any pet odours, dust and grime.

■ **Tidy the garden** Do some outdoor housework – make sure the grass and hedges are trimmed and that the flowerbeds look attractive. Make the most of outdoor space by staging it with table and chairs.

■ **Lighten up** Maximise the light in all the rooms by ensuring the windows are sparkling and curtains are open and some lights are on. It may even be worth redecorating in lighter shades to increase the impression of airy spaciousness.

■ **Give rooms a role** The function of each room should be obvious, so make sure a three-bedroom house has three proper bedrooms, for example. If necessary, add a bed to a former junk room or a table to a dining room.

■ **Create a good atmosphere** On the day prospective buyers come to view, add welcoming touches such as vases of fresh flowers, scented candles or a fire in the grate.

DO YOU NEED A SOLICITOR?

Solicitors' fees for conveyancing are one of the major costs in buying and selling property. In theory, you can do it yourself. Plenty of help is available on the Internet and through books, and the standard legal forms cost only a few pounds.

DIY drawbacks Although conveyancing is largely a form-filling exercise, a mistake can be costly. Mortgage lenders may not deal with someone who is not legally qualified, or may impose higher charges. If it all goes wrong, you could end up paying a solicitor to sort out your mess.

Shop around If you don't have the courage for DIY conveyancing, at least take advantage of the competitiveness of the conveyancing market. It is easy to get a range of quotes from the Internet (see *Resources*, right) or by phone from local firms. Online quotes to sell a £200,000 house and buy a £250,000 house in England and Wales range between £450 and £600 (plus stamp duty of £2,500 and Land registry fee of about £200). Some companies offer nil charges if the transaction does not go through and a guarantee of no extra charges. Note that you may pay around £200 more for each leasehold transaction, depending on their complexity.

Go out of town If you live in a major city, get a quote from a solicitor in a more rural area as prices can be much lower.

Fix the price Some solicitors work on a time basis, others may quote a fixed price. Agree the terms at the outset so you know where you stand. If your bill is higher than expected, complain to the firm promptly. If you are not satisfied, contact Legal Complaints Service ✉ (see *Resources*, right).

RESOURCES

HELPFUL INFORMATION

■ Royal Institute of Chartered Surveyors **www.rics.org** 0870 333 1600 ✉.

■ Find a local estate agent at National Association of Estate Agents **www.naea.co.uk** 01926 496800 ✉.

■ The Ombudsman for Estate Agents **www.oea.co.uk** 01722 333306 ✉.

■ Surveyors Ombudsman Service **www.surveyors-ombudsman.org.uk** 0845 050 8181 ✉.

■ Sell online with **www.houseweb.com** 0845 003 0717 ✉, **www.thelittlehousecompany. co.uk** 0800 083 4241 ✉ and **www.privatehouse move.co.uk** ✉.

■ For advice, try Citizens Advice Bureau **www.adviceguide.org.uk** ✉ or **www.direct.gov.uk** ✉.

■ To find a solicitor, contact the Law Society **www.lawsociety.org.uk** 020 7242 1222 ✉.

■ Legal Complaints Service **www.legal complaints.org.uk** 0845 608 6565 ✉.

■ Get conveyancing quotes from **www.reallymoving.com** ✉, **www.onlineconveyancing. co.uk** ✉ and **www.easier2move.co.uk** 0845 4600 800 ✉.

■ *Which?* has useful information about selling your home yourself at **www.which.co.uk** ✉, and sells *Buy, Sell and Move House* via the website or through bookstores.

DO YOU NEED A SURVEY?

Most people don't get a building survey (formerly known as a full structural survey) of the house they want to buy. Although this may not be a problem for most buyers, for others the survey cost might have saved them the several thousand pounds they had to spend on structural problems.

SURVEYS FOR LESS

If you decide on a building survey, make sure you get your money's worth. Ask questions about what will be included, and have the surveyor comment on specific matters of interest, although bear in mind that extra work may add to the cost.

Discounted surveys Your lender's surveyor may carry out a survey for you at a discount by doing the survey at the same time as the lender's valuation report. It might be better to get your own totally independent survey, however.

Finding a surveyor To find a surveyor consult the Royal Institute of Chartered Surveyors on 0870 333 1600 ✉. Their website **www.rics.org** also has information on surveys.

WATCH POINTS IS A FULL SURVEY NEEDED?

If you are buying any of the following, get a building survey to avoid paying to fix problems after the sale. A full survey may mean you can negotiate on the sale price, or decide not to go ahead with a sale at all. Consider a building survey if your property is:
- a property built before 1900 – it may have developed significant faults over the years;
- a listed building;
- a building of unusual construction – a timber-built or thatched house of any age warrants a full survey;
- a house you plan to renovate or change;
- a house that has been renovated or altered;
- a place with obvious problems, such as signs of damp, very old electrics or a damaged roof.

AT RISK FROM FLOODING?

Check to see if the house you are considering buying is at risk from flooding. You can get information about the risk of flooding at a specific postcode from The Environment Agency at **www.environment-agency.gov.uk** 08708 506 506 ✉ and at **www.homecheck.co.uk** 0844 844 9966 ✉. Home Check brings together information from The Environment Agency, The Health Protection Agency and the British Geological Survey.

Different surveys and their costs

SMART MOVES

REPORT AND VALUATION	HOMEBUYERS' SURVEY	BUILDING SURVEY
Gives a basic description only – the number of rooms and the type of construction. Also gives an estimated valuation.	Looks at easily visible features – measurements of rooms, any obvious defects or repairs needed such as damp, rot or woodworm. Includes a valuation.	Detailed survey – may lift carpets, look in loft, test electrics and plumbing. Can answer specific questions, such as 'Could we knock down a wall?' No valuation but you can request one.
Cost: around £250.	**Cost: £400–£600.**	**Cost: from £500–£1,000+.**
Needed: always.	**Needed: optional.**	**Needed: optional. Shows**
Required by lender.	**Highlights obvious problems.**	**underlying problems.**

GET MONEY OFF THE ASKING PRICE

We're not suggesting that you do your own buildings' survey. But check the following to get an idea of the condition of the property. There are three strong reasons to do this.

■ It may indicate a full survey is needed.

■ You may discover things that will turn out to be costly or persuade you not to go ahead with the purchase.

■ You may find ammunition for getting the seller to drop the price, so don't be put off by problems. Cost the repairs carefully by calling in a specialist and estimating any inconvenience costs. Show your calculations to the vendor and lower your offer.

WHERE?	WHAT'S THE PROBLEM?	CALL A SURVEYOR
OUTSIDE **WALLS AND ROOF**	■ Is the brickwork in good repair? Cracks could indicate subsidence. ■ Will you have to pay for expensive external decoration? ■ Crumbling mortar? The walls might need an expensive repointing job. ■ Is the roof in good order? Damaged slates could indicate leaks. ■ Are gutters and drains damaged or blocked? ■ Are the windows in good order – or will they need replacing? REDUCE YOUR OFFER BY £1,000–£10,000	✔ ✔ ✔
THE GARDEN	■ Who is responsible for the hedges and fences? (See the deeds.) ■ Are there fences? If not, you may have to pay for them. ■ Might those large trees close to the house cause subsidence? REDUCE YOUR OFFER BY £500–£1,000	✔
INSIDE **DECOR**	■ Is the decoration dated, extreme or very shabby? ■ Could brand new redecorating be an attempt to hide defects? REDUCE YOUR OFFER BY £2,000–£5,000	
ELECTRICS AND PLUMBING	■ Can you trust old-style switches and obvious DIY wiring? Definitely not. ■ Do the taps work? How long does hot water take to come through?. ■ Check the central heating boiler works. How old is it and has it been regularly serviced? REDUCE YOUR OFFER BY £1,000–£4,000	✔ ✔ ✔
WALLS AND CEILINGS	■ Do those ceiling stains indicate leaks? If so there are probably plumbing or roof problems. ■ Are those cracks just settlement or something more sinister? ■ Is that musty smell damp? And is the wood panelling covering defects? REDUCE YOUR OFFER BY £2,000–£10,000	✔ ✔
RUNNING EXPENSES **BILLS**	■ Are fuel bills, council tax or insurance very expensive? Check the cost of running the house. REDUCE YOUR OFFER BY £500–£1,000	
GENERAL UPKEEP	■ How much will the beech hedge surrounding the large garden cost to cut each year? It could be over £300. ■ Do you realise a thatched roof will need replacing every 15–20 years – and could cost from £15,000–£20,000. ■ Are you prepared for the maintenance costs of that swimming pool? REDUCE YOUR OFFER BY £300–£20,000	✔
LOCAL KNOWLEDGE	■ Check on possible problems such as noise nuisance from traffic. Chat to the neighbours or check out the local council website. Visit **www.upmystreet.com** ✉ for local area information.	

CUT THE COST OF MORTGAGES

A mortgage is a means of borrowing money to finance a property purchase. As with any other loan, you have to pay interest to the lender until the loan is repaid. Mortgages are available from sources such as banks, building societies, Internet lenders and specialist mortgage companies.

FINDING THE BEST MORTGAGE

You can find out about available mortgages through specialist magazines or the Internet and approach the lender direct, or ask a mortgage broker to find you the right deal. **A better deal?** Brokers should trawl the whole market for you and point out the pros and cons of different loans. They may also get cheaper deals than you could by going direct. You should always buy your mortgage with advice. This means the adviser will make sure the mortgage is suitable for you and you have redress if you are sold the wrong

---

Know your mortages

REPAYMENT
You pay some capital and some interest off with each monthly payment, until the whole loan is paid off at the end of the term (usually 25 years).
Good for: Steady and reliable repayment of the whole mortgage.

SMART MOVES

INTEREST ONLY
Your monthly payment covers interest only, leaving the capital outstanding at the end of the loan. In order to pay off the capital, you should take out a savings plan (ISA, pension or life policy) at the start. This, in theory, should grow enough to cover the capital. Endowment mortgages – a type of interest-only mortgage using a life policy to make the repayment at the end of the mortgage – have been controversial in recent years as many policyholders have ended

up with a shortfall.
Good for: Risk takers. Can be cheaper than a repayment and may result in a lump sum at the end.

FLEXIBLE
Many standard mortgages let you make over and under payments within certain limits each year. Some flexible mortgages offer even more flexibility.
Good for: Borrowers whose financial status may change.

TRACKER
The rate varies and is fixed at a certain level above or below the Bank of England base rate. Watch out for collars though – a minimum rate the mortgage will not drop lower than.
Good for: Housebuyers who want to benefit from any drops in the base rate.

DISCOUNT
For a specified term, you pay interest at a discount on the lender's standard variable rate (SVR), after

which you pay at the SVR. Redemption penalties may apply.
Good for: People who want to benefit from lower rates at the start of the term.

FIXED
The interest rate is fixed for a period – usually two, five or ten years. Redemption penalties usually apply.
Good for: Buyers worried by rising rates who need security at the start. Will miss out on base-rate falls.

OFFSET ACCOUNT
Using money in your savings or current account to reduce the size of your mortgage and the interest you pay. Also, as you are effectively overpaying each month your mortgage should be paid off early.
Good for: Buyers with a healthy current or savings account. Especially beneficial for higher rate taxpayers. Mortgage interest rates not as competitive.

mortgage. The adviser will give you advice and make a recommendation of what is a suitable mortgage. Find an independent mortgage adviser at **www.unbiased.co.uk** ✉.

Avoid high fees Most mortgage brokers will charge you for advice about a mortgage. Some will charge a percentage of the value of the mortgage. This could be 1% or more, so a £150,000 mortgage could cost £1,500 or more just for the advice. However lots of advisers don't charge a fee for advice as they receive a commission from the lender you get your mortgage from. Before getting advice about a mortgage ask how much the adviser will charge. Watch out for them trying to sell you unnecessary insurance.

Compare total cost When comparing mortgage deals compare the total cost over the life of the mortgage or the length of a discounted rate. When you compare deals you need to include set-up fees, legal costs and any other charges. If you simply choose the lowest rate you could end up paying more over the length of the mortgage.

PAYING YOUR MORTGAGE OFF EARLY

For most people their mortgage is their biggest expense each month. If you can afford to, making overpayments to your mortgage will mean you pay off your mortgage early and incur less interest. If you have other debts, like credit cards, store cards or loans, at much higher rates of interest you should pay these off first before paying extra off your mortgage. If you have savings one way to pay your mortgage off early is to make lump sum payments off your mortgage. Most mortgages let you pay off a certain amount of your mortgage each year without penalty. Check with your lender. Of course only do this if you won't need your savings in future as you probably won't be able to access your money again without increasing the size of your mortgage or taking out a separate loan. Another option is an offset mortgage. (See *Know your mortgages*, left, or *Saving, Borrowing and Investing* chapter, page 324.)

WATCH POINTS BEWARE HIDDEN COSTS

Don't be seduced by lenders' advertising. Seemingly attractive deals may not suit your circumstances. The lowest APR may not be the best deal for you.

■ **Set-up fees** Set-up or arrangement fees on mortgages have increased in recent years. When you are comparing mortgages you need to take fees and the interest rate into account and compare the total cost of mortgage deals.

■ **Small deposits** Some lenders will charge you a mortgage indemnity guarantee (MIG) fee if you have a small deposit. Avoid deals that carry this extra expense. Not so common as deposits required have increased because of the global credit crisis.

■ **Insure cheaply** Lenders may try to persuade you to buy their house insurance. You are likely to get it cheaper if you shop around. Also watch out for advisers selling you protection insurance. Mortgages are

ASK YOURSELF

IS IT WORTH SWITCHING OFTEN TO GET THE BEST DEAL?

■ It may be. Keep your eye on market rates and the Bank of England Base Rate compared to what you are paying. Take into account costs of switching mortgage and exit penalties before moving your mortgage.

DO REDEMPTION PENALTIES APPLY?

■ Redemption penalties will probably mean it is not worth switching more often than every two or three years.

WILL I PROLONG MY MORTGAGE?

■ If you start a new 25-year mortgage each time you switch, you are postponing the day when you pay off your loan. When you take a new mortgage you can reduce the term of the mortgage in line with how long you have had it already.

RESOURCES

MORGAGE COSTS

The Internet is a good starting point for finding information on mortgages, and many sites offer calculators to work out how much you can borrow and what your mortgage will cost.

■ The *Which?* Mortgage finder is one of the best mortgage searches and lets you search from a wide range of mortgages and tailor the search to your requirements **www. which.co.uk/reviews/mortga ges/mortgage-finder**

■ For fee-free mortgage advice try **www.charcol. co.uk** 0845 034 2100 ✉ or London and Country **www.lcplc.co.uk** 0800 953 0304 ✉.

■ Comparison sites also provide information on mortgages. Try: **www.moneyfacts.co.uk** ✉, **www.moneysupermarket. com** ✉ and **www.uswitch.com** ✉.

complicated enough on their own. Make an appointment with an IFA to review your protection or see a protection insurance specialist. See *Family Affairs*, page 111 *Resources*.

■ **Expensive moves** Beware of redemption penalties if you move your mortgage during the penalty period. These are normally a percentage of the mortgage, for example 3%, but could be higher. When taking out a deal don't choose a mortgage with a penalty that lasts longer than the discounted or fixed rate.

■ **Cash costs** A number of lenders offer cashback – they give you back a percentage of the mortgage as a cash refund when you take out the mortgage. These may seem appealing, but interest rates will be higher and there may be hefty redemption penalties that last for several years. Also these mortgages often have high set-up fees.

SAVE MONEY WITH 'SWITCH AND SAVE'

If you have had your mortgage for several years and are paying your lender's SVR (standard variable rate), you could save thousands of pounds by switching to a cheaper deal.

HAS YOUR MORTGAGE DEAL RUN OUT?

This simple question could slash thousands off your mortgage. Although your discounted mortgage may have been a good deal to start with, you could probably save by switching at the end of the discounted period. The table below shows that a borrower currently paying 6% could save £116 a month by moving to a two-year discounted 4% deal, which is almost £2,800 over the discount period. However you need to take into account the cost of moving mortgage, including set-up and legal costs.

Change lenders See if your existing lender will give you a better deal to save you the cost and hassle of moving to a new lender. However the best deals tend to be reserved for new customers. Also bear in mind that because of the global credit crisis lenders are being more choosy who they lend to and some fees and charges have increased. You may also need a larger deposit than you paid with your current lender.

Avoid charges When you switch, you pay off the existing mortgage and take out a new one. This entails a number of charges, so find a lender who will pay them.

WATCH POINTS SWITCHING COSTS

Before you rush into switching your mortgage, check to see whether you will really save.

■ **Short-lived savings** Most really cheap deals are for a short period, say two years. They may carry big penalties to make it harder for you to move again. You also need to take into account set-up costs and legal fees, etc.

EFFECTS OF INTEREST RATE CHANGES

£100,000 repayment mortgage over 25 years

INTEREST RATE %

MONTHLY REPAYMENT

Interest Rate %	Monthly Repayment
2.0	£424
2.5	£449
3.0	£474
3.5	£501
4.0	£528
4.5	£556
5.0	£585
5.5	£614
6.0	£644

Source: **www.moneymadeclear.fsa.gov.uk**

■ **Total charges** There will be a valuation charge (£220) and legal costs (£400), and there may also be a discharge fee from your existing lender (£100) and a booking fee on a fixed-rate mortgage (£300). This all adds up to nearly £1,000, or 1% of a £100,000 mortgage – a percentage that will seriously reduce the benefit of a rate switch, although some deals will pay for all of these.

■ **Rates vs fees** The larger your mortgage, the less significant the fees will be in percentage terms. Someone with a big mortgage might save more by switching to a low rate and paying fees, while a smaller borrower could find it more cost-effective to go for an interest rate that is not as low but where one-off costs are paid by the lender. However, anyone taking out a mortgage should compare the total cost of deals, including all fees and charges. It makes sense to get advice from an independent mortgage broker.

■ **Find the alternatives** Shopping around is crucial. Even if you use a broker, ask them to look at several deals. Also do some research yourself and be prepared.

■ **The right deal** While you are going to the trouble and cost of switching, think whether a different type of mortgage would benefit you, too – repayment rather than interest only perhaps, or offset rather than conventional.

BARGAIN HOMES

If you are not in a position to spend vast sums of money on becoming a home owner, or are simply looking for a good buy, then try your luck at an auction or go for a property that other buyers find unattractive.

TOP TIPS BUYING CHEAPER AT AUCTION

■ **Make a dry run** Attend an auction as a practice outing and pick up tips on how to do it. Learn the jargon: the reserve price is the minimum price the seller will accept; the guide price what the auctioneer thinks the house might fetch.

■ **Plan ahead** Start getting auction catalogues as early as possible from local auction houses and subscription services with details of sales nationwide. Check property details carefully and make a list of properties you are interested in.

■ **Visit the property** If you can, go and see the property and arrange an internal visit. Many people buy at auction without a viewing and can get some nasty shocks.

■ **Hold back on professional fees** Only pay the legal and surveying costs on a property on which you are reasonably sure of making a successful bid. If you are unsuccessful, these costs of several hundred pounds will be wasted.

■ **Don't underestimate** Do not assume you will pay less at auction. There are many types of property for sale at auction, not just repossessed and dilapidated houses.

■ **Have a mortgage offer in place** You will need a 10% deposit ready on the auction day. You will also need a mortgage offer in place to pay the remainder in time – normally 20 working days from the auction.

■ **Legally binding** Make sure you bid on the right property. Bids at auction are binding.

RESOURCES

PROPERTY FOR SALE
■ You can search for property for sale at:
www.latesthomes.co.uk ✉
www.findaproperty.com ✉
www.rightmove.co.uk ✉
www.primelocation.com ✉
www.fish4.co.uk ✉.
■ Another interesting and useful site is **www.propertysnake.co.uk** ✉, which not only lists properties for sale but also shows you if the price has been reduced and for how long the property has been on the market.

THE LOCAL AREA
■ You can find out about a local area at:
www.upmystreet.com ✉.
It includes information about schools, crime and council services, as well as property prices.

keep it simple

MAKE AN OFFER
Houses can be sold privately before an auction sale – so if you are keen you could try making a pre-sale offer through the auctioneer. Or, if the lot fails to make its reserve and is not sold, try approaching the auctioneer after the sale with an offer.

BUY ON A BUDGET

Joint purchase One option is to buy jointly with a friend or group of friends. You will need to be 'tenants in common' rather than the 'joint tenants' arrangement that is more usual between couples. This makes things easier should one of you die. You will also need to have an arrangement that sets out how the property is owned and a legal agreement about what is to happen if one of you wants to sell.

Shorter leases You could look for a flat which has a shorter than normal lease to save money on the purchase price. Most leasehold flats start with a 99-year lease, but mortgage lenders may lend on shorter leases, down to about 60 or 70 years. Once you have owned the flat for two years in most cases you are entitled to get a lease extension. The lease extension will be for 90 years on top of the number of years remaining on the lease. You will need to pay for the lease extension, maybe another £15,000 on a flat that cost £120,000 at the outset. Use a solicitor who specialises in short-lease properties. If you are unhappy with the price you are quoted you can challenge it. The Leasehold Advisory Service can provide help and guidance at **www.lease-advice.org** or 020 7374 5380 ✉. Don't forget to renew the lease after two years, otherwise you could find the place very hard to sell and even harder to mortgage.

MOVING ECONOMIES

Whether you use a professional mover or do it yourself, you can make big savings if you know the ropes.

CHOOSE A CHEAPER MOVER

When selecting a removal firm, get several quotes. Decide where you are prepared to economise.

Shop around A range of quotes on a fairly standard move can vary by hundreds of pounds. You can get different quotes from Internet sites such as **www.reallymoving.com** ✉. If you live in a big city, consider hiring a company from an outlying area – it will sometimes be cheaper.

Agree a price Expect to pay several hundred pounds for a professional removal firm. The total will depend on the firm, how many possessions you have, how far you have to go and whether anything needs special handling. A typical bill is around £600; negotiate a lower price by agreeing to handle some special items yourself.

Move early in the week Removal firms are less busy then, and you may get a cheaper rate. Avoid Fridays, which are the busiest days for removals.

Book as early as you can Some firms charge more for bookings made at short notice.

Provide parking Make sure a parking space has been cleared as near your house as possible. Costs may rise if movers have to park at a distance.

Check professional associations If possible, choose a firm that is a member of the British Association of Removers (BAR) ✉. BAR has approval for its code of conduct from the Office of Fair Trading and has more than 500 members.

TOP TIPS PAY LESS FOR MOVERS

■ **Declutter first** Don't pay to move things you don't want in the new house. Take them to charity shops or ask special furniture charities to pick them up. Or make money selling items at a car boot or garage sale. Sell stuff to the new buyer. Put stuff in storage temporarily – move it in a bit at a time.

■ **Save £200 on packing up** If you use a professional removal firm, save money by handling some or all of the packing yourself. You will be charged more the more packing the remover has to do.

■ **Save £70 on packaging** Some companies offer complete kits with self-assembly boxes, bubble wrap and tape for £30–£70. Or you could use old newspapers for wrapping, and linen or towels for protecting valuables.

■ **Move your own garden tools** Consider moving the contents of your garden shed or garage yourself and storing them at your new address to keep costs down. This only makes sense if you are moving nearby and you can store them at your new property or move them the day you move.

■ **Move into storage** Another option is to move some or all of your belongings into storage. Lots of companies offer secure storage of belongings for small or large amounts for short or longer periods of time. This can be handy if your moving dates are not on the same day for some reason.

GO THE DIY ROUTE

With a little forethought, preparation and elbow grease, big savings can be made by shunning the professionals and moving all your possessions yourself. If you or a friend are happy driving a 35-cwt van, and you can rally the troops to help you lug your wardrobe downstairs, it is perfectly feasible. By using a cheap but reliable van rental service (preferably one that has been recommended), making as few trips as possible and travelling at off-peak times, you are sure to save a small fortune.

Van hire Costs will depend on the size of van and how long you need it, so try to keep both to a minimum, but be realistic. Get a quote and check it is inclusive of all charges. You will need to show your driving licence so don't send it off to the DVLC to have the address changed before your moving day.

Use the Internet Compare costs of van hire and find a competitive quote. Big-name companies in city centres will cost more than independent hire places outside the city.

RESOURCES

GET THE BEST PRICES

■ To get a range of quotes on moving go to **www.reallymoving.com** ✉.

■ The British Association of Removers lists removal firms at **www.bar.co.uk** or 01923 699480 ✉.

■ One of the biggest firms with a range of packing services is Pickfords at **www.pickfords.co.uk** ✉.

■ To hire a van suitable for removals try a local directory. Also try Hertz **www.hertzvans.co.uk** ✉ and Practical Car & Van Rental at **www.practical.co.uk** or 0121 772 8599 ✉.

■ Buy your own packing materials online at **www.bigbrownbox.co.uk** ✉, **www.theboxstore.co.uk** 0800 007 5220 ✉, **www.removalboxes.org** 01294 313348 ✉.

SMART MOVES

Savings on the day

Use common sense to make sure you don't lose out on moving day.

Have a moving party Get your friends to help with carrying boxes and any last-minute packing.

Take it away Remove everything that you are not contractually obliged to leave behind, within reason. Don't forget ornaments, pot plants, curtains and lampshades. Check in lofts and cellars.

Switch off Don't end up paying for utilities that your buyers will end up using – notify all the relevant companies and take notes of meter readings.

Switch on Changing utilities suppliers could get you a better deal. (See *Household finance*, page 292.)

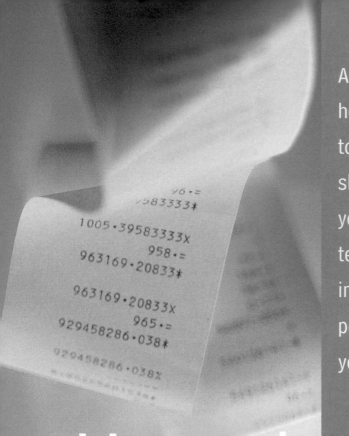

Are you at the mercy of your household bills? It doesn't have to be like that. You can cut hefty slices out of what you pay for your gas and electricity, telephone services and insurance. At a time when every penny counts, take control of your finances and save money.

Household
finance

BALANCING THE BOOKS

Get a clear picture of your household finances by putting together a budget showing your income and expenditure (see overleaf). If you find you are overspending, the good news is that by shopping around you can save hundreds of pounds on your household expenses – such as utilities and telephone bills – without noticing any difference to your lifestyle.

IMPROVE CASH FLOW – SAVE £30 A MONTH

Every time you go overdrawn at the bank it can cost you as much as £25, plus the interest charges you incur – as much as 30% on an unauthorised overdraft. If several direct debits are unpaid or a cheque is bounced you could be charged more than £30 each time. Make a budget to see all your outgoings clearly, and time the payment of bills to coincide with money coming into your account. Ask your bank to set up an authorised overdraft in case of emergencies.

SETTLE YOUR BILLS TO SUIT YOU

Notice when your utility bills – gas, electricity, phone, water – arrive and see if the timing suits you. Perhaps you've been

keep it simple

ALLOW FOR SAVINGS
If you haven't already got an emergency fund, put some money aside each month so you build up a fund of at least three times your monthly income in case of emergencies. You also need to be saving at least 10% of your gross income towards a pension for your retirement.

CASE STUDY

REGAINING CONTROL

Londoners Richard and Caroline Stanswick, 38 and 33, both worked in the banking industry. But their joint current account was regularly overdrawn by much more than they'd reckoned on. Before pay day, they would often be more than £1,000 in the red. 'We both knew we had to sort it out,' says Richard.

Looking at past bank statements, Caroline added up how much the couple had paid in overdraft fees and interest. It came to £156 in one year alone. 'It was such a waste!' she says. 'But it finally prompted us to work out what was going wrong.'

The couple set everything out on paper – how much money they had coming in and how much they'd been spending based on their habits over the past six months. 'The whole thing made us aware of how we were throwing money away by failing to plan,' says Caroline.

At the same time, the couple switched their electricity and gas supply to a cheaper provider and plumped for a lower cost phone service. Within three months, they were managing to spend well within their

monthly income of £3,650, saving around £150 a year in overdraft interest, £180 in energy costs and an estimated £200 in phone charges.

SMART MOVES

Work out a monthly budget

Make your household budget in four easy steps. Being able to list all your debits and credits will make it much easier for you to analyse and control what you spend and when you are spending it.

1 TOTAL INCOME
Add up all the money that you can expect to receive during the month. Note when it goes into your account so that you can better plan when you make various payments.

■ Regular pay cheques and bonuses, or pension payments
■ Part-time or freelance income
■ Interest
■ Dividends
■ Other income such as rent on properties, benefit payments or income from a trust

2 FIXED EXPENSES
Next, total all the regular payments you make during the month.

■ Mortgage or rent
■ Electricity, gas, water
■ Home telephone
■ Insurance: home, contents and car
■ Insurance: life, medical, income protection
■ Internet service, cable or satellite dish
■ Mobile phone
■ Pension, savings, investments
■ Debt payments such as car loans or other hire purchase
■ Commuting expenses
■ Memberships and subscriptions

3 VARIABLE EXPENSES
Now add up all the payments you make that vary from month to month.

■ Food, beverages, household products
■ Car maintenance: petrol, oil, upkeep
■ Home maintenance and improvement
■ Furnishings, appliances
■ Clothing
■ Personal grooming
■ Recreation: eating out, sports and cultural events, movies
■ Holidays
■ Gifts and contributions
■ Health care not covered by insurance

4. THE MOMENT OF TRUTH
Subtract all your fixed and variable expenditure from your total monthly income. If you spot any problems, see where savings can be made or how cash flow can be improved. This chapter will show you how to cut at least 10% from your electricity, gas, home telephone and insurance bills alone; look in the Index for hundreds of ways to make more savings every month.

Even if your budget is not tight, any excess cash floating around in your current account can be put to better use in a high-interest savings account.

So it pays to have firm control of your monthly finances, and a detailed budget is the only way to do that.

Internet resources
There are also budget planners that you can download from the Internet. There's a simple-to-use Budget Planner at MoneySavingExpert.com (**www.moneysavingexpert.com** ✉). It suggests that you gather together bank and credit card statements for the past three months first, plus three months' worth of food shopping receipts. Or the Financial Services Authority has one at **www.moneymadeclear.fsa.gov.uk/campaigns/budgeting.html** ✉.

At Thisismoney.co.uk (**www.thisismoney.co.uk** ✉) there's a household budget calculator that lets you track where your money goes each month. Again, you'll have to collect together bills, payslips, and details on your expenditure.

receiving your quarterly telephone bills just when your bank balance is at its weakest. In this case, set up monthly direct debits on your bills. Having a regular amount coming out of your account just after you get paid will give you much more control over your expenditure and is the first step towards cutting back. However, if you pay your bills at the end of the month and keep an eye on your account you can keep the money in your account for longer and earn interest on it.

THE ADVANTAGES OF DIRECT DEBIT

When you pay by direct debit, you benefit from your supplier's money-off policy for this method of payment. You could also get around £50 off if you buy both gas and electricity from the same supplier. If you don't already pay your utility bills by monthly direct debit, it is a good idea to switch for this reason. And, of course, your suppliers want you to agree to this pre-arranged payment as it makes business more predictable for them. However keep an eye on your bills and make sure your direct debits aren't too high. And check that you are not being charged interest for paying a bill over 12 months – insurance, for example, may be cheaper to pay in a one-off payment if you can afford to do this, rather than making 12 monthly payments that incur an interest charge.

Regular income, regular payments If you have a regular monthly income, then having your bills paid each month – and at a predictable, year-round level – will help you to keep on top of your money matters and avoid overspending.

BENEFITS OF PAYING QUARTERLY

If you can easily handle the quarterly bills when they arrive, there is an advantage in staying with this method of payment.

Earn some interest By paying your bills quarterly, you can hang on to your money for slightly longer before handing it over to the utility companies. In this way you can take advantage of your bank or building society's interest rates.

ESTIMATED BILLS

It's tempting, if you get an estimated gas or electricity bill, to call the freephone number and give your actual meter reading to the company. But you can be clever about this.

Free credit If the estimated reading is below your actual reading, isn't the company actually giving you free credit? As long as you can afford the higher bill that will come when they do eventually read the meter, why not let it lie for a while?

ARE YOU PAYING TOO MUCH?

You should still monitor your bills once a direct debit has been arranged to make sure that the amount you're paying isn't too high. If this is the case, you will have built up a credit, which most suppliers do not repay automatically. You will need to request a refund and adjust your direct debit accordingly. Some suppliers do refund the credit automatically, but only when it reaches a certain amount.

RESOURCES

COMPARE PRICES

■ The following websites will help you to compare prices and switch energy suppliers:
www.confused.com ✉,
www.energyhelpline.com
0800 074 0745 ✉,
www.energylinx.co.uk
0800 849 7077 ✉,
www.homeadvisoryservice.com 0845 1800 300 ✉,
www.saveonyourbills.co.uk 0800 055 3800 ✉,
www.simplyswitch.com 08000 111 395 ✉,
www.switchandgive.com (up to £30 donation to charity) ✉
www.switchwithwhich.co.uk ✉,
www.energyshop.com
0845 330 7247 ✉,
www.ukpower.co.uk
0845 009 1780 ✉,
www.unravelit.com ✉,
www.uswitch.com ✉.

■ Ofgem is the regulator for the gas and electricity industries **www.ofgem.gov.uk** ✉. If you have a complaint about gas or electricity contact Consumer Direct **www.consumerdirect.gov.uk** 08454 04 05 06 ✉.

CHOOSING A FUEL SUPPLIER

In the late 1990s, the government broke the monopolies on the provision of electricity and gas. Before that, you didn't have any choice about who sold you either form of energy – it had to be the local provider. Now you can choose – and save on average around £100. But depending on who you are with currently and how much energy you use this figure could be even higher.

SWITCHING SUPPLIERS

There are now dozens of gas and electricity suppliers in Britain. Fierce competition between energy companies leads to lower prices for the consumer. The pipes and cables running into your house may be owned by a separate company from the one supplying your energy, so you don't need any new pipework or wiring to switch providers.

Shop around The supplier you choose can be based at the other end of the country. For example, a couple in Kent could buy their electricity from ScottishPower if they happened to offer the cheapest deal.

Check the Internet The Internet is the best place to get information about how much you could save on your energy bills. There are several websites that give detailed price comparisons (see *Resources*, left), which are based on the suppliers where you live and the amount of energy your household uses. Often these sites will switch you online, although you will have to sign paperwork at a later stage.

How do they make money? Comparison sites receive a payment each time you switch to a new gas or electricity company. However, these payments don't influence which companies the sites recommend or affect the price you pay. The Consumer Focus Confidence Code sets standards of how gas and electricity comparison sites operate, so check that the site you use is signed up to it (Consumer Focus has taken over the role from Energywatch).

CUT YOUR ELECTRICITY BILL

If a family spends £494 a year on electricity with Power Company A, they could save the following amounts simply by changing their supplier to Power Company B.

SUPPLIER		SAVING
COMPANY B	(Direct Debit)	£71
COMPANY B	(Online)	£138
COMPANY B	(Online Direct Debit)	£178

CASE STUDY

AN OFFER THEY COULDN'T REFUSE

Sandy and Gill McBain had bought their electricity supply from Scottish Hydro-Electric for years. In Aberdeen, many of their friends did the same. But a year ago, when a work colleague of Sandy's mentioned she'd saved money by changing to another company, Sandy did some research into the matter.

'We found out that we could save £80 by switching our electricity over to British Gas – paying £470 instead of the £550 we were shelling out at the time. If we'd been using gas, too, we were told we would save another £100 a year. But Scottish Power had a better service rating, so we went with them instead.'

The savings still added up to around £70 a year. Then, a few weeks ago, the McBains were contacted by their old supplier. Did they want a special deal for returning

customers? They'd have no standing charge to pay and an even lower tariff than with Scottish Power. So they switched back and saved even more. 'Staying faithful to one company really doesn't pay,' says Sandy.

CHANGE YOUR PLAN

When you've done your research and got a good idea of how much less you could be paying, have a word with your current energy provider.

Same company, different plan Some companies have ten or more different plans and may be able to offer you a different plan from the one you're on that will match the savings you would make if you switched. So you can benefit from the savings without the bother of forms to sign and a different bill format to get used to.

Other benefits Some energy providers offer plans that include benefits such as no standing charge, or give Air Miles or other incentives.

ELECTRICITY FOR NIGHT OWLS

If you can organise your household to use power-hungry appliances such as washing machines and dishwashers at night by putting them on a timer, you could cut money on your electricity bill.

Change to a cheaper tariff Electricity companies in Britain offer cheap rate power for seven hours during the night (1am to 8am) – for this reason, these cheaper tariffs are called Economy 7. If you change to Economy 7, you pay around a quarter of the normal unit price for power used at night, depending on the supplier. However charges for daytime use are higher than standard rates. Compare the costs of standard and Economy 7 tariffs.

QUALITY OF SERVICE

Most of the websites give star ratings for the quality of service provided by the energy suppliers. It may be worth paying attention to this. But as long as you don't tie yourself into a long-term contract, you can easily switch to another supplier if you're dissatisfied. On the other hand, if you are prepared to sign up for a certain period, you may get an even better deal on the energy you buy.

RUN ONLY FULL LOADS

Use your dishwasher and washing machine only if there is a full load. These appliances are some of the most energy-intensive in your home. Only rinse dishes in the dishwasher if you really need to.

A NEW BOILER

You could save up to £200 a year fitting a new efficient condensing boiler. Also by fitting thermostats on your radiators.

USE A BOWL

When washing up or preparing vegetables in the sink, don't let the tap run.

FIT A SAVE-A-FLUSH

This water-saving device saves 1 litre (2 pints) of water every time you flush. It costs about £1 and could save you 10% on your water bill.

BOILER SERVICING

By not servicing your boiler regularly you risk having to spend money on a costly emergency call-out if it stops working in the depths of winter.

KEEP COOL WATER IN A COVERED JUG

Put the jug in the fridge so you don't have to run the tap for a long time to get a cold drink. Change the water every day.

CHECK YOUR CISTERNS EVERY THREE MONTHS

Faulty ball or float valves in toilets and header tanks waste water.

SAVE WATER AND ENERGY

There are some simple things you can do to save money on heating and lighting your house. You can get a free energy check from the Energy Saving Trust ✉. It will show you how you could save up to £250 a year on your household bills.

USE A BUCKET OF WATER TO WASH YOUR CAR

If you are on a water meter save water when cleaning your car by using a bucket of soapy water and a sponge rather than a hosepipe. Or use the hose briefly just to rinse off the soap.

FIX DRIPPING TAPS

A dripping tap could fill half a bath in a week. If it is the hot-water tap, it will also waste energy and cost you money.

TAKE A SHOWER

A quick shower uses 20% of the water a bath does, but watch out – power showers use about the same amount of hot water as a bath.

TURN DOWN YOUR THERMOSTAT

Just one degree lower cuts heating bills by 10% – or 10p in the pound.

BLOCK CHIMNEYS

If you're not using your fireplace, block the chimney with newspaper to prevent heat loss.

STANDBY COSTS MONEY

TVs, DVDs, sound systems and especially computers all use electricity on standby. Get in the habit of switching them off and save £10 a year.

TURN YOUR CENTRAL HEATING OFF HALF AN HOUR EARLY

The house will stay warm until you are in bed. In an average 3-bed semi you'll save at least £20 a year.

INSULATION

If you don't have insulation in your loft you could be wasting more than £100 a year through heat escaping. You should also lag your hot water tank and pipes.

DRAUGHTPROOFING

A cheap, cost-effective way to save money is to draughtproof your home. In a typical home 20% of heat is lost through poor ventilation and draughts.

WALL AND FLOOR INSULATION

As well as insulating your roof and installing double-glazing you should insulate your walls and floors. Saving your another £100 per year.

INSTALL DOUBLE-GLAZING

If you don't have double-glazing you could be losing more than £100 of energy through your windows each year.

REDUCE YOUR HOT WATER TEMPERATURE

Turn it down to 60°C (140°F) and save between £10 and £20 a year.

TURN OFF LIGHTS

Get your family into the habit of turning off electrical devices when they leave a room.

CLOSE YOUR CURTAINS

Stop heat escaping, especially if you don't have double-glazed windows.

THE BEST PRICES FOR OIL AND SOLID FUEL

The market for heating oil and solid fuels is smaller and less competitive than for gas and electricity, but there are still considerable savings to be made.

SAVING ON HEATING OIL

If you use oil to heat your home, you have always been able to shop around. But are you making the most of that freedom?

Phone around When your oil tank is getting low, don't just order your next supply from the company you used last time. Phone around to find the cheapest price.

Check money-off vouchers If your usual supplier has sent you a money-off voucher to keep your custom, factor this into your calculation, although it won't necessarily make their oil any cheaper for you than the most competitive price from your ring-around.

Put in a big order Wait until your oil tank is low before ordering more fuel – you get a cheaper rate for orders over 1,000 litres (220 gallons). But don't let it run out altogether or you could face a bill from a heating engineer for bleeding the air out of your boiler.

Club together with neighbours It is not usually feasible to have a very large domestic tank as they're expensive, take up a lot of room and tougher environmental regulations will apply – which spells even more cost for you. But you can club together with neighbours to order your oil together. If you can order 5,000 litres (1,100 gallons) at a time between, say, five households, you'll each save around 7% on the cost of your oil.

keep it simple

STOCK UP FOR WINTER
Coal and other solid fuels are cheaper in the summer, so think ahead. By buying between June and September, you could pay less than if you leave it until the autumn.

GET A BETTER DEAL FOR OIL AND COAL

The best place to find heating oil and solid fuel is local directories, like *Yellow Pages* and *Thomson Local*. These directories are now available online **www.yell.com** ✉ and **www.thomsonlocal.com** ✉.

Heating oil Turn to the 'Oil Fuel Distributors' listing or search online and find the numbers of five suppliers. Tell them how much oil you want to buy and how soon you need it, and ask for their best price. This will be a per-litre price. Then ask if there are any discounts available. **www.heatingoil.co.uk** ✉ is an online service to help you find cheap oil. Use its postcode search to see if it covers your area. Another service is **www.boilerjuice.com** ✉.

Coal Prices for coal vary more widely between suppliers than heating oil prices – so there is even more reason to shop around. As with oil, the directories are your best starting point for checking prices. Choose five local coal merchants and phone around for the best price. Do the same each time your bunker is nearly down to the base and you could save yourself around £20 on ½ tonne of house coal.

CHEAPER CHATTING

Competition in the phone market has increased dramatically in recent years. As a result, it is pretty complicated to work out the best option to use for your home phone. What will be best depends on who provides your landline, how many calls you make, when you make them and who you are phoning. For example, calling mobiles from a landline is rarely a good idea. You could save money by 'bundling' your phone, TV and broadband into one package.

Compare the options Several websites can help you compare the different options, including mobile phones. Some of the best are: **www.omio.com** ✉ and **www.niftylist.co.uk** ✉ for mobiles; **www.uswitch.com** ✉, **www.moneysupermarket.com** ✉, **www.homephonechoices.co.uk** ✉, **www.simplyswitch.com** 08000 111 395 ✉ and **www.simplifydigital.co.uk** 0800 1388 388 ✉ for broadband, home phone and digital TV.

MOBILES
You could be wasting money on a mobile you don't use enough or are making too many calls outside of your contract allowance and running up huge bills. Either way there are ways to take control of your mobile phone bills.

If you already have a phone a pay as you go contract (PAYG) could save you money as you just pay for the calls and texts you make. If you need a new phone then a contract is probably the best way of getting a new phone. If you choose the best deal and get the right mix of minutes and texts or other services, you could get a new phone and 100 minutes of phone calls a month for less than £10 a month.

HOW TO SWITCH MOBILE PHONE
Work out if you need a new contract phone You may be better off with a PAYG phone. If you don't use it often then a PAYG phone may be the best option as you aren't locked into a contract and pay for calls as you go along.

Haggle with current phone company Before switching to a new phone company ask your existing phone company if it can offer you an upgrade handset and a better deal. Some companies will be keen to keep your business and offer free upgrades or better-than-advertised deals. They may also match a deal you have found elsewhere, saving you the hassle of switching.

Need a new handset? Shop around for the handset you want with a suitable mixture of minutes and texts.

Transfer your number If you want to take your new number to your new phone ask your existing phone company for a port authorisation code (PAC). This is valid for 30 days and your new phone provider will use it to transfer over your old number.

MAKE MONEY FROM YOUR OLD MOBILE
You can make money by recycling any old mobile phones you have. There are several companies that will give you

money for your old phone or donate money to charity. How much you will get for your old phone depends on how old it is, if it's a popular handset and if it works. To get the best price, try several companies, such as: **www.envirofone.com** 0870 979 9652 ✉, **www.mazumamobile.com** 0845 872 3000 ✉ and **www.mobile2cash.co.uk** 020 8274 4044 ✉.

BUNDLES

You can save money on your communication needs by bundling your home phone, broadband and digital TV into one package from the same provider. You can get bundles from BT, Sky and Virgin.

USE A CHEAPER 'OVERRIDE' SERVICE

You can sign up with various companies to use their service for some calls only. So if you have family living overseas, choose a company that gives a good rate for calls to that country. Just dial the four- or five-digit prefix they give you and connect through their service. They'll bill you for those calls separately from BT.

USE CHEAPER 'NORMAL' NUMBERS

Many companies use 0845/0870/0871 numbers (see below), which can be expensive and are rarely included in any inclusive minutes offered with your phone provider's package. But companies often give normal geographical phone numbers on their literature for callers from abroad. Use these even when you're in the UK – as normal rate calls, they will be included in your monthly call allowances.

BROADBAND

Broadband has now almost totally replaced slower dial-up services. Smaller broadband providers tend to give better service than the big brands so don't be afraid of trying a brand you may not have heard of. You can include broadband in bundles, see above, or as a standalone product. Most broadband services run at a speed of 1 to 8mbps. For most people, 1 or 2mbps should be sufficient. There will also be a usage allowance, typically of 1 or 2gb per month. Some providers give unlimited downloads. **Check the speed of your connection** at **www.broadbandspeedchecker.co.uk** ✉ or **www.speedtest.net** ✉. You can switch broadband supplier (see *Cheaper Chatting*, page 301, for some places to compare and switch broadband).

TOP TIPS CUT YOUR PHONE CHARGES

Think before you pick up the phone. Use all the benefits that your tariff offers and avoid making unnecessary and expensive calls, which all mount up.

■ **Don't call mobiles from a landline** If you must do it, keep the call short or ask the person you are speaking to if they have a landline you could call. Mobile to mobile is often cheaper than landline to mobile.

■ **Look carefully at your bills** Notice which calls were expensive so you can be aware of the cost when you are making them next time.

CASE STUDY

DONNA MINIMISES HER BILL

When Donna Ware moved 100 miles away from home and got a flat of her own in Hartlepool, the phone was one of the main things she appreciated, as she could chat to her friends as long as she liked.

'Before, Mum or my brother Joe were always knocking on the door after ten minutes,' she says.

But never having had to deal with the phone bills before, she had no idea how much she was paying. When the first quarterly bill came through, it was for £452.

'My jaw dropped! I could afford it, but I didn't want another one like it.'

A friend at work told her to try some other phone companies. But she didn't like the idea of switching and she still had enough paperwork to deal with following the purchase of the flat. She called BT and asked if there was anything she could do. They offered to put her on their Unlimited Anytime Plan. For £4.85 a month, plus her line rental, she then had unlimited calls

(some calls have a maximum length of an hour) to any UK landlines. It also includes free calls to 0845 and 0870 numbers. Her bill dropped dramatically. She is also charged a much lower rate to mobiles.

■ **Use cheap rates** Find out the times of your call provider's cheap rates. BT's cheap rate begins at 6pm and ends at 8am. Wait until 6pm to make evening calls.

■ **No 09 calls** Never call 09 premium-rate numbers.

■ **Avoid scams** Don't be tempted by scams that require you to call a number to find out if you have won a prize. The call will usually end up costing you £10 or more.

■ **Answer your phone** If you let people leave messages and call them back, then you will have to pay for the call.

■ **Get a chatter's plan** If you want to talk to friends for ages, sign up with a package that lets you do this for free.

■ **Stop before you start** Before you dial, ask yourself if you really need to make that call.

DIRECTORY ENQUIRIES

■ Free directory enquiries are available from Free Directory Enquiries 0800 100 100 and The Number 0800 118 3733. With both the service is free as they charge an advert each time you call.

■ If you have access to the Internet, you can find the information you need without paying any extra. Go to one of the following: **www.192.com** ✉, **www.118.com** ✉ or **www.thephonebook.bt.com** ✉.

■ Or try **www.yell.com** ✉ (Yellow Pages online) and **www.thomsonlocal.com** ✉ (Thomson Local online) for free access to its listings.

GET WISE TO COUNCIL TAX

Every year, your local council sets the level of tax residents have to pay. But this doesn't mean there's nothing you can do about your bill. Check that you are paying the correct amount for both your home and your situation. If you aren't, you could save over £100 a year.

DISCOUNTS AVAILABLE

There are various discounts that you might be entitled to when paying your council tax, so don't miss out.

Home alone Are you the only adult occupant of your home? If so, you are entitled to a 25% discount on the full rate of council tax. Let the council know if your circumstances change – the discount can usually be backdated if necessary.

Other discounts You may be able to reduce your council tax bill, if the property is empty, you are disabled, you are a student or a student nurse. For furnished second or holiday homes you will receive second home's discount of between 10% and 50%. Empty homes get a discount of up to 50% if property is empty and unfurnished for six months or more.

IS YOUR PROPERTY CORRECTLY VALUED?

All homes are categorised by the government according to the market value they would have had on a certain date. This is only updated every 15 years or so, so work out if your property is currently in the correct band.

Ask your neighbours Check by asking neighbours with houses of similar value what band they are in. If your house is in a higher band, it may be worth querying the valuation. You can check which band your property and your neighbour's property is in and challenge it if necessary at the Valuation Office Agency **www.voa.gov.uk** 0845 602 1507 ✉.

If your valuation is downgraded This could mean a windfall for you. The last round of valuations was probably more than 15 years ago. You could then be eligible for ten years' worth of rebates on your council tax. But beware – if you challenge your valuation, the valuation could be lifted into a higher band and you could face a hefty retrospective council tax bill. So think carefully before trying this.

PAYING YOUR BILL COST-EFFECTIVELY

What is the most cost-effective way of paying your bill? Your council will usually give you two choices: monthly direct debit or the whole bill in one go.

Gain interest with direct debit It is rarely worth paying the bill all in one go. Council tax is a large amount of money – often around £1,000 or more. The interest you could earn on £1,000 is about £30 a year before tax, so the longer it stays in your account, the more you will gain. If you pay by monthly direct debit you will generally be given two or more payment dates to choose from each month, and the money will trickle out month by month throughout the year.

ASK YOURSELF

AM I EXEMPT FROM COUNCIL TAX?

If you fall into any of these categories, you do not have to pay Council Tax:

- full-time students
- student nurses
- resident hospital patients
- apprentices and youth training trainees
- people in care homes
- those who are severely mentally impaired
- 18- and 19-year-olds who are at or have just left school
- careworkers working for low pay
- monks and nuns
- people in prison

INSURING YOUR HOME AND POSSESSIONS

Insuring your home is vital to enable you to recover financially in the event of misfortune, which could otherwise cost you tens of thousands of pounds. Buildings insurance covers the structure and fittings of your home, while house contents insurance covers your possessions. Buildings insurance will be a stipulation of any mortgage agreement.

A GOOD DEAL ON BUILDINGS INSURANCE

Your current insurer might not be giving you the best deal, so get quotes from several other companies and use an online comparison service.

Consider remortgaging If your mortgage lender insists you use their insurance company for your buildings cover, think about changing to a lender who'll leave you free to choose your own insurer. You will need to take into account the cost of moving mortgage and any early repayment penalties.

Charges for switching Some mortgage lenders charge you if you switch insurer, so take this into account when you work out the savings you'd be making with a new policy.

Ask your insurer for a better deal Before changing insurer, speak to your existing insurer and see if they will give you a better deal. Having a few lower quotes up your sleeve can be persuasive. If they cut your premiums by enough, you can save the hassle of changing company.

Buy from the same company You might be able to save £50 or more a year by buying your contents and buildings insurance from the same company. Some insurers may even give buildings or contents for free if you buy the other.

Increase your excess and save 20% Ask your insurer to recommend savings you can make. They might tell you that if you double your excess, they will take £50 a year off your premium, for example. Of course if you need to make a claim you will have to pay more as an excess.

Claim-free years count Ask for lower premiums – if you have several years of claim-free insurance you will be entitled to a discount of 30% or more.

WATCH POINTS PERILS OF UNDERINSURING

It's important to keep your insurer up to date with the rebuild cost of your home (see below). If disaster struck, it could badly damage your finances, too.

■ **Keep up to date** To calculate the rebuild cost of your home you need to know its dimensions, which you then multiply by the current building cost for each square foot – this depends on where you live and the age of your house. As a guide, visit the website of the Association of British Insurers at **http://abi.bcis.co.uk** ✉, which has a Rebuilding Cost Calculator to help you work it out.

■ **Don't be caught out** In recent years many homes have been flooded. The damage to homes is devastating, leaving some people unable to afford the necessary repairs. Buildings insurance covers flooding, but once you have been flooded it

ASK YOURSELF

DOES IT NEED INSURING?

It's easy to be scared into insuring everything but there's no point in paying premiums to insure items that are cheap to replace or unlikely to get damaged. And there might be cheaper ways of protecting your more expensive items.

■ **Covering antiques** Do you have items of antique furniture worth more than £2,000? Check the single item limit of any contents insurance policy. If a piece is worth more than that, ask each insurer you approach how much they would charge to insure it. It may be cheaper to find an insurer with a higher single item limit.

■ **Frozen assets** If you have a large chest freezer, the value of the frozen food could be substantial, so choose a policy that covers it. A small freezer may contain only £25 worth of food at any time and not be worth insuring.

■ **Save £70** Accidental damage insurance can add £70 a year to a combined buildings and contents policy. If you have children or are keen on DIY, then you might benefit from this extra cover. Otherwise, consider saving the cost of these premiums.

INSURANCE FOR BUNGEE - JUMPING, MRS PATTERSON ?!

will be more expensive to insure your home and if you live in an area where flooding is likely you may struggle to get insurance at all. You can check if you live in a flood area at **www.environment-agency.gov.uk** 08708 506 506 ✉.

CHECK THE FINE PRINT

Before you search for the best deal on insuring the contents of your home, have a good look around your house or flat. Work out, roughly, how much it would cost you to replace everything you own should it all be destroyed.

Value expensive items There are many different options in contents policies, and often a limit on what the insurer will pay out for single items. If you have an antique piece of furniture, it could easily exceed this. Jewellery, too, can be worth more than a claim would pay out. Make sure these items are valued and listed when you buy the policy, or you could lose out.

Check conditions of cover Check that you are abiding by the conditions of your insurance. For instance, it might be a condition of the cover that you have locks on your windows, and that keys are taken out of the inside of doors. If you don't comply with these conditions, the insurer could refuse to honour a claim.

Check out your coverage

SMART MOVES

- What is the policy excess?
- Does the sum insured cover jewellery?
- Is new-for-old cover standard when making a claim?

- What cover is there for accidental damage?
- Do you have to pay an extra premium for bicycles to be covered away from the home?
- Is the food in your freezer covered?
- What is covered if a burst pipe causes damage?

- Will your business equipment be covered?
- Are you covered abroad?
- Will the policy pay out for third-party liability claims?
- Does the policy include a legal helpline? This can save you upwards of £60 on the fees you would pay for specialist legal advice.

HOW TO LOWER PREMIUMS

Buying contents and buildings insurance together can give you a discount on two separate policies.

Get the right amount of cover Make sure you don't over or underinsure your belongings or property. You will waste money or risk not having cover in the event of a claim.

Don't pay for extras you don't need Accidental damage and legal expenses may not be necessary.

Join a local Neighbourhood Watch scheme if there is one or set one up if there isn't.

Burglar alarm Some insurers will only give a discount on a monitored burglar alarm system.

Window locks Make sure you have window locks on all accessible windows and five-lever locks on final exit doors.

FACTORS AFFECTING PREMIUMS

Where you live Insurers rate different postcodes in terms of risk based on claims and if it is in an area affected by subsidence or flooding, for example.

Age/lifestyle Insurers often give older people discounts. However be wary of special deals on insurance for older people as there is no guarantee that you will get a good price. As with all insurance, shop around.

Sum insured and cover Make sure you get the right level of cover and only pay for extras like legal expenses and personal possessions cover if you really need them.

DON'T STAY LOYAL TO THE SAME INSURER

Each year, when your insurance comes up for renewal, do some research to see if you could be getting a better deal elsewhere.

Try the Internet Many comparison sites will search lots of insurers and give you quotes in just a few minutes. Save yourself time by having all the information about your property and contents to hand.

Contact insurers direct Pick five insurers from *Yellow Pages* ✉ or *Thomson Local* ✉ or online and phone them up in turn. When they give you a quote, ask them for a reference number and write it down. Otherwise, if you decide to buy that policy later you could have to give them the same information all over again.

Use a broker This is an easy way to search for the best quote from several insurers at the same time. But don't be lulled into thinking that a call to a broker means you don't have to go any further. The list of insurance companies that brokers use is far from comprehensive. The direct insurers won't be included, and they often offer the best value of all.

RESOURCES

USEFUL CONTACTS
The Association of British Insurers is the trade association for the UK's insurance industry, representing about 400 companies. Contact them for information at **www.abi.org.uk** or 020 7600 3333 ✉. Several comparison sites will let you search and buy house insurance, **www.confused.com** ✉ **www.gocompare.com** ✉ **www.moneysupermarket. com** ✉ **www.uswitch.com** ✉

COMPARING QUOTES FOR BUILDINGS/CONTENTS INSURANCE

This table shows the cheapest three quotes for buildings and contents insurance for a 3-bed detached house in Sussex built in 1930, with a building rebuild cost of £150,000 and £40,000 of contents for standard cover, with accidental damage and personal possessions cover. Premiums are based on three years' no claims discount.

INSURER	PREMIUM	EXCESS
www.quotelinedirect.co.uk	£179	£200
www.homequotedirect.co.uk	£188	£50
www.onlyinsurance.com	£196	£50

INSURER	WITH ACCIDENTAL DAMAGE	EXCESS
www.policyshop-insurance.co.uk	£200	£50
www.quotelinedirect.co.uk	£216	£200
www.homequotedirect.co.uk	£228	£50

INSURER	WITH PERSONAL POSSESSIONS	EXCESS
www.quotelinedirect.co.uk	£194	£200
www.policyshop-insurance.co.uk	£200	£50
www.homequotedirect.co.uk	£205	£50

Tax and state benefits

Although many taxes are unavoidable, you can avoid paying more than you should if you understand how they work and make sure you get any benefits you are entitled to.

MAKE INCOME TAX WORK FOR YOU

Although everyone with an income above a set amount must pay income tax, you can save money by ensuring you are given the correct tax code and claiming all the allowances and credits to which you are entitled. To do this, you need to understand the basics of the taxation system.

WHAT TAXES DO WE PAY

We all pay several different taxes on our income, shopping, houses and investments. These are some of the main taxes.

Income tax This is paid on all sorts of income – earned income for employed and self-employed people, income from savings, pension income, rental and investment income.

National Insurance Builds up entitlement to state benefits, like the State Pension.

VAT (Value Added Tax) Paid when you buy a number of goods and services. From 1 December 2008 it has been cut to 15%; from 1 January 2010 it will go back to 17.5%.

Capital Gains Tax A tax of 18% on certain assets you give away or sell that have increased in value. You are not taxed on the first £9,600 (2008/2009) each year. You won't be taxed on some assets, (see page 316).

Stamp Duty Is paid on most house purchases above a certain amount. Stamp Duty is payable on a sliding scale up to 4% on purchases over £500,000. It is also payable on shares and some securities.

Inheritance Tax When you die your estate may be liable to Inheritance Tax depending on how much you leave behind. IHT is charged at 40% on amounts above certain limits (see *Family Affairs*, page 114 for more details).

Council Tax Charged by Local Authorities based on the value of your property (see *Household Finance*, page 304).

Excise duty Paid on car fuel, alcohol and tobacco.

IPT A tax on insurance premiums. The standard rate is 5% but it is 17.5% for travel insurance and some other insurances.

HOW INCOME TAX WORKS

By law, we have to pay a proportion of the money we earn in income tax. Each person has a personal tax-free allowance – £6,035 in 2008/2009 (in 2009/2010 it will be £6,475) – that they can earn before tax has to be paid. Above that level, two bands apply. You will be charged 20% on income from £0 to £34,800 and then 40% on all income above this. Remember income tax is charged on the amount above your personal allowance not your whole income.

Employed or self-employed? If you are employed, tax is deducted from your salary along with National Insurance contributions. If you are self-employed, you must declare what you have earned in each tax year by the end of the following January, and pay the tax you owe. Failure to pay by 31 January will mean a fine of £100.

Self-assessment HM Revenue and Customs (HMRC) runs the self-assessment system. You fill in a multi-page tax form

---

GET AN EXTRA £4,250 TAX-FREE EACH YEAR

If you're a homeowner with spare rooms, you may be able to rent them out tax-free. Under the government's 'rent-a-room' scheme, you can charge rent of up to £4,250 tax-free, within a given tax year. This only applies where the property is your main residence and the lodger shares facilities with you.

RESOURCES

CHECKING TAX RATES

To check current rates of income tax, and where the bands begin, see **www.hmrc.gov.uk/rates/it. htm** ✉.

■ Make sure you're not paying too much tax. Check your payslip and tax code details on this website: **www.digita.com/ taxcentral/home/calculators/ default.asp** ✉.

RESOURCES

WHERE IS YOUR LOCAL TAX OFFICE?

Correspondence from the HMRC will display the address of your local tax office at the top. You will also find the phone number in your local phonebook, or go to **www.hmrc.gov.uk** ✉.

MORE THAN ONE JOB?

If you have more than one job you will get a tax code for each job. HMRC will allocate your personal allowance against the job it deems to be your main job. You can ask your tax office to split your personal tax allowance between your employments. If you earn less than your personal allowance, you should not have to pay any tax.

A POOL CAR MEANS NO TAX

If you use a car for work, try to make sure it is a pool car. There is no tax payable on this at all. To qualify, the car must be available to – and be used by – more than one employee. Normally, it shouldn't be kept overnight at or near an employee's home. If the car is used privately, this must be incidental to business use.

and submit it or complete it online. Self-assessment is for people with more complex tax affairs, including the self-employed, business partners, company directors and higher-rate tax payers. Millions of people fall into the self-assessment system. Although this is more work it could save you money, so if you think you could be self-assessed contact your local tax office (see *Resources*, left).

The phone number can be found in your local phonebook or at **www.hmrc.gov.uk** ✉.

TOP TIPS SAVING TAX

Financial experts estimate that millions of people may be paying more tax than they need to in one way or another. Make sure you are not one of them.

■ **Check your tax code** If you're employed, HM Revenue and Customs (HMRC) gives you a tax code, which your employer uses to deduct tax from your pay. Check this code on your payslip or your coding notice (see below, and *Resources*, page 309). In 2006, half a million people paid too much tax because their tax code was incorrect – on average an overpayment of £290 each.

■ **People over 65** Pensioners should always check they've been given their higher age income tax allowances. HMRC doesn't always notice 65th birthdays, but being 65 at any time in a tax year qualifies you for a higher allowance. Check your code straight away, and query anything you don't understand with your local tax office.

■ **Understand banding** Make sure you understand the rules governing the top rate of tax you have to pay as this affects the savings schemes suitable for you. Although income on interest from your savings counts towards your banding, remember that tax is applied to your income only after allowances and credits that apply to you have been deducted. Also, if you are a higher-rate tax payer, you need to claim relief on personal or stakeholder pension contributions or you will miss out.

CHECKING YOUR TAX CODE

Your code is normally a number followed by a letter. The number is based on the tax-free income you can earn in a tax year. Multiply it by 10 to see how much you can earn without paying income tax in a year. The letter is for your employer and shows how it should be adjusted if the government makes tax changes.

Avoid emergency tax code You'll be put on an emergency tax code if HMRC doesn't have enough information about your previous job. If you are put on an emergency code rectify it as soon as possible. The emergency code is based on the personal allowance for people under 65. Even if this is your correct allowance, you may pay too much tax for a while. This happens because the emergency code doesn't take into account what income you have earned and how much tax you may or may not have paid in the rest of that tax year. You can make sure you are on the correct code by checking your payslip details on the website listed in the *Resources* box on page 309. If you think there has been a mistake, contact your HMRC office.

UNDERSTANDING TAX CODES

LETTER	MEANING
L	The basic personal allowance.
P	The full personal allowance for those aged 65–74.
V	The full Personal Allowance for those aged 65–74, plus the full Married Couples' allowance if you are liable at the basic rate of tax.
Y	The full personal allowance for those aged 75 or over.
T	If there are other items the HMRC needs to review in your tax code.
K	The total allowances in your code are less than the total deductions to be taken away from your allowances.

Other codes that can be used: **BR** If all your income is taxed at the basic rate of income tax (20%); **D0** If all your income is taxed at the higher rate (40%); **NT** If no tax is going to be taken from your income or pension.

The cost of the wrong tax code If you carry on earning money and have an incorrect tax code, you could end up paying too much or too little tax. This could mean you are effectively lending HMRC money that could be earning interest in your account. If you are underpaying tax each month more will be taken out each month next year.

Look beyond the current year If you're on the wrong tax code, it may have been wrong last year, too. Make sure that it's put right, and you could be in for a welcome tax rebate.

TOP TIPS SAVINGS FOR MARRIED COUPLES

Although a Married Couple's Allowance now only applies to older couples, money-conscious couples can still save on tax by splitting their assets in the most tax-efficient way.

■ **Divide your assets** Married couples can pay less tax by making full use of their tax-free personal allowances. If one of you is a top-rate taxpayer and the other a basic rate or non-taxpayer, halve your tax liability by transferring income-yielding assets, such as building society deposits or shares, to the lower earner. Instead of paying 40% tax, as a couple you could be paying 20% or less. As married couples do not pay capital gains tax when transferring assets between them, it is a good way to reduce your joint income tax bill. Ownership of the assets passes to the other party.

■ **Halve joint assets** If you are married, only enter half of the income from assets held jointly on your tax return.

■ **Older couples can benefit** If you were married before 5 December 2005 and one of you was born before 1935, the husband can claim Married Couple's Allowance. If you were married after 5 December 2005 the person with the higher income can claim but the tax bill is reduced by 10% of the Married Couple's Allowance.

■ **Claim tax back** Once you have divided your assets, remember to claim back any tax that has already been paid on bank and building society accounts by completing form R85, available from your bank or building society.

SAVE ON WORK-RELATED TRAVEL

A company car could be a perk worth having. Although a company car is taxable as a 'benefit in kind', the tax you pay could be less than the purchase and running costs you would incur if you owned your own car. Obviously the more mileage you do, the more you will benefit. But to reduce tax liability choose a fuel-efficient car (see *Keep it simple*, page 317). And even if you don't have a company car, you can still save on work-related travel by claiming a mileage allowance from your employer, who should pay you a reasonable allowance (around 40p per mile for 2008/2009).

SMART MOVES

REDUCING TAX FOR THE SELF-EMPLOYED

It is a common assumption that there are huge tax advantages to being self-employed. But self-employed people have many expenses, such as transport costs and electricity bills, that don't apply to employees. Although these expenses are non-taxable, they can still add up to a hefty sum. To minimise tax bills, all business expenses should be claimed for and tax forms completed on time.

TOP TIPS TAX FOR THE SELF-EMPLOYED

If you run your own business, control what work is done, put your own money at risk and suffer losses then you are probably classed as self-employed for tax purposes. If you are unsure check with HMRC, which also runs courses for the newly self-employed. Make sure you claim all the allowable expenses you can. Business expenses can be offset against tax, which reduces your taxable income. HMRC doesn't give a list of expenses you can claim but gives guidance on what's allowable. It states that allowable expenditure relates to day-to-day running costs of your business. Where expenditure relates to business and private use only the part relating to the business is allowed.
You should be able to claim for the following:
■ **Your home office** If you work from home, put in a claim for the proportion of the household bills that relate to your workspace, such as the cost of water, light, heat, power, property insurance, council tax, rent and security. This can be based on the number of rooms or floor area.
■ **Admin costs** Claim for all your administrative costs, such as phone bills and stationery.
■ **Reading material** You can claim for the cost of relevant trade and professional journals. A lot more of your reading may be for work purposes than you realise. If you take a daily paper to keep up with the business news and this is relevant to your job, then this may be a deductible expense.
■ **Travel** Put in a claim for travel and hotel accommodation costs related to your business.
■ **Loans** You can also include interest on bank and other loans that relate to your business.
■ **Repairs** The cost of repairs and maintenance of business equipment are also legitimate expenses.
■ **Motoring expenses** These include AA or RAC membership, petrol or diesel and parking charges. You may be able to claim for driving to social occasions if the primary purpose is to meet work contacts or new customers.
■ **Record everything** You must keep accurate records of all your expenses if they are to be allowable for tax purposes. See **www.hmrc.gov.uk** ✉ and **www.businesslink.gov.uk** ✉ for more useful information.

MAKE USE OF YOUR CAPITAL ALLOWANCES

If you have a small or medium-sized firm and you buy capital items such as furniture or equipment, you can claim allowances each year. Generally you can claim up to 20% of the cost of capital items each year until you have claimed for the full value of the item.

WATCH POINTS PAYING YOUR TAX ON TIME

Don't join the millions who have to pay £100 fines for being late returning their self-assessment forms.

■ **Pay on time to avoid a fine** You must get your completed tax return to the tax office by the end of September following the tax year (the tax year ends on 5 April) if you want HMRC to calculate your tax, or by the end of January if you calculate it yourself. All money owed must be paid by the end of January. If you don't, you will pay a fine of £100 and be charged interest on the amount you owe the Revenue.

■ **Late payers risk paying more** If you leave your return until the end of January and you miscalculate your tax liability, you could have to pay a fine and interest for the amount you owe. In this case, it's safer to overestimate it but better still to have done your return by the end of September so it will be calculated for you.

■ **Avoid overpayment** Tax bills must be paid on time, and once you are established as self-employed for tax purposes you will be asked to make payments on account. This is usually two payments a year – one before the end of January and one before the end of July – which together equate roughly to the amount of tax payable for the previous tax year. If your income drops substantially, you can ask to have your payment on account reduced.

SAVING TOWARDS YOUR TAX BILL

Whether you pay less tax when you're self-employed or not, at least you are allowed to hang on to it for longer. Often, you don't have to pay the tax for months or even more than a year after the income has been generated. This gives you the opportunity to put that money to work in the meantime.

Save the right amount A good habit to get into is to put aside a certain percentage of all gross earned income to cover income tax and National Insurance contributions. Provided you are likely to fall into the basic rate tax bracket – earning £37,400 or less in one tax year (2009-2010) – then putting aside a quarter of gross earned income should cover your subsequent tax bill. Once you have two years' experience of how much tax you actually pay, you will be able to get a better idea of how much you need to put aside. It may be as little as a fifth.

Use a high-interest account The money you put aside for tax is best kept in an easily accessible savings account, paying as high a rate of interest as possible. The interest you can earn on your tax money is substantial. For example, if you earned £28,000 during the year and gradually put a quarter of this away each month in an account paying 4.5% in interest, you could earn around £160 before tax in interest on the money before you have to pay it to HMRC. Another option is to use this saved money to reduce your mortgage using an offset mortgage where savings reduce the size of your mortgage and the interest you pay (see *Saving, Borrowing and Investing* page 326).

Keep invoicing

Invoice clients as early as possible. Check when they normally pay invoices and submit your invoice so it will be ready to be paid at this date. Many companies pay as late as possible, but don't accept this without a fight. Make sure that the client has actually received the invoice, and then chase them up just before the due date, not after it.

RESOURCES

FOR THE SELF-EMPLOYED
■ HMRC ✉ has a special helpline for the newly self-employed on 0845 915 4515. It also has a line for the self-employed who have queries about NICs (National Insurance Contributions) on 0845 915 4655. The Self-Assessment helpline is on 0845 900 0444 and the Tax and Benefit helpline on 0845 608 6000. Alternatively, you can write to your local tax office (see **www.hmrc.gov. uk/local/index.htm**. Always quote your UTR number (Unique Taxpayer Reference number).

■ The FSB (Federation of Small Businesses) has a website that includes advice about tax at **www.fsb.org.uk** 01253 336000 ✉.

TAX CREDITS – KNOW YOUR ENTITLEMENTS

The government pays out large sums of money to people who are looking after children or those who work but are on low incomes. Tax credits are made by HMRC, but you won't receive this extra help automatically so it's important to understand whether you are eligible, how to claim if you are, and to get your claim in as soon as possible.

WHAT ARE TAX CREDITS?

Tax credits are intended to support families and make working worthwhile for them, especially when the high cost of childcare is enough to make having a job pretty pointless for many parents. There are two types of tax credit: Working Tax Credit and Child Tax Credit. Tax credits don't reduce how much tax you pay, they just give you extra money.

WORKING TAX CREDIT

Working Tax Credit supports working people who are on a low income by topping up their earnings. There are extra amounts for working households in which someone has a disability. You can claim it if you are employed or self-employed, and it includes support for the cost of childcare.

Who qualifies? If you are on a low income, you might qualify for Working Tax Credit if you are undertaking 16 or more hours a week of paid work and are working for at least 4 weeks. You also need to be 16 or over and responsible for at least one child; 16 or over and have a disability. You might also qualify if you're 25 or over and work for 30 hours a week or more. You may also qualify for help with the cost of childcare. If you get the childcare element of Working Tax Credit it will be paid to the person who is responsible for the child or children as well as Child Tax Credit.

WHO QUALIFIES FOR CHILD TAX CREDIT?

Child Tax Credit is paid to the main carer of the child/children and is not dependent on whether the carer works. To receive Child Tax Credit, you must be responsible for at least one child who is 16 or younger, or 16–19 and in full-time education, or has left school, doesn't have a job yet or has registered for work.

HOW TO FIND OUT HOW MUCH YOU WILL GET

Find out how much you will be entitled to from Child Tax Credit and Working Tax Credit by using the calculator at **www.hmrc.gov.uk/taxcredits/calculator.htm** and you can also register and apply online.

WORKING TAX CREDIT PER YEAR

RATES AND THRESHOLDS	APRIL 2008	APRIL 2009
Basic element	£1,800	£1,890
Couple and loan parent	£1,770	£1,860
30 hour	£735	£775
Disabled worker	£2,405	£2,530

CHILDCARE ELEMENT OF WORKING TAX CREDIT PER YEAR

	APRIL 2008	APRIL 2009
Maximum for one child	£175	£175
Maximum cost for two or more children	£300	£300
Percentage of costs covered	80%	80%

CHILD TAX CREDIT PER YEAR

	APRIL 2008	APRIL 2009
Child Tax Credit family	£545	£545
Family, baby addition	£545	£545
Child	£2,085	£2,235
Disabled child	£2,540	£2,670

Source: HMRC, January 2009

HOW TO CLAIM

You can claim tax credits in two ways: either phone the HMRC's Tax Credit Helpline on 0845 300 3900 and ask for a claim pack or go to **www.hmrc.gov.uk/taxcredits** and apply by post or in person.

MAKING A LATE CLAIM

If you discover that you have been eligible for tax credits for some time but haven't claimed them, or that you should have received more in tax credits, HMRC will backdate your claim for up to three months or the date you became eligible. You must make your claim by 5 July. You can tell HMRC of your change of circumstances either by using their website or phoning their Tax Credits helpline (see *Resources*, left).

WATCH POINTS AVOID FINES FOR OVERPAYMENTS

Tell HMRC as soon as your circumstances change. If the changes cause you to be paid tax credits to which you are no longer entitled, you could be liable for a £300 fine, as well as having to repay all the money you owe, back to the time when the change in circumstances occurred.

Here are some typical scenarios that would mean you could be receiving too much in tax credits:

■ There has been a change to your status as a single person or as part of a couple.

■ You have not made any childcare payments for more than four consecutive weeks.

■ There has been a reduction of more than £10 a week in the cost of your childcare for more than four weeks in a row.

Watch your pension

You can get a State Pension Forecast by contacting the Future Pension Centre (part of The Pension Service) **www.thepension service.gov.uk** or 0845 3000 168. Have to hand your NI number, your spouse or ex-spouse's details, and dates of marriage and divorce, if applicable.

GET THE BENEFIT

At some point during your working life, you may be offered a choice between a fringe benefit, such as a company car, or the equivalent in salary. Although you have to pay income tax on fringe benefits, you don't have to pay National Insurance contributions on them, so it can be worth taking the benefit rather than the salary to save on NICs.

REDUCE NATIONAL INSURANCE AND OTHER TAXES

Most people have to pay NICs (National Insurance contributions) when they work. The class and level of contributions changes throughout your working life, but what you pay counts towards certain benefits, including your state old-age pension when you retire.

WHICH CLASS OF NI DO YOU PAY?
Class 1 – paid by employed people.
Class 2 – flat rate contribution paid by the self-employed.
Class 3 – voluntary contributions and pay for basic state pension and bereavement benefits.
Class 4 – profit-related contributions paid by self-employed people who also pay Class 2 contributions.

HOW MUCH NI DO YOU HAVE TO PAY?
It depends on your earnings. There is an Earnings Threshold of £110 a week (check the current level), and an Upper Earnings Limit of £770. Between these levels, you pay Class 1 contributions at the rate of 11%. For earnings above the top limit, you pay 1%. For example, if you earned £615 a week, you would pay 0% on the first £110, 11% on £111–£615. To find out more about NI, ask HMRC for a leaflet, or get one at **www.hmrc.gov.uk/thelibrary/leaflets.htm**.

DON'T PAY TWICE
If you have two jobs, National Insurance contributions will be deducted from both. But there is an annual maximum amount that you should pay in NICs, so you can apply for a refund if the combined deductions will exceed this. Or, if you know in advance that you will pay too much, you can apply for a refund by obtaining a deferment certificate by the start of the tax year.

DON'T LOSE OUT ON CAPITAL GAINS TAX
If any asset you have grows in value and you then sell it, the difference between the acquisition cost and the selling price – the capital gain – is taxable.
Annual exemption Everyone is entitled to an exemption of £9,600 (in 2008/2009). This is the amount of capital gains you can make before CGT (Capital Gains Tax) applies.
Don't be afraid Many people fear that CGT will seriously erode any revenue from a sale. But there are various types of relief available, and costs such as fees are allowable against the gain. A self-assessment tax return must be filed if you are in a capital gains situation.

WHICH CAPITAL GAINS TAX RATE APPLIES?

Take your taxable income plus any taxable gains (after relief and allowable costs) less £9,600 exemption to find the relevant range, then check the rate.	RANGE	RATE
	0-£34,800	20%
	over £34,800	40%

TOP TIPS PAY LESS CGT

Couples can avoid CGT by splitting assets sensibly. You can also offset losses against gains to reduce your liability and time any gains so that they are spread over several tax years.

■ **Divide to maximise exemptions** If you have assets that have built up a capital gain, transfer them between you and your spouse and use both annual exemptions.

■ **Lowest rate tax** The rate of CGT that is levied depends on the income tax band of the person concerned. So try to ensure that the spouse paying income tax at the lower rate is the one who ends up with the taxable gains.

■ **Think ahead** For example, if you have lost money on the stock market recently (there are few investors who have not), you can carry your losses forward to future tax years and offset them against any gains you might realise.

■ **Report losses** To offset losses against gains, you need to report any loss to HMRC within 5 years and 10 months of the date when the loss occurred. If you want to carry forward losses, you must notify HMRC of your intention within six years, but once you have done this, there is no time limit on when you have to use the losses that you have brought forward to offset gains.

■ **Timed gains** If you know you are going to make taxable gains, be clever with timing. If in 2008/2009 you will sell assets and make more than £9,600 in capital gains from it, split it into two transactions. Dispose of one portion within that tax year and the other in the next. This way, you'll use the exemptions for two tax years.

■ **Give assets to charity** Assets you give to a charity, or a similar organisation, like a local authority, are normally free of CGT.

■ **ISA trick** Participants in employee share schemes who sell shares after exercising their options may have to pay CGT. To avoid this, they can use the 90-day period from the date they exercised the share option to transfer the shares into an ISA (see page 329), where they can then be sold tax-free.

INHERITANCE TAX (IHT)

Your estate doesn't pay this tax until after your death. There are plenty of ways you can keep it to a minimum for those you leave behind, (see *Family affairs*, page 114).

keep it simple

HOW MUCH WILL YOUR COMPANY CAR COST YOU

From 2008 there are new rules around company cars and fuel benefits. Use HMRC's online calculator at **www.hmrc. gov.uk/calcs/cars.htm** to see how much your company car will cost you in tax. For example, it could cost a higher rate taxpayer who gets a £10,000 car with fuel paid for in 2009/2010 with a CO_2 figure of 140 almost £1,600 in car and fuel tax. A less efficient car with a CO_2 figure of 240 would cost almost £3,500 a year.

Figures from HMRC calculator.

GETTING VALUE FROM YOUR ACCOUNTANT

RESOURCES

ACCOUNTANTS AND SOFTWARE

■ You can find an accountant through The Institute of Chartered Accountants in England and Wales **www.icaew.com** ✉, The Institute of Chartered Accountants of Scotland **www.icas.org.uk** 0131 347 0100 ✉, the Association of Taxation Technicians **www.att.org.uk** 020 7235 2544 ✉, The Chartered Institute of Taxation **www.tax.org.uk** 020 7235 9381 ✉, The Association of Chartered Certified Accountants **www.accaglobal.com** ✉.

Having the expertise of an accountant on your side can, in some circumstances, save you hundreds or even thousands of pounds in tax. On the other hand, you do have to pay for the service. Is it worth employing one? Unfortunately the only way to find out is to try one and at least the initial consultation should be free.

DECIDE WHETHER YOU'LL SAVE

Try to find an accountant who is recommended by someone you trust. Arrange a meeting; find out if they will be able to save you money and how much their fees would be. It may be that you are already well aware of how to minimise your tax bill and the fees could not justify the convenience of having an accountant prepare your tax return for you.

HELP FOR DIY ACCOUNTANTS

If you decide that your affairs are sufficiently straightforward and that you have the necessary skills to do your own accounting, you can get help from the HMRC ✉ or using financial software (see *Resources*, right).

LEARN FROM THE EXPERT

If you use an accountant to complete your tax return, be canny about it. Take a good look at how they have done it, and which expenses they have been able to claim for you. Use the accountant as your tutor – then consider saving yourself the fee next year by doing it yourself.

TOP TIPS MINIMISING ACCOUNTANCY COSTS

To keep your accountant's fees to a minimum, do a little research before hiring one. As there is no set scale of fees, fee scales vary considerably, so it pays to get at least three quotes for the services you require.

■ **Fixed rates often cheaper** Accountancy services may be charged for by the hour, with costs such as phone calls and letters being itemised separately. Some will charge a fixed annual fee, which can be paid monthly. If you can find a suitable firm which charges a fixed rate for particular services, such as completing an annual tax return for you, this is often a cost-effective option.

■ **Hire a junior and save** Charges may vary depending on the seniority of the accountant involved, so you may be able to save by having a more junior member of staff deal with your account, as long as you are happy to work this way.

■ **Beware of price hikes** Check that charges will not rise steeply after the first year – many reputable firms are willing to give you a guarantee that this won't happen.

■ **Shop out of town** As with many professionals, accountants in London and other major cities usually charge more than those in smaller towns, so it may be worth going to one from a different area or using an online service. A smaller firm may give you a more personal service, too.

■ **Don't pay a rush fee** If you give your accountant plenty of time to do the work you require, you are likely to pay less than if you need work completed quickly.

■ **Be organised** Your accountant will charge more for records that require a lot of additional work. By keeping clear records yourself, and particularly if you use a software package recommended by your accountant, you can minimise the work that they have to do and reduce costs.

■ **Deduct fees** Remember that your accountant's fees are a business expense and can be used to reduce your tax bill.

BEFORE HIRING AN ACCOUNTANT

Use the initial consultation to ask these questions:

■ Are they qualified? Look for the words 'chartered' or 'certified'.

■ Who are their other clients? It's helpful if the accountant has experience with people in similar circumstances or other businesses the same size as yours, or in the same field.

■ How do they charge? Hourly fees are most common, but you may be able to arrange a fixed fee for a certain job such as a tax return.

■ Can you work with this person? Take a moment to consider whether this person has understood and responded to your requests. If you feel the communication is poor, try a different accountant.

DO YOU NEED AN ACCOUNTANT?

If your financial affairs are fairly simple, you can probably save the cost of hiring an accountant by doing the work yourself. On the other hand, if your affairs are complex – for example, if you are self-employed or want tax advice – the money a properly trained accountant can save you will usually repay the cost of hiring one.

LEVEL OF SERVICE	SUITABLE FOR	COST
DIY ACCOUNTANCY	Employed people with no complicating factors such as a requirement for tax advice.	Your time, plus any potential savings you miss due to lack of expertise.
BOOKKEEPING	Small businesses who require help with keeping track of their finances.	from £25+ an hour
BASIC ACCOUNTING	Clients who wish to keep costs down, using a newly qualified accountant or using an Internet-based service.	from £75 an hour
FULL ACCOUNTING	Clients with complex affairs who want a full service that includes tax advice.	from £125 an hour

MAKING THE MOST OF STATE BENEFITS

Every year, hundreds of millions of pounds in benefits cash reportedly goes unclaimed. Through lack of knowledge, many people who are entitled to benefits don't even apply. Don't miss out. Find out what there is, and if you qualify for benefits, take them – they're yours!

KNOW WHAT YOU CAN CLAIM

You can check if you are entitled to benefits using an online questionnaire at **http://campaigns.direct.gov.uk/benefitsadviser**. Benefits are paid out either by Jobcentre Plus ✉, Department for Work and Pensions ✉, HMRC ✉ or local authorities. All depend on your circumstances, but some are paid regardless of income. Use *Resources* (left) or contact your local Jobcentre Plus ✉ office to find out which benefits apply to you.

- Attendance Allowance
- Bereavement Allowance
- Bereavement Payment
- Carer's Allowance
- Child Benefit
- Child Tax Credit
- Constant Attendance Allowance
- Cold Weather Payments
- Community Care Grants
- Council Tax Benefit
- Crisis Loans
- Disability Living Allowance
- Employment and Support Allowance
- Guardian's Allowance
- Funeral Payments
- Incapacity Benefit
- Income Support
- Jobseeker's Allowance
- Maternity Allowance
- Pension Credit
- Social Fund
- Statutory Maternity Pay
- Statutory Paternity Pay
- War Widow's or Widower's Pension
- Widowed Parent's Allowance
- Working Tax Credit

DEALING WITH UNEMPLOYMENT

If you become unemployed, take action as quickly as you can. To minimise any loss of income, claim benefits as soon as possible and take your finances in hand.

Put in your claim Contact your local Jobcentre Plus ✉ right away and claim any applicable benefits. If you have a mortgage or rent to pay, ask about help with mortgage interest or Housing Benefit. Check on the progress of your claim every few days.

Identify your priorities Make sure you can pay the most important bills – rent, council tax, electricity, gas and TV licence. If you can't pay your utility bills, your Jobcentre Plus ✉ may be able to help. If there is anything else you can't pay, let the company concerned know as soon as possible. Then get advice from your local Citizens Advice Bureau ✉, which can help work out a payment plan with any creditors. (See *Saving, Borrowing and Investing* chapter for more information about dealing with debt problems.

Get a new job Once your finances are safe, start job hunting, making use of all the resources and advice available. Visit your Jobcentre Plus ✉, and use the library to look in a variety of local area newspapers. Online sites let you search for jobs, you can also load your CV so prospective employers can look for you.

HELP FOR THE SICK OR DISABLED

If you find yourself unable to work due to sickness or disability, find out which benefits apply to your situation and claim as soon as you can. If you're too ill to make a claim yourself, get help from someone you trust or ask your doctor to contact Social Services for you.

Incapacity Benefit If you already receive incapacity benefit you will continue to receive it for the next few years. It has now been replaced by Employment and Support Allowance.

Accommodation costs For help with your rent or mortgage, ask the Jobcentre Plus ✉ about how to apply for Housing Benefit or assistance with your mortgage interest.

Check your entitlements Check out the list opposite to make sure you've claimed all the benefits to which you're entitled. If your income is about to fall, you need to make sure the essentials are secure.

Help for the disabled Find out if you qualify for the 'disabled element' of the Working Tax Credit. This is for people who meet the conditions for Working Tax Credit and have an illness or disability that puts them at a disadvantage in getting a job. To find out more, visit HMRC's website **www.hmrc.gov.uk/taxcredits** or phone the helpline on 0845 300 3900 ✉. You may be able to claim Disability Living Allowance, which is a Jobcentre Plus ✉ benefit for people under 65 who need a lot of help with personal care because of a physical or mental illness or disability. Or you may be able to claim it if you have a disability that means you need help getting around.

MATERNITY BENEFITS

When you're going to have a baby, your employer has certain obligations and there are benefits you can claim. If you're fortunate, your firm will have more generous maternity benefits than the legal minimum.

Statutory Maternity Pay This is for women who've been in the same job throughout their pregnancy, and whose earnings average £90 a week or more. It's paid for 26 weeks and is paid to you by your employer. You are entitled to it even if you don't intend to go back to work after having the baby, and you don't have to pay it back. It's paid for a maximum of 39 weeks. For the first six weeks you receive 90% of your previous pay, and after that you get the basic rate of around £117 a week.

Get personalised information about maternity leave and pay from **http://tiger.direct.gov.uk/cgi-bin/maternity.cgi**.

BENEFITS FOR THE SICK

Get in contact with the Social Services department of your local council to see if they can help with:
- Bus and train fares
- Home helps
- Day centres and social clubs
- Occupational health
- Meals on wheels
- Special housing
- Special equipment for adapting your home
- Help with home care fees
- Laundry
- Blue Badge Parking Scheme

Notify your employer Tell your employer, in writing, at least 28 days before the start of maternity leave. Say that you are pregnant, the expected week of childbirth and the date you intend to start maternity leave.

Maternity Allowance This benefit is for women who don't qualify for Statutory Maternity Pay, for example because they have changed jobs during pregnancy or are self-employed. It is worth around £117 a week at present, and lasts for 39 weeks. Ask your Jobcentre Plus ✉ for details.

Help with housing You might also be eligible for Council Tax Benefit and Housing Benefit (see below).

Get a Sure Start If you or your partner are getting Income Support, Jobseeker's Allowance or some types of Tax Credit, you qualify for a £500 Sure Start grant from the Social Fund to cover purchases for the baby. You don't have to pay it back and it doesn't matter if you already have savings.

CHILD BENEFIT

A tax-free benefit you can claim for your child. Normally paid every four weeks, but it can be paid weekly. It is not means-tested and you can claim if your child is under 16 or is over 16 and in relevant education or training, or is 16 or 17 and is registered for work, education or training with an approved body. The amount you get depends on if it is your first or other children. From April 2009 a family with two children under 16 will receive more than £1,726 a year.

CHILD BENEFIT PER WEEK		
RATES	APRIL 2008	APRIL 2009
Eldest/only child	£18.80	£20
Other children	£12.55	£13.20

HELP WITH HOUSING

The two benefits given to those who need help with costs related to accommodation are paid by the local council. They are means-tested and depend on your type of housing.

Council Tax Benefit (CTB) You might qualify if you are on a low income, have little savings or all your council tax is paid for you. If you have more than £16,000, you usually won't get any. Contact your local council for a claim form.

Housing Benefit In some areas this is called Local Housing Allowance. You may be eligible if you pay rent to a private landlord and are on a very low income. As with CTB, if you have savings this will affect how much housing benefit you can get. And the amount you receive depends on a number of factors, such as whether other people live with you and whether the rent is reasonable for your accommodation. The most you can get is your total rent.

CLAIM PENSION CREDIT – GAIN UP TO £215 PER WEEK

Nearly half of all pensioners are entitled to Pension Credit (see table, right) but many of those eligible don't claim. There are two parts to Pension Credit. Minimum Income Guarantee (MIG) and Savings Credit. People over 60 may be eligible for MIG and 65+ for Savings Credit. Single people can have their income topped up to £124.05 per week and couples up to £189.35 per week (2008/2009). Savings Credit is up to £19.71 for single people and £26.13 for couples per week. Contact your local Pension Service **www.thepensionservice.gov. uk** or use the freephone number 0800 99 1234 ✉ for help with claiming. Have your NI number and details of income and savings to hand.

COMMON BENEFITS YOU MAY QUALIFY FOR

BENEFIT	WHAT IS IT?	WHO CAN CLAIM?	WHAT YOU MAY RECEIVE (PER WEEK)
JOBSEEKER'S ALLOWANCE	Benefit for the unemployed – divided into contribution-based and income-based benefits.	Unemployed or those working less than 16 hrs a week. They must be available for work.	For single people aged 25 and over, the benefit is worth around £60.50.
DISABILITY LIVING ALLOWANCE	Available for the disabled. It's split into two parts, mobility and care, which attract different rates.	Those under 65 who are disabled.	Maximum total for care and mobility components £113.75 a week, minimum total for both £33.50.
COUNCIL TAX BENEFIT	A benefit that can pay some or all of your Council Tax.	Those on low incomes.	Some or even all of your Council Tax may be rebated.
MATERNITY ALLOWANCE	Benefit lasting 18 weeks, for women expecting a baby.	Women who don't qualify for Statutory Maternity Pay.	Approx £117 per week.
PENSION CREDIT	Divided into two parts – Minimum Income Guarantee (MIG) and Savings Credit.	MIG is for the over 60s. Savings Credit is for the 65+ whose income exceeds the set level due to savings or pensions.	MIG for single people is £124.05; couples get £189.35. Savings Credit is up to £19.71 or £26.13 for couples.

BENEFITS FOR THE BEREAVED

If you lose a partner you may be entitled to bereavement benefits.

Help for younger spouses Regardless of age, you should be entitled to a tax-free one-off payment of £2,000. Bereavement Payment is based on your late spouse's NI contributions. You can get it if you're under 60 for women and 65 for men, or if your spouse died before being entitled to a Retirement Pension. You may be entitled to it if they died because of their job and didn't make NI contributions.

Widowed Parent's Allowance If you're a parent and have a dependent child who you receive child benefit for and your spouse dies you may be able to get Widowed Parent's Allowance. You can also claim if you are expecting your late partner's baby. Again you can claim if your partner died in their job and didn't pay NICs. If entitled you will receive £90.70 a week in 2008/2009.

For the over 45s If you lose a partner and are not bringing up children, you might be eligible for weekly Bereavement Allowance. In 2008, the weekly maximum was £90.70. To get it, you have to be 45 or older when your spouse died or when your Widowed Parent's Allowance ended. The amount you receive varies depending on your age – £27.21 a week for a 45-year-old, £58.96 for a 50-year-old and the full £90.70 if you are 55 and older until State Pension age.

WHERE DO YOU MAKE CLAIMS?

Check the phone book for your local Jobcentre Plus ✉. See the Directory at the back of this book for further help in finding government and local offices.

Saving, borrowing and investing

There are a few fundamental financial truths that don't change over time. If you master them and stay on top of current trends, you can maximise your assets and provide for a secure future.

SURER SAVING AND BETTER BANKING

Even if you only have a small amount of spare cash, there are ways of making savings grow into worthwhile amounts. And check your banking habits – they're probably so familiar that you fail to notice the fees your bank takes.

KEEP SOME CASH ON HAND

Keep enough money available so that you can pay regular bills and cope with unexpected expenses.

Rainy-day savings You never know when you might need cash at short notice, to repair the car or a leaking roof or to cover the cost of sickness and redundancy. It's vital to create a savings fund to protect yourself and your family.

Cover necessities Even cutting out luxuries, the average person needs around £850 a month to cover food, travel and household bills (excluding mortgages and rent).

Emergency funds You should save at least three, ideally six, months' salary in an instant-access savings account for an emergency. This will also save you from having to use expensive credit when you can least afford it.

GET THE BEST RATE FOR YOUR SAVINGS

Keep an eye on your cash. If your current account starts showing a healthy surplus, shift some of the money into a savings account to make it work harder for you.

Introductory bonus Many savings accounts offer an introductory bonus of 0.5% or 1% for the first six or 12 months, but after this rate has ended you might get a pretty ordinary return. Either choose an account with a good long-term rate or keep an eye on rates and, if necessary, move your money at the end of the introductory period.

Give notice Check out accounts with 30 or 60 days' notice of withdrawal. These may give a higher interest rate but they mean you can't access your funds for a month or two.

ISA allowance If you pay tax, use your annual cash ISA allowance to invest up to £3,600 a year in a special savings account and you won't pay any income tax on your interest. Rates can be pretty good, as banks and building societies compete for new customers. Some of the best rates are offered by online banks and building societies.

Fluctuating interest rates If you expect interest rates to rise, consider a tracker account that pledges to match any future increases for a set period. If you expect interest rates to fall, you could fix your interest rate for one, three or five years. But if rates rise, you could lose out. Don't tie up money in a fixed-rate account if you might need it later as there will probably be penalties for early withdrawals.

Minimum payments Some accounts insist you pay a minimum sum of £50 to £250 into your account each month. Only open this type of account if you're sure you won't miss a payment, or you won't get that attractive interest rate. If you have a lump sum you will be better off investing it in one go even in an account with a lower rate.

LOYALTY DOESN'T PAY

Look at your existing savings account. It may have been a best buy when you took it out, but it could be bottom of the barrel now. Banks and building societies regularly launch high-profile savings accounts with eye-catching rates of interest, then sneakily let rates dwindle. Some savings accounts offer as little as 0.1% interest. If you've never switched your bank account you could get a better deal by switching and it's easier than you think.

CASE STUDY

SAVE A HEALTHY £3,400 A YEAR

Until his girlfriend pointed out how much money he was frittering away, Alan Brown, 28, had nothing left at the end of each month to put aside for savings. By trimming back on crisps, chocolate, alcohol and cigarettes, Alan is now saving nearly £3,400 a year. With the average pint of lager now costing £2.60, one pint fewer a day saves Alan £949 a year. And by stopping his 20-a-day smoking habit, he is now a whopping £2,117 a year better off. Also gone are his daily 40p packet of crisps and 45p chocolate bar (saving him a further £350 a year). Now, as well as feeling healthier, Alan has healthy savings, too.

CLEAR DEBTS BEFORE SAVING

Instead of putting spare cash in a savings account, use it to pay off your mortgage or other debts, like credit cards or loans. Many mortgages let you make overpayments up to a certain amount each year, say 10%. You might be paying 5% on a lender's standard variable mortgage rate, whereas you will get little more than 2% or 3% on its best savings rate. It makes even more sense to pay off credit card and store card debt. Many credit cards charge more than 20% while store cards can charge up to 30%.

KEEP AN EYE ON YOUR SAVINGS

Once you've decided to invest some money, keep track of how it's performing and change to a better deal if necessary. **Compare ISA rates** Check out www.moneyfacts.co.uk ✉ and www.moneysupermarket.com ✉ for savings and cash ISA comparison tables, or read the money section in your weekend newspaper. Switch if your rate doesn't match up. **No branches** Telephone, postal and online accounts may offer more competitive rates because they don't have the cost of a branch network. **Annual equivalent rate (AER)** This rate puts accounts on a level playing field by showing the annual amount you receive, regardless of when you take the money. It also includes the impact of introductory bonuses.

PROTECTION FOR YOUR SAVINGS

As a result of the worldwide banking crisis in 2008 more people are aware of The Financial Services Compensation Scheme (FSCS). The FSCS protects UK savers and will pay up to £50,000 if a bank goes bust. You are only covered up to £50,000 in an individual bank or group of banks so check if the bank is protected in its own name or part of a group. To be covered banks need to be regulated by the FSA in the UK. Some banks operating in the UK only have partial cover under the FSCS. To be sure you are protected only invest £50,000 with banks or building societies fully covered by the FSCS. For more information go to www.fscs.org.uk or 020 7892 7300 ✉. Check if a company is regulated by the FSA at www.fsa.gov.uk or 0845 606 1234 ✉.

MAKE THE MOST OF YOUR BANK ACCOUNT

Many people have a current account with one of the four big high street banks – Barclays, HSBC, NatWest and Lloyds

---

SMART MOVES

Be flexible with offset mortgages

There are two types of mortgage that let you link money in your savings or bank account with your mortgage so your mortgage is reduced and you pay less interest. Current account mortgages combine your mortgage, bank account and savings account into one account. Offset mortgages do the same thing but the money is held in separate accounts. With both types instead of receiving interest on your savings or money in your bank account the size of your mortgage is reduced. As you don't pay tax on the interest on your savings they are particularly beneficial for people with large savings and higher rate taxpayers. But these mortgages aren't suitable for everyone as mortgage rates tend to be higher than standard mortgages. Compare the benefits of offsetting with the overall cost of the mortgage.

THE BENEFITS OF OFFSET MORTGAGES

This type of mortgage will benefit homeowners with:
■ high levels of savings;
■ large sums of money in their credit account earning negligible interest;
■ high credit card or personal loan bills – you repay the debt at the much lower mortgage rate;
■ higher-rate tax – a mortgage rate of 5.45% is equivalent to a return of 9.08% for this group;
■ fluctuating incomes – reduce your account or borrow back, according to your earnings;
■ the desire to pay off their mortgage early – offsetting your savings and overpaying will clear your mortgage years early and save thousands of pounds in interest.

TSB – and never think of changing. The banks know this and don't work hard to keep your custom. They typically pay a miserable 0.1% interest on current accounts but hit you with heavy penalties if you go overdrawn.

Find a better deal *Which? Magazine* ✉ regularly reviews bank accounts and explains how easy it is to switch to get a better credit interest rate on money in your account or a better overdraft rate, go to **www.weownthebanks.co.uk**.

Online banks Cahoot and Smile, and building society Nationwide, do well for customer satisfaction and good value products in *Which?* customer satisfaction surveys that it runs each year. Alliance & Leicester, now part of the Santander group, also offers several good-value bank accounts.

Don't go overdrawn It makes sense to set up an overdraft facility in case of emergencies even if you never use it. Setting up an overdraft before you go overdrawn could save you lots of money as most banks will charge around 12%, but around 25% if you don't tell them first. They will also hit you with high fees for unauthorised borrowing, for example, each unpaid standing order or cheque will cost an average of £32, plus daily or monthly charges while you are overdrawn.

Beware surcharging ATMs You can withdraw cash for free on a debit card from most ATMs. However there are a growing number of so-called convenience ATMs that charge up to £2 when you take cash out. ATMs that charge have to display the cost of withdrawing cash on the machine and on the screen so watch out. Or ask for cashback when you make purchases in shops.

Check your statements Check your bank and credit card statements each month for any fraudulent or duplicate transactions. Also keep an eye on how much you owe and the interest rates you are earning on savings.

EARN CASH FROM YOUR CREDIT CARD

If you pay off your credit card balance every month, swap your current card for a cashback card, available from American Express, Alliance & Leicester, Barclaycard, Bank of Ireland and Smile. The amount you get on spending on your card ranges from 0.5 to 1.5%. For example, buying a TV costing £1,000 on a credit card with 1% cashback would give you £10 cashback. Spending £1,000 a month on credit card purchases would earn you £120 a year on the same card. Cashback is normally credited to your credit card account once a year. Another option is a credit card that gives points or Air Miles.

USE WINDFALL CASH WISELY

When you have a windfall – a bonus from work, a gift, or cash from overtime – use the rule of thirds to determine how you'll use it.

One third for the past Use one third to pay off debt.

One third for the present Use a third to improve your home or your lifestyle.

One third for the future Put the final third into some sort of savings or investment for the future.

BANK CHARGES BEING INVESTIGATED

The Office of Fair Trading is currently investigating whether unauthorised overdraft charges levied by banks are fair. If you have incurred unauthorised bank charges you may be able to claim some or all of your money back. For more information you can download complaint letters from *Which?* at **www.weownthebanks.co.uk**.

DON'T TAKE CASH OUT ON YOUR CREDIT CARD

You face an extra charge if you draw cash on your credit card, ranging from 2% to 2.5% of the money you withdraw. Credit card companies also normally charge interest immediately, rather than waiting for the standard 56 days, as with shop purchases. Avoid drawing cash on credit cards except in emergencies.

TAX-EFFICIENT SAVINGS

The taxman doesn't just want to take a bite of your income, he's also after your savings. But there's plenty you can do to keep his hands off your money, whether it's taking steps to safeguard your earnings or making sure that any money you invest pays the best possible returns.

PLAY THE PERFECT PARTNERS GAME

If your spouse or partner is in a lower tax band than you are, consider shifting your savings into their name as they will pay less tax on the interest.

Significant savings A top-rate taxpayer earning 4% a year on savings worth £15,000 would get interest worth £600 a year but lose £240 of that to the taxman. They could save that by shifting the money into the name of their non-taxpaying spouse. If their partner pays basic rate tax, they

TAX-EFFICIENT SAVINGS		
SAVINGS VEHICLE	**ANNUAL MAXIMUM**	**PURPOSE**
Individual Savings Account (ISA)	Invest up to £7,200 a year in a stocks and shares ISA. Alternatively, invest up to £3,600 in a cash ISA and the balance in a stocks and shares ISA.	An ISA can be used for almost every investment purpose, from long-term stock market savings to a tax-free deposit account. All returns are free of most income tax and all capital gains tax. Investing in stocks and shares is risky and value can go up and down plus there are charges.
Friendly Society bonds	Invest a maximum £25 a month or £270 a year in a tax-free bond run by mutual organisations called friendly societies.	Most commonly used by parents and grandparents investing for children in so-called 'baby bonds'. You have to maintain your monthly investment for a minimum of 10 years. Watch out for high charges, especially early on – with many bonds the entire first-year contributions could be swallowed up in charges. But some now charge just 1% a year.
National Savings and Investments	You can invest up to £60,000 in tax-free savings certificates.	Savings certificates, Children's Bonus Bonds and Premium Bonds all pay tax-free interest or prizes. Backed by the government and so low risk.
Stakeholder pensions	Pension savings plan that allows you to invest as much as you like each year. You get tax relief on contributions up to 100% of your earnings each year or £3,600 whichever is greater subject to an annual allowance (£245,000 for 2009-2010).	Must be used to buy an annuity before the age of 75. You can take out a 25% tax-free cash lump sum when you retire. Thereafter, you may have to pay income tax on your annuity income.

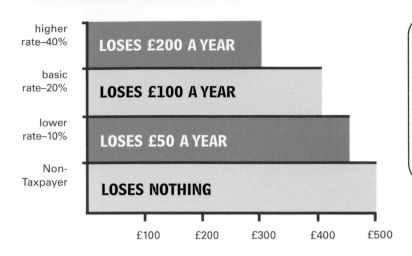

HOW TAX ERODES YOUR RETURN

higher rate–40%	LOSES £200 A YEAR
basic rate–20%	LOSES £100 A YEAR
lower rate–10%	LOSES £50 A YEAR
Non-Taxpayer	LOSES NOTHING

£100   £200   £300   £400   £500

This chart shows how much savers in different tax brackets receive in interest on £10,000 in a savings account that pays 5% a year. Only non-taxpayers receive the full £500 of interest, with the taxman not getting a penny. So other forms of saving may be a smarter option.

can still make savings. In this case, shifting that £15,000 into their partner's name would reduce the tax bill from £240 to £120.

Word of warning Make sure a relationship is solid before transferring your life savings – you risk losing everything if an untrustworthy partner were to run off with your fortune.
Reclamation Non-taxpayers should make sure they don't get taxed by mistake. Complete HMRC form R85, available from your bank or building society, to reclaim tax automatically deducted from your savings. Why give it to the taxman when you don't have to?

USE YOUR ISA ALLOWANCE

Use your Individual Savings Account (ISA) allowance. You can invest up to £7,200 a year in a stocks and shares ISA free of tax, with a choice of where the money is invested. Or you can invest up to £3,600 a year in a cash ISA. You can then invest the balance up to £7,200 in a stocks and shares ISA. Couples can shelter a total of £14,400 a year in ISAs.
Cash ISA The safest way to use your ISA allowance is to invest in a cash ISA. You can save up to £3,600 a year. If you have savings sitting in a deposit account, and you haven't used your ISA allowance for this year, then transfer them into a cash ISA; interest is tax-free and rates are competitive. Shifting £3,600 of savings into a cash ISA paying 4.5% saves a higher-rate taxpayer £65 a year and a basic-rate taxpayer £32.

MAKE A SOUND INVESTMENT

Saving tax is important, but it's even more important to choose the investment that's right for your personal circumstances. As any financial adviser will tell you, never let the tax tail wag the investment dog.

FAMILY FINANCES

A well-planned saving strategy will help the whole family prepare for the future. Get more for your money by starting to invest while your children are small, and save even more by claiming all your tax breaks and entitlements.

SET UP A CHILD SAVINGS ACCOUNT
A good way of teaching your children about the value of money, and making sure they don't squander it when they get older, is to set up a savings account in their name.
Best interest rates Almost every bank or building society offers children's savings accounts, often giving away goodies such as stickers, cuddly toys and birthday cards. Don't be distracted by free gifts – go for the best interest rate. The delights of compound interest will hopefully prove more attractive than fluffy toys in the longer run.

STOCKS AND SHARES FOR THE LONG TERM
You might think the risky nature of the stock market makes it the wrong place to invest money for your children, but the reverse may be true. Stocks and shares are very risky in the short to medium term, but over long periods such as 10 or 20 years they have tended to outperform other types of investment. If you start saving when your child is born, you are setting the money aside for at least 18 years – enough time to override short-term volatility.
Spread the risk You can choose the safer option by saving in a fund such as a unit trust or investment trust. Some investment fund managers promote funds targeted at parents and grandparents who wish to invest

CASE STUDY

SET UP FOR LIFE
Helen Kirby, 20, is delighted that her parents had the foresight to start saving on her behalf shortly after she was born. 'They didn't have much cash to spare but decided the best way to save was little and often. So they put £20 a month for me in a high-interest savings account – they didn't really notice the money leaving their account, but its value was gradually mounting in mine.' Over time they increased the monthly sum to £40, and now the savings account holds more than £10,000. This is proving a real boon now that Helen is studying at university. 'Most of my friends have already racked up large debts, but I've got this financial cushion to fall back on.'
Helen's parents always taught her the value of money and how to look after it wisely. 'They set up another account in my name when I was 12 for spare pocket or Christmas money. The account only holds a few hundred pounds, but the lesson it taught me about handling my cash was invaluable.' Helen isn't just relying on her parents – she has a part-time job working in a local coffee shop one afternoon a week and every Saturday. 'This brings in a bit of extra money and helps keep things ticking over. Some of my friends expect to graduate with five-figure debts, but I'm hoping to keep mine to just a few thousand pounds. Then I want to start saving for a deposit on my first flat.'

on behalf of children, but there is absolutely no reason why you should plump for these. What really counts is the underlying performance of the investment. Ignore marketing gimmicks – make your choice in exactly the same way as for any other investment.

LOW-RISK NATIONAL SAVINGS

A Children's Bonus Bond from National Savings is a low-risk, tax-efficient savings account targeted at children. The headline interest rate may be better than it seems, because all returns are free of tax for child and parents, provided you hold the bond for five years. You can invest up to £3,000 in each bond issue.

SAVE WITH A CHILD TRUST FUND

Every child born after 1 September 2002 claiming Child Benefit will receive at least £250 (£500 for low income families) from the government to be invested in a special saving account they will be able to access when they reach 18.

Lump sum The state will pay £250 (£500 for low-income families) into a fund held in the child's name. A further payment is made when the child is seven years old.

How it works You will receive your voucher within a month of starting to claim Child Benefit and you have 12 months to open a Child Trust Fund account or the government will do it for you. Accounts can be opened at banks, building societies or friendly societies. You and family members and friends can also contribute to the fund up to an annual limit of £1,200.

Types of account There are three types of Child Trust Fund: stakeholder accounts; accounts that invest in shares; and, savings accounts. Share-based child trust funds are much riskier than cash funds as the value of the investment can go down as well as up. Stakeholder child trust funds are also invested in shares, but are managed more cautiously than other share-based funds and have maximum charges of 1.5% per year. You don't pay tax on income and gains from funds until the child reaches 18. You can get details at **www.direct.gov.uk** ✉ and **www.childtrustfund.gov.uk** 0845 302 1470 ✉.

Free to switch Keep an eye on your children's investments. You can switch from cash to shares or vice versa to get a better return.

AVOID TAX ON CHILD SAVINGS

Children have the same tax allowances as adults and so can earn £6,475 (from April 2009) in savings interest each year before paying tax. To prevent parents using their children as a tax dodge, the Inland Revenue will tax parents on any interest above £100 a year – £200 if the original investment came from both parents. But this doesn't apply to accounts opened by friends and other family members.

Set up a trust Parents who want to make bigger investments can protect themselves from tax using a 'bare

trust', which states you are holding the assets in trust for the child and managing them on their behalf until they turn 18. All income and growth is then taxed as belonging to the child, so they can use their full personal allowance.

Grandparents' gifts Providing they live for seven years afterwards, grandparents can give their grandchildren any amount of money free of inheritance tax.

Coming of age From the age of 16, your child can use their £3,600 cash ISA allowance for low-risk, tax-free savings. From 18, they can use their full £7,200 allowance on stocks and shares as well as cash.

MEETING THE COST OF EDUCATION

With charges going up all the time, it's good to know that there are several ways you can make up for any shortfall in your savings.

Child benefit Don't forget that this continues up to the age of 19 if your child stays on at school. In addition, means-tested education maintenance allowances (EMAs) of up to £1,500 a year are available.

Bursaries If your child plans to study an NHS-approved medical or dental course, they may be entitled to bursaries that cover tuition fees in the final years of their course. The NHS Student Grants Unit will supply details. For other courses, there are opportunity bursaries for students from low-income families without a history of higher education. All three Armed Forces also offer bursaries to undergraduates and scholarship schemes to sixth-formers.

Sponsorship Some companies will fund the cost of a university course – especially in engineering, science and technology – based on an agreement that the student will work for the company for a specified period upon completion of their course.

Debt clearance Some employers offer to repay university debts as part of the salary package. If your child goes on to work as a teacher in a subject with a shortage, they could qualify for government help with repaying their loan.

TOP TIPS TRACKING DOWN LOST ASSETS

Nobody likes losing money, but families in Britain are currently letting up to £15 billion slip through their fingers. That's £245 for every man, woman and child in the UK. The money is lying unclaimed in old savings accounts, insurance policies, share certificates, pension schemes and Premium Bonds. Assets can be lost when people move house, lose paperwork or die without telling relatives where their documents are kept. But there are ways of tracking assets down, either free of charge or for a small fee.

■ **Get help tracking down your assets** You can search bank and building society accounts and National Savings and Investments for lost accounts for free using online service **www.mylostaccount.org.uk** ✉. The Unclaimed Assets Register will help you locate life policies, pensions and unit trusts for a £25 search fee (see *Resources*, left, for details).

■ **Do your own search** Save money by searching for lost accounts yourself. Contact the relevant bank, insurer, investment company, National Savings or former employer.

BEST WAYS TO BORROW

Borrowing money has become a way of life for many people, with lenders offering credit cards, store cards and personal loans. However rates range from 0% to more than 30%, which makes a huge difference to your monthly bill, so get the cheapest possible interest rate. What are your credit options? Because of the global credit crisis banks are more choosy who they lend to and rates have increased.

CREDIT CARDS CAN BE CHEAP – OR DEAR

Spending on plastic is easy, but can be pricey. Your credit card probably charges you on average around 17% APR on borrowing on purchases and even more on cash withdrawals. Unless you clear your outstanding balance each month, switch to a hungrier, leaner rival.

0% introductory rate for balance transfers Many credit cards offer 0% for balance transfers for 12 months or more. Most cards also charge balance transfer fees of 2.5% to 3% of the amount transferred. If you do a balance transfer unless you have a card that also charges 0% for purchases don't use your card to make purchases. At the end of the period the standard rate will be charged so, if you can, switch to another card.

0% on new purchases Some credit cards come with an introductory 0% rate on new purchases lasting for 6 months or more. Again at the end of the introductory period the much higher standard rate will be charged.

Low balance transfer rates for life Some cards offer low rates for balance transfers of around 5% or 6% and last until you pay off the debt. Not all cards charge balance transfer fees so shop around for the best deal. Visit comparison websites like **www.moneyfacts.co.uk** ✉, **www.moneysupermarket.com** ✉ and **www.uswitch.com** ✉ or check weekend newspapers and financial magazines for the latest best buys.

WATCH POINTS CREDIT CARD DRAWBACKS

Credit card providers now include summary boxes on marketing literature, highlighting details usually hidden in the small print. Always watch out for the following:

■ **APR (Annual Percentage Rate)** charged on purchases This is the most important figure for those who don't clear their balances. Look out for 0% introductory charges, but don't pay a rip-off rate when you revert to the standard APR.

■ **Interest rate for balance transfers** This is the interest rate you pay on money transferred from a previous card, and isn't always the same as the rate for purchases. But be warned: a card charging 0% on balance transfers but a high APR on purchases will probably use your monthly payment to clear the 0% balance first, while your spending attracts hefty interest. So don't spend if you do a balance transfer. Also watch out for balance transfer fees of 2.5% to 3%.

■ **The rate you actually pay** Sometimes companies charge APRs according to your credit rating, which means you could pay much more than the advertised rate.

SHOULD I TAKE THE RISK TO RAISE CASH?
You can use your house to borrow money using a secured loan or remortgage; this is often used to consolidate debt. However it is very risky as you risk losing your house if you are unable to keep up repayments. As loans are taken out for long periods, up to 25 years, the amount of interest you pay increases dramatically even if you are being charged a relatively low rate. Also, as a result of the global credit crisis there is less money available and lenders have tightened their lending criteria and interest rates have increased.

■ **Interest-free period** Most credit cards don't charge any interest for up to around 56 days after making a purchase. But a few charge interest immediately, which means you still pay interest even if you clear your balance every month.

■ **Loyalty and cashback schemes** Some credit cards offer rewards such as Air Miles or points. Cashback credit cards give you a percentage of your spending back once a year – normally between 0.5% and 1.5%.

■ **Penalties** Most credit cards now charge £12 if you make a late payment or exceed your credit limit.

■ **Minimum payments** If you only repay the minimum amount each month it will take years to pay your debt and you incur more interest. Pay off as much as you can each month.

■ **Credit card cheques** If your card company sends you credit card cheques they are probably best ripped up. They cost more than using your credit card to make purchases and you have less protection if something goes wrong.

LOANS BEAT CREDIT CARDS
Personal loans are normally cheaper than credit cards, with the cheapest loans charging around 8% (at the start of 2009). Unlike credit cards, the amount you pay each month and the interest rate are fixed when you take out the loan. The longer you borrow for the more interest you pay. Shop around – your bank or building society won't necessarily give you the best deal.

GOING INTO THE RED? TELL YOUR BANK
If you seem likely to exceed your bank account funds and go overdrawn, always warn your bank. If you don't, you could pay twice as much interest on your overdraft as you would on a personal loan plus have to pay other charges.

CREDIT REFERENCE AGENCIES
Your financial record, including details of all borrowings, arrears and defaults, is kept on file at three credit reference agencies – Experian, Equifax and Call Credit. Banks and building societies access these records when deciding whether to lend you money.

A credit rating pays Whereas a bad credit rating can cost you dearly, having no credit rating at all (because you've never borrowed money or had a credit card) can be just as detrimental. You are most likely to be granted a loan or credit card if you have a proven record of paying back credit and debt responsibly.

OVERCOME A BAD CREDIT RATING
Millions of people trapped in costly home loans or paying spiralling loan rates from a loan shark have a damaged credit rating, and many face problems securing a mortgage or remortgage from the major high street lenders. And because of the impact of the global credit crisis banks are being more choosy who they lend to and interest rates have increased.

Mortgages are available Don't despair, there are some reputable lenders that may give you a mortgage, even if you

have mortgage arrears, county court judgements (CCJs), discharged bankruptcy, a poor credit rating or no proof of income. You will pay more than the most competitive rates, but it may not be as expensive as you think. Consult an independent mortgage broker to help you find the best deal.
Restore your standing Sub-prime or non-standard mortgages also allow you to repair your battered credit rating. After a year or two of regular payments, you may be able to remortgage to a lower rate from a different lender.

BENEFIT BY JOINING A CREDIT UNION

If you are struggling to get a loan from a mainstream organisation because of previous credit problems, or are tired of your hard-earned cash going to banks the annual profits of which run into billions, then you should consider joining your local credit union.

What are they? Credit unions are non-profit-making organisations owned by their members, which offer basic savings and loan services. There are about 600 credit unions in the UK, usually serving a local community, a church, trade union or workers in the same industry.

Cheap credit Interest on a loan from a credit union is capped by law at 26.8% APR although many charge 12.7% APR or less. This means someone borrowing £1,000 over a year would pay no more than £67 in interest.

Savers' rates Profits from loans help pay the interest on savers' deposits. Savings rates are typically 2% or 3%, although some can be as high as 8%.

Other benefits Savings include free life insurance, and can give your main beneficiary double the amount you have saved if you die. Like banks and building societies, credit unions are covered by the Financial Services Compensation Scheme, so in the unlikely event that your union goes bust, up to £50,000 of your savings will be refunded.

PAY LESS FOR YOUR PERSONAL LOAN

■ Beware rates quoted in adverts – you could pay much more, depending on your credit rating.
■ Many people like the option to repay their loan early, so watch out for redemption penalties.
■ Shop around to find the best deal. Some of the best rates are available online.
■ Payment protection insurance on loans is very expensive and you may already be covered elsewhere. A standalone insurance policy will be much better value. If you are worried about unemployment or illness cover consider other protection, like income protection.

WHAT TO DO IF YOU HAVE DEBT PROBLEMS

First of all, accept that you have a problem and take steps to find the help you need to tackle it.

Get free advice and counselling Personal problems often contribute to debt, and even the most conscientious people can run into problems following redundancy or divorce. A variety of organisations give free counselling services to help you to find ways of paying off your debts (see *Resources*, left). Reputable debt agencies won't make you feel guilty, and they will help you to put things right. Avoid companies that charge a fee for helping people in debt as this will only add to your costs.

Contact your creditors Don't hide from your creditors – they have seen it all before and will view you more positively if you contact them and explain your situation rather than if you just don't pay your bills. They may also be more sympathetic than you fear, particularly utility companies (gas, electricity, water, etc) and financial services companies, who have a social obligation to help you with your problem.

Remember you have rights, too Don't be bullied by heavy-handed or threatening creditors and debt collectors. The courts are there to protect your interests as well as help creditors get their money.

Action plan for clearing your debt

The quicker you pay your debts the less they will cost you in the long run.

Make a budget Draw up a personal budget to see how much you are earning and spending each month, and make cutbacks.

Prioritise your debt Pay your mortgage or rent to keep the roof over your head. Then meet utility bills and try to maintain hire purchase agreements, such as a car to get you to work. Finally, look at debts such as credit and store cards.

Draw up a repayment plan If you can't afford to pay all your monthly bills negotiate a debt-management plan with your creditors. This involves paying as much as you can after covering all your essentials. Many companies prefer this to taking you to court, which is expensive and time-consuming.

Pay bills promptly Don't let bills stack up or the debt spiral will begin again.

Top up your income This might include taking a part-time job, freelancing or renting out a room in your home. Check that you are receiving the state benefits you're entitled to.

Maximise your resources Do you have any unwanted but valuable possessions you could turn into cash?

Pay bills by direct debit It's relatively painless as you don't see the money leaving your account and can save you money.

Consolidate your debts Consider moving expensive borrowings into cheaper forms of debt, such as a 0% introductory credit card rate or a remortgage. But if you are in serious financial difficulties further borrowing is probably not the answer.

Say no Don't enter into any instant credit agreements you can't afford, no matter how enticing they seem.

CASE STUDY

GETTING TO GRIPS WITH MOUNTING DEBTS

Andy Johnstone, 27, knew he had to take charge of his debts when he found that he owed more than £10,000 on his credit cards. Andy had put off clearing his credit cards for years, simply switching the outstanding balance to new cards with 0% introductory rates. 'I was earning £22,000 a year, which meant the debts were half my annual income. So I really had to take control.'

There are several organisations that help people deal with their debts, and Andy contacted National Debtline (see *Resources*, opposite). 'I was embarrassed to call them at first, but they didn't judge me and gave me a lot of useful advice.'

They suggested he start by drawing up a list of his regular outgoings, and this helped him identify where he was spending his money – a simple step that might have helped him to avoid debt in the first place. Its advisers also suggested ways of boosting his income, such as taking a part-time job, and Andy now works three nights a week in a local pub, getting paid to serve drinks rather than spending money buying them. Andy has now cut up his credit cards and set up regular standing orders to repay £300 a month, the maximum he could afford.

Once his debts are cleared, he wants to get into the saving habit to put down a deposit on a flat. 'That may be a few years away – and something I couldn't have imagined a few months ago – but at least I'm starting to take control of my finances now.'

SAVVY SOLUTIONS FOR STUDENT DEBT

The interest rate charged on a student loan is very low compared with other loans in the marketplace.

Therefore if your child has graduated with other borrowing, such as credit card debt or a bank overdraft, any money earned would be better placed clearing these debts before paying back the student loan.

TOP TIPS ECONOMIES TO HELP YOU SAVE

Here are some financial 'housekeeping tips' to keep your expenses down, allowing you to pay off your debts more quickly.

■ **Prune direct debits** Do you use that gym membership or magazine subscription?

■ **Switch your utility supplier** You can cut the cost of gas and electricity by 25% (see *Household finance*, page 296).

■ **Check overpayments on direct debits** If you have a direct debit for your gas, electricity or telephone, check whether you have overpaid. Your provider could owe you hundreds of pounds and be getting interest on your money.

■ **Shop around for cheaper life insurance** You could save money switching to a new insurer. Make sure you have new cover in place before cancelling an existing policy.

■ **Switch house or car insurer** Switching your house and motor insurance could cut your premiums by more than 30%.

■ **Find cheaper phone deals** Hunt for a cheaper mobile phone tariff or cancel it and save £15 to £50 a month.

■ **Pay promptly** Set up a direct debit so you avoid paying store cards or credit cards late.

HOW TO INVEST

Choosing the right way to invest your money can make it grow quicker and not at too much risk. However, choose the wrong way to invest and you risk losing money and taking too much risk.

SHOULD YOU INVEST?

It only makes sense to invest money if you have paid off any other debts, like credit cards and loans (excluding your mortgage). You also need to make sure you and your family are protected if you are unable to work because of illness or accident, or if you were to die.

Check life and income policies Before investing any money make sure you have life insurance if you have family that depend on your income, and income protection or other insurance to provide an income if you are unable to work because of illness. Check what cover you have in place already or if you get any protection from your employer.

Emergency fund Everyone should also have an emergency fund of at least three month's income, and ideally six, and it makes sense to hold off investing until you have a pension in place for a secure retirement.

How best to invest Once you have all of this in place then you can think about investing your money and how best to do it. Stocks and shares may give the highest returns over the long-term, but they are also the most volatile and you risk losing a large part of your money in a downturn.

WHAT ARE YOU INVESTING FOR

You need to think about why you want to invest money and how long you are investing for. You will need a different strategy if you are saving for your retirement or your children's education as opposed to saving for a holiday or to buy a car. When it comes to money nothing is risk-free. By doing nothing with your money it will be worth less next year than it is this year because of inflation. And while stocks and shares have given the best growth over the long

RESOURCES

INVESTMENT GROWTH OVER THE PAST 35 YEARS	CASH	GILTS	PROPERTY	SHARES
Number of years as best performing asset	2	5	11	17
Number of years as worst performing asset	12	9	6	8
Value of £1,000 investment after 35 years	£15,434	£37,471	£60,138	£95,444
Value adjusted for inflation	£1,525	£3,702	£5,942	£9,430
Average annual return	8.1%	10.9%	12.4%	13.9%
Average annual return adjusted for inflation	1.2%	3.8%	5.2%	6.6%

Source: Barclays Capital Equity-Gilt Study and Investment Property Databank; Hargreaves Lansdown/*Which? Money* August 2008

term you risk losing your money in a downturn. If you aren't prepared to take any risk then don't invest in stocks and shares. It makes sense to have a mixture of types of investments to minimise your risk. The closer you are to retirement the less you should have in stocks and shares and more in safer investments like bonds and cash, or perhaps avoid stocks and shares altogether.

TYPES OF INVESTMENT

There are four main types of investment. Choosing the right one at the right time of your life should help you have a secure financial future.

Cash Investing in savings accounts, cash ISAs and National Savings and Investments is free from investment risk and perfect for fairly small amounts for the short-term, say up to five years. Apart from ISAs, interest is taxable. Interest rates are normally variable, but you can invest in fixed-rate accounts or ones that follow the Bank of England base rate. Another option is guaranteed income and growth bonds. Like fixed rate accounts you get a set return after a number of years or a fixed amount each year for two or three years. Your money is safe unless you want to access it before the bond matures.

Fixed-interest securities Investments like corporate bonds and gilts give better returns than cash savings. Corporate bonds are loans to companies that are repaid at the end of a set period and pay a set amount of interest. As the value of bonds go up and down because they are bought and sold on the stock market, if you need to get your money back before the end of the bond you may get less than you invested. Gilts work the same as corporate bonds, but they are loans to the government. Gilts have lower returns than corporate bonds as the government is unlikely to default on the debt. Gilts can be index-linked or level term. Both gilts and corporate bonds can be invested in individually or as part of an investment fund, where your money is pooled with other investors and managed by a fund manager. Investing in a fund is more risky as your capital is not guaranteed.

Property Buy to let has been a popular way for many people to invest in property over the past decade. However, as the recent downturn in the housing market has demonstrated it is a very risky business. Buy to let is buying a property to rent out. As a result of the global credit crisis many lenders have withdrawn buy-to-let mortgages, interest rates have risen and bigger deposits are required. Another way to invest in property is in a property fund where the fund is invested in commercial property. Property is a risky long-term investment of at least 10 years.

Shares This is the most risky way to invest your money. You can invest in individual shares or through an investment fund. Over the long term, shares have provided the best returns beating all other investments. However, as you can see in the table (left) this is not always the case.

WHERE IS YOUR FUND INVESTED?

If you spread your investments you minimise risk. The same applies for investments in shares in investment funds.

keep it simple

MANAGE YOUR INVESTMENTS
Investments need to be reviewed regularly, especially as the older you are the less you should have invested in stocks and shares and the more in safer investments like cash and bonds or gilts, as you have less time to recoup any losses. If you have only a small nest egg or don't want any risk at all, avoid the stock market altogether.

FINANCIAL ADVICE
Before you invest your hard-earned money in anything more risky than cash you should get some financial advice. An independent financial adviser can help you review your finances and advise how best to invest your money to maximise return in line with your attitude to risk and plans.

BE YOUR OWN INVESTOR

Investing in individual companies by buying shares is the most risky way to invest and isn't for the faint-hearted or anyone who isn't prepared to risk losing money.

COULD YOU GO IT ALONE?

Ask yourself the following questions if you are considering becoming your own investment manager.

■ Are you willing to monitor markets daily for new opportunities and watch out for threats to your existing portfolio?

■ Do you know how to analyse the information in a company report?

■ Do you have any specialist knowledge of an industry or company to help boost returns?

Reply 'no' to more than one of these, and you should probably employ a stockbroker to make the decisions on your behalf.

ONLINE SHARE DEALING SLASHES COSTS

You can save money on your share dealing by using an online or telephone-based broker. There are now dozens of stockbrokers allowing you to trade online in real-time and slashing fees from around £50 for each share trade to around £10 or even less. You can compare your existing broker and consider around 100 online stockbrokers at **www.moneysupermarket.com** ✉.

Percentage or flat-rate fees? If you expect to trade relatively small amounts, investing less than £1,000 at a time, look for percentage-based fees, but check minimum charges. Investors trading larger sums might do better using one of a number of sites that charges flat rates.

Hidden costs When comparing costs, make sure you compare total cost including transaction charges and monthly or annual fees. Some websites charge a monthly or quarterly fee that can add from £20 to £80 a year to your costs. There may also be inactivity fees unless you make regular trades.

Online brokers As well as offering popular online share dealing services, online stockbrokers give free information, news and analysis on share trading.

TAKE UP SHARE OPTIONS

Millions of workers can benefit from having shares in their own company under schemes offering a combination of tax breaks and free or cut-price shares. The two most popular schemes are Save As You Earn and Share Incentive Plan (SIP). If you work for a company that offers such a plan, don't miss out on it.

Save As You Earn This gives you the right (known as a share option) to buy shares at a fixed price using money you have saved into the scheme. You can save up to £250 a month for three or five, and sometimes seven years. Interest

RESOURCES

FREE INFORMATION

If you sign up to an online stockbroker, its website will normally give you access to all kinds of investment information. But you can get free information from a number of other websites, too, although you may have to pay a subscription for their more advanced services:
ADVFN **www.advfn.com** ✉
Bloomberg
www.bloomberg.com ✉
Fool **www.fool.co.uk** ✉
UKCityMedia
www.ukcitymedia.co.uk ✉.
Compare sharedealing costs at
Moneysupermarket.com
www.moneysupermarket. com ✉.

and any bonus you get at the end of the savings scheme is tax-free. You also don't pay Income Tax or National Insurance on the difference between the fixed price you pay for the shares and the actual share price. Unless you put the shares into an ISA when you get them you may have to pay Capital Gains Tax when you sell the shares.

Share Incentive Plans (SIP) With a SIP you receive shares and if you keep them in the plan for five years you don't have to pay Income Tax, National Insurance or Capital Gains Tax if you sell them after that. With a SIP you could be given up to £3,000 of free shares per tax year or up to two partnership shares for each one you buy.

HOW MUCH IT MIGHT COST

Someone who makes two share transactions of £500 a month for a year could be charged at the following rates.

CHEAPEST	CHARGE PER TRADE	ADMIN CHARGES	TOTAL COST
The Share Centre	£7.50	£2.50 + VAT/quarter	£191
Hoodless Brennan	£8.00	Nil	£192

EXPENSIVE	CHARGE PER TRADE	ADMIN CHARGES	TOTAL COST
Citibank Sharedealing	£16.50	£10 + VAT/quarter	£443
Abbey Sharedealing Certificate Trader	£22.50	Nil	£540

Source: Moneysupermarket.com January 2009

CASE STUDY

QUITTING WHILE HE WAS AHEAD

David Allen, 55, thought he could beat the investment professionals and started to trade stocks and shares online. He invested £2,500 – £500 each in a bank, an insurance company, an oil giant, a pharmaceuticals company and a small technology firm. The bank and insurer both grew 20% within weeks, and the technology firm grew a mighty 35%. Within three months, his portfolio had risen 20% to £3,000. Dazzled by this early success, David became impatient, cashing in slow-moving stock and trading it for new stock without doing his research properly. Then one of his companies tumbled a massive 50%. This movement cost him £250 and, more annoyingly, he had decided against investing in a stock that rose 75%. David soon realised he was becoming obsessed. He was devoting

so much time and energy to his new hobby that his wife was complaining. So he decided that there was more to life than share dealing and decided to call it a day while he was still in profit, banking a £400 gain, closing the account and resuming a normal existence.

When times are hard saving for your future may be the last thing on your mind, but in order to have a financially secure future you need to do something about it now. A bit of planning today could make the difference between living comfortably and living in poverty.

Planning for retirement

UNDERSTANDING THE BASIC STATE PENSION

Before looking after your financial future you need to make sure your financial present is secure as well. If you have dependants you need to make sure you have life insurance in place. You should also have an emergency fund of at least three and preferably six months' salary in case of emergencies. And you need to do something to protect you and your family if you were off work sick or made redundant for a short or longer time, for example an income protection policy could be suitable. (See *Family Affairs*, page 110 for more details of how to protect you and your family.)

Although times are hard we all need to think about our financial future. This is even more important as we are living longer than ever before, so any money we save for our retirement has to stretch even further. Even if you will receive the Basic State Pension when you retire this probably won't be enough to live on, so if you haven't already done something to safeguard your financial future, do so today. The longer your money has to grow the better the chance you will have enough to live on.

BASIC STATE PENSION

If you have made enough National Insurance Contributions (NICs) during your working life you will receive some Basic State Pension. However the amount you receive probably won't be enough for you to live on comfortably.

Who gets the full pension? If you are retiring before April 2010, to get the maximum pension a man must have 44 years of qualifying NICs and a woman needs 39 years. Anyone retiring after April 2010 will need 30 years of NICs.

How much will I get? From April 2009 the Basic State Pension is £95.25 a week for a single person and £152.30 for a couple. This is just under £5,000 per year for a single person and almost £8,000 for couples.

When will I be able to claim Basic State Pension? Currently men can claim the Basic State Pension from 65 and women at 60. However women's retirement age will rise in stages to 65 in 2020.

Check up on your benefits To find out how much Basic State Pension you are entitled to, contact the forecasting unit at The Pension Service ✉. The call could be one of the most valuable you ever make. If you have any gaps you may be able to fill them with voluntary contributions, boosting your state retirement income. Call 0845 3000 168 or visit **www.thepensionservice.gov.uk**; have your NI number ready.

HOW MUCH WILL YOU NEED

Once you have found out how much you will get from the state you need to think about how much you will need to live on in retirement. You should think about what bills you will need to pay when you retire and which ones you will no longer have to worry about. For example, your mortgage

Hedging your bets

To ensure you have enough money in retirement, your best bet is to combine a number of different pension savings options:

- Basic State Pension and additional state pension benefits;
- final salary or money-purchase occupational pension;
- personal pension, including stakeholders;
- other investments, including ISAs, stocks and shares, bonds, cash;
- property, including your own home.

SMART MOVES

PROS AND CONS OF EQUITY RELEASE

ADVANTAGES

■ Allows you to tap into your most valuable asset to improve your lifestyle.

■ You can live in your home for many years, and can even move house.

■ Look for a 'no negative equity guarantee', which means never owing more than your house is worth.

■ Good for homeowners without children or who don't want to leave an inheritance and can enjoy their money while alive.

DISADVANTAGES

■ You don't get the full value of your home, but a percentage depending on your age.

■ You won't enjoy the full benefit of any future rises in house price values.

■ Equity release is complex, and you don't know how much you will end up owing.

■ Much – or all – of your family's inheritance will be depleted.

■ More complicated and expensive than downsizing.

■ Can affect benefits and could mean you pay more income tax.

CASH IN ON YOUR HOME

Many pensioners are living in poverty despite owning an asset worth tens, or even hundreds, of thousands of pounds – their home. Equity release is an increasingly popular solution, but it's not suitable for everybody and choosing the wrong type could mean you can't move home or could end up owing more than the value of your home. Experts warn that equity release should only be considered as a last resort. Another safer way of releasing equity from your home is to downsize and move to a smaller property.

DOWNSIZING

One way to release money from a property you own is to sell it and move to a smaller property. You could use the money you release to fund your retirement and buy a pension annuity. The benefit of downsizing over equity release is that you still own 100% of your house and don't have a new debt to worry about. Of course you have to take into account the cost of moving (estate agent fees, legal fees and the costs of surveys and removals). But at a time of falling house prices, using equity release to release cash tied up in your home is increasingly risky.

EQUITY RELEASE

There are two types of equity release scheme (also called home income plans) and both types allow people to release money from their property without having to move home or downsize. Most are only available to people aged over 55. With both types, the money you borrow and interest are repaid when the house is finally sold, either after you die or when you move into long-term nursing care.

Lifetime mortgage With a lifetime mortgage you release between 20% and 50% of the value of your property. Interest rates are fixed at around 6% or 7%. You pay nothing until the loan is repaid with interest when the property is sold, you die or move permanently into a care home. The main drawback is that the amount you owe quickly grows and you won't know how much you owe. You could be left with insufficient equity if you need to move or want to use the remaining equity for something else.

With a lifetime mortgage a drawdown scheme means you only take cash when you need it. This reduces the amount you owe and the interest that is accruing.

Home reversion plan With this option, you sell a percentage of your property at less than the market value. You continue to live in your house rent-free, as a part tenant rather than owner. When you die or move into care – with relatives or a nursing home – your policy provider receives a percentage of the proceeds. The rest goes into your estate.

HOW MUCH DO YOU GET?

On a home reversion plan you won't get the full value of your property, because you retain the right to live there for many years. But the older you are, the more money you will get. For example, if you are 70 years old, you could raise £40,000 on a £100,000 property. Compare quotes from different companies. If choosing a lifetime mortgage, shop around for the lowest interest rate. Get some independent financial advice to help you choose the right scheme.

WHAT PROTECTION DO YOU HAVE?

Choose a scheme from a provider who is a members of the industry body Safe Home Income Plans (SHIP) ✉. Members of SHIP all offer a guarantee that you won't owe more than the sale value of your home – a 'no negative equity guarantee'. Get some independent financial advice before signing up and make sure you understand the terms and conditions fully.

HOW DO YOU CHOOSE THE BEST DEAL?

Equity release is complicated so you must speak to an independent financial adviser and your solicitor if you have one. Discuss your plans with your family and beneficiaries, as you are spending their inheritance. Take time to consider your options and don't be rushed into anything.

ALTERNATIVES TO EQUITY RELEASE

Equity release is very risky and should be an option of last resort. You are selling part of your home for less than the market value and will miss out on future growth in its value. Other options may be more suitable.

Move house A much simpler solution is to sell up, move to a smaller property and invest and live off the difference. Your home may now be too big if you are still in the family home but your children have moved away. However, moving is stressful and upsetting so think carefully before you decide to leave your home. You won't pay any capital gains tax when you sell your own home, but once you re-invest the money you are liable to pay income tax on the interest. You should therefore use your tax-free allowances such as ISAs and your personal allowances.

Remortgaging You could raise an ordinary mortgage against your property, taking a relatively small proportion of its value, say £20,000 or £30,000, on what is known as an 'interest-only' basis. This means you repay the interest every month but not the capital (which can be repaid from your estate when you die). The advantage over equity release is that the debt doesn't grow in value as you pay the interest each month, the disadvantage is that you need enough spare funds to repay the monthly interest.

Get help Your beneficiaries could help you out financially, knowing they will eventually profit from a share in the property. If you decide to follow this route, make sure all your beneficiaries accept the situation and you aren't creating a family dispute. Get a solicitor to draw up a proper agreement.

keep it simple

SAVE WITH AN ISA
Instead of a pension, you can save up to £7,200 under your ISA allowance and take all returns free of most income tax and all capital gains tax. If you have lost faith in the stock market, play it safe by saving up to £3,600 a year in a mini-cash ISA.

GET ADVICE

■ Contact the Women and Pensions Helpline at The Pensions Advisory Service 0845 600 0806 or **www.pensionsadvisory service.org.uk** ✉. From April 2010, the number of qualifying years of National Insurance needed to get a full State Pension is being reduced to 30 years, which should make it easier for some men and women to get a full pension.

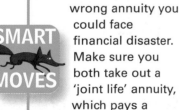

Buy a joint life annuity
Even if you and your partner have saved for years, if you buy the wrong annuity you could face financial disaster. Make sure you both take out a 'joint life' annuity, which pays a reduced amount after the first partner dies, usually half or two-thirds of the full amount. Take the open market option, seek out the best quote and get independent financial advice (see page 350).

WOMEN AND PENSIONS

Women still tend to get a worse deal in retirement – a typical woman's pension is just two-thirds of a typical man's. Most women earn less than men during their working life and are more likely to work part-time and take career breaks to have children. Many still rely on men to save on their behalf, which costs them dearly in the long run.

MARRIED WOMEN'S ENTITLEMENTS
Marriage qualifies you for State Pension benefits based on your husband's entitlement, plus a share of any workplace or personal pension benefits. Even if you divorce, you are due up to half your husband's assets, including pension up to the time of divorce. Your share depends on how long you were together, how old you are and whether you have children.

You can either transfer a share of his pension into your name or offset assets, taking the house, for example, but leaving his pension fund intact.

WATCH POINTS UNMARRIED PARTNERS
More women choose to cohabit with their partner than ever before, but this could prove financially disastrous as it gives you no protection under family law.
■ **Understand your position** You can live with a man for 30 years and have children together, but if he decides to leave, he doesn't have to give you anything. All you get is a share of any assets held in joint names.
■ **Check pension rights** If your relationship is stable, check what happens to your partner's occupational pension if he dies, either before or after retirement. Is your name down for death-in-service benefits or a percentage of his pension fund?

STATE PENSION BENEFITS
Like men, women don't automatically get the full Basic State Pension but a sum depending on their NI contributions.
Carers' benefits Since 1975, women taking time off work to look after children, and carers looking after a sick or elderly relative, have also accumulated benefits under the home responsibilities protection scheme, which treats them as if they have been making contributions. From 2010 this will be replaced by a new weekly National Insurance credit for those caring for children up to 12 years of age and those caring for a severely disabled person for more than 20 hours a week.
Married and divorced Married women receive up to 60% of their husband's State Pension, but only after he retires at age 65. However the 60% is not in addition to the pension you may be entitled to, but instead of it. From 2010 the requirement for your husband to be drawing his pension no longer applies.
If your husband dies you get his pension. If you divorce, your entitlement will include your husband's NI contributions during your marriage.
Nothing for partners Unmarried women won't earn any State Pension benefits entitlement in their partner's name.

A LATE CAREER CHANGE

The over-50s can enjoy a career change the same as younger workers. DirectGov **www.direct.gov.uk** ✉ gives professional help through Jobcentre Plus **www.jobcentreplus.gov.uk** ✉. Learn Direct **www.learndirect.co.uk** ✉ offers information on 620 Learndirect courses to help you get up to speed with computers, office skills and self-development.

JOB HUNTING

Contacts are often best when looking for a job later in life, rather than applying for advertised positions. Jobcentre Plus ✉ and Careers Advice **http://careersadvice.direct.gov.uk** 0800 100 900 ✉ can help to match your skills and interests to job opportunities.

'NEW DEAL' CAN HELP

New Deal 50 Plus is a government-funded scheme that offers personal advice and financial support to older job-seekers claiming income-replacement benefits for six months or more. Go to **www.jobcentreplus.gov.uk** ✉ or call the helpline 0845 6060 234.

WORKING FOR LONGER

Those who continue to work beyond the state retirement age are the fastest-growing part of the work force. Some people shudder at the idea, but rising life expectancy and low incomes will compel many more to do it.

WORKING PART TIME

Many people carry on working after normal retirement age. An option is to work part time. Consider working in a local shop or café, which can be both sociable and fun as well as financially sound.

OVER 50S' SUPPORT

The Over 50s section at Directgov **www.direct.gov.uk** ✉ gives information and advice on work-related issues, including part-time work and volunteering.

MAXIMISING YOUR RETIREMENT INCOME

If you're retiring shortly, are already in retirement or simply don't have the spare cash to build worthwhile savings, you'll need to find innovative ways of getting by. As well as working for longer, there are other options you might consider, depending on your individual circumstances.

DELAY CLAIMING TO BOOST YOUR PENSION

You can still carry on working after reaching State Pension age and either claim your pension or delay claiming in return for receiving a higher pension when it is finally paid or receive a lump sum. This may prove tempting if your salary is enough to live on but your pension benefits are minimal.

What you get now Since 6 April 2005 you can put off claiming your State Pension and get an extra 10% for each year that you delay. There is now no limit on how long you can wait before starting to claim your State Pension. You get an extra 1% for every five weeks you delay – 10.4% increase to your weekly state pension each year. If you put off claiming your State Pension for a year or more you can choose to receive a lump sum payment.

If you have already retired If you retired before 6 April 2005 and have started to claim your State Pension you can stop receiving it so you can build up a higher pension or a lump sum payment. You can only do this once and only if you are living in the UK. You may also be able to do this if you are living in the European Economic Area or Switzerland.

CASE STUDY

FRANK SPICES UP HIS WORKING LIFE

After 30 years working as an insurance agent, Frank Deacon, 62, seized the opportunity to retire three years early. But rather than quietly draw his pension, he decided it was time for a fresh challenge, and launched a handmade pickles business with his wife, June.

'I didn't fancy spending the next 25 years watching telly and playing golf, I had too much life in me for that. June has always enjoyed making food, and is a dab hand at jams and pickles, so we decided to turn it into a business.'

Frank used his sales experience to promote June's pickles and relishes to independent food shops and delicatessens. 'I visit food fares and farmers' markets around the country and try to get specialist shops to display our stock. This is harder work than my desk job, but it's much more rewarding.' The business is now taking off, helped by the growing interest in quality British food – and new premises. 'Our kitchen was small and we were tired of the smell of pickles. It just shows that it's never too late to do something you really enjoy,' Frank says.

If you retired before 6 April 2005 and haven't started claiming your State Pension yet, your pension grew by the old rate of around 7.5% per year until April 2005 and then at the new rate of 10.4% per year.

Other pension types You could also benefit from drawing your money-purchase or personal pension at a later date, but this depends how stock markets perform in the interim. If they take off, you will benefit; if they slump, you could be in an even worse position.

WATCH POINTS RETIRING ABROAD

Moving abroad when you retire may seem like a dream come true. However, you need to think carefully about your pension, healthcare and the impact of exchange rates on your finances.

■ **Will you get your pension?** You can still receive your State Pension if you retire overseas in countries within the European Economic Area (EEA), or other countries with social security agreements with Britain, including Barbados, Cyprus, Jamaica, Turkey and America. And you may be able to receive your pension paid directly into your foreign bank account. In these countries, you should get exactly the same pension as you would in the UK. But this doesn't apply elsewhere. If you spend six months or more of the year in the UK you are entitled to have your full State Pension plus increases each year.

■ **Keep everyone informed** Let the Pension Service ✉ know your new address as soon as possible. Also let your personal pension or company pension scheme know where you are. However your pension should continue to be paid in full and you should be entitled to increases regardless of which country you live in. Make sure your pension will be paid into a foreign bank or a UK bank.

■ **Avoid NI shortfall** Many people who head overseas before the state retirement age unwittingly lose out. If you leave before making enough National Insurance Contributions you could miss out on the State Pension. Contact the Pension Service ✉ to see about making voluntary contributions to maintain your 100% entitlement to the State Pension.

■ **Get tax advice** If you have accumulated your personal or company pension fund in Britain it may still be taxed by HMRC ✉. If you spend 183 days or more in the UK, or your visits average 91 days or more every year over four years, you will pay tax in Britain. Otherwise, you will pay tax in your new country of residence. Rules are complex, so take specialist tax advice or contact the HMRC.

■ **Exchange-rate problems** If your pension is paid in sterling, you will face a currency risk. Consider switching some of your savings into your new home currency to protect against adverse movement in exchange rates.

FOOD AND DRINK

A LOT OF ORGANICS
Unit 55, Milford Road, Reading RG1 8LG
0845 094 6498
www.alotoforganics.co.uk

ARBLASTER & CLARKE
College Street, Petersfield GU31 4AE
01730 263111
www.winetours.co.uk

ASDA
0845 300 1111
www.asda.co.uk

BASC
(British Assoc. for Game & Conservation)
Marford Mill, Rossett, Wrexham LL12 0HL
01244 573000
www.basc.org.uk

CHATEAU ONLINE
www.uk.chateauonline.com

THE CHOCOLATE SOCIETY
Unit 6, Acton Park Estate,
London W3 7QE
0845 230 8868
www.chocolate.co.uk

CHOCOLATE TRADING CO
Byron Street, Macclesfield SK11 7QA
08700 508 244
www.chocolatetradingco.com

COOKS KNIVES
Unit 5, Geisher Road, Callander FK17 8LX
01877 332703
www.cooks-knives.co.uk

COSTCO WHOLESALE
Hartspring Lane, Watford WD25 8JS
01923 213113
www.costco.co.uk

CULINAIRE
01293 550563
www.kitchenknivesdirect.co.uk

DAY TRIPPER
239 Stoke Newington Church Street,
London N16 9HP
020 7254 7772
www.day-tripper.net

DECANTER
www.decanter.com/learning/
wine_clubs.php

DELI ROSSLYN
56 Rosslyn Hill, London NW3 1ND
020 7794 9210
www.delirosslyn.co.uk

DISCOUNT COFFEE
Strutherhill Estate, Larkhall ML9 2PJ
0845 225 5000
www.discountcoffee.co.uk

DONALD RUSSELL
Harlaw Road, Inverurie AB51 4FR
01467 629666
www.donaldrusselldirect.com

EVERYWINE
0800 072 0011
everywine.co.uk

FARMERS' MARKETS
0845 45 88 420
www.farmersmarkets.net

FARM SHOPPING
0845 45 88 420
www.farmshopping.net

FERRY ONLINE
www.ferryonline.co.uk

THE FISH SOCIETY
Fish, FREEPOST, Surrey GU8 5TG
0800 279 3474
www.thefishsociety.co.uk

FISSLER/SALAMANDER COOKSHOP
57 High Street, Wimborne BH21 1HS
0845 6800 258
www.fisslercookware.co.uk
www.salamandercookshop.com

FOOD FIRST
2 Chalk Hill Road, London W6 8DW
www.foodfirst.co.uk

FOOD STANDARDS AGENCY
125 Kingsway, London WC2B 6NH
020 7276 8000
www.food.gov.uk

FREEDOM FOOD
See RSPCA (General Resources)

FRESHAMPERS
01962 773771
www.freshampers.com

GOURMET WORLD
01993 774741
www.gourmet-world.co.uk

HARTS OF STUR
Station Rd, Sturminster Newton DT10 1BD
0800 371 355
www.hartsofstur.com

HOTEL CHOCOLAT
Mint House, Royston SG8 5HL
08444 93 13 13
www.hotelchocolat.co.uk

HOUSE OF CHEESE
13 Church Street, Tetbury GL8 8JG
01666 502865
www.houseofcheese.co.uk

LAITHWAITES
New Aquitaine House, Exeter Way,
Theale, Reading RG7 4PL
0845 194 7755
www.laithwaites.co.uk

LOCAL FOOD WEB
www.localfoodweb.co.uk

LOVE FOOD HATE WASTE
0808 1002040
www.lovefoodhatewaste.com

MAJESTIC WINE
Otterspool Way, Watford WD25 8WW
01923 298200
www.majestic.co.uk

MAKRO UK
0844 445 7445
www.makro.co.uk

MARTIN'S SEAFRESH
St Columb Business Centre, Barn Lane
St Columb Major, Cornwall TR9 6BU
0800 0272066
www.martins-seafresh.co.uk

MERCHANT GOURMET
2 Rollins Street, London SE15 1EW
020 7635 4096
www.merchantgourmet.com

MYSUPERMARKET
www.mysupermarket.co.uk

OCADO
FREEPOST 13498, PO BOX 362,
Hatfield AL9 7BR
0845 399 1122
www.ocado.com

PICK-YOUR-OWN
0845 45 88 420
www.pickyourown.info

RECIPES4US
www.recipes4us.co.uk

RED MONKEY COFFEE
Bache Farm, Westhope, near Ludlow,
Shropshire SY7 9LG
www.redmonkeycoffee.com

THE SUNDAY TIMES WINE CLUB
New Aquitaine House, Exeter Way,
Theale, Reading RG7 4PL
www.sundaytimeswineclub.co.uk

SAINSBURY'S
33 Holborn, London E1N 2HT
0845 602 3860
www.sainsburys.com

SCOTCH WHISKY
www.scotchwhisky.net

TRAIDCRAFT
Kingsway, Gateshead NE11 0NE
0845 330 8900
www.traidcraftshop.co.uk

TROLLYDOLLY
www.trollydolly.co.uk

THE VEGETARIAN SOCIETY
Parkdale, Dunham Road, Altrincham,
Cheshire WA14 4QG
0161 925 2000
www.vegsoc.org

VIRGIN WINES
St James' Mill, Whitefriars,
Norwich NR3 1TN
0870 164 2031
www.virginwines.com

WAITROSE
Doncastle Road, Bracknell RG12 8YA
0800 188 884
www.waitrose.com

WINE & SPIRIT EDUCATION TRUST
39-45 Bermondsey Street, London SE1 3XF
020 7089 3800
www.wset.co.uk

THE WINE ANORAK
020 8890 7330
www.wineanorak.com

WINE COURSES
www.freewinecourse.com

THE WINE EDUCATION SERVICE
Vanguard Business Centre, Alperton Lane,
Western Avenue, Greenford UB6 8AA
020 8991 8212/3
www.wine-education-service.co.uk

WINE 2 LAY DOWN
0845 873 9300
www.wine2laydown.com

WOMEN'S INSTITUTE
104 New Kings Road, London SW6 4LY
020 7371 9300
www.thewi.org.uk

LOOKING GOOD

ALEXON SALE SHOPS
(see page 48)

THE ANERLEY FROCK EXCHANGE
122 Anerley Road, London SE20 8DL
020 8778 2030

AQUASCUTUM FACTORY SHOPS
01536 205086
www.aquascutum.co.uk

ARMSTRONGS
83 The Grassmarket, Edinburgh EH1 2HJ
0131 220 5557
www.armstrongsvintage.co.uk

ASH SAMTANI CLOTHING
00852 2367 4285
www.samtani.com

ASOS
www.asos.com

AVON
0845 601 4040
www.avon.uk.com

BANG BANG
Goodge Street, London W1T 2PJ
020 7631 4191

BARNADO'S
Tanners Lane, Barkingside, Essex IG6 1QG
020 8550 8822
www.barnados.org.uk

BEATNIK EMPORIUM
Above Bar, Southampton 023 8063 3428
www.beatnikemporium.com

BIG FOR MEN MENSWEAR
97 Canterbury Road, Westbrook, Margate,
Kent CT9 5AX
01843 297788
www.bigformen.com

BODY SHOP
Building 4, Hawthorn Road, Wick,
Littlehampton BN17 7LT
0800 0929090
www.thebodyshop.co.uk

BRAND ALLEY
020 3060 1651
www.brandalley.co.uk

BRITISH HEART FOUNDATION
180 Hampstead Road, London NW1 7AW
020 7554 0000
www.bhf.org.uk

THE BRITISH JEWELLER'S ASSOCIATION
10 Vyse Street, Birmingham B18 6LT
0121 237 1110
www.bja.org.uk

BROWN BAG CLOTHING
PO Box 403, Macclesfield SK10 4WR
01625 858491
www.bbclothing.co.uk

THE BURBERRY FACTORY OUTLET
29–53 Chatham Place, London E9 6LP
020 8328 4287

BUY COSMETICS
FREEPOST ANG20402, London W1E 9BR
0871 871 9682
www.buycosmetics.com

CANCER RESEARCH UK
PO Box 123, London WC2A 3PX
020 7121 6699
www.cancerresearchuk.org

CATALINK
Gresham Court, Station Approach,
Wendens Ambo, Essex CB11 4LG
08700 46 98 48
www.catalink.com

CATWALK QUEEN
www.catwalkqueen.tv

CLARK'S FACTORY SHOPS
Rye Lane, Peckham, London SE15 5EX
020 7732 2530

CLARKS VILLAGE
Farm Road, Street, Somerset BA16 0BB
01458 840064
www.clarksvillage.co.uk

COSMETICS 4 LESS
www.cosmetics4less.net

CREATIVE BEADCRAFT
Asheridge Business Centre, Chesham,
Bucks HP5 2PT
01494 778818
www.creativebeadcraft.co.uk

CRUSAID
Churton Street, London SW1
020 7539 3800
www.crusaid.org.uk

THE DANBURY DRESS AGENCY
121 Main Road, Danbury CM3 4DL
01245 225525
www.danburydressagency.co.uk

DEBENHAMS
1 Welbeck Street, London W1G 0AA
08445 616 161
www.debenhams.com

DESIGNER DISCOUNT
PO Box 7007, Nottingham NG7 5FN
0871 508 1277
www.designerdiscount.co.uk

DESIGNER EXCHANGE
3 Royal Exchange Court, Glasgow G1 3DB
0141 221 6898

DESIGNER SALES UK
Wick Street, Firle, Lewes BN8 6NB
01273 858464
www.designersales.co.uk

THE DESIGNER WAREHOUSE SALES
5-6 Islington Studios, London N7 7NU
020 7697 9888
www.dwslondon.co.uk

DOROTHY PERKINS
www.dorothyperkins.co.uk

ELITE DRESS AGENCY
35 King Street West, Manchester M3 2PW
0161 832 3670
www.elitedressagency.co.uk

ELVI
Honeywell Building, Burnt Meadow Road,
North Moons Moat, Redditch B98 9PA
01527 400450
www.elvi.co.uk

ESSENTIALLY OILS
8–10 Mount Farm, Junction Road,
Churchill, Chipping Norton OX7 6NP
0845 130 4400
www.essentiallyoils.com

EVANS
0844 984 0262
www.evans.co.uk

FARA
662 Fulham Road, London SW6 5RX
020 7371 0141

FASHION WORLD
0871 231 4000
www.fashionworld.co.uk

FRAGRANCE DIRECT
Byrons Lane, Macclesfield SK11 7JW
01625 432565
www.fragrancedirect.co.uk

FREEMANS
Amberley Street, Sheffield S9 2FS
0871 987 1030
www.freemans.com

THE GALLERIA OUTLET CENTRE
The Galleria, Comet Way, Hatfield AL10 0XR
01707 278301
www.thegalleria.co.uk

GET AHEAD HATS
www.getaheadhats.co.uk

THE GOOD DEAL DIRECTORY
PO Box 75, Rochester, Kent ME2 2DB
01367 860016
www.gooddealdirectory.co.uk

HAIR-DVD.COM
24 Audrey Street, Ossett WF5 0JN
www.hair-dvd.com

HIRE SOCIETY
25c Lombard Road, London SW19 3TZ
0871 437 0271
www.hire-society.com

KAYS
08448 111 800
www.kays.com

KITBAG
0845 408 4345
www.kitbag.co.uk

LANDS END
FREEPOST Mid 15304, Oakham,
Rutland LE15 6ZW
0845 0123 000
www.landsend.co.uk

LA REDOUTE
Horbury Road, Wakefield WF90 8AA
0844 842 2222
www.redoute.co.uk

LAURA ASHLEY DISCOUNT SHOPS
(see page 48)

L'HOMME DESIGNER EXCHANGE
50 Blandford Street, London W1U 7HX
020 7224 3266

TIM LITTLE SHOES
020 7736 1999
www.timlittle.com

THE LOFT
35 Monmouth Street,
London WC2H 9DD
020 7240 3807

LONDON FASHION DESIGNER SALE
020 7794 1636
www.designerfashionsales.co.uk

LONDON FASHION WEEKEND
0871 230 1558
www.londonfashionweekend.co.uk

NATIONAL FOOTBALL MUSEUM
Sir Tom Finney Way, Preston PR1 6PA
01772 908 442
www.nationalfootballmuseum.com

NECTAR
0844 811 0 811
www.nectar.com

REAL NAPPY CAMPAIGN
0845 850 0606
www.realnappycampaign.com

ROSPA (THE ROYAL SOCIETY FOR THE PREVENTION OF ACCIDENTS)
353 Bristol Road, Edgbaston B5 7ST
0121 248 2000
www.rospa.com
www.childcarseats.org.uk

SAFEKIDS
www.safekids.co.uk

SMILECHILD
www.smilechild.co.uk

SO MUCH EASIER
www.somucheasier.co.uk

SURREY OUTDOOR LEARNING AND DEVELOPMENT
The Coach House, Headley Lane, Mickleham, Dorking RH5 6DQ
01372 378901
www.surreycc.gov.uk

THE TRAINLINE
PO Box 1111, Edinburgh EH11 3AF
0870 010 1296
www.thetrainline.com

TRICYCLE
269 Kilburn High Road, London NW6 7JR
020 7372 6611
www.tricycle.co.uk

UK CHILDREN'S DIRECTORY
www.ukchildrensdirectory.com

UK SHOPPING CATALOGUES
www.ukshoppingcatalogues.co.uk

WORKING FAMILIES
1-3 Berry Street, London EC1V 0AA
0800 013 0313
www.workingfamilies.org.uk

YMCA
640 Forest Road, London E17 3DZ
www.ymca.org.uk

FAMILY AFFAIRS

AGE CONCERN
1268 London Road, London SW16 4ER
0800 00 99 66
www.ageconcern.org.uk

CARE CHOICES
4 Valley Court, Lower Road, Croydon SG8 0HF
01223 207770
www.carechoices.co.uk

COMMISSION FOR SOCIAL CARE INSPECTION (CSCI)
33 Greycoat Street, London SW1P 2QF
0845 015 0120
www.csci.org.uk

HELP THE AGED
207–221 Pentonville Road, London N1 9UZ
020 7278 1114
www.helptheaged.org.uk

THE INSTITUTE OF PROFESSIONAL WILLWRITERS
Trinity Point, New Road, Halesowen B63 3HY
08456 442042
www.ipw.org.uk

LIFEINSURANCE.CO.UK
0845 108 0505
www.lifeinsurance.co.uk

MONEYNET.CO.UK
020 8313 9030
www.moneynet.co.uk

THE NURSING HOME FEES AGENCY
St Leonards House, Mill Street, Eynsham, Oxford OX29 4BR
0800 99 88 33
www.nhfa.co.uk

SENIOR RAILCARD
ATOC, 40 Bernard Street, London WC1N 1BY
08448 714 036
www.senior-railcard.co.uk

THE SOCIETY OF WILL WRITERS
Eagle House, Exchange Road, Lincoln LN6 3JZ
01522 687888
www.willwriters.com

TV LICENSING
Bristol BS98 1TL
0844 800 6790
www.tvlicensing.co.uk
Accommodation for Residential Care (ARC) concessionary licence: 0844 800 5808

THE WILL SITE
0845 126 0891
www.thewillsite.co.uk

ANIMAL MATTERS

THE BLUE CROSS
Shilton Road, Burford, Oxon OX18 4PF
01993 822651
www.bluecross.org.uk

BREEDER DIRECTORY
www.breederdirectory.co.uk

CATCHAT
PO Box 358, Ramsgate, Kent CT12 6YP
www.catchat.org

CATS PROTECTION
Chelwood Gate, Haywards Heath RH17 7TT
08707 708 649
www.cats.org.uk

THE DOG RESCUE PAGES
www.dogpages.org.uk

DOGS' TRUST
17 Wakley Street, London EC1V 7RQ
020 7837 0006
www.dogstrust.org.uk

GOVERNING COUNCIL OF THE CAT FANCY
5 King's Castle Business Park, The Drove, Bridgwater, Somerset TA6 4AG
01278 427575
www.gccfcats.org

THE KENNEL CLUB
1 Clarges Street, London W1J 8AB
0870 606 6750
www.the-kennel-club.org.uk
www.doggenetichealth.org
www.discoverdogs.org.uk

K9 DIRECTORY
www.k9directory.com

NATIONAL PETSITTERS
PO Box 1433, Oxford OX4 9AU
0845 2398544
www.dogsit.com

OUR CATS
Orion House, Barn Hill, Stamford PE9 2AE
01780 758 504
www.ourcats.co.uk

PDSA
Whitechapel Way, Priorslee, Telford TF2 9PQ
01952 290999
Special request scheme: 0800 731 2502
www.pdsa.org.uk

PET PLANET
10 Lindsay Square, Deans Industrial Estate, Livingston EH54 8RL
0845 345 0723
www.petplanet.co.uk

PETS AT HOME
Epsom Avenue, Stanley Green, Handforth, Cheshire SK9 3RN
0800 328 4204
www.petsathome.com

PET-SUPERMARKET
54a Aidan Court, Bede Industrial Estate Jarrow, Tyne and Wear NE32 3EF
0870 626 02 19
www.pet-supermarket.co.uk

PET TRAVEL SCHEME (PETS)
(see also DEFRA, General Resources)
0870 241 1710

PET VACCINATION CLINICS
Coventry: 024 7659 4242
Nuneaton: 024 7638 6855
Birmingham: 0121 783 5085
Wythall: 01564 823825
Rayleigh, Essex: 01268 745180
www.petvaccinationclinic.com

PUCHI PETWEAR
14 Hartley Old Road, Purley CR8 4HG
020 8405 7999
www.puchipetwear.com

UKPETSITTER/SAFE HANDS BY ANIMAL ANGELS
0845 2600488
www.ukpetsitter.co.uk

URBAN PUP
3 Wellington Park, Malone Road, Belfast, Northern Ireland BT9 6DJ
02890 385 799
www.urbanpup.com

SPECIAL OCCASIONS

ALTON TOWERS
(see General Resources)

BIRSTALL GARDEN CENTRE
27–35 Sibson Road, Birstall, Leicester LE4 4DX
0800 085 0005
www.birstall.co.uk

THE BRITISH CHRISTMAS TREE GROWERS ASSOCIATION
13 Wolrige Road, Edinburgh EH16 6HX
0131 664 1100
www.christmastree.org.uk

BUNCHES
Unit 19, Hazelford Way, Newstead Village,
Nottinghamshire NG15 0DQ
0800 626 249
www.bunches.co.uk

CADBURY
PO Box 12, Bournville, Birmingham B30 2LU
0121 451 4444; Cadbury World: 0845 450 3599
www.cadbury.co.uk

CHRISTMAS SHOP
Hay's Galleria, London Bridge City,
Tooley Street, London SE1 2HD
020 7378 1998
www.haysgalleria.co.uk

CHRISTMASTIME UK
Castle Farm, Fillingham, Gainsborough,
Lincolnshire DN21 5BX
01427 667270
www.christmastimeuk.com

CHRISTMAS TREE LAND
The Old Coach House, Hattonburn Farm,
Milnathort, Scotland KY13 0SA
01577 865500
www.christmastreeland.co.uk

CHRISTMAS TREES DIRECT
0845 3700 333
www.xmastreesdirect.co.uk

CO-DRINKS2U.COM
www.co-opdrinks2u.com

CROCUS
0844 557 2233
www.crocus.co.uk

DISCOUNT WINES
www.discountwines.com

E GREETINGS
www1.egreetings.com

EVITE
www.evite.co.uk

FORESTRY COMMISSION
231 Corstorphine Road, Edinburgh EH12 7AT
0131 334 0303
www.forestry.gov.uk

JUST CANDLES
Bentalls Business Park, Basildon SS14 3BN
01268 533866
www.just-candles.net

KIDS PARTY SURVIVAL GUIDE
www.kidspartysurvivalguide.com

LINCOLN CHRISTMAS MARKET
City Hall: 01522 881188
www.lincoln.gov.uk

LONGLEAT
Warminster, Wiltshire BA12 7NW
01985 844400
www.longleat.co.uk

MADAME TUSSAUDS
Marylebone Road, London NW1 5LR
0870 999 0046 or 0870 400 3000
www.madametussauds.com

MAJESTIC WINE
(see Food and Drink)

NETMUMS
www.netmums.com

NORMANDIE WINE WAREHOUSE
71 Avenue Carnot, Cherbourg, France
+33 (0)2 33 43 39 79
www.normandie-wine.com

ODDBINS
31-33 Weir Road, London SW19 8UG
0800 917 4093
www.oddbins.com

PARTY STUFF ONLINE
01908 261 280
www.partystuffonline.co.uk

PRICE'S CANDLES
16 Hudson Road, Bedford MK41 0LZ
01234 264500
www.prices-candles.co.uk

THORPE PARK
Staines Road, Chertsey, Surrey KT16 8PN
0870 444 44 66
www.thorpepark.com

VIRGIN WINES
(see Food and Drink)

WAITROSE WINE DIRECT
0800 188 881
www.waitrosewine.com

WEDDING GUIDE UK
80–81 Tottenham Court Rd, London W1T 4TE
020 7291 7600
www.weddingguide.co.uk

LEISURE AND HOBBIES

ABEBOOKS
www.abebooks.co.uk

ACE CAMERAS
16 Green Street, Bath BA1 2JZ
01225 466975
www.acecameras.co.uk

ACCOR SERVICES
0800 247 1233
www.luncheonvouchers.co.uk

AMATEUR ROWING ASSOCIATION
6 Lower Mall, London W6 9DJ
020 8237 6700
www.ara-rowing.org

AMDRAM
PO Box 536, Norwich MLO, NR6 7JZ
www.amdram.co.uk

**ANTIQUES, COLLECTABLES,
MEMORABILIA & HOBBIES**
Britannia House, Leagrave Rd, Luton LU3 1RJ
01582 488385
www.antiqueswebsite.co.uk

ANTIQUES TRADE GAZETTE
115 Shaftesbury Avenue, London WC2H 8AF
020 7420 6600
www.antiquestradegazette.com

ART AND CRAFT WORLD
Paperclix House, Sandybrook Lane,
St Lawrence, Jersey JE3 1LJ
01534 867901
www.artandcraftworld.com

ART DISCOUNT
Graphics Hse, Charnley Rd, Blackpool FY1 4PE
0845 230 5510
www.artdiscount.co.uk

ARTS COUNCIL
14 Great Peter Street, London SW1P 3NQ
0845 300 6200
www.artscouncil.org.uk
Take it away:020 7973 6452
www.artscouncil.org.uk/takeitaway

**ASSOCIATION OF BRITISH RIDING
SCHOOLS**
38/40 Queen Street, Penzance TR18 4BH
01736 369440
www.abrs-info.org

ASSOCIATION OF CYCLE TRADERS
31a High Street, Tunbridge Wells TN1 1XN
08704 288 404
www.thecyclingexperts.co.uk

THE AUDIENCE CLUB
104 Albany Road, London SE5 0DA
020 7708 5770
www.theaudienceclub.com

THE ART FUND
7 Cromwell Place, London SW7 2JN
020 7225 4800
www.artfund.org

BARTER BOOKS
Alnwick Station, Northumberland NE66 2NP
01665 604888
www.barterbooks.co.uk

BBC GARDENERS' WORLD
201 Wood Lane, London W12 7TQ
020 8433 3959
www.gardenersworld.com

BBC LEARNING
(see also BBC, General Resources)
www.bbc.co.uk/languages
www.bbc.co.uk/learning

BEANS OF BICESTER
86 Sheep Street, Bicester,
Oxon OX26 6LP
01869 246451
www.beansonline.co.uk

BFI (BRITISH FILM INSTITUTE)
South Bank, London SE1 8XT
020 7928 3232
www.bfi.org.uk

BOOK A TABLE
www.bookatable.com

THE BOOK PEOPLE
Park Menai, Bangor LL57 4FB
0845 602 40 40
www.thebookpeople.co.uk

BOOKS PRICE
www.booksprice.co.uk

**BRING YOUR OWN BOTTLE
DIRECTORY/WINE-PAGES**
0141 416 4958
www.wine-pages.com/byoblist.shtml

**CADE'S CAMPING, TOURING AND
MOTOR CARAVAN SITE GUIDE**
Marwain House, Clarke Road, Mount Farm,
Milton Keynes MK1 1LG
0844 504 9500
www.cades.co.uk

CASH CONVERTERS
www.cashconverters.co.uk

**CENTRAL COUNCIL OF CHURCH
BELL RINGERS**
35A High Street, Andover SP10 1LJ
01264 366620
www.cccbr.org.uk

CHELSEA FLOWER SHOW
Royal Hospital, Chelsea,
London SW3
020 7649 1885
www.rhs.org.uk/whatson/index.htm

ANYWORK ANYWHERE
www.anyworkanywhere.com

APARTMENTS.CZ
Divadelní 24, 110 00 Praha 1, Czech Republic
+420 224 990 990
www.apartments.cz

BABYGOES2
01273 230669
www.babygoes2.com

BEST AT HOLIDAYS
10-12 Berners Mews London W1T 3AP
0871 282 4304
www.bestatholidays.co.uk

BIG FREE GUIDE
www.bigfreeguide.com

BRITTANY FERRIES
Millbay, Plymouth, Devon PL1 3EW
0871 244 0744
www.brittany-ferries.co.uk

**THE CAMPING AND
CARAVANNING CLUB**
Greenfields House, Westwood Way,
Coventry CV4 8JH
0845 130 7632
www.campingandcaravanningclub.co.uk

CAMPING AND CARAVANNING UK
www.camping.uk-directory.com

CANVAS HOLIDAYS
0845 268 0827
www.canvasholidays.co.uk

CARIBBEAN CONNECTION
17 West Park, Harrogate HG1 1BJ
01423 534596
www.caribbeanconnection.com

CHALETFINDER
Stalcot, Taberbacle Walk, Stroud GL5 3UJ
01453 766094
www.chaletfinder.co.uk

CHEAP FLIGHTS
www.cheapflights.co.uk

CHEAP HOTELS WORLDWIDE
0871 717 7397
www.cheaphotelsworldwide.co.uk

CHEAP ONLINE FLIGHTS
www.cheaponlineflights.com

CHEEP TRAVEL
www.cheeptravel.co.uk

CIVIL AVIATION AUTHORITY (CAA)
CAA House, 45-59 Kingsway,
London WC2B 6TE
01293 573725
www.caa.co.uk

CONSORT TRAVEL
Sunway House, Canklow Meadows,
Rotherham S60 2XR
0844 844 0470
www.consorttravel.com

CONTOURS WALKING HOLIDAYS
3 Berrier Road, Greystoke CA11 0UB
01768 480451
www.contours.co.uk

COSMOS/MONARCH HOLIDAYS
17 London Road, Bromley BR1 1DE
0871 423 8568
www.cosmos.com

COUCHSURFING
www.couchsurfing.com

CREDIT CHOICES
United House, North Road, London N7 9DP
www.creditchoices.co.uk

CRUISE CONTROL CRUISES
www.cruisecontrolcruises.co.uk

CRUISE DEALS
Mariner Street, Swansea SA1 5BA
0800 107 2323
www.cruisedeals.co.uk

CRUISE DIRECT
85 Oswald Street, Glasgow G1 4PA
0800 093 0622
www.cruisedirect.co.uk

THE CRUISE PEOPLE
88 York Street, London W1H 1QT
0800 526 313
www.cruisepeople.co.uk

CUNARD
0845 678 0013
www.cunard.co.uk

CYBERCAFES
www.cybercafes.com

DALTONS HOLIDAYS
11th Floor, CI Tower, St George's Square,
New Malden, Surrey KT3 4JA
020 7955 3786
www.daltonsholidays.com

EASYJET
www.easyjet.com

EBOOKERS
0871 223 5000
www.ebookers.com

ECO HOLIDAYING
Daresbury Point, Green Wood Drive,
Manor Park, Cheshire WA7 1UP
www.ecoholidaying.co.uk

ECOTOUR DIRECTORY
www.ecotourdirectory.com

EUROCAMP
Hartford Manor, Greenbank Lane,
Northwich, Cheshire CW8 1HW
0844 406 0402
www.eurocamp.co.uk

EUROPA
www.europa-pages.com/uk/
budget_accommodation.html

**EUROPEAN HEALTH INSURANCE
CARD**
EHIC Enquiries, PO Box 1114,
Newcastle upon Tyne NE99 2TL
0845 606 2030
www.ehic.org.uk

EUROSTAR
102 George Street,
Croydon CR9 1AJ
08705 186 186
www.eurostar.com

EXPEDIA
0871 226 0808
www.expedia.co.uk

FAMILYHOLIDAYS.BIZ
0131 208 1589
www.familyholidays.biz

FAIRFX
13-14 Great St Thomas Apostle,
London EC4V 2BB
www.fairfx.com

FAMILY TRAVEL
www.family-travel.co.uk

FARM STAY UK
www.farmstayuk.co.uk

FEDERATION OF TOUR OPERATORS
30 Park Street, London SE1 9EQ
020 3117 0590
www.fto.co.uk

FERRY SAVERS
0844 576 8835
www.ferrysavers.co.uk

FIRST CHOICE
Peel Cross Road, Salford M5 4DN
0871 200 7799
www.firstchoice.co.uk

FLYBE
Exeter International Airport EX5 2HL
0871 700 2000
Flybe.com

FRED OLSEN CRUISE LINES
Fred Olsen House, Whitehouse Road,
Ipswich IP1 5LL
01473 742424
www.fredolsencruises.com

FRIENDS OF WORLD HERITAGE
www.friendsofworldheritage.org

GAZETTEERS
0800 015 4850
www.gazetteers.com

GLOBAL FLIGHT
2, Rue du Bac, F31700 Blagnac, France
+33 (0)5-61-71-16-57
www.globalflight.net

HAVEN HOLIDAYS
1 Park Lane, Hemel Hempstead HP2 4TU
0871 230 1930
www.haven.com

HOLIDAY AUTOS
www.holidayautos.co.uk

HOLIDAY CARS DIRECT
0870 112 8101
www.holidaycarsdirect.com

HOLIDAYGITES
Le Bourg, 17210 Chatenet, France
www.holidaygites.co.uk

HOLIDAY-RENTALS
200 Shepherds Bush Road, London W6 7NL
020 8846 3444
www.holiday-rentals.co.uk

HILLSCAPE WALKING HOLIDAYS
Blaen Y Ddôl, Pontrhydygroes,
Ystrad Meurig SY25 6DS
01974 282640
www.wales-walking.co.uk

HOMELINK INTERNATIONAL
01962 886882
www.homelink.org.uk

HOTELS.COM
0871 200 0171
www.hotels.co.uk

IBIS HOTELS
www.ibishotel.com

IGLU CRUISE
165 The Broadway, London, SW19 1NE
020 8544 6620
www.iglucruise.com

INFO TRANSPORT
www.infotransport.co.uk

KELKOO TRAVEL
http://travel.kelkoo.co.uk

KIDS IN TOW
0845 470 7558
www.kidsintow.co.uk

KING'S COLLEGE LONDON
London WC2R 2LS
020 7836 5454
Accommodation:020 7848 1700
www.kcl.ac.uk

LATE DEALS
0800 027 3157
www.latedeals.co.uk

LATEROOMS.COM
www.laterooms.com

LONDON FOR FREE
www.londonforfree.net

LONDON WALKS
PO Box 1708, London NW6 4LW
020 7624 3978
www.walks.com

LOW COST BEDS
0800 111 6270
www.lowcostbeds.com

MASTERCARD
www.mastercard.com
http://www.mastercard.com/us/pers
onal/en/cardholderservices/atmlocat
ions/index.html

MSN.MONEY
0870 60 10 100
www.money.msn.co.uk

MY VOUCHER CODES
0800 112 3000
www.myvouchercodes.co.uk

NORWEGIAN CRUISE LINE (NCL)
0845 658 8010
www.uk.ncl.com

ONE TRAVEL
www.onetravel.co.uk

ORANGE
Pay monthly: 07973 100 150
PAYG: 07973 100 450
www.orange.co.uk

OVERSEAS JOBCENTRE
www.overseasjobcentre.co.uk

P&O CRUISES
Richmond House, Terminus Terrace,
Southampton SO14 3PN
0845 678 00 14
www.pocruises.com

PARK AND SAVE AIRPORT PARKING
0870 733 0542
www.parkandsave.co.uk

PASSENGER SHIPPING ASSOCIATION
41-42 Eastcastle Street, London W1W 8DU
020 7436 2449
www.the-psa.co.uk
www.discover-cruises.co.uk

PERSONAL DEVELOPMENT OVERSEAS (POD)
Linden Cottage, The Burgage, Prestbury,
Cheltenham GL52 3DJ
01242 250901
www.thepodsite.co.uk

PREMIER INN
Oakley House, Oakley Road, Luton LU4 9QH
0870 242 8000
www.premierinn.com

PROJECTS ABROAD
Aldsworth Parade, Goring BN12 4TX
01903 708300
www.projects-abroad.co.uk

QJUMP
PO Box 222333, Edinburgh EH11 3AF
www.qjump.co.uk

RAMBLERS WORLDWIDE HOLIDAYS
Lemsford Mill, Lemsford Village,
Welwyn Garden City AL8 7TR
01707 331133
www.ramblersholidays.co.uk

REBTEL
www.rebtel.com

RESPONSIBLE TRAVEL
01273 600030
www.responsibletravel.com

ROOMS TO BOOK
0870 240 7060
www.roomstobook.co.uk

ROYAL CARIBBEAN INTERNATIONAL
Building 2, Aviator Park, Station Road,
Addlestone, Surrey KT15 2PG
0845 165 8414
www.royalcaribbean.com

RYANAIR
www.ryanair.com

SAGA HOLIDAYS
Middelburg Square, Folkestone CT20 1AZ
0800 096 0089
www.saga.co.uk

SYHA (SCOTTISH YOUTH HOSTEL ASSOCIATION)
7 Glebe Crescent, Stirling FK8 2JA
01786 891400
www.syha.org.uk

SIBLU HOLIDAYS
20 Black Friars Lane, London EC4V 6HD
0871 911 22 88
www.siblu.com

SKYPE
www.skype.com

SKYSCANNER
www.skyscanner.net

SPECIAL FARES
www.specialfares.net

STAY4FREE
www.stay4free.com

TAKE THE FAMILY
www.takethefamily.com

TELETEXT HOLIDAYS
www.teletextholidays.co.uk

THOMAS COOK
0871 895 0055
www.thomascook.com

3 MOBILE
PO Box 333, Glasgow G2 9AG
0800 358 6946
www.three.co.uk

TOTAL STAY
0844 493 9115
www.totalstay.com

TOURIST OFFICES (ANTOR)
www.tourist-offices.org.uk

TRAILFINDERS
0845 054 6060
www.trailfinders.com

TRAVELBAG
0871 703 4700
www.travelbag.co.uk

TRAVEL INDEPENDENT
www.travelindependent.info

TRAVEL INSURANCE GUIDE
www.travelinsuranceguide.org.uk

TRAVELINSURANCEGUIDE.CO.UK
www.travelinsuranceguide.co.uk

TRAVEL INSURANCE-WEB
19 Bartlett Street, Croydon CR2 6TB
0870 033 9985
www.travelinsuranceweb.com

TRAVELOCITY
0871 472 5116
www.travelocity.co.uk

TRAVELSPHERE
Compass House, Rockingham Road,
Market Harborough LE16 7QD
0870 240 2426
www.travelsphere.co.uk

TRAVELSUPERMARKET.COM
www.travelsupermarket.com

UK HOTELS
www.ukhotels-net.com

VILLASTOGO
0845 241 7733
www.villastogo.com

VIRGIN HOLIDAYS
The Galleria, Station Road, Crawley,
West Sussex RH10 1WW
0844 557 5825
www.virginholidays.co.uk

VOUCHER CODES
020 8124 4266
www.vouchercodes.com

VOYANA CRUISE
Buckingham House East, The Broadway,
Stanmore, Middlesex HA7 4EB
0800 970 4509
www.voyanacruise.com

WOMEN WELCOME WOMEN
88 Easton Street, High Wycombe HP11 1LT
01494 465441
www.womenwelcomewomen.org.uk

WORKING ABROAD
Old School House, Pendomer, Yeovil,
Somerset BA22 9PH
01935 864458
www.workingabroad.com

WORLD TRAVEL GUIDE
Media House, Azalea Drive, Swanley,
Kent BR8 8HU
www.worldtravelguide.net

WORLD WALKS
5 Tebbit Mews, Winchcombe Street,
Cheltenham GL52 2NF
01242 254353
www.worldwalks.com

WORLDWIDE INSURE
01892 833338
www.worldwideinsure.com

CONSERVATORIES ONLINE
0845 603 6078
conservatoriesonline.co.uk

COUNCIL FOR REGISTERED GAS INSTALLERS (CORGI)
1 Elmwood, Chineham Park,
Crockford Lane, Basingstoke RG24 8WG
0870 401 2300
www.trustcorgi.com

COVENTRY DEMOLITION COMPANY
Ryton Fields Farm, Wolston Lane,
Ryton on Dunsmore CV8 3ES
0800 294 8603
www.coventry-demolition.co.uk

CROWN PAINTS
Hollins Road, Darwen, Lancashire BB3 0BG
0870 2401127
www.crownpaints.co.uk

CUPRINOL
Wexham Road, Slough,
Berkshire SL2 5DS
0870 444 11 11
www.cuprinol.co.uk

DECORATING DIRECT
FREEPOST Decorating Direct
www.decoratingdirect.co.uk

DIRECT DOORS
Bay 5 Eastfield Industrial Estate, Penicuik,
Edinburgh EH26 8HA
01968 671 681
www.directdoors.com

DISCOUNTED CARPET UNDERLAY
41 Hedon Road, Hull
01482 215008
www.discounted-carpet-underlay.co.uk

DIY DOCTOR
39 Magnolia Close, Frome BA11 2TT
www.diydoctor.org.uk

DIY FIXIT
www.diyfixit.co.uk

DIYNOT
www.diynot.com

DIY TOOLS
15-37 Caryl Street, Liverpool L8 5SQ
0870 750 1549
www.diytools.co.uk

DOOR FURNITURE DIRECT
26–30 Oxton Road, Birkenhead CH41 2QJ
0151 652 3136
www.doorfurnituredirect.co.uk

DOORS DIRECT
01423 50 20 40
www.doorsdirect.co.uk

DOORS SELECT
Unit 55 Dinting Vale Business Park,
Dinting Vale, Glossop SK13 6JD
01457 867079
www.doorsselect.co.uk

DRAPER TOOLS
Hursley Road, Chandlers Ford S053 1YF
023 8026 6355
www.draper.co.uk

DRAUGHT PROOFING ADVISORY ASSOCIATION
PO Box 12, Haslemere, Surrey GU27 3AH
01428 654011
http://dubois.vital.co.uk/database/ceed/wall.html

DULUX
ICI Paints, Wexham Road, Slough SL2 5DS
0870 444 11 11
www.dulux.co.uk

ELECTRICAL CONTRACTORS ASSOC.
34 Palace Court, London W2 4HY
020 7313 4800
www.eca.co.uk

ESTIMATORS ONLINE
0845 650 2208
www.estimators-online.com

FEDERATION OF MASTER BUILDERS
14–15 Great James Street, London WC1N 3DP
020 7242 7583
www.fmb.org.uk

FLOORING LAMINATE
77 Totteridge Road, Enfield EN3 6NG
www.flooringlaminate.co.uk

FOCUS DIY
Gawsworth House, Westmere Drive,
Crewe, Cheshire CW1 6XB
0800 436 436
www.focusdiy.co.uk

GLASS AND GLAZING FEDERATION
44–48 Borough High Street, London SE1 1XB
0870 042 4255
www.ggf.org.uk

HAMMERITE
ICI Paints, Wexham Road, Slough SL2 5DS
0870 444 11 11
www.hammerite.com/uk

HANDLE WORLD
Unit 2, Holme Bank Mills, Station Road,
Mirfield, West Yorkshire WF14 8NA
01924 481713
www.handleworld.co.uk

HARLEQUIN
Chelsea Harbour Design Centre, SW10 0XE
0844 5430200
www.harlequin.uk.com

HOMESOURCES
Sutton Business Centre, Restmor Way,
Hackbridge Road, Wallington SM6 7AH
020 8747 5055
www.homesources.co.uk

INSTITUTE OF PLUMBING AND HEATING ENGINEERING
01708 472791
www.plumbers.org.uk

INSTITUTION OF ENGINEERING AND TECHNOLOGY
Michael Faraday House, Stevenage SG1 2AY
01438 313 311
www.theiet.org

JUST DOORS
24 Church Street, Bicester, Oxon OX26 6AZ
0870 200 1010
www.justdoors.co.uk

KERSHAWS DOOR WAREHOUSE
5 Main Street, Woodside Road
Wyke, Bradford BD12 8BN
0845 126 0270 or 01274 604488
www.door-warehouse.co.uk

THE KITCHEN BATHROOM BEDROOM SPECIALISTS ASSOC.
Unit L4A, Mill 3, Pleasley Vale Business
Park, Mansfield NG19 8RL
01623 818808
www.ksa.co.uk

KITCHENS.CO.UK
www.kitchens.co.uk

KITCHEN REFURBS
Unit 9 Harrier Park, Didcot OX11 7PL
0800 781 4798
www.kitchenrefurbs.co.uk

THE KITCHEN DOCTOR
1 Sevenoaks Road, Pratts Bottom BR6 7SF
01689 850000
www.thekitchendoctor.com

LIGHTING-DIRECT
Unit 4, Colne Way Court, Colne Way,
Watford, Hertfordshire WD24 7NE
0844 8044 944
www.lighting-direct.co.uk

LIGHTING SUPERSTORE
Unit G11, Avonside Enterprise Park,
Melksham, Wiltshire SN12 8BS
01225 704442
www.thelightingsuperstore.co.uk

LIGHTSAVER
58 Aston Church Road, Birmingham B7 5RX
0845 600 3112
www.lightsaver.co.uk

LOCAL AUTHORITY BUILDING CONTROL
137 Lupus Street, London SW1V 3HE
0844 561 6136
www.labc-services.co.uk

LOW CARBON BUILDINGS PROGRAMME
0800 915 0990
www.lowcarbonbuildings.org.uk

MARLBOROUGH TILES
Elcot Lane, Marlborough, Wiltshire SN8 2AY
01672 512422
www.marlboroughtiles.com

NATIONAL ASSOCIATION OF ESTATEAGENTS (NAEA)
6 Tournament Court, Edgehill Drive,
Warwick CV34 6LG
01926 496800
www.naea.co.uk

NATIONAL BRANDS FURNITURE
Cambridge: 01223 835100
Liverpool: 0151 521 8967
www.national-brands.co.uk

NATIONAL FEDERATION OF BUILDERS
55 Tufton Street, London SW1P 3QL
08450 578 160
www.builders.org.uk

NATIONAL HOME IMPROVEMENT COUNCIL
31 Worship Street, London EC2A 2DY
020 7448 3853
www.nhic.org.uk

THE NATURAL SLATE COMPANY
161 Ballards Lane, London, N3 1LJ
Flooring: 020 8371 1485
Roofing: 01262 606070
www.theslatecompany.net

1926 TRADING COMPANY
High March Ind. Estate, Daventry NN11 4HB
0800 587 2027
www.1926trading.co.uk

ORIGINAL BOX SASH WINDOWS CO.
29–30 The Arches, Alma Rd, Windsor SL4 1QZ
0800 169 3198
www.boxsash.com

PAINTING AND DECORATING ASSOC.
32 Coton Road, Nuneaton CV11 5TW
024 7635 3776
www.paintingdecoratingassociation.co.uk

PILKINGTON'S
PO Box 4, Clifton Junction, Manchester M27 8LP
0161 727 1111
www.pilkingtons.com

PLUMB CENTER
(see Build Center)
0870 1622 557
www.plumbcenter.co.uk

PLUMBWORLD
Millennium Court, Enterprise Way,
Evesham, Worcs WR11 1GS
01386 768498
www.plumbworld.co.uk

PROTECH DIRECT
Bermingham House, Blue Bridge Centre
Horndale Avenue, Newton Aycliffe DL5 6DS
01283 511122
www.thebbgroup.co.uk

ROYAL INSTITUTE OF BRITISH ARCHITECTS
66 Portland Place, London W1B 1AD
020 7580 5533
www.architecture.com

ROYAL TOWN PLANNING INSTITUTE
41 Botolph Lane, London EC3R 8DL
020 7929 9494
www.rtpi.org.uk

RUGS UK
93 Highgate, Kendal LA9 4EN
0808 108 9657
www.rugsuk.com

SALVO
020 8400 6222
www.salvo.co.uk

SCREWFIX
Trade House, Mead Ave, Yeovil BA22 8RT
0500 41 41 41
www.screwfix.com

SMALL CLAIMS COURT SUPPORT
Claim Link, 8 Reed Court, Longwell Green,
Bristol BS30 7DX
0117 370 4385
www.small-claims-court-support.co.uk

TECHNICAL PAINT SERVICES
27 Southcote Road, Bournemouth BH1 3SH
0845 230 1244
www.technicalpaintservices.co.uk

TERRA FIRMA TILES
High Street, Stockbridge SO20 6HF
01264 810315
www.terrafirmatiles.co.uk

THE TILE ASSOCIATION
83 Copers Cope Road, Beckenham BR3 1NR
020 8663 0946
www.tiles.org.uk

THE TILE WAREHOUSE
131 Derby Road, Stapleford,
Nottingham NG9 7AS
0115 939 0209
www.thetilewarehouse.com

TOOLBANK
Crossways Business Park, Dartford DA2 6QE
0800 068 6238
www.toolbank.co.uk

TOPPS TILES
Thorpe Way Grove Park, Leicester LE19 1SU
0800 023 4703
www.topstiles.co.uk

UK FLOORING DIRECT
Unit 1-5 Croftmead, Ansley Village,
Nuneaton, Warwickshire CV10 9PX
0845 263 6586
www.ukflooringdirect.co.uk

WALLPAPER COVERINGS DIRECT
Oozewood Road, Royton OL2 5SQ
0870 170 9669
www.wallcoveringsdirect.co.uk

WALLPAPER DIRECT
01323 430886
http://wallpaperdirect.co.uk

WALLPAPER ORDERS
Oozewood Road, Royton OL2 5SQ
0870 170 9660
www.wallpaperorders.co.uk

WICKES
Rhosili Road, Brackmills Industrial Estate,
Northampton NN4 7JE
0845 279 9898
www.wickes.co.uk

WORLD'S END TILES
Silverthorne Road, London SW8 3HE
020 7819 2100
www.worldsendtiles.co.uk

BUYING AND RUNNING A CAR

AA
Stockport Road, Cheadle SK8 2DY
0870 600 0371
www.theaa.com

AUTOEBID
www.autoebid.com

AUTO CHECK
Talbot House, Talbot Str., Nottingham NG80 1TH
0870 013 1696
www.autocheck.co.uk

AUTO FINDERS
Riverside Business Pk, Bakewell DE45 1GS
01629 814985
www.autofinders.ltd.uk

AUTO TRADER
0845 345 3450
www.autotrader.co.uk

BREAKERLINK
5 Church Farm Barns, The Street,
Bramerton, Norwich, Norfolk NR14 7DW
09045 140173
www.breakerlink.com

BREAKERYARD
0905 232 3000
www.breakeryard.com

CAR CLUBS/CAR PLUS
0845 217 8996
www.carclubs.org.uk

CARCRAFT
0845 094 7000
www.carcraft.co.uk

CARGIANT
Hythe Road, London NW10 6RJ
0844 482 4100
www.cargiant.co.uk

CAR SPARE FINDER
Springbank, Ampleforth, York YO62 4DB
0907 004 3339
www.carsparefinder.co.uk

CAR SUPERMARKETS
4 Watchgate, Newby Road, Hazel Grove,
Stockport SK7 5DB
0161 482 7650
www.car-supermarkets.com

FRIENDS OF THE EARTH
26-28 Underwood Street, London N1 7JQ
020 7490 1555
www.foe.co.uk

GLASS'S GUIDE
1 Princes Road, Weybridge KT13 9TU
www.glass.co.uk

HPI CHECK
Dolphin House, New Street, Salisbury SP1 2PH
01722 422 422
www.hpicheck.com

INSTITUTE OF ADVANCED MOTORISTS
510 Chiswick High Road, London W4 5RG
020 8996 9600
www.iam.org.uk

JAMJAR CARS
Cyan Building, Adwick Park,
Wath-Upon-Dearne, Rotherham S63 5AD
0845 608 1133
www.jamjar.com

MOTORPOINT
7 Gregory Boulevard, Nottingham NG7 6LB
0845 4133000
www.motorpoint.co.uk

NATIONAL CARSHARE
PO Box 6311, Bournemouth BH11 0AW
0871 8718 880
www.nationalcarshare.co.uk

PARKER'S CAR PRICE GUIDE
21 Holborn Viaduct, London EC1A 2DY
www.parkers.co.uk

PASS PLUS
Driving Standards Agency, 112 Upper
Parliament Street, Nottingham NG1 6LP
0115 936 6504
www.passplus.org.uk

PETROLPRICES.COM
www.petrolprices.com

RAC
Great Park Rd, Bradley Stoke, Bristol BS32 4QN
08705 722 722
www.rac.co.uk

RETAIL MOTOR INDUSTRY FEDERATION (RMIF)
201 Great Portland Street, London W1W 5AB
08457 58 53 50
www.rmif.co.uk

THATCHAM
The Motor Insurance Repair Research
Centre, Colthrop Way, Thatcham RG19 4NR
01635 868855
www.thatcham.org/abigrouprating

USED CAR EXPERT
www.usedcarexpert.co.uk

VEHICLE CERTIFICATION AGENCY
Eastgate Road, Bristol BS5 6XX
0117 951 5151
www.vca.gov.uk

WE BUY ANY CAR
www.webuyanycar.com

WHAT CAR?
Teddington Studios, Teddington TW11 9BE
020 8267 5688
www.whatcar.com

WHIZZGO
Leeming House, Vicar Lane, Leeds LS2 7JF
08444 77 99 66
www.whizzgo.co.uk

ZIPCAR
167 Borough High Street, London SE1 1HR
020 7669 4000
www.zipcar.co.uk

BUYING AND SELLING PROPERTY

BIG BROWN BOX
0845 226 6915
www.bigbrownbox.co.uk

THE BOXSTORE
0800 007 5220
www.theboxstore.co.uk

BRITISH ASSOCIATION OF REMOVERS
62 Exchange Road, Watford WD18 0TG
01923 699 480
www.bar.co.uk

CHARCOL
0845 034 2100
www.charcol.co.uk

EASIER2MOVE
4 Walls Yard, South Street,
Rochford SS4 1GR
0845 4600 800
www.easier2move.co.uk

FIND A PROPERTY
www.findaproperty.com

FISH4
www.fish4.co.uk

HERTZ VANS
www.hertzvans.co.uk

HMRC STAMP TAXES CALCULATOR
http://sdccalculator.hmrc.gov.uk

HOME CHECK
0844 844 9966
www.homecheck.co.uk

HOUSEPRICES.CO.UK
www.houseprices.co.uk

HOUSE WEB
PO Box 122, Royston SG8 8YD
0845 003 0720/17
www.houseweb.co.uk

LATESTHOMES
020 8457 4777
www.latesthomes.co.uk

THE LAW SOCIETY
113 Chancery Lane, London WC2A 1PL
020 7242 1222
www.lawsociety.org.uk

LEASEHOLD ADVISORY SERVICE
1 Worship Street,
London EC2A 2DX
020 7374 5380
www.lease-advice.org

LEGAL COMPLAINTS SERVICE
8 Dormer Place, Leamington Spa CV32 5AE
0845 608 6565
www.legalcomplaints.org.uk

LONDON AND COUNTRY
0800 953 0304
www.lcplc.co.uk

NATIONAL ASSOCIATION OF ESTATE AGENTS
6 Tournament Court, Edgehill Drive,
Warwick CV34 6LG
01926 496800
www.naea.co.uk

NETHOUSEPRICES
46 High Street, Ringwood BH24 1AG
www.nethouseprices.com

OMBUDSMAN FOR ESTATE AGENTS
4 Bridge Street, Salisbury SP1 2LX
01722 333306
www.oea.co.uk

ONLINE CONVEYANCING
Windsor House, Pepper Str., Chester CH1 1DF
01244 408300
www.onlineconveyancing.co.uk

PICKFORDS
www.pickfords.co.uk

PRACTICAL CAR AND VAN RENTAL
1/23 Little Broom Street, Camp Hill,
Birmingham B12 0EU
0121 772 8599
www.practical.co.uk

PRIME LOCATION
www.primelocation.com

PRIVATE HOUSE MOVE
www.privatehousemove.co.uk

PROPERTY PRICE ADVICE
020 7647 8614
www.propertypriceadvice.co.uk

PROPERTY SNAKE
www.propertysnake.co.uk

REALLY MOVING
224 London Road, St Albans AL1 1JB
0870 870 4851
www.reallymoving.com

REMOVAL BOXES
30 Ballot Road, Irvine, Ayrshire KA12 0HW
01294 313348
www.removalboxes.org

RIGHT MOVE
www.rightmove.co.uk

SHOOSMITHS
08700 86 87 88
www.property-conveyancing-online.co.uk

SURVEYOR'S OMBUDSMAN SERVICE
PO Box 1021, Warrington WA4 9FE
0845 050 8181
www.surveyors-ombudsman.org.uk

THE LITTLE HOUSE COMPANY
30 St Mary Axe, London EC3A 8BF
0800 083 42 41
www.thelittlehousecompany.co.uk

UNBIASED.CO.UK
www.unbiased.co.uk

UP MY STREET
www.upmystreet.com

ZOOPLA!
www.zoopla.co.uk

HOUSEHOLD FINANCE

BOILER JUICE
www.boilerjuice.com

BROADBAND SPEED CHECKER
213 Redland Road, Bristol BS6 7YT
www.broadbandspeedchecker.co.uk

DIRECTORY ENQUIRIES SERVICES
Freedirectory: 0800 100 100
The Number 0800 118 3733
www.192.com
www.118.com
www.thephonebook.bt.com
www.ukphonebook.com

ENERGY HELPLINE
30 Great Guildford Street, London SE1 0HS
0800 074 0745
www.energyhelpline.com

ENERGYLINX
Hilton House, Whins Road, Alloa FK10 3SA
0800 849 7077
www.energylinx.co.uk

THE ENERGY SHOP
0845 330 7247
www.theenergyshop.com

ENVIROFONE
Guildford House, Heather Close, Lyme
Green Business Pk, Macclesfield SK11 0LR
0870 979 9652
www.envirofone.com

HEATING OIL
www.heatingoil.co.uk

HOME ADVISORY SERVICE
10-11 Queens Terrace, Southampton SO14 3BP
0845 1800 300
www.homeadvisoryservice.com

HOME PHONE CHOICES
United House, North Road, London N7 9DP
www.homephonechoices.co.uk

MAZUMA MOBILE
1 Colne Way Crt, Colne Way, Watford WD24 7NE
0845 872 3000
www.mazumamobile.com

MOBILE2CASH
020 8274 4044
www.mobile2cash.co.uk

NIFTY LIST
www.niftylist.co.uk

OFGEM
9 Millbank, London SW1P 3GE
020 7901 7000
www.ofgem.gov.uk

OMIO
www.omio.com

SAVE ON YOUR BILLS
52 St Enoch's Square Glasgow G1 4AA
0800 055 3800
www.saveonyourbills.co.uk

SIMPLIFY DIGITAL
1 Lyric Square, London W6 0NB
0800 1388 388
www.simplifydigital.co.uk

SIMPLY SWITCH
0800 011 1366
www.simplyswitch.com

SPEEDTEST
www.speedtest.net

SWITCHANDGIVE
www.switchandgive.com

THIS IS MONEY
www.thisismoney.co.uk

UKPOWER
The Granary, Upton Estate, Banbury OX15 6HU
0845 009 1780
www.ukpower.com

VALUATION OFFICE AGENCY
0845 602 1507
www.voa.gov.uk

WHICH? SWITCH
www.switchwithwhich.co.uk

TAX AND STATE BENEFITS

ADVFN
www.advfn.co.uk

ASSOCIATION OF CHARTERED CERTIFIED ACCOUNTANTS
29 Lincoln's Inn Fields, London WC2A 3EE
020 7059 5000
www.accaglobal.com

ASSOC. OF TAXATION TECHNICIANS
12 Upper Belgrave Street, London SW1X 8BB
020 7235 2544
www.att.org.uk

BLOOMBERG
www.bloomberg.com

BUSINESS DEBTLINE
0800 197 6026
www.bdl.org.uk

CHARTERED INSTITUTE OF TAXATION
12 Upper Belgrave Street, London SW1X 8BB
020 7235 9381
www.tax.org.uk

DIGITA
Liverton Business Park, Exmouth EX8 2NR
01395 270 311
www.digita.com/taxcentral/home/cal
culators/default.asp

ENTITLED TO
www.entitledto.co.uk

FEDERATION OF SMALL BUSINESSES
Blackpool Business Park, Blackpool FY4 2FE
01253 336000
www.fsb.org.uk

INSTITUTE OF CHARTERED ACCOUNTANTS
England and Wales:
PO Box 433, London EC2R 6EA
020 7920 8100
www.icaew.com
Scotland:
21 Haymarket Yards, Edinburgh EH12 5BH
0)131 347 0100
www.icas.org.uk

JOB SITES ONLINE
www.jobsite.co.uk
http://jobs.guardian.co.uk

http://business.timesonline.co.uk
www.monster.co.uk
www.jobcrawler.co.uk
www.jobcentreplus.gov.uk
www.totaljobs.com

MATERNITY ACTION
28 Charles Square, London N1 6HT
020 7324 4740
www.maternityaction.org.uk

DIRECTGOV/MATERNITY RIGHTS
(see also Directgov, General Resources)
http://tiger.direct.gov.uk/cgi-
bin/maternity.cgi

TAX CREDITS
(see HMRC, General Resources)
www.inlandrevenue.gov.uk/taxcredits

SAVING, BORROWING AND INVESTING

BEST INVEST
6 Chesterfield Gardens,
London W1J 5BQ
0845 053 3175
www.bestinvest.com

CALLCREDIT
One Park Lane, Leeds LS3 1EP
0113 244 1555
www.callcredit.plc.uk

CHILD TRUST FUND
Waterview Park, Mandarin Way,
Washington NE38 8QG
0845 302 1470
www.childtrustfund.gov.uk

CITYWIRE
www.citywire.co.uk

CONSUMER CREDIT COUNSELLING SERVICE
Wade House, Merrion Centre,
Leeds LS2 8NG
0800 138 1111
www.cccs.co.uk

CREDIT EXPERT (EXPERIAN)
PO Box 7710, Nottingham NG80 7WE
0800 656 9000
www.creditexpert.co.uk

EQUIFAX
PO Box 1140, Bradford BD1 5US
www.equifax.co.uk

FINANCIAL SERVICES COMPENSATION SCHEME (FSCS)
7th Floor, Lloyds Chambers,
Portsoken Street, London E1 8BN
www.fscs.org.uk

FOOL
www.fool.co.uk

THE INSOLVENCY SERVICE
Insolvency: 0845 602 9848
Redundancy: 0845 145 0004
www.insolvency.gov.uk

INTERACTIVE INVESTOR
0845 88 00 267
www.iii.co.uk

LOST ACCOUNTS
British Bankers' Assoc: 020 7216 8909
Building Societies Assoc: 020 7520 5900
National Savings & Investments: 0845 964 5000
www.mylostaccount.org.uk

MONEY EXTRA
1st Floor, City Wharf, New Bailey Street,
Manchester M3 5ER
0845 122 8878
www.moneyextra.com

NATIONAL DEBTLINE
0808 808 4000
www.nationaldebtline.co.uk

THE UNCLAIMED ASSETS REGISTER
PO Box 9501, Nottingham NG80 1WD
0870 241 1713
www.uar.co.uk

UKCITYMEDIA
www.ukcitymedia.co.uk

WHICH? CAMPAIGNS
www.weownthebanks.co.uk

PLANNING FOR RETIREMENT

ANNUITY BUREAU
020 8686 0660
www.annuity-bureau.co.uk

ANNUITY DIRECT
The Innovation Centre, St Cross Business
Park, Monks Brook, Newport PO30 5WB
0500 50 65 75
www.annuitydirect.co.uk

ANTIQUES COLLECTORS' CLUB
Sandy Lane, Old Martlesham IP12 1PJ
www.antique-acc.com

ANTIQUES TRADE GAZETTE
(see Special Occasions)

BONHAMS
Montpelier Street, London SW7 1HH
020 7393 3900
www.bonhams.com

CHRISTIE'S
8 King Street, London SW1Y 6QT
020 7839 9060
www.christies.co.uk

FSA
(see also General Resources)
www.moneymadeclear.fsa.gov.uk

HARGREAVES LANSDOWN
0845 345 0800
www.h-l.co.uk

THE PENSIONS ADVISORY SERVICE
0845 601 2923
www.pensionsadvisoryservice.org.uk

THE SALE ROOM
www.thesaleroom.com

SELLING ANTIQUES
14-18 Heddon Street, London W1B 4DA
www.sellingantiques.co.uk

SHIP (SAFE HOME INCOME PLANS)
83 Victoria Street, London SW1H OHW
0870 241 6060
www.ship-ltd.org

SOTHEBY'S
34/35 New Bond Street, London W1A 2AA
020 7293 5000
www.sothebys.com

2YOUNG2RETIRE
Margintrip Hse, Thorpe Way, Banbury OX16 4SP
www.2young2retire.co.uk

INDEX

This index refers you to the main subjects and SECTIONS in the book. See also the detailed tables of contents at the beginning of each chapter, and the Directory of Addresses beginning on page 358 for contact information on the sources and suppliers named in the book.

ACKNOWLEDGMENTS

Cartoons Special thanks to Paul Bommer for supplying all
cartoons throughout the book

Photographs
8-9 www.moneysupermarket.com, **10** Digital Vision, **12** Corbis/
John Feingersh, **21** RD © **27** RD ©/Ken Field, **29** RD © **31** RD
©, **37** Getty Images/Photodisc, **38** Getty Images/Photodisc,
42-43 Image Source, **47** Digital Vision, **55** Punchstock/
bilderlounge **58** Digital Vision, **59** Getty Images/Photodisc,
60-61 Getty Images/Photodisc, **64** Digital Vision, **66** RD ©/
Ulrich Kopp, **77** Stockbyte **91** Digital Vision, **94** Digital Vision,
99 Digital Vision, **103** Digital Vision, **107** Digital Vision,
110 Digital Vision, **120** Digital Vision, **127** Getty Images/
Photodisc, **129** Getty Images/ Photodisc, **130** Digital Vision,
135 Digital Vision, **139** RD © **140** Digital Vision, **145** RD ©
(GID WSW058_2F), **148** Getty Images/Photodisc, **152** Getty
Images/Photodisc, **161** Digital Vision, **162** Digital Vision,
164 Digital Vision, **167** Getty Images/ Photodisc, **172** Getty
Images/ Photodisc, **175** Digital Vision, **179** Shutterstock, Inc/Yuri
Arcurs, **186** Digital Vision, **190** Shutterstock, Inc, **196** RD
©/Debbie Patterson, **203** Jess Walton, **207** Shutterstock, Inc/Jiri
Miklo, **212** Getty Images/Photodisc, **214** RD ©/ Sarah Cuttle,
216 RD ©/ Debbie Patterson, **220** Getty Images/Photodisc,
224 Getty Images/Photodisc, **227** Shutterstock, Inc/Yuri Arcurs,
232 Digital Vision, **236** RD ©/Colin Bowling & Paul Forrester,
240 Getty Images/Photodisc, **245** RD ©/ Colin Bowling & Paul
Forrester, **246** Digital Vision, **254** RD ©/Colin Bowling & Paul
Forrester, **257** RD © (GID 051ASK01A), **260** Stockbyte, **274**
Digital Vision, **279** Punchstock/Thinkbyte, **280** Digital Vision,
290 Hemera Technologies Inc., **292** Digital Vision, **295** Digital
Vision, **298** Comstock, **301** iStockphoto.com/Phil Date,
308 Getty Images/Photodisc, **316** Getty Images/Photodisc, ·
321 Getty Images/Photodisc, **324** Getty Images/Photodisc,
329 Getty Images/Photodisc, **331** Digital Vision, **342** Getty
Images/ Photodisc, **348** Digital Vision, **355** Getty Images/
Photodisc.

Originated by **Creative Plus Publishing Limited,
2nd floor, 151 High Street, Billericay, Essex, CM12 9AB**

Project Manager Sue Joiner
Writers Carol Davis, Kerensa Deane, Jane Egginton,
Rachel Fixsen, Katharine Gurney, Vicky Huntley,
Harvey Jones, David Leck, Barry Plows, Gisela Roberts,
Christine Stopp, Wendy Sweetser
Indexer Diana Lecore
Editors Dawn Bates, Sue Churchill, Judy Fovargue,
Margaret Maino, Patsy North, Gisela Roberts
Sub Editor Bea Agombar
Proofreader Ron Pankhurst
Design Kerrie Blake, Jane McKenna

For **The Reader's Digest Association Limited**
Project editor Lisa Thomas
Editor Diane Cross
Art editor Simon Webb
Finance consultant and writer Mike Naylor

Reader's Digest General Books
Editorial Director Julian Browne
Art Director Anne-Marie Bulat
Managing Editor Nina Hathway
Head of Book Development Sarah Bloxham
Picture Resource Manager Christine Hinze
Pre-press Account Manager Dean Russell
Product Production Manager Claudette Bramble
Senior Production Controller Katherine Tibbals

Colour origination Colour Systems, London
Printed and bound in Europe by Arvato Iberia

Concept code UK1731/IC
Book code 400-422 UP0000-1
ISBN 978 0 276 44530 9
Oracle code 250013336S.00.24